PEARSON ALWAYS LEARNING

Haleh Azimi • Kyle Goehner

In Conversation

A Thematic Reader for Critical Thinking

Second Custom Edition

Cover Art by Mitra Azimi
Photographs by Farhad Azimi

Pearson Learning Solutions, 330 Hudson Street, New York,
New York 10013
A Pearson Education Company
www.pearsoned.com

Printed in the United States of America

1 2 3 4 5 6 7 8 9 10 v092 18 17 16 15

000200010272019838

JHA/KE

PEARSON

ISBN 10: 1-323-30671-4
ISBN 13: 978-1-323-30671-0

CONTENTS

UNIT 6 ECONOMICS AND SPORTS 291

UNIT 7 CRIMINAL JUSTICE 323

CITATIONS FOR INCLUDED WORKS 400

TELEVISION AND CHILDREN REFERENCES 403

ACKNOWLEDGMENTS

Haleh and Kyle would like to thank the many people whose assistance made this reader a possibility. Sharon Hayes motivated us to pursue this opportunity, and we hope this reader rewards her belief in us. Elizabeth Blackert's immense positivity helped keep us optimistic and on schedule. Rachele Lawton provided insightful commentary and a keen editing eye. Her valuable contributions can not be overstated, and, because she is not editing this part, they will go unstated fear of misusing the adjective "wondrous." Greg Campbell graciously edited the work under deadline and this reader is much better for it.

Haleh Azimi's parents have been tremendously supportive to her throughout her life, and she looks up to both in so many ways. Mitra and Farhad Azimi have great artistic talent, and their cover and images warrant this claim. Laylee Stalter and Mina Krul are to be thanked for encouraging Haleh's work on this project. Jackson and Brennan cannot be forgotten for their patience while their mom multi-tasked long hours on this project, while balancing play time with them. Finally, Haleh cannot thank her colleague, and very dear friend, (and wonderful cook) Kyle Goehner enough for working tirelessly on this project with her. Kyle, your overall leadership and thoughtful nature while working on this project made this entire reader come to life.

Kyle Goehner's parents have supported him through so many things, this reader being no exception. Britt Goehner's eye for accuracy has not dimmed as he enjoys his retirement. Rebecca Sickenberger allowed late nights, a covered dining room table, and an overworked coffee pot. Her unwavering belief in this project and joyful attitude made this a much better process. Derek Jeter provided an example of excellence that this reader aims for. And most of all, thanks to Haleh Azimi, who dealt with emails at unreasonable times, hastily assembled lunches featuring cold soups, and a file naming system that made sense only to Kyle. Haleh, your leadership, attention to detail, creative thinking, and friendship were invaluable during this process.

COPYRIGHT ACKNOWLEDGMENTS

Grateful acknowledgment is made to the following sources for permission to reprint material copyrighted or controlled by them:

"Against School: How Public Education Cripples Our Kids, and Why," by John Taylor Gatto, reprinted by permission of *Harper's Magazine,* September 2003.

"Social Class and the Hidden Curriculum of Work," by Jean Anyon, reprinted from *Journal of Education* 162, no.1 (1980), permission of Jessica Anyon and the Journal of Education.

"It Takes a Mentor," by Thomas L. Friedman, reprinted by permission of the *New York Times Magazine,* September 9, 2014.

"Why Poor Students Struggle," by Vicki Madden, reprinted by permission of the *New York Times Magazine,* September 21, 2014.

"American Schools Are Training Kids for a World That Doesn't Exist," by David Edwards, reprinted from *Wired,* October 17, 2014.

"Education Gap Grows between Rich and Poor, Studies Say," by Sabrina Tavernise, reprinted by permission of the *New York Times Magazine,* February 9, 2012.

"States Listen as Parents Give Rampant Testing an F," by Lizette Alvarez, reprinted by permission of the *New York Times Magazine,* November 9, 2014.

"Segregation Now," by Nikole Hannah-Jones, reprinted by permission of *ProPublica,* April 16, 2014.

"Unequal Opportunity: Race and Education," by Linda Darling-Hammond, reprinted from *Brookings Review* (spring 1998), permission of The Brookings Institution.

"U.S. to Focus on Equity in Assigning of Teachers," by Motoko Rich, reprinted by permission of the *New York Times Magazine,* November 10, 2014.

"Them That's Got Shall Get," by Nathalie Baptiste, reprinted by permission of the *American Prospect,* October 13, 2014.

"The Case for Reparations," by Ta-Nehisi Coates, reprinted from the Tribune Content Agency, June 2014.

"What If Black America Were a Country?" by Theodore R Johnson, reprinted from the Tribune Content Agency, October 14, 2014.

"Wealth Gap Rise to Record Highs between Whites, Blacks, Hispanics," by Rakesh Kochhar, Richard Fry, and Paul Taylor, reprinted from Pew Research Center for the People & the Press, June 26, 2011.

"A World Not Neatly Divided," by Amartya Sen, reprinted by permission of the *New York Times Magainze,* November 23, 2001.

"1776 and All That," by Edward Hoagland, reprinted from the *Nation,* July 3, 2002.

"The Politics of Pidgin English in Cameroon," by Dibussi Tande, reprinted from *Scribbles* from the Den.

"Education Gap Grows between Rich and Poor, Studies Say," by Sabrina Tavernise, reprinted by permission of the *New York Times Magazine,* February 9, 2012.

"The Rise of Asian Americans," reprinted by Pew Research Center for the People & the Press, April 04, 2013.

"How Economic Inclusion Can Lead to Success," by Anise D Wiley-Little, reprinted from the Tribune Content Agency, January 9, 2014.

"Black Men and Public Space," by Brent Staples, reprinted by permission of the author.

"The Unsafety Net: How Social Media Turned Against Women," by Catherine Buni and Soraya Chemaly, reprinted from the *Atlantic Monthly,* October 9, 2014.

"How the Cult of Internet Openness Enables Misogyny," by Astra Taylor, reprinted by permission of *Mother Jones*, April 10, 2014.

"How to Rid Twitter of Misogyny—and Make It Fit for Debate," by Simon Jenkins, reprinted by permission of the *Guardian*, July 31, 2013.

"Why Women Aren't Welcome on the Internet," by Amanda Hess, reprinted from *Pacific Standard*, January 6, 2014.

"Technology's Man Problem," by Claire Cain Miller, reprinted by permission of the *New York Times Magazine*, April 5, 2014.

"The Glaring Gender Dilemma Silicon Valley Venture Capitalists Are Hiding From," by Vivek Wadhwa, reprinted by permission of the *Washington Post*, October 7, 2014.

"Popular Culture Can Inspire and Entice Girls in Technology," by Reshma Saujani, reprinted from the *New York Times Magazine*, May 12, 2014.

"A Female Writer's New Milestone: Her First Death Threat," by Annie Gaus, reprinted by permission of the *Daily Beast*, December 1, 2014. Daily Beast

"This Is What Tech's Ugly Gender Problem Really Looks Like," by Issie Lapowsky, reprinted by permission of Conde Nast Publications, Inc., July 28, 2014.

"How to Stop the Bullies," by Emily Bazelon, reprinted from the *Atlantic Monthly*, February 23, 2013.

"New Study Exposes Gender Bias in Tech Job Listings," by Klint Finley, reprinted by permission of Conde Nast Publications, Inc., March 11, 2013.

"5 Modern Diseases Grown by Factory Farming," by Monica Nickelburg, reprinted by permission of the *Week Publications, Inc.*, November 7, 2013.

"How Junk Food Can End Obesity," by David H Freedman, reprinted from the *Atlantic Monthly*, June 19,2013.

"Is Obesity an Addiction?" by Paul J Kenny, reprinted by permission of the *Scientific American*, August 20, 2013.

"Still a Fast-Food Nation: Eric Schlosser Reflects on 10 Years Later," by Eric Schlosser, reprinted by permission of Houghton Mifflin Harcourt Publishing, March 12, 2012.

"Hormones in Food: Should You Worry?" by Carina Storrs, reprinted from the *Huffington Post*, January 31, 2011.

"The Dangers of Eating Late at Night," by Jamie A Koufman, reprinted by permission of the *New York Times Magazine*, October 25, 2014.

"Dirty Secrets of the Food Processing Industry," by Sally Fallon, reprinted from the *Weston A. Price Foundation*, February 10, 2012, by permission of the author.

"Organic Shmorganic," by Melinda Wenner Moyer, reprinted by permission of *Slate*, January, 28 2014.

"How a National Food Policy Could Save Millions of American Lives," by Mark Bittman, Michael Pollan, Ricardo Salvador, and Olivier De Schutter, reprinted from the *Washington Post*, November 7, 2014 by permission of the author.

"Gap in Diet Quality between Wealthiest and Poorest Americans Doubles, Study Finds," by Tracey McMillan, reprinted by permission of the *National Geographic*, September 2, 2014.

"What It Means to Be Popular (When Everything Is Popular)," by Adam Sternbergh, reprinted by permission from the *New York Times Magazine*.

"Hong Kongs Pop Culture of Protest," by Nury Vittachi, reprinted by permission of the *New York Times Magazine*, October 14, 2014.

"How Magic Conquered Pop Culture," by Lev Grossman, reprinted by permission of *Time, Inc.*, August 19, 2014.

"The Growing Transgender Presence in Pop Culture," reprinted by permission of the *New York Times Magazine*, March 13, 2014.

"Vox Is the Carmelo Anthony of Bad Pop-Culture Metaphors," by Benjamin Freed, reprinted from the *Washingtonian Magazine*, October 10, 2014.

"Television and Children," by Kyla Boyse and Brad Bushman, reprinted from the University of Michigan Health System, August 2010.

"The Effects of Television Violence on Children," by Dale Kunkel, PhD, reprinted from the American Psychological Association, June 26, 2007.

"New Starts on Live Free or Die Survivor and Utopia," by Jon Caramanica, reprinted by permission of the *New York Times Magazine,* November 23, 2014.

"What It Means to Be Popular (When Everything Is Popular)," by Adam Sternbergh, reprinted by permission from the *New York Times Magazine.*

"Marston, Gender Identity and Casting the Modern Wonder Woman," by Noah Berlatsky, reprinted from *Comic Book Resources/Boiling Point,* August 5, 2014.

"America's Game," by Michael Nelson, reprinted by permission of the Claremont Institute, February 7, 2014.

"Some College Athletes Will Now Get Paid—a Little," by Sean Gregory, reprinted by permission of *Time, Inc.,* August 7, 2014.

"People Are Making a Lot of Money in College Sports, Just Not the Athletes," by Tyler Kingkade, reprinted by permission of the *Huffington Post,* April 13, 2014.

"Myth: College Sports Are a Cash Cow," by David Welch Suggs, Jr., Ph.D, reprinted from the *Presidency,* (spring 2012).

"NCAA approaching $1 billion per year amid challenges by players," by Haoyun Se and Mark Alesia, reprinted by permission of the *Indianapolis Star,* March 27, 2014.

"The Economics of College Football: A Look at the Top-25 Teams' Revenues and Expenses," by Alicia Jessop, reprinted by permission of *Forbes,* August 31, 2013.

"NCAA must adapt or move aside," by Christopher L Gasper, reprinted from *The Boston Globe,* April 15, 2014.

"College Sports Aren't Like Slavery. They're Like Jim Crow," by Brando Simeo Starkey, reprinted by permission of the *New Republic,* October 31, 2014.

"What Death Penalty Opponents Don't Get," by James Ridgeway and Jean Casella, reprinted from the *Marshall Project,* November 30, 2014.

"Death by Deadline, Part One," by Ken Armstrong, reprinted from the *Marshall Project,* November 15, 2014.

"Death by Deadline, Part Two," by Ken Armstrong, reprinted from the *Marshall Project,* November 16, 2014.

"The Science of Why Cops Shoot Young Black Men," by Chris Mooney, reprinted by permission of *Mother Jones,* December 1, 2014.

"Criminal Lockup: How Lockup Quotas and 'Low-Crime Taxes' Guarantee Profits for Private Prison Corporations," reprinted from In the *Public Interest,* September 2013.

"The Prison Industry in the United States: Big Business or a New Form of Slavery?" by Vicki Pelaez, reprinted from *Global Research,* March 31, 2014.

"How Lack of Police Training Can Be Deadly for the Mentally Ill," by Aaron Ernst, reprinted form Al Jazeera American Press, April 23, 2014.

"Breaking the School-to-Prison Pipeline: Rethinking 'Zero Tolerance'," by Bryce Wilson Stucki, reprinted from the *American Prospect,* June 10, 2014.

"Race, Disability and the School-to-Prison Pipeline," by Julianne Hing, reprinted from *Color Lines,* May 13, 2014.

"Trial by Fire. Did Texas Execute an Innocent Man?" by David Grann, reprinted from the *New Yorker,* September 7, 2009.

UNIT 1

Education

INTRODUCTION

A little over a hundred years ago, fewer than 10% of Americans had a high school diploma. In 2010, fewer than ten percent of Americans *did not* have a high school diploma. This has to be considered a great success. Yet, the history of the massive spread of education presents us with questions about fairness and concerns about how that education is delivered in the American school system.

Several generations of Americans have seen the connection between increased education and economic advancement. In order to formalize our system of education, public schools were created and schooling became mandatory. Teacher education was formalized, buildings were erected, and curricula were developed. America aimed at educating all of its citizens to be productive members of society. With the advent of the post-industrial economy, a high school diploma now failed to put a middle class life in reach for most Americans. Through the GI Bill, the government sent many soldiers returning home from the Second World War to college. The country reset its goals: everyone should have a college degree.

Yet, as of 2013, just a third of Americans have a college degree. And the effects of our education system's failings are evident. Forty-five million Americans live in poverty. Over two and a half million are behind bars, with almost another five million on probation or parole. We spent a century building up a school system for everyone—why are so many failing to obtain an education?

These readings explore the failings of our education system. Too often, if you are poor, your educational prospects are as well. The struggles of poor students are difficult to quantify, but the results are plain to see. If you are poor, your school looks different than if you are wealthy; your school treats you differently than if you are wealthy; and your diploma is worth less than if you are wealthy.

School for all does not mean equal schooling for all; this especially applies if you are a minority in America. Across parts of the country, schools are looking more and more like they did in the Jim Crow south. The correlation between race and class means that minority-dominated schools are often poor schools. And poor schools too often get poor results for the majority of their students.

Many times, and in many ways, we have attempted to address these failings. Our readings explore some of these avenues, and where they have succeeded. But, too often, legislation like "No Child Left Behind" or "Race to the Top" have failed to bring any meaningful change. Therefore, this unit tries to answer the following two questions: *If America is the land of opportunity, and opportunity is found through education, why are we failing so many of our students? Also what are the factors that are causing America to fail those who strive for an education—and what can be done about it?*

This reader was compiled and composed in Baltimore, Maryland. Here in 2010, four out of ten students dropped out of school before receiving their high school diploma. For Baltimore the answers to those questions are pressing.

SOCIAL CLASS AND THE HIDDEN CURRICULUM OF WORK

by Jean Anyon

Jean Anyon was a Professor of Education Policy in the Graduate Center at the City University of New York. In 2010 she won the lifetime achievement award from the American Education Research Association for her work examining the influences that determine how our educational system functions.

In this 1980 article from the *Journal of Education*, Jean Anyon studies four different types of schools: the *working class school*, the *middle class school*, the *affluent/professional school*, and the *executive elite school*. Each treat their students in different ways, use distinct assignments, grade differently, and have varied expectations and classroom time. Why is this the case?

• • • • • • • • • • • • • • • •

Scholars in political economy and the sociology of knowledge have recently argued that public schools in complex industrial societies like our own make available different types of educational experience and curriculum knowledge to students in different social classes. Bowles and Gintis (1976), for example, have argued that students from different social class backgrounds are rewarded for classroom behaviors that correspond to personality traits allegedly rewarded in the different occupational strata—the working classes for docility and obedience, the managerial classes for initiative and personal assertiveness. Basil Bernstein (1977), Pierre Bourdieu (Bourdieu and Passeron, 1977), and Michael W. Apple (1979), focusing on school knowledge, have argued that knowledge and skills leading to social power and reward (e.g., medical, legal, managerial) are made available to the advantaged social groups but are withheld from the working classes, to whom a more "practical" curriculum is offered (e.g., manual skills, clerical knowledge). While there has been considerable argumentation of these points regarding education in England, France, and North America, there has been little or no attempt to investigate these ideas empirically in elementary or secondary schools and classrooms in this country.[1]

This article offers tentative empirical support (and qualification) of the above arguments by providing illustrative examples of differences in student *work* in classrooms in contrasting social class communities. The examples were gathered as part of an ethnographical study of curricular, pedagogical and pupil evaluation practices in five elementary schools.* The article attempts a theoretical contribution as well, and assesses student work in the light of a theoretical approach to social class analysis. The organization is as follows: the methodology of the ethnographical study is briefly described; a theoretical approach social class is offered; income and other characteristics of the parents in each school are provided, and examples from the study that illustrate work tasks and interaction in each school are presented; then the concepts used to define social class are applied to the examples in

---

*The research was funded by Rutgers University Research Council and will be reported in detail elsewhere.

order to assess the theoretical meaning of classroom events. It will be suggested that there is a "hidden curriculum" in school work that has profound implication for the theory—and consequence—of everyday activity in education.

METHODOLOGY

The methods used to gather data were classroom observation; interviews of students, teachers, principals, and district administrative staff; and assessment of curriculum and other materials in each classroom and school. All classroom events to be discussed here involve the fifth grade in each school. All schools but one departmentalize at the fifth grade level. Except for that school where only one fifth grade teacher could be observed, all the fifth grade teachers (that is, two or three) were observed as the children moved from subject to subject. In all schools the art, music, and gym teachers were also observed and interviewed. All teachers in the study were described as "good" or "excellent" by their principals. All except one new teacher had taught for more than four years. The fifth grade in each school was observed by the investigator for ten three-hour periods between September 15, 1978 and June 20, 1979.

Before providing the occupations, incomes, and other relevant social characteristics of the parents of the children in each school, I will offer a theoretical approach to defining social class.

SOCIAL CLASS

One's occupation and income level contribute significantly to one's social class, but they do not define it. Rather, social class is a series of relationships. A person's social class is defined here by the way that person relates to the process in society by which goods, services, and culture are produced.[2] One relates to several aspects of the production process primarily through one's work. One has a relationship to the system of ownership, to other people (at work and in society) and to the content and process of one's own productive activity. One's relationship to all three of these aspects of production determines one's social class; that is, all three relationships are necessary and none is sufficient for determining a person's relation to the process of production in society.

Ownership Relations. In a capitalist society, a person has a relation to the system of private ownership of capital. Capital is usually thought of as being derived from physical property. In this sense capital is property which is used to produce profit, interest, or rent in sufficient quantity so that the result can be used to produce more profit, interest, or rent that is, more capital. Physical capital may be derived from money, stocks, machines, land, or the labor of workers (whose labor, for instance, may produce products that are sold by others for profit). Capital, however, can also be symbolic. It can be the socially legitimated knowledge of how the production process works, its financial, managerial, technical, or other "secrets." Symbolic capital can also be socially legitimated skills—cognitive (e.g., analytical), linguistic, or technical skills that provide the ability to, say, produce the dominant scientific, artistic, and other culture, or to manage the systems of industrial and cultural production. Skillful application of symbolic capital may yield social and cultural power, and perhaps physical capital as well.

The ownership relation that is definitive for social class is one's relation to physical capital. The first such relationship is that of capitalist. To be a member of the capitalist class in the present-day United States, one must participate in the ownership of the apparatus of production in society. The number of such persons is relatively small: while one person in tens owns some stock, for example, a mere 1.6 percent of the population owns 82.2 percent of *all* stock, and the wealthiest one-fifth owns almost all the rest (see New York Stock Exchange, 1975; Smith and Franklin, 1974; Lampman, 1962).

At the opposite pole of this relationship is the worker. To be in the United States working class a person will not ordinarily own physical capital; to the contrary, his or her work will be wage or salaried labor that is either a *source* of profit (i.e., capital) to others, or that makes it possible for others to *realize* profit. Examples of the latter are white-collar clerical workers in industry and distribution (office and sales) as well as wage and salaried workers in the institutions of social and economic legitimation and service (e.g., in state education and welfare institutions).[3] According to the criteria to be developed here, the number of persons who presently comprise the working class in the United States is between 50 percent and 60 percent of the population (see also Wright, 1978; Braverman, 1974; Levison, 1974).

In between the defining relationship of capitalist and worker are the middle classes, whose relationship to the process of production is less clear, and whose relationship may indeed exhibit contradictory characteristics. For example, social service employees have a somewhat contradictory relationship to the process of production because, although their income may be at middle-class levels, some characteristics of their work are working-class (e.g., they may have very little control over their work). Analogously, there are persons at the upper income end of the middle class, such as upper-middle-class professionals, who may own quantities of stocks and will therefore share characteristics of the capitalist class. As the next criterion to be discussed makes clear, however, to be a member of the present-day capitalist in the United States, one must also participate in the social *control* of this capital.

Relationships Between People. The second relationship which contributes to one's social class is the relation one has to authority and control at work and in society.[4] One characteristic of most working-class jobs is that there is no built-in mechanism by which the worker can control the content, process, or speed of work. Legitimate decision making is vested in personnel supervisors, in middle or upper management, or, as in an increasing number of white-collar working-class (and most middle-class) jobs, by bureaucratic rule and regulation. For upper-middle-class professional groups there is an increased amount of autonomy regarding work. Moreover, in middle- and upper-middle-class positions there is an increasing chance that one's work will also involve supervising the work of others. A capitalist is defined within these relations of control in an enterprise by having a position which participates in the direct control of the entire enterprise. Capitalists do not directly control workers in physical production and do not directly control ideas in the sphere of cultural production. However, more crucial to control, capitalists make the decisions over how resources are used (e.g., where money is invested) and how profit is allocated.

Relations Between People and Their Work. The third criterion which contributes to a person's social class is the relationship between that person and his or her own productive activity—the type of activity that constitutes his or her work. A working-class job is often characterized by work that is routine and mechanical and that is a small, fragmented part of a larger process with which workers are not usually acquainted. These working-class jobs are usually blue-collar, manual labor. A few skilled jobs such as plumbing and printing are not mechanical, however, and an increasing number of working-class jobs are *white*-collar. These white-collar jobs, such as clerical work, may involve work that necessitates a measure of planning and decision making, but one still has no built-in control over the content. The work of some middle- and most upper-middle-class managerial and professional groups is likely to involve the need for conceptualization and creativity, with many professional jobs demanding one's full creative capacities. Finally, the work that characterizes the capitalist position is that this work is almost entirely a matter of conceptualization (e.g., planning and laying-out) that has as its object management and control of the enterprise.

One's social class, then, is a result of the relationships one has, largely through one's work, to physical capital and its power, to other people at work and in society, and to one's own productive activity. Social class is a lived, developing process. It is not an abstract category, and it is not a fixed, inherited position (although one's family background is, of course, important). Social class is perceived as a complex of social relations that one develops as one grows up—as one acquires and develops certain bodies of knowledge, skills, abilities, and traits, and as one has contact and opportunity in the world.[5] In sum, social class describes relationships which we as adults have developed, may attempt to maintain and in which we participate every working day. These relationships in a real sense define our material ties to the world. An important concern here is whether these relationships are developing in children in schools within particular social class contexts.

THE SAMPLE OF SCHOOLS

With the above discussion as a theoretical backdrop, the social class designation of each of the five schools will be identified, and the income, occupation, and other relevant available social characteristics of the student and their parents will be described. The first three schools are in a medium-sized city district in northern New Jersey, and the other two are in a nearby New Jersey suburb.

The first two schools I will call *Working-class Schools.* Most of the parents have blue-collar jobs. Less than a third of the fathers are skilled the majority are in unskilled or semiskilled jobs. During the period of the study (1978–1979) approximately 15 percent of the fathers were unemployed. The large majority (85 percent) of the families are white. The following occupations are typical: platform, storeroom, and stockroom workers; foundrymen, pipe welders, and boilermakers; semiskilled and unskilled assembly-line operatives; gas station attendants, auto mechanics, maintenance workers, and security guards. Less than 30 percent of the women work, some part-time and some full-time, on assembly lines, in storerooms and stockrooms, as waitresses, barmaids, or sales clerks. Of the fifth grade parents, none of the wives of the skilled workers had jobs. Approximately 15 percent of the families in each school are at or below the federal "poverty" level;[6] most of the rest of the family incomes at or below $12,000, except some of the skilled workers whose in are higher. The incomes of the majority of the families in these two schools (i.e., at or below $12,000) are typical of 38.6 percent of the families in the United States (U.S. Bureau of the Census, 1979, p. 2, table A).

The third school is called the *Middle-class School,* although because of neighborhood residence patterns, the population is a mixture of several social classes. The parents' occupations can be divided into three groups: a small group of blue-collar "rich," who are skilled, well-paid workers such as printers, carpenters, plumbers, and construction workers. The second group is composed of parents in working-class and middle-class white-collar jobs: women in office jobs, technicians, supervisors in industry, and parents employed by the city (such as firemen, policemen, and several of the school's teachers). The third group is composed of occupations such as personnel directors in local firms, accountants, "middle management," and a few small capitalists (owners of shops in the area). The children of several local doctors attend this school. Most family incomes are between $13,000 and $25,000 with a few higher. This income range is typical of 38.9 percent of the families in the United States (U.S. Bureau of the Census, 1979, p. 2, table A).

The fourth school has a parent population that is at the upper income level of the upper middle class, and is predominantly professional. This school will be called the *Affluent Professional School.* Typical jobs are: cardiologist, interior designer, corporate lawyer or engineer, executive in advertising or television. There are some families who are not as affluent as the majority (e.g., the family of the superintendent of the district's schools, and the one or two families in which the fathers are skilled workers). In addition, a few of the families are more affluent than the majority, and can be classified in the capitalist class (e.g., a partner in a prestigious Wall Street stock brokerage firm). Approximately 90 percent of the children in this school are white. Most family incomes are between $40,000 and $80,000. This income span represents approximately 7 percent of the families in the United States.

In the fifth school the majority of the families belong to the capitalist class. This school will be called the *Executive Elite School* because most of the fathers are top executives (e.g., presidents and vice presidents) in major U.S.-based multinational corporations—for example, ATT, RCA, City Bank, American Express, U.S. Steel. A sizable group of fathers are top executives in financial firms on Wall Street. There are also a number of fathers who list their occupations as "general counsel" to a particular corporation, and these corporations are also among the large multinationals. Many of the mothers do volunteer work in the Junior League, Junior Fortnightly, or other service groups; some are intricately involved in town politics; and some are themselves in well-paid occupations. There are no minority children in the school. Almost all family incomes are over $100,000 with some in the $500,000 range. The incomes in this school represent less than 1 percent of the families in the United States (see Smith and Franklin, 1974).

Since each of the five schools is only one instance of elementary education in a particular social class context, I will not generalize beyond the sample. However, the examples of school work which follow will characteristics of education in each social setting that appear to have theoretical and social significance and to be worth investigation in a larger number of schools.

SOCIAL CLASS AND SCHOOL WORK

There are obvious similarities among United States schools and classrooms. There are school and classroom rules, teachers who ask questions and attempt to exercise control and who give work and homework. There are textbooks and tests. All of these were found in the five schools. Indeed, there were other curricular similarities as well: all schools and fifth grades used the same math book and series (*Mathematics Around Us,* Scott Foresman, 1978); all fifth grades had a least one boxed set of an individualized reading program available in the room (although the variety and amounts of teaching materials in the classrooms increased as the social class of the school population increased); and, all fifth grade language arts curricula included aspects of grammar, punctuation and capitalization.[7]

This section provides examples of work and work-related activities in each school that bear on the categories used to define social class. Thus, examples will be provided concerning students' relation to capital (e.g., as manifest in any symbolic capital that might be acquired through school work); students' relation to persons and types of authority regarding school work; and students' relation to their own productive activity. The section first offers the investigator's interpretation of what school work *is* for children in each setting, and then presents events and interactions that illustrate that assessment.

The Working-class Schools. In the two working-class schools, work is following the steps of a procedure. The procedure is usually mechanical, involving rote behavior and very little decision making or choice. The teachers rarely explain why the work is being assigned, how it might connect to other assignments, or what the idea is that lies behind the procedure or gives it coherence and perhaps meaning or significance. Available textbooks are not always used, and the teachers often prepare their own dittos or put work examples on the board. Most of the rules regarding work are designations of what the children are to do; the rules are steps to follow. These steps are told to the children by the teachers and often written on the board. The children are usually told to copy the steps as notes. These notes are to be studied. Work is often evaluated not according to whether it is right or wrong, but according to whether the children followed the right steps.

The following examples illustrate these points. In math, when two-digit division was introduced, the teacher in one school gave a four-minute lecture on what the terms are called (i.e., which number is the divisor, dividend, quotient, and remainder). The children were told to copy these names in their notebooks. Then the teacher told them the steps to follow to do the problems, saying, "This is how you do them." The teacher listed the steps on the board, and they appeared several days later as a chart hung in the middle of the front wall: "Divide; Multiply; Subtract; Bring Down." The children often did examples of two-digit division. When the teacher went over the examples with them, he told them for each problem what the procedure was, rarely asking them to conceptualize or explain it themselves: "3 into 22 is 7; do your subtraction and one is left over." During the week that two-digit division was introduced (or at any other time), the investigator did not observe any discussion of the idea of grouping involved in division, any use of manipulables, or any attempt to relate two-digit division to any other mathematical process. Nor was there any attempt to relate the steps to an actual or possible thought process of the children. The observer did not hear the terms dividend, quotient, etc., used again. The math teacher in the other working-class school followed similar procedures regarding two-digit division, and at one point her class seemed confused. She said, "You're confusing yourselves. You're tensing up. Remember, when you do this it's the same steps over and over again—and that's the way division always is." Several weeks later, after a test, a group of her children "still didn't get it," and she made no attempt to explain the concept dividing things into groups, or to give them manipulables for their own investigation. Rather, she went over the steps with them again and told them that they "needed more practice."

In other areas of math, work is also carrying out often unexplained, fragmented procedures. For example, one of the teachers led the children through a series of steps to make a one-inch grid on their paper *without* telling them that they were making a one-inch grid, or that it would be used to study scale. She said, "Take your ruler. Put it across the top. Make a mark at every number. Then move your ruler down to the bottom. No, put it across the bottom. Now make a mark on top of every number. Now draw a line from . . ." At this point a girl said that she had a faster way to do it and the teacher said, "No, you don't; you don't even know what I'm making yet. Do it this way, or it's wrong." After they had made the lines up and down and across, the teacher told them she wanted them to make a figure by connecting some dots and to measure that, using the scale of one inch equals one mile. Then they were to cut it out. She said, "Don't cut until I check it."

In both working-class schools, work in language arts is mechanics of punctuation (commas, periods, question marks, exclamation points), capitalization, and the four kinds of sentences. One teacher explained to me, "Simple punctuation is all they'll ever use." Regarding punctuation, either a teacher or a ditto stated the rules for where, for example, to put commas. The investigator heard no classroom discussion of the aural context of punctuation (which, of course, is what gives each mark its meaning). Nor did the investigator hear any statement or inference that placing a punctuation mark could be a decision-making process, depending, for example, on one's intended meaning. Rather, the children were told to follow the rules. Language arts did not involve creative writing. There were several writing assignments throughout the year, but in each instance the children were given a ditto, and they wrote answers to questions on the sheet. For example, they wrote their "autobiography" by answering such questions as "Where were you born?" "What is your favorite animal?" on a sheet entitled, "All About Me."

In one of the working-class schools the class had a science period several times a week. On the three occasions observed, the children were not called upon to set up experiments or to give explanations for facts or concepts. Rather, on each occasion the teacher told them in his owns words what the book said. The children copied the teacher's sentences from the board. Each day that preceded the day they were to do a science experiment, the teacher told them to copy the directions from the book for the procedure they would carry out the next day, and to study the list at home that night. The day after each experiment, the teacher went over what they had "found" (they did the experiments as a class, and each was actually a class demonstration led by the teacher). Then the teacher wrote what they "found" on the board, and the children copied that in their notebooks. Once or twice a year there are science projects. The project is chosen and assigned by the teacher from a box of three-by-five-inch cards. On the card the teacher has written the question to be answered, books to use, and how much to write. Explaining the cards to the observer, the teacher said, "It tells them exactly what to do, or they couldn't do it."

Social studies in the working-class schools is also largely mechanical, rote work that was given little explanation or connection to larger contexts. In one school, for example, although there was a book available, social studies work was to copy the teacher's notes from the board. Several times a week for a period of several months, the children copied these notes. The fifth grades in the district were to study U.S. history. The teacher used a booklet she had purchased called "The Fabulous Fifty States." Each day she put information from the booklet in outline form on the board and the children copied it. The type of information did not vary: the name of the state, its abbreviation, state capital, nickname of the state, its main products, main business, and a "Fabulous Fact" (e.g., "Idaho grew 27 billion potatoes in one year. That's enough potatoes for each man, woman and . . ."). As the children finished copying the sentences, the teacher erased them and wrote more. Children would occasionally go to the front to pull down the wall map in order to locate the states they were copying, and the teacher did not dissuade them. But the observer never saw her refer to the map; nor did the observer ever hear her make other than perfunctory remarks concerning the information the children were copying. Occasionally the children colored in a ditto and cut it out to make a stand-up figure (representing, for example, a man roping a cow in the Southwest). These were referred to by the teacher as their social studies "projects."

Rote behavior was often called for in classroom oral work. When going over math and language arts skills sheets, for example, as the teacher asked for the answer to each problem, he fired the questions rapidly, staccato, and the scene reminded the observer of a sergeant drilling recruits: above all, the questions demanded that you stay at attention: "The next one? What do I put here? . . . Here? Give us the next." Or "How many commas in this sentence? Where do I put them . . . The next one?"

The (four) fifth grade teachers observed in the working-class schools attempted to control classroom time and space by making decisions without consulting the children and without explaining the basis for their decisions. The teacher's control thus often seemed capricious. Teachers for instance, very often ignored the bells to switch classes—deciding among themselves to keep the children after the period was officially over, to continue with the work, or for disciplinary reasons, or so they (the teachers) could stand in the hall and talk. There were no clocks in the rooms in either school, and the children often asked, "What period is this?" "When do we go to gym?" The children had no access to materials. These were handed out by teachers and closely guarded. Things in the room "belonged" to the teacher: "Bob, bring me my garbage can." The teachers continually gave the children orders. Only three times did the investigator hear a teacher in either working-class school preface a directive with an unsarcastic "please," or "let's" or "would you." Instead the teachers said, "Shut up," "Shut your mouth," "Open your book," "Throw your *gum* away—if you want to rot your teeth, do it on your *own* time." Teachers made every effort to control the movement of the children, and often shouted, "Why are you out of your *seat*??!!" If the children got permission to leave the room they had to take a written pass with the date and time.

The control that the teachers have is less than they would like. It is a result of constant struggle with the children. The children continually resist the teachers' orders and the work itself. They do not directly challenge the teachers' authority or legitimacy, but they make indirect tempts to sabotage and resist the flow of assignments:

TEACHER:	I will put some problems on the board. You are to divide.
CHILD:	We got to divide?
TEACHER:	Yes.
SEVERAL CHILDREN:	(Groan) Not again. Mr. B, we done this yesterday.
CHILD:	Do we put the date?
TEACHER:	Yes. I hope we remember we work in silence. You're supposed to do it on white paper. I'll explain it later.
CHILD:	Somebody broke my pencil. (Crash—a child falls out of his chair.)
CHILD:	(repeats) Mr. B., somebody broke my *pencil!*
CHILD:	Are we going to be here all morning?

(TEACHER COMES TO THE OBSERVER, SHAKES HIS HEAD AND GRIMACES, THEN SMILES.)

The children are successful enough in their struggle against work that there are long periods where they are not asked to *do* any work, but just to sit and be quiet.[8] Very often the work that the teachers assign is "easy," that is, not demanding, and thus receives less resistance. Sometimes a compromise is reached where, although the teachers insist that the children continue to work, there is a constant murmur of talk. The children will be doing arithmetic examples, copying social studies notes, or doing other dittos, and all the while there is muted but spirited conversation—about somebody's broken arm, an afterschool disturbance the day before, etc. Sometimes the teachers themselves join in the conversation because, as one teacher explained to me, "It's a relief from the routine."

Middle-class School. In the middle-class school, work is getting the answer. If one accumulates enough right answers one gets a good grade. One must follow the directions in order to get the right answers, but the directions often call for some figuring, some choice, some decision making. For example, the children must often figure out by themselves what the directions ask them to do, and how to get the answer: what do you do first, second, and perhaps third? Answers are usually found in books or by listening to the teacher. Answers are usually words, sentences, numbers, or facts and dates; one writes them on paper, and one should be neat. Answers must be in the right order, and one can not make them up.

The following activities are illustrative. Math involves some choice: one may do two-digit division the long way, or the short way, and there are some math problems that can be done "in your head." When the teacher explains how to do two-digit division, there is recognition that a cognitive process is involved; she gives several ways, and says, "I want to sure you understand what you're doing—so you get it right"; and, when they go over the homework, she asks the *children* to tell how they did the problem and what answer they got.

In social studies the daily work is to read the assigned pages in the textbook and to answer the teacher's questions. The questions are almost always designed to check on whether the students have read the assignment and understood it: who did so-and-so; what happened after that; when did it happen, where, and sometimes, why did it happen? The answers are in the book and in one's understanding of the book; the teacher's hints when one doesn't know the answer are to "read it again," or to look at the picture or at the rest of the paragraph. One is to search for the answer in the "context," in what is given.

Language arts is "simple grammar, what they need for everyday life." The language arts teacher says, "They should learn to speak properly, to write business letters and thank-you letters, and to understand what nouns and verbs and simple subjects are." Here, as well, the actual work is to choose the right answers, to understand what is given. The teacher often says, "Please read the next sentence and then I'll question you about it." One teacher said in some exasperation to a boy who was fooling around in class, "If you don't know the answers to the questions I ask, then you can't stay in this *class!* (pause) You *never* know answers to the questions I ask, and it's not fair to me—and certainly not to you!"

Most lessons are based on the textbook. This does not involve a critical perspective on what is given there. For example, a critical perspective in social studies is perceived as dangerous by these teachers because it may lead to controversial topics; the parents might complain. The children, however, are often curious, especially in social studies. Their questions are tolerated, and usually answered perfunctorily. But after a few minutes the teacher will say, "All right, we're not going any farther. Please open your social studies workbook." While the teachers spend a lot of time explaining and expanding on what the textbooks say, there is little attempt to analyze how or why things happen, or to give thought to how pieces of a culture, or, say, a system of numbers or elements of a language fit together or can be analyzed. What has happened in the past, and what exists now may not be equitable or fair, but (shrug) that is way things are, and one does not confront such matters in school. For example, in social studies after a child is called on to read a passage about the pilgrims, the teacher summarizes the paragraph and then says, "So you can see how strict they were about everything." A child asks "Why?" "Well, because they felt that if you weren't busy you'd get into trouble." Another child asks, "Is it true that they burned women at the stake?" The teacher says, "Yes, if a woman did anything strange, they hanged them. [sic] What would a woman do, do you think, to make them burn them? [sic] See if you can come up with better answers than my other [social studies] class." Several children offer suggestions, to which the teacher nods but does not comment. Then she says, "OK, good," and calls on the next child to read.

Work tasks do not usually request creativity. Serious attention is rarely given in school work to *how* the children develop or express their own feelings and ideas, either linguistically or in graphic form. On the occasions when creativity or self-expression is requested, it is peripheral to the main activity, or it is "enrichment," or "for fun." During a lesson on what similes are, for example, the teacher explains what they are, puts several on the board, gives some other examples herself, and then asks the children if they can "make some up." She calls on three children who give similes, two of which are actually in the book they have open before them. The teacher does not comment on this, and then asks several others to choose similes from the list of phrases in the book. Several do so correctly, and she says, "Oh *good!* You're picking them out! See how *good* we are?" Their homework is to pick out the rest of the similes from the list.

Creativity is not often requested in social studies and science projects, either. Social studies projects, for example are given with directions to "find information on your topic," and write it up. The children are not supposed to copy, but to "put it in your own words." Although a number of the projects subsequently went beyond the teacher's direction to find information and had quite expressive covers and inside illustrations, the teacher's evaluative comments had to do with the amount of information, whether they had "copied," and if their work was neat.

The style of control of the three fifth grade teachers observed in this school varied from somewhat easygoing to strict, but in contrast to the working-class schools, the teachers' decisions were usually based on external rules and regulations, for example, on criteria that were known or available to the children. Thus, the teachers always honor the bells for changing classes, and they usually evaluate children's work by what is in the textbooks and answer booklets.

There is little excitement in school work for the children and the assignments are perceived as having little to do with their interests and feelings. As one child said, what you do is "store facts in your head like cold storage—until you need it later for a test, or your job." Thus, doing well is important because there are thought to be *other* likely rewards: a good job, or college.[9]

Affluent Professional School. In the affluent professional school, work is creative activity carried out independently. The students are continually asked to express and apply ideas and concepts. Work involves individual thought and expressiveness, expansion and illustration of ideas, and choice of appropriate method and material. (The class is not considered an open classroom, and the principal explained that because of large number of discipline problems in the fifth grade this year they did not departmentalize. The teacher who agreed to take part in the study said she is "more structured" this year than she usually is.) The products of work in this class are often written stories, editorials and essays, or representations of ideas in mural, graph, or craft form. The products of work should not be like everybody else's and should show individuality. They should exhibit good design, and (this is important), they must also fit empirical reality. Moreover, one's work should attempt to interpret or "make sense" of reality. The relatively few rules to be followed regarding work are usually criteria for, or limits on, individual activity. One's product is usually evaluated for the quality of its expression and for the appropriateness of its conception to the task. In many cases one's own satisfaction with the product is an important criterion for its evaluation. When right answers are called for, as in commercial materials like SRA (Science Research Associates) and math, it is important that the children decide on an answer as a result of thinking about the idea involved in what they're being asked to do. Teacher's hints are to "think about it some more."

The following activities are illustrative. The class takes home a sheet requesting each child's parents to fill in the number of cars they have, the number of television sets, refrigerators, games, or rooms in the house, etc. Each child is to figure the average number of a type of possession owned by the fifth grade. Each child must compile the "data" from all the sheets. A calculator is available in the classroom to do the mechanics of finding the average. Some children decide to send sheets to the fourth grade families for comparison. Their work should be "verified" by a classmate before it is handed in.

Each child and his or her family has made a geoboard. The teacher asks the class to get their geoboards from the side cabinet, to take a handful of rubber bands, and then to listen to what she would like them to do. She says, "I would like you to design a figure and then find the perimeter and area. When you have it, check with your neighbor. After you've done that, please transfer it to graph paper and tomorrow I'll ask you to make up a question about it for someone. When you hand it in, please let know whose it is, and who verified it. Then I have something else for you to do that's really fun. (pause) Find the average number of chocolate chips in three cookies. I'll give you three cookies, and you'll have to *eat* your way through, I'm afraid!" Then she goes around the room and gives suggestions, praise, and admonitions that they are getting noisy. They work sitting, or standing up at their desks, at benches in the back, or on the floor. A child hands the teacher his paper and she comments, "I'm not accepting this paper. Do a better design." To another child she says, "That's fantastic! But you'll never find the area. Why don't you draw a figure inside [the big one] and subtract to get the area?"

The school district requires the fifth grades to study ancient civilizations (in particular, Egypt, Athens, and Sumer). In this classroom, the emphasis is on illustrating and re-creating the culture of the people of ancient times. The following are typical activities: The children made an 8mm film on Egypt, which one of the parents edited. A girl in the class wrote the script, and the class acted it out. They put the sound on themselves. They read stories of those days. They wrote essays and stories depicting the lives of the people and the societal and occupational divisions. They chose from a list of projects, all of which involved graphic representations of ideas: for example, "Make a mural depicting the division of labor in Egyptian society."

Each child wrote and exchanged a letter in hieroglyphics with a fifth grade in another class, and they also exchanged stories they wrote in cuneiform. They made a scroll and singed the edges so it looked authentic. They each chose an occupation and made an Egyptian plaque representing that occupation, simulating the appropriate Egyptian design. They carved their design on a cylinder of wax, pressed the wax into clay, and then baked the clay. Although one girl did not choose an occupation, but carved instead of series of gods and slaves, the teacher, said "That's all right, Amber, it's beautiful." As they were working the teacher said, "Don't cut into your clay until you're satisfied with your design."

Social studies also involves almost daily presentation by the children of some event from the news. The teacher's questions ask the children to expand what they say, to give more details, and to be more specific. Occasionally she adds some remarks to help them see connections between events.

The emphasis on expressing and illustrating ideas in social studies is accompanied in language arts by an emphasis on creative writing. Each child wrote a rhebus story for a first grader whom they had interviewed to see what kind of story the child liked best. They wrote editorials on pending decisions by the school board, and radio plays, some of which were read over the school intercom from the office, and one of which was performed in the auditorium. There is no language arts textbook because, the teacher said, "The principal wants us to be creative." There is not much grammar, but there is punctuation. One morning when the observer arrived the class was doing a punctuation ditto. The teacher later apologized for using the ditto. "It's just for review," she said. "I don't teach punctuation that way. We use their language." The ditto had three unambiguous rules for where to put commas in a sentence. As the teacher was going around to help the children with the ditto, she repeated several times, "Where you put commas depends on how you say the sentence; it depends on the situation and what you want to say." Several weeks later the observer saw another punctuation activity. The teacher had printed a five-paragraph story on an oak tag and then cut it into phrases. She read whole story to the class from the book, then passed out the phrases. The group had to decide how the phrases could best be put together again. (They arranged the phrases on the floor.) The point was not to replicate the story, although that was not irrelevant, but to "decide what you think the best way is." Punctuation marks on cardboard pieces were then handed out and the children discussed, and then decided, what mark was best at each place they thought one was needed. At the end of each paragraph the teacher asked, "Are you satisfied with the way the paragraphs are now? Read it to yourself and see how it sounds." Then she read the original story again, and they compared to two.

Describing her goals in science to the investigator, the teacher said, "We use ESS (Elementary Science Study). It's very good because it gives a hands-on experience—so they can make *sense* out of it. It doesn't matter whether it [what they find] is right or wrong. I bring them together and there's value in discussing their ideas."

The products of work in this class are often highly valued by the children and the teacher. In fact, this was the only school in which the investigator was not allowed to take original pieces of the children's work for her files. If the work was small enough, however, and was on paper, the investigator could duplicate it on the copying machine in the office.

The teacher's attempt to control the class involves constant negotiation. She does not give direct orders unless she is angry because the children have been too noisy. Normally, she tries to get them to foresee the consequences of their actions and to decide accordingly. For example, lining them up to go see a play written by the sixth graders, she says, "I presume you're lined up by someone with whom you want to sit. I hope you're lined up by someone you won't get in trouble with." The following two dialogues illustrate the process of negotiation between student and teacher.

TEACHER: Tom, you're behind in your SRA this marking period.

TOM: So what!

TEACHER: Well, last time you had a hard time catching up.

TOM: But I have my [music] lesson at 10:00.

TEACHER: Well, that doesn't mean you're going to sit here for twenty minutes.

TOM: Twenty minutes! OK. (He goes to pick out a SRA booklet and chooses one, puts it back, then takes another, and brings it to her.)

TEACHER: OK, this is the one you want, right?

TOM: Yes.

TEACHER: OK. I'll put tomorrow's date on it so you can take it home tonight or finish it tomorrow if you want.

■ ■ ■ ■ ■

TEACHER: To a child who is wandering around during reading) Kevin why don't you do *Reading for Concepts*?

KEVIN: No, I don't like *Reading for Concepts.*

TEACHER: Well, what are you going to do?

KEVIN: (pause) I'm going to work on my DAR. (The DAR had sponsored an essay competition on "Life in the American Colonies.")

One of the few rules governing the children's movement is that no more than three children may be out of the room at once. There is a school rule that anyone can go to the library at any time to get a book. In the fifth grade I observed, they sign their name on the chalkboard and leave. There are no passes. Finally, the children have a fair amount of officially sanctioned say over what happens in the class. For example, they often negotiate what work is to be done. If the teacher wants to move on to the next subject, but the children say they are not ready, they want to work on their present projects some more, she very often lets them do it.

Executive Elite School. In the executive elite school, work is developing one's analytical intellectual powers. Children are continually asked to reason through a problem, to produce intellectual products that are both logically sound and of top academic quality. A primary goal of thought is to conceptualize rules by which elements may fit together in systems, and then to apply these rules in solving a problem. School work helps one to achieve, to excel, to prepare for life.

The following are illustrative. The math teacher teaches area and perimeter by having the children derive formulae for each. First, she helps them, through discussion at the board, to arrive at $A = W \times L$ as a formula (not *the* formula) for area. After discussing several, she says, "Can anyone make up a formula for perimeter? Can you figure that out yourselves? (pause) Knowing what we know, can we think of a formula?" She works out three children's suggestions at the board, saying to two, "Yes, that's a good one," and then asks the class if they can think of any more. No one volunteers. To prod them, she says, "If you use rules and good reasoning, you get many ways. Chris, can you think up a formula?"

She discusses two-digit division with the children as a decision-making process. Presenting a new type of problem to them, she asks, "What's the *first* decision you'd make if presented with this kind of example? What is the first thing you'd *think*? Craig?" Craig says "To find my first partial quotient." She responds, "Yes, that would be your first decision. How would you do that?" Craig explains, and then the teacher says, "OK, we'll see how that works for you." The class tries his way. Subsequently, she comments on the merits and shortcomings of several other children's decisions. Later, she tells the investigator that her goals in math are to develop their reasoning and mathematical thinking and that, unfortunately, "there's no *time* for manipulables."

While right answers are important in math, they are not "given" by the book or by the teacher, but may be challenged by the children. Going over some problems in late September the teacher says, "Raise your hand if you do not agree." A child says, "I don't agree with 64." The teacher responds, "OK, there's a question about 64. (to class) Please check it. Owen, they're disagreeing with you. Kristen, they're checking yours." The teacher emphasized this repeatedly during September and October with statements like, "Don't be afraid to say if you disagree. In the last [math] class, somebody disagreed, and they were right. Before you disagree, check yours, and if you still think we're wrong, then we'll check it out. By Thanksgiving, the children did not often speak in terms of right and wrong math problems, but of whether they agreed with the answer that had been given.

There are complicated math mimeos with many word problems. Whenever they go over the examples, they discuss how each child has set up the problem. The children must explain it precisely. On one occasion the teacher said, "I'm more—just as interested in *how* you set up the problem as in what answer you find. If you set up a problem in a good way, the answer is *easy* to find."

Social studies work is most often reading and discussion of concepts and independent research. There are only occasional artistic, expressive, or illustrative projects. Ancient Athens and Sumer are, rather, societies to analyze. The following questions are typical of those which guide the children's independent research: "What mistakes did Pericles make after the war?" "What mistakes did the citizens of Athens make?" "What are the elements of a civilization?" "How did Greece build an economic empire?" "Compare the way Athens chose its leaders with the way we choose ours." Occasionally the children are asked to make up sample questions for their social studies tests. On an occasion when the investigator was present the social studies teacher rejected a child's question by saying, "That's just fact. If I asked you that question on a test, you'd complain it was just memory! Good questions ask for concepts."

In social studies—but also in reading, science, and health—the teachers initiate classroom discussions of current social issues and problems. These discussions occurred on every one of the investigator's visits, and a teacher told me, "These children's opinions are important—it's important that they learn to reason things through." The classroom discussions always struck the observer as quite realistic and analytical, dealing with concrete social issues like the following: "Why do workers strike?" "Is that right or wrong?" "Why do we have inflation, and what can be done to stop it?" "Why do companies put chemicals in food when the natural ingredients are available?" etc. Usually the children did not have to be prodded to give their opinions. In fact, their statements and the interchanges between them struck the observer as quite sophisticated conceptually and verbally, and well-informed. Occasionally the teachers would prod with statements such as, "Even if you don't know [the answers], if you think logically about it, you can figure it out." And "I'm asking you [these] questions to help you think this through."

Language arts emphasizes language as a complex system, one that should be mastered. The children are asked to diagram sentences of complex grammatical construction, to memorize irregular verb conjugations [he lay, he has lain, etc. . . .), and to use the proper participles, conjunctions, and interjections, in their speech. The teacher (the same one who teaches social studies) told them, "It is not enough to get these right on tests; you must use what you learn [in grammar classes] in your written and oral work. I will grade you on that."

Most writing assignments are either research reports and essays for social studies, or experiment analyses and write-ups for science. There is only an occasional story or other "creative writing" assignment. On the occasion observed by the investigator (the writing of a Halloween story), the points the teacher stressed in preparing the children to write involved the structural aspects of a story rather than the expression of feelings or other ideas. The teacher showed them a filmstrip, "The Seven Parts of a Story," and lectured them on plot development, mood setting, character development, consistency, and the use of a logical or appropriate ending. The stories they subsequently wrote were, in fact, well-structured, but many were also personal and expressive. The teacher's evaluative comments, however, did not refer to the expressiveness or artistry, but were all directed toward whether they had "developed" the story well.

Language arts work also involved a large amount of practice in presentation of the self and in managing situations where the child was expected to be in charge. For example, there was a series of assignments in which each child had to be a "student teacher." The child had to plan a lesson in grammar, outlining, punctuation, or other language arts topics and explain the concept to the class. Each child was to prepare a worksheet or game and a homework assignment as well. After each presentation, the teacher and other children gave a critical appraisal of the "student teacher's" performance. Their criteria were: whether the student spoke clearly; whether the lesson was interesting; whether the student made any mistakes; and whether he or she kept control of the class. On an occasion when a child did not maintain control, the teacher said, "When you're up there, you have authority, and you have to use it. I'll back you up."

The teacher of math and science explained to the observer that she likes the ESS program because "the children can manipulate variables. They generate hypotheses and devise experiments to solve the problem. Then they have to explain what they found."

The executive elite school is the only school where bells do not demarcate the periods of time. The two fifth grade teachers were very strict about changing classes on schedule, however, as specific plans for each session had been made. The teachers attempted to keep tight control over the children during lessons, and the children were sometimes flippant, boisterous, and occasionally rude. However, the children may be brought into line by reminding them that "it is up to you." "You must control yourself," "you are responsible for your work," you must "set your priorities." One teacher told a child, "You are the only driver of your car—and only you can regulate your speed." A new teacher complained to the observer that she had thought "these children" would have more control.

While strict attention to the lesson at hand is required, the teachers make relatively little attempt to regulate the movement of the children at other times. For example, except for the kindergartners, the children in this school do not have to wait for the bell to ring in the morning; they may go to their classroom when they arrive at school. Fifth graders often came early to read, to finish work, or to catch up. After the first two months of school the fifth grade teachers did not line the children up to change classes or to go to gym, etc., but, when the children were ready and quiet, they were told they could go—sometimes without the teachers.

In the classroom, the children could get materials when they needed them and took what they needed from closets and from the teacher's desk. They were in charge of the office at lunchtime. During class they did not have to sign out or ask permission to leave the room; they just got up and left. Because of the pressure to get work done, however, they did not leave the room very often. The teachers were very polite to the children, and the investigator heard no sarcasm, no nasty remarks, and few direct orders. The teachers never called the children "honey," or "dear," but always called them by name. The teachers were expected to be available before school, after school, and for part of their lunch time to provide extra help if needed.

DISCUSSION AND CONCLUSION

One could attempt to identify physical, educational, cultural, and interpersonal characteristics of the environment of each school that might contribute to an empirical explanation of the events and interactions. For example, the investigator could introduce evidence to show that the following *increased* as the social class of the community increased (with the most marked differences occurring between the two districts): increased variety and abundance of teaching materials in the classroom; increased time reported spent by the teachers on preparation; higher social class background and more prestigious educational institutions attended by teachers and administrators; more stringent board of education requirements regarding teaching methods; more frequent and demanding administrative evaluation of teachers; increased teacher support services such as in-service workshops; increased parent expenditure for school equipment over and above district or government funding; higher expectations of student ability on the part of parents, teachers, and administrators; higher expectations and demands regarding student achievement on the part of teachers, parents, and administrators; more positive attitudes on the part of the teachers as to the probable occupational futures of the children; an increase in the children's acceptance of classroom assignments; increased intersubjectivity between students and teachers; and increased cultural congruence between school and community.

All of these—and other—factors may contribute to the character and scope of classroom events. However, what is of primary concern here is not the immediate causes of classroom activity (although these are in themselves quite important). Rather, the concern is to reflect on the deeper social meaning, the wider theoretical significance, of what happens in each social setting. In an attempt to assess the theoretical meaning of the differences among the schools, the work tasks and milieu in each will be discussed in light of the concepts used to define social class.

What potential relationships to the system of ownership of symbolic and physical capital, to authority and control, and to their own productive activity are being developed in children in each school? What economically relevant knowledge, skills, and predispositions are being transmitted in each classroom, and for what future relationship to the system of production are they appropriate? It is of course true that a student's future relationship to the process of production in society is determined by the combined effects of circumstances beyond elementary schooling. However, by examining elementary school activity in its social class context in the light of our theoretical perspective on social class, we can see certain potential relationships already developing. Moreover, in this structure of developing relationships lies theoretical—and social—significance.

The *working-class* children are developing a potential *conflict* relationship with capital. Their present school work is appropriate preparation for future wage labor that is mechanical and routine. Such work, insofar as it denies the human capacities for creativity and planning, is degrading; moreover, when performed in industry, such work is a source of profit to others. This situation produces industrial conflict over wages, working conditions, and control. However, the children in the working-class schools are not learning to be docile and obedient in the face of present or future degrading conditions or financial exploitation. They are developing abilities and skills of resistance. These methods are highly similar to the "slowdown," subtle sabotage and other modes of indirect resistance carried out by adult workers in the shop, on the department store sales floor, and in some offices.[10] As these types of resistance develop in school, they are highly constrained and limited in their ultimate effectiveness. Just as the children's resistance prevents them from learning socially legitimated knowledge and skills in school and is therefore ultimately debilitating, so is this type of resistance ultimately debilitating in industry. Such resistance in industry does not succeed in producing, nor is it intended to produce, fundamental changes in the relationships of exploitation or control. Thus, the methods of resistance that the working-class children are developing in school are only temporarily, and *potentially*, liberating.

In the *middle-class school* the children are developing somewhat different potential relationships to capital, authority, and work. In this school the work tasks and relationships are appropriate for a future relation to capital that is *bureaucratic*. Their school work is appropriate for white-collar working-class and middle-class jobs in the supportive institutions of United

States society. In these jobs one does the paperwork, the technical work, the sales and the social service in the private and state bureaucracies. Such work does not usually demand that one be creative, and one is not often rewarded for critical analysis of the system. One is rewarded, rather, for knowing the answers to the questions one is asked, for knowing where or how to find the answers, and for knowing which form, regulation, technique, or procedure is correct. While such work does not usually satisfy human needs for engagement and self-expression, one's salary can be exchanged for objects or activities that attempt to meet these needs.

In the *affluent professional school* the children are developing a potential relationship to capital that is instrumental and expressive and involves substantial negotiation. In their schooling these children are acquiring *symbolic capital*: they are being given the opportunity to develop skills of linguistic, artistic, and scientific expression and creative elaboration of ideas into concrete form. These skills are those needed to produce, for example, culture (e.g., artistic, intellectual, and scientific ideas and other "products"). Their schooling is developing in these children skills necessary to become society's successful artists, intellectuals, legal, scientific, and technical experts and other professionals. The developing relation of the children in this school to their work is creative and relatively autonomous. Although they do not have control over which ideas they develop or express, the creative act in itself affirms and utilizes the human potential for conceptualization and design that is in many cases valued as intrinsically satisfying.

Professional persons in the cultural institutions of society (in, say, academe, publishing, the nonprint media, the arts, and the legal and state bureaucracies) are in an expressive relationship to the system of ownership in society because the ideas and other products of their work are often an important means by which material relationships of society are given ideological (e.g., artistic, intellectual, legal, and scientific) expression. Through the system of laws, for example, the ownership relations of private property are elaborated and legitimated in legal form; through individualistic and meritocratic theories in psychology and sociology, these individualistic economic relations are provided scientific "rationality" and "sense." The relationship to physical capital of those in society who create what counts as the dominant culture or ideology also involves substantial negotiation. The producers of symbolic capital often do not control the socially available physical capital nor the cultural uses to which it is put. They must therefore negotiate for money for their own projects. However, skillful application of one's cultural capital may ultimately lead to social (for example, state) power and to financial reward.

The *executive elite school* gives its children something that none of the other schools does: knowledge of and practice in manipulating the socially legitimated tools of analysis of systems. The children are given the opportunity to learn and to utilize the intellectually and socially prestigious grammatical, mathematical, and other vocabularies and rules by which elements are arranged. They are given the opportunity to use these skills in the analysis of society and in control situations. Such knowledge and skills are a most important kind of *symbolic capital*. They are necessary for control of a production system. The developing relationship of the children in this school to their work affirms and develops in them the human capacities for analysis and planning and helps to prepare them for work in society that would demand these skills. Their schooling is helping them to develop the abilities necessary for ownership and control of physical capital and the means of production in society.

The foregoing analysis of differences in school work in contrasting social class contexts suggests the following conclusion: the "hidden curriculum" of school work is tactic preparation for relating to the process of production in a particular way. Differing curricular, pedagogical, and pupil evaluation practices emphasize different cognitive and behavioral skills in each social setting and thus contribute to the development in the children of certain potential relationships to physical and symbolic capital, to authority, and to the process of work. School experience, in the sample of schools discussed here, differed qualitatively by social class. These differences may not only contribute to the development in the children in each social class of certain types of economically significant relationships and not others, but would thereby help to *reproduce* this system of relations in society. In the contribution to the reproduction of unequal social relations lies a theoretical meaning, and social consequence, of classroom practice.

The identification of different emphases in classrooms in a sample of contrasting social class contexts implies that further research should be conducted in a large number of schools to investigate the types of work tasks and interactions in each, to see if they differ in the ways discussed here, and to see if similar potential relationships are uncovered. Such research could have as a product the further elucidation of complex but not readily apparent connections between everyday activity in schools and classrooms and the unequal structure of economic relationships in which we work and live.

NOTES

1. But see, in a related vein, Apple and King (1977) and Rist (1973).
2. The definition of social class delineated here is the author's own, but it relies heavily on her interpretation of the work of Eric Olin Wright (1978), Pierre Bourdieu (Bourdieu and Passeron, 1977) and Raymond Williams (1977).
3. For discussion of schools as agencies of social and economic legitimation see Althusser (1971); see also Anyon (1978; 1979).
4. While relationships of control in society will not be discussed here, it can be said that they roughly parallel the relationships of control in the workplace, which will be the focus of this discussion. That is, working-class and many middle-class persons have less control than members of the upper-middle and capitalist classes do, not only over conditions and processes of their work, but over their nonwork lives as well. In addition, it is true that persons from the middle and capitalist classes, rather than workers, are most often those who fill the positions of state and other power in United States society.
5. Occupations may change their relation to the means of production over time, as the expenditure and ownership of capital change, as technology, skills, and the social relations of work change. For example, some jobs which were middle-class, managerial positions in 1900 and which necessitated conceptual laying-out and planning are now working-class and increasingly mechanical: e.g., quality control in industry, clerical work, and computer programming (see Braverman, 1974).
6. The U.S. Bureau of the Census defines "poverty" for a nonfarm family of four as a yearly income of $6,191 a year or less. U.S. Bureau of the Census, *Statistical Abstract of the United States: 1978* (Washington, D.C.: U.S. Government Printing Office, 1978, p. 465, table 754).
7. For other similarities alleged to characterize United States classrooms and schools, but which will not be discussed here, see Dreeben (1968), Jackson (1968), and Sarasan (1971).

8. Indeed, strikingly little teaching occurred in either of the working-class schools; this curtailed the amount that the children were taught. Incidentally, it increased the amount of time that had to be spent by the researcher to collect data on teaching style and interaction.

9. A dominant feeling, expressed directly and indirectly by teachers in this school, was boredom with their work. They did, however, in contrast to the working-class schools, almost always carry out lessons during class times.

10. See, for example, discussions in Levison (1974), Aronowitz (1978), and Benson (1978).

REFERENCES

Althusser, L. Ideology and ideological state apparatuses. In L. Althusser, *Lenin and philosophy and other essays.* Ben Brewster, Trans. New York: Monthly Review Press, 1971.

Anyon, J. Elementary social studies textbooks and legitimating knowledge. *Theory and Research in Social Education,* 1978, *6,* 40–55.

Anyon, J. Ideology and United States history textbooks. *Harvard Educational Review,* 1979, *49,* 361–386.

Apple, M. W. *Ideology and curriculum.* Boston: Routledge and Kegan Paul, 1979.

Apple, M. W., & King, N. What do schools teach? *Curriculum Inquiry,* 1977, *6,* 341–358.

Aronowitz, S. Marx, Braverman, and the logic of capital. *The Insurgent Sociologist,* 1978, *8,* 126–146.

Benson, S. The clerking sisterhood: rationalization and the work culture of saleswomen in American department stores, 1890–1960. *Radical America,* 1978, *12,* 41–55.

Bernstein, B. *Class, codes and control, Vol. 3. Towards a theory of educational transmission.* 2nd ed. London: Routledge and Kegan Paul, 1977.

Bourdieu, P. and Passeron, J. *Reproduction in education, society, and culture.* Beverly Hills, Calif.: Sage, 1977.

Bowles, S. & Gintis, H. *Schooling in capitalist America: educational reform and the contradictions of economic life.* New York: Basic Books, 1976.

Braverman, H. *Labor and monopoly capital: the degradation of work in the twentieth century.* New York: Monthly Review Press, 1974.

Dreeben, R. *On what is learned in school.* Reading, Mass.: Addison-Wesley, 1968.

Jackson, P. *Life in classrooms.* Holt, Rinehart & Winston, 1968.

Lampman, R. J. *The share of top wealth-holders in national wealth, 1922–1956:* A study of the National Bureau of Economic Research. Princeton, N.J.: Princeton University Press, 1962.

Levison, A. *The working class majority.* New York: Penguin Books, 1974.

New York Stock Exchange. *Census.* New York: New York Stock Exchange, 1975.

Rist, R. C. *The urban school: a factory for failure.* Cambridge, Mass.: MIT Press, 1973.

Sarasan, S. *The culture of school and the problem of change.* Boston: Allyn and Bacon, 1971.

Smith, J. D., and Franklin, S. The concentration of personal wealth, 1922–1969. *American Economic Review,* 1974, *64,* 162–167.

U.S. Bureau of the Census. *Current population reports.* Series P–60, no. 118. Money income in 1977 of families and persons in the United States. Washington, D.C.: U.S. Government Printing Office, 1979.

U.S. Bureau of the Census. *Statistical abstract of the United States: 1978.* Washington, D.C.: U.S. Government Printing Office, 1978.

Williams, R. Marxism and literature. New York: Oxford University Press, 1977.

Wright, E. O. *Class, crisis and the state.* London: New Left Books, 1978.

CRITICAL THINKING QUESTIONS

1. Jean Anyon describes four different types of schools. Which type of school do you think you spent the majority of your education attending? Why do you say that? Prove your case. Has your attendance at this type of school affected the skills you were taught or the expectations you have for your own educational or occupational goals?

2. Compare your school from answer one to a different type of school that Anyon discusses. Describe the second type. How was it different from your school? What was an advantage it had over your school? A disadvantage?

3. Jean Anyon argues that students are "being prepared to occupy particular rungs on the social ladder." What does that mean? How do the schools function like this, according to Jean Anyon? Do you agree? What do teachers in the different types of schools *expect* from their students? Why do you think these expectations matter?

4. How do you define "the hidden curriculum of work?" Why does Jean Anyon argue that different schools have different, hidden curricula? Who benefits from this? Who does this hurt? What can be done to fix this situation?

AGAINST SCHOOL

by John Gatto*

John Gatto was a public school teacher with over thirty years of experience. Later, he authored books and several articles on education in America in which he critiques the education system. In 1989, 1990, and 1991, Gatto was named Teacher of the Year in New York City; and in 1991, he was recognized as New York State Teacher of the Year.

In this article, John Gatto argues that schools are no longer designed to teach, but to train. The forces of industrialization have created a school system based upon a factory model, not aiming for education, but something else. What is this system aiming for, and who benefits?

. . . .

HOW PUBLIC EDUCATION CRIPPLES OUR KIDS, AND WHY

I taught for thirty years in some of the worst schools in Manhattan, and in some of the best, and during that time I became an expert in boredom. Boredom was everywhere in my world, and if you asked the kids, as I often did, *why* they felt so bored, they always gave the same answers: They said the work was stupid, that it made no sense, that they already knew it. They said they wanted to be doing something real, not just sitting around. They said teachers didn't seem to know much about their subjects and clearly weren't interested in learning more. And the kids were right: their teachers were every bit as bored as they were.

Boredom is the common condition of schoolteachers, and anyone who has spent time in a teachers' lounge can vouch for the low energy, the whining, the dispirited attitudes, to be found there. When asked why *they* feel bored, the teachers tend to blame the kids, as you might expect. Who wouldn't get bored teaching students who are rude and interested only in grades? If even that. Of course, teachers are themselves products of the same twelve-year compulsory school programs that so thoroughly bore their students, and as school personnel they are trapped inside structures even more rigid than those imposed upon the children. Who, then, is to blame?

We all are. My grandfather taught me that. One afternoon when I was seven I complained to him of boredom, and he batted me hard on the head. He told me that I was never to use that term in his presence again, that if I was bored it was my fault and no one else's. The obligation to amuse and instruct myself was entirely my own, and people who didn't know that were childish people, to be avoided if possible. Certainly not to be trusted. That episode cured me of boredom forever, and here and there over the years I was able to pass on the lesson to some remarkable student. For the most part, however, I found it futile to challenge the official notion that boredom and childishness were the natural state of affairs in the classroom. Often I had to defy custom, and even bend the law, to help kids break out of this trap.

The empire struck back, of course; childish adults regularly conflate opposition with disloyalty. I once returned from a medical leave to discover that all evidence of my having been granted the leave had been purposely destroyed, that my job had been terminated, and that I no longer possessed even a teaching license. After nine months of tormented effort I was able to retrieve the license when a school secretary testified to witnessing the plot unfold. In the meantime my family suffered more than I care to remember. By the time I finally retired in 1991, I had more than enough reason to think of our schools—with their long-term, cell-block-style, forced confinement of both students and teachers—as virtual factories of childishness. Yet I honestly could not see why they had to be that way. My own experience had revealed to me what many other teachers must learn along the way, too, yet keep to themselves for fear of reprisal: if we wanted to we could easily and inexpensively jettison the old, stupid structures and help kids take an education rather than merely receive a schooling. We could encourage the best qualities of youthfulness—curiosity, adventure, resilience, the capacity for surprising insight—simply by being more flexible about time, texts, and tests, by introducing kids to truly competent adults, and by giving each student what autonomy he or she needs in order to take a risk every now and then.

But we don't do that. And the more I asked why not, and persisted in thinking about the "problem" of schooling as an engineer might, the more I missed the point: What if there is no "problem" with our schools? What if they are the way they are, so expensively flying in the face of common sense and long experience in how children learn things, not because they are doing something wrong but because they are doing something right? Is it possible that George W. Bush accidentally spoke the truth when he said we would "leave no child behind"? Could it be that our schools are designed to make sure not one of them ever really grows up?

Do we really need school? I don't mean education, just forced schooling: six classes a day, five days a week, nine months a year, for twelve years. Is this deadly routine really necessary? And if so, for what? Don't hide behind reading, writing, and arithmetic as a rationale, because 2 million happy homeschoolers have surely put that banal justification to rest. Even if they hadn't, a considerable number of well-known Americans never went through the twelve-year wringer our kids currently go through, and they turned out all right. George Washington, Benjamin Franklin, Thomas Jefferson, Abraham Lincoln? Someone taught them, to be sure, but they were not products of a school system, and not one of them was ever "graduated" from a secondary school. Throughout most of American history, kids generally didn't go to high school, yet the unschooled rose to be admirals, like Farragut; inventors, like Edison; captains of industry, like Carnegie and Rockefeller; writers, like Melville and Twain and Conrad; and even scholars, like Margaret Mead. In fact, until pretty recently people who reached the age of thirteen weren't looked upon as children at all. Ariel Durant, who co-wrote an enormous, and very good, multivolume history of the world with her husband, Will, was happily married at fifteen, and who could reasonably claim that Ariel Durant was an uneducated person? Unschooled, perhaps, but not uneducated.

We have been taught (that is, schooled) in this country to think of "success" as synonymous with, or at least dependent upon, "schooling," but historically that isn't true in either an intellectual or a financial sense. And plenty of people throughout the world today find a way to educate themselves without resorting to a system of compulsory secondary schools that all too often resemble prisons. Why, then, do Americans confuse education with just such a system? What exactly is the purpose of our public schools?

Mass schooling of a compulsory nature really got its teeth into the United States between 1905 and 1915, though it was conceived of much earlier and pushed for throughout most of the nineteenth century. The reason given for this enormous upheaval of family life and cultural traditions was, roughly speaking, threefold:

1. To make good people.
2. To make good citizens.
3. To make each person his or her personal best.

These goals are still trotted out today on a regular basis, and most of us accept them in one form or another as a decent definition of public education's mission, however short schools actually fall in achieving them. But we are dead wrong. Compounding our error is the fact that the national literature holds numerous and surprisingly consistent statements of compulsory schooling's true purpose. We have, for example, the great H. L. Mencken, who wrote in *The American Mercury* for April 1924 that the aim of public education is not

> to fill the young of the species with knowledge and awaken their intelligence. . . . Nothing could be further from the truth. The aim . . . is simply to reduce as many individuals as possible to the same safe level, to breed and train a standardized citizenry, to put down dissent and originality. That is its aim in the United States . . . and that is its aim everywhere else.

Because of Mencken's reputation as a satirist, we might be tempted to dismiss this passage as a bit of hyperbolic sarcasm. His article, however, goes on to trace the template for our own educational system back to the now vanished, though never to be forgotten, military state of Prussia. And although he was certainly aware of the irony that we had recently been at war with Germany, the heir to Prussian thought and culture, Mencken was being perfectly serious here. Our educational system really is Prussian in origin, and that really is cause for concern.

The odd fact of a Prussian provenance for our schools pops up again and again once you know to look for it. William James alluded to it many times at the turn of the century. Orestes Brownson, the hero of Christopher Lasch's 1991 book, *The True and Only Heaven,* was publicly denouncing the Prussianization of American schools back in the 1840s. Horace Mann's "Seventh Annual Report" to the Massachusetts State Board of Education in 1843 is essentially a paean to the land of Frederick the Great and a call for its schooling to be brought here. That Prussian culture loomed large in America is hardly surprising, given our early association with that utopian state. A Prussian served as Washington's aide during the Revolutionary War, and so many German-speaking people had settled here by 1795 that Congress considered publishing a German-language edition of the federal laws. But what shocks is that we should so eagerly have adopted one of the very worst aspects of Prussian culture: an educational system deliberately designed to produce mediocre intellects, to hamstring the inner life, to deny students appreciable leadership skills, and to ensure docile and incomplete citizens—all in order to render the populace "manageable."

It was from James Bryant Conant—president of Harvard for twenty years, WWI poison-gas specialist, WWII executive on the atomic-bomb project, high commissioner of the American zone in Germany after WWII, and truly one of the most influential figures of the twentieth century—that I first got wind of the real purposes of American schooling. Without Conant, we would probably not have the same style and degree of standardized testing that we enjoy today, nor would we be blessed with gargantuan high schools that warehouse 2,000 to 4,000 students at a time, like the famous Columbine High in Littleton, Colorado. Shortly after I retired from teaching I picked up Conant's 1959 book-length essay,

The Child the Parent and the State, and was more than a little intrigued to see him mention in passing that the modern schools we attend were the result of a "revolution" engineered between 1905 and 1930. A revolution? He declines to elaborate, but he does direct the curious and the uninformed to Alexander Inglis's 1918 book, *Principles of Secondary Education,* in which "one saw this revolution through the eyes of a revolutionary."

Inglis, for whom a lecture in education at Harvard is named, makes it perfectly clear that compulsory schooling on this continent was intended to be just what it had been for Prussia in the 1820s: a fifth column into the burgeoning democratic movement that threatened to give the peasants and the proletarians a voice at the bargaining table. Modern, industrialized, compulsory schooling was to make a sort of surgical incision into the prospective unity of these underclasses. Divide children by subject, by age-grading, by constant rankings on tests, and by many other more subtle means, and it was unlikely that the ignorant mass of mankind, separated in childhood, would ever reintegrate into a dangerous whole.

Inglis breaks down the purpose—the actual purpose—of modem schooling into six basic functions, any one of which is enough to curl the hair of those innocent enough to believe the three traditional goals listed earlier:

1. The *adjustive* or *adaptive* function. Schools are to establish fixed habits of reaction to authority. This, of course, precludes critical judgment completely. It also pretty much destroys the idea that useful or interesting material should be taught, because you can't test for reflexive obedience until you know whether you can make kids learn, and do, foolish and boring things.

2. The *integrating* function. This might well be called "the conformity function," because its intention is to make children as alike as possible. People who conform are predictable, and this is of great use to those who wish to harness and manipulate a large labor force.

3. The *diagnostic and directive* function. School is meant to determine each student's proper social role. This is done by logging evidence mathematically and anecdotally on cumulative records. As in "your permanent record." Yes, you do have one.

4. The *differentiating* function. Once their social role has been "diagnosed," children are to be sorted by role and trained only so far as their destination in the social machine merits—and not one step further. So much for making kids their personal best.

5. The *selective* function. This refers not to human choice at all but to Darwin's theory of natural selection as applied to what he called "the favored races." In short, the idea is to help things along by consciously attempting to improve the breeding stock. Schools are meant to tag the unfit—with poor grades, remedial placement, and other punishments—clearly enough that their peers will accept them as inferior and effectively bar them from the reproductive sweepstakes. That's what all those little humiliations from first grade onward were intended to do: wash the dirt down the drain.

6. The *propaedeutic* function. The societal system implied by these rules will require an elite group of caretakers. To that end, a small fraction of the kids will quietly be taught how to manage this continuing project, how to watch over and control a population deliberately dumbed down and declawed in order that government might proceed unchallenged and corporations might never want for obedient labor.

That, unfortunately, is the purpose of mandatory public education in this country. And lest you take Inglis for an isolated crank with a rather too cynical take on the educational enterprise, you should know that he was hardly alone in championing these ideas. Conant himself, building on the ideas of Horace Mann and others, campaigned tirelessly for an American school system designed along the same lines. Men like George Peabody, who funded the cause of mandatory schooling throughout the South, surely understood that the Prussian system was useful in creating not only a harmless electorate and a servile labor force but also a virtual herd of mindless consumers. In time a great number of industrial titans came to recognize the enormous profits to be had by cultivating and tending just such a herd via public education, among them Andrew Carnegie and John D. Rockefeller.

There you have it. Now you know. We don't need Karl Marx's conception of a grand warfare between the classes to see that it is in the interest of complex management, economic or political, to dumb people down, to demoralize them, to divide them from one another, and to discard them if they don't conform. Class may frame the proposition, as when Woodrow Wilson, then president of Princeton University, said the following to the New York City School Teachers Association in 1909: "We want one class of persons to have a liberal education, and we want another class of persons, a very much larger class, of necessity, in every society, to forgo the privileges of a liberal education and fit themselves to perform specific difficult manual tasks." But the motives behind the disgusting decisions that bring about these ends need not be class-based at all. They can stem purely from fear, or from the by now familiar belief that "efficiency" is the paramount virtue, rather than love, liberty, laughter, or hope. Above all, they can stem from simple greed.

There were vast fortunes to be made, after all, in an economy based on mass production and organized to favor the large corporation rather than the small business or the family farm. But mass production required mass consumption, and at the turn of the twentieth century most Americans considered it both unnatural and unwise to buy things they didn't actually need. Mandatory schooling was a godsend on that count. School didn't have to train kids in any direct sense to think they should consume nonstop, because it did something even better: it encouraged them not to think at all. And that left them sitting ducks for another great invention of the modem era—marketing.

Now, you needn't have studied marketing to know that there are two groups of people who can always be convinced to consume more than they need to: addicts and children. School has done a pretty good job of turning our children into addicts, but it has done a spectacular job of turning our children into children. Again, this is no accident. Theorists from Plato to Rousseau to our own Dr. Inglis knew that if children could be cloistered with other children, stripped of responsibility and independence, encouraged to develop only the trivializing emotions of greed, envy, jealousy, and fear, they would grow older but never truly grow up. In the 1934 edition of his once well-known book *Public Education in the United States,* Ellwood P. Cubberley detailed and praised the way the strategy of successive school enlargements had extended childhood by two to six years, and forced schooling was at that point still quite new. This same Cubberley—who was dean of Stanford's School of Education, a textbook editor at Houghton Mifflin, and Conant's friend and correspondent at Harvard—had written the following in the 1922 edition of his book *Public School Administration*: "Our schools are . . . factories in which the raw products (children) are to be shaped and fashioned. . . . And it is the business of the school to build its pupils according to the specifications laid down."

It's perfectly obvious from our society today what those specifications were. Maturity has by now been banished from nearly every aspect of our lives. Easy divorce laws have removed the need to work at relationships; easy credit has removed the need for fiscal self-control; easy entertainment has removed the need to learn to entertain oneself; easy answers have removed the need to ask questions. We have become a nation of children, happy to surrender our judgments and our wills to political exhortations and commercial blandishments that would insult actual adults. We buy televisions, and then we buy the things we see on the television. We buy computers, and then we buy the things we see on the computer. We buy $150 sneakers whether we need them or not, and when they fall apart too soon we buy another pair. We drive SUVs and believe the lie that they constitute a kind of life insurance, even when we're upside-down in them. And, worst of all, we don't bat an eye when Ari Fleischer tells us to "be careful what you say," even if we remember having been told somewhere back in school that America is the land of the free. We simply buy that one too. Our schooling, as intended, has seen to it.

Now for the good news. Once you understand the logic behind modern schooling, its tricks and traps are fairly easy to avoid. School trains children to be employees and consumers; teach your own to be leaders and adventurers. School trains children to obey reflexively; teach your own to think critically and independently. Well-schooled kids have a low threshold for boredom; help your own to develop an inner life so that they'll never be bored. Urge them to take on the serious material, the *grown-up* material, in history, literature, philosophy, music, art, economics, theology—all the stuff schoolteachers know well enough to avoid. Challenge your kids with plenty of solitude so that they can learn to enjoy their own company, to conduct inner dialogues. Well-schooled people are conditioned to dread being alone, and they seek constant companionship through the TV, the computer, the cell phone, and through shallow friendships quickly acquired and quickly abandoned. Your children should have a more meaningful life, and they can.

First, though, we must wake up to what our schools really are: laboratories of experimentation on young minds, drill centers for the habits and attitudes that corporate society demands. Mandatory education serves children only incidentally; its real purpose is to turn them into servants. Don't let your own have their childhoods extended, not even for a day. If David Farragut could take command of a captured British warship as a preteen, if Thomas Edison could publish a broadsheet at the age of twelve, if Ben Franklin could apprentice himself to a printer at the same age (then put himself through a course of study that would choke a Yale senior today), there's no telling what your own kids could do. After a long life, and thirty years in the public school trenches, I've concluded that genius is as common as dirt. We suppress our genius only because we haven't yet figured out how to manage a population of educated men and women. The solution, I think, is simple and glorious. Let them manage themselves.

CRITICAL THINKING QUESTIONS

1. Gatto references Farragut, Edison, Carnegie, Rockefeller, Melville, Twain, Conrad, and Mead as "Unschooled, perhaps, but not uneducated." What does the author mean by this? Is there any validity to his argument? From your own experience, who is someone who may be considered unschooled, but not uneducated? Why do you think that person fits that role?

2. John Gatto argues that schools operate like factories *and* like prisons. Choose one of these models and answer the following questions about it: How does a school operate in that way? Why does he argue that schools need to operate like this? What is an example from your own educational experience, and how does it connect your school to the factory or prison model?

3. Gatto references the six basic functions of schools according to Inglis' perspective. In what ways are these six basic functions different from the three 19th century goals: "to make Good people; to make good citizens; to make each person his or her personal best?" What do the six basic functions of mandatory public education say about American society?

4. Gatto speaks to the fact that our society has created a "nation of children happy to surrender our judgments and our wills . . ." He argues that our culture is one in which things come easily. How does Gatto connect this with our society being "immature?" How do these statements link to Gatto's arguments about the U.S. education system?

AMERICAN SCHOOLS ARE TRAINING KIDS FOR A WORLD THAT DOESN'T EXIST

by David Edwards

David Edwards is a writer and a teacher based out of Harvard University. In 2010, he joined the prestigious National Academy of Engineering. His research recently has shifted to education, and his work is changing the model for the way ideas are delivered in a college setting.

In this 2014 article from *Wired* magazine, David Edwards argues that, despite falling test scores in relation to other countries, Americans are not getting any dumber. The education system is just preparing Americans for a world that no longer exists. No longer can a student learn all she needs to know in college and then go out and "do" their profession; in the new economy, "learning" and "doing" cannot be separated. How, then, should we be teaching our students?

. . . .

ARE AMERICANS GETTING DUMBER?

Our math skills are falling. Our reading skills are weakening. Our children have become less literate than children in many developed countries. But the crisis in American education may be more than a matter of sliding rankings on world educational performance scales.

Our kids learn within a system of education devised for a world that increasingly does not exist.

To become a chef, a lawyer, a philosopher or an engineer, has always been a matter of learning what these professionals do, how and why they do it, and some set of general facts that more or less describe our societies and our selves. We pass from kindergarten through twelfth grade, from high school to college, from college to graduate and professional schools, ending our education at some predetermined stage to become the chef, or the engineer, equipped with a fair understanding of what being a chef, or an engineer, actually is and will be for a long time.

We "learn," and after this we "do." We go to school and then we go to work.

This approach does not map very well to personal and professional success in America today. Learning and doing have become inseparable in the face of conditions that invite us to discover.

Over the next twenty years the earth is predicted to add another two billion people. Having nearly exhausted nature's ability to feed the planet, we now need to discover a new food system. The global climate will continue to change. To save our coastlines, and maintain acceptable living conditions for more than a billion people, we need to discover new science, engineering, design, and architectural methods, and pioneer economic models that sustain their implementation and maintenance. Microbiological threats will increase as our traditional techniques of anti-microbial defense lead to greater and greater resistances, and to thwart these we must discover new approaches to medical treatment, which we can afford, and implement in ways that incite compliance and good health. The many rich and varied human cultures of the earth will continue to mix, more rapidly than they ever have, through mass population movements and unprecedented information exchange, and to preserve social harmony we need to discover new cultural referents, practices, and environments of cultural exchange. In such conditions the futures of law, medicine, philosophy, engineering, and agriculture—with just about every other field—are to be rediscovered.

AMERICANS NEED TO LEARN HOW TO DISCOVER

Being dumb in the existing educational system is bad enough. Failing to create a new way of learning adapted to contemporary circumstances might be a national disaster. The good news is, some people are working on it.

Against this arresting background, an exciting new kind of learning is taking place in America. Alternatively framed as maker classes, after-school innovation programs, and innovation prizes, these programs are frequently not framed as learning at all. Discovery environments are showing up as culture and entertainment, from online experiences to contemporary art installations and new kinds of culture labs. Perhaps inevitably, the process of discovery—from our confrontation with challenging ambiguous data, through our imaginative responses, to our iterative and error-prone paths of data synthesis and resolution—has turned into a focus of public fascination.

Discovery has always provoked interest, but *how* one discovers may today interest us even more. Educators, artists, designers, museum curators, scientists, engineers, entertainment designers and others are creatively responding to this new reality, and, together, they are redefining what it means to learn in America.

At Harvard University, where I teach, Peter Galison, in History of Science, asks his students to make films, to understand science; Michael Chu, in business, brings students to low income regions to learn about social entrepreneurship; Michael Brenner, in Engineering and Applied Science, invites master chefs to help students discover the science of cooking; and Doris Sommer, in Romance Languages, teaches aesthetics by inviting students to effect social and political change through cultural agency. Similarly, in the course I teach, How to Create Things and Have Them Matter, students are asked to look, listen, and discover, using their own creative genius, while observing contemporary phenomena that matter today.

Because that's what discoverers do.

A NEW KIND OF LEARNING LAB

Learning by an original and personal process of discovery is a trend on many US university campuses, like Stanford University, MIT, and Arizona State University. It also shows up in middle school, high school and after school programs, as in the programs supported by the ArtScience Prize, a more curricular intensive version of the plethora of innovation prizes that have sprung up in the last years around the world. Students and participants in these kinds of programs learn something even more valuable than discovering a fact for themselves, a common goal of "learning discovery" programs; they learn the thrill of discovering the undiscovered. Success brings not just a good grade, or the financial reward of a prize. It brings the satisfaction that one can realize dreams, and thrive, in a world framed by major dramatic questions. And this fans the kind of passion that propels an innovator along a long creative career.

Discovery, as intriguing process, has become a powerful theme in contemporary culture and entertainment. In art and design galleries, and many museums, artists and designers, like Olafur Eliasson, Mark Dion, Martin Wattenberg, Neri Oxman and Mathieu Lehanneur, invite the public to explore contemporary complexities, as in artist Mark Dion's recent collaborative work with the Alaskan SeaLife Center and Anchorage Museum on plastic fragments in the Pacific Ocean. Often they make visitors discovery participants, as in Martin Wattenberg's Apartment, where people enter words that turn into architectural forms, or sorts of memory palaces. In a more popular way, television discovery and reality programs, from Yukon Men to America's Got Talent, present protagonists who face challenges, encounter failure, and succeed, iteratively and often partially, while online the offer is even more pervasive, with games of discovery and adventure immersing young people in the process of competing against natural and internal constraints.

All this has led to the rise of the culture lab.

Culture labs conduct or invite experiments in art and design to explore contemporary questions that seem hard or even impossible to address in more conventional science and engineering labs. Their history, as public learning forum, dates from the summer of 2007, when the Wellcome Collection opened in King's Cross London, to invite the incurably curious to probe contemporary questions of body and mind through contemporary art and collected object installations. A few months later, in the fall 2007, Le Laboratoire opened in Paris, France, to explore frontiers of science through experimental projects in contemporary art and design, and translate experimental ideas from educational, through cultural, to social practice. And in the winter 2008 Science Gallery opened in downtown Dublin to bring contemporary science experimentation to the general public (and students of Trinity College) with installations in contemporary art and design. Other culture labs have opened since then, in Amsterdam, Kosovo, Madrid and other European, American, Asian, African and Latin American cities. In the USA, culture labs especially thrive on campuses, like MIT's famous Media Lab, Harvard's iLab, and the unique metaLAB, run by Jeffrey Schnapp within Harvard's Berkman Center. These will now be joined by a public culture lab, Le Laboratoire Cambridge, which opens later this month near MIT and Harvard, bringing to America the European model with a program of public art and design exhibitions, innovation seminars, and future-of-food sensorial experiences.

The culture lab is the latest indication that learning is changing in America. It cannot happen too fast.

We may not be getting dumber in America. But we need to get smarter in ways that match the challenges we now face. The time is now to support the role of learning in the pursuit of discovery and to embrace the powerful agency of culture.

CRITICAL THINKING QUESTIONS

1. David Edwards writes that, "the futures of law, medicine, engineering, and agriculture—with just about every other field—are to be rediscovered." Why does he think these fields need to be rediscovered in relation to globalization? How has your educational background either prepared or failed to prepare you to discover things?

2. How would you summarize what David Edwards means by "learning by discovery"? Why is this increasingly important? Describe a discovery-based learning experience, inside or outside of school, that you have had. If you are unable to think of one, design one for something you know well enough to teach others.

3. Edwards writes, "We learn, and after this we do. We go to school and then we go to work." Is this systematic approach to our education system making it so that "Americans are getting dumber"? Why or why not? How could the introduction of culture labs change this?

4. **Connection.** Jean Anyon describes four different types of schools. What type of school would be most likely to adopt "learning by discovery"? Why would this school be able to do so and the other three types of schools less likely to do so? How does this reinforce Jean Anyon's central argument?

STATES LISTEN AS PARENTS GIVE RAMPANT TESTING AN F

by Lizette Alvarez

Lizette Alvarez has written for the the New York *Daily News*, the *Miami Herald* and most recently for the *The New York Times* as their Miami Bureau chief. In 1993, she won the Pulitzer Prize for her coverage of Hurricane Andrew.

In this 2014 article for *The New York Times*, Lizette Alvarez writes about the current testing-crisis hitting Florida. Since the introduction of the "No Child Left Behind" legislation in 2001, high-stakes, standardized testing has become an increasingly common way to evaluate both schools and teachers. What Alvarez's reporting finds is that the system is not making students, teachers, or parents happy. Why, then, are some schools in Florida scheduling sixty days of testing each year?

• • • • • • • • • • • • • • •

ROYAL PALM BEACH, Fla.—Florida embraced the school accountability movement early and enthusiastically, but that was hard to remember at a parent meeting in a high school auditorium here not long ago.

Parents railed at a system that they said was overrun by new tests coming from all levels—district, state and federal. Some wept as they described teenagers who take Xanax to cope with test stress, children who refuse to go to school and teachers who retire rather than promote a culture that seems to value testing over learning.

"My third grader loves school, but I can't get her out of the car this year," Dawn LaBorde, who has three children in Palm Beach County schools, told the gathering, through tears. Her son, a junior, is so shaken, she said, "I have had to take him to his doctor." She added: "He can't sleep, but he's tired. He can't eat, but he's hungry."

One father broke down as he said he planned to pull his second grader from school. "Teaching to a test is destroying our society," he said.

Where once these frustrations were voiced in murmurs, this year not only parents but also educators across Florida are rebelling. They have joined a national protest in which states have repealed their graduation test requirements, postponed the consequences of testing for the Common Core—national standards in more than 40 states—and rolled back the number of required exams.

In August, Education Secretary Arne Duncan added to the chorus when he wrote in a blog post that "testing issues today are sucking the oxygen out of the room in a lot of schools," and that teachers needed more time to adapt to new standards and tests.

Last month, state school chiefs and the heads of large city districts were the latest to express their concerns by committing to review the panoply of tests students must take.

In Florida, which tests students more frequently than most other states, many schools this year will dedicate on average 60 to 80 days out of the 180-day school year to standardized testing. In a few districts, tests were scheduled to be given every day to at least some students.

The furor in Florida, which cuts across ideological, party and racial lines, is particularly striking for a state that helped pioneer accountability through former Gov. Jeb Bush. Mr. Bush, a possible presidential contender, was one of the first governors to introduce high-stakes testing and an A-to-F grading system for schools. He continues to advocate test-based accountability through his education foundation. Former President George W. Bush, his brother, introduced similar measures as governor of Texas and, as president, embraced No Child Left Behind, the law that required states to develop tests to measure progress.

The concerns reach well beyond first-year jitters over Florida's version of Common Core, which is making standards tougher and tests harder. Frustrations also center on the increase this year in the number of tests ordered by the state to fulfill federal grant obligations on teacher evaluations and by districts to keep pace with the new standards. The state mandate that students use computers for standardized tests has made the situation worse because computers are scarce and easily crash.

"This is a spinning-plates act like the old 'Ed Sullivan Show,'" said David Samore, the longtime principal at Okeeheelee Community Middle School in Palm Beach County. "What you are seeing now are the plates are starting to fall. Principals, superintendents, kids and teachers can only do so much. They never get to put any plates down."

School districts across Florida have started to pare back the number of district-mandated tests. Palm Beach County announced recently that it would cut dozens of tests this year.

"This is the proverbial perfect storm of testing that has hit not only Florida but all the states," said Alberto M. Carvalho, the influential superintendent of Miami-Dade County Schools, the fourth-largest district in the country, who was named the 2014 national superintendent of the year. "This is too much, too far, too fast, and it threatens the fabric of real accountability."

Mr. Carvalho has joined other superintendents and school board members in the state in calling for a delay in the use of new tests, including the not yet validated Florida Standards Assessment—a Common Core variant, with tougher standards than the last assessment used—to grade the state's schools, teachers and students.

Despite continued support in the Republican-dominated State Legislature for high-stakes testing, there are signs that Florida is headed for a showdown with opponents of an education system that many say is undermining its original mission: to improve student learning, help teachers and inform parents.

Responding to the growing outcry, Gov. Rick Scott in late August called for Education Commissioner Pam Stewart to investigate standardized tests, many of them state-mandated.

Robert A. Schaeffer, the public education director for FairTest, a standardized-test watchdog organization, said, "The numbers and consequences of these tests have driven public opinion over the edge, and politicians are scrambling to figure out how to deal with that."

Much has changed this year in Florida. As part of the federal Race to the Top grant obligation, the state will require end-of-the-year tests for every subject to help evaluate teachers whose pay and job will be tied to scores. In Miami-Dade County, there are 1,600 courses. School districts are obligated to write the course exams, but the Legislature did not give them money for the task, so districts are far behind in developing them.

On top of routine classroom tests, students face an increase in district-led diagnostic tests to keep tabs on student progress. Some teachers are testing children biweekly. This is in addition to high school Advanced Placement, SAT and ACT tests.

But there is another requirement that has made testing more difficult in Florida. The state ordered all students, including those in elementary school, to take standardized tests on computers as of this year. But again, the state did not give districts extra money for computers or technology help.

Because schools do not have computers for every student, tests are staggered throughout the day, which translates to more hours spent administering tests and less time teaching.

Students who are not taking tests often occupy their time watching movies. The staggered test times also mean computer labs are not available for other students.

The overlay of this year's tougher Common Core-like standards—which has led to drops in test scores in cities like New York—also has students in a panic over falling grades. Teachers, too, are worried about how the scores will affect their evaluations. In Florida, students who fail the test can be held back in third grade or fail to graduate from high school.

The frustration over testing has spilled across the state. The Lee County School Board led the charge in August when it voted to opt out of state-mandated standardized testing during an emotional meeting in Fort Myers. It rescinded the vote shortly after it learned of the penalties the district would face. Miami-Dade just canceled one set of district-ordered interim exams to allow teachers and students more time in the classroom.

In Gainesville, one kindergarten teacher, Susan Bowles, explained to parents on her Facebook page that she would refuse to give state-ordered diagnostic reading tests. The kindergartners were obligated to take the tests one by one on a computer. After the first go-round, Ms. Bowles calculated it would eat up three weeks of teaching time.

Her public stance galvanized even more parents and educators. Not long after her posting, Ms. Stewart, the education commissioner, suspended that particular test for younger pupils. Parents and teachers across the state began to air their grievances, detail by detail.

"The emotional effect on students, teachers and parents has been damaging; the manifestation of sadness and frustration is real," Mr. Carvalho said of the headlong rush into more tests. "And the state should pay attention to it."

CRITICAL THINKING QUESTIONS

1. Describe the efforts Jeb Bush took as Governor of Florida dealing with high stakes testing. Describe the actions his brother, President George W. Bush, took at the federal level. Describe at least three concerns the article raises with these pushes for standardized testing.

2. According to the article, one parent stated, "Teaching to the test is destroying our society." Is this parent's claim justifiable? Why or why not? Who is, in fact, impacted in our society by all of this testing? How does this connect to your own school experiences—what effect did standardized testing have on you and your peers? Do you think standardized testing is effective?

3. Carvalho notes that "The emotional effect on students, teachers and parents has been damaging . . . and the state should pay attention to it." What do you think the state of Florida needs to do to respond appropriately to meet the needs of its three primary stakeholders (students, parents, and teachers) regarding the education system?

4. **Connection.** How have computers affected the rollout of standardized tests? John Gatto, in *Against Schools*, makes an argument that schools act like factories. How does the use of computers, as described in Lizette Alvarez's article, seem like something that would happen in a factory? Why are the Florida schools forced to act this way?

UNEQUAL OPPORTUNITY: RACE AND EDUCATION

by Linda Darling-Hammond

Linda Darling-Hammond, a Professor of Education at Stanford University and former president of the American Educational Research Association, is a leader in policy changes that impact teachers and the education system. Darling-Hammond is a leader in education policy, and she served as a leader on President Obama's education policy team.

In this 1998 report from the Brookings Institute, Darling-Hammond worries about the unequal allocation of opportunity to our students. Job opportunities in the new economy are more and more dependent on knowledge and education, and, how a society distributes these resources should be a major concern. She finds that in every metric, from teacher training to class size, from math curriculum to the availability of reading materials, minority students in America are not being provided equal opportunities in school. What are some of the key failings in our system with regard to race and education, and how can we fix them?

• • • • • • • • • • • • • • •

W.E.B. DuBois was right about the problem of the 21st century. The color line divides us still. In recent years, the most visible evidence of this in the public policy arena has been the persistent attack on affirmative action in higher education and employment. From the perspective of many Americans who believe that the vestiges of discrimination have disappeared, affirmative action now provides an unfair advantage to minorities. From the perspective of others who daily experience the consequences of ongoing discrimination, affirmative action is needed to protect opportunities likely to evaporate if an affirmative obligation to act fairly does not exist. And for Americans of all backgrounds, the allocation of opportunity in a society that is becoming ever more dependent on knowledge and education is a source of great anxiety and concern.

At the center of these debates are interpretations of the gaps in educational achievement between white and non-Asian minority students as measured by standardized test scores. The presumption that guides much of the conversation is that equal opportunity now exists; therefore, continued low levels of achievement on the part of minority students must be a function of genes, culture, or a lack of effort and will (see, for example, Richard Herrnstein and Charles Murray's *The Bell Curve* and Stephan and Abigail Thernstrom's *America in Black and White*).

The assumptions that undergird this debate miss an important reality: educational outcomes for minority children are much more a function of their unequal access to key educational resources, including skilled teachers and quality curriculum, than they are a function of race. In fact, the U.S. educational system is one of the most unequal in the industrialized world, and students routinely receive dramatically different learning opportunities based on their social status. In contrast to European and Asian nations that fund schools centrally and equally, the wealthiest 10 percent of U.S. school districts spend nearly 10 times more than the poorest 10 percent, and spending ratios of 3 to 1 are common within states. Despite stark differences in funding, teacher quality, curriculum, and class sizes, the prevailing view is that if students do not achieve, it is their own fault. If we are ever to get beyond the problem of the color line, we must confront and address these inequalities.

THE NATURE OF EDUCATIONAL INEQUALITY

Americans often forget that as late as the 1960s most African-American, Latino, and Native American students were educated in wholly segregated schools funded at rates many times lower than those serving whites and were excluded from many higher education institutions entirely. The end of legal segregation followed by efforts to equalize spending since 1970 has made a substantial difference for student achievement. On every major national test, including the National Assessment of Educational Progress, the gap in minority and white students' test scores narrowed substantially between 1970 and 1990, especially for elementary school students. On the Scholastic Aptitude Test (SAT), the scores of African-American students climbed 54 points between 1976 and 1994, while those of white students remained stable.

Even so, educational experiences for minority students have continued to be substantially separate and unequal. Two-thirds of minority students still attend schools that are predominantly minority, most of them located in central cities and funded well below those in neighboring suburban districts. Recent analyses of data prepared for school finance cases in Alabama, New Jersey, New York, Louisiana, and Texas have found that on every tangible measure—from qualified teachers to curriculum offerings—schools serving greater numbers of students of color had significantly fewer resources than schools serving mostly white students. As William L. Taylor and Dianne Piche noted in a 1991 report to Congress: Inequitable systems of school finance inflict disproportionate harm on minority and economically disadvantaged students. On an inter-state basis, such students are concentrated in states, primarily in the South, that have the lowest capacities to finance public education. On an intra-state basis, many of the states with the widest disparities in educational expenditures are large industrial states. In these states, many minorities and economically disadvantaged students are located in property-poor urban districts which fare the worst in educational expenditures (or) in rural districts which suffer from fiscal inequity.

Jonathan Kozol's 1991 *Savage Inequalities* described the striking differences between public schools serving students of color in urban settings and their suburban counterparts, which typically spend twice as much per student for populations with many fewer special needs. Contrast MacKenzie High School in Detroit, where word processing courses are taught without word processors because the school cannot afford them, or East St. Louis Senior High School, whose biology lab has no laboratory tables or usable dissecting kits, with nearby suburban schools where children enjoy a computer hookup to Dow Jones to study stock transactions and science laboratories that rival those in some industries. Or contrast Paterson, New Jersey, which could not afford the qualified teachers needed to offer foreign language courses to most high school students, with Princeton, where foreign languages begin in elementary school.

Even within urban school districts, schools with high concentrations of low-income and minority students receive fewer instructional resources than others. And tracking systems exacerbate these inequalities by segregating many low-income and minority students within schools. In combination, these policies leave minority students with fewer and lower-quality books, curriculum materials, laboratories, and computers; significantly larger class sizes; less qualified and experienced teachers; and less access to high-quality curriculum. Many schools serving low-income and minority students do not even offer the math and science courses needed for college, and they provide lower-quality teaching in the classes they do offer. It all adds up.

WHAT DIFFERENCE DOES IT MAKE?

Since the 1966 Coleman report, Equality of Educational Opportunity, another debate has waged as to whether money makes a difference to educational outcomes. It is certainly possible to spend money ineffectively; however, studies that have developed more sophisticated measures of schooling show how money, properly spent, makes a difference. Over the past 30 years, a large body of research has shown that four factors consistently influence student achievement: all else equal, students perform better if they are educated in smaller schools where they are well known (300 to 500 students is optimal), have smaller class sizes (especially at the elementary level), receive a challenging curriculum, and have more highly qualified teachers.

Minority students are much less likely than white children to have any of these resources. In predominantly minority schools, which most students of color attend, schools are large (on average, more than twice as large as predominantly white schools and reaching 3,000 students or more in most cities); on average, class sizes are 15 percent larger overall (80 percent larger for non-special education classes); curriculum offerings and materials are lower in quality; and teachers are much less qualified in terms of levels of education, certification, and training in the fields they teach. And in integrated schools, as UCLA professor Jeannie Oakes described in the 1980s and Harvard professor Gary Orfield's research has recently confirmed, most minority students are segregated in lower-track classes with larger class sizes, less qualified teachers, and lower-quality curriculum.

Research shows that teachers' preparation makes a tremendous difference to children's learning. In an analysis of 900 Texas school districts, Harvard economist Ronald Ferguson found that teachers' expertise—as measured by scores on a licensing examination, master's degrees, and experience—was the single most important determinant of student achievement, accounting for roughly 40 percent of the measured variance in students' reading and math achievement gains in grades 1–12. After controlling for socioeconomic status, the large disparities in achievement between black and white students were almost entirely due to differences in the qualifications of their teachers. In combination, differences in teacher expertise and class sizes accounted for as much of the measured variance in achievement as did student and family background.

Ferguson and Duke economist Helen Ladd repeated this analysis in Alabama and again found sizable influences of teacher qualifications and smaller class sizes on achievement gains in math and reading. They found that more of the difference between the high- and low-scoring districts was explained by teacher qualifications and class sizes than by poverty, race, and parent education.

Meanwhile, a Tennessee study found that elementary school students who are assigned to ineffective teachers for three years in a row score nearly 50 percentile points lower on achievement tests than those assigned to highly effective teachers over the same period. Strikingly, minority students are about half as likely to be assigned to the most effective teachers and twice as likely to be assigned to the least effective.

Minority students are put at greatest risk by the American tradition of allowing enormous variation in the qualifications of teachers. The National Commission on Teaching and America's Future found that new teachers hired without meeting certification standards

(25 percent of all new teachers) are usually assigned to teach the most disadvantaged students in low-income and high-minority schools, while the most highly educated new teachers are hired largely by wealthier schools. Students in poor or predominantly minority schools are much less likely to have teachers who are fully qualified or hold higher-level degrees. In schools with the highest minority enrollments, for example, students have less than a 50 percent chance of getting a math or science teacher with a license and a degree in the field. In 1994, fully one-third of teachers in high-poverty schools taught without a minor in their main field and nearly 70 percent taught without a minor in their secondary teaching field.

Studies of underprepared teachers consistently find that they are less effective with students and that they have difficulty with curriculum development, classroom management, student motivation, and teaching strategies. With little knowledge about how children grow, learn, and develop, or about what to do to support their learning, these teachers are less likely to understand students' learning styles and differences, to anticipate students' knowledge and potential difficulties, or to plan and redirect instruction to meet students' needs. Nor are they likely to see it as their job to do so, often blaming the students if their teaching is not successful.

Teacher expertise and curriculum quality are interrelated, because a challenging curriculum requires an expert teacher. Research has found that both students and teachers are tracked: that is, the most expert teachers teach the most demanding courses to the most advantaged students, while lower-track students assigned to less able teachers receive lower-quality teaching and less demanding material. Assignment to tracks is also related to race: even when grades and test scores are comparable, black students are more likely to be assigned to lower-track, nonacademic classes.

WHEN OPPORTUNITY IS MORE EQUAL

What happens when students of color do get access to more equal opportunities? Studies find that curriculum quality and teacher skill make more difference to educational outcomes than the initial test scores or racial backgrounds of students. Analyses of national data from both the High School and Beyond Surveys and the National Educational Longitudinal Surveys have demonstrated that, while there are dramatic differences among students of various racial and ethnic groups in course-taking in such areas as math, science, and foreign language, for students with similar course-taking records, achievement test score differences by race or ethnicity narrow substantially.

Robert Dreeben and colleagues at the University of Chicago conducted a long line of studies documenting both the relationship between educational opportunities and student performance and minority students' access to those opportunities. In a comparative study of 300 Chicago first graders, for example, Dreeben found that African-American and white students who had comparable instruction achieved comparable levels of reading skill. But he also found that the quality of instruction given African-American students was, on average, much lower than that given white students, thus creating a racial gap in aggregate achievement at the end of first grade. In fact, the highest-ability group in Dreeben's sample was in a school in a low-income African-American neighborhood. These children, though, learned less during first grade than their white counterparts because their teacher was unable to provide the challenging instruction they deserved.

When schools have radically different teaching forces, the effects can be profound. For example, when Eleanor Armour-Thomas and colleagues compared a group of exceptionally effective elementary schools with a group of low-achieving schools with similar demographic characteristics in New York City, roughly 90 percent of the variance in student reading and mathematics scores at grades 3, 6, and 8 was a function of differences in teacher qualifications. The schools with highly qualified teachers serving large numbers of minority and low-income students performed as well as much more advantaged schools.

Most studies have estimated effects statistically. However, an experiment that randomly assigned seventh grade "at-risk" students to remedial, average, and honors mathematics classes found that the at-risk students who took the honors class offering a pre-algebra curriculum ultimately outperformed all other students of similar backgrounds. Another study compared African-American high school youth randomly placed in public housing in the Chicago suburbs with city-placed peers of equivalent income and initial academic attainment and found that the suburban students, who attended largely white and better-funded schools, were substantially more likely to take challenging courses, perform well academically, graduate on time, attend college, and find good jobs.

WHAT CAN BE DONE?

This state of affairs is not inevitable. Last year the National Commission on Teaching and America's Future issued a blueprint for a comprehensive set of policies to ensure a "caring, competent, and qualified teacher for every child," as well as schools organized to support student success. Twelve states are now working directly with the commission on this agenda, and others are set to join this year. Several pending bills to overhaul the federal Higher Education Act would ensure that highly qualified teachers are recruited and prepared for students in all schools. Federal policymakers can develop incentives, as they have in medicine, to guarantee well-prepared teachers in shortage fields and high-need locations. States can equalize education spending, enforce higher teaching standards, and reduce teacher shortages, as Connecticut, Kentucky, Minnesota, and North Carolina have already done. School districts can reallocate resources from administrative superstructures and special add-on programs to support better-educated teachers who offer a challenging curriculum in smaller schools and classes, as restructured schools as far apart as New York and San Diego have done. These schools, in communities where children are normally written off to lives of poverty, welfare dependency, or incarceration, already produce much higher levels of achievement for students of color, sending more than 90 percent of their students to college. Focusing on what matters most can make a real difference in what children have the opportunity to learn. This, in turn, makes a difference in what communities can accomplish.

AN ENTITLEMENT TO GOOD TEACHING

The common presumption about educational inequality—that it resides primarily in those students who come to school with inadequate capacities to benefit from what the school has to offer—continues to hold wide currency because the extent of inequality in opportunities to learn is largely unknown. We do not currently operate schools on the presumption that students might be entitled to decent teaching and schooling as a matter of course. In fact, some state and local defendants have countered school finance and desegregation cases with assertions that such remedies are not required unless it can be proven that they will produce equal outcomes. Such arguments against equalizing opportunities to learn have made good on DuBois's prediction that the problem of the 20th century would be the problem of the color line.

But education resources do make a difference, particularly when funds are used to purchase well-qualified teachers and high-quality curriculum and to create personalized learning communities in which children are well known. In all of the current sturm und drang about affirmative action, "special treatment," and the other high-volatility buzzwords for race and class politics in this nation, I would offer a simple starting point for the next century's efforts: no special programs, just equal educational opportunity.

CRITICAL THINKING QUESTIONS

1. Several studies cited in the article reference the way minority students are considered at-risk within the education system. For you, what are the **five** most concerning issues revealed by these studies, and why are they concerning? What organizations wrote these studies?

2. How does Ronald Ferguson define teacher expertise? Why is it so important? Why does he control for "socioeconomic status" in his studies? What does this mean, and why would it be important to do this?

3. In the "What Can Be Done?" section, Lisa Darling-Hammond lists several recommendations. What are the four that you thought were most important? Select two of them and explain how, if they were addressed, a school district would increase its effectiveness. Add an additional reform you think is necessary that wasn't found in the article. Why would your reform help close the racial achievement gap?

4. **Connection.** Linda Darling-Hammond writes that, "tracking systems exacerbate these inequalities." How do you define the tracking system in schools? What is your opinion of tracking students? Go back to John Gatto's six hidden functions of education. Explain two functions and connect them to Darling-Hammond's concerns about tracking.

WHY POOR STUDENTS STRUGGLE

by Vicki Madden

Vicki Madden has written for *The New York Times* and often presents on issues of educational management. She worked for many years in New York City at several schools, including the Brooklyn School for Collaborative Studies. She served as an instructional leader and was a member of a school pedagogical leadership group from 2007–2013.

In this 2014 article from *The New York Times*, Madden recounts her own difficulties as a college student and compares them to her own students' difficulties. Her students grow up in some of the most difficult parts of America's largest city; she grew up with a goat in her backyard. She connects these struggles by exploring the role poverty and culture play in students' success at the college level. With more and more impoverished and first-time students coming to college, what can be done to ensure that poor students aren't struggling because they are poor?

• • • • • • • • • • • • • • •

I was rushing to change trains at Delancey Street in downtown Manhattan earlier this year when a tall young man stepped in front of me, blocking my way through the crowd. He said my name and I looked up.

"Kelvin!" I cried. As we hugged, I considered what month it was. March. Why wasn't he upstate at school? He knew what I was thinking.

"I'm taking a year off. Everybody told me I should go to college, but I didn't really know what I was doing there."

I told him that I had taken a year off from college myself. And that when my son was unhappy at his small-town college, I had recommended a transfer to Hunter College, a return to the city. I suggested he get in touch with the college counselor at the secondary school in Brooklyn where I'd taught him. "Josh can help you with a transfer," I said.

He nodded, but I walked away unconvinced that he would ask for help. A couple of months later, another former student came out from behind the cash register at a grocery store in Brooklyn to hug me and reassure me that she would be back in college in September—she just needed to earn some money. As we caught up, she told me that yet another classmate had left a top-tier college in Maine.

The effort to increase the number of low-income students who graduate from four-year colleges, especially elite colleges, has recently been front-page news. But when I think about my students, and my own story, I wonder whether the barriers, seen and unseen, have changed at all.

In spite of our collective belief that education is the engine for climbing the socioeconomic ladder—the heart of the "American dream" myth—colleges now are more divided by wealth than ever. When lower-income students start college, they often struggle to finish for many reasons, but social isolation and alienation can be big factors. In "Rewarding Strivers: Helping Low-Income Students Succeed in College," Anthony P. Carnevale and Jeff Strohl analyzed federal data collected by Michael Bastedo and Ozan Jaquette of the University of Michigan School of Education; they found that at the 193 most selective colleges, only 14 percent of students were from the bottom 50 percent of Americans in terms of socioeconomic status. Just 5 percent of students were from the lowest quartile.

I know something about the lives behind the numbers, which are largely unchanged since I arrived at Barnard in 1978, taking a red-eye flight from Seattle by myself. The other students I encountered on campus seemed foreign to me. Their parents had gone to Ivy League schools; they played tennis. I had never before been east of Nebraska. My mother raised five children while she worked for the post office, and we kept a goat in our yard to reduce the amount of garbage we'd have to pay for at the county dump.

My former students are attending Franklin and Marshall, Barnard, Bard, Colby. They are so much more worldly than I was. They've grown up in New York City, so they've hung out on the High Line, eaten sushi, visited museums and colleges on class trips. Their adjustment to college life in small towns hits different bumps than mine did.

When a miscommunication about paperwork or a parent's slight rise in income leads to a reduction in financial aid, however small, that can be enough for a student to consider withdrawing. If you don't have $700, it might as well be a million.

Kids at the most selective colleges often struggle academically, but they are capable of doing the work. The real key is whether they feel comfortable going to professors to ask for help or teaming up with other students in study groups and to manage the workload. At that school in Brooklyn, I taught history, leading students through writing 10-page position papers with proper citations, as well as presenting and defending their work to a panel of adults. Other teachers did the same in their subjects. Through the college application process, these students had help with every step—including convincing their parents that going away to school would be a good thing.

But once those from lower socioeconomic backgrounds arrive on campus, it's often the subtler things, the signifiers of who they are and where they come from, that cause the most trouble, challenging their very identity, comfort and right to be on that campus. The more elite the school, the wider that gap. I remember struggling with references to things I'd never heard of, from Homer to the Social Register. I couldn't read *The New York Times*—not because the words were too hard, but because I didn't have enough knowledge of the world to follow the articles. Hardest was the awareness that my own experiences were not only undervalued but often mocked, used to indicate when someone was stupid or low-class: No one at Barnard ate Velveeta or had ever butchered a deer.

Urban students face different slights but ones with a more dangerous edge. One former student was told by multiple people in his small Pennsylvania college town not to wear a hoodie at night, because it made him look "sketchy." Standing out like that—being himself—could put him at risk.

To stay four years and graduate, students have to come to terms with the unspoken transaction: exchanging your old world for a new world, one that doesn't seem to value where you came from. The transition is not just about getting a degree and making more money. If that was all socioeconomics signified, it would not be such a strong predictor of everything from SAT scores and parenting practices to health and longevity.

Perhaps because I came from generations of people who had left their families behind and pushed west from Ireland, West Virginia and Montana, I suffered few pangs at the idea of setting out for a new land with better opportunities. I wanted the libraries, summer houses and good wine more than anything that I then valued about my own history.

In college, I read Richard Rodriguez's memoir, "Hunger of Memory," in which he depicts his alienation from his family because of his education, painting a picture of the scholarship boy returned home to face his parents and finding only silence. Being young, I didn't understand, believing myself immune to the idea that any gain might entail a corresponding loss. I was keen to exchange my Western hardscrabble life for the chance to be a New York City middle-class museumgoer. I've paid a price in estrangement from my own people, but I was willing. Not every 18-year-old will make that same choice, especially when race is factored in as well as class.

As the income gap widens and hardens, changing class means a bigger difference between where you came from and where you are going. Teachers like me can help prepare students academically for college work. College counselors can help with the choices, the federal financial aid application and all the bureaucratic details. But how can we help our students prepare for the tug of war in their souls?

CRITICAL THINKING QUESTIONS

1. In her article, Vicki Madden discusses barriers, "seen and unseen," as to why low-income students fail to graduate from college. What is one "seen" barrier she mentions? How does that hold back low-income students? What is one unseen barrier? How does that function to keep low-income students from graduating from school?
2. Why did Vicki Madden find difficulty reading *The New York Times*? How does this connect to her upbringing? Many articles in this reader are from *The New York Times*. Do any of these struggles resonate with you? Why or why not?
3. What was the "tug of war in (her) soul" that Madden describes feeling when she was in college? Who were the two sides of the tug of war? How might this play out for the low-income students she describes in her essay? Do you feel a tug of war? Why or why not?
4. Define the "American Dream." Does the "American Dream" still include the idea that earning a college degree will help one climb the "socioeconomic ladder?" Why do you feel your work here in college may improve your socioeconomic status?

SEGREGATION NOW

by Nikole Hannah-Jones

Nikole Hannah-Jones is an award-winning investigative reporter for *ProPublica* in New York City. Hannah Jones is specifically interested in writing on civil rights topics, and her reporting has been featured on *Face the Nation, This American Life, NPR, The Atlantic Wire, Huffington Post* and many other popular media outlets.

In this 2014 essay from *ProPublica*, Hannah-Jones describes the changes to the Tuscaloosa school district, starting with the 1954 *Brown v. Board of Education* decision through the present day. Through three interconnecting stories, she tells of the dramatic rise and fall of Central High School. She argues that, for many parts of the country, segregation *now* is different only in how it is enacted. In 1954, the Supreme Court ruled that separate schools meant inherently unequal schools. Why have places like Tuscaloosa forgotten this lesson?

• • • • • • • • • • • • • • • •

Though James Dent could watch Central High School's homecoming parade from the porch of his faded-white bungalow, it had been years since he'd bothered. But last fall, Dent's oldest granddaughter, D'Leisha, was vying for homecoming queen, and he knew she'd be poking up through the sunroof of her mother's car, hand cupped in a beauty-pageant wave, looking for him.

So, at about 4:30 in the afternoon on October 18, Dent, age 64, made his way off the porch and to the curb along Martin Luther King Jr. Boulevard in the West End of Tuscaloosa, Alabama. Soon he could hear the first rumblings of the band.

There was a time, little more than a decade ago, when the Central High School homecoming parade brought out the city. The parade started in the former state capital's lively downtown and seemed to go on for miles. The horns of one of the state's largest marching bands, some 150 members strong, would bounce off the antebellum mansions along the streets. Revelers—young and old, black and white, old money and no money—crowded the sidewalks to watch the elaborate floats and cheer a football team feared across the region.

Central was not just a renowned local high school. It was one of the South's signature integration success stories. In 1979, a federal judge had ordered the merger of the city's two largely segregated high schools into one. The move was clumsy and unpopular, but its consequences were profound. Within a few years, Central emerged as a powerhouse that snatched up National Merit Scholarships and math-competition victories just as readily as it won trophies in football, track, golf. James Dent's daughter Melissa graduated from Central in 1988, during its heyday, and went on to become the first in her family to graduate from college.

But on that sunlit day last October, as Dent searched for Melissa's daughter in the procession coming into view, he saw little to remind him of that era. More caravan than parade, Central's homecoming pageant consisted of a wobbly group of about 30 band members, some marching children from the nearby elementary schools, and a dozen or so cars with handwritten signs attached to their sides. The route began in the predominantly black West End and ended a few blocks later, just short of the railroad tracks that divide that community from the rest of the city.

The reason for the decline of Central's homecoming parade is no secret. In 2000, another federal judge released Tuscaloosa City Schools from the court-ordered desegregation mandate that had governed it for a single generation. Central had successfully achieved integration, the district had argued—it could be trusted to manage that success going forward.

Freed from court oversight, Tuscaloosa's schools have seemed to move backwards in time. The citywide integrated high school is gone, replaced by three smaller schools. Central retains the name of the old powerhouse, but nothing more. A struggling school serving the city's poorest part of town, it is 99 percent black. D'Leisha, an honors student since middle school, has only marginal college prospects. Predominantly white neighborhoods adjacent to Central have been gerrymandered into the attendance zones of other, whiter schools.

Tuscaloosa's schools today are not as starkly segregated as they were in 1954, the year the Supreme Court declared an end to separate and unequal education in America. No all-white schools exist anymore—the city's white students generally attend schools with significant numbers of black students. But while segregation as it is practiced today may be different than it was 60 years ago, it is no less pernicious: in Tuscaloosa and elsewhere, it involves the removal and isolation of poor black and Latino students, in particular, from everyone else. In Tuscaloosa today, nearly one in three black students attends a school that looks as if *Brown v. Board of Education* never happened.

Tuscaloosa's school resegregation—among the most extensive in the country—is a story of city financial interests, secret meetings, and angry public votes. It is a story shaped by racial politics and a consuming fear of white flight. It was facilitated, to some extent, by the city's black elites. And it was blessed by a U.S. Department of Justice no longer committed to fighting for the civil-rights aims it had once championed.

Certainly what happened in Tuscaloosa was no accident. Nor was it isolated. Schools in the South, once the most segregated in the country, had by the 1970s become the most integrated, typically as a result of federal court orders. But since 2000, judges have released hundreds of school districts, from Mississippi to Virginia, from court-enforced integration, and many of these districts have followed the same path as Tuscaloosa's—back toward segregation. Black children across the South now attend majority-black schools at levels not seen in four decades. Nationally, the achievement gap between black and white students, which greatly narrowed during the era in which schools grew more integrated, widened as they became less so.

RESEGREGATING U.S. SCHOOLS

In recent years, a new term, apartheid schools—meaning schools whose white population is 1 percent or less, schools like Central—has entered the scholarly lexicon. While most of these schools are in the Northeast and Midwest, some 12 percent of black students in the South and nearly a quarter in Alabama now attend such schools—a figure likely to rise as court oversight continues to wane. In 1972, due to strong federal enforcement, only about 25 percent of black students in the South attended schools in which at least nine out of 10 students were racial minorities. In districts released from desegregation orders between 1990 and 2011, 53 percent of black students now attend such schools, according to an analysis by *ProPublica.*

The Dent family, from grandfather to granddaughter, has lived out integration's fleeting wonder, a fact that hardened James Dent's face as he stood on that Tuscaloosa curb last October. The parade—just 15 minutes old, and yet almost over—quickly brought D'Leisha before him. Nene, as her family calls her, beamed and waved. Dent waved back and looked around to share the moment. But besides his wife and his stepson, no one else was there.

James

In the hours after the parade, James Dent sat back in a worn wingback chair in the cramped but tidy house he and his wife rent in the West End. As dusk brought out the whirring of cicadas, he quietly flipped through a photo album devoted to D'Leisha's many accomplishments. She's the class president, a member of the mayor's youth council, a state champion in track and field. Later that night, she would be named homecoming queen as well.

Dent never went to college. One of 13 children born into the waning days of Jim Crow, he took his place in the earliest of integrated American institutions: the military. He served four years in the Air Force, including a year in Vietnam, before returning to the West End to spend the next 40 mixing cement for a living. The work was steady, but the pay meager.

Thin, with chestnut skin, and seldom seen without a Vietnam-vet cap, Dent is a reserved man, not prone to soapboxes. But after a long silence, he gently suggested that maybe his granddaughter deserved a little more than a 12-car salute at a brief and sparsely attended parade. When D'Leisha graduates this spring, she will have spent her entire public education in segregated schools. Just like he had.

"I think about it all the time, and ain't nothing I can do about it," he said. "It ain't going to get no better." He said he just hoped she was learning as much as the city's white students were, then grew quiet again. If integration was going to prove so brief, what, he wondered, had all the fighting been for?

Tucked along the Black Warrior River some 60 miles southwest of Birmingham, Tuscaloosa has a racial history marked by contradictions. The city is home to three colleges, the University of Alabama among them, and a pioneering psychiatric hospital. Its civic leaders have, at times, been called progressive. A *New York Times* reporter covering civil rights in the 1950s described Tuscaloosa as a "clean, prosperous city that has long been proud of its good race relations."

And yet, of course, the phrase good race relations was misleading: the city operated under the dictates of Jim Crow until the passage of the Civil Rights Act of 1964. Black people took their first breaths in segregated hospital rooms, worshipped in segregated churches, and, when they died, were buried in segregated graveyards. The imperial wizard of the United Klans of America, responsible for the Birmingham church bombing that killed four little girls, called Tuscaloosa home during the civil-rights era. Historians and older black residents say the city avoided the ugliest violence of that time because black people mostly stayed in their place.

Unlike many other southern cities, Tuscaloosa has a long tradition of educating black children. When the city founded its public-school system in 1885, it opened both white and black schools. That year, the new school board provided maps, tables, blackboards, and crayons for 274 white children and 173 black children.

But that does not mean that Tuscaloosa's schools were equal before their integration, or that the city would accommodate integration willingly (as the infamous riots foiling the attempted integration of the University of Alabama in 1956 attested).

James Dent entered first grade at the "colored" Central Elementary not long after the Supreme Court issued its landmark *Brown v. Board of Education* decision in 1954. "We conclude that, in the field of public education, the doctrine of 'separate but equal' has no place," Chief Justice Earl Warren wrote. "Separate educational facilities are inherently unequal." And yet—so ferocious and effective was the southern pushback against desegregation—Dent would never attend school with a white classmate.

The *Brown* ruling did not hinge on the inferior resources allotted black students under many segregated educational systems. As Warren pointed out in his decision, many southern officials, in an effort to forestall integration, had been investing heavily in bringing black schools up to white standards, so that by the time the Court agreed to hear *Brown*, school facilities and teacher salaries in many black public schools had "been equalized, or [were] being equalized."

"We must look instead," Warren wrote, "to the effect of segregation itself." He wrote that to separate black children "from others of similar age and qualifications solely because of their race generates a feeling of inferiority as to their status in the community that may affect their hearts and minds in a way unlikely ever to be undone." The justices noted that education was "perhaps the most important function of state and local governments" and that the integration of schools was essential to the integration of black citizens into society as a whole.

The ruling came with a heavy compromise. Warren understood the storm of resistance likely to confront the decision. He believed only a united Court could contain southern rage, but some of the justices wanted to go slow. So, instead of laying out an explicit framework for desegregation, the Court acknowledged that the "variety of local conditions" made dismantling Jim Crow schools a complicated matter, and ultimately placed the burden of enforcing its ruling on district courts. It gave the lower courts no guidance other than to say that desegregation should proceed "with all deliberate speed."

In some ways, the Court's hesitancy to mandate immediate desegregation is understandable. The racial caste system the Court suddenly deemed illegal not only predated the nation itself but had been sanctioned by that very judicial body for six decades.

Yet while the Court dragged its feet on what to do, southern officials were moving quickly. Virginia Governor Thomas B. Stanley vowed to use "every legal means" to "continue segregated schools." Alabama joined other southern states in passing laws allowing or requiring school boards to shut schools to avoid having even a handful of black children sit in classrooms with white ones. Some states helped fund the all-white academies popping up across the South. State officials encouraged white parents to remove their children from public schools, helping to set off the white flight that continues to plague school systems today. Two years after the *Brown* ruling, not a single black child attended school with white children in eight of the 11 former Confederate states, including Alabama.

Dent doesn't recall hearing his parents ever discuss his new right to an integrated education. His mother, a domestic who cleaned white people's houses, provided the family with its only stable income; his father worked odd jobs as he could find them. Dent and his parents and 12 siblings were often on the move, sometimes crashing with relatives.

School did not come easily to Dent, an athletic boy with a serious face, nor did he particularly like it. Mostly, it reminded him of how poor his family was. "I remember going to school barefoot" as a young child, Dent told me. "I'd be so embarrassed, I'd try to play hooky."

By the time he started his freshman year in high school, in 1964, a full decade after *Brown*, just 2.3 percent of the nearly 3 million school-aged black children in the old

Confederate South attended school alongside white children. None of those children lived in Tuscaloosa. At Dent's school, Druid High, students learned from hand-me-down textbooks and lagged behind their white counterparts on achievement tests. The curriculum pushed students toward learning a trade instead of preparing for college.

Even so, Dent's experience at Druid reveals a truth often lost in the history of school integration. Though its resources were not as rich as those of the all-white Tuscaloosa High, Druid was a source of pride within the city's black community. Its students soaked up lessons from a committed staff of all-black teachers, many of whom were exceptionally talented, in part because teaching was among the only professional careers open to black southerners at the time. What the school lacked in racial diversity, it made up for in economic variety: the children of domestic workers walked the halls with the children of college professors. Condoleezza Rice was one of Dent's schoolmates.

McDonald Hughes, Druid's tall, stern principal, instilled a sense of discipline and of possibility in his students. "He'd grab you by the shoulders," Dent recalled with a laugh. "He wanted you to succeed."

Just before Dent's freshman year, Congress had passed the Civil Rights Act of 1964. The law barred school districts that discriminated against black students from receiving federal education funding, which would soon be increased by more than $1 billion. Under the law, the feds for the first time could sue defiant districts. The sweeping legislation brought about the rarest of moments in American history: all three branches of government were aligned on civil rights. Backed by the courts and Congress, the Johnson administration set the Justice Department to aggressively pursuing desegregation.

James Dent would never feel the impact of these changes: Druid High remained untouched until well after his graduation. Throughout the South, school officials, realizing they could not avoid integration altogether, sought "race neutral" means to control it. Some adopted plans for "neighborhood schools," with attendance zones carefully drawn around racially distinct parts of town. As a result, token integration replaced absolute segregation in many places. All-white schools started disappearing, but all-black schools remained common.

Still, by 1968, one out of three southern black kids was going to school with white children. That same year, the Supreme Court revealed its growing impatience when it ordered school officials to produce plans that promised "realistically to work, and realistically to work now," eliminating segregation "root and branch." Three years later, the Court emphasized that desegregation plans should be judged by their effectiveness in eliminating racially identifiable schools.

The dominoes, at last, had begun to fall.

Melissa

Melissa Dent, James's first child, was born in 1969, around the time the National Education Association and the Department of Justice persuaded a federal court to force Tuscaloosa to comply with a statewide desegregation order. As she began to toddle and then run around, revealing herself to be an athlete, like her father, the South was quickly changing: by the early '70s, more than 90 percent of black children were attending desegregated schools.

Even so, Melissa Dent began her education at the same all-black elementary school that her father had attended. In 1975, the Department of Justice and the NAACP Legal Defense Fund hauled the district back into court, not long before a federal agency placed the Tuscaloosa system on its list of the nation's worst civil-rights offenders. The case landed on the docket of Judge Frank McFadden, a Yale Law–educated former Wall Street attorney born in Oxford, Mississippi.

McFadden, now 88, with a shock of white hair, still practices law in Montgomery, and he recently described the predicament he found himself in some 40 years ago. The Supreme Court had been right in striking down legal segregation, McFadden said. The details of the Jim Crow era—how the words white supremacy were written on Alabama's Democratic Party ballot, or how even which line you stood in at the liquor store depended on your race—remained vivid for the former judge. "Separate but equal was a joke, a horrible joke," he said.

But by the time the Tuscaloosa case hit his desk, McFadden said, *Brown* had stood as the law of the land for two decades and the legal barriers to integration had been eliminated. "The plaintiffs were contending that the absence of integration equals the presence of segregation, and they are not necessarily the same." The Justice Department and the Legal Defense Fund were asserting that "if there was a racial imbalance in the student body, then that in and of itself established segregation, and some remedy had to happen."

McFadden disagreed. "What was being sought in the Tuscaloosa case when it came to me was a forced integration," he said. "If you read my orders in the Tuscaloosa case and what I said in the courtroom, it was simply this: *Brown v. Board of Education* said you cannot send a child to a specific school because of his or her race, and that is precisely what affirmative action was requiring to be done."

McFadden admitted to me that much of the segregation once required by law remained, even though the laws no longer did. He noted that segregation had its roots in slavery, and that white attitudes toward black Americans had hardened over the centuries.

But when asked how the country could have addressed the resistance to integration if the courts hadn't forced it, he turned philosophical. "You would have sunk the first slave ship, cut that all out, and not brought them in here," he said, his honeyed Oxford drawl softening the bite in his words. "How one would accomplish desegregation in an ideal world, I don't have that answer." He raised his age-speckled hands, palms up. "But before you have that ideal, human beings have to change attitudes."

The Tuscaloosa case and others like it were hard, McFadden said. He ultimately decided that Tuscaloosa's efforts, centered on the creation of neighborhood-based schools, were sufficient, because he believed the school segregation that remained resulted from housing patterns. But the Supreme Court had already made clear that disproportionately black schools in districts with a history of legal segregation were highly suspicious, and that housing-based segregation could not justify all-black schools in these districts. In overruling McFadden, the federal appeals court noted that the virtually all-black Druid High was not even two miles from the mostly white Tuscaloosa High. McFadden eventually presided over a series of changes, including the creation of Central as the city's sole public high school.

In the fall of 1979, Central High School opened to serve all public high school students in the district—no matter their race, no matter whether they lived in the city's public housing projects or in one of the mansions along the meandering Black Warrior River. The megaschool, a creative solution to a complex problem, resulted from many hours of argument and negotiation in McFadden's chambers. It was spread across two campuses—ninth- and 10th-graders at the former black high school, now called Central West; 11th- and 12th-graders at the old white high school, called Central East. (The judge's order also created three single-grade middle schools.)

All traces of the segregated system, from the mascots to the school colors of the two former schools, were discarded. All of Tuscaloosa's public-high-school students would now unite under the red-and-white banner of the Falcons. As one of the biggest schools in the state, Central would offer classes in subjects ranging from Latin to forensics.

Over the years, Central racked up debate-team championships. Its math team dominated at state competitions. The cheerleaders tumbled their way to nationals, and the Falcons football team trounced local competitors so badly, some refused to play against it. Central students were regularly named National Merit Scholars. In 2001, the state found Central's projected dropout rate to be less than half Alabama's average.

"Central and its resources could reach any child," said Robert Coates, a former principal of the school.

The school was hardly perfect. Black students were disproportionately funneled into vocational classes, and white students into honors classes. Some parents complained that competitive opportunities were limited to just the very best students and athletes because the school, at 2,300 students, was so large. And the white flight that had begun when the courts first ordered the district to desegregate continued, slowly, after the formation of the mega-school. But despite these challenges, large numbers of black students studied the same robust curriculum as white students, and students of both races mixed peacefully and thrived.

Desegregation had been wrenching and complicated, but in Tuscaloosa and across the country, it achieved undeniable results. During the 1970s and '80s, the achievement gap between black and white 13-year-olds was cut roughly in half nationwide. Some scholars argue that desegregation had a negligible effect on overall academic achievement. But the overwhelming body of research shows that once black children were given access to advanced courses, well-trained teachers, and all the other resources that tend to follow white, middle-income children, they began to catch up.

A 2014 study conducted by Rucker Johnson, a public-policy professor at the University of California at Berkeley, published by the National Bureau of Economic Research, found desegregation's impact on racial equality to be deep, wide, and long-lasting. Johnson examined data on a representative sample of 8,258 American adults born between 1945 and 1968, whom he followed through 2011. He found that black Americans who attended schools integrated by court order were more likely to graduate, go on to college, and earn a degree than black Americans who attended segregated schools. They made more money: five years of integrated schooling increased the earnings of black adults by 15 percent. They were significantly less likely to spend time in jail. They were healthier.

Notably, Rucker also found that black progress did not come at the expense of white Americans—white students in integrated schools did just as well academically as those in segregated schools. Other studies have found that attending integrated schools made white students more likely to later live in integrated neighborhoods and send their own children to racially diverse schools.

Melissa Dent attended her first integrated class as a middle-schooler, in 1980, as a result of the court order. But by the time she graduated from Central eight years later, integration in the South had already reached its high-water mark. The percentage of black and white students attending school together would never be greater.

At Central, Dent quickly made a name for herself as a premier athlete. Her track team took the state title twice, and she was named Alabama's top female high-school track performer in 1987. More important, the school introduced her to people from different backgrounds. Neither her mother nor her father had gone to college, yet her classmates—some of whose fathers were attorneys or business owners—planted that seed. "All my friends were talking about college and wanting to do better," she told me. "I've always been ambitious, and I wanted to do better too."

As part of the first generation born outside the constraints of Jim Crow, Dent has not lived out a Horatio Alger Jr. fable. Much like the story of integration, her story is one of fits and starts, of grinding progress and battles to hang on to the gains. In her sophomore year of college, she got pregnant. She came back home and had her baby. But she then returned to school, walking onto the track team at the University of Alabama and graduating in 1995.

Now 45 and a single mother of four, she works on the assembly line at the Mercedes-Benz plant just outside of town. Her work is physically taxing, but she fought to get the factory gig, a coveted job in the area, because it paid more than she'd ever earned as a teaching assistant, the job she had after college. Unlike her father, she owns her West End home, a brick fixer-upper she bought eight years ago, after falling in love with its den and big backyard.

Dent called herself "average, very average," as a student, but like her own parents, she hopes that education will take her children further than it has taken her.

Her children's academic medals and certificates clutter the living-room walls in her house. It is clear in conversation that Melissa never expected to count the opportunity for a quality education among the things she would be unable to provide for her children. She said she'd assumed that she'd be the bridge between her father's Jim Crow generation and a new generation for whom integration was natural.

Dent said her high-school class had formed a lasting bond. Even now, she said, if she called on any of her white fellow alums, like the prominent lawyer she'd reconnected with during a recent class reunion, they would remember her. She believes D'Leisha, a child every bit as outgoing as her mother is reserved, would have formed a rainbow coalition of friends if she'd attended the old Central, and made connections that could have helped her in the future.

D'Leisha

A few minutes before first period on a Wednesday last October, D'Leisha Dent, a 17-year-old senior, waded through Central High's halls, toes with chipped blue polish peeking out from her sandals, orange jeans hugging solid legs that had helped make her the three-time state indoor shot-put champion.

She eventually broke free from a tangle of girls to enter Tyrone Jones's Advanced Placement English class and take her seat at the front. She dropped two black bags taut with notebooks and binders beside her desk.

Jones didn't waste time setting the boisterous class to task. The AP exam was approaching. Students who didn't score high enough wouldn't get college credit for the class. Even though the 17 girls and boys gathered in front of him made up Central's brightest, their practice essay about a poem hadn't gone so well.

D'Leisha raised her hand, her brow furrowed. How many kids had made the cutoff last year? she asked. Only two students had, but the teacher dodged the question. "I really do believe all of you can make those scores," he said.

He passed out an essay question about D. H. Lawrence's novel *The Rainbow.* As the students began to write, a girl sitting to his left scrunched up her nose and raised her hand. She couldn't spell a word she wanted to use in her essay. Jones told her to look it up in one of the heavy red dictionaries in the baskets below their desks.

"You know what I don't understand?" the girl said, a pen poised at her lips. "You always tell us to look up the word. How are we supposed to look a word up if we don't know to spell it?"

Jones stopped. His eyes scanned each of the 17 brown faces looking expectantly back at him. Then he gave an answer that seemed to sum up their educational experience. "What do we say about struggling?" he asked. "You have to work through the struggle."

After Melissa Dent graduated, in 1988, Central continued as one of the state's standout high schools. But over time, local leaders grew more concerned about the students who didn't attend the school than those who did.

White students once accounted for a majority of the Tuscaloosa school district's students. But by the mid-1990s, they made up less than a third. Total enrollment had dropped from 13,500 in 1969 to 10,300 in 1995. Many white parents had decided to send their children to nearly all-white private schools or to move across the city line to access the heavily white Tuscaloosa County Schools.

Tuscaloosa's business leaders and elected officials had witnessed the transformation of other southern cities after their school districts had reached a tipping point—the point at which white parents become unsettled by the rising share of black students in a school, and pull their children from the school en masse. School districts in cities such as Birmingham and Richmond had seen their integration efforts largely mooted: just about all the white students had left. As white families had moved out to the suburbs, eroding the tax base, both the schools and the cities themselves had suffered. Many officials in Tuscaloosa obsessed about the rippling consequences of continued white flight. "Money follows kids, and the loss of white students was very, very critical," said Shelley Jones, who is white and served as a school-board member in the 1990s, and later as the chair.

Tuscaloosa's residential population stagnated during the '90s, and the school situation took on special urgency in 1993: Tuscaloosa was vying for the Mercedes-Benz plant where Melissa Dent now works, which officials hoped would draw people to the city. Just a few years earlier, Tuscaloosa had lost out on a bid for a Saturn plant. In an interview early this year, Johnnie Aycock, who at the time headed the Chamber of Commerce of West Alabama, suggested the schools had scared Saturn away. "We learned that lesson. We learned that lesson completely."

Publicly, the city's movers and shakers said the lack of neighborhood schools made the district unattractive and that schools languished in disrepair because the district had to await court approval for every little decision. Behind closed doors, they argued that if they did not create some schools where white students made up the majority—or near it—they'd lose the white parents still remaining.

Districts under desegregation orders aren't supposed to take actions that increase racial separation. And so the city's leadership decided the desegregation order needed to go, and they believed the time was ripe for a court to agree.

In the early 1990s, an increasingly conservative Supreme Court had issued several crucial rulings that made it much easier for school systems to get out from under court supervision. The Court ruled that desegregation orders were never meant to be permanent, but rather were a "temporary measure to remedy past discrimination," and that school decisions should return to local control once a district had shown a "good faith" effort to eliminate segregation. Because of changing racial demographics and housing patterns, the Court also ruled that districts no longer had to prove that they'd eliminated segregation "root and branch," just that they'd done so to the "extent practicable." Once released, a school board could assign students however it chose, as long as no proof existed that it did so for discriminatory reasons.

In 1993, Tuscaloosa's school board fired a test shot. It filed papers in federal court seeking to build a new elementary school called Rock Quarry, deep in a nearly all-white part of town separated from the rest of the city by the Black Warrior River. If a judge accepted the school, that might signal a willingness to end the order altogether.

"You could see what the city and the school district were doing. They were going to have a racially and economically segregated school system," said Janell Byrd, one of the NAACP Legal Defense Fund attorneys who represented the plaintiffs at the time.

The case landed in the courtroom of Judge Sharon Blackburn, a recent George H. W. Bush appointee who had gone to college in Tuscaloosa. In 1995, Blackburn held a five-day hearing to decide the question of Rock Quarry. School officials promised that the new school's student body, though whiter than the district's overall school population, would be half black.

The roster of witnesses lined up behind the school board shocked many in the black community. It included some of the city's most influential black leaders, including a city councilman, a state senator, and Judge John England Jr., whose credentials carried force. England had been a member of the first integrated class at the University of Alabama Law School, and he'd fought discrimination his whole career as a litigator, before taking on roles as a city-council member and then as a county judge.

England testified as to how the city's racial views had changed over the years. Building a school "across the river," England told the court, was "the best thing for the community as a whole."

Rumors spread within the community that England's and others' support had been part of a secret arrangement with white leaders. Dennis Parker, another Legal Defense Fund attorney, asked England during his testimony whether he'd said at a public meeting that a deal had been struck to improve a West End school in exchange for support for a new school in the whitest part of town. England denied that any such deal had been made, and Blackburn gave the nod to the new school. Soon thereafter, the school board voted to go back to court to seek release from federal oversight.

The Legal Defense Fund had by that time started supporting the release of districts from federal court orders, settling cases in return for promises that the districts would voluntarily continue some desegregation efforts. It had seen the writing on the wall: "There seemed almost a fatigue with the cases" on the part of judges, "and a desire to get them finished," Parker told me. And beginning in the Reagan administration, which cut off federal desegregation funding, the Justice Department had started to walk away from the court orders.

A negotiated agreement, supported by the Legal Defense Fund and the Justice Department, to end Tuscaloosa's federal desegregation order was brought before Judge Blackburn in 1998. School leaders publicly pledged to continue desegregation efforts, and Superintendent Bob Winter said that no new schools, which might lead to less integration, were planned.

Still, Blackburn, before making what she called the most significant ruling of her time on the bench, ordered a hearing. About 50 people showed up, and many urged her to reject the settlement. Emotions were raw. "I wouldn't be up here if I didn't think someone was trying to harm my children," Chykeitha Roshell told the local paper.

Before granting the request to free the district, Blackburn seemed to speak to Tuscaloosa's black community. "I don't know any of you all, and you don't know me," she said. "I grew up in Alabama in the '60s, in a small town in south Alabama . . . You can't know my views about segregation and how strongly I feel about our state and our history of racial injustice." She acknowledged the crowd's sentiment, saying, "You don't understand why I'm doing this, and you think I'm wrong. But I'm doing what I believe the law requires me to do." And with that, Blackburn announced that the 30-year-old desegregation order had come to an end.

In an interview last fall in his chambers at the Tuscaloosa County Courthouse, Judge England said on the record for the first time that he had privately agreed to support the Rock Quarry school during the trial—which would ultimately lead to the district's release from federal oversight—only with the assurance of investment in West End schools, though he denied having made a quid pro quo deal. (Several others confirmed that white business, school, and city officials met privately with select black leaders to gain support for the district's efforts to end the court order and free it to return to neighborhood schools, in exchange for new black schools and development in the West End.) The day of our interview, the story had broken nationally that England's step-granddaughter had been snubbed by the white sororities at the University of Alabama—among the nation's last remaining segregated Greek systems. The judge, a university trustee, was in a foul mood.

His retelling of the events leading up to the dismissal revealed none of the optimism he'd displayed on the stand all those years ago, but rather a steely pragmatism and no small measure of disillusionment. Under the court order, England said, black students had ridden buses all over the city chasing an ever-receding white population. Desegregation had not ended the stigmatization of black children, England said. It had reinforced it.

England had believed that if the school system continued to grow more black, financial support for schools within the white community would fall off and the city would struggle to attract commerce. Further, he'd thought that the school district would eventually free itself of federal oversight with or without the support of black leaders.

"There was a desire to have a school built across the river, where a number of white students were in private school," he said. "The business community wanted to be able to say Tuscaloosa City Schools would not be an inner-city school system."

At least the prospect of his cooperation, along with that of other black elites, offered leverage. So England and a handful of others made a Faustian bargain. In exchange for their support for building new schools in the whitest part of town, he said, white leaders promised to build some state-of-the-art schools in Tuscaloosa's West End, providing local development to a part of town with little more than factories and dollar stores. "They kept their word to build schools on this side, we kept ours," England said. "White folks got your schools. Black folks, you got yours."

In an interview last fall, Byrd said evidence of a secret agreement would have been "significant" during the trial, and had she had proof, "I certainly would have tried to get it into evidence."

For his part, England knew this arrangement meant consigning hundreds of black students to segregated schools. And he never disputed that integration had brought real academic benefits. But he saw few options and had also grown nostalgic about his own years in Jim Crow schools. "I would put the education I got against anyone's," he said. "The answer cannot be 'The only way to get good schools is to have white people in them.'"

The hearings opened a rift in Tuscaloosa's black community, dividing longtime friends. Many still accuse the judge and others of selling out, a charge that snapped the judge upright in his chair.

"Those people had their right to their viewpoint as I had mine," he said, his voice rising. "I thought I saw the whole picture." England said he still stands behind the decision he made to support Rock Quarry. But as far as segregation was concerned, he added, "I don't know what happened the last 13 years."

What happened was rapid and continual resegregation, in particular the sequestration of poor black students in nearly hopeless schools—something that didn't surprise Parker from the LDF.

"We said that it was planned and the judge just did not want to hear it." (Blackburn did not respond to numerous interview requests.)

It is no small irony that efforts to woo the very plant that allows Melissa Dent to earn enough to support her family also played a part in ensuring that her children would attend nearly all-black schools.

In 1999, less than a year after Blackburn's public hearing, the school board voted to abandon its three single-grade, citywide middle schools in favor of more traditional middle schools. It carved out two integrated schools to serve sixth- through eighth-graders in the northern, central, and eastern parts of the city, and returned Westlawn Middle, in the West End, to its familiar historic state: virtually all black.

The school board commissioned a biracial committee to figure out what to do about the high school. White parents, the commission suggested in its May 2000 report, would not want their children to attend schools once they turned 70 percent black. By its reasoning, the district had already reached the tipping point. The only way to create the necessary school ratios in a district where black students outnumbered white students almost three to one was to cluster a large number of black children in schools without white students.

The commission pointed to a handful of studies showing that smaller schools benefited low-income students. It did not note that Westlawn Middle School was floundering: the state's Department of Education had already placed the school under a warning for low achievement.

After the commission issued its report, the district created a plan for two large integrated high schools—Northridge, in the whitest and most affluent part of town, and Paul W. Bryant, along the city's eastern edge—as well as a much smaller high school that would retain the name Central. School officials drew Central's proposed attendance zone compactly around the West End, saying that an all-black high school couldn't be avoided, because the district couldn't help where people lived.

While a vocal group of white parents and community leaders supported the high-school breakup, large numbers of black and white residents fought against it. A poll of a few dozen parents who'd pulled their kids from the schools showed that most of them supported a shift to neighborhood high schools. But in a wider poll of more than 200 parents in the district, and another of Central's teachers and other staff, most respondents wanted the mega-school to remain intact. Robert Coates had just been named principal of the Central East campus, and he warned the board that if it went forward with the plan to split the schools, the new Central would be "relegated as a low-performing school from day one."

Nonetheless, in August 2000, the seven-member board ordered Central's dismantling, 21 years after its creation. One black member joined the board's four white ones in voting in favor. Under the plan, some black students would continue to be bused north of the river, though many of them were from black neighborhoods filled with two-parent, two-garage homes, as Ernestine Tucker, a current school-board member, puts it. Overall, the vote ensured that nearly a third of the district's black students would spend their entire 13 years of public education in completely segregated schools.

And so the district built its new high schools—but white parents did not flock to them. By 2007, white enrollment had fallen to 22 percent, and school leaders once again insisted something had to be done. The superintendent presented a plan that would send hundreds of black children who were still being bused to high-performing, integrated schools back to failing schools closer to their homes. The idea was that this latest plan would do what the breaking-apart of Central hadn't: draw back white parents.

The redistricting plan roiled the community, still raw over the breakup of the integrated middle and high schools less than a decade earlier. A racially mixed group of local academics and parents fired off searing editorials and showed up at meetings to protest.

But some parents were unhappy with the plan for a different set of reasons. The historic district around the University of Alabama, a predominantly white and middle-class area that's home to college professors and other professionals, lies south of the river. The district's plan would re-assign children in this neighborhood to their closest schools, which were heavily black.

The day before the school board voted, the president of the historic district association sent an e-mail to his fellow association members assuring them that after "lengthy negotiations with the school board attorney" and "discussions with school board members and the superintendent," students in the district would be able to continue to attend the north-of-the-river schools. The school board's final proposal did indeed reflect that change. The final plan also allowed children from a tiny triangle conspicuously carved from the West End—encompassing a country club and its surrounding neighborhood—to attend school north of the river.

On May 3, 2007, as the school board prepared to vote on the new plan, a few members said they had been unaware of the negotiations, and fought unsuccessfully to delay the decision. The plan passed in a bitterly divided vote, 5–3. One white school-board member, Virginia Powell, who represented the historic district around the university, joined the board's two black members in voting no. Powell said that the appeasement of white parents had trumped doing what was best educationally for the district. "It was totally orchestrated. It was awful, I felt powerless," Powell told me recently. "I remember sitting in church after one of the votes. It was a Wednesday-night supper and no one would sit with me, because I voted with the black members. It made me realize where people stood."

Since the vote, the black population at Rock Quarry, one of the district's highest-performing elementary schools—the one that school officials had promised would be 50-50 in its racial composition—has fallen from 24 percent to 9 percent. The U.S. Department of Education's Office of Civil Rights has opened an investigation into allegations of racial discrimination in how the district assigns students, including the 2007 redistricting plan.

When President George W. Bush came into office, approximately 595 school districts nationwide—including dozens of non-southern districts—remained under court-ordered desegregation, according to a *ProPublica* analysis of data on school desegregation orders compiled by Stanford University education professor Sean Reardon. By the end of Bush's second term, that number had plummeted to 380. Nearly 60 percent of all the districts that have been released from their desegregation orders since 1967 were released under Bush, whose administration pressed the Justice Department to close those cases wherever possible. The trend has slowed under the Obama administration, but it has continued. Today, about 340 districts remain under court order.

ProPublica examined 24 years of demographic data compiled by the National Center for Education Statistics and found that districts grew steadily more segregated after their desegregation orders ended. A 2012 Stanford study examined school districts with at least 2,000 students that had been released from court order since 1990, finding that, typically, these districts grew steadily more segregated after their release. A separate 2011 study in the *American Economic Journal* found that within 10 years of being released, school districts on average unwound about 60 percent of the integration they had achieved under court order.

One troubling truth is that, as witnessed in Tuscaloosa, backing away from integration doesn't typically arrest or reverse the outflow of white students from diverse school districts. The Stanford researchers found that school systems' white populations slightly declined after court orders ended. Many districts nonetheless continue to embrace the type of gerrymandering at play in Tuscaloosa. After comprehensively examining attendance zones across the country, Meredith Richards at the University of Pennsylvania's Institute of Education Sciences found in a recent study that they are nearly as irregular as legislative districts.

Some districts, of course, have gerrymandered to increase integration. Kentucky's Jefferson County Public Schools, serving Louisville, are often held up as an example. The battle for desegregation had been violent there, but eventually the community came to value its integrated schools. When the superintendent began pressing to end the district's elementary-school busing program, Jefferson County's business leaders met with residents but came to a very different conclusion from the one reached in Tuscaloosa. They decided to support continued integration efforts, because they deemed integrated schools good for business. Even though its court supervision ended in 2000, Jefferson County remains one of the most integrated urban districts in the country.

But Jefferson County is the rarest of cases. Few communities seem able to summon the political will to continue integration efforts. And the Obama administration, while saying integration is important, offers almost no incentives that would entice school districts to increase it. Instead, Richards says, districts have typically gerrymandered "to segregate, particularly whites from blacks," and that gerrymandering is "getting worse over time" as federal oversight diminishes. According to an analysis by *ProPublica,* the number of apartheid schools nationwide has mushroomed from 2,762 in 1988—the peak of school integration—to 6,727 in 2011.

When school officials make decisions that funnel poor children of color into their own schools, they promise to make those separate schools equal. But that promise is as false today as it was in 1954. Indeed, in some ways all-black schools today are worse than Druid High was back in the 1950s, when poor black students mixed with affluent and middle-class ones, and when many of the most talented black residents of Tuscaloosa taught there.

High-poverty, segregated black and Latino schools account for the majority of the roughly 1,400 high schools nationwide labeled "dropout factories"—meaning fewer than 60 percent of the students graduate. School officials often blame poor performance on the poverty these kids grow up in. But most studies conclude that it's the concentration of poor students in the same school that hurts them the most. Low-income students placed in middle-income schools show marked academic progress.

As a school's black population increases, the odds that any given teacher there will have significant experience, full licensure, or a master's degree all decline. Teacher turnover at segregated schools is typically high. And black students, overall, are less likely than any other group of students to attend schools with Advanced Placement courses and high-level classes like calculus.

The achievement gap for black students grows the longer they spend in segregated schools. When they start 8th grade, black students are already three years behind their white counterparts in math and reading.

"You go into these places rapidly re-segregating districts . . . and they say, 'We are going to focus on raising test scores at every school. We are really committed to standards,'" said

Gary Orfield, co-director of UCLA's Civil Rights Project. "It doesn't work. They don't know how to raise the test scores in segregated schools." Orfield warned the Tuscaloosa school board in 2000 as it prepared to vote that its plan wouldn't stem white flight.

The night the Tuscaloosa school board voted to split up the old Central, board member Bryan Chandler pledged that there would be no winners and losers. Yet while Northridge offered students a dozen Advanced Placement classes, the new Central went at least five years without a single one. Journalism awards stretch wall to wall in Northridge's newspaper classroom, but for the better part of a decade, Central students didn't have a school newspaper or a yearbook. Until last year, Central didn't even offer physics.

The same superintendent who oversaw the 2007 redistricting reportedly called Tuscaloosa's all-black schools a "dumping ground" for bad teachers who'd been let go from other district schools. Teachers hired from outside Tuscaloosa were, for many years, allowed to apply to specific schools, and some would not apply to black schools.

By the time students get to Central, most have spent nine years in low-performing, virtually all-black schools. More than 80 percent of them come from families with incomes low enough to qualify them for free or reduced-price school lunches.

Earlier this year, the state of Alabama designated Central and Westlawn Middle School as failing, because they'd performed in the lowest 6 percent of the state's schools for at least three of the previous six years.

D'Leisha arrived at Central in 2010, the same year as its new principal, Clarence Sutton Jr., who'd attended the integrated version of the school as Melissa Dent's classmate. A year later, the district hired a new superintendent, Paul McKendrick.

Sitting in his office, at a desk six inches deep in papers and reports, McKendrick, a bespectacled man, quiet but forceful, said the black, mostly poor kids of the West End had been separated and written off. A recent audit of Central had found that 80 percent of students were not on the college track. The low test scores that have plagued the school don't stem from "a child problem," he told me. "You may have some children that have special needs or cognitive issues, but you are not going to say a whole group of kids" has "lost intelligence in some way."

Though its students may arrive bearing more burdens, in many ways Central is like any other high school. It's got its jocks, its nerds, its mean girls and band geeks. D'Leisha herself is the all-American girl—the homecoming queen dating a football player. But students and staff say most people see only one thing about Central: it's all black. And that still bears a stigma. The school is housed in a lovely modern brick building outside of the West End on the very spot of the old white high school, within view of the towering University of Alabama football stadium. Much of the neighbor-hood surrounding it is middle-class and predominantly white. Too many times, Sutton told me, his students have asked why the kids who live across the street don't attend their school. Most have never had a white classmate or neighbor, he said, leaving them unprepared to navigate a country where those in charge are usually white.

The principal struggles to explain to students how the segregation they experience is any different from the old version simply because no law requires it. "It is hard, it is a tough conversation, and it is a conversation I don't think we as adults want to have."

Standing one day last fall outside the counselor's office at Central, D'Leisha looked up at the college bulletin board. It was dominated by National Guard and Army flyers, with some brochures for small Alabama colleges tucked among them. Students with D'Leisha's grades and tough honors coursework often come home to mailboxes stuffed with glossy college brochures. But most days, nothing showed up in the mail for her, and no colleges had come calling. She had taken the ACT college-entrance exam twice already. The first time she scored a 16, the second time a 17. Her mother's alma mater, the University of Alabama, expects a 21, the national average. Many four-year colleges will not even consider students who score below an 18.

"My biggest fear right now is the ACT," D'Leisha said. "I don't have a good score. It's been on my mind a lot." She described an ACT study session she'd attended last summer at a community college. "We were with kids from Northridge, and they knew things we didn't know," she said. "They had done things we hadn't done." D'Leisha wound a lock of hair around and around her index finger as she mulled what she just said. "I guess I'll just have to catch on fast, study, all that."

Because D'Leisha excels in school and everything else she's involved in, her teachers and counselors don't worry about whether she's on the right track. They're stretched thin trying to keep in class the seniors—roughly 35 percent of them—who fail to graduate each year. But in December, at home texting with her boyfriend, D'Leisha admitted that she'd filled out only one college application. Lately, she said, she'd been looking more closely at those military brochures, just as her grandfather had, something that angers her mother. "I am kind of clueless how to get stuff done for college," D'Leisha told me, looking down and fidgeting with her phone. "They are supposed to be helping us, but they think because I am the class president I know what to do. Sometimes I don't speak up, because I know people have expectations of me."

For black students like D'Leisha—the grandchildren of the historic *Brown* decision—having to play catch-up with their white counterparts is supposed to be a thing of the past. The promise was that students of all colors would be educated side by side, and would advance together into a more integrated, equitable American society. Polls show Americans embracing this promise in the abstract, but that rarely translates into on-the-ground support for integration efforts.

At no point in the history of our country have half of black children attended majority white schools. Even now in Tuscaloosa, a secret deal to give the district land to build a new school, which would requires another redistricting, recently came to light. Proponents say it's necessary to ease overcrowding in the only majority-white schools, though 1,500 seats sit unfilled across the district.

Late last year, D'Leisha took the ACT for the third time, but her score dropped back to 16. So early on a Saturday in February, she got up quietly, forced a few bites of a muffin into her nervous stomach, and drove once again to the community college where the test is administered. A few weeks later, she got her score: 16 again. She contemplated a fifth attempt, but could see little point.

A few months earlier, D'Leisha had talked about how much she looked forward to meeting people from different cultures at college and sitting in a racially mixed classroom for the first time. But her college hopes are thinner now than she'd expected then. As of this writing, they largely hinge on the tenuous promise of a coach at a small, historically black college outside of Birmingham, who has told her that the school will have a place for her despite her score. No official offer of admission has yet arrived.

CRITICAL THINKING QUESTIONS

1. In 1954, "The supreme court declared an end to separate and unequal education in America." How has desegregation of our schools in America affected schools such as the ones in Tuscaloosa? Describe Dent's school experience compared to the school experience of D'Leisha, Dent's granddaughter.

2. According to the author, "In Tuscaloosa today, nearly 1 in 3 Black students attends a school that looks as if *Brown v. Board of Education* never happened." What is the *Brown v. Board of Education* court case? Provide evidence from the article to support the author's claims. Did your K–12 experience look similar or different to the Tuscaloosa schools?

3. Judge McFadden heard a case from those concerned with the "new apartheid" in Southern public schools. They, along with the Justice department argue that the "absence of integration equals the presence of segregation." Explain what they mean by the argument, and how the "absence of integration" could apply to Central HS this year. Judge McFadden argues that the only solution to the current lack of diversity in schools is forced integration. Do you agree? If so, why? If not, what are some other solutions?

4. Hannah-Jones believes that school integration is important for the success of all students. She writes that, "most studies show that it's the concentration of poor students in the same school that hurts them the most." Towards the end of her essay, she gives several reasons why students in diverse schools perform better. Find three and explain the author's reasoning. Do you wish your school had been more diverse? Why or why not?

U.S. TO FOCUS ON EQUITY IN ASSIGNING OF TEACHERS

by Motoko Rich

Motoko Rich, a reporter for *The New York Times*, writes about the nation's K–12 education system. She brings a diverse perspective, having grown up in New Jersey, California, and Japan. Previously, Rich wrote about workforce training, unemployment, housing and retirement for *The Wall Street Journal*.

Teachers are the most visible symbols of the classroom we have. It makes sense that, as a society, we turn to them when our schools are failing. And there are many ideas about how to improve teacher performance. But as Motoko Rich points out in this 2014 article from *The New York Times*, many of the teachers who are failing to reach their students are located in poor school districts. Are the ineffective teachers all gathering in certain school districts, or are the school districts in some way failing the teachers?

• • • • • • • • • • • • • • •

The Obama administration is directing states to show how they will ensure that all students have equal access to high-quality teachers, with a sharp focus on schools with a high proportion of the poor and racial minorities.

In a letter to state superintendents released Monday, Deborah S. Delisle, an assistant secretary at the Department of Education, said states must develop plans by next June that make sure that public schools comply with existing federal law requiring that "poor and minority children are not taught at higher rates than other children by inexperienced, unqualified or out-of-field teachers."

States last submitted plans to address such inequities in 2006, but data shows that large disparities persist.

"It is important to remind our states that one step in front of the other is the way to begin to deliver for all our students," said Catherine Lhamon, assistant secretary for civil rights, in a conference call with reporters. "We are all dismayed by the lack of compliance and lack of satisfaction and delivery on this point."

The Education Department will send each state data collected by the department's Office for Civil Rights showing rates of teacher experience, certification, absenteeism and salary by school as well as student access to taxpayer-funded preschool and advanced courses in math and science.

The administration is also urging states to look at teacher evaluations to determine whether those who receive lower ratings are disproportionately assigned to schools with high proportions of racial minorities and students in poverty.

But the only requirement of states is that they ensure that teachers are equitably distributed based on experience and credentials.

Education advocates said such measures could limit improvements in the quality of instruction in struggling schools.

"There are going to be inexperienced teachers who are quite effective," said Timothy Daly, the president of TNTP, formerly the New Teacher Project, a nonprofit that recruits teachers, "and there are going to be some experienced teachers who are quite ineffective."

In an increasingly rare show of agreement with the Obama administration, Randi Weingarten, the president of the American Federation of Teachers, the country's second largest teachers' union, welcomed the guidance.

"We're supporting this process because the rhetoric around this process has changed from 'Just come up with the data and we will sanction you if the data doesn't look right,'" Ms. Weingarten said in a telephone interview, "to 'What's the plan to attract and support and retain qualified and well-prepared teachers for the kids who need it most.'"

But other education advocates said they were concerned that the guidance could lack teeth. "The very real risk is that this just becomes a big compliance paperwork exercise," said Daria Hall, K–12 policy director at the Education Trust, a nonprofit group that advocates for racial minority students and low-income children, "and nothing actually happens on behalf of kids."

Terry Holliday, Kentucky's commissioner of education, said states could set policies that would make some federal funding contingent on districts complying with the guidance. "The feds, kind of between the lines, are saying, 'States, we want you to take more action'" and "'You can certainly utilize all of these federal funding streams to incentivize or penalize.'"

School administrators said that given union contracts and other factors, simply looking at how teachers are placed is not sufficient.

It is not enough to "just find the best teachers and best principals and put them where they need to be," said Joshua Starr, superintendent of Montgomery County Public Schools in Maryland. He said districts needed to think about creating supportive school cultures.

"A teacher works in an ecosystem," he said.

CRITICAL THINKING QUESTIONS

1. What are the six ways the Office for Civil Rights evaluates for school quality? Which one of these do you think is the most important, and why is it the most important? What is another factor you think they should look at, and why?

2. Who is Randi Weingarten? Why has she decided to support the evaluation process? What are three steps you think could help "attract and support and retain qualified and well prepared teachers for the kids who need it most?"

3. According to Rich, the Obama administration is putting pressure on states to help "students have equal access to high-quality teachers, with a sharp focus on schools with a high proportion of the poor and racial minorities." However, Joshua Starr, superintendent of the Montgomery County Public Schools in Maryland, indicates, "It is not enough to just find the best teachers and best principals and put them where they need to be . . . districts need to think about creating supportive school cultures." Why is there a need to think beyond staffing schools with strong teachers and leaders? What other supports are necessary to run a productive school?

4. **Connection.** Use at least two other readings from this section in your answer. Joshua Starr, a superintendent from Maryland, argues that "a teacher works in an ecosystem." What is an ecosystem and how do you think this term is applied to schools? What are three factors raised in other readings that you think affect the ecosystem that teachers work in? Why do you think each of these affects the performance of teachers?

UNIT 2

Economics and Race

INTRODUCTION

President Lyndon B. Johnson was born one of five children in Stonewall, Texas. His early life was marked by desperate poverty. Through work and education, he set a course for Washington, DC. He hated the poverty he encountered as a youth and felt motivated to play a part in ending it. From the House of Representatives to the Senate, from Vice President to President, Lyndon Johnson is a modern example of someone attaining the *American Dream.*

Harlon Dalton, who teaches law at Yale University, believes that the *American Dream* has a three part argument. The first is that we are judged by our merits—what we do or say, who we are, and how we act. The second is that we all have an equal opportunity to develop our merits. The third part is that our merit is judged above all other considerations in economic decisions. The readings in this section question all three of those arguments.

Lyndon Johnson found great success here in America through hard work and his natural ability to lead/govern. He was also a white man. His truth is not a universal truth. The American Dream concept leaves out what many call "America's Original Sin." Author Jim Wallis famously wrote in 1986 that "The United States of America was established as a white society, founded upon the near genocide of another race and then the enslavement of yet another." The economic exploitation of two races is undoubtedly still at work in explaining who has resources—and who doesn't—in America today. This country has always had a difficult relationship with race that we struggle to talk about. Many would even deny that it is still a factor in economic advancement.

Yet if race is not a factor in economic advancement, why is white household wealth 13 times that of African-American household wealth—and why has that number been increasing over the past decade? Why do white students complete college at a higher rate, and why do their college degrees have a higher value on the market? Why is the median household income for an African American family $27,000 less than that of a white family?

This section aims to explore the connection between race and economic advancement. America has a complicated history with race—and things are still complicated. Some ethnic groups are thriving; others are falling behind. President Lyndon Johnson knew that African American poverty was not white poverty; he said, "many of its causes and many of its cures are the same. But there are differences—deep, corrosive, obstinate differences—radiating painful roots into the community, the family, the nature of the individual." Merit, to borrow Harlon Dalton's term, is spread evenly across all people. And yet our economic results are so uneven. This unit tries to answer the following two questions: *If America is a land where merit causes economic advancement, why is economic advancement so unequally distributed? What is the connection between poverty and race in America?*

In a country whose founding document's second clause is that, "all men are created equal," these sustained economic disparities must be addressed. And we cannot fully understand these economic injustices until we have grappled with the issue of race. As President Johnson said, "until justice is blind to color, until education is unaware of race, until opportunity is unconcerned with the color of men's skins, emancipation will be a proclamation but not a fact."

THEM THAT'S GOT SHALL GET

by Nathalie Baptiste

Nathalie Baptiste is a Hatian-American who lives in the Washington, D.C. area. She holds a BA and an MA in International Studies. Baptiste often writes on topics related to Latin America and the Caribbean.

In her 2014 article for the *The American Prospect*, Nathalie Baptiste argues that the 2008 economic crisis did not hit everyone equally. Her title, "Them That's Got Shall Get" summarizes this nicely; them that's got—the large financial institutions in America—shall get more. In many cases they got more due to the staggering loss of African-American wealth during the economic crisis. But why did African Americans enter the crisis with less wealth than white Americans, and why did they lose more to a worldwide economic tsunami?

• • • • • • • • • • • • • • •

Two years after we last investigated the the foreclosure crisis in the most affluent black county in America, things aren't exactly looking up—except, maybe, for the banks.

Driving through Prince George's County, Maryland, it's not obvious that its towns and cities are at the epicenter of the foreclosure crisis in the Washington, D.C., region. In the town of Bowie, for instance, large colonial-style homes with attached two-car garages, spacious apartment buildings designed for families, and modern shopping centers line the streets. As in any other middle-class community, school-aged children chase each other in front yards while their parents monitor from the porch, and twentysomethings in workout gear jog the tree-lined streets. There's no shortage of schools, community centers and places of worship, and if any homes are abandoned, it's not glaringly obvious.

What sets Prince George's County apart from other upscale regions is that most of its citizens are black. No other majority-black counties in the United States are even comparable in terms of numbers of educated citizens and middle-class incomes, but when the economy crumbled, so did the dreams of many homeowners living in Prince George's. And despite promises of help by President Barack Obama and lawmakers, seven years after the housing bubble burst, the county's foreclosure crisis has only slowed, not abated.

As the wealthiest black-majority county in the United States, Prince George's has long represented the pinnacle of black success. The county's median household income is $73,568—a full $20,000 more than the median household income of the United States as a whole. Only 7.1 percent of U.S. firms are black-owned, but in Prince George's that number stands at a whopping 54.5 percent.

A full 29.5 percent of people over the age of 25 hold bachelor's degrees—slightly higher than the 28.5 percent rate for all persons in the United States. Known colloquially as just P.G., the county is filled with lawyers, entrepreneurs, teachers, and federal employees. In popular lore, Prince George's was proof that, while blacks still lagged behind in education, wealth and employment, the black community was finally catching up.

But in 2007, the bursting of the housing bubble triggered an economic recession that rippled throughout the global economy. For years, the housing market had been booming; in

2007 the U.S. median price for a house hit a record high of $247,900. By 2009, though, that number had fallen to $216,700. For Prince George's County, however, the decline was much more stark. In 2009 the median price for a house dropped by nearly $100,000, from $343,000 to just $245,000.

Although the foreclosure crisis left no part of the country untouched, in the Washington, D.C., area—which, overall, weathered the crisis well—Prince George's County bore the brunt. The reason? Subprime lending.

A subprime mortgage is a loan that carries a higher interest rate than prime mortgages. Prime mortgages are often given to lenders with the best credit histories, while subprime mortgages are designed for borrowers with flawed credit histories. The higher interest rate that comes with subprime mortgages is intended to pay the lender for taking on a risky borrower. In 2009, one quarter of all mortgages in Prince George's County were subprime.

By 2011, the foreclosure rate in Prince George's county had reached 5.3 percent, twice the rate for the Washington, D.C., region overall. Approximately 15 percent of homeowners in Prince George's County received notices of intent to foreclose (NOI) that year. On average, the median borrower receiving an NOI was 79 days behind on his or her mortgage payment, and owed an average of $6,400 in late mortgage payments, as well as fees and penalties.

Across the nation, black homeowners were disproportionately affected by the foreclosure crisis, with more than 240,000 blacks losing homes they had owned. Black homeowners in the D.C. region were 20 percent more likely to lose their homes compared to whites with similar incomes and lifestyles. (See the December 2012 issue of *The American Prospect*, "The Collapse of Black Wealth," by Monica Potts.) The foreclosure crisis also affected blacks of all income brackets; high-earning blacks were 80 percent more likely to lose their homes than their white counterparts, making the homeowners of Prince George's County prime targets.

Even the most stable of P.G. County homeowners wound up with subprime mortgages, presumably made to believe that subprime was their only option. Not even a good credit score would have spared blacks from these discriminatory lending practices. The Center for Responsible Lending found that during the housing boom, 6.2 percent of whites with a credit score of 660 and higher received high-interest mortgages but 21.4 percent of blacks with a score of 660 or higher received these same loans.

It turned out that several of the major banks had been purposely giving people of color subprime mortgages, including borrowers who would have qualified for a prime loan. The City of Baltimore took Wells Fargo to court, bringing some of the banking giant's abhorrent lending practices to light. One former employee testified that in 2001, Wells Fargo created a unit that would be responsible for pushing expensive refinance loans on black customers, especially those living in Baltimore, southeast Washington, D.C., and Prince George's County—all locations with large black populations.

According to court testimony, some of the loan officers at Wells Fargo spoke of these subprime loans as "ghetto loans," and referred to their black customers as "mud people." There was even a cash incentive for loan officers to aggressively market subprime mortgages in minority neighborhoods. In the end, the Justice Department found that 4,500 homeowners in Baltimore and the Washington, D.C., region had been affected by these flat-out racist lending practices.

Specifically targeted for subprime loans among the minority demographic were black women. Women of color are the most likely to receive subprime loans while white men are the least likely; the disparity grows with income levels. Compared to white men earning the same level of income, black women earning less than the area median income are two and a half times more likely to receive subprime. Upper-income black women were nearly five times more likely to receive subprime purchase mortgages than upper-income white men.

The services of data collection agencies made it easy for lenders who were able to buy information about a potential borrower's age, race and income. Armed with that information, it was easy for lenders to target moderate-to-high income women of color.

Without admitting to any wrongdoing, Wells Fargo finally settled with the City of Baltimore in 2012. Still, Wells Fargo agreed to pay to the tune of $175 million dollars; $50 million of the settlement went towards helping community members in the Washington, D.C., region, as well as those in seven other metropolitan areas, make down payments on new homes. The settlement, however, was hardly a fix for the loss of family wealth suffered by those who lost their homes.

Family wealth describes all the assets of a family: the members' financial holdings, their property, and any businesses they may own. For many homeowning families, the home comprises most of the family's wealth. When such a family loses its home, other forms of wealth—savings, stock shares—are often used to cover the costs of the crisis. In the Great Recession, according to a working paper by Signe-Mary McKernan and colleagues for the Urban Institute, the wealth of U.S. families overall was reduced by 28.5 percent. But for blacks, the authors found, the decline was far greater: a loss of 47.6 percent.

The relative lack of black wealth is a complex problem with roots going back to slavery, exacerbated by decades of institutional racism. In 2010, the median wealth for white families was $124,000; for black families it was a mere $16,000, according to the Urban Institute. As blacks moved into the middle class, the housing boom held out the promise of a chance to build prosperity. The wealth gap between blacks and whites was by no means created by the recession, but after the economy collapsed, the gap worsened drastically.

From 2005 to 2009, the net worth of black households declined by 53 percent while the net worth of white households declined by 16 percent, according to Social & Demographic Trends researchers at the Pew Research Center. At the peak of the housing boom, 49 percent of blacks owned homes while the same measure for whites hovered around 75 percent.

Historically, the wealth gap between whites and blacks can be traced back to the ability to own land; for a number of years blacks were prohibited from owning land, and once homeownership became the primary way to own property black people were often barred from that, too.

In response to the Great Depression, the Federal Housing Administration was created through the National Housing Act of 1934. The purpose of the FHA was to regulate interest rates and mortgage terms. While this new government agency created an opportunity for whites to become homeowners and begin accumulating wealth, government-sanctioned racism kept blacks out of the housing market. The FHA regularly denied mortgages to black people and limited loans to new residential areas on the outskirts of the city, where the white population tended to live; this contributed to the decay of inner city neighborhoods as middle-class residents left to build new homes in the suburbs. Federal policy also dictated that the home values of predominantly black neighborhoods were to be lower than in neighborhoods that were mostly white. Even though that law is no longer on the books, its legacy remains: Homes in black neighborhoods still have lower values than homes in white neighborhoods with similar incomes.

The Federal Housing Administration also practiced redlining, the practice in which lenders would deny or limit financial services based on race, regardless of other financial qualifications. The term redlining comes from the practice of drawing red lines on maps to mark the black neighborhoods where banks would not invest. The FHA was firm in its racial bias; in one of its publications, the agency even declared that neighborhoods should not be racially integrated. Finally, by 1968 as part of the Civil Rights Act, the Fair Housing Act was implemented. It was a victory for blacks nationwide, but the damage had already been done. While white families had been building wealth for decades, blacks found themselves behind. In the years after housing act's passage, the wealth gap would certainly shrink, but never come close to closing.

In the 1970s, black migration from Washington, D.C., to Prince George's County began to pick up speed. As developers created suburban landscapes out of the farms of this once-rural area, black families began moving to Prince George's from the city to enjoy the lower housing costs. In response, real estate agents began practicing what is known as blockbusting, selling a house to a black family then urging all the white families to move out because the presence of blacks in the neighborhood would allegedly cause property values to decline.

The blockbusting era coincided with the integration of schools in Prince George's County, which began in 1973 with a court-mandated busing plan. The desegregation of the schools led to a massive white flight—the term given to describe extensive white out-migration from neighborhoods in response to blacks beginning to move in. All of these factors led to Prince George's becoming a majority-black county.

Throughout the 1980s and 1990s, the black population in Prince George's continued to grow; the housing values did not plummet as real estate agents had predicted. Instead, the county grew wealthier. By purchasing homes, black homeowners began to gain their own wealth, thinking to ensure wealth for their children. Passing down wealth through homes has long been a practice of the middle class.

The foreclosure crisis not only caused blacks to lose their homes and their slice of the American dream; it will also present new challenges to the next generation as the likelihood of receiving wealth passed down from their parents is disappearing very quickly. When it comes to inherited wealth, blacks often don't receive any, according to Valerie Wilson, director of the Economic Policy Institute's Program on Race, Ethnicity, and the Economy. Often, Wilson told me in an interview in her Washington, D.C., office, the home is the only substantial asset a black family has, and many will use their homes to finance the education of their children, or retirement for the homeowners, who, by the time they've reached the end of their lives, consequently have very little accumulated wealth.

After the economic crash and subsequent subprime meltdown, the closing of the wealth gap between blacks and whites, which accelerated during the housing boom, began to reverse, eroding years of progress—and there doesn't seem to be an easy way to fix the problem.

"I don't think you can do it with any one thing," said Wilson. "The most immediate [solution] would be a transfer of cash—reparations—but even with that I don't know that the gap would stay closed." Inequities exist in much more than just wealth; there are also disparities in education, wages and employment, she explained. "All of these things would still eat away at wealth, even if we could wipe the slate clean and equalize. We'd really have to address structural racism and inequality in this country."

As the foreclosure crisis continued to eat away at black wealth, the Obama administration introduced a couple of programs intended to alleviate the suffering of homeowners. The Home Affordable Modification Program (HAMP) was created to provide eligible homeowners with loan modifications on their mortgage debt. This program is designed to provide relief to borrowers who are facing foreclosure. To meet eligibility requirements, applicants must prove financial hardship, have obtained their mortgage on or before January 1, 2009; owe no more than $729,750 on their primary residences or a one-to-four unit rental property; and, finally, applicants must not have been "convicted in the last 10 years of felony larceny, theft, fraud, or forgery, money laundering or tax evasion, in connection with a mortgage or real estate transaction."

If HAMP is helping Prince George's homeowners, it's certainly not helping enough.

The program is widely considered a failure. Nationwide, 1.3 million people received loan modifications, but 350,000 of those people again defaulted on their mortgages and lost their homes. In the Washington, D.C., metro area, the redefault rate was at 26 percent in mid-2013.

North Carolina Republican Patrick McHenry sought to address the program's shortcomings by introducing the HAMP Termination Act of 2011. But Representative Donna Edwards, who represents the 4th Congressional District of Maryland, comprising parts of Prince George's County and neighboring Anne Arundel County, was in no mood to give up. In a speech on the House floor arguing against McHenry's measure, Edwards spoke of how the Neighborhood Stabilization Program, part of HAMP, provided $12 million dollars to Prince George's County, helping communities in her district resell abandoned homes. She lamented that the HAMP program wasn't able to help as many homeowners as it originally planned, but felt that doing away with the program altogether was an injustice to her constituents, and struggling homeowners nationwide. McHenry's measure passed the House, but never saw a vote in the Senate.

Three years later, the congresswoman still remains firm in her support for HAMP. "Some of my colleagues don't want to expand programs that would give relief to homeowners," Edwards explained in a telephone interview, "but I'm a big fan of that, because these are people who are getting up and going to work every day, and we need them in the economy. And part of them being in the economy is being able to pay their mortgages."

When a homeowner applies for loan modification, the application must first go through the bank. Edwards told the *Prospect* that the slow processing of loan modification applications is making the foreclosure crisis worse on homeowners in her district.

"The banks are taking forever to respond, and by the time they do, the fees and expenses add up," she said. "The homeowner is in more of a bind, sometimes waiting a year to get the paperwork straightened out." Not only are late fees adding up; some homeowners are still stuck paying their old mortgages while waiting for a resolution.

Edwards's staff find themselves fielding calls from desperate constituents who are stymied by the banks' glacial pace in processing paperwork. When the congressional office calls the bank with the same request as the homeowner, the process is suddenly sped up, Edwards said, proving that the process for evaluating applications could easily be improved.

"I do think that there has to be some kind of accountability mechanism placed on the banks," Edwards said. "Some accountability for what the banks are doing, and how fast they're doing it, would be really helpful for homeowners."

It's been six years since the beginning of the foreclosure crisis and five years since the recession technically ended and the recovery period began. Nationally, the foreclosure crisis is easing. But in Maryland foreclosures recently hit a high. Initially, Maryland was in 16th place in number of foreclosures, but by 2013, the state had skyrocketed to third in the nation; the number of filings increased by a staggering 250 percent between 2013 and 2014 with Prince George's County seeing a 50 percent increase of foreclosure in this year.

The new wave of foreclosures is not a new crisis but a continuation of the old one. In 2011 and 2012, the rate of foreclosures in Maryland slowed, but this was the result of a new law that went into effect on July 1, 2010. Placing pressure on lenders, the Foreclosure Mediation Law created a new timeline for home foreclosures. Under the new law, when a lender notifies a homeowner of the possibility of foreclosure, the lender is also required to provide information on loan modifications, or any other type of assistance. The mediation law created a backlog and Maryland is just now beginning to see all the foreclosures that were previously stalled. The original intention of the law was to help members of the community stay in their homes, but instead, for many, it appears to merely put a pause on foreclosures.

The recent uptick in foreclosures led to a bill sponsored by State Senator Anthony Muse, a Democrat representing Prince George's 26th legislative district that would place a moratorium on all home foreclosures in Maryland. The bill also called for legal examinations of those who were foreclosed on illegally. The bill is still pending.

It's safe to say that the foreclosure crisis is nowhere near over for Prince George's County.

The big banks, the creators of the financial crisis, were bailed out and are now making record profits. Those most victimized by the economic downturn, blacks—and black women in particular—were saddled with haphazardly created programs that have not lived up to their promises.

As Prince George's County continues to suffer from the foreclosure crisis, the loss of wealth by so many of its residents is felt far beyond its borders. For those still within those borders, it must be asked, when will these homeowners begin to see real relief?

CRITICAL THINKING QUESTIONS

1. According to the author, "the relative lack of black wealth is a complex problem with roots going back to slavery, exacerbated by decades of institutional racism." Using three statistics or numbers from the article, provide evidence that would support that argument. How has the distribution of lending for houses unfairly targeted African Americans? Why do you think this might have been the case?
2. What is redlining? How does it operate? How did (does?) the process of redlining limit the accumulation of wealth in African-American communities? Why do you think banks would make this choice?
3. What is the risk of a subprime mortgage over other mortgage options? What makes a subprime mortgage a "discriminatory lending practice" according to the author? What does the practice of aggressive marketing of subprime mortgages in minority neighborhoods, especially African-American neighborhoods, say about our society? How do practices such as this one impact economic stability for minority populations?
4. Describe State Senator Anthony Muse's bill. If it were passed, how would it help stop the wealth gap from growing? Who would this bill harm? If you were in the Maryland Senate, would you vote for or against the bill—and why?

THE CASE FOR REPARATIONS

by Ta-Nehisi Coates

Ta-Nehisi Coates is a writer, journalist, and educator from Baltimore, MD. Currently, he is a senior editor for *The Atlantic.* His reporting encompasses topics of racism, politics, culture, and education. Coates has worked for *The Village Voice, Washington City Paper* and *Time Magazine.* He published a memoir, *The Beautiful Struggle: A Father, Two Sons, and an Unlikely Road to Manhood.* Most recently, Coates joined the City University of New York as its journalist-in-residence in fall 2014.

In this 2014 cover story for *The Atlantic,* Coates makes an argument for reparations for African Americans. He argues that you do not need to look to the slavery period to find cause for financially compensating African Americans; you can look to the bankers of the 21st century and the racism of the 20th century, and he argues that the cumulative effect of government policies that have too often favored white Americans is too large to deny any longer. Yet, many think the struggles of African Americans are an issue to be fixed through hard work or changing cultural norms; even President Obama has argued this. Why are we so reluctant to face the case for reparations?

• • • • • • • • • • • • • • • •

Two hundred fifty years of slavery. Ninety years of Jim Crow. Sixty years of separate but equal. Thirty-five years of racist housing policy. Until we reckon with our compounding moral debts, America will never be whole.

> *And if thy brother, a Hebrew man, or a Hebrew woman, be sold unto thee, and serve thee six years; then in the seventh year thou shalt let him go free from thee. And when thou sendest him out free from thee, thou shalt not let him go away empty: thou shalt furnish him liberally out of thy flock, and out of thy floor, and out of thy winepress: of that wherewith the LORD thy God hath blessed thee thou shalt give unto him. And thou shalt remember that thou wast a bondman in the land of Egypt, and the LORD thy God redeemed thee: therefore I command thee this thing today.*
>
> —Deuteronomy 15:12–15

> *Besides the crime which consists in violating the law, and varying from the right rule of reason, whereby a man so far becomes degenerate, and declares himself to quit the principles of human nature, and to be a noxious creature, there is commonly injury done to some person or other, and some other man receives damage by his transgression: in which case he who hath received any damage, has, besides the right of punishment common to him with other men, a particular right to seek reparation.*
>
> —John Locke, "Second Treatise"

> *By our unpaid labor and suffering, we have earned the right to the soil, many times over and over, and now we are determined to have it.*
>
> —Anonymous, 1861

I. "SO THAT'S JUST ONE OF MY LOSSES"

Clyde Ross was born in 1923, the seventh of 13 children, near Clarksdale, Mississippi, the home of the blues. Ross's parents owned and farmed a 40-acre tract of land, flush with cows, hogs, and mules. Ross's mother would drive to Clarksdale to do her shopping in a horse and buggy, in which she invested all the pride one might place in a Cadillac. The family owned another horse, with a red coat, which they gave to Clyde. The Ross family wanted for little, save that which all black families in the Deep South then desperately desired—the protection of the law.

In the 1920s, Jim Crow Mississippi was, in all facets of society, a kleptocracy. The majority of the people in the state were perpetually robbed of the vote—a hijacking engineered through the trickery of the poll tax and the muscle of the lynch mob. Between 1882 and 1968, more black people were lynched in Mississippi than in any other state. "You and I know what's the best way to keep the nigger from voting," blustered Theodore Bilbo, a Mississippi senator and a proud Klansman. "You do it the night before the election."

The state's regime partnered robbery of the franchise with robbery of the purse. Many of Mississippi's black farmers lived in debt peonage, under the sway of cotton kings who were at once their landlords, their employers, and their primary merchants. Tools and necessities were advanced against the return on the crop, which was determined by the employer. When farmers were deemed to be in debt—and they often were—the negative balance was then carried over to the next season. A man or woman who protested this arrangement did so at the risk of grave injury or death. Refusing to work meant arrest under vagrancy laws and forced labor under the state's penal system.

Well into the 20th century, black people spoke of their flight from Mississippi in much the same manner as their runagate ancestors had. In her 2010 book, *The Warmth of Other Suns,* Isabel Wilkerson tells the story of Eddie Earvin, a spinach picker who fled Mississippi in 1963, after being made to work at gunpoint. "You didn't talk about it or tell nobody," Earvin said. "You had to sneak away."

When Clyde Ross was still a child, Mississippi authorities claimed his father owed \$3,000 in back taxes. The elder Ross could not read. He did not have a lawyer. He did not know anyone at the local courthouse. He could not expect the police to be impartial. Effectively, the Ross family had no way to contest the claim and no protection under the law. The authorities seized the land. They seized the buggy. They took the cows, hogs, and mules. And so for the upkeep of separate but equal, the entire Ross family was reduced to sharecropping.

This was hardly unusual. In 2001, the Associated Press published a three-part investigation into the theft of black-owned land stretching back to the antebellum period. The series documented some 406 victims and 24,000 acres of land valued at tens of millions of dollars. The land was taken through means ranging from legal chicanery to terrorism. "Some of the land taken from black families has become a country club in Virginia," the AP reported, as well as "oil fields in Mississippi" and "a baseball spring training facility in Florida."

Clyde Ross was a smart child. His teacher thought he should attend a more challenging school. There was very little support for educating black people in Mississippi. But Julius Rosenwald, a part owner of Sears, Roebuck, had begun an ambitious effort to build schools for black children throughout the South. Ross's teacher believed he should attend the local Rosenwald school. It was too far for Ross to walk and get back in time to work in the fields. Local white children had a school bus. Clyde Ross did not, and thus lost the chance to better his education.

Then, when Ross was 10 years old, a group of white men demanded his only childhood possession—the horse with the red coat. "You can't have this horse. We want it," one of the white men said. They gave Ross's father $17.

"I did everything for that horse," Ross told me. "Everything. And they took him. Put him on the racetrack. I never did know what happened to him after that, but I know they didn't bring him back. So that's just one of my losses."

The losses mounted. As sharecroppers, the Ross family saw their wages treated as the landlord's slush fund. Landowners were supposed to split the profits from the cotton fields with sharecroppers. But bales would often disappear during the count, or the split might be altered on a whim. If cotton was selling for 50 cents a pound, the Ross family might get 15 cents, or only five. One year Ross's mother promised to buy him a $7 suit for a summer program at their church. She ordered the suit by mail. But that year Ross's family was paid only five cents a pound for cotton. The mailman arrived with the suit. The Rosses could not pay. The suit was sent back. Clyde Ross did not go to the church program.

It was in these early years that Ross began to understand himself as an American—he did not live under the blind decree of justice, but under the heel of a regime that elevated armed robbery to a governing principle. He thought about fighting. "Just be quiet," his father told him. "Because they'll come and kill us all."

Clyde Ross grew. He was drafted into the Army. The draft officials offered him an exemption if he stayed home and worked. He preferred to take his chances with war. He was stationed in California. He found that he could go into stores without being bothered. He could walk the streets without being harassed. He could go into a restaurant and receive service.

Ross was shipped off to Guam. He fought in World War II to save the world from tyranny. But when he returned to Clarksdale, he found that tyranny had followed him home. This was 1947, eight years before Mississippi lynched Emmett Till and tossed his broken body into the Tallahatchie River. The Great Migration, a mass exodus of 6 million African Americans that spanned most of the 20th century, was now in its second wave. The black pilgrims did not journey north simply seeking better wages and work, or bright lights and big adventures. They were fleeing the acquisitive warlords of the South. They were seeking the protection of the law.

Clyde Ross was among them. He came to Chicago in 1947 and took a job as a taster at Campbell's Soup. He made a stable wage. He married. He had children. His paycheck was his own. No Klansmen stripped him of the vote. When he walked down the street, he did not have to move because a white man was walking past. He did not have to take off his hat or avert his gaze. His journey from peonage to full citizenship seemed near-complete. Only one item was missing—a home, that final badge of entry into the sacred order of the American middle class of the Eisenhower years.

In 1961, Ross and his wife bought a house in North Lawndale, a bustling community on Chicago's West Side. North Lawndale had long been a predominantly Jewish neighborhood, but a handful of middle-class African Americans had lived there starting in the '40s. The community was anchored by the sprawling Sears, Roebuck headquarters. North Lawndale's Jewish People's Institute actively encouraged blacks to move into the neighborhood, seeking to make it a "pilot community for interracial living." In the battle for integration then being fought around the country, North Lawndale seemed to offer promising terrain. But out in the tall grass, highwaymen, nefarious as any Clarksdale kleptocrat, were lying in wait.

Three months after Clyde Ross moved into his house, the boiler blew out. This would normally be a homeowner's responsibility, but in fact, Ross was not really a homeowner. His payments were made to the seller, not the bank. And Ross had not signed a normal mortgage. He'd bought "on contract": a predatory agreement that combined all the responsibilities of homeownership with all the disadvantages of renting—while offering the benefits of neither. Ross had bought his house for $27,500. The seller, not the previous homeowner but a new kind of middleman, had bought it for only $12,000 six months before selling it to Ross. In a contract sale, the seller kept the deed until the contract was paid in full—and, unlike with a normal mortgage, Ross would acquire no equity in the meantime. If he missed a single payment, he would immediately forfeit his $1,000 down payment, all his monthly payments, and the property itself.

The men who peddled contracts in North Lawndale would sell homes at inflated prices and then evict families who could not pay—taking their down payment and their monthly installments as profit. Then they'd bring in another black family, rinse, and repeat. "He loads them up with payments they can't meet," an office secretary told *The Chicago Daily News* of her boss, the speculator Lou Fushanis, in 1963. "Then he takes the property away from them. He's sold some of the buildings three or four times."

Ross had tried to get a legitimate mortgage in another neighborhood, but was told by a loan officer that there was no financing available. The truth was that there was no financing for people like Clyde Ross. From the 1930s through the 1960s, black people across the country were largely cut out of the legitimate home-mortgage market through means both legal and extralegal. Chicago whites employed every measure, from "restrictive covenants" to bombings, to keep their neighborhoods segregated.

Their efforts were buttressed by the federal government. In 1934, Congress created the Federal Housing Administration. The FHA insured private mortgages, causing a drop in interest rates and a decline in the size of the down payment required to buy a house. But an insured mortgage was not a possibility for Clyde Ross. The FHA had adopted a system of maps that rated neighborhoods according to their perceived stability. On the maps, green areas, rated "A," indicated "in demand" neighborhoods that, as one appraiser put it, lacked "a single foreigner or Negro." These neighborhoods were considered excellent prospects for insurance. Neighborhoods where black people lived were rated "D" and were usually considered ineligible for FHA backing. They were colored in red. Neither the percentage of black people living there nor their social class mattered. Black people were viewed as a contagion. Redlining went beyond FHA-backed loans and spread to the entire mortgage industry, which was already rife with racism, excluding black people from most legitimate means of obtaining a mortgage.

Explore Redlining in Chicago

"A government offering such bounty to builders and lenders could have required compliance with a nondiscrimination policy," Charles Abrams, the urban-studies expert who helped create the New York City Housing Authority, wrote in 1955. "Instead, the FHA adopted a racial policy that could well have been culled from the Nuremberg laws."

The devastating effects are cogently outlined by Melvin L. Oliver and Thomas M. Shapiro in their 1995 book, *Black Wealth/White Wealth*:

> Locked out of the greatest mass-based opportunity for wealth accumulation in American history, African Americans who desired and were able to afford home ownership found

> themselves consigned to central-city communities where their investments were affected by the "self-fulfilling prophecies" of the FHA appraisers: cut off from sources of new investment[,] their homes and communities deteriorated and lost value in comparison to those homes and communities that FHA appraisers deemed desirable.

In Chicago and across the country, whites looking to achieve the American dream could rely on a legitimate credit system backed by the government. Blacks were herded into the sights of unscrupulous lenders who took them for money and for sport. "It was like people who like to go out and shoot lions in Africa. It was the same thrill," a housing attorney told the historian Beryl Satter in her 2009 book, *Family Properties.* "The thrill of the chase and the kill."

The kill was profitable. At the time of his death, Lou Fushanis owned more than 600 properties, many of them in North Lawndale, and his estate was estimated to be worth $3 million. He'd made much of this money by exploiting the frustrated hopes of black migrants like Clyde Ross. During this period, according to one estimate, 85 percent of all black home buyers who bought in Chicago bought on contract. "If anybody who is well established in this business in Chicago doesn't earn $100,000 a year," a contract seller told *The Saturday Evening Post* in 1962, "he is loafing."

Contract sellers became rich. North Lawndale became a ghetto.

Clyde Ross still lives there. He still owns his home. He is 91, and the emblems of survival are all around him—awards for service in his community, pictures of his children in cap and gown. But when I asked him about his home in North Lawndale, I heard only anarchy.

"We were ashamed. We did not want anyone to know that we were that ignorant," Ross told me. He was sitting at his dining-room table. His glasses were as thick as his Clarksdale drawl. "I'd come out of Mississippi where there was one mess, and come up here and got in another mess. So how dumb am I? I didn't want anyone to know how dumb I was.

"When I found myself caught up in it, I said, 'How? I just left this mess. I just left no laws. And no regard. And then I come here and get cheated wide open.' I would probably want to do some harm to some people, you know, if I had been violent like some of us. I thought, 'Man, I got caught up in this stuff. I can't even take care of my kids.' I didn't have enough for my kids. You could fall through the cracks easy fighting these white people. And no law."

But fight Clyde Ross did. In 1968 he joined the newly formed Contract Buyers League—a collection of black homeowners on Chicago's South and West Sides, all of whom had been locked into the same system of predation. There was Howell Collins, whose contract called for him to pay $25,500 for a house that a speculator had bought for $14,500. There was Ruth Wells, who'd managed to pay out half her contract, expecting a mortgage, only to suddenly see an insurance bill materialize out of thin air—a requirement the seller had added without Wells's knowledge. Contract sellers used every tool at their disposal to pilfer from their clients. They scared white residents into selling low. They lied about properties' compliance with building codes, then left the buyer responsible when city inspectors arrived. They presented themselves as real-estate brokers, when in fact they were the owners. They guided their clients to lawyers who were in on the scheme.

The Contract Buyers League fought back. Members—who would eventually number more than 500—went out to the posh suburbs where the speculators lived and embarrassed them by knocking on their neighbors' doors and informing them of the details of the contract-lending trade. They refused to pay their installments, instead holding monthly payments in an escrow account. Then they brought a suit against the contract sellers, accusing them of buying properties and reselling in such a manner "to reap from members of the Negro race large and unjust profits."

In return for the "deprivations of their rights and privileges under the Thirteenth and Fourteenth Amendments," the league demanded "prayers for relief"—payback of all moneys paid on contracts and all moneys paid for structural improvement of properties, at 6 percent interest minus a "fair, non-discriminatory" rental price for time of occupation. Moreover, the league asked the court to adjudge that the defendants had "acted willfully and maliciously and that malice is the gist of this action."

Ross and the Contract Buyers League were no longer appealing to the government simply for equality. They were no longer fleeing in hopes of a better deal elsewhere. They were charging society with a crime against their community. They wanted the crime publicly ruled as such. They wanted the crime's executors declared to be offensive to society. And they wanted restitution for the great injury brought upon them by said offenders. In 1968, Clyde Ross and the Contract Buyers League were no longer simply seeking the protection of the law. They were seeking reparations.

II. "A DIFFERENCE OF KIND, NOT DEGREE"

According to the most-recent statistics, North Lawndale is now on the wrong end of virtually every socioeconomic indicator. In 1930 its population was 112,000. Today it is 36,000. The halcyon talk of "interracial living" is dead. The neighborhood is 92 percent black. Its homicide rate is 45 per 100,000—triple the rate of the city as a whole. The infant-mortality rate is 14 per 1,000—more than twice the national average. Forty-three percent of the people in North Lawndale live below the poverty line—double Chicago's overall rate. Forty-five percent of all households are on food stamps—nearly three times the rate of the city at large. Sears, Roebuck left the neighborhood in 1987, taking 1,800 jobs with it. Kids in North Lawndale need not be confused about their prospects: Cook County's Juvenile Temporary Detention Center sits directly adjacent to the neighborhood.

North Lawndale is an extreme portrait of the trends that ail black Chicago. Such is the magnitude of these ailments that it can be said that blacks and whites do not inhabit the same city. The average per capita income of Chicago's white neighborhoods is almost three times that of its black neighborhoods. When the Harvard sociologist Robert J. Sampson examined incarceration rates in Chicago in his 2012 book, *Great American City,* he found that a black neighborhood with one of the highest incarceration rates (West Garfield Park) had a rate more than 40 times as high as the white neighborhood with the highest rate (Clearing). "This is a staggering differential, even for community-level comparisons," Sampson writes. "A difference of kind, not degree."

In other words, Chicago's impoverished black neighborhoods—characterized by high unemployment and households headed by single parents—are not simply poor; they are "ecologically distinct." This "is not simply the same thing as low economic status," writes Sampson. "In this pattern Chicago is not alone."

The lives of black Americans are better than they were half a century ago. The humiliation of WHITES ONLY signs are gone. Rates of black poverty have decreased. Black teen-pregnancy rates are at record lows—and the gap between black and white teen-pregnancy rates has shrunk significantly. But such progress rests on a shaky foundation, and fault lines are everywhere. The income gap between black and white households is roughly the same today as it was in 1970. Patrick Sharkey, a sociologist at New York University, studied children born from 1955 through 1970 and found that 4 percent of whites and 62 percent of blacks across America had been raised in poor neighborhoods. A generation later, the same study showed, virtually nothing had changed. And whereas whites born into affluent neighborhoods tended to remain in affluent neighborhoods, blacks tended to fall out of them.

This is not surprising. Black families, regardless of income, are significantly less wealthy than white families. The Pew Research Center estimates that white households are worth roughly 20 times as much as black households, and that whereas only 15 percent of whites have zero or negative wealth, more than a third of blacks do. Effectively, the black family in America is working without a safety net. When financial calamity strikes—a medical emergency, divorce, job loss—the fall is precipitous.

And just as black families of all incomes remain handicapped by a lack of wealth, so too do they remain handicapped by their restricted choice of neighborhood. Black people with upper-middle-class incomes do not generally live in upper-middle-class neighborhoods. Sharkey's research shows that black families making $100,000 typically live in the kinds of neighborhoods inhabited by white families making $30,000. "Blacks and whites inhabit such different neighborhoods," Sharkey writes, "that it is not possible to compare the economic outcomes of black and white children."

The implications are chilling. As a rule, poor black people do not work their way out of the ghetto—and those who do often face the horror of watching their children and grandchildren tumble back.

Even seeming evidence of progress withers under harsh light. In 2012, the Manhattan Institute cheerily noted that segregation had declined since the 1960s. And yet African Americans still remained—by far—the most segregated ethnic group in the country.

With segregation, with the isolation of the injured and the robbed, comes the concentration of disadvantage. An unsegregated America might see poverty, and all its effects, spread across the country with no particular bias toward skin color. Instead, the concentration of poverty has been paired with a concentration of melanin. The resulting conflagration has been devastating.

One thread of thinking in the African American community holds that these depressing numbers partially stem from cultural pathologies that can be altered through individual grit and exceptionally good behavior. (In 2011, Philadelphia Mayor Michael Nutter, responding to violence among young black males, put the blame on the family: "Too many men making too many babies they don't want to take care of, and then we end up dealing with your children." Nutter turned to those presumably fatherless babies: "Pull your pants up and buy a belt, because no one wants to see your underwear or the crack of your butt.") The thread is as old as black politics itself. It is also wrong. The kind of trenchant racism to which black people have persistently been subjected can never be defeated by making its victims more respectable. The essence of American racism is disrespect. And in the wake of the grim numbers, we see the grim inheritance.

The Contract Buyers League's suit brought by Clyde Ross and his allies took direct aim at this inheritance. The suit was rooted in Chicago's long history of segregation, which had created two housing markets—one legitimate and backed by the government, the other lawless and patrolled by predators. The suit dragged on until 1976, when the league lost a jury trial. Securing the equal protection of the law proved hard; securing reparations proved impossible. If there were any doubts about the mood of the jury, the foreman removed them by saying, when asked about the verdict, that he hoped it would help end "the mess Earl Warren made with *Brown v. Board of Education* and all that nonsense."

The Supreme Court seems to share that sentiment. The past two decades have witnessed a rollback of the progressive legislation of the 1960s. Liberals have found themselves on the defensive. In 2008, when Barack Obama was a candidate for president, he was asked whether his daughters—Malia and Sasha—should benefit from affirmative action. He answered in the negative.

The exchange rested upon an erroneous comparison of the average American white family and the exceptional first family. In the contest of upward mobility, Barack and Michelle Obama have won. But they've won by being twice as good—and enduring twice as much. Malia and Sasha Obama enjoy privileges beyond the average white child's dreams. But that comparison is incomplete. The more telling question is how they compare with Jenna and Barbara Bush—the products of many generations of privilege, not just one. Whatever the Obama children achieve, it will be evidence of their family's singular perseverance, not of broad equality.

III. "WE INHERIT OUR AMPLE PATRIMONY"

In 1783, the freedwoman Belinda Royall petitioned the commonwealth of Massachusetts for reparations. Belinda had been born in modern-day Ghana. She was kidnapped as a child and sold into slavery. She endured the Middle Passage and 50 years of enslavement at the hands of Isaac Royall and his son. But the junior Royall, a British loyalist, fled the country during the Revolution. Belinda, now free after half a century of labor, beseeched the nascent Massachusetts legislature:

> The face of your Petitioner, is now marked with the furrows of time, and her frame bending under the oppression of years, while she, by the Laws of the Land, is denied the employment of one morsel of that immense wealth, apart whereof hath been accumilated by her own industry, and the whole augmented by her servitude.
>
> WHEREFORE, casting herself at your feet if your honours, as to a body of men, formed for the extirpation of vassalage, for the reward of Virtue, and the just return of honest industry—she prays, that such allowance may be made her out of the Estate of Colonel Royall, as will prevent her, and her more infirm daughter, from misery in the greatest extreme, and scatter comfort over the short and downward path of their lives.

Belinda Royall was granted a pension of 15 pounds and 12 shillings, to be paid out of the estate of Isaac Royall—one of the earliest successful attempts to petition for reparations. At the time, black people in America had endured more than 150 years of enslavement, and the idea that they might be owed something in return was, if not the national consensus, at least not outrageous.

"A heavy account lies against us as a civil society for oppressions committed against people who did not injure us," wrote the Quaker John Woolman in 1769, "and that if the particular case of many individuals were fairly stated, it would appear that there was considerable due to them."

As the historian Roy E. Finkenbine has documented, at the dawn of this country, black reparations were actively considered and often effected. Quakers in New York, New England, and Baltimore went so far as to make "membership contingent upon compensating one's former slaves." In 1782, the Quaker Robert Pleasants emancipated his 78 slaves, granted them 350 acres, and later built a school on their property and provided for their education. "The doing of this justice to the injured Africans," wrote Pleasants, "would be an acceptable offering to him who 'Rules in the kingdom of men.'"

Edward Coles, a protégé of Thomas Jefferson who became a slaveholder through inheritance, took many of his slaves north and granted them a plot of land in Illinois. John Randolph, a cousin of Jefferson's, willed that all his slaves be emancipated upon his death, and that all those older than 40 be given 10 acres of land. "I give and bequeath to all my slaves their freedom," Randolph wrote, "heartily regretting that I have been the owner of one."

In his book *Forever Free,* Eric Foner recounts the story of a disgruntled planter reprimanding a freedman loafing on the job:

PLANTER: "You lazy nigger, I am losing a whole day's labor by you."
FREEDMAN: "Massa, how many days' labor have I lost by you?"

In the 20th century, the cause of reparations was taken up by a diverse cast that included the Confederate veteran Walter R. Vaughan, who believed that reparations would be a stimulus for the South; the black activist Callie House; black-nationalist leaders like "Queen Mother" Audley Moore; and the civil-rights activist James Forman. The movement coalesced in 1987 under an umbrella organization called the National Coalition of Blacks for Reparations in America (N'COBRA). The NAACP endorsed reparations in 1993. Charles J. Ogletree Jr., a professor at Harvard Law School, has pursued reparations claims in court.

But while the people advocating reparations have changed over time, the response from the country has remained virtually the same. "They have been taught to labor," the *Chicago Tribune* editorialized in 1891. "They have been taught Christian civilization, and to speak the noble English language instead of some African gibberish. The account is square with the ex-slaves."

Not exactly. Having been enslaved for 250 years, black people were not left to their own devices. They were terrorized. In the Deep South, a second slavery ruled. In the North, legislatures, mayors, civic associations, banks, and citizens all colluded to pin black people into ghettos, where they were overcrowded, overcharged, and undereducated. Businesses discriminated against them, awarding them the worst jobs and the worst wages. Police brutalized them in the streets. And the notion that black lives, black bodies, and black wealth were rightful targets remained deeply rooted in the broader society. Now we have half-stepped away from our long centuries of despoilment, promising, "Never again." But still we are haunted. It is as though we have run up a credit-card bill and, having pledged to charge no more, remain befuddled that the balance does not disappear. The effects of that balance, interest accruing daily, are all around us.

Broach the topic of reparations today and a barrage of questions inevitably follows: Who will be paid? How much will they be paid? Who will pay? But if the practicalities, not the justice, of reparations are the true sticking point, there has for some time been the beginnings of a solution. For the past 25 years, Congressman John Conyers Jr., who represents the Detroit area, has marked every session of Congress by introducing a bill calling for a congressional study of slavery and its lingering effects as well as recommendations for "appropriate remedies."

A country curious about how reparations might actually work has an easy solution in Conyers's bill, now called HR 40, the Commission to Study Reparation Proposals for African Americans Act. We would support this bill, submit the question to study, and then assess the possible solutions. But we are not interested.

"It's because it's black folks making the claim," Nkechi Taifa, who helped found N'COBRA, says. "People who talk about reparations are considered left lunatics. But all we are talking about is studying [reparations]. As John Conyers has said, we study everything. We study the water, the air. We can't even study the issue? This bill does not authorize one red cent to anyone."

That HR 40 has never—under either Democrats or Republicans—made it to the House floor suggests our concerns are rooted not in the impracticality of reparations but in something more existential. If we conclude that the conditions in North Lawndale and black America are not inexplicable but are instead precisely what you'd expect of a community that for centuries has lived in America's crosshairs, then what are we to make of the world's oldest democracy?

One cannot escape the question by hand-waving at the past, disavowing the acts of one's ancestors, nor by citing a recent date of ancestral immigration. The last slaveholder has been dead for a very long time. The last soldier to endure Valley Forge has been dead much longer. To proudly claim the veteran and disown the slaveholder is patriotism à la carte. A nation outlives its generations. We were not there when Washington crossed the Delaware, but Emanuel Gottlieb Leutze's rendering has meaning to us. We were not there when Woodrow Wilson took us into World War I, but we are still paying out the pensions. If Thomas Jefferson's genius matters, then so does his taking of Sally Hemings's body. If George Washington crossing the Delaware matters, so must his ruthless pursuit of the runagate Oney Judge.

In 1909, President William Howard Taft told the country that "intelligent" white southerners were ready to see blacks as "useful members of the community." A week later Joseph Gordon, a black man, was lynched outside Greenwood, Mississippi. The high point of the lynching era has passed. But the memories of those robbed of their lives still live on in the lingering effects. Indeed, in America there is a strange and powerful belief that if you stab a black person 10 times, the bleeding stops and the healing begins the moment the assailant drops the knife. We believe white dominance to be a fact of the inert past, a delinquent debt that can be made to disappear if only we don't look.

There has always been another way. "It is in vain to alledge, that *our ancestors* brought them hither, and not we," Yale President Timothy Dwight said in 1810.

> We inherit our ample patrimony with all its incumbrances; and are bound to pay the debts of our ancestors. *This* debt, particularly, we are bound to discharge: and, when the righteous Judge of the Universe comes to reckon with his servants, he will rigidly exact the payment at our hands. To give them liberty, and stop here, is to entail upon them a curse.

IV. "THE ILLS THAT SLAVERY FREES US FROM"

America begins in black plunder and white democracy, two features that are not contradictory but complementary. "The men who came together to found the independent United States, dedicated to freedom and equality, either held slaves or were willing to join hands with those who did," the historian Edmund S. Morgan wrote. "None of them felt entirely comfortable about the fact, but neither did they feel responsible for it. Most of them had inherited both their slaves and their attachment to freedom from an earlier generation, and they knew the two were not unconnected."

When enslaved Africans, plundered of their bodies, plundered of their families, and plundered of their labor, were brought to the colony of Virginia in 1619, they did not initially endure the naked racism that would engulf their progeny. Some of them were freed. Some of them intermarried. Still others escaped with the white indentured servants who had suffered as they had. Some even rebelled together, allying under Nathaniel Bacon to torch Jamestown in 1676.

One hundred years later, the idea of slaves and poor whites joining forces would shock the senses, but in the early days of the English colonies, the two groups had much in common. English visitors to Virginia found that its masters "abuse their servantes with intollerable oppression and hard usage." White servants were flogged, tricked into serving beyond their contracts, and traded in much the same manner as slaves.

This "hard usage" originated in a simple fact of the New World—land was boundless but cheap labor was limited. As life spans increased in the colony, the Virginia planters found in the enslaved Africans an even more efficient source of cheap labor. Whereas indentured servants were still legal subjects of the English crown and thus entitled to certain protections, African slaves entered the colonies as aliens. Exempted from the protections of the crown, they became early America's indispensable working class—fit for maximum exploitation, capable of only minimal resistance.

For the next 250 years, American law worked to reduce black people to a class of untouchables and raise all white men to the level of citizens. In 1650, Virginia mandated that "all persons except Negroes" were to carry arms. In 1664, Maryland mandated that any Englishwoman who married a slave must live as a slave of her husband's master. In 1705, the Virginia assembly passed a law allowing for the dismemberment of unruly slaves—but forbidding masters from whipping "a Christian white servant naked, without an order from a justice of the peace." In that same law, the colony mandated that "all horses, cattle, and hogs, now belonging, or that hereafter shall belong to any slave" be seized and sold off by the local church, the profits used to support "the poor of the said parish." At that time, there would have still been people alive who could remember blacks and whites joining to burn down Jamestown only 29 years before. But at the beginning of the 18th century, two primary classes were enshrined in America.

"The two great divisions of society are not the rich and poor, but white and black," John C. Calhoun, South Carolina's senior senator, declared on the Senate floor in 1848. "And all the former, the poor as well as the rich, belong to the upper class, and are respected and treated as equals."

In 1860, the majority of people living in South Carolina and Mississippi, almost half of those living in Georgia, and about one-third of all Southerners were on the wrong side of Calhoun's line. The state with the largest number of enslaved Americans was Virginia, where in certain counties some 70 percent of all people labored in chains. Nearly one-fourth of all white Southerners owned slaves, and upon their backs the economic basis of America—and much of the Atlantic world—was erected. In the seven cotton states, one-third of all white income was derived from slavery. By 1840, cotton produced by slave labor constituted 59 percent of the country's exports. The web of this slave society extended north to the looms of New England, and across the Atlantic to Great Britain, where it powered a great economic transformation and altered the trajectory of world history. "Whoever says Industrial Revolution," wrote the historian Eric J. Hobsbawm, "says cotton."

The wealth accorded America by slavery was not just in what the slaves pulled from the land but in the slaves themselves. "In 1860, slaves as an asset were worth more than all of

America's manufacturing, all of the railroads, all of the productive capacity of the United States put together," the Yale historian David W. Blight has noted. "Slaves were the single largest, by far, financial asset of property in the entire American economy." The sale of these slaves—"in whose bodies that money congealed," writes Walter Johnson, a Harvard historian—generated even more ancillary wealth. Loans were taken out for purchase, to be repaid with interest. Insurance policies were drafted against the untimely death of a slave and the loss of potential profits. Slave sales were taxed and notarized. The vending of the black body and the sundering of the black family became an economy unto themselves, estimated to have brought in tens of millions of dollars to antebellum America. In 1860 there were more millionaires per capita in the Mississippi Valley than anywhere else in the country.

Beneath the cold numbers lay lives divided. "I had a constant dread that Mrs. Moore, her mistress, would be in want of money and sell my dear wife," a freedman wrote, reflecting on his time in slavery. "We constantly dreaded a final separation. Our affection for each was very strong, and this made us always apprehensive of a cruel parting."

Forced partings were common in the antebellum South. A slave in some parts of the region stood a 30 percent chance of being sold in his or her lifetime. Twenty-five percent of interstate trades destroyed a first marriage and half of them destroyed a nuclear family.

When the wife and children of Henry Brown, a slave in Richmond, Virginia, were to be sold away, Brown searched for a white master who might buy his wife and children to keep the family together. He failed:

> The next day, I stationed myself by the side of the road, along which the slaves, amounting to three hundred and fifty, were to pass. The purchaser of my wife was a Methodist minister, who was about starting for North Carolina. Pretty soon five waggon-loads of little children passed, and looking at the foremost one, what should I see but a little child, pointing its tiny hand towards me, exclaiming, "There's my father; I knew he would come and bid me good-bye." It was my eldest child! Soon the gang approached in which my wife was chained. I looked, and beheld her familiar face; but O, reader, that glance of agony! may God spare me ever again enduring the excruciating horror of that moment! She passed, and came near to where I stood. I seized hold of her hand, intending to bid her farewell; but words failed me; the gift of utterance had fled, and I remained speechless. I followed her for some distance, with her hand grasped in mine, as if to save her from her fate, but I could not speak, and I was obliged to turn away in silence.

In a time when telecommunications were primitive and blacks lacked freedom of movement, the parting of black families was a kind of murder. Here we find the roots of American wealth and democracy—in the for-profit destruction of the most important asset available to any people, the family. The destruction was not incidental to America's rise; it facilitated that rise. By erecting a slave society, America created the economic foundation for its great experiment in democracy. The labor strife that seeded Bacon's rebellion was suppressed. America's indispensable working class existed as property beyond the realm of politics, leaving white Americans free to trumpet their love of freedom and democratic values. Assessing antebellum democracy in Virginia, a visitor from England observed that the state's natives "can profess an unbounded love of liberty and of democracy in consequence of the mass of the people, who in other countries might become mobs, being there nearly altogether composed of their own Negro slaves."

V. THE QUIET PLUNDER

The consequences of 250 years of enslavement, of war upon black families and black people, were profound. Like homeownership today, slave ownership was aspirational, attracting not just those who owned slaves but those who wished to. Much as homeowners today might discuss the addition of a patio or the painting of a living room, slaveholders traded tips on the best methods for breeding workers, exacting labor, and doling out punishment. Just as a homeowner today might subscribe to a magazine like *This Old House,* slaveholders had journals such as *De Bow's Review,* which recommended the best practices for wringing profits from slaves. By the dawn of the Civil War, the enslavement of black America was thought to be so foundational to the country that those who sought to end it were branded heretics worthy of death. Imagine what would happen if a president today came out in favor of taking all American homes from their owners: the reaction might well be violent.

"This country was formed for the white, not for the black man," John Wilkes Booth wrote, before killing Abraham Lincoln. "And looking upon *African slavery* from the same standpoint held by those noble framers of our Constitution, I for one have ever considered *it* one of the greatest blessings (both for themselves and us) that God ever bestowed upon a favored nation."

In the aftermath of the Civil War, Radical Republicans attempted to reconstruct the country upon something resembling universal equality—but they were beaten back by a campaign of "Redemption," led by White Liners, Red Shirts, and Klansmen bent on upholding a society "formed for the *white*, not for the black man." A wave of terrorism roiled the South. In his massive history *Reconstruction*, Eric Foner recounts incidents of black people being attacked for not removing their hats; for refusing to hand over a whiskey flask; for disobeying church procedures; for "using insolent language"; for disputing labor contracts; for refusing to be "tied like a slave." Sometimes the attacks were intended simply to "thin out the niggers a little."

Terrorism carried the day. Federal troops withdrew from the South in 1877. The dream of Reconstruction died. For the next century, political violence was visited upon blacks wantonly, with special treatment meted out toward black people of ambition. Black schools and churches were burned to the ground. Black voters and the political candidates who attempted to rally them were intimidated, and some were murdered. At the end of World War I, black veterans returning to their homes were assaulted for daring to wear the American uniform. The demobilization of soldiers after the war, which put white and black veterans into competition for scarce jobs, produced the Red Summer of 1919: a succession of racist pogroms against dozens of cities ranging from Longview, Texas, to Chicago to Washington, D.C. Organized white violence against blacks continued into the 1920s—in 1921 a white mob leveled Tulsa's "Black Wall Street," and in 1923 another one razed the black town of Rosewood, Florida—and virtually no one was punished.

The work of mobs was a rabid and violent rendition of prejudices that extended even into the upper reaches of American government. The New Deal is today remembered as a model for what progressive government should do—cast a broad social safety net that protects the poor and the afflicted while building the middle class. When progressives wish to express their disappointment with Barack Obama, they point to the accomplishments of Franklin Roosevelt. But these progressives rarely note that Roosevelt's New Deal, much like the democracy that produced it, rested on the foundation of Jim Crow.

"The Jim Crow South," writes Ira Katznelson, a history and political-science professor at Columbia, "was the one collaborator America's democracy could not do without." The marks of that collaboration are all over the New Deal. The omnibus programs passed under the Social Security Act in 1935 were crafted in such a way as to protect the southern way of life. Old-age insurance (Social Security proper) and unemployment insurance excluded farmworkers and domestics—jobs heavily occupied by blacks. When President Roosevelt signed Social Security into law in 1935, 65 percent of African Americans nationally and between 70 and 80 percent in the South were ineligible. The NAACP protested, calling the new American safety net "a sieve with holes just big enough for the majority of Negroes to fall through."

The oft-celebrated G.I. Bill similarly failed black Americans, by mirroring the broader country's insistence on a racist housing policy. Though ostensibly color-blind, Title III of the bill, which aimed to give veterans access to low-interest home loans, left black veterans to tangle with white officials at their local Veterans Administration as well as with the same banks that had, for years, refused to grant mortgages to blacks. The historian Kathleen J. Frydl observes in her 2009 book, *The GI Bill,* that so many blacks were disqualified from receiving Title III benefits "that it is more accurate simply to say that blacks could not use this particular title."

In Cold War America, homeownership was seen as a means of instilling patriotism, and as a civilizing and anti-radical force. "No man who owns his own house and lot can be a Communist," claimed William Levitt, who pioneered the modern suburb with the development of the various Levittowns, his famous planned communities. "He has too much to do."

But the Levittowns were, with Levitt's willing acquiescence, segregated throughout their early years. Daisy and Bill Myers, the first black family to move into Levittown, Pennsylvania, were greeted with protests and a burning cross. A neighbor who opposed the family said that Bill Myers was "probably a nice guy, but every time I look at him I see $2,000 drop off the value of my house."

The neighbor had good reason to be afraid. Bill and Daisy Myers were from the other side of John C. Calhoun's dual society. If they moved next door, housing policy almost guaranteed that their neighbors' property values would decline.

Whereas shortly before the New Deal, a typical mortgage required a large down payment and full repayment within about 10 years, the creation of the Home Owners' Loan Corporation in 1933 and then the Federal Housing Administration the following year allowed banks to offer loans requiring no more than 10 percent down, amortized over 20 to 30 years. "Without federal intervention in the housing market, massive suburbanization would have been impossible," writes Thomas J. Sugrue, a historian at the University of Pennsylvania. "In 1930, only 30 percent of Americans owned their own homes; by 1960, more than 60 percent were home owners. Home ownership became an emblem of American citizenship."

That emblem was not to be awarded to blacks. The American real-estate industry believed segregation to be a moral principle. As late as 1950, the National Association of Real Estate Boards' code of ethics warned that "a Realtor should never be instrumental in introducing into a neighborhood . . . any race or nationality, or any individuals whose presence will clearly be detrimental to property values." A 1943 brochure specified that such potential undesirables might include madams, bootleggers, gangsters—and "a colored man of means who was giving his children a college education and thought they were entitled to live among whites."

The federal government concurred. It was the Home Owners' Loan Corporation, not a private trade association, that pioneered the practice of redlining, selectively granting loans and insisting that any property it insured be covered by a restrictive covenant—a clause in the deed forbidding the sale of the property to anyone other than whites. Millions of dollars flowed from tax coffers into segregated white neighborhoods.

"For perhaps the first time, the federal government embraced the discriminatory attitudes of the marketplace," the historian Kenneth T. Jackson wrote in his 1985 book, *Crabgrass Frontier*, a history of suburbanization. "Previously, prejudices were personalized and individualized; FHA exhorted segregation and enshrined it as public policy. Whole areas of cities were declared ineligible for loan guarantees." Redlining was not officially outlawed until 1968, by the Fair Housing Act. By then the damage was done—and reports of redlining by banks have continued.

The federal government is premised on equal fealty from all its citizens, who in return are to receive equal treatment. But as late as the mid-20th century, this bargain was not granted to black people, who repeatedly paid a higher price for citizenship and received less in return. Plunder had been the essential feature of slavery, of the society described by Calhoun. But practically a full century after the end of the Civil War and the abolition of slavery, the plunder—quiet, systemic, submerged—continued even amidst the aims and achievements of New Deal liberals.

VI. MAKING THE SECOND GHETTO

Today Chicago is one of the most segregated cities in the country, a fact that reflects assiduous planning. In the effort to uphold white supremacy at every level down to the neighborhood, Chicago—a city founded by the black fur trader Jean Baptiste Point du Sable—has long been a pioneer. The efforts began in earnest in 1917, when the Chicago Real Estate Board, horrified by the influx of southern blacks, lobbied to zone the entire city by race. But after the Supreme Court ruled against explicit racial zoning that year, the city was forced to pursue its agenda by more-discreet means.

Like the Home Owners' Loan Corporation, the Federal Housing Administration initially insisted on restrictive covenants, which helped bar blacks and other ethnic undesirables from receiving federally backed home loans. By the 1940s, Chicago led the nation in the use of these restrictive covenants, and about half of all residential neighborhoods in the city were effectively off-limits to blacks.

It is common today to become misty-eyed about the old black ghetto, where doctors and lawyers lived next door to meatpackers and steelworkers, who themselves lived next door to prostitutes and the unemployed. This segregationist nostalgia ignores the actual conditions endured by the people living there—vermin and arson, for instance—and ignores the fact that the old ghetto was premised on denying black people privileges enjoyed by white Americans.

In 1948, when the Supreme Court ruled that restrictive covenants, while permissible, were not enforceable by judicial action, Chicago had other weapons at the ready. The Illinois state legislature had already given Chicago's city council the right to approve—and thus to veto—any public housing in the city's wards. This came in handy in 1949, when a new federal housing act sent millions of tax dollars into Chicago and other cities around the country. Beginning in 1950, site selection for public housing proceeded entirely on the grounds of segregation. By the 1960s, the city had created with its vast housing projects what the historian Arnold R. Hirsch calls a "second ghetto," one larger than the old Black Belt but just as impermeable. More than 98 percent of all the family public-housing units built in Chicago between 1950 and the mid-1960s were built in all-black neighborhoods.

Governmental embrace of segregation was driven by the virulent racism of Chicago's white citizens. White neighborhoods vulnerable to black encroachment formed block associations for the sole purpose of enforcing segregation. They lobbied fellow whites not to sell. They lobbied those blacks who did manage to buy to sell back. In 1949, a group of Englewood Catholics formed block associations intended to "keep up the neighborhood." Translation: keep black people out. And when civic engagement was not enough, when government failed, when private banks could no longer hold the line, Chicago turned to an old tool in the American repertoire—racial violence. "The pattern of terrorism is easily discernible," concluded a Chicago civic group in the 1940s. "It is at the seams of the black ghetto in all directions." On July 1 and 2 of 1946, a mob of thousands assembled in Chicago's Park Manor neighborhood, hoping to eject a black doctor who'd recently moved in. The mob pelted the house with rocks and set the garage on fire. The doctor moved away.

In 1947, after a few black veterans moved into the Fernwood section of Chicago, three nights of rioting broke out; gangs of whites yanked blacks off streetcars and beat them. Two years later, when a union meeting attended by blacks in Englewood triggered rumors that a home was being "sold to niggers," blacks (and whites thought to be sympathetic to them) were beaten in the streets. In 1951, thousands of whites in Cicero, 20 minutes or so west of downtown Chicago, attacked an apartment building that housed a single black family, throwing bricks and firebombs through the windows and setting the apartment on fire. A Cook County grand jury declined to charge the rioters—and instead indicted the family's NAACP attorney, the apartment's white owner, and the owner's attorney and rental agent, charging them with conspiring to lower property values. Two years after that, whites picketed and planted explosives in South Deering, about 30 minutes from downtown Chicago, to force blacks out.

When terrorism ultimately failed, white homeowners simply fled the neighborhood. The traditional terminology, *white flight,* implies a kind of natural expression of preference. In fact, white flight was a triumph of social engineering, orchestrated by the shared racist presumptions of America's public and private sectors. For should any nonracist white families decide that integration might not be so bad as a matter of principle or practicality, they still had to contend with the hard facts of American housing policy: When the mid-20th-century white homeowner claimed that the presence of a Bill and Daisy Myers decreased his property value, he was not merely engaging in racist dogma—he was accurately observing the impact of federal policy on market prices. Redlining destroyed the possibility of investment wherever black people lived.

VII. "A LOT OF PEOPLE FELL BY THE WAY"

Speculators in North Lawndale, and at the edge of the black ghettos, knew there was money to be made off white panic. They resorted to "block-busting"—spooking whites into selling cheap before the neighborhood became black. They would hire a black woman to walk up and down the street with a stroller. Or they'd hire someone to call a number in the neighborhood looking for "Johnny Mae." Then they'd cajole whites into selling at low prices, informing them that the more blacks who moved in, the more the value of their homes would decline, so better to sell now. With these white-fled homes in hand, speculators then turned to the masses of black people who had streamed northward as part of the Great Migration, or who were desperate to escape the ghettos: the speculators would take the houses they'd just bought cheap through block-busting and sell them to blacks on contract.

To keep up with his payments and keep his heat on, Clyde Ross took a second job at the post office and then a third job delivering pizza. His wife took a job working at Marshall Field. He had to take some of his children out of private school. He was not able to be at home to supervise his children or help them with their homework. Money and time that Ross wanted to give his children went instead to enrich white speculators.

"The problem was the money," Ross told me. "Without the money, you can't move. You can't educate your kids. You can't give them the right kind of food. Can't make the house look good. They think this neighborhood is where they supposed to be. It changes their outlook. My kids were going to the best schools in this neighborhood, and I couldn't keep them in there."

Mattie Lewis came to Chicago from her native Alabama in the mid-'40s, when she was 21, persuaded by a friend who told her she could get a job as a hairdresser. Instead she was hired by Western Electric, where she worked for 41 years. I met Lewis in the home of her neighbor Ethel Weatherspoon. Both had owned homes in North Lawndale for more than 50 years. Both had bought their houses on contract. Both had been active with Clyde Ross in the Contract Buyers League's effort to garner restitution from contract sellers who'd operated in North Lawndale, banks who'd backed the scheme, and even the Federal Housing Administration. We were joined by Jack Macnamara, who'd been an organizing force in the Contract Buyers League when it was founded, in 1968. Our gathering had the feel of a reunion, because the writer James Alan McPherson had profiled the Contract Buyers League for *The Atlantic* back in 1972.

Weatherspoon bought her home in 1957. "Most of the whites started moving out," she told me. "'The blacks are coming. The blacks are coming.' They actually said that. They had signs up: DON'T SELL TO BLACKS."

Before moving to North Lawndale, Lewis and her husband tried moving to Cicero after seeing a house advertised for sale there. "Sorry, I just sold it today," the Realtor told Lewis's husband. "I told him, 'You know they don't want you in Cicero,'" Lewis recalls. "'They ain't going to let nobody black in Cicero.'"

In 1958, the couple bought a home in North Lawndale on contract. They were not blind to the unfairness. But Lewis, born in the teeth of Jim Crow, considered American piracy—black people keep on making it, white people keep on taking it—a fact of nature. "All I wanted was a house. And that was the only way I could get it. They weren't giving black people loans at that time," she said. "We thought, 'This is the way it is. We going to do it till we die, and they ain't never going to accept us. That's just the way it is.'

"The only way you were going to buy a home was to do it the way they wanted," she continued. "And I was determined to get me a house. If everybody else can have one, I want one too. I had worked for white people in the South. And I saw how these white people were living in the North and I thought, 'One day I'm going to live just like them.' I wanted cabinets and all these things these other people have."

Whenever she visited white co-workers at their homes, she saw the difference. "I could see we were just getting ripped off," she said. "I would see things and I would say, 'I'd like to do this at my house.' And they would say, 'Do it,' but I would think, 'I can't, because it costs us so much more.'"

I asked Lewis and Weatherspoon how they kept up on payments.

"You paid it and kept working," Lewis said of the contract. "When that payment came up, you knew you had to pay it."

"You cut down on the light bill. Cut down on your food bill," Weatherspoon interjected.

"You cut down on things for your child, that was the main thing," said Lewis. "My oldest wanted to be an artist and my other wanted to be a dancer and my other wanted to take music."

Lewis and Weatherspoon, like Ross, were able to keep their homes. The suit did not win them any remuneration. But it forced contract sellers to the table, where they allowed some members of the Contract Buyers League to move into regular mortgages or simply take over their houses outright. By then they'd been bilked for thousands. In talking with Lewis and Weatherspoon, I was seeing only part of the picture—the tiny minority who'd managed to hold on to their homes. But for all our exceptional ones, for every Barack and Michelle Obama, for every Ethel Weatherspoon or Clyde Ross, for every black survivor, there are so many thousands gone.

"A lot of people fell by the way," Lewis told me. "One woman asked me if I would keep all her china. She said, 'They ain't going to set you out.'"

VIII. "NEGRO POVERTY IS NOT WHITE POVERTY"

On a recent spring afternoon in North Lawndale, I visited Billy Lamar Brooks Sr. Brooks has been an activist since his youth in the Black Panther Party, when he aided the Contract Buyers League. I met him in his office at the Better Boys Foundation, a staple of North Lawndale whose mission is to direct local kids off the streets and into jobs and college. Brooks's work is personal. On June 14, 1991, his 19-year-old son, Billy Jr., was shot and killed. "These guys tried to stick him up," Brooks told me. "I suspect he could have been involved in some things . . . He's always on my mind. Every day."

Brooks was not raised in the streets, though in such a neighborhood it is impossible to avoid the influence. "I was in church three or four times a week. That's where the girls were," he said, laughing. "The stark reality is still there. There's no shield from life. You got to go to school. I lived here. I went to Marshall High School. Over here were the Egyptian Cobras. Over there were the Vice Lords."

Brooks has since moved away from Chicago's West Side. But he is still working in North Lawndale. If "you got a nice house, you live in a nice neighborhood, then you are less prone to violence, because your space is not deprived," Brooks said. "You got a security point. You don't need no protection." But if "you grow up in a place like this, housing sucks. When they tore down the projects here, they left the high-rises and came to the neighborhood with that gang mentality. You don't have nothing, so you going to take something, even if it's not real. You don't have no street, but in your mind it's yours."

We walked over to a window behind his desk. A group of young black men were hanging out in front of a giant mural memorializing two black men: IN LOVIN MEMORY QUENTIN AKA "Q," JULY 18, 1974 ♥ MARCH 2, 2012. The name and face of the other man had been spray-painted over by a rival group. The men drank beer. Occasionally a car would cruise past, slow to a crawl, then stop. One of the men would approach the car and make an exchange, then the car would drive off. Brooks had known all of these young men as boys.

"That's their corner," he said.

We watched another car roll through, pause briefly, then drive off. "No respect, no shame," Brooks said. "That's what they do. From that alley to that corner. They don't go no farther than that. See the big brother there? He almost died a couple of years ago. The one drinking the beer back there . . . I know all of them. And the reason they feel safe here is cause of this building, and because they too chickenshit to go anywhere. But that's their mentality. That's their block."

Brooks showed me a picture of a Little League team he had coached. He went down the row of kids, pointing out which ones were in jail, which ones were dead, and which ones were doing all right. And then he pointed out his son—"That's my boy, Billy," Brooks said. Then he wondered aloud if keeping his son with him while working in North Lawndale had hastened his death. "It's a definite connection, because he was part of what I did here. And I think maybe I shouldn't have exposed him. But then, I had to," he said, "because I wanted him with me."

From the White House on down, the myth holds that fatherhood is the great antidote to all that ails black people. But Billy Brooks Jr. had a father. Trayvon Martin had a father. Jordan Davis had a father. Adhering to middle-class norms has never shielded black people from plunder. Adhering to middle-class norms is what made Ethel Weatherspoon a lucrative target for rapacious speculators. Contract sellers did not target the very poor. They targeted black people who had worked hard enough to save a down payment and dreamed of the emblem of American citizenship—homeownership. It was not a tangle of pathology that put a target on Clyde Ross's back. It was not a culture of poverty that singled out Mattie Lewis for "the thrill of the chase and the kill." Some black people always will be twice as good. But they generally find white predation to be thrice as fast.

Liberals today mostly view racism not as an active, distinct evil but as a relative of white poverty and inequality. They ignore the long tradition of this country actively punishing black success—and the elevation of that punishment, in the mid-20th century, to federal policy. President Lyndon Johnson may have noted in his historic civil-rights speech at Howard University in 1965 that "Negro poverty is not white poverty." But his advisers and their successors were, and still are, loath to craft any policy that recognizes the difference.

After his speech, Johnson convened a group of civil-rights leaders, including the esteemed A. Philip Randolph and Bayard Rustin, to address the "ancient brutality." In a strategy paper, they agreed with the president that "Negro poverty is a special, and particularly destructive, form of American poverty." But when it came to specifically addressing the "particularly destructive," Rustin's group demurred, preferring to advance programs that addressed "all the poor, black and white."

The urge to use the moral force of the black struggle to address broader inequalities originates in both compassion and pragmatism. But it makes for ambiguous policy. Affirmative action's precise aims, for instance, have always proved elusive. Is it meant to make amends for the crimes heaped upon black people? Not according to the Supreme Court. In its 1978 ruling in *Regents of the University of California v. Bakke*, the Court rejected "societal discrimination" as "an amorphous concept of injury that may be ageless in its reach into the past." Is affirmative action meant to increase "diversity"? If so, it only tangentially relates to the specific problems of black people—the problem of what America has taken from them over several centuries.

This confusion about affirmative action's aims, along with our inability to face up to the particular history of white-imposed black disadvantage, dates back to the policy's origins. "There is no fixed and firm definition of affirmative action," an appointee in Johnson's Department of Labor declared. "Affirmative action is anything that you have to do to get results. But this does not necessarily include preferential treatment."

Yet America was built on the preferential treatment of white people—395 years of it. Vaguely endorsing a cuddly, feel-good diversity does very little to redress this.

Today, progressives are loath to invoke white supremacy as an explanation for anything. On a practical level, the hesitation comes from the dim view the Supreme Court has taken of the reforms of the 1960s. The Voting Rights Act has been gutted. The Fair Housing Act might well be next. Affirmative action is on its last legs. In substituting a broad class struggle for an anti-racist struggle, progressives hope to assemble a coalition by changing the subject.

The politics of racial evasion are seductive. But the record is mixed. Aid to Families With Dependent Children was originally written largely to exclude blacks—yet by the 1990s it was perceived as a giveaway to blacks. The Affordable Care Act makes no mention of race, but this did not keep Rush Limbaugh from denouncing it as reparations. Moreover, the act's expansion of Medicaid was effectively made optional, meaning that many poor blacks in the former Confederate states do not benefit from it. The Affordable Care Act, like Social Security, will eventually expand its reach to those left out; in the meantime, black people will be injured.

"All that it would take to sink a new WPA program would be some skillfully packaged footage of black men leaning on shovels smoking cigarettes," the sociologist Douglas S. Massey writes. "Papering over the issue of race makes for bad social theory, bad research, and bad public policy." To ignore the fact that one of the oldest republics in the world was erected on a foundation of white supremacy, to pretend that the problems of a dual society are the same as the problems of unregulated capitalism, is to cover the sin of national plunder with the sin of national lying. The lie ignores the fact that reducing American poverty and ending white supremacy are not the same. The lie ignores the fact that closing the "achievement gap" will do nothing to close the "injury gap," in which black college graduates still suffer higher unemployment rates than white college graduates, and black job applicants without criminal records enjoy roughly the same chance of getting hired as white applicants *with* criminal records.

Chicago, like the country at large, embraced policies that placed black America's most energetic, ambitious, and thrifty countrymen beyond the pale of society and marked them as rightful targets for legal theft. The effects reverberate beyond the families who were robbed to the community that beholds the spectacle. Don't just picture Clyde Ross working three jobs so he could hold on to his home. Think of his North Lawndale neighbors—their children, their nephews and nieces—and consider how watching this affects them. Imagine yourself as a young black child watching your elders play by all the rules only to have their possessions tossed out in the street and to have their most sacred possession—their home—taken from them.

The message the young black boy receives from his country, Billy Brooks says, is "'You ain't shit. You not no good. The only thing you are worth is working for us. You will never own anything. You not going to get an education. We are sending your ass to the penitentiary.' They're telling you no matter how hard you struggle, no matter what you put down, you ain't shit. 'We're going to take what you got. You will never own anything, nigger.'"

IX. TOWARD A NEW COUNTRY

When Clyde Ross was a child, his older brother Winter had a seizure. He was picked up by the authorities and delivered to Parchman Farm, a 20,000-acre state prison in the Mississippi Delta region.

"He was a gentle person," Clyde Ross says of his brother. "You know, he was good to everybody. And he started having spells, and he couldn't control himself. And they had him picked up, because they thought he was dangerous."

Built at the turn of the century, Parchman was supposed to be a progressive and reformist response to the problem of "Negro crime." In fact it was the gulag of Mississippi, an object of terror to African Americans in the Delta. In the early years of the 20th century, Mississippi Governor James K. Vardaman used to amuse himself by releasing black convicts into the surrounding wilderness and hunting them down with bloodhounds. "Throughout the American South," writes David M. Oshinsky in his book *Worse Than Slavery*, "Parchman Farm is synonymous with punishment and brutality, as well it should be . . . Parchman is the quintessential penal farm, the closest thing to slavery that survived the Civil War."

When the Ross family went to retrieve Winter, the authorities told them that Winter had died. When the Ross family asked for his body, the authorities at Parchman said they had buried him. The family never saw Winter's body.

And this was just one of their losses.

Scholars have long discussed methods by which America might make reparations to those on whose labor and exclusion the country was built. In the 1970s, the Yale Law professor Boris Bittker argued in *The Case for Black Reparations* that a rough price tag for reparations could be determined by multiplying the number of African Americans in the population by the difference in white and black per capita income. That number—$34 billion in 1973, when Bittker wrote his book—could be added to a reparations program each year for a decade or two. Today Charles Ogletree, the Harvard Law School professor, argues for something broader: a program of job training and public works that takes racial justice as its mission but includes the poor of all races.

To celebrate freedom and democracy while forgetting America's origins in a slavery economy is patriotism à la carte.

Perhaps no statistic better illustrates the enduring legacy of our country's shameful history of treating black people as sub-citizens, sub-Americans, and sub-humans than the wealth gap. Reparations would seek to close this chasm. But as surely as the creation of the wealth gap required the cooperation of every aspect of the society, bridging it will require the same.

Perhaps after a serious discussion and debate—the kind that HR 40 proposes—we may find that the country can never fully repay African Americans. But we stand to discover much about ourselves in such a discussion—and that is perhaps what scares us. The idea of reparations is frightening not simply because we might lack the ability to pay. The idea of reparations threatens something much deeper—America's heritage, history, and standing in the world.

The early American economy was built on slave labor. The Capitol and the White House were built by slaves. President James K. Polk traded slaves from the Oval Office. The laments about "black pathology," the criticism of black family structures by pundits and intellectuals, ring hollow in a country whose existence was predicated on the torture of black fathers, on the rape of black mothers, on the sale of black children. An honest assessment of America's relationship to the black family reveals the country to be not its nurturer but its destroyer.

And this destruction did not end with slavery. Discriminatory laws joined the equal burden of citizenship to unequal distribution of its bounty. These laws reached their apex in the mid-20th century, when the federal government—through housing policies—engineered the wealth gap, which remains with us to this day. When we think of white supremacy, we picture COLORED ONLY signs, but we should picture pirate flags.

On some level, we have always grasped this.

"Negro poverty is not white poverty," President Johnson said in his historic civil-rights speech.

> Many of its causes and many of its cures are the same. But there are differences—deep, corrosive, obstinate differences—radiating painful roots into the community and into the family, and the nature of the individual. These differences are not racial differences. They are solely and simply the consequence of ancient brutality, past injustice, and present prejudice.

We invoke the words of Jefferson and Lincoln because they say something about our legacy and our traditions. We do this because we recognize our links to the past—at least when they flatter us. But black history does not flatter American democracy; it chastens it. The popular mocking of reparations as a harebrained scheme authored by wild-eyed lefties and intellectually unserious black nationalists is fear masquerading as laughter. Black nationalists have always perceived something unmentionable about America that integrationists dare not acknowledge—that white supremacy is not merely the work of hotheaded demagogues, or a matter of false consciousness, but a force so fundamental to America that it is difficult to imagine the country without it.

And so we must imagine a new country. Reparations—by which I mean the full acceptance of our collective biography and its consequences—is the price we must pay to see ourselves squarely. The recovering alcoholic may well have to live with his illness for the rest of his life. But at least he is not living a drunken lie. Reparations beckons us to reject the intoxication of hubris and see America as it is—the work of fallible humans.

Won't reparations divide us? Not any more than we are already divided. The wealth gap merely puts a number on something we feel but cannot say—that American prosperity was ill-gotten and selective in its distribution. What is needed is an airing of family secrets, a settling with old ghosts. What is needed is a healing of the American psyche and the banishment of white guilt.

What I'm talking about is more than recompense for past injustices—more than a handout, a payoff, hush money, or a reluctant bribe. What I'm talking about is a national reckoning that would lead to spiritual renewal. Reparations would mean the end of scarfing hot dogs on the Fourth of July while denying the facts of our heritage. Reparations would mean the end of yelling "patriotism" while waving a Confederate flag. Reparations would mean a revolution of the American consciousness, a reconciling of our self-image as the great democratizer with the facts of our history.

X. "THERE WILL BE NO 'REPARATIONS' FROM GERMANY"

We are not the first to be summoned to such a challenge.

In 1952, when West Germany began the process of making amends for the Holocaust, it did so under conditions that should be instructive to us. Resistance was violent. Very few Germans believed that Jews were entitled to anything. Only 5 percent of West Germans surveyed reported feeling guilty about the Holocaust, and only 29 percent believed that Jews were owed restitution from the German people.

"The rest," the historian Tony Judt wrote in his 2005 book, *Postwar*, "were divided between those (some two-fifths of respondents) who thought that only people 'who really committed something' were responsible and should pay, and those (21 percent) who thought 'that the Jews themselves were partly responsible for what happened to them during the Third Reich'."

Germany's unwillingness to squarely face its history went beyond polls. Movies that suggested a societal responsibility for the Holocaust beyond Hitler were banned. "The German soldier fought bravely and honorably for his homeland," claimed President Eisenhower, endorsing the Teutonic national myth. Judt wrote, "Throughout the fifties West German officialdom encouraged a comfortable view of the German past in which the Wehrmacht was heroic, while Nazis were in a minority and properly punished."

Konrad Adenauer, the postwar German chancellor, was in favor of reparations, but his own party was divided, and he was able to get an agreement passed only with the votes of the Social Democratic opposition.

Among the Jews of Israel, reparations provoked violent and venomous reactions ranging from denunciation to assassination plots. On January 7, 1952, as the Knesset—the Israeli parliament—convened to discuss the prospect of a reparations agreement with West Germany, Menachem Begin, the future prime minister of Israel, stood in front of a large crowd, inveighing against the country that had plundered the lives, labor, and property of his people. Begin claimed that all Germans were Nazis and guilty of murder. His condemnations then spread to his own young state. He urged the crowd to stop paying taxes and claimed that the nascent Israeli nation characterized the fight over whether or not to accept reparations as a "war to the death." When alerted that the police watching the gathering were carrying tear gas, allegedly of German manufacture, Begin yelled, "The same gases that asphyxiated our parents!"

Begin then led the crowd in an oath to never forget the victims of the Shoah, lest "my right hand lose its cunning" and "my tongue cleave to the roof of my mouth." He took the crowd through the streets toward the Knesset. From the rooftops, police repelled the crowd with tear gas and smoke bombs. But the wind shifted, and the gas blew back toward the Knesset, billowing through windows shattered by rocks. In the chaos, Begin and Prime Minister David Ben-Gurion exchanged insults. Two hundred civilians and 140 police officers were wounded. Nearly 400 people were arrested. Knesset business was halted.

Begin then addressed the chamber with a fiery speech condemning the actions the legislature was about to take. "Today you arrested hundreds," he said. "Tomorrow you may arrest thousands. No matter, they will go, they will sit in prison. We will sit there with them. If necessary, we will be killed with them. But there will be no 'reparations' from Germany."

Survivors of the Holocaust feared laundering the reputation of Germany with money, and mortgaging the memory of their dead. Beyond that, there was a taste for revenge. "My soul would be at rest if I knew there would be 6 million German dead to match the 6 million Jews," said Meir Dworzecki, who'd survived the concentration camps of Estonia.

Ben-Gurion countered this sentiment, not by repudiating vengeance but with cold calculation: "If I could take German property without sitting down with them for even a minute but go in with jeeps and machine guns to the warehouses and take it, I would do that—if, for instance, we had the ability to send a hundred divisions and tell them, 'Take it.' But we can't do that."

The reparations conversation set off a wave of bomb attempts by Israeli militants. One was aimed at the foreign ministry in Tel Aviv. Another was aimed at Chancellor Adenauer himself. And one was aimed at the port of Haifa, where the goods bought with reparations money were arriving. West Germany ultimately agreed to pay Israel 3.45 billion deutsche marks, or more than $7 billion in today's dollars. Individual reparations claims followed—for psychological trauma, for offense to Jewish honor, for halting law careers, for life insurance, for time spent in concentration camps. Seventeen percent of funds went toward purchasing ships. "By the end of 1961, these reparations vessels constituted two-thirds of the Israeli merchant fleet," writes the Israeli historian Tom Segev in his book *The Seventh Million*. "From 1953 to 1963, the reparations money funded about a third of the total investment in Israel's electrical system, which tripled its capacity, and nearly half the total investment in the railways."

Israel's GNP tripled during the 12 years of the agreement. The Bank of Israel attributed 15 percent of this growth, along with 45,000 jobs, to investments made with reparations money. But Segev argues that the impact went far beyond that. Reparations "had indisputable psychological and political importance," he writes.

Reparations could not make up for the murder perpetrated by the Nazis. But they did launch Germany's reckoning with itself, and perhaps provided a road map for how a great civilization might make itself worthy of the name.

Assessing the reparations agreement, David Ben-Gurion said:

> For the first time in the history of relations between people, a precedent has been created by which a great State, as a result of moral pressure alone, takes it upon itself to pay compensation to the victims of the government that preceded it. For the first time in the history of a people that has been persecuted, oppressed, plundered and despoiled for hundreds of years in the countries of Europe, a persecutor and despoiler has been obliged to return part of his spoils and has even undertaken to make collective reparation as partial compensation for material losses.

Something more than moral pressure calls America to reparations. We cannot escape our history. All of our solutions to the great problems of health care, education, housing, and economic inequality are troubled by what must go unspoken. "The reason black people are so far behind now is not because of now," Clyde Ross told me. "It's because of then." In the early 2000s, Charles Ogletree went to Tulsa, Oklahoma, to meet with the survivors of the 1921 race riot that had devastated "Black Wall Street." The past was not the past to them. "It was amazing seeing these black women and men who were crippled, blind, in wheelchairs," Ogletree told me. "I had no idea who they were and why they wanted to see me. They said, 'We want you to represent us in this lawsuit.'"

A commission authorized by the Oklahoma legislature produced a report affirming that the riot, the knowledge of which had been suppressed for years, had happened. But the lawsuit ultimately failed, in 2004. Similar suits pushed against corporations such as Aetna (which insured slaves) and Lehman Brothers (whose co-founding partner owned them) also have thus far failed. These results are dispiriting, but the crime with which reparations activists charge the country implicates more than just a few towns or corporations. The crime indicts the American people themselves, at every level, and in nearly every configuration. A crime that implicates the entire American people deserves its hearing in the legislative body that represents them.

John Conyers's HR 40 is the vehicle for that hearing. No one can know what would come out of such a debate. Perhaps no number can fully capture the multi-century plunder of black people in America. Perhaps the number is so large that it can't be imagined, let alone calculated and dispensed. But I believe that wrestling publicly with these questions matters as much as—if not more than—the specific answers that might be produced. An America that asks what it owes its most vulnerable citizens is improved and humane. An America that looks away is ignoring not just the sins of the past but the sins of the present and the certain sins of the future. More important than any single check cut to any African American, the payment of reparations would represent America's maturation out of the childhood myth of its innocence into a wisdom worthy of its founders.

In 2010, Jacob S. Rugh, then a doctoral candidate at Princeton, and the sociologist Douglas S. Massey published a study of the recent foreclosure crisis. Among its drivers, they found an old foe: segregation. Black home buyers—even after controlling for factors like creditworthiness—were still more likely than white home buyers to be steered toward subprime loans. Decades of racist housing policies by the American government, along with decades of racist housing practices by American businesses, had conspired to concentrate African Americans in the same neighborhoods. As in North Lawndale half a century earlier, these neighborhoods were filled with people who had been cut off from mainstream financial institutions. When subprime lenders went looking for prey, they found black people waiting like ducks in a pen.

"High levels of segregation create a natural market for subprime lending," Rugh and Massey write, "and cause riskier mortgages, and thus foreclosures, to accumulate disproportionately in racially segregated cities' minority neighborhoods."

Plunder in the past made plunder in the present efficient. The banks of America understood this. In 2005, Wells Fargo promoted a series of Wealth Building Strategies seminars. Dubbing itself "the nation's leading originator of home loans to ethnic minority customers," the bank enrolled black public figures in an ostensible effort to educate blacks on building "generational wealth." But the "wealth building" seminars were a front for wealth theft. In 2010, the Justice Department filed a discrimination suit against Wells Fargo alleging that the bank had shunted blacks into predatory loans regardless of their creditworthiness. This was not magic or coincidence or misfortune. It was racism reifying itself. According to *The New York Times*, affidavits found loan officers referring to their black customers as "mud people" and to their subprime products as "ghetto loans."

"We just went right after them," Beth Jacobson, a former Wells Fargo loan officer, told *The Times*. "Wells Fargo mortgage had an emerging-markets unit that specifically targeted black churches because it figured church leaders had a lot of influence and could convince congregants to take out subprime loans."

In 2011, Bank of America agreed to pay $355 million to settle charges of discrimination against its Countrywide unit. The following year, Wells Fargo settled its discrimination suit for more than $175 million. But the damage had been done. In 2009, half the properties in Baltimore whose owners had been granted loans by Wells Fargo between 2005 and 2008 were vacant; 71 percent of these properties were in predominantly black neighborhoods.

CRITICAL THINKING QUESTIONS

1. Coates writes that, "Contract sellers became rich. North Lawndale became a ghetto." What is contract selling? How is that different from how the white community in Chicago often bought their homes? How was it hurtful to the African-American community in Chicago—how did it help turn North Lawndale into a ghetto? Clyde Ross joined the Contract Buyers League in 1968 to combat this predatory business practice. What was the purpose of this organization, and how did it function?

2. In a sentence for each one, describe the social, political, and economic climates of the state of Mississippi in the 1920s. As it relates to African Americans, how do the social, political, and economic climates of your home state compare?

3. Coates writes, "It was in these early years that Ross began to understand himself as an American." How would you define Ross's perception and understanding of being American while living in Mississippi? In what way did Ross's life change when living in California and Chicago? Did his social, political, and economic lifestyle improve, worsen, or stay the same?

4. Walter Johnson, a Harvard Historian, writes that American slaves were those "in whose bodies that money congealed." How did slave's bodies help money come together? Who did it come together for? Please provide three arguments or examples from the text.

THE RISE OF ASIAN AMERICANS

by Pew Research

The Pew Research Center is a nonpartisan American organization that provides information on social issues, public opinion, and trends that shape the Unites States and the world.

In 2012, President Obama announced a shifting focus in American Foreign policy—a "pivot to East Asia." These economic powers—China, Japan, Singapore, Malaysia, and others—were growing in importance, raising the standards of living for their citizens. For the past century and a half, many would leave these countries and arrive in America to find the land of opportunity a hostile place. Forced to work long hours, live in ethnically-distinct neighborhoods, and denied rights, an Asian immigrant's life for most of our country's history seemed dire. This is not the case anymore—Asian Americans are rising socially and integrating faster than any other ethnic group. Why is this the case, and what does it say about economics and race in America?

. . . .

OVERVIEW

Asian Americans are the highest-income, best-educated and fastest-growing racial group in the United States. They are more satisfied than the general public with their lives, finances and the direction of the country, and they place more value than other Americans do on marriage, parenthood, hard work and career success, according to a comprehensive new nationwide survey by the Pew Research Center.

A century ago, most Asian Americans were low-skilled, low-wage laborers crowded into ethnic enclaves and targets of official discrimination. Today they are the most likely of any major racial or ethnic group in America to live in mixed neighborhoods and to marry across racial lines. When newly minted medical school graduate Priscilla Chan married Facebook founder Mark Zuckerberg last month, she joined the 37% of all recent Asian-American brides who wed a non-Asian groom.[1]

These milestones of economic success and social assimilation have come to a group that is still majority immigrant. Nearly three-quarters (74%) of Asian-American adults were born abroad; of these, about half say they speak English very well and half say they don't.

Asians recently passed Hispanics as the largest group of new immigrants to the United States. The educational credentials of these recent arrivals are striking. More than six-in-ten (61%) adults ages 25 to 64 who have come from Asia in recent years have at least a bachelor's degree. This is double the share among recent non-Asian arrivals, and almost surely makes the recent Asian arrivals the most highly educated cohort of immigrants in U.S. history.

Compared with the educational attainment of the population in their country of origin, recent Asian immigrants also stand out as a select group. For example, about 27% of adults ages 25 to 64 in South Korea and 25% in Japan have a bachelor's degree or more.[2] In contrast, nearly 70% of comparably aged recent immigrants from these two countries have at least a bachelor's degree.

Recent Asian immigrants are also about three times as likely as recent immigrants from other parts of the world to receive their green cards—or permanent resident status—on the

Meet the New Immigrants: Asians Overtake Hispanics

% of immigrants, by year of arrival, 2000-2010

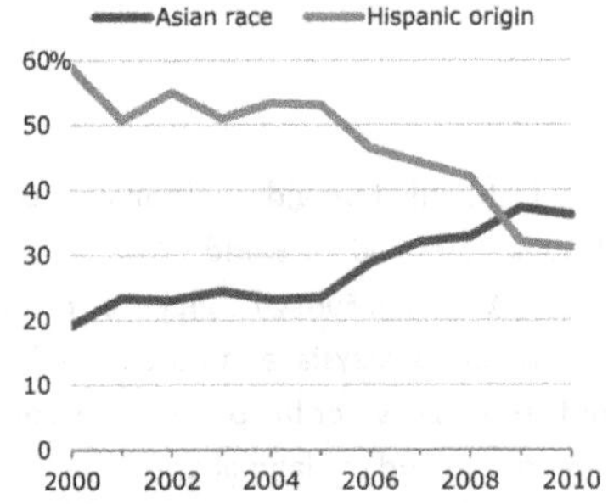

Note: Based on total foreign-born population, including adults and children. Asians include mixed-race Asian population, regardless of Hispanic origin. Hispanics are of any race. The 2010 ACS includes only partial-year arrivals for 2010; arrivals for 2010 adjusted to full-year totals based on analysis of 2005-2009 ACS data on partial-year arrivals.

Source: Pew Research Center analysis of 2010 American Community Survey, Integrated Public Use Microdata Sample (IPUMS) files

PEW RESEARCH CENTER

Asian Americans Lead Others In Education, Income

% with a bachelor's degree or more, among ages 25 and older, 2010

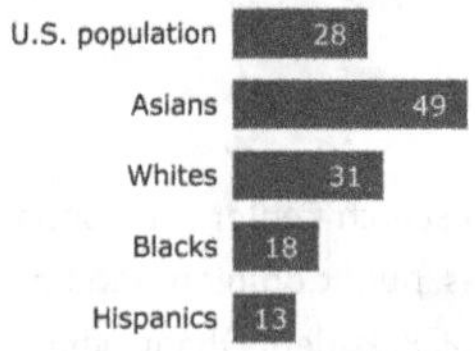

Median household income, 2010

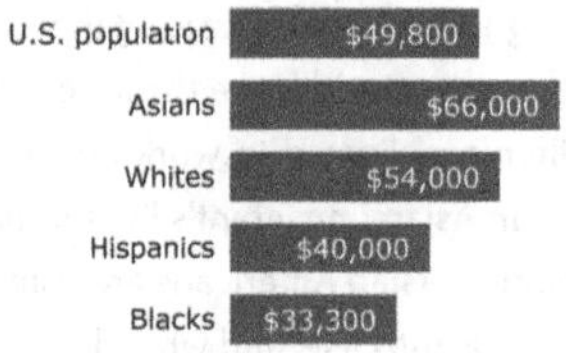

Note: Asians include mixed-race Asian population, regardless of Hispanic origin. Whites and blacks include only non-Hispanics. Hispanics are of any race. Household income is based on householders ages 18 and older; race and ethnicity are based on those of household head.

Source: Pew Research Center analysis of 2010 American Community Survey, Integrated Public Use Microdata Sample (IPUMS) files

PEW RESEARCH CENTER

basis of employer rather than family sponsorship (though family reunification remains the most common legal gateway to the U.S. for Asian immigrants, as it is for all immigrants).

The modern immigration wave from Asia is nearly a half century old and has pushed the total population of Asian Americans—foreign born and U.S. born, adults and children—to a record 18.2 million in 2011, or 5.8% of the total U.S. population, up from less than 1% in 1965.[3] By comparison, non-Hispanic whites are 197.5 million and 63.3%, Hispanics 52.0 million and 16.7% and non-Hispanic blacks 38.3 million and 12.3%.

Asian Americans trace their roots to any of dozens of countries in the Far East, Southeast Asia and the Indian subcontinent. Each country of origin subgroup has its own unique history, culture, language, religious beliefs, economic and demographic traits, social and political values, and pathways into America.

But despite often sizable subgroup differences, Asian Americans are distinctive as a whole, especially when compared with all U.S. adults, whom they exceed not just in the share with a college degree (49% vs. 28%), but also in median annual household income ($66,000 versus $49,800) and median household wealth ($83,500 vs. $68,529).[4]

They are noteworthy in other ways, too. According to the Pew Research Center survey of a nationally representative sample of 3,511 Asian Americans, conducted by telephone from Jan. 3 to March 27, 2012, in English and seven Asian languages, they are more satisfied than the general public with their lives overall (82% vs. 75%), their personal finances (51% vs. 35%) and the general direction of the country (43% vs. 21%).

They also stand out for their strong emphasis on family. More than half (54%) say that having a successful marriage is one of the most important things in life; just 34% of all American adults agree. Two-thirds of Asian-American adults (67%) say that being a good parent is one of the most important things in life; just 50% of all adults agree.

Their living arrangements align with these values. They are more likely than all American adults to be married (59% vs. 51%); their newborns are less likely than all U.S. newborns to have an unmarried mother (16% vs. 41%); and their children are more likely than all U.S. children to be raised in a household with two married parents (80% vs. 63%).

They are more likely than the general public to live in multi-generational family households. Some 28% live with at least two adult generations under the same roof, twice the share of whites and slightly more than the share of blacks and Hispanics who live in such households. U.S. Asians also have a strong sense of filial respect; about two-thirds say parents should have a lot or some influence in choosing one's profession (66%) and spouse (61%).

The Asian-American Work Ethic

% saying ...

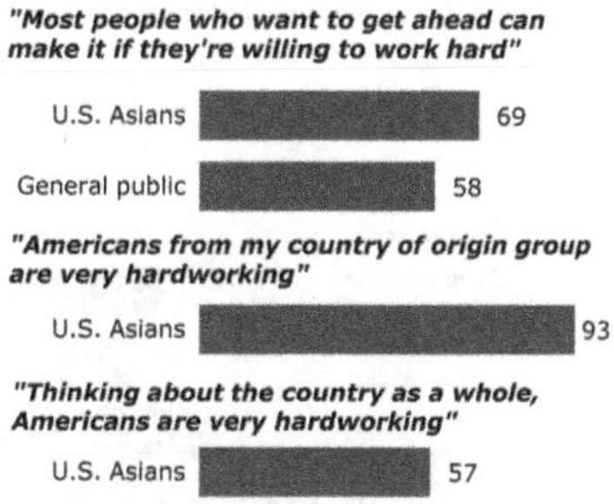

2012 Asian-American Survey. Q12b, 21, 70. Those who did not provide a country of origin were asked about "Asian Americans."

PEW RESEARCH CENTER

Asian Americans have a pervasive belief in the rewards of hard work. Nearly seven-in-ten (69%) say people can get ahead if they are willing to work hard, a view shared by a somewhat smaller share of the American public as a whole (58%). And fully 93% of Asian Americans describe members of their country of origin group as "very hardworking"; just 57% say the same about Americans as a whole.

By their own lights, Asian Americans sometimes go overboard in stressing hard work. Nearly four-in-ten (39%) say that Asian-American parents from their country of origin subgroup put too much pressure on their children to do well in school. Just 9% say the same about all American parents. On the flip side of the same coin, about six-in-ten Asian parents put too little pressure on their children to succeed in school, while just 9% say the same about Asian-American parents. (The publication last year of "Battle Hymn of the Tiger Mother," a comic memoir about strict parenting by Yale Law Professor Amy Chua, the daughter of immigrants, triggered a spirited debate about cultural differences in parenting norms.)

The immigration wave from Asia has occurred at a time when the largest sending countries have experienced dramatic gains in their standards of living. But few Asian immigrants are looking over their shoulders with regret. Just 12% say that if they had to do it all over again, they would remain in their country of origin. And by lopsided margins, Asian Americans say the U.S. is preferable to their country of origin in such realms as providing economic

Who's a "Tiger Mom"?

% of U.S. Asians saying (American parents/Asian-American parents) put ... pressure on their children to do well in school

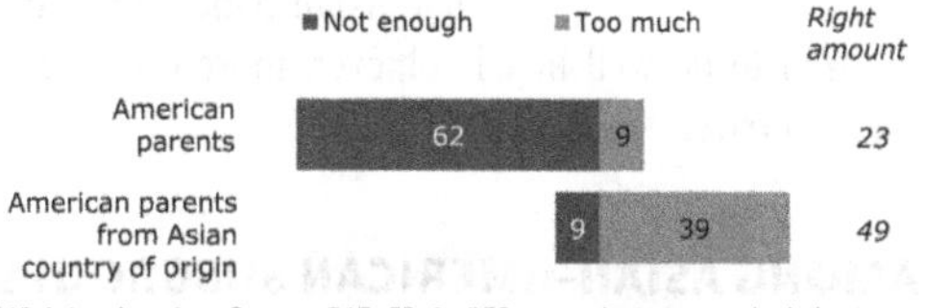

2012 Asian-American Survey. Q17, 53. In Q53 respondents were asked about parents from their country of origin group (Chinese-American parents, Korean-American parents, etc.). Those who did not provide a country of origin were asked about "Asian-American parents." Responses of "Don't know/Refused" not shown.

PEW RESEARCH CENTER

For Most Asians, U.S. Offers a Better Life

% saying ...

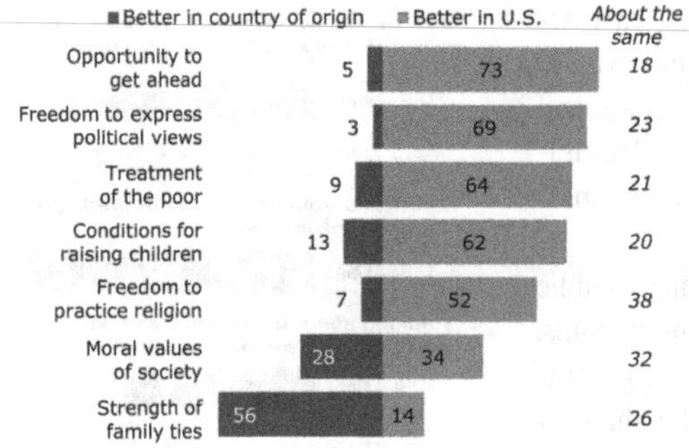

2012 Asian-American Survey. Q54a-g. Responses of "Don't know/Refused" not shown.

PEW RESEARCH CENTER

opportunity, political and religious freedoms, and good conditions for raising children. Respondents rated their country of origin as being superior on just one of seven measures tested in the survey—strength of family ties.

(The survey was conducted only among Asian Americans currently living in the U.S. As is the case with all immigration waves, a portion of those who came to the U.S. from Asia in recent decades have chosen to return to their country of origin. However, return migration rates are estimated to be lower for immigrants from Asia than for other immigrants, and naturalization rates—that is, the share of eligible immigrants who become U.S. citizens—are higher.)

ASIANS IN THE U.S. AND IN ASIA

Intergenerational Mobility among Asians in the U.S. and in Asia

% saying their current standard of living is "much better" than their parents' was at a comparable age

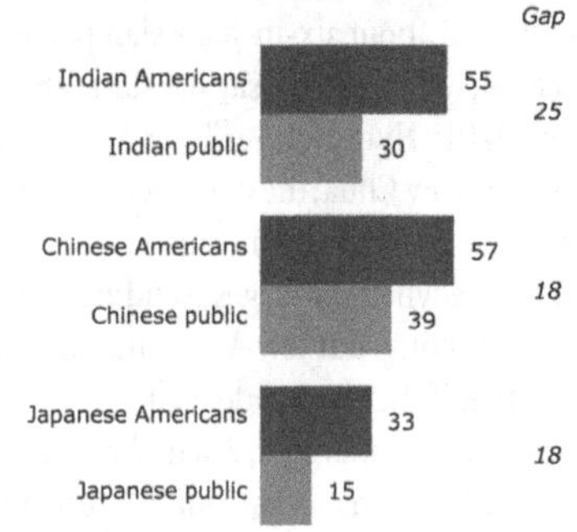

Data for Indian Americans, Chinese Americans and Japanese Americans are from the 2012 Asian-American survey. Q10. Data for the Indian, Chinese and Japanese publics are from surveys conducted in those countries in 2012 by the Pew Research Center's Global Attitudes Project.

PEW RESEARCH CENTER

When findings from this survey are compared with recent surveys conducted by the Pew Research Center's Global Attitudes Project among Asians in major Asian countries, a mixed picture emerges. For example, adults living in China are more satisfied with the way things are going in their country than Chinese Americans are with the way things are going in the United States. By contrast, the publics of India and Japan have a more downbeat view of the way things are going in their countries than their counterpart groups do about the U.S.

Across the board, however, U.S. Asians are more likely than Asians in Asia to say their standard of living is better than that of their parents at a similar stage of life. U.S. Asians also exceed Asians in their belief that hard work leads to success in life. And while many U.S. Asians say that Asian-American parents place too much pressure on their children to do well in school, even more Chinese and Japanese say this about parents in their countries.

DIFFERENCES AMONG ASIAN-AMERICAN SUBGROUPS

The Pew Research Center survey was designed to contain a nationally representative sample of each of the six largest Asian-American groups by country of origin—Chinese Americans,

Filipino Americans, Indian Americans, Vietnamese Americans, Korean Americans and Japanese Americans. Together these groups comprise at least 83% of the total Asian population in the U.S.[5]

The basic demographics of these groups are different on many measures. For example, Indian Americans lead all other groups by a significant margin in their levels of income and education. Seven-in-ten Indian-American adults ages 25 and older have a college degree, compared with about half of Americans of Korean, Chinese, Filipino and Japanese ancestry, and about a quarter of Vietnamese Americans.

On the other side of the socio-economic ledger, Americans with Korean, Vietnamese, Chinese and "other U.S. Asian"[6] origins have higher shares in poverty than does the U.S. general public, while those with Indian, Japanese and Filipino origins have lower shares.[7]

The Largest U.S. Asian Groups

The six largest country of origin groups each number more than a million people

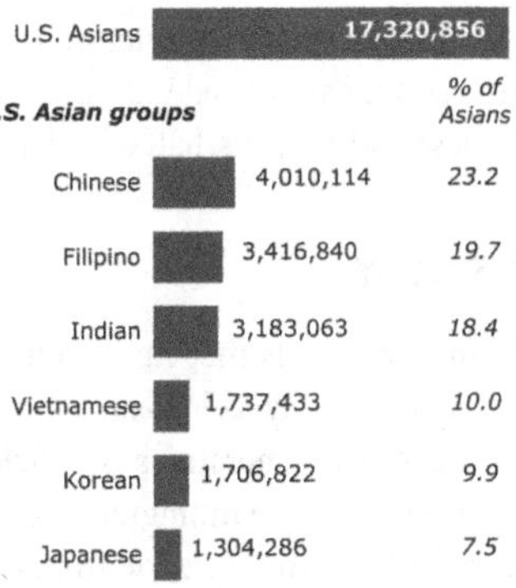

Note: Based on the total Asian-race population, including adults and children. There is some overlap in the numbers for the six largest Asian groups because people with origins in more than one group—for example, "Chinese and Filipino"—are counted in each group to which they belong.

Source: Pew Research Center analysis based on Elizabeth M. Hoeffel et al., *The Asian Population: 2010*, U.S. Census Bureau, March 2012.

PEW RESEARCH CENTER

Their geographic settlement patterns also differ. More than seven-in-ten Japanese and two-thirds of Filipinos live in the West, compared with fewer than half of Chinese, Vietnamese and Koreans, and only about a quarter of Indians.

The religious identities of Asian Americans are quite varied. According to the Pew Research survey, about half of Chinese are unaffiliated, most Filipinos are Catholic, about half of Indians are Hindu, most Koreans are Protestant and a plurality of Vietnamese are Buddhist. Among Japanese Americans, no one group is dominant: 38% are Christian, 32% are unaffiliated and 25% are Buddhist. In total, 26% of Asian Americans are unaffiliated, 22% are Protestant (13% evangelical; 9% mainline), 19% are Catholic, 14% are Buddhist, 10% are Hindu, 4% are Muslim and 1% are Sikh. Overall, 39% of Asian Americans say religion is very important in their lives, compared with 58% of the U.S. general public.

There are subgroup differences in social and cultural realms as well. Japanese and Filipino Americans are the most accepting of interracial and intergroup marriage; Koreans, Vietnamese and Indians are less comfortable. Koreans are the most likely to say discrimination against their group is a major problem, and they are the least likely to say that their group gets along very well with other racial and ethnic groups in the U.S. In contrast, Filipinos have the most upbeat view of intergroup relations in the U.S.

The Japanese are the only group that is majority U.S. born (73% of the total population and 68% of adults); all other subgroups are majority foreign born.

Their pathways into the U.S. are different. About half of all Korean and Indian immigrants who received green cards in 2011 got them on the basis of employer sponsorship, compared with about a third of Japanese, a fifth of Chinese, one-in-eight Filipinos and just 1% of Vietnamese. The Vietnamese are the only major subgroup to have come to the U.S. in large numbers as political refugees; the others say they have come mostly for economic, educational and family reasons.

Asian Americans have varying degrees of attachment to relatives in their home countries—likely reflecting differences in the timing and circumstances of their immigration.

For example, though they are among the least well-off financially, Vietnamese Americans are among the most likely (58%) to say they have sent money to someone in Vietnam in the past year. About half of Filipinos (52%) also say they sent remittances home in the past year. By contrast, Japanese (12%) and Koreans (16%) are much less likely to have done this.

They have different naturalization rates. Fully three-quarters of the foreign-born Vietnamese are naturalized U.S. citizens, compared with two-thirds of Filipinos, about six-in-ten Chinese and Koreans, half of Indians and only a third of Japanese.

HISTORY

Asian immigrants first came to the U.S. in significant numbers more than a century and a half ago—mainly as low-skilled male laborers who mined, farmed and built the railroads. They endured generations of officially sanctioned racial prejudice—including regulations that prohibited the immigration of Asian women; the Chinese Exclusion Act of 1882, which barred all new immigration from China; the Immigration Act of 1917 and the National Origins Act of 1924, which extended the immigration ban to include virtually all of Asia; and the forced relocation and internment of about 120,000 Japanese Americans after the Japanese attack on Pearl Harbor in 1941.

Large-scale immigration from Asia did not take off until the passage of the landmark Immigration and Nationality Act of 1965. Over the decades, this modern wave of immigrants from Asia has increasingly become more skilled and educated. Today, recent arrivals from Asia are nearly twice as likely as those who came three decades ago to have a college degree, and many go into high-paying fields such as science, engineering, medicine and finance. This evolution has been spurred by changes in U.S. immigration policies and labor markets; by political liberalization and economic growth in the sending countries; and by the forces of globalization in an ever-more digitally interconnected world.

These trends have raised the education levels of immigrants of all races in recent years, but Asian immigrants exceed other race and ethnic groups in the share who are either college students or college graduates.

The Immigrant Education Gap

% with at least a bachelor's degree, ages 25-64, 1980-2010

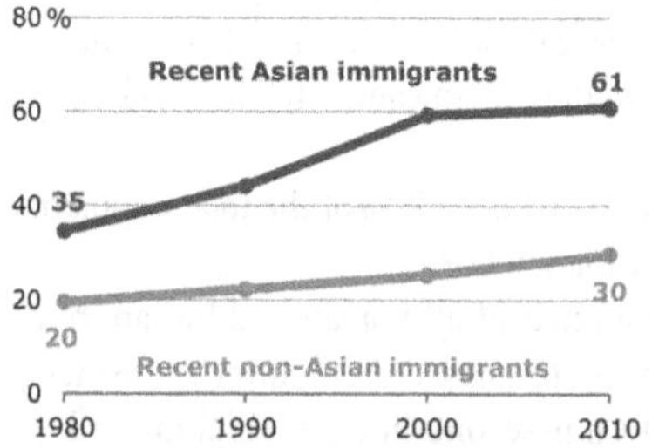

Note: Except for 1980, "recent immigrants" refers to those who came to live in the U.S. in the past three years prior to the survey. In 1980, the reference period was 1975-1980.

Source: Pew Research Center analysis of the 1980, 1990 and 2000 Decennial Censuses and 2010 American Community Survey, Integrated Public Use Microdata Sample (IPUMS) files

PEW RESEARCH CENTER

Education Characteristics of Recent Immigrants, by Race and Ethnicity, 2010

% among adults

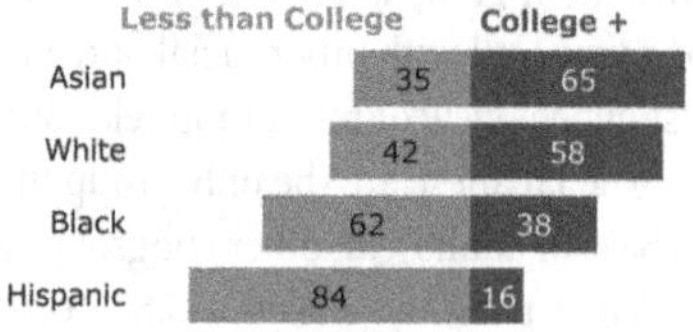

Note: Recent immigrants refer to those who came to the U.S. in the past three years prior to the survey date (since 2007). "College +" includes those who are either currently in a four-year college or graduate school or have completed their bachelor's degree or advanced degrees. Asian includes mixed-race Asian population, regardless of Hispanic origin. White and black include only non-Hispanics. Hispanics are of any race.

Source: Pew Research Center analysis of 2010 American Community Survey, Integrated Public Use Microdata Sample (IPUMS) files

PEW RESEARCH CENTER

NATIVE BORN AND FOREIGN BORN

Throughout the long history of immigration waves to the U.S., the typical pattern has been that over time the second generation (i.e., the children of immigrants) surpasses the immigrant generation in key measures of socio-economic well-being and assimilation, such as household income, educational attainment and English fluency.

It is not yet possible to make any full intergenerational accounting of the modern Asian-American immigration wave; the immigrants themselves are still by far the dominant group and the second generation has only recently begun to come into adulthood in significant numbers. (Among all second-generation Asians, the median age is just 17; in other words, about half are still children.)

But on the basis of the evidence so far, this immigrant generation has set a bar of success that will be a challenge for the next generation to surpass. As of now, there is no difference in the share of native-and foreign-born Asian Americans ages 25 and older who have a college degree (49% for each group), and there is only a modest difference in the median annual earnings of full-time workers in each group ($50,000 for the native born; $47,000 for the foreign born). The two groups also have similar shares in poverty and homeownership rates.

Not surprisingly, when it comes to language fluency, there are significant differences between the native-and foreign-born adults. Only about half (53%) of the foreign born say they speak English very well, compared with 95% of the U.S. born. Family formation patterns are also quite different. The U.S. born are much less likely than the foreign born to be married (35% vs. 67%), a difference largely driven by the fact that they are a much younger group. (Among adults, the median age is 30, versus 44 for the foreign born.)

Characteristics of Native- and Foreign-born Asian-American Adults, 2010

% (unless otherwise noted)

	U.S. Asians	Native born	Foreign born
Share of Asian population	100.0	25.9	74.1
Citizen	69.6	100.0	58.9
Median age *(in years)*	41	30	44
Married	59.0	34.9	67.4
Fertility (women ages 18-44)			
Had a birth in the past 12 months	6.8	4.8	7.7
Of these, % unmarried	14.6	31.1	9.6
Educational attainment (ages 25+)			
Less than high school	13.9	4.7	16.3
High school or more	86.1	95.3	83.7
Bachelor's degree or more	49.0	49.4	48.9
Median annual personal earnings			
Full-time, year-round workers	$48,000	$50,000	$47,000
Household annual income			
Median	$66,000	$67,400	$65,200
Average household size *(persons)*	3.1	2.6	3.2
Homeownership rate	58.1	57.4	58.3
In poverty	11.9	11.1	12.2
Speaks English less than "very well"	36.5	5.3	47.5

Note: Asians include mixed-race Asian population, regardless of Hispanic origin. Unmarried women include those who are divorced, separated, widowed or never married. "High school or more" includes those who attained at least a high school diploma or an equivalent, such as a General Education Development (GED) certificate. "Speaks English less than 'very well'" includes those who say they speak English "well" or "not well" or who don't speak English at all.

Source: Pew Research Center analysis of 2010 American Community Survey, Integrated Public Use Microdata Sample (IPUMS) files

PEW RESEARCH CENTER

There are also differences between the native born and foreign born in the share of recent mothers who are unmarried. About three-in-ten (31%) U.S.-born Asian women who had children recently are unmarried, compared with just 10% of all recent foreign-born Asian-American mothers. Among the U.S. population as a whole, about four-in-ten recent American mothers are unmarried. Even as births to single mothers have become more widespread in recent decades, Pew Research surveys find that a sizable majority of Americans believe this growing phenomenon has been bad for society. So in the eyes of the public, this appears to be a case of "downward assimilation" by second generation and later generations of Asian Americans to an increasingly prevalent—but still frowned upon—U.S. pattern of behavior.[8]

On a more positive note, U.S.-born Asians are more upbeat than the foreign born about their relations with other racial and ethnic groups, and they are more receptive to the growing practice of racial and ethnic intermarriage.

PERCEPTIONS OF DISCRIMINATION

For the most part, today's Asian Americans do not feel the sting of racial discrimination or the burden of culturally imposed "otherness" that was so much a part of the experience of their predecessors who came in the 19th and early 20th centuries.

About one-in-five Asian Americans say they have personally been treated unfairly in the past year because they are Asian, and one-in-ten say they have been called an offensive name. Older adults are less likely than young and middle-aged adults to report negative personal experience with bias.

Compared with the nation's two largest minority groups—Hispanics and blacks—Asian Americans appear to be less inclined to view discrimination against their group as a major problem.[9] Just 13% of Asian Americans say it is, while about half (48%) say it is a minor problem, and a third (35%) say it is not a problem.

About six-in-ten say that being Asian American makes no difference when it comes to getting a job or gaining admission to college. Of those who do say it makes a difference, a slightly higher share say that members of their group are helped rather than hurt by their race. Those with less education are more prone than those with more education to say that being an Asian American is an advantage.

Does Being Asian American Help or Hurt with College, Career?

% saying being of their U.S. Asian group helps, makes no difference or hurts when it comes to ...

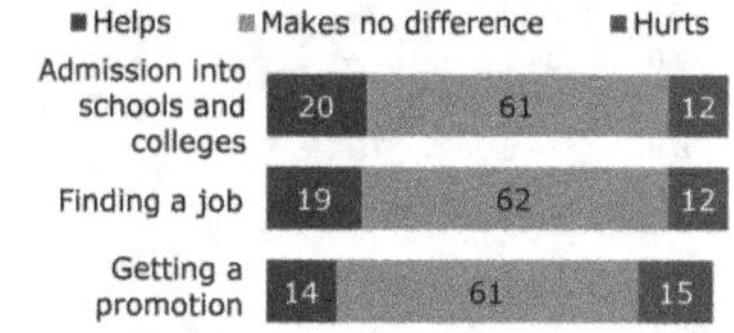

2012 Asian-American Survey. Q46a-c. Responses of "Don't know/Refused" not shown.

PEW RESEARCH CENTER

GROUP RELATIONS

Overall, more than eight-in-ten Asian Americans say their group gets along either very or pretty well with whites; roughly seven-in-ten say the same about relations with Hispanics and just over six-in-ten say that about their relations with blacks. Korean Americans stand out for their negative views on their group's relations with blacks. Fully half say these two groups don't get along well; while 39% say they get along pretty well and just 4% say they get along very well. In several cities across the country, there has been a history of tension

Getting Along across Group Boundaries

% saying their U.S. Asian group and each of the following get along ...

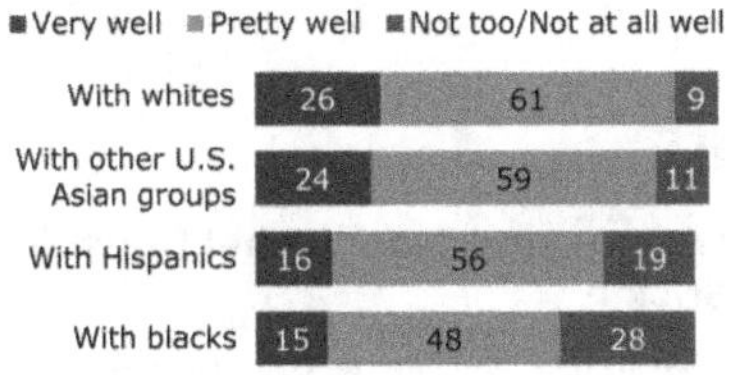

2012 Asian-American Survey. Q49a-d. Responses of "Don't know/Refused" not shown.

PEW RESEARCH CENTER

Intermarriage Rates for Asians

% of Asian newlyweds (2008-2010) married to ...

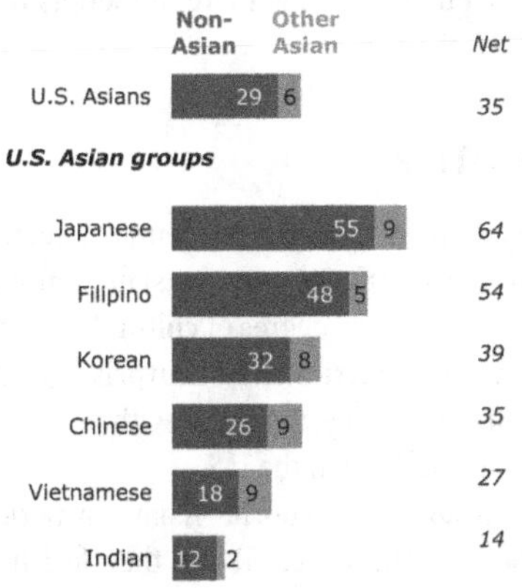

Notes: "Newlyweds" refers to people ages 15 and older who got married in the year prior to the survey, and their marital status was "married, spouse present." U.S. Asians and each U.S. Asian group include non-Hispanic single-race Asians who are from only one group; "Non Asian" includes Hispanics and single- or multiple-race non-Hispanics except single-race Asians; "Other Asian" includes non-Hispanics from other single-Asian or multiple-Asian groups. "Net" was computed prior to rounding.

Source: Pew Research Center analysis of 2008-2010 American Community Survey, Integrated Public Use Microdata Sample (IPUMS) files

PEW RESEARCH CENTER

Residential Segregation, 2010

% from each group living in census tracts where the majority of residents are from their racial/ethnic group

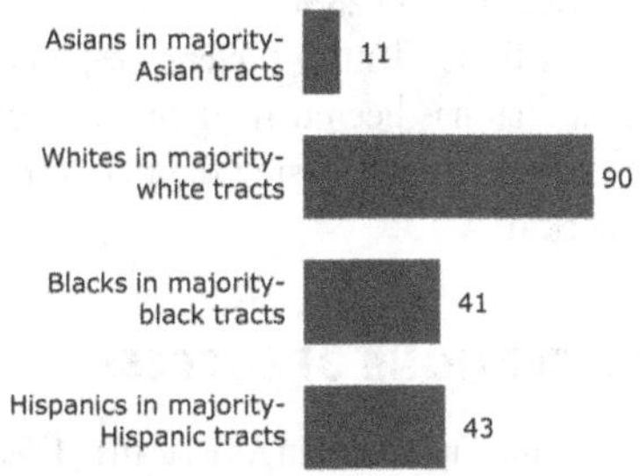

Note: Based on total population, including adults and children. Asians, whites and blacks are single-race, non-Hispanic. Hispanics are of any race. See footnote on this page for definition of census tract.

Source: Pew Research Center tabulations of 2010 Decennial Census SF1 data

PEW RESEARCH CENTER

between Koreans and blacks, often arising from friction between Korean shopkeepers and black customers in predominantly black neighborhoods.

About four-in-ten Asian Americans say their circle of friends is dominated by Asians from the same country of origin, while 58% say it is not. Among U.S.-born Asians, however, just 17% say that all or most of their friends are from their same country of origin group.

Asian-American newlyweds are more likely than any other major racial or ethnic group to be intermarried. From 2008 to 2010, 29% of all Asian newlyweds married someone of a different race, compared with 26% of Hispanics, 17% of blacks and 9% of whites. There are notable gender differences. Asian women are twice as likely as Asian men to marry out. Among blacks, the gender pattern runs the other way—men are more than twice as likely as women to marry out. Among whites and Hispanics, there are no differences by gender.

Among Asian-American newlyweds, Japanese have the highest rate of intermarriage and Indians have the lowest. More than half of recent Japanese newlyweds married a non-Asian; among recent Indian newlyweds, just one-in-eight did.

Asian Americans were once highly concentrated into residential enclaves, exemplified by the establishment of "Chinatowns" and other Asian communities in cities across the country. Today, however, Asian Americans are much more likely than any other racial group to live in a racially mixed neighborhood. Just 11% currently live in a census tract in which Asian Americans are a majority.[10] The comparable figures are 41% for blacks, 43% for Hispanics and 90% for whites. (This comparison should be treated with caution: Each of the other groups is more numerous than Asians, thereby creating larger potential pools for racial enclaves.)

IDENTITY

Despite high levels of residential integration and out-marriage, many Asian Americans continue to feel a degree of cultural separation from other Americans. Not surprisingly, these feelings are highly correlated with nativity and duration of time in the U.S.

Among U.S.-born Asian Americans, about two-thirds (65%) say they feel like "a typical American." Among immigrants, just 30% say the same, and this figure falls to 22% among immigrants who have arrived since 2000.

"Asian-American" Label Doesn't Stick

% saying they most often describe themselves as ...

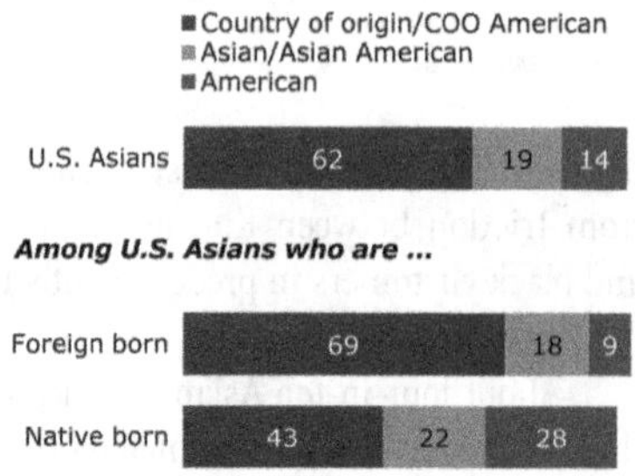

2012 Asian-American Survey. Q42. Only respondents who identified a country of origin (COO) were asked this question; percentages shown here are based on total sample. Responses of "Depends" and "Don't know/Refused" not shown.

PEW RESEARCH CENTER

The Asian-American label itself doesn't hold much sway with Asian Americans. Only about one-in-five (19%) say they most often describe themselves as Asian-American or Asian. A majority (62%) say they most often describe themselves by their country of origin (e.g., Chinese or Chinese American; Vietnamese or Vietnamese American, and so on), while just 14% say they most often simply call themselves American. Among U.S.-born Asians, the share who most often call themselves American rises to 28%.

In these identity preferences, Asian Americans are similar to Hispanics, the other group that has been driving the modern immigration wave. Hispanics are more likely to identify themselves using their country of origin than to identify as a Hispanic or as an American.[11]

PERCEPTIONS OF SUCCESS

About four-in-ten Asian Americans (43%) say Asian Americans are more successful than other racial and ethnic minorities in the U.S. A similar share of Asian Americans (45%) say they are about as successful, and just 5% say they are less successful.

Asian Americans and Hispanics: How Well Are We Doing Compared with Other Minorities?

% of group saying, compared with other racial and ethnic minority groups in the U.S., Asian Americans/Hispanic Americans have been ... successful

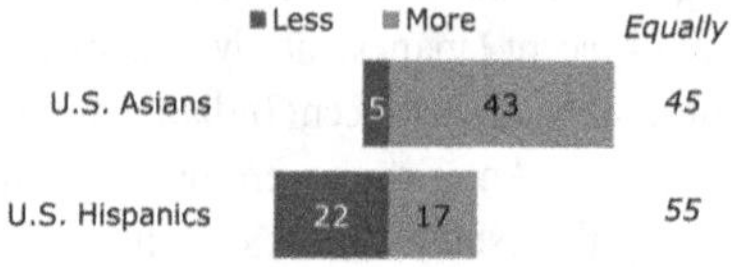

2012 Asian-American Survey. Q47. Responses of "Depends" and "Don't know/Refused" not shown. U.S. Hispanic results from November 2011 survey by the Pew Hispanic Center.

PEW RESEARCH CENTER

Native-born and foreign-born Asian Americans have similar views about their groups' success relative to other minorities. Recent immigrants, however, tend to be somewhat less upbeat in these assessments than are immigrants who came before 2000: 36%

of the former versus 48% of the latter say their group has been more successful than other minority groups in the U.S.

Members of the nation's other large immigrant group—Hispanics—are less than half as likely as Asian Americans to say their group is more successful than other racial and ethnic minorities, and they are four times as likely to say they are less successful.[12]

On a personal level, Asian Americans are more satisfied than the general public with their financial situations and their standard of living. When measured against how well their parents were doing at the same stage of life, about half (49%) say they are doing much better, and a quarter say they are doing somewhat better. By contrast, only about a third of all Americans say they are doing much better than their parents at a similar stage of life.

There are only minor differences between Asian Americans and the general public in their expectations about the upward mobility of their children. Some 31% of Asian Americans believe that when their children are the age they are now, their children will have a much better standard of living, 22% say somewhat better, 19% say about the same, and 19% say somewhat or much worse.

On this measure, there are sizable differences among U.S. Asian subgroups. Nearly half of Vietnamese Americans (48%) say they expect their children eventually to have a much better standard of living than they themselves have now. About a third of Koreans and Indians feel this way, as do one-in-four Chinese and Filipinos, and just one-in-five Japanese. Overall, the foreign born are more optimistic than the native born about their children's future standard of living relative to their own at the present.

POLITICAL AND SOCIAL ATTITUDES

Compared with the general public, Asian Americans are more likely to support an activist government and less likely to identify as Republicans. Half are Democrats or lean Democratic, while only 28% identify with or lean toward the GOP. Among all American adults, 49% fall in the Democratic camp and 39% identify with or lean toward the Republican Party. Indian Americans are the most heavily Democratic Asian subgroup (65%), while Filipino Americans and Vietnamese Americans are the most evenly split between the two parties.

President Obama gets higher ratings from Asian Americans than from the general public—54% approve of the way he is handling his job as president, compared with 44% of the general public. In 2008, Asian-American voters supported Obama over Republican John McCain by 62% to 35%, according to Election Day exit polls.[13]

On balance, Asian Americans prefer a big government that provides more services (55%) over a smaller government than provides fewer services (36%). In contrast, the general public Filipino prefers a smaller government over a bigger government, by 52% to 39%.

Asian Americans Lean Democratic

% saying their party identification is ...

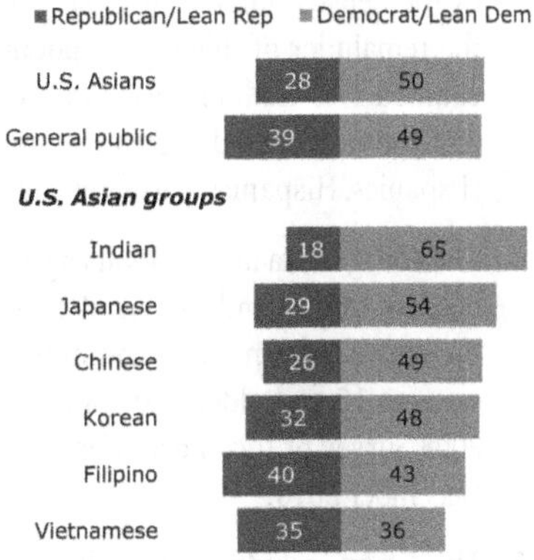

2012 Asian-American Survey. PARTY, PARTYLN. Those who refused to lean are not shown. General public results from February 2012 survey by the Pew Research Center for the People & the Press

PEW RESEARCH CENTER

Sampler of Key Demographic and Survey Findings

% of adults (unless otherwise noted)

	Median household income	College degree or higher*	Foreign born	Recent inter-marriage rate	Majority or plurality religion	Satisfied with life	Satisfied with direction of country	Personal finances (Excellent/ Good)	Belief in hard work**
U.S. Asians	$66,000	49	74	29	Christian	82	43	51	69
General public	$49,800	28	16	15	Christian	75	21	35	58
U.S. Asian groups									
Chinese	$65,050	51	76	26	Unaffiliated	84	41	55	61
Filipino	$75,000	47	69	48	Catholic	82	30	50	72
Indian	$88,000	70	87	12	Hindu	84	47	67	75
Vietnamese	$53,400	26	84	18	Buddhist	82	56	29	83
Korean	$50,000	53	78	32	Protestant	83	48	45	64
Japanese	$65,390	46	32	55	*No plurality*	81	36	57	59

* ages 25 and older
** share that agrees that "most people who want to get ahead can make it if they're willing to work hard"

Source: The four items to the left are from Pew Research Center analysis of 2010 American Community Survey, Integrated Public Use Microdata Sample (IPUMS) files. The five items to the right are from the Pew Research Center 2012 Asian-American Survey.

PEW RESEARCH CENTER

While they differ on the role of government, Asian Americans are close to the public in their opinions about two key social issues. By a ratio of 53% to 35%, Asian Americans say homosexuality should be accepted by society rather than discouraged. And on the issue of abortion, 54% of Asian Americans say it should be legal in all or most cases, while 37% say it should be illegal.

NOTES

1. The share for recent Asian-American grooms is lower (17%). Overall, 29% of recent Asian newlyweds between 2008 and 2010 married a non-Asian.
2. Organisation for Economic Co-operation and Development (OECD). Education at a Glance 2011: OECD Indicators. Based on 2009 data.
3. This is the first official estimate of the size of the Asian-American population produced by the Census Bureau since the 2010 Census; it was released in May 2012. Throughout the remainder of this report, population counts are based on the 2010 Census, which counted 17.3 million Asian Americans. Totals for Asian Americans include Hispanics and those of mixed race; totals for whites and blacks include only single-race non-Hispanics. Hispanics are of any race.
4. The college data are for adults ages 25 and older. Household income is based on householders ages 18 and older and comes from Pew Research Center analysis of the Census Bureau's 2010 American Community Survey. Household wealth is based on householders ages 15 and older and comes from Pew Research Center analysis of Wave 7 of the 2008 Survey of Income and Program Participation panel, conducted from September–December 2010.
5. This figure includes almost all Asians with origins in the six major country groups, but is not a complete count. The available 2010 ACS data from which it is drawn include specific counts only for Asians with origins in one major group or with origins in the most common combinations of race or country group.

6. "Other U.S. Asians" are a diverse population that includes numerous subgroups of less than a million people. Seven of these subgroups number more than 100,000 people—Bangladeshis, Burmese, Cambodians, Hmong, Laotians, Pakistanis and Thais.
7. Revised July 12, 2012, to change "poverty rate" to "% in poverty" or "share in poverty," and to add a definition to Notes on Terminology.
8. See Pew Research Center Social & Demographic Trends project. 2010. "The Decline of Marriage and Rise of New Families." Washington, D.C.: November.
9. For more details on how Asian Americans' perceptions of discrimination compare with those of other minority groups, see Chapter 3.
10. A census tract is a small, relatively permanent subdivision of a county that often follows generally accepted neighborhood boundaries and has an average of 4,200 residents. The Census Bureau delineated about 73,000 tracts for the 2010 Census.
11. Taylor, Paul, et al. 2012. "When Labels Don't Fit: Hispanics and Their Views of Identity." Washington, D.C.: Pew Hispanic Center, April. The question wording differed slightly from the Asian-American survey; see Chapter 2 for a fuller explanation.
12. Ibid.
13. 2008 national exit polls conducted by Edison Media Research for the National Election Pool.

CRITICAL THINKING QUESTIONS

1. Discuss the history of Asian immigration—this section discusses several dates, but which two do you think are the most important and why? In what ways have Asians assimilated in America? How have these examples of assimilation become "milestones of economic success" for Asian Americans?
2. The study notes that only five percent of Asian Americans "say they are less successful" than other racial or ethnic minorities. What three statistics could you cite from the study that would help create that perception? How would those statistics indicate that Asian Americans are a successful minority group?
3. What are the basic demographic differences between the six Asian American groups that the Pew Research Center survey uncovered? What group has the highest level of income? What group has the highest level of poverty? Supply two reasons that you believe this variation might exist.
4. **Connection.** The survey summarizes its findings on discrimination: "for the most part, today's Asian Americans do not feel the sting of racial discrimination or the burden of culturally imposed "otherness" that was so much a part of the experience of their predecessors who came in the 19th and early 20th centuries." In "Them That's Got Shall Get," Nathalie Baptiste argues that African Americans have continued to suffer racial discrimination through the current economic recovery. Using three points of data from the Pew Report, discuss why Asian Americans might feel better about their place and role in American society than other minorities?

A WORLD NOT NEATLY DIVIDED

by Amartya Sen

Amartya Sen, an Indian economist and philosopher, is the chancellor of Nalanda University located in northeast India. He also teaches at a number of elite institutions, including Cambridge, Harvard, and Trinity College. Sen was awarded the Nobel Memorial Prize in Economic Sciences in 1998 for his work in welfare economics.

Amartya Sen wrote this article shortly after the September 11, 2011 attacks. The attackers came from several countries, and many tried to simplify the complex causes and nature of the attacks by talking about "the Muslim world." In this essay from *The New York Times,* Sen explains that trying to see a certain part of the world, or certain types of people as being homogenous, which means all the same, can hurt much more than it helps. Why, then, do we continue to do it?

• • • • • • • • • • • • • • •

CAMBRIDGE, England—When people talk about clashing civilizations, as so many politicians and academics do now, they can sometimes miss the central issue. The inadequacy of this thesis begins well before we get to the question of whether civilizations must clash. The basic weakness of the theory lies in its program of categorizing people of the world according to a unique, allegedly commanding system of classification. This is problematic because civilizational categories are crude and inconsistent and also because there are other ways of seeing people (linked to politics, language, literature, class, occupation or other affiliations).

The befuddling influence of a singular classification also traps those who dispute the thesis of a clash: To talk about "the Islamic world" or "the Western world" is already to adopt an impoverished vision of humanity as unalterably divided. In fact, civilizations are hard to partition in this way, given the diversities within each society as well as the linkages among different countries and cultures. For example, describing India as a "Hindu civilization" misses the fact that India has more Muslims than any other country except Indonesia and possibly Pakistan. It is futile to try to understand Indian art, literature, music, food or politics without seeing the extensive interactions across barriers of religious communities. These include Hindus and Muslims, Buddhists, Jains, Sikhs, Parsees, Christians (who have been in India since at least the fourth century, well before England's conversion to Christianity), Jews (present since the fall of Jerusalem), and even atheists and agnostics. Sanskrit has a larger atheistic literature than exists in any other classical language. Speaking of India as a Hindu civilization may be comforting to the Hindu fundamentalist, but it is an odd reading of India.

A similar coarseness can be seen in the other categories invoked, like "the Islamic world." Consider Akbar and Aurangzeb, two Muslim emperors of the Mogul dynasty in India. Aurangzeb tried hard to convert Hindus into Muslims and instituted various policies in that direction, of which taxing the non-Muslims was only one example. In contrast, Akbar reveled in his multiethnic court and pluralist laws, and issued official proclamations insisting that no one "should be interfered with on account of religion" and that "anyone is to be allowed to go over to a religion that pleases him."

If a homogeneous view of Islam were to be taken, then only one of these emperors could count as a true Muslim. The Islamic fundamentalist would have no time for Akbar; Prime

Minister Tony Blair, given his insistence that tolerance is a defining characteristic of Islam, would have to consider excommunicating Aurangzeb. I expect both Akbar and Aurangzeb would protest, and so would I. A similar crudity is present in the characterization of what is called "Western civilization." Tolerance and individual freedom have certainly been present in European history. But there is no dearth of diversity here, either. When Akbar was making his pronouncements on religious tolerance in Agra, in the 1590s, the Inquisitions were still going on; in 1600, Giordano Bruno was burned at the stake, for heresy, in Campo dei Fiori in Rome.

Dividing the world into discrete civilizations is not just crude. It propels us into the absurd belief that this partitioning is natural and necessary and must overwhelm all other ways of identifying people. That imperious view goes not only against the sentiment that "we human beings are all much the same," but also against the more plausible understanding that we are diversely different. For example, Bangladesh's split from Pakistan was not connected with religion, but with language and politics.

Each of us has many features in our self-conception. Our religion, important as it may be, cannot be an all-engulfing identity. Even a shared poverty can be a source of solidarity across the borders. The kind of division highlighted by, say, the so-called "antiglobalization" protesters—whose movement is, incidentally, one of the most globalized in the world—tries to unite the underdogs of the world economy and goes firmly against religious, national or "civilizational" lines of division.

The main hope of harmony lies not in any imagined uniformity, but in the plurality of our identities, which cut across each other and work against sharp divisions into impenetrable civilizational camps. Political leaders who think and act in terms of sectioning off humanity into various "worlds" stand to make the world more flammable—even when their intentions are very different. They also end up, in the case of civilizations defined by religion, lending authority to religious leaders seen as spokesmen for their "worlds." In the process, other voices are muffled and other concerns silenced. The robbing of our plural identities not only reduces us; it impoverishes the world.

CRITICAL THINKING QUESTIONS

1. Amartya Sen argues that we each have "the plurality of our identities." Arising from the word "plural" or more than one, what do you make of his argument that we have "a plurality of identities?" What are some different identities that you have? For you, one identity might be that of a student. If people saw you only as a student, what would they miss? How do you think people "viewing you" as a homogeneous being affects you?

2. Classifications, such as "The Islamic World" or "The Western World," adopt an "impoverished version of humanity as unalterably divided." What does this statement mean? Why does Sen argue that classifications act this way? Do you think this way of classifying groups is so common? If so, why?

3. Sen describes what it means to provide a homogeneous view of Islam. What example does he provide? Identify a group of your choice according to race, ethnicity, or political affiliation, and provide a homogeneous view of that group. How does your representation of that group limit or empower that group?

4. **Connection.** Amartya Sen is making an argument for thinking about people in many ways and the power of embracing that diversity. In "The Case for Reparations," Ta-Nehisi Coates describes the many ways in which African Americans have been excluded from what it means to be an American. Sen argues that, when we ignore our diversity—our plural identity as a country—it "reduces us; it impoverishes" all of us. What are at least three ways that the exclusion of African Americans, and other ethnic minorities, from the idea of "America" hurts all Americans? Defend each reason.

WEALTH GAPS RISE TO RECORD HIGHS

by Pew Research

The Pew Research Center is a nonpartisan American organization that provides information on social issues, public opinion, and trends that shape the Unites States and the world.

President Obama has stated that his economic goals are to grow the economy while ensuring that we "remain a free and prosperous land of opportunity." The data presented in this pew report, however, indicate that this "land of opportunity" isn't as prosperous for everyone. Pew presents data point after data point that demonstrates, on any important economic measure, ethnic and racial minorities are lagging behind white America in attainment. How can we consider our land "free" if the economic costs for certain groups are higher than for others?

• • • • • • • • • • • • • • • •

WEALTH GAPS RISE TO RECORD HIGHS BETWEEN WHITES, BLACKS AND HISPANICS

by Rakesh Kochhar, Richard Fry, and Paul Taylor

EXECUTIVE SUMMARY

The median wealth of white households is 20 times that of black households and 18 times that of Hispanic households, according to a Pew Research Center analysis of newly available government data from 2009.

These lopsided wealth ratios are the largest since the government began publishing such data a quarter century ago and roughly twice the size of the ratios that had prevailed between these three groups for the two decades prior to the Great Recession that ended in 2009.

The Pew Research analysis finds that, in percentage terms, the bursting of the housing market bubble in 2006 and the recession that followed from late 2007 to mid-2009 took a far greater toll on the wealth of minorities than whites. From 2005 to 2009, inflation-adjusted median wealth fell by 66% among Hispanic households and 53% among black households, compared with just 16% among white households.

As a result of these declines, the typical black household had just $5,677 in wealth (assets minus debts) in 2009; the typical Hispanic household had $6,325 in wealth; and the typical white household had $113,149.

Moreover, about a third of black (35%) and Hispanic (31%) households had zero or negative net worth in 2009, compared with 15% of white

Median Net Worth of Households, 2005 and 2009

in 2009 dollars

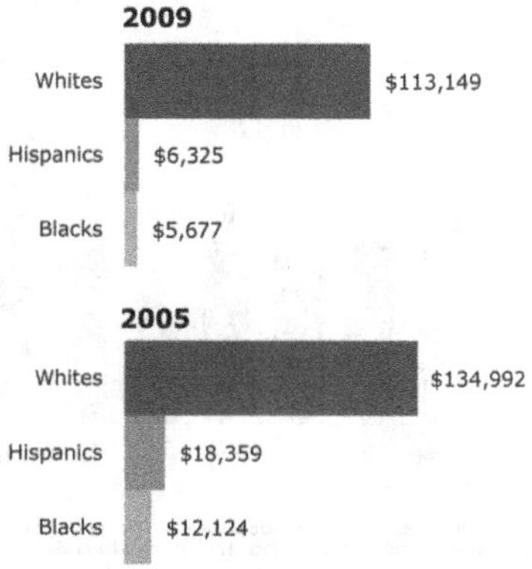

Source: Pew Research Center tabulations of Survey of Income and Program Participation data

PEW RESEARCH CENTER

Percentage Change in Median Net Worth of Households, 2005 to 2009

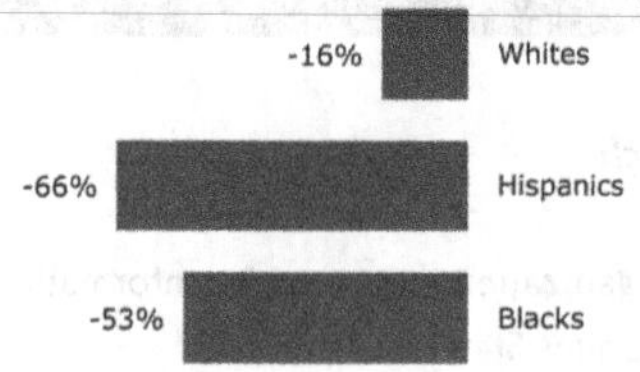

Source: Pew Research Center tabulations of Survey of Income and Program Participation data

PEW RESEARCH CENTER

households. In 2005, the comparable shares had been 29% for blacks, 23% for Hispanics and 11% for whites.

Hispanics and blacks are the nation's two largest minority groups, making up 16% and 12% of the U.S. population respectively.

These findings are based on the Pew Research Center's analysis of data from the Survey of Income and Program Participation (SIPP), an economic questionnaire distributed periodically to tens of thousands of households by the U.S. Census Bureau. It is considered the most comprehensive source of data about household wealth in the United States by race and ethnicity. The two most recent administrations of SIPP that focused on household wealth were in 2005 and 2009. Data from the 2009 survey were only recently made available to researchers.[1]

Plummeting house values were the principal cause of the recent erosion in household wealth among all groups, with Hispanics hit hardest by the meltdown in the housing market.

From 2005 to 2009, the median level of home equity held by Hispanic homeowners declined by half—from $99,983 to $49,145—while the homeownership rate among Hispanics was also falling, from 51% to 47%. A geographic analysis suggests the reason: A disproportionate share of Hispanics live in California, Florida, Nevada and Arizona, which were in the vanguard of the housing real estate market bubble of the 1990s and early 2000s but that have since been among the states experiencing the steepest declines in housing values.

Wealth Ratios: A 25-Year History

The chart below shows the Pew Research Center's estimates of the wealth ratios for 2009 and those published by the Census Bureau for 1984 to 2004. As the chart demonstrates, the white-to-black and white-to-Hispanic wealth ratios were much higher in 2009 than they had been at any time since 1984, the first year for which the Census Bureau published wealth estimates by race and ethnicity based on SIPP data.

Media Wealth Ratios, 1984 to 2009

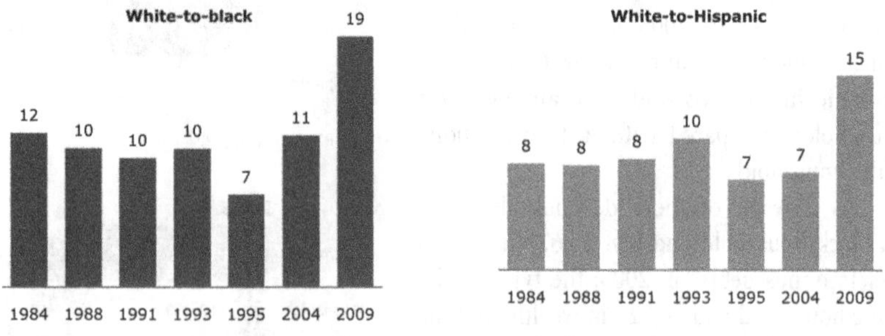

Notes: Blacks and whites include Hispanics. The Survey of Income and Program Participation was redesigned for the 1996 panel. The redesign may have affected the comparability of the data from 1998 and later years with the data from earlier panels.

Sources: For 2009: Pew Research Center tabulations of Survey of Income and Program Participation data from the 2008 panel; for 1984 to 2004: various U.S. Census Bureau P-70 *Current Population Reports*.

PEW RESEARCH CENTER

An Alternative Approach to Measuring the Wealth Gap Trend

This report measures the changing wealth gaps between whites, Hispanics and blacks using ratios. An alternative approach would be to measure the changes in absolute levels rather than ratios. By that yardstick, the median wealth gaps between these groups *decreased* from 2005 to 2009. For example, in 2005, the median wealth of white households was $116,632 more than the median wealth of Hispanic households. By 2009, the difference had shrunk to $106,824. The same is true for the white-black difference in median wealth. This means that white households experienced a greater absolute drop in their wealth. However, because the wealth base for white households is so much far larger than it is for Hispanics and blacks, the proportional decrease in wealth was much less for whites. That is reflected in the sharp rise of the white-to-Hispanic and white-to-black wealth ratios reported in this study.

Note that the ratios shown in the chart for 2009 differ slightly from the 2009 estimates used in the rest of this report: 19-to-1 for the white-to-black ratio, compared with 20-to-1 elsewhere in the report, and 15-to-1 for the white-to-Hispanic ratio, compared with 18-to-1 elsewhere in the report. That is because, in order to make the estimates in the chart consistent over time, the 2009 figures were adjusted to allow the racial groups "white" and "black" to include Hispanic members of these groups, consistent with methods used by the Census Bureau from 1984 to 2004. In the rest of this report, the white, black (and Asian) racial groups include only the non-Hispanic components of these populations. (Changes in racial identification methods and a redesign of SIPP in 1996 may also have had an impact on the comparability of the wealth ratios over time).

White and black homeowners also saw the median value of their home equity decline during this period, but not by as much as Hispanics. Among white homeowners, the decline was from $115,364 in 2005 to $95,000 in 2009. Among black homeowners, it was from $76,910 in 2005 to $59,000 in 2009. There was little or no change during this period in the homeownership rate for whites and blacks; it fell from 47% to 46% among blacks and was unchanged at 74% among whites.[2]

Household wealth is the accumulated sum of assets (houses, cars, savings and checking accounts, stocks and mutual funds, retirement accounts, etc.) minus the sum of debt (mortgages, auto loans, credit card debt, etc.). It is different from household income, which measures the annual inflow of wages, interest, profits and other sources of earning. Wealth gaps between whites, blacks and Hispanics have always been much greater than income gaps.

The 2005 to 2009 time frame allows for a before-and-after look at the impact of the Great Recession. However, those dates do not align perfectly with the downturn, which ran from December 2007 to June 2009, according to the National Bureau of Economic Research.

In 2005, both the stock and housing markets were still rising. Thus, had the base year for these measurements of wealth been closer to the top of these markets in 2006 or 2007, the recorded declines are likely to have been even steeper.

Moreover, since the official end of the recession in mid-2009, the housing market in the U.S. has remained in a slump while the stock market has recaptured much of the value it lost from 2007 to 2009. Given that a much higher share of whites than blacks or Hispanics own stocks—as well as mutual funds and 401(k) or individual retirement accounts (IRAs)—the stock market rebound since 2009 is likely to have benefited white households more than minority households.

Other Key Findings from the Report

Hispanics: The net worth of Hispanic households decreased from $18,359 in 2005 to $6,325 in 2009. The percentage drop—66%—was the largest among all groups. Hispanics derived nearly two-thirds of their net worth in 2005 from home equity and are more likely to reside in areas where the housing meltdown was concentrated. Thus, the housing downturn had a deep impact on them. Their net worth also diminished because of a 42% rise in median levels of debt they carried in the form of unsecured liabilities (credit card debt, education loans, etc.).

Blacks: The net worth of black households fell from $12,124 in 2005 to $5,677 in 2009, a decline of 53%. Like Hispanics, black households drew a large share (59%) of their net worth from home equity in 2005. Thus, the housing downturn had a strong impact on their net worth. Blacks also took on more unsecured debt during the economic downturn, with the median level rising by 27%.

Whites: The drop in the wealth of white households was modest in comparison, falling 16% from $134,992 in 2005 to $113,149 in 2009. White households were also affected by the housing crisis. But home equity accounts for relatively less of their total net worth (44% in 2005), and that served to lessen the impact of the housing bust. Median levels of unsecured debt among whites rose by 32%.

Asians: In 2005 median Asian household wealth had been greater than the median for white households, but by 2009 Asians lost their place at the top of the wealth hierarchy. Their net worth fell from $168,103 in 2005 to $78,066 in 2009, a drop of 54%. Like Hispanics, they are geographically concentrated in places such as California that were hit hard by the housing market meltdown. The arrival of new Asian immigrants since 2004 also contributed significantly to the estimated decline in the overall wealth of this racial group. Absent the immigrants who arrived during this period, the median wealth of Asian households is estimated to have dropped 31% from 2005 to 2009. Asians account for about 5% of the U.S. population.

No Assets: About a quarter of all Hispanic (24%) and black (24%) households in 2009 had no assets other than a vehicle, compared with just 6% of white households. These percentages are little changed from 2005.

Medians and Means: Just as the gap in median household wealth among racial and ethnic groups rose from 2005 to 2009, so too did the gap in mean household wealth. However, the mean differences are not as dramatic as the median differences. (A median is the midpoint that separates the upper half from the lower half of a given group; a mean is an average, and, in this case, the average is driven upward by households with high net worth). In 2005, mean white household wealth was 2.3 times that of Hispanics and 3 times that of blacks. By 2009, it was 3.7 times that of both Hispanics and blacks.

Wealth Disparities within Racial and Ethnic Groups: During the period under study, wealth disparities increased not only between racial and ethnic groups, they also rose *within* each group. Even though the wealthiest 10% of households within each group suffered a loss in wealth from 2005 to 2009, their share of their group's overall wealth rose during this period. The increase was the greatest among Hispanics, with the top 10% boosting their share of all Hispanic household wealth from 56% in 2005 to 72% in 2009. Among whites, the share of wealth owned by the top 10% rose from 46% in 2005 to 51% in 2009. These trends indicate that those in the top 10% of the wealth ladder were relatively less impacted by the economic downturn than those in the remaining 90%.

Terminology

References to whites, blacks and Asians are to the non-Hispanic components of those populations. The only exception to this rule is when historical comparisons are drawn with data published by the Census Bureau.

- "Asian" refers to (non-Hispanic) persons reporting their racial origin as Asian alone and does not include native Hawaiians or other Pacific Islanders. "Black" refers to black alone, and "white" refers to white alone.
- The racial and ethnic identity of a household is determined on the basis of the racial and ethnic identity of the head of the household.
- Household "net worth" is the sum of the market value of assets owned by every member of the household minus their liabilities (debt).

Unless otherwise stated, all estimates in this report are expressed in 2009 dollars.

SIPP Net Worth

SIPP data include the following assets and liabilities:

Assets

- Financial institution accounts
  - Savings accounts
  - Money market deposit accounts
  - Certificates of deposit (CD)
  - Interest-earning checking accounts
  - Regular checking accounts
- Other interest-earnings assets
  - U.S. government securities
  - Municipal or corporate bonds
  - U.S. savings bonds
- Stocks and mutual fund shares
- Business or profession
- Motor vehicles
- Owned home
- Rental property
- Vacation homes and other real estate
- IRA and Keogh accounts
- 401(k) and Thrift Saving Plans
- Mortgages held for sale of real estate
- Amount due from sale of business or property
- Other financial assets

Liabilities

- Secured liabilities
  - Margin and broker accounts
  - Debt on business or profession
  - Vehicle loans
  - Mortgages on own home
  - Mortgages on rental property
  - Mortgages on other homes or real estate
- Unsecured liabilities
  - Credit card and store bills
  - Student loans
  - Doctor, dentist, hospital, and nursing home bills
  - Loans from individuals
  - Loans from financial institutions
  - Other unsecured liabilities

Major assets not captured by SIPP are equities in defined-benefit pension plans, the cash value of life insurance policies, the value of household furnishings and jewelry, and future claims on Social Security. Thus, wealth estimates from SIPP are typically less than the estimates from the Survey of Consumer Finances.

About the Report

This report presents net worth and asset ownership figures from wave 6 of the 2004 panel of the Survey of Income Program and Participation (SIPP) and wave 4 of the 2008 SIPP panel. These waves were conducted at the end of 2005 and 2009, respectively. SIPP is a longitudinal survey of households conducted by the U.S. Census Bureau. By design, SIPP oversamples low-income households and thus surveys large numbers of minority households. SIPP has periodically collected detailed wealth data since 1984 and is considered an authoritative source on the wealth of American households. As with any survey, estimates from SIPP are subject to sampling and nonsampling errors.

This report was edited and the overview written by Paul Taylor, executive vice president of the Pew Research Center and director of its Social and Demographic Trends project. Senior researcher Rakesh Kochhar and senior economist Richard Fry researched and wrote the report. Research assistant Seth Motel helped with the preparation of charts. The report was number-checked by Motel and Pew Research Center staff member Gabriel Velasco. The report was copy-edited by Marcia Kramer. The Center is grateful for the expeditious assistance of Nasrin Dalirazar of the Housing and Household Economic Statistics Division of the U.S. Census Bureau on the definition of SIPP net worth components, weighting issues, and the replication of wealth tabulations published by the Census Bureau.

NOTES

1. Data on the wealth of households are also collected in the Survey of Consumer Finances (SCF) and the Panel Survey of Income Dynamics (PSID), neither with as large a sample size as SIPP. The SCF was last conducted in 2010 and the PSID last collected wealth data in 2009. However, the final sets of data from those surveys were not available as of the writing of this report.

2. The homeownership rates cited in this report are derived from SIPP data. They differ from homeownership rates published by the Census Bureau from other data sources.

CRITICAL THINKING QUESTIONS

1. The report makes a distinction between "household wealth" and "household income." Define each of these terms. According to Pew, which is the larger issue: the wealth gap or the income gap? Why might that be the case?
2. The report notes that, "during the period under study (2005–2009), wealth disparities increased not only between racial and ethnic groups, they arose within each group." What does "wealth disparities" mean? What does it mean that it increased within ethnic groups—for example, for those identifying themselves as Hispanic? What do you think might be a cause of this, and why would that cause an increase in wealth disparity?
3. Compare the median wealth of whites, African Americans, and Hispanics in 2005 and 2009. Why is there such a discrepancy in wealth ratios between these three racial groups? The report claims that wealth ratios are "lopsided." What does this mean? What would wealth ratios that were not lopsided look like?
4. **Connection.** Both this report and Nathalie Baptiste's article describe an increase in the differences in wealth between African Americans and white Americans. Drawing from both articles, explain three reasons why this gap has increased since 2005.

1776 AND ALL THAT

by Edward Hoagland

Edward Hoagland, an American essayist and novelist, has been widely praised by highly accomplished authors like John Updike and Joyce Carol Oates. Hoagland graduated from Harvard in 1954. He has taught at The New School, Rutgers, Sarah Lawrence, the City University of New York, the University of Iowa, Columbia, and Brown.

In "1776 and All That," published in *The Nation* in 2002, Edward Hoagland argues that we look to the Revolution of 1776 but forget it's lessons. In this wide ranging essay, he names a number of American sins—mostly foreign, but some domestic—that he thinks have led us away from our founding promise; indeed, contradictions were found inside that promise. How can a country work on improving itself if it is unable to face its past?

• • • • • • • • • • • • • • •

The country is riven and ailing, with a guns-plus-butter nuttiness in some of its governing echelons and the sort of lapsed logic implicit in the collapse of trust in money-center capitalism, which has been an undergirding theory of a good deal of the work that many people do. The tallest buildings, real profit centers, fall, as "wogs" and "ragheads" defy us, perhaps comparably to how the "gooks" in Vietnam did (from whose example Osama bin Laden may have learned that we could be defeated). But that was on foreign soil, and we believed that we had pulled our punches and beaten ourselves, and so remained triumphalist for the remainder of the twentieth century, as we had been practically since Reconstruction.

Now we're not so sure. For the first time since the War of 1812 we have been damaged in continental America by foreigners, having made other people hate us, though we had never needed to pay attention to such matters before. Proxies could fight the malcontents for us in places like Central America, and the Japanese and Germans, would-be conquerors, had not felt much real animus, becoming close, amicable allies after the war. Our first World War II hero, Colin Kelly, three days after Pearl Harbor, flew his B-17 bomber (as media myth had it) in kamikaze fashion to hit a Japanese cruiser, before the Japanese made a practice of it. To give your life for your country, like Nathan Hale, is an ideal that's since evaporated.

Obese individually and as a nation, and trying to stall the aging process, we talk instead of cars and taxes, sports and movies, cancer and entitlements, but with a half-unmentioned inkling too of what more ominously may be in store—a premonition that our righteous confidence might have served us just a bit too well. We never agonized a lot about killing off the Indians, or our slaving history either, once that was over, or being the only nuclear power ever to incinerate multitudes of people. We've hardly seemed to notice when free enterprise segues into simple greed, because our religious beginnings countenanced rapacity, as long as you tithed. Settling the seaboard in official belts of piety, whether Puritan, Anglican, Quaker or Dutch Reformed (only the frontier tended to be atheistic), we seized land and water with abandon, joined by Catholics, Lutherans, Methodists and what have you, westward ho. Each group encouraged its rich men to creep like a camel through the eye of the needle, and political freedoms were gradually canted away from the pure ballot box toward influence-buying.

We swallowed all of that because the New World dream envisioned everybody working hard and getting fairly rich, except when undertows of doubt pervaded our prosperity, as in the 1930s and 1960s; or now when, feeling gridlocked, we wonder if we haven't gone too far and used the whole place up. We seem to need some kind of condom invented just for greed—a latex sac where spasms of that particular vice can be ejaculated, captured and contained. Like lust, it's not going to go away. Nor will Monopoly games do the trick, any more than pornographic videos erase impulses that might result in harm. The old phrase patrons of prostitutes used to use—"getting your ashes hauled"—said it pretty well, and if we could persuade people to think of greed, as well, that way and expel its destructiveness perhaps into a computer screen, trapping the piggishness in cyberspace might save a bit of Earth. The greediest guys would not be satisfied, but greed might be looked on as slightly outré.

Some vertigo or "near death" experience of global warming may be required to trip the necessary degree of alarm. The droughts and water wars, a polar meltdown and pelagic crisis—too much saltwater and insufficient fresh. In the meantime, dried-up high plains agriculture and Sunbelt golf greens in the Republicans' heartlands will help because African famines are never enough. We need a surge of altruism, artesian decency. The oddity of greed nowadays is that it is so often solo—in the service of one ego—not ducal or kingly, as the apparatus of an unjust state. Overweening possession, such as McMansions and so on, will be loony in the century we are entering upon—ecologically, economically, morally, commonsensically. But how will we realize this, short of disastrous procrastination? Hurricanes and centrifugal violence on the home front, not to mention angry Arabs flying into the World Trade Center? That astounded us: both the anger and the technological savvy. These camel-herding primitives whom we had manipulated, fleeced, romanticized and patronized for generations, while pumping out their oil and bottling them up in monarchies and emirates that we cultivated and maintained, while jeering at them with casual racism in the meantime, when we thought of it, for not having democracies like ours. To discover that satellite TV, the Internet and some subversive preaching should suddenly provide them access to divergent opinions disconcerts if it doesn't frighten us, as does their willingness to counterpose rudimentary suicide missions to the helicopter gunships and F-16s we provide the Israelis. "Don't they value life?"

They won't be the last. The Vietcong were as culturally different from the Palestinians as we are and yet succeeded in winning a country for themselves, at a tremendous but bearable cost, which the Palestinians will also undoubtedly do. Self-sacrifice can be a match for weaponry, not because the Americans or Israelis value Asian or Arab life—at key junctures and for essentially racist reasons they have not—but because of the value they place on their own citizenry. As many as fifty Vietnamese lives were lost for every American's, but that was not a high enough ratio for us, even though, unlike some Israelis, we don't ascribe to ourselves a biblical imprimatur. So we let them have their land, and the domino calamities that had been famously predicted did not result.

To equate our own revolution with anybody else's is quite offensive to us. Mostly, in fact, we prefer to forget that we had a revolutionary past and kicked thousands of wealthy Tories into Canada, seizing their property. We were slow to condemn apartheid in South Africa, having scarcely finished abolishing our own at the time, and have been slow in general to support self-governance in the warmer climates or to acknowledge suffering among people whose skins are beiger than ours. And if our income per capita is sixty or eighty times theirs, that doesn't strike us as strange. We are a bootstrap country, after all. They should pay us heed. And the whole United Nations is "a cesspool," according to a recent New York City mayor.

But primitive notions like those of Ed Koch invite a primitive response. And box-cutters in the hands of Taliban fundamentalists are not our main problem. We have gratuitously destroyed so much of nature that the Taliban's smashing up of Buddhist statues, as comparative vandalism, will someday seem quite minuscule. We have also denatured our own nominal religions: that is, taken the bite of authenticity out of Christianity, for instance. Our real problem, I think, is a centrifugal disorientation and disbelief. There is a cost to cynicism (as in our previous activities in Afghanistan), and the systematic demonizing of communitarianism during the cold war made it harder afterward for us to reject as perverse the double-talking profiteering implicit in phenomena like Enron, when we had thought that anything was better than collective regulation and planning.

But ceasing to believe in revolutionary democracy—whether of the secular or Christian (or Emersonian) variety—has proven costly. A decent regard for the welfare of other people, in international as well as local life, is going to be more than just a matter of private virtue. In a shrinking world it may be a survival tool. Fanaticism doesn't carry as far unless catastrophic economic conditions lurk in the background, as we learned in the case of Germany between the two world wars but then, when non-Caucasians were involved, forgot. Our foreign aid budget, once the cold war ended, collapsed into spectacular stinginess, and our sole response to September 11 has been police work. This can probably erase Al Qaeda—which became after its instant victory that one morning quite superfluous anyway—but not the knowledge of our vulnerability to any handful of smart and angry plotters in this technological age. We might see an explosion of those.

Our national self-absorption (in which the focus seems more on trying to stay young than helping the young) may give capitalism a bad name. Simple hedonism and materialism was not the point of crossing the ocean. Our revolution was better than that. It was to paint the world anew.

CRITICAL THINKING QUESTIONS

1. The article's title—"1776 and All That"—refers to the American Revolution. According to Edward Hoagland, we think our revolution was special because we forget some things about our country. What are three of the things he mentions that we forget? How would you explain them to someone who was unfamiliar with those topics?

2. Hoagland thinks something catastrophic, like global warming, might be needed to "trip the necessary degree of alarm." Why does he think an alarm needs to be sounded? What does he think we need? Do you think an alarm needs to be sounded in the United States? Why or why not?

3. The Viet Cong "succeeded in winning a country" for themselves; the author believes the Palestinians will "also undoubtedly do so." Pretend you are writing six sentences to someone who knows nothing about either of those groups. What are six things a person would need to know to understand why that group needed (or needs) to win a country for itself.

4. **Connection.** Edward Hoagland's argument is summarized towards the end of the essay: "our national self-absorption . . . may give capitalism a bad name . . . Our revolution was better than that. It was to paint the world anew." Do you think self-absorption is a problem in America? Provide two reasons to support your stance. Jamartya Sen, in "A World Not Neatly Divided," argues that as a nation, we are too self-absorbed to see the complexities of other cultures. How might this lack of understanding of other cultures abroad affect minority populations and their economic success here at home?

EDUCATION GAP GROWS BETWEEN RICH AND POOR, STUDIES SAY

by Sabrina Tavernise

Sabrina Tavernise is an American journalist who writes for *The New York Times*. She previously reported for the newspaper from Iraq, Lebanon, and Russia. She received an honorable mention in the 2003 Kurt Schork awards for her coverage of Russia.

In this selection from *The New York Times*, Travernise explores the two largest causes of the education gap in the United States: an income gap and a racial gap. For much of the 20th century, the differences in achievement between racial groups were larger than any gap that existed within racial groups. Just recently, however, things have changed. For the first time, when looking at the chances for future success, the economics of the parent are more important than the race of the child. Still, we must wonder—why is there any kind of education gap at all?

• • • • • • • • • • • • • • •

WASHINGTON—Education was historically considered a great equalizer in American society, capable of lifting less advantaged children and improving their chances for success as adults. But a body of recently published scholarship suggests that the achievement gap between rich and poor children is widening, a development that threatens to dilute education's leveling effects.

It is a well-known fact that children from affluent families tend to do better in school. Yet the income divide has received far less attention from policy makers and government officials than gaps in student accomplishment by race.

Now, in analyses of long-term data published in recent months, researchers are finding that while the achievement gap between white and black students has narrowed significantly over the past few decades, the gap between rich and poor students has grown substantially during the same period.

"We have moved from a society in the 1950s and 1960s, in which race was more consequential than family income, to one today in which family income appears more determinative of educational success than race," said Sean F. Reardon, a Stanford University sociologist. Professor Reardon is the author of a study that found that the gap in standardized test scores between affluent and low-income students had grown by about 40 percent since the 1960s, and is now double the testing gap between blacks and whites.

In another study, by researchers from the University of Michigan, the imbalance between rich and poor children in college completion—the single most important predictor of success in the work force—has grown by about 50 percent since the late 1980s.

The changes are tectonic, a result of social and economic processes unfolding over many decades. The data from most of these studies end in 2007 and 2008, before the recession's full impact was felt. Researchers said that based on experiences during past recessions, the recent downturn was likely to have aggravated the trend.

"With income declines more severe in the lower brackets, there's a good chance the recession may have widened the gap," Professor Reardon said. In the study he led, researchers analyzed 12 sets of standardized test scores starting in 1960 and ending in 2007. He compared children from families in the 90th percentile of income—the equivalent of around $160,000 in 2008, when the study was conducted—and children from the 10th percentile, $17,500 in 2008. By the end of that period, the achievement gap by income had grown by 40 percent, he said, while the gap between white and black students, regardless of income, had shrunk substantially.

Both studies were first published last fall in a book of research, *Whither Opportunity?* compiled by the Russell Sage Foundation, a research center for social sciences, and the Spencer Foundation, which focuses on education. Their conclusions, while familiar to a small core of social sciences scholars, are now catching the attention of a broader audience, in part because income inequality has been a central theme this election season.

The connection between income inequality among parents and the social mobility of their children has been a focus of President Obama as well as some of the Republican presidential candidates.

One reason for the growing gap in achievement, researchers say, could be that wealthy parents invest more time and money than ever before in their children (in weekend sports, ballet, music lessons, math tutors, and in overall involvement in their children's schools), while lower-income families, which are now more likely than ever to be headed by a single parent, are increasingly stretched for time and resources. This has been particularly true as more parents try to position their children for college, which has become ever more essential for success in today's economy.

A study by Sabino Kornrich, a researcher at the Center for Advanced Studies at the Juan March Institute in Madrid, and Frank F. Furstenberg, scheduled to appear in the journal *Demography* this year, found that in 1972, Americans at the upper end of the income spectrum were spending five times as much per child as low-income families. By 2007 that gap had grown to nine to one; spending by upper-income families more than doubled, while spending by low-income families grew by 20 percent.

"The pattern of privileged families today is intensive cultivation," said Dr. Furstenberg, a professor of sociology at the University of Pennsylvania.

The gap is also growing in college. The University of Michigan study, by Susan M. Dynarski and Martha J. Bailey, looked at two generations of students, those born from 1961 to 1964 and those born from 1979 to 1982. By 1989, about one-third of the high-income students in the first generation had finished college; by 2007, more than half of the second generation had done so. By contrast, only 9 percent of the low-income students in the second generation had completed college by 2007, up only slightly from a 5 percent college completion rate by the first generation in 1989.

James J. Heckman, an economist at the University of Chicago, argues that parenting matters as much as, if not more than, income in forming a child's cognitive ability and personality, particularly in the years before children start school.

"Early life conditions and how children are stimulated play a very important role," he said. "The danger is we will revert back to the mindset of the war on poverty, when poverty was just a matter of income, and giving families more would improve the prospects of their children. If people conclude that, it's a mistake."

Meredith Phillips, an associate professor of public policy and sociology at the University of California, Los Angeles, used survey data to show that affluent children spend 1,300 more hours than low-income children before age 6 in places other than their homes, their day care centers, or schools (anywhere from museums to shopping malls). By the time high-income children start school, they have spent about 400 hours more than poor children in literacy activities, she found.

Charles Murray, a scholar at the American Enterprise Institute whose book, *Coming Apart: The State of White America, 1960–2010,* was published Jan. 31, described income inequality as "more of a symptom than a cause."

The growing gap between the better educated and the less educated, he argued, has formed a kind of cultural divide that has its roots in natural social forces, like the tendency of educated people to marry other educated people, as well as in the social policies of the 1960s, like welfare and other government programs, which he contended provided incentives for staying single.

"When the economy recovers, you'll still see all these problems persisting for reasons that have nothing to do with money and everything to do with culture," he said.

There are no easy answers, in part because the problem is so complex, said Douglas J. Besharov, a fellow at the Atlantic Council. Blaming the problem on the richest of the rich ignores an equally important driver, he said: two-earner household wealth, which has lifted the upper middle class ever further from less educated Americans, who tend to be single parents.

The problem is a puzzle, he said. "No one has the slightest idea what will work. The cupboard is bare."

CRITICAL THINKING QUESTIONS

1. According to Traversine, "The achievement gap between white and black students has narrowed significantly . . . while the gap between rich and poor students has grown substantially." Why has family income recently increased as a predictor of educational success rather than race? Provide one piece of *data*—a number—that would support why this argument might be true. How do you explain this—why might race as a factor have decreased since the 1950s?

2. Heckman argues that "The danger is we will revert back to the mindset of the war on poverty when poverty was just a matter of income, and giving families more would improve the prospects of their children." Why does Heckman feel this is a danger, and what does he imply children need in order to close the education gap between the rich and the poor?

3. Summarize Sabino Kornrich's research. Connect this data to Furstenberg's concept of "intensive cultivation." What does Furstenberg mean by "intensive cultivation" and why aren't most low-income students exposed to "intensive cultivation?" How do you think these differences affect children who are in school today?

4. **Connection.** Despite the increasing importance of the income gap, a racial achievement gap still exists. Ta-Nehisi Coates, Nathalie Baptiste, and the Pew Study "Wealth Gaps Rise," all mention the importance of a wealth gap. How could the existence of a racial achievement gap create and maintain a wealth gap? What are two ways you think education could be used as a tool to reduce the wealth gap?

HOW ECONOMIC INCLUSION CAN LEAD TO SUCCESS

by Anise Wiley-Little

Anise Wiley-Little has been Assistant Vice President and Chief Diversity Officer for Allstate, a large insurance company. She also served as Director of Diversity and Work/Life for the same organization. Wiley-Little is a human resources expert, where she focuses on compensation, organizational development and design, policy compliance, and technology optimization.

In this selection from Wiley-Little, she works to understand how we can create diversity in businesses and organizations. Some of the remedies she points to—like a strong mentoring program—can happen when a person obtains a job. But too often, jobs are scarce for racial minorities in this country. What are some things that can be done to reduce and, hopefully, even eliminate this institutional barrier?

• • • • • • • • • • • • • • • •

The key to a better career for people of color is to address opportunity "much earlier than college or the workplace," the author of "Profitable Diversity" suggests.

Diversity had an early foundation in equity in regard to race and gender, but as it evolves, ask if it's now more about poverty and class. As progress with diversity is elevated, keep an open mind by looking for greater advancements in the field because a clear vision of what is really happening around us is necessary. Fairness is what is sought as we strive for greater achievement. Most everyone wants to play by the same rules and have a fair shot, but is that possible?

Regardless of race, where is crime most pervasive? Typically, the most social challenges are found in economically impoverished areas. Regardless of gender or race, whom do we find successful people spending their time with? Most often, other people within their own economic class.

According to the National Center for Children in Poverty's report [http://www.nccp.org/publications/pdf/text_1034.pdf] "Improving the Odds for Adolescents July 2011," low-income children continue to feel the effects of poverty throughout their working lives, including poor employment outcomes. The United States is one of the few places that, despite the situation you are born into, you can move yourself from poverty to prosperity. But those numbers are small. In the UK, this has been addressed through the Deputy Prime Minister's Social Mobility Strategy through the *Business Compact,* which encourages the hiring of those from all socio-economic backgrounds.

THE NUMBERS TELL THE STORY OF CHANGE

Is it time to think about diversity in a new paradigm? The number of low-income individuals is growing in rural areas. The Rural School and Community Trust's report [http://www.ruraledu.org/articles.php?id=2820] "Why Rural Matters 2011–2012: The Condition of Rural

Education in the 50 States" notes increased rates of poverty in rural America, some due to the growing Hispanic populations in the South, Southeast, and Appalachia. Poverty overall has grown in the Southwest, South, and Midwest.

The recognition of poverty and class leads us to the next level of discussion, which is to ask who is focusing on these broader issues. How can social scientists and the government begin to raise the profile of the conversation so that we can intentionally shape the years to come? It can be said that the business case is clear, but when we have to continually justify the existence of diversity and its advantages or disadvantages, the business case development, which may be clear to some, continues to hold an elusive promise for others.

It's true that the wealth gap continues to widen between whites and minorities according to the new census data. The Pew Research Center says the median wealth of white households in 2009 was $113,149, compared to $6,325 for Hispanics, and $5,677 for blacks.

Poverty rates among minorities continue to rise for all groups except for Asians. Women may represent a significant portion of the U.S. workforce, but their wages are still struggling to meet parity. They are still at 77 percent of what men make according to the U.S. census in September of 2010. The median earnings for women of color, except Asians at 90 percent, are even lower.

THE LACK OF OPPORTUNITY

The difference is opportunity. To affect this lack, it must start early, much earlier than college or upon entry to the workplace, which is where most organizations want to spend their time and money. The only place that touches most children consistently is school, which is where change begins. This is where our investment should begin. However, organizations want instant gratification by investing in diversity recruiting from colleges or providing internships to the underprivileged. With the lack of that investment earlier in the cycle, those without opportunity start life at a disadvantage.

Yes, some will pull themselves up despite their life circumstances, yet others, even if they do pull themselves to a better place, have faced a more challenging road. Corporate Voices for Working Families [http://corporatevoices.wordpress.com/], the leading national business membership organization representing the private sector on public policy issues, supports business and education partnerships that encourage organizations to start early in the process and ultimately impact talent management. Their research is developing a numbers-based business case compelling business leaders to take the lead in early development of a diverse talent pipeline.

SOCIAL JUSTICE

There has been little consistency in the recent research of diversity and social justice. Some practitioners believe there is no longer room for social justice in the diversity equation, while others believe we must think outside the box to expand our understanding of diversity. Profitable diversity can be seen as a measure of success that provides an advantage, which may be in dollars, to a greater good as well as increased innovation, efficiency, or collaboration. In order to move closer to any of these benefits of diversity, we must fully explore the tenets that may impact how we think about it, including the economics.

ACCESS

One could easily argue that the white person in poverty without access to industry and jobs should also be a focus of diversity, rather than the Latino individual in the suburbs of a large city who has access to the many possibilities of education and culture. Institutional barriers still exist, although circumstances can and do have an impact on the long-term effects of one's success. Money or birthright can elevate your class and provide you the privilege of access.

Consider the following scenario: In certain situations, a white child raised in poverty may have more opportunities or face less scrutiny because of being born white, but both the white child of poverty and the Latino child of privilege each face unique issues. In evaluating differences, shouldn't all differences including economic be explored for potential bias?

THE ECONOMICS

The premise of socioeconomic issues being a level of diversity does not ignore the complex history of the United States or the current issues of immigration affecting more than simply those crossing the borders of Texas, California, or Arizona. It is imperative to acknowledge miscegenation laws that placed blacks at the bottom of the class system, lower than white indentured servants who had lived peacefully with blacks before those laws.

My own parents, who were both born in Little Rock, Arkansas, were in high school during the time of the Little Rock Nine and experienced firsthand the racial tension, social upheaval, and civil unrest. Given that we are not yet a "post-racial" society as some may suggest, there must be an acknowledgment of systemic bias and overt or subtle racism that impacts under-represented groups regardless of their class. This premise only allows that diversity has many layers of complexity.

Even armed with education, navigating corporate America and the many unspoken rules can be challenging for anyone, but even more so for one with limited exposure, access, or sponsorship. Charles Murray explores the white lower class and the declining middle class in his book [http://www.amazon.com/Coming-Apart-State-America-1960-2010/dp/030745343X] *Coming Apart: The State of White America, 1960–2010.* The privileged majority will remain powerful for many generations to come because of the wealth they hold, often due to the complicated acquisition of land by their forefathers that blacks and others, even those well educated and privileged, will never have access to. There is only so much prime oceanfront property to be acquired.

SPONSORSHIP

If you have already been exposed to travel, executive role models, and quality life and education, you may have a natural, authentic executive presence that provides you a head start. Family history or legacy can translate into appropriate connections. This could also be interpreted as the dark side of assimilation, but we know that mentoring is not enough; it's about sponsorship, who you know and who knows you. In most programs that want to see the advancement of the diverse population, participants tend to be over-mentored and under-sponsored based upon access.

Most will need to seek their own sponsors outside of the structured talent management process. These are the relationships that form naturally when an executive is willing to tell you the real story, speak up for you in the succession meeting, give you that risky assignment, and be there if you fail because he or she feels a positive connection to you. When you are comfortable in a particular circle of people, this may be an invisible advantage. People like you or with the same experiences or lifestyle can be drawn to you regardless of race or gender or orientation without realizing why. When we talk about hiring in our own image, it's not always limited simply to race, gender, generation, or sexual orientation.

Everything practical tells us that we should pay attention to many dimensions of diversity, including some that don't commonly come to mind. In an age of cultural diversity, fast-paced ethnic growth, and increased understanding of the LGBT community, our socio-economic class is also a necessary part of what we bring to the table that defines how and who we are.

CRITICAL THINKING QUESTIONS

1. In the section titled "Access," Wiley-Little argues that both poor white people and privileged Latino people both face "unique issues" in succeeding. She says, "both might face institutional barriers." What are two issues a privileged Latino person might face that a poor white person would not? What are two types of access that might be limiting for a poor white person?
2. What is your definition of diversity in the 21st century? Wiley-Little makes the argument that diversity is important to organizations—do you agree? Why or why not? Is it possible for minority groups to "have a fair shot" in our society? If so, how? If not, why not?
3. Why is our socio-economic class "a necessary part of what we bring to the table that defines . . . who we are?" What do you consider your socio-economic class? What are two ways your socio-economic status could benefit a potential employer?
4. **Connection.** Wiley-Little writes, "The privileged majority will remain powerful for many generations to come because of the wealth they hold, often due to the complicated acquisition of land by their forefathers that blacks and others, even those well educated and privileged, will never have access to. There is only so much prime oceanfront property to be acquired." Ta-Nehisi Coates outlined several ways in which African Americans specifically faced "institutional barriers" that held many back from advancing economically. What are some of the solutions that Wiley-Little points to in her article? And how do you think two of them would address some of the wrongs that Coates brings to light?

UNIT 3

Technology

INTRODUCTION

There is a classic cartoon from *The New Yorker* composed by Pete Steiner in 1993. Two dogs are talking while one is behind a computer screen. The dog behind the computer screen tells the dog on the floor, "on the Internet, nobody knows you're a dog."

That has been one of the blessings of the Internet—It allows people to hide behind their communication in a way that has never before been possible. For anyone from the gay kid in rural Alabama who finds a message board with comments from other teens like him, to the rap music fan in northeastern Minnesota who connects with other fans through YouTube comments, the promise of technology to bring people together and eliminate barriers is obvious. The protesters such as those in Egypt and Tunisia used Twitter to organize revolutions that brought democracy, if only for a time, to large numbers of people who were suffering under dictatorships.

These are examples of people who found what was lacking in the offline world in the world of the Internet. Unfortunately, too much of the "real" world is now subject to the "realities" of the online world, influencing all aspects of our lives. The previous unit contained the reading, "The Case for Reparations," in which the author argued that centuries of institutional violence against African Americans created conditions in which poverty is endemic. An anonymous commenter on this article wrote, "black people should b happy to have been slaves [sic]." Racism isn't the only form of discrimination to go digital. This unit explores how one half of Internet users—women—have become second class citizens on the Internet.

We celebrate those visionaries who have created our online institutions—Bill Gates of Microsoft, Mark Zuckerberg of Facebook, Sergey Brin of Google—with magazine covers and billions of dollars in revenue. But the online space they have created is unfriendly to women. Could it be because these visionaries are mostly men?

Readings in this unit explore women who are working hard to disrupt the male dominated nature of the technology industry. They encounter sexism from their classmates, their potential investors, their coworkers, and their supervisors. Technology companies claim to be able to solve the world's problems—from education to traffic, from connecting with friends to ordering food—yet their companies are struggling to solve the hostile work environment they create for many women.

While the demographics of the technology companies are troubling, what may be worse is how many women are treated online. From dating sites to social media sites, from comments on their blogs to the videos available on media sharing sites, the Internet can be seen as a series of frightening, possibly dangerous locations in which to be a woman. Sexism and misogyny have existed offline for centuries, but this new misogyny is different. It is more immediate—the threatening tweet comes to your phone, mere inches from where you are sleeping. It is more graphic—the ability to send images, or use words you would say at a bar increases the isolation many women can feel online. It is also most frequent, as you are now a target not just for people who are near you, but for anyone who is angered at your gender and has an Internet connection.

On the Internet, nobody knows if you are a dog. They also don't know if you are an angry young man who is typing horrible things because you broke up with your girlfriend and that you will feel guilty in the morning for the things you wrote on your Facebook wall. Nobody knows how serious you are when you tell a women you have never met, "I kill bitches like you." The uncertainty is frightening; the uncertainty creates a hostile environment. Is it possible that, because nobody knows if you are a dog since you are anonymous, you feel more emboldened to say terrible things? In the unit we try to understand the following: *Does the structure of the Internet itself amplify sexism? What is sexism like online compared to the sexism women have dealt with for centuries? And can an industry that is full of sexist behavior and harassment help?*

In high school, 74% of women express an interest in STEM related fields. Yet, fewer than 25% obtain a college degree in one. Women are being discouraged from careers that they could excel in, and this lack of diversity in our new public square hurts us all.

WHY WOMEN AREN'T WELCOME ON THE INTERNET

by Amanda Hess

Amanda Hess, a freelance writer, reports on sex, Hollywood, and technology. Additionally, Hess is a regular contributor to *Slate's* sister publication *Double X*.

In this 2014 article published in *The Pacific Standard*, Amanda Hess outlines the many ways in which women face harassment online. The Internet—which thinks of itself as an open and free meritocracy—is actually a difficult place to be a proactive and prominent woman. She identifies a harassment free Internet as the next civil rights issue. When so much of our daily lives—from social connections to work appointments to emails from the babysitter—exists online, what responsibility do the law and law enforcement have to make that a safe space?

• • • • • • • • • • • • • • • •

"Ignore the barrage of violent threats and harassing messages that confront you online every day." That's what women are told. But these relentless messages are an assault on women's careers, their psychological bandwidth, and their freedom to live online. We have been thinking about Internet harassment all wrong.

I was 12 hours into a summer vacation in Palm Springs when my phone hummed to life, buzzing twice next to me in the dark of my hotel room. I squinted at the screen. It was 5:30 a.m., and a friend was texting me from the opposite coast. "Amanda, this twitter account. Freaking out over here," she wrote. "There is a twitter account that seems to have been set up for the purpose of making death threats to you."

I dragged myself out of bed and opened my laptop. A few hours earlier, someone going by the username "headlessfemalepig" had sent me seven tweets. "I see you are physically not very attractive. Figured," the first said. Then: "You suck a lot of drunk and drug fucked guys cocks." As a female journalist who writes about sex (among other things), none of this feedback was particularly out of the ordinary. But this guy took it to another level: "I am 36 years old, I did 12 years for 'manslaughter', I killed a woman, like you, who decided to make fun of guys cocks." And then: "Happy to say we live in the same state. Im looking you up, and when I find you, im going to rape you and remove your head." There was more, but the final tweet summed it up: "You are going to die and I am the one who is going to kill you. I promise you this."

My fingers paused over the keyboard. I felt disoriented and terrified. Then embarrassed for being scared, and, finally, pissed. On the one hand, it seemed unlikely that I'd soon be defiled and decapitated at the hands of a serial rapist-murderer. On the other hand, headlessfemalepig was clearly a deranged individual with a bizarre fixation on me. I picked up my phone and dialed 911.

Two hours later, a Palm Springs police officer lumbered up the steps to my hotel room, paused on the outdoor threshold, and began questioning me in a steady clip. I wheeled through the relevant background information: I am a journalist; I live in Los Angeles; sometimes, people don't like what I write about women, relationships, or sexuality; this was not the first time that someone had responded to my work by threatening to rape and kill me. The cop anchored his hands on his belt, looked me in the eye, and said, "What is Twitter?"

Staring up at him in the blazing sun, the best answer I could come up with was, "It's like an e-mail, but it's public." What I didn't articulate is that Twitter is the place where I laugh, whine, work, schmooze, procrastinate, and flirt. It sits in my back pocket wherever I go and lies next to me when I fall asleep. And since I first started writing in 2007, it's become just one of the many online spaces where men come to tell me to get out.

The examples are too numerous to recount, but like any good journalist, I keep a running file documenting the most deranged cases. There was the local cable viewer who hunted down my email address after a television appearance to tell me I was "the ugliest woman he had ever seen." And the group of visitors to a "men's rights" site who pored over photographs of me and a prominent feminist activist, then discussed how they'd "spend the night with" us. ("Put em both in a gimp mask and tied to each other 69 so the bitches can't talk or move and go round the world, any old port in a storm, any old hole," one decided.) And the anonymous commenter who weighed in on one of my articles: "Amanda, I'll fucking rape you. How does that feel?"

None of this makes me exceptional. It just makes me a woman with an Internet connection. Here's just a sampling of the noxious online commentary directed at other women in recent years. To Alyssa Royse, a sex and relationships blogger, for saying that she hated *The Dark Knight:* "you are clearly retarded, i hope someone shoots then rapes you." To Kathy Sierra, a technology writer, for blogging about software, coding, and design: "i hope someone slits your throat and cums down your gob." To Lindy West, a writer at the women's website Jezebel, for critiquing a comedian's rape joke: "I just want to rape her with a traffic cone." To Rebecca Watson, an atheist commentator, for blogging about sexism in the skeptic community: "If I lived in Boston I'd put a bullet in your brain." To Catherine Mayer, a journalist at *Time* magazine, for no particular reason: "A BOMB HAS BEEN PLACED OUTSIDE YOUR HOME. IT WILL GO OFF AT EXACTLY 10:47 PM ON A TIMER AND TRIGGER DESTROYING EVERYTHING."

A woman doesn't even need to occupy a professional writing perch at a prominent platform to become a target. According to a 2005 report by the Pew Research Center, which has been tracking the online lives of Americans for more than a decade, women and men have been logging on in equal numbers since 2000, but the vilest communications are still disproportionately lobbed at women. We are more likely to report being stalked and harassed on the Internet—of the 3,787 people who reported harassing incidents from 2000 to 2012 to the volunteer organization Working to Halt Online Abuse, 72.5 percent were female. Sometimes, the abuse can get physical: A Pew survey reported that five percent of women who used the Internet said "something happened online" that led them into "physical danger." And it starts young: Teenage girls are significantly more likely to be cyberbullied than boys. Just appearing as a woman online, it seems, can be enough to inspire abuse. In 2006, researchers from the University of Maryland set up a bunch of fake online accounts and then dispatched them into chat rooms. Accounts with feminine usernames incurred an average of 100 sexually explicit or threatening messages a day. Masculine names received 3.7.

There are three federal laws that apply to cyberstalking cases; the first was passed in 1934 to address harassment through the mail, via telegram, and over the telephone, six decades after Alexander Graham Bell's invention. Since the initial passage of the Violence Against Women Act, in 1994, amendments to the law have gradually updated it to apply to new technologies and to stiffen penalties against those who use them to abuse. Thirty-four states have cyberstalking laws on the books; most have expanded long-standing laws against stalking and criminal threats to prosecute crimes carried out online.

But making quick and sick threats has become so easy that many say the abuse has proliferated to the point of meaninglessness, and that expressing alarm is foolish. Reporters who take death threats seriously "often give the impression that this is some kind of shocking event for which we should pity the 'victims,'" my colleague Jim Pagels wrote in *Slate* this fall, "but anyone who's spent 10 minutes online knows that these assertions are entirely toothless." On Twitter, he added, "When there's no precedent for physical harm, it's only baseless fear mongering." My friend Jen Doll wrote, at *The Atlantic Wire,* "It seems like that old 'ignoring' tactic your mom taught you could work out to everyone's benefit. . . . These people are bullying, or hope to bully. Which means we shouldn't take the bait." In the epilogue to her book *The End of Men,* Hanna Rosin—an editor at *Slate*—argued that harassment of women online could be seen as a cause for celebration. It shows just how far we've come. Many women on the Internet "are in positions of influence, widely published and widely read; if they sniff out misogyny, I have no doubt they will gleefully skewer the responsible sexist in one of many available online outlets, and get results."

So women who are harassed online are expected to either get over ourselves or feel flattered in response to the threats made against us. We have the choice to keep quiet or respond "gleefully."

But no matter how hard we attempt to ignore it, this type of gendered harassment—and the sheer volume of it—has severe implications for women's status on the Internet. Threats of rape, death, and stalking can overpower our emotional bandwidth, take up our time, and cost us money through legal fees, online protection services, and missed wages. I've spent countless hours over the past four years logging the online activity of one particularly committed cyberstalker, just in case. And as the Internet becomes increasingly central to the human experience, the ability of women to live and work freely online will be shaped, and too often limited, by the technology companies that host these threats, the constellation of local and federal law enforcement officers who investigate them, and the popular commentators who dismiss them—all arenas that remain dominated by men, many of whom have little personal understanding of what women face online every day.

This summer, Caroline Criado-Perez became the English-speaking Internet's most famous recipient of online threats after she petitioned the British government to put more female faces on its bank notes. (When the Bank of England announced its intentions to replace social reformer Elizabeth Fry with Winston Churchill on the £5 note, Criado-Perez made the modest suggestion that the bank make an effort to feature at least one woman who is not the Queen on any of its currency.) Rape and death threats amassed on her Twitter feed too quickly to count, bearing messages like "I will rape you tomorrow at 9 p.m. . . . Shall we meet near your house?"

Then, something interesting happened. Instead of logging off, Criado-Perez retweeted the threats, blasting them out to her Twitter followers. She called up police and hounded Twitter for a response. Journalists around the world started writing about the threats. As more and more people heard the story, Criado-Perez's follower count skyrocketed to near 25,000. Her supporters joined in urging British police and Twitter executives to respond.

Under the glare of international criticism, the police and the company spent the next few weeks passing the buck back and forth. Andy Trotter, a communications adviser for the British police, announced that it was Twitter's responsibility to crack down on the messages. Though Britain criminalizes a broader category of offensive speech than the U.S. does, the sheer volume of threats would be too difficult for "a hard-pressed police service" to investigate, Trotter said. Police "don't want to be in this arena." It diverts their attention from "dealing with something else."

Meanwhile, Twitter issued a blanket statement saying that victims like Criado-Perez could fill out an online form for each abusive tweet; when Criado-Perez supporters hounded Mark Luckie, the company's manager of journalism and news, for a response, he briefly shielded his account, saying that the attention had become "abusive." Twitter's official recommendation to victims of abuse puts the ball squarely in law enforcement's court: "If an interaction has gone beyond the point of name calling and you feel as though you may be in danger," it says, "contact your local authorities so they can accurately assess the validity of the threat and help you resolve the issue offline."

In the weeks after the flare-up, Scotland Yard confirmed the arrest of three men. Twitter—in response to several online petitions calling for action—hastened the rollout of a "report abuse" button that allows users to flag offensive material. And Criado-Perez went on receiving threats. Some real person out there— or rather, hundreds of them—still liked the idea of seeing her raped and killed.

The Internet is a global network, but when you pick up the phone to report an online threat, whether you are in London or Palm Springs, you end up face-to-face with a cop who patrols a comparatively puny jurisdiction. And your cop will probably be a man: According to the U.S. Bureau of Justice Statistics, in 2008, only 6.5 percent of state police officers and 19 percent of FBI agents were women. The numbers get smaller in smaller agencies. And in many locales, police work is still a largely analog affair: 911 calls are immediately routed to the local police force; the closest officer is dispatched to respond; he takes notes with pen and paper.

After Criado-Perez received her hundreds of threats, she says she got conflicting instructions from police on how to report the crimes, and was forced to repeatedly "trawl" through the vile messages to preserve the evidence. "I can just about cope with threats," she wrote on Twitter. "What I can't cope with after that is the victim-blaming, the patronising, and the police record-keeping." Last year, the American atheist blogger Rebecca Watson wrote about her experience calling a series of local and national law enforcement agencies after a man launched a website threatening to kill her. "Because I knew what town [he] lived in, I called his local police department. They told me there was nothing they could do and that I'd have to make a report with my local police department," Watson wrote later. "[I] finally got through to someone who told me that there was nothing they could do but take a report in case one day [he] followed through on his threats, at which point they'd have a pretty good lead."

The first time I reported an online rape threat to police, in 2009, the officer dispatched to my home asked, "Why would anyone bother to do something like that?" and declined to file a report. In Palm Springs, the officer who came to my room said, "This guy could be sitting in a basement in Nebraska for all we know." That my stalker had said that he lived in my state, and had plans to seek me out at home, was dismissed as just another online ruse.

Of course, some people are investigated and prosecuted for cyberstalking. In 2009, a Florida college student named Patrick Macchione met a girl at school, then threatened to kill her on Twitter, terrorized her with lewd videos posted to YouTube, and made hundreds of calls to her phone. Though his victim filed a restraining order, cops only sprung into action after a county sheriff stopped him for loitering, then reportedly found a video camera in his backpack containing disturbing recordings about his victim. The sheriff 's department later worked with the state attorney's office to convict Macchione on 19 counts, one of which was cyberstalking (he successfully appealed that count on grounds that the law hadn't been enacted when he was arrested); Macchione was sentenced to four years in prison. Consider also a recent high-profile case of cyberstalking investigated by the FBI. In the midst of her affair with General David Petraeus, biographer Paula Broadwell allegedly created an anonymous email account for the purpose of sending harassing notes to Florida socialite Jill Kelley. Kelley reported them to the FBI, which sniffed out Broadwell's identity via the account's location-based metadata and obtained a warrant to monitor her email activity.

In theory, appealing to a higher jurisdiction can yield better results. "Local law enforcement will often look the other way," says Dr. Sameer Hinduja, a criminology professor at Florida Atlantic University and co-director of the Cyberbullying Research Center. "They don't have the resources or the personnel to investigate those crimes." County, state, or federal agencies at least have the support to be more responsive: "Usually they have a computer crimes unit, savvy personnel who are familiar with these cases, and established relationships with social media companies so they can quickly send a subpoena to help with the investigation," Hinduja says.

But in my experience and those of my colleagues, these larger law enforcement agencies have little capacity or drive to investigate threats as well. Despite his pattern of abusive online behavior, Macchione was ultimately arrested for an unrelated physical crime. When I called the FBI over headlessfemalepig's threats, a representative told me an agent would get in touch if the bureau was interested in pursuing the case; nobody did. And when Rebecca Watson reported the threats targeted at her to the FBI, she initially connected with a sympathetic agent—but the agent later expressed trouble opening Watson's file of screenshots of the threats, and soon stopped replying to her emails. The Broadwell investigation was an uncommon, and possibly unprecedented, exercise for the agency. As University of Wisconsin-Eau Claire criminal justice professor Justin Patchin told *Wired* at the time: "I'm not aware of any case when the FBI has gotten involved in a case of online harassment."

After I received my most recent round of threats, I asked Jessica Valenti, a prominent feminist writer (and the founder of the blog Feministing), who's been repeatedly targeted with online threats, for her advice, and then I asked her to share her story. "It's not really one story. This has happened a number of times over the past seven years," she told me. When rape and death threats first started pouring into her inbox, she vacated her apartment for a week, changed her bank accounts, and got a new cell number. When the next wave of threats came, she got in touch with law enforcement officials, who warned her that though the men emailing her were unlikely to follow through on their threats, the level of vitriol indicated that she should be vigilant for a far less identifiable threat: silent "hunters" who lurk behind the tweeting "hollerers." The FBI advised Valenti to leave her home until the threats blew over, to never walk outside of her apartment alone, and to keep aware of any cars or men who might show up repeatedly outside her door. "It was totally impossible advice," she says. "You have to be paranoid about everything. You can't just not be in a public place."

And we can't simply be offline either. When *Time* journalist Catherine Mayer reported the bomb threat lodged against her, the officers she spoke to—who thought usernames were secret codes and didn't seem to know what an IP address was—advised her to unplug. "Not one of the officers I've encountered uses Twitter or understands why anyone would wish to do so," she later wrote. "The officers were unanimous in advising me to take a break from Twitter, assuming, as many people do, that Twitter is at best a time-wasting narcotic."

All of these online offenses are enough to make a woman *want* to click away from Twitter, shut her laptop, and power down her phone. Sometimes, we do withdraw: Pew found that from 2000 to 2005, the percentage of Internet users who participate in online chats and discussion groups dropped from 28 percent to 17 percent, "entirely because of women's fall off in participation." But for many women, steering clear of the Internet isn't an option. We use our devices to find supportive communities, make a living, and construct safety nets. For a woman like me, who lives alone, the Internet isn't a fun diversion—it is a necessary resource for work and interfacing with friends, family, and, sometimes, law enforcement officers in an effort to feel safer from both online and offline violence.

The Polish sociologist Zygmunt Bauman draws a distinction between "tourists" and "vagabonds" in the modern economy. Privileged tourists move about the world "on purpose," to seek "new experience" as "the joys of the familiar wear off." Disempowered vagabonds relocate because they have to, pushed and pulled through mean streets where they could never hope to settle down. On the Internet, men are tourists and women are vagabonds. "Telling a woman to shut her laptop is like saying, 'Eh! Just stop seeing your family,'" says Nathan Jurgenson, a social media sociologist (and a friend) at the University of Maryland.

What does a tourist look like? In 2012, Gawker unmasked "Violentacrez," an anonymous member of the online community Reddit who was infamous for posting creepy photographs of underage women and creating or moderating subcommunities on the site with names like "chokeabitch" and "rapebait." Violentacrez turned out to be a Texas computer programmer named Michael Brusch, who displayed an exceedingly casual attitude toward his online hobbies. "I do my job, go home, watch TV, and go on the Internet. I just like riling people up in my spare time," he told Adrian Chen, the Gawker reporter who outed him. "People take things way too seriously around here."

Abusers tend to operate anonymously, or under pseudonyms. But the women they target often write on professional platforms, under their given names, and in the context of their real lives. Victims don't have the luxury of separating themselves from the crime. When it comes to online threats, "one person is feeling the reality of the Internet very viscerally: the person who is being threatened," says Jurgenson. "It's a lot easier for the person who made the threat—and the person who is investigating the threat—to believe that what's happening on the Internet isn't real."

When authorities treat the Internet as a fantasyland, it has profound effects on the investigation and prosecution of online threats. Criminal threat laws largely require that victims feel tangible, immediate, and sustained fear. In my home state of California, a threat must be "unequivocal, unconditional, immediate, and specific" and convey a "gravity of purpose and an immediate prospect of execution of the threat" to be considered a crime. If police don't know whether the harasser lives next door or out in Nebraska, it's easier for them to categorize the threat as non-immediate. When they treat a threat as a boyish hoax, the implication is that the threat ceases to be a criminal offense.

So the victim faces a psychological dilemma: How should she understand her own fear? Should she, as many advise, dismiss an online threat as a silly game, and not bother to inform the cops that someone may want to—ha, ha—rape and kill her? Or should she dutifully report every threat to police, who may well dismiss her concerns? When I received my most recent rape and death threats, one friend told me that I should rest assured that the anonymous tweeter was unlikely to take any physical action against me in real life; another noted that my stalker seemed like the type of person who would fashion a coat from my skin, and urged me to take any action necessary to land the stalker in jail.

Danielle Citron, a University of Maryland law professor who focuses on Internet threats, charted the popular response to Internet death and rape threats in a 2009 paper published in the *Michigan Law Review.* She found that Internet harassment is routinely dismissed as "harmless locker-room talk," perpetrators as "juvenile pranksters," and victims as "overly sensitive complainers." Weighing in on one online harassment case, in an interview on National Public Radio, journalist David Margolick called the threats "juvenile, immature, and obnoxious, but that is all they are . . . frivolous frat-boy rants."

Of course, the frat house has never been a particularly safe space for women. I've been threatened online, but I have also been harassed on the street, groped on the subway, followed home from the 7-Eleven, pinned down on a bed by a drunk boyfriend, and raped on a date. Even if I sign off Twitter, a threat could still be waiting on my stoop.

Today, a legion of anonymous harassers are free to play their "games" and "pranks" under pseudonymous screen names, but for the women they target, the attacks only compound the real fear, discomfort, and stress we experience in our daily lives.

If American police forces are overwhelmingly male, the technology companies that have created the architecture of the online world are, famously, even more so. In 2010, according to the information services firm CB Insights, 92 percent of the founders of fledgling Internet companies were male; 86 percent of their founding teams were exclusively male. While the number of women working across the sciences is generally increasing, the percentage of women working in computer sciences peaked in 2000 and is now on the decline. In 2012, the Bureau of Labor Statistics found, women made up just 22.5 percent of American computer programmers and 19.7 percent of software developers. In a 2012 study of 400 California companies, researchers at the University of California–Davis, found that just seven percent of the highest-paid executives at Silicon Valley companies were women.

When Twitter announced its initial public offering in October, its filings listed an all-male board. Vijaya Gadde, Twitter's general counsel, was the only woman among its executive officers. When Vivek Wadhwa, a fellow at Stanford's Rock Center for Corporate Governance, suggested that the gender imbalance on Twitter's board was an issue of "elite arrogance" and "male chauvinistic thinking," Twitter CEO Dick Costolo responded with a joking tweet, calling Wadhwa "the Carrot Top of academic sources."

Most executives aren't intentionally boxing women out. But the decisions these men make have serious implications for billions of people. The gender imbalance in their companies compromises their ability to understand the lives of half their users.

Twitter "has a history of saying 'too bad, so sad'" when confronted with concerns about harassment on its platform, says Citron, the University of Maryland law professor who studies the emerging legal implications of online abuse against women. The culture of the platform has typically prioritized freewheeling discussion over zealous speech policing. Unlike Facebook, Twitter doesn't require people to register accounts under their real names. Users are free to enjoy the frivolity—and the protection—that anonymous speech provides. If a user runs afoul of Twitter's terms of service, he's free to create a new account under a fresh handle. And the Communications Decency Act of 1996 protects platforms like Twitter from being held legally responsible for what individuals say on the site.

The advent of the "report abuse" button is a development Citron finds "very heartening." Allowing people to block an abuser's account helps women avoid having to be faced with vile and abusive tweets. But our problems can't all be solved with the click of a button. In some cases, the report-abuse button is just a virtual Band-Aid for a potentially dangerous real-world problem. It can undermine women by erasing the trail of digital evidence. And it does nothing to prevent these same abusers from opening a new account and continuing their crimes.

When I received those seven tweets in Palm Springs, a well-meaning friend reported them as abusive through Twitter's system, hoping that action on the platform's end would help further my case. A few hours later, the tweets were erased from the site without comment (or communication with me). Headlessfemalepig's Twitter feed was replaced with a page noting that the account had been suspended. Luckily, I had taken screenshots of the tweets, but to the cops working with a limited understanding of the platform, their sudden disappearance only confused the issue. The detective assigned to my case asked me to send him links pointing to where the messages lived online—but absent a subpoena of Twitter's records, they were gone from law enforcement's view. If someone had reported the threats before I got a chance to see them, I might not even have been able to indicate their existence at all. Without a proper investigation, I am incapable of knowing whether headlessfemalepig is a one-time offender or the serial stalker who has followed me for many years. Meanwhile, nothing's stopping headlessfemalepig from continuing to tweet away under a new name.

It shouldn't be Twitter's responsibility to hunt down and sanction criminals who use its service—that's what cops are (supposedly) for. Twitter has to balance its interests in addressing abusive behavior with its interests in protecting our private information (or that of, say, political dissidents), which means keeping a tight lid on users' IP addresses and refusing to offer up deleted material to civilians. When I asked how Twitter balances those demands, Nu Wexler, who leads public policy communications for the company, pointed me to a chart published by the Electronic Frontier Foundation—an advocacy group dedicated to defending the free speech and privacy rights of Internet users—that illustrates the platform's "commitment to user privacy." The chart, titled "Who Has Your Back: Which Companies Help Protect Your Data From the Government?," awards Twitter high marks for fighting for users' privacy rights in court and publishing a transparency report about government data requests.

A high score awarded by the Electronic Frontier Foundation communicates to users that their Internet activity will be safe from overreaching government snoops—and post–Edward Snowden, that concern is more justified than ever. But in some cases, the impulse to protect our privacy can interfere with the law's ability to protect us when we're harassed. Last year, the Electronic Frontier Foundation came out against an amendment to the Violence Against Women Act. Until recently, the law criminalized abusive, threatening, and harassing speech conveyed over a telephone line, provided the abuser placed the call; the new law, passed in March, applies to any electronic harassment targeted at a specific person, whether it's made over the telephone or by another means. Critics of the legislation pulled out the trope that the Internet is less real than other means of communication. As the Foundation put it, "a person is free to disregard something said on Twitter in a way far different than a person who is held in constant fear of the persistent ringing of a telephone intruding in their home."

The Electronic Frontier Foundation—and the tech companies that benefit from its ratings—are undoubtedly committed to fighting government First Amendment abuses. But when they focus their efforts on stemming the spread of anti-harassment laws from outdated media, like landline telephones, to modern means like Twitter, their efforts act like a thumb on the scale, favoring some democratic values at the expense of others. "Silicon Valley has the power to shape society to conform to its values, which prioritize openness and connectivity," Jurgenson says. "But why are engineers in California getting to decide what constitutes harassment for people all around the world?"

Tech companies are, of course, fully aware that they need a broad base of users to flourish as billion-dollar businesses. Today women have the bargaining power to draft successful petitions calling for "report abuse" buttons, but our corporate influence is limited, and alternative venues for action are few. Local police departments "have no money," Jurgenson says, and "it feels unlikely that the government is going to do more anytime soon, so we're forced to put more pressure on Twitter." And while an organized user base can influence the decisions of a public, image-conscious company like Twitter, many platforms—like the dedicated "revenge porn" sites that have proliferated on the Web—don't need to appease women to stay popular. "I call this the myth of the market," Citron says. "There's definitely a desire for anti-social behavior. There are eyeballs. And there are users who are providing the content. The market isn't self-correcting, and it's not going to make this go away."

In a 2009 paper in the *Boston University Law Review,* Citron proposed a new way of framing the legal problem of harassment on the Internet: She argued that online abuse constitutes "discrimination in women's employment opportunities" that ought to be better addressed by the U.S. government itself. Title VII of the Civil Rights Act of 1964, which outlawed discrimination based on race, religion, or gender, was swiftly applied to members of the Ku Klux Klan, who hid behind hoods to harass and intimidate black Louisianans from voting and pursuing work. Anonymous online harassment, Citron argued, similarly discourages women from "writing and earning a living online" on the basis of their gender. "It interferes with their professional lives. It raises their vulnerability to offline sexual violence. It brands them as incompetent workers and inferior sexual objects. The harassment causes considerable emotional distress."

On the Internet, women are overpowered and devalued. We don't always think about our online lives in those terms—after all, our days are filled with work to do, friends to keep up with, Netflix to watch. But when anonymous harassers come along—saying they would like to rape us, or cut off our heads, or scrutinize our bodies in public, or shame us for our sexual habits—they serve to remind us in ways both big and small that we can't be at ease online. It is precisely the banality of Internet harassment, University of Miami law professor Mary Anne Franks has argued, that makes it "both so effective and so harmful, especially as a form of discrimination."

The personal and professional costs of that discrimination manifest themselves in very real ways. Jessica Valenti says she has stopped promoting her speaking events publicly, enlisted security for her public appearances, signed up for a service to periodically scrub the Web of her private information, invested in a post-office box, and begun periodically culling her Facebook friend list in an attempt to filter out readers with ulterior motives. Those efforts require a clear investment of money and time, but the emotional fallout is less directly quantifiable. "When people say you should be raped and killed for years on end, it takes a toll on your soul," she says. Whenever a male stranger approaches her at a public event, "the hairs on the back of my neck stand up." Every time we call the police, head to court to file a civil protection order, or get sucked into a mental hole by the threats that have been made against us, zeroes drop from our annual incomes. Says Jurgenson, "It's a monetary penalty for being a woman."

Citron has planted the seed of an emerging debate over the possibility of applying civil rights laws to ensure equal opportunities for women on the Internet. "There's no silver bullet for addressing this problem," Citron says. But existing legislation has laid the groundwork for potential future reforms. Federal civil rights law can punish "force or threat[s] of force" that interfere with a person's employment on the basis of race, religion, or national origin. That protection, though, doesn't currently extend to threats targeted at a person's gender. However, other parts of the Civil Rights Act frame workplace sexual harassment as discriminatory, and require employers to implement policies to both prevent and remedy discrimination in the office. And Title IX of the Education Amendments of 1972 puts the onus on educational institutions to take action against discrimination toward women. Because Internet harassment affects the employment and educational opportunities of women, laws could conceivably be amended to allow women to bring claims against individuals.

But it's hard to get there from here. As Citron notes, the Internet is not a school or a workplace, but a vast and diffuse universe that often lacks any clear locus of accountability. Even if online threats are considered a civil rights violation, who would we sue? Anonymous tweeters lack the institutional affiliation to make monetary claims worthwhile. And there is the mobbing problem: One person can send just one horrible tweet, but then many others may pile on. A single vicious tweet may not clear the hurdle of discriminatory harassment (or repetitive abuse). And while a mob of individuals each lobbing a few attacks clearly looks and feels like harassment, there is no organized group to take legal action against. Bringing separate claims against individual abusers would be laborious, expensive, and unlikely to reap financial benefits. At the same time, amending the Communications Decency Act to put the onus on Internet platforms to police themselves could have a serious chilling effect on all types of speech, discriminatory or otherwise.

Citron admits that passing new civil rights legislation that applies to a new venue—the Internet—is a potentially Sisyphean task. But she says that by expanding existing civil rights laws to recognize the gendered nature of Internet threats, lawmakers could put more pressure on law enforcement agencies to take those crimes seriously. "We have the tools already," Citron says. "Do we use them? Not really." Prosecuting online threats as bias-motivated crimes would mean that offenders would face stronger penalties, law enforcement agencies would be better incentivized to investigate these higher-level crimes—and hopefully, the Internet's legions of anonymous abusers would begin to see the downside of mouthing off.

Our laws have always found a way to address new harms while balancing long-standing rights, even if they do it very slowly. Opponents of the Civil Rights Act of 1964 characterized its workplace protections as unconstitutional and bad for business. Before workplace sexual harassment was reframed as discriminatory under Title VII, it was written off as harmless flirting. When Title IX was first proposed to address gender discrimination in education, a Senate discussion on the issue ended in laughter when one senator cracked a co-ed football joke. Until domestic violence became a national policy priority, abuse was dismissed as a lovers' quarrel. Today's harmless jokes and undue burdens are tomorrow's civil rights agenda.

My serial cyberstalker began following me in 2009. I was on the staff of an alt-weekly when a mini-controversy flared up on a blog. One of the blog's writers had developed a pattern of airing his rape fantasies on the site; I interviewed him and the site's other contributors and published a story. Then I started receiving rape threats of my own. Their author posted a photo of me on his blog and wrote, "Oh, sure, you might say she's pretty. Or you might say she looks sweet or innocent. But don't let looks fool you. This woman is pure evil." (To some harassers, you're physically not very attractive; to others, you're beautiful.) "I thought I'd describe her on my blog as 'rape-worthy,' but ultimately decided against it," he added. "Oops! I've committed another thought crime!"

In the comments section below the article, threats popped up under a dozen fake names and several phony IP addresses—which usually point to a device's precise location, but can be easily faked if you have the right software. "Amanda, I'll fucking rape you," one said. "How's that feel? Like that? What's my IP address, bitch?" On his Twitter account, my stalker wrote that he planned to buy a gun—apparently intending to defend his First Amendment rights by exercising the Second.

Then, one night when my boyfriend and I were in our apartment, my cell phone started ringing incessantly. I received a series of voicemails, escalating in tone from a stern "You cut the shit right fucking now" to a slurred "You fucking dyke . . . I will fuck you up." For the first time ever, I called the police. When an officer arrived at my house, I described the pattern of abuse. He expressed befuddlement at the "virtual" crime, handed me his card, and told me to call if anyone came to my house—but he declined to take a report.

Without police support, I opted to file a civil protection order in family court. I posted a photograph of my stalker at my office's front desk. When the local sheriff's department failed to serve him court papers, I paid $100 for a private investigator to get the job done. It took me five visits to court, waiting for my case to be called up while sitting quietly across the aisle from him in the gallery as dozens of other local citizens told a domestic violence judge about the boyfriends and fathers and ex-wives who had threatened and abused them. These people were seeking protection from crowbar-wielding exes and gun-flashing acquaintances—more real crimes the justice system had failed to prosecute. By the time the judge finally called up my protection order for review, I had missed a half-dozen days of work pursuing the case. I was lucky to have a full-time job and an understanding boss—even if he didn't understand the threats on the same level I did. And because my case was filed under new anti-stalking protections—protections designed for cases like mine, in which I was harassed by someone I didn't have a personal relationship with—I was lucky to get a court-appointed lawyer, too. Most victims don't.

My harasser finally acquiesced to the protection order when my lawyer showed him that we knew the blog comments were coming from his computer—he had made a valiant attempt to obscure his comments, but he'd slipped up in a couple of instances, and we could prove the rape threats were his. When the judge approved the order, she instructed my harasser that he was not allowed to contact me in any way—not by email, Twitter, phone, blog comment, or by hiring a hot air balloon to float over my house with a message, she said. And he had to stay at least 100 feet away from me at all times. The restraining order would last one year.

Soon after the order expired, he sent an email to my new workplace. Every once in a while, he re- establishes contact. Last summer, he waded into the comments section of an article I wrote about sex website creator Cindy Gallop, to say, "I would not sacrifice the physiological pleasure of ejaculating inside the woman for a lesser psychological pleasure. . . . There is a reason it feels better to do it the right way and you don't see others in the ape world practicing this behavior." A few months later, he reached out via LinkedIn. ("Your stalker would like to add you to his professional network.") A few days before I received the threats in Palm Springs, he sent me a link via Twitter to a story he wrote about another woman who had been abused online. Occasionally, he sends his tweets directly my way—a little reminder that his "game" is back on.

It's been four years, but I still carry the case files with me. I record every tweet he sends me in a Word document, forward his emails to a dedicated account, then print them out to ensure I'll have them ready for police in analog form if he ever threatens me again (or worse). Whenever I have business travel to the city where he lives, I cart my old protection order along, even though the words are beginning to blur after a dozen photocopies. The stacks of paper are filed neatly in my apartment. My anxieties are harder to organize.

CRITICAL THINKING QUESTIONS

1. Describe what Caroline Criado-Perez was trying to do with British Currency. How were her efforts received online? How did she respond on Twitter? With the police? What was the ultimate outcome of her case—what happened to some of the men?
2. Amanda Hess writes that "gendered harassment—and the sheer volume of it—has severe implications for women's status on the Internet." What does the term "gendered harassment" mean? What are some of the implications that this type of harassment has on women in the field of technology and online reporting?
3. Provide an example from this article of when local police enforcement was unable to deal with online threats. Why does local law enforcement struggle to deal with these cases? Identify two changes in the law that you think would make local law enforcement better able to deal with online threats.
4. The journalist, Hess, was threatened by "headlessfemalepig" in a Tweet. Do you think this type of harassment is a common occurrence toward women who have technology related careers? Explain your point of view by providing evidence from the reading.

THE UNSAFETY NET: HOW SOCIAL MEDIA TURNED AGAINST WOMEN

by *Catherine Buni and Soraya Chemaly*

Catherine Buni is a writer and editor whose work has appeared in *The New York Times, Outside,* and *The Writer.* Her co-author, Soraya Chemaly, is a writer and media critic. Soraya Chemaly is a board member of the Women's Media Center.

In this 2015 article from *The Atlantic,* the authors explore the rampant sexism that exists on our social media sites. This problem is multi-faceted and complex. The users are posting sexist content. But why do they feel free to do so? The companies want to create safe spaces for people to gather online. But their best policies are overly complex and ineffective. Those who invest in social media websites don't want to be associated with hateful speech, but they often have no idea about what is actually happening on these sites. Social media is supposed to be your life, online—how did it get so ugly and violent for the women who use it?

• • • • • • • • • • • • • • •

In December 2012, an Icelandic woman named Thorlaug Agustsdottir discovered a Facebook group called "Men are better than women." One image she found there, Thorlaug wrote to us this summer in an email, "was of a young woman naked chained to pipes or an oven in what looked like a concrete basement, all bruised and bloody. She looked with a horrible broken look at whoever was taking the pic of her curled up naked." Thorlaug wrote an outraged post about it on her own Facebook page.

Before long, a user at "Men are better than women" posted an image of Thorlaug's face, altered to appear bloody and bruised. Under the image, someone commented, "Women are like grass, they need to be beaten/cut regularly." Another wrote: "You just need to be raped." Thorlaug reported the image and comments to Facebook and requested that the site remove them.

"We reviewed the photo you reported," came Facebook's auto reply, "but found it does not violate Facebook's Community Standards on hate speech, which includes posts or photos that attack a person based on their race, ethnicity, national origin, religion, sex, gender, sexual orientation, disability, or medical condition."

Instead, the Facebook screeners labeled the content "Controversial Humor." Thorlaug saw nothing funny about it. She worried the threats were real.

Some 50 other users sent their own requests on her behalf. All received the same reply. Eventually, on New Year's Eve, Thorlaug called the local press, and the story spread from there. Only then was the image removed.

In January 2013, *Wired* published a critical account of Facebook's response to these complaints. A company spokesman contacted the publication immediately to explain that Facebook screeners had mishandled the case, conceding that Thorlaug's photo "should have been taken down when it was reported to us." According to the spokesman, the company tries to address complaints about images on a case-by-case basis within 72 hours, but with millions of reports to review every day, "it's not easy to keep up with requests." The spokesman, anonymous to *Wired* readers, added, "We apologize for the mistake."

• • •

If, as the communications philosopher Marshall McLuhan famously said, television brought the brutality of war into people's living rooms, the Internet today is bringing violence against women out of it. Once largely hidden from view, this brutality is now being exposed in unprecedented ways. In the words of Anne Collier, co-director of ConnectSafely.org and co-chair of the Obama administration's Online Safety and Technology Working Group, "We are in the middle of a global free speech experiment." On the one hand, these online images and words are bringing awareness to a longstanding problem. On the other hand, the amplification of these ideas over social media networks is validating and spreading pathology.

We, the authors, have experienced both sides of the experiment firsthand. In 2012, Soraya, who had been reporting on gender and women's rights, noticed that more and more of her readers were contacting her to ask for media attention and help with online threats. Many sent graphic images, and some included detailed police reports that had gone nowhere. A few sent videos of rapes in progress. When Soraya wrote about these topics, she received threats online. Catherine, meanwhile, received warnings to back up while reporting on the cover-up of a sexual assault.

All of this raised a series of troubling questions: Who's proliferating this violent content? Who's controlling its dissemination? *Should* someone be? In theory, social media companies are neutral platforms where users generate content and report content as equals. But, as in the physical world, some users are more equal than others. In other words, social media is more symptom than disease: A 2013 report from the World Health Organization called violence against women "a global health problem of epidemic proportion," from domestic abuse, stalking, and street harassment to sex trafficking, rape, and murder. This epidemic is thriving in the petri dish of social media.

While some of the aggression against women online occurs between people who know one another, and is unquestionably illegal, most of it happens between strangers. Earlier this year, *Pacific Standard* published a long story by Amanda Hess about an online stalker who set up a Twitter account specifically to send her death threats.

Across websites and social media platforms, everyday sexist comments exist along a spectrum that also includes illicit sexual surveillance, "creepshots," extortion, doxxing, stalking, malicious impersonation, threats, and rape videos and photographs. The explosive use of the Internet to conduct human trafficking also has a place on this spectrum, given that three-quarters of trafficked people are girls and women.

A report, "Misogyny on Twitter," released by the research and policy organization Demos this June, found more than 6 million instances of the word "slut" or "whore" used in English on Twitter between December 26, 2013, and February 9, 2014. (The words "bitch" and "cunt" were not measured.) An estimated 20 percent of the misogyny study Tweets appeared, to researchers, to be threatening. An example: "*@XXX @XXX You stupid ugly fucking slut I'll go to your flat and cut your fucking head off you inbred whore.*"

A second Demos study showed that while male celebrities, female journalists, and male politicians face the highest likelihood of online hostility, women are significantly more likely to be targeted specifically because of their gender, and men are overwhelmingly those doing the harassing. For women of color, or members of the LGBT community, the harassment is amplified. "In my five years on Twitter, I've been called 'nigger' so many times that it barely registers as an insult anymore," explains attorney and legal analyst Imani Gandy. "Let's just say that my 'nigger cunt' cup runneth over."

At this summer's VidCon, an annual nationwide convention held in Southern California, women vloggers shared an astonishing number of examples. The violent threats posted beneath YouTube videos, they observed, are pushing women off of this and other platforms in disproportionate numbers. When Anita Sarkeesian launched a Kickstarter to help fund a feminist video series called *Tropes vs. Women*, she became the focus of a massive and violently misogynistic cybermob. Among the many forms of harassment she endured was a game where thousands of players "won" by virtually bludgeoning her face. In late August, she contacted the police and had to leave her home after she received a series of serious violent online threats.

Danielle Keats Citron, law professor at the University of Maryland and author of the recently released book *Hate Crimes in Cyberspace,* explained, "Time and time again, these women have no idea often who it is attacking them. A cybermob jumps on board, and one can imagine that the only thing the attackers know about the victim is that she's female." Looking at 1,606 cases of "revenge porn," where explicit photographs are distributed without consent, Citron found that 90 percent of targets were women. Another study she cited found that 70 percent of female gamers chose to play as male characters rather than contend with sexual harassment.

This type of harassment also fills the comment sections of popular websites. In August, employees of the largely female-staffed website Jezebel published an open letter to the site's parent company, Gawker, detailing the professional, physical, and emotional costs of having to look at the pornographic GIFs maliciously populating the site's comments sections everyday. "It's like playing whack-a-mole with a sociopathic Hydra," they wrote, insisting that Gawker develop tools for blocking and tracking IP addresses. They added, "It's impacting our ability to do our jobs."

For some, the costs are higher. In 2010, 12-year-old Amanda Todd bared her chest while chatting online with a person who'd assured her that he was a boy, but was in fact a grown man with a history of pedophilia. For the next two years, Amanda and her mother, Carol Todd, were unable to stop anonymous users from posting that image on sexually explicit pages. A Facebook page, labeled "Controversial Humor," used Amanda's name and image—and the names and images of other girls—without consent. In October 2012, Amanda committed suicide, posting a YouTube video that explained her harassment and her decision. In April 2014, Dutch officials announced that they had arrested a 35-year-old man suspected to have used the Internet to extort dozens of girls, including Amanda, in Canada, the United Kingdom, and the United States. The suspect now faces charges of child pornography, extortion, criminal harassment, and Internet luring.

Almost immediately after Amanda shared her original image, altered versions appeared on pages, and videos proliferated. One of the pages was filled with pictures of naked pre-pubescent girls, encouraging them to drink bleach and die. While she appreciates the many online tributes honoring her daughter, Carol Todd is haunted by "suicide humor" and pornographic content now forever linked to her daughter's image. There are web pages dedicated to what is now called "Todding." One of them features a photograph of a young woman hanging.

Meanwhile, extortion of other victims continues. In an increasing number of countries, rapists are now filming their rapes on cell phones so they can blackmail victims out of reporting the crimes. In August, after a 16-year-old Indian girl was gang-raped, she explained, "I was afraid. While I was being raped, another man pointed a gun and recorded me with his cellphone camera. He said he will upload the film on the Net if I tell my family or the police."

In Pakistan, the group Bytes for All—an organization that previously sued the government for censoring YouTube videos—released a study showing that social media and mobile tech are causing real harm to women in the country. Gul Bukhari, the report's author, told Reuters, "These technologies are helping to increase violence against women, not just mirroring it."

In June 2014, a 16-year-old girl named Jada was drugged and raped at a party in Texas. Partygoers posted a photo of her lying unconscious, one leg bent back. Soon, other Internet users had turned it into a meme, mocking her pose and using the hashtag #jadapose. Kasari Govender, executive director of the Vancouver-based West Coast Legal Education and Action Fund (LEAF), calls this kind of behavior "cybermisogyny." "Cyberbullying," she says, "has become this term that's often thrown around with little understanding. We think it's important to name the forces that are motivating this in order to figure out how to address it."

In an unusually bold act, Jada responded by speaking publicly about her rape and the online abuse that followed. Supporters soon took to the Internet in her defense. "There's no point in hiding," she told a television reporter. "Everybody has already seen my face and my body, but that's not what I am and who I am. I'm just angry."

• • •

After Facebook removed Thorlaug's altered image and the rape threats, she felt relieved, but she was angry too. "These errors are going to manifest again," she told *Wired*, "if there isn't clear enough policy."

Yet, at the time of Thorlaug's report, Facebook *did* have a clear policy. Its detailed Community Standards for speech, often considered the industry's gold standard, were bolstered by reporting tools that allowed users to report offensive content, and Thorlaug had used these tools as instructed. But serious errors were still manifesting regularly.

Not long after Thorlaug's struggle to remove her image, a Facebook user posted a video documenting the gang rape of a woman by the side of a road in Malaysia. The six minutes of graphic footage were live for more than three weeks, during which Facebook moderators declined repeated requests for removal. It had been viewed hundreds of times before a reader of Soraya's forwarded the video to her with a request for help. We notified a contact on Facebook's Safety Advisory Board, and only then was the video taken offline.

Around the same time, another Icelandic woman, Hildur Lilliendahl Viggósdóttir, decided to draw attention to similar problems by creating a page called "Men who hate women," where she reposted examples of misogyny she found elsewhere on Facebook. Her page was suspended four times—not because of its offensive content, but because she was reposting images without written permission. Meanwhile, the original postings—graphically depicting rape and glorifying the physical abuse of women—remained on Facebook. As activists had been noting for years, pages like these were allowed by Facebook to remain under the category of "humor." Other humorous pages live at the time had names like "I kill bitches like you," "Domestic Violence: Don't Make Me Tell You Twice," "I Love the Rape Van," and "Raping Babies Because You're Fucking Fearless."

• • •

Jillian C. York, director for international freedom of expression at the Electronic Frontier Foundation, is one of many civil libertarians who believe Facebook and other social media platforms should not screen this, or any, content at all. "It of course must be noted that the company—like any company—is well within its rights to regulate speech as it sees fit," she wrote in a May 2013 piece in *Slate* in response to growing activism. "The question is not *can* Facebook censor speech, but rather, *should it*?" She argues that censoring any content "sets a dangerous precedent for special interest groups looking to bring their pet issue to the attention of Facebook's censors."

When the problem involves half the world's population, it's difficult to classify it as a "pet issue." What's more, there are free speech issues on both sides of the regulated content equation. "We have the expressive interests of the harassers to threaten, to post photos, to spread defamation, rape threats, lies on the one hand," explains Citron. "And on the other hand you have the free speech interests, among others, of the victims, who are silenced and are driven offline."

These loss-of-speech issues tend to draw less attention and sympathy than free speech rights. However, as Citron points out, sexual hostility has already been identified as a source of real harm: Title VII demands that employers regulate such hostility in the workplace. These policies exist, Citron says, because sexual hostility "is understood as conduct interfering with life opportunities."

For online harassers, this is often an overt goal: to silence female community members, whether through sexual slurs or outright threats. It's little surprise that the Internet has become a powerful tool in intimate partner violence: A 2012 survey conducted by the National Network to End Domestic Violence (NNEDV) found that 89 percent of local domestic violence programs reported victims who were experiencing technology-enabled abuse, often across multiple platforms.

For their part, social media companies often express commitment to user safety, but downplay their influence on the broader culture. Administrators repeatedly explain that their companies, while very concerned with protecting users, are not in the business of policing free speech. As Twitter co-founder Biz Stone phrased it in a post titled "Tweets Must Flow," "We strive not to remove Tweets on the basis of their content." The company's guidelines encourage readers to unfollow the offensive party and "express your feelings [to a trusted friend] so you can move on."

None of this was of much help to Caroline Criado-Perez, a British journalist and feminist who helped get a picture of Jane Austen on the £10 banknote. The day Bank of England made the announcement, Criado-Perez began receiving more than 50 violent threats per hour on Twitter. "The immediate impact was that I couldn't eat or sleep," she told *The Guardian* in 2013. She asked Twitter to find some way to stop the threats, but at the time the company offered no mechanism for reporting abuse. Since then, the company has released a reporting button, but its usefulness is extremely limited: It requires that every tweet be reported separately, a cumbersome process that gives the user no way of explaining that she is a target of ongoing harassment. (The system currently provides no field for comments.)

And yet companies like Facebook, Twitter, and YouTube do moderate content and make quasi-governmental decisions regarding speech. Some content moderation is related to legal obligations, as in the case of child pornography, but a great deal more is a matter of cultural interpretation. Companies have disclosed that governments rely on them to implement censorship requests—earlier this year, for example, Twitter blocked tweets and accounts deemed "blasphemous" by the Pakistani government. (In response to these government incursions, a coalition of academics, legal scholars, corporations, non-profit organizations, and schools came together in 2008 to form the Global Network Initiative, a non-governmental organization dedicated to privacy and free expression.)

When it comes to copyright and intellectual property interests, companies are highly responsive, as Hildur's "Men who hate women" experience highlighted. But, says Jan Moolman, who coordinates the Association of Progressive Communications's women's rights division, "'garden variety' violence against women—clearly human rights violations—frequently get a lukewarm response until it becomes an issue of bad press."

For that reason, when social media companies fail to respond to complaints and requests, victims of online harassment frequently turn to individuals who can publicize their cases. Trista Hendren, an Oregon-based blogger, became an advocate for other women after readers from Iceland, Egypt, Australia, India, Lebanon, and the UK began asking her to write about their experiences. "I was overwhelmed," she told us. In December 2012, Hendren and several collaborators created a Facebook page called RapeBook where users could flag and report offensive content that the company had refused to take down.

By April 2013, people were using RapeBook to post pictures of women and pre-pubescent girls being raped or beaten. Some days, Hendren received more than 500 anonymous, explicitly violent comments—"I will skull-fuck your children," for instance. Facebook users tracked down and posted her address, her children's names, and her phone number and started to call her.

By that time, Hendren had abandoned any hope that using Facebook's reporting mechanisms could help her. She was able, however, to work directly with a Facebook moderator to address the threats and criminal content. She found that the company sincerely wanted to help. Their representatives discussed the posts with her on a case-by-case basis, but more violent and threatening posts kept coming, and much of the content she considered graphic and abusive was allowed to remain.

Eventually, Hendren told us, she and Facebook became locked in disagreement over what constituted "safety" and "hate" on the site. Facebook's people, she said, told her they didn't consider the threats to her and her family credible or legitimate. Hendren, however, was concerned enough to contact the police and the FBI. The FBI started an investigation; meanwhile Hendren, physically and emotionally spent, suspended her Facebook account. "I was the sickest I have ever been," she said. "It was really disgusting work. We just began to think, 'Why are we devoting all our efforts on a volunteer basis to do work that Facebook—with billions of dollars—should be taking care of?'"

Hendren contacted Soraya, who continued to press Facebook directly. At the same time, Soraya and Laura Bates, founder of the Everyday Sexism Project, also began comparing notes on what readers were sending them. Bates was struck by surprising ad placements. At the time, a photo captioned "The bitch didn't know when to shut up" appeared alongside ads for Dove and iTunes. "Domestic Violence: Don't Make Me Tell You Twice"—a page filled with photos of women beaten, bruised, and bleeding—was populated by ads for Facebook's COO Sheryl Sandberg's new bestselling book, *Lean In: Women, Work, and the Will to Lead.*

In early May, Bates decided to tweet at one of these companies. "Hi @Finnair here's your ad on another domestic violence page—will you stop advertising with Facebook?" FinnAir responded immediately: "It is totally against our values and policies. Thanks @r2ph! @everydaysexism. Could you send us the URL please so that we can take action?"

Soraya, Bates, and Jaclyn Friedman, the executive director of Women, Action, and Media, a media justice advocacy group, joined forces and launched a social media campaign designed to attract advertisers' attention. The ultimate goal was to press Facebook to recognize explicit violence against women as a violation of its own prohibitions against hate speech, graphic violence, and harassment. Within a day of beginning the campaign, 160 organizations and corporations had co-signed a public letter, and in less than a week, more than 60,000 tweets were shared using the campaign's #FBrape hashtag. Nissan was the first company to pull its advertising dollars from Facebook altogether. More than 15 others soon followed. The letter emphasized that Facebook's refusal to take down content that glorified and trivialized graphic rape and domestic violence was actually hampering free expression—it was "marginaliz[ing] girls and women, sidelin[ing] our experiences and concerns, and contribut[ing] to violence against us."

On May 28, Facebook issued a public response:

> In recent days, it has become clear that our systems to identify and remove hate speech have failed to work as effectively as we would like . . . We have been working over the past several months to improve our systems to respond to reports of violations, but the guidelines used by these systems have failed to capture all the content that violates our standards. We need to do better—and we will.

• • •

For all its shortcomings, Facebook is doing more than most companies to address online aggression against women. Cindy Southworth, vice president of development and innovation at the National Network to End Domestic Violence, has served on Facebook's Safety Advisory Board since 2010. "[My organization] gets calls from Google, Twitter, Microsoft—but Facebook and Airbnb are the only ones who've put us on an advisory board," she told us.

This is huge progress, she says. By inviting experts who understand the roots of violence against women and children and are familiar with emerging strategies to prevent it, tech is more likely to innovate improvements. The once profusely applied "Controversial Humor" label in Facebook is no longer in use. The company now officially recognizes gender-based hate as a legitimate concern, and its representatives continue to work closely with advocates like Southworth and the coalition that formed during the #FBRape campaign. There are ongoing efforts to improve user safety and identify content that is threatening, harassing, hateful, or discriminatory.

Southworth calls the company's representatives "thoughtful, passionate, concerned, and straddling the line between free speech and safety." But, sometimes, progress feels slow. "The teams who handle these cases are just swamped," she explained.

When Emily Bazelon, author of a book and a March 2013 *Atlantic* story about Internet bullies, visited Facebook's headquarters, the young men she saw working as moderators were spending roughly 30 seconds assessing each reported post, millions of reports a week. Outsourced speech moderation has become a booming industry. Like Facebook's own moderation process, the operations of these companies are opaque by design.

TaskUs, with bases in Santa Monica, California, and several locations in the Philippines, provides moderation for iPhone and Android apps such as Whisper, Secret, and Yik Yak. The company advertises "a bulletproof system to ensure that no one—not a single person—is hurt physically or mentally by the actions of another user in an anonymous app community." Yet TaskUs doesn't disclose its standards of speech, its hiring practices, its training process, or working conditions. "Unfortunately," we were told when we inquired, "we're bound by confidentiality from discussing details of process including hiring and training. We can speak generally about how we handle the moderation process but our clients are not comfortable with us exposing anything proprietary (and they consider the moderation and training processes proprietary)."

While private companies protect their practices, nonprofits like The Internet Watch Foundation don't. IWF, based in Cambridge, England, screens images of child sexual abuse for Facebook, Google, and Virgin Media, among others. IWF staff watch, analyze, categorize, and report abusive images—70 percent of them involve children under 10. Data collected by police across England and Wales in 2012 suggest that 150 million child pornography images were in distribution in the UK alone that year. By comparison, in 1995, when the reach of the Internet was far narrower, only about 7,000 child pornography images were in online circulation.

IWF's analysts see everything, said Heidi Kempster, IWF's director of business affairs, during a conversation this summer. Kempster was candid about IWF's business practices: The group screens rigorously during its hiring processes, conducting psychological interviews that establish everything from family history and relationship-building skills to views on pornography. The company also requires monthly individual counseling and quarterly group counseling, as well as expert consultation—with police, attorneys, or judges—and breaks as needed. IWF analysts, said Kempster, "look at shocking and violent images all day every day. There are days that are tough. They have to take time out."

Over the past two years, Facebook has taken steps to improve its reporting system. Matt Steinfeld, a spokesperson for Facebook, spoke to us about Facebook's Compassion Research, a bullying prevention project developed in conjunction with Yale's Center for Emotional Intelligence. The tools developed through this program have more than tripled the rate at which users send a message directly to the person who posted the offensive material, asking for the removal of photos or comments. Now, in 85 percent of those requests, the person who posted the photo takes the photo down or sends a reply.

Still, the company hasn't yet come up with a reliable approach for dealing with the other 15 percent of cases. "We've always recognized that there is going to be content that won't be moderated through compassion tools," said Steinfeld. "We're not going to tell the people who is right and who is wrong."

The opacity maintained around moderation means sites are not obligated to honor the reports they receive and any decision to remove content can be legitimized, as Kate Crawford of Microsoft Research and MIT, and Tarleton Gillespie at Cornell University, observed in an August study on social media reporting tools. In other words, "given that flags remain open to interpretation and can be gamed, they can also be explained away when the site prefers to ignore them."

In conversations this summer, Matt Steinfeld, a spokesperson for Facebook, maintained that his own company's standards are clearly defined. "There's this misconception that there's an algorithm," he said during one conversation in July, "but there's a human who's given objective standards" for responding to individual complaints.

When we spoke with Microsoft's Crawford about her research, she described the limitations of these seemingly objective standards. "The flag is being asked to do too much," she said. "It's a fundamentally narrow mechanism: the technical version of 'I object.' And while some platforms claim that flags are 'objective' data about which content to remove, they are part of a profoundly human decision-making process about what constitutes appropriate speech in the public domain."

Researchers and industry experts are beginning to consider the effects of that context. Ninety percent of tech employees are men. At the most senior levels, that number goes up to 96 percent. Eight-nine percent of startup leadership teams are all male. Google recently announced that it is implementing programs to, in the words of a *New York Times* report, "fight deep-set cultural biases and an insidious frat-house attitude that pervades the tech business." A computer simulation used by the company illustrated how an industry-wide 1-percent bias against women in performance evaluations might have led to the significant absence of women in senior positions.

Many Silicon Valley leaders—such as Twitter co-founder Jack Dorsey, who recently acknowledged a "leadership crisis" among women in tech—have been investing in programs they hope will encourage girls to enter, and remain, in STEM fields. However, the fact that companies better understand the need to encourage girls and women doesn't necessarily mean they're welcomed. Despite the presence of visible, active and prominent women in the industry, according to one recent study, 56 percent of the women who do enter tech leave the industry, frequently stating that they were pushed out by sexism. This attrition rate is twice that of their male peers. As Vivek Wadha, author of *Innovating Women,* recently pointed out, only 2.7 percent of 6,517 companies that received venture funding from 2011 to 2013 had female chief executives.

It's not hard to imagine how unconscious biases might affect systems architecture, including the ways companies handle moderation requests. It is notable that Ello, a new ad-free social network, launched without private profiles, a block button, or a reporting mechanism. (After much criticism, those features were added.) Its designers appear to be seven young white men whose features, appearing on the beta website, are obscured by smiley faces. The Ello site reads, "We reserve the right to enforce or not to enforce these rules in whatever way we see fit, at our sole discretion. According to our lawyer, we should also tell you that Ello's rules and policies do not create a duty or contractual obligation for us to act in any particular manner. And we reserve the right to change these rules at any time. So please play nice, be respectful, and have fun."

• • •

Sandy Garossino, a former British Columbia prosecutor who has worked on dozens of cases of cyber extortion and online child pornography, is concerned about the implications of today's industry practices and policies, not only for children but for adults. "Right now, the slightest calibrations are going to have a profound effect on the future," she told us.

In late June, the U.S. Supreme Court announced it would hear the case of Anthony Elonis, a man with five charges of sexual harassment, who was imprisoned after threatening to kill his wife on Facebook. Elonis insists that his Facebook posts were not real threats but protected speech. Tara Elonis, his estranged wife—possibly aware that most female murder victims are killed by intimate partners—said that there was nothing unthreatening about her husband's Facebook posts and that they forced her to take necessary, costly precautions. "If I only knew then what I know now," read one, "I would have smothered your ass with a pillow, dumped your body in the back seat, dropped you off in Toad Creek, and made it look like a rape and murder."

"Although threats are traditional categories of excluded speech," explains First Amendment legal scholar Susan Williams, "there is very little take on actually defining what a true threat is in constitutional terms." This lack of definition is what plagues social media companies seeking scalable solutions for moderating content and keeping users safe. Following legal precedent they, too, avoid defining what makes a comment a threat and instead hone in on whether or not there's one specific target. However, as Williams explains, "threats can be one of those environmental factors that reduce the autonomy of whole classes of persons."

In a recent high-profile case, intimate photographs of 100 celebrities—all of whom were women—were stolen and shared without consent. Google is now facing the possibility of a $100 million lawsuit, brought by over a dozen of the women whose privacy was violated, for refusing to remove the stolen photographs. In a letter dated October 1, the women's attorneys wrote that "Google has exhibited the lowest standards of ethical business conduct, and has acted dishonorably by perpetrating unlawful activity that exemplifies an utter lack of respect for women and privacy. Google's 'Don't be evil' motto is a sham."

In response, Google removed tens of thousands of the hacked celebrity photographs. Meanwhile, social media companies have been far less responsive to similar demands from ordinary citizens. "Hey @google, what about my photos?" tweeted revenge porn victim Holly Jacobs in the aftermath of the celebrity scandal. It remains to be seen how the courts will rule in the case of Meryam Ali, a Houston woman who filed a $123 million lawsuit against Facebook for failing to remove a false profile that showed her face superimposed on pornographic images. As writer Roxanne Gay poignantly observed in *The Guardian*, "What these people are doing is reminding women that, no matter who they are, they are still women. They are forever vulnerable."

In late August, Drew Curtis, founder of the content aggregator FARK, announced that the company had added "misogyny" to its moderation guidelines. FARK no longer allows rape jokes or threats. It also prohibited posts that call groups of women "whores" or "sluts," or suggest that a woman who suffered a crime is somehow asking for it. In a note to readers, Curtis wrote, "This represents enough of a departure from pretty much how every other large Internet community operates that I figure an announcement is necessary." Responding in *Slate*, Amanda Hess praised FARK's new policy but also pointed out its limitations: Just underneath his announcement, users posted dozens of comments about rape, whores, and "boobies."

Announcements like FARK's are important, particularly for catalyzing discussion, but policy changes alone can't solve such a complex problem. Kate Crawford of MIT and Microsoft urges tech innovators to think about solutions "as pluralistically as possible." She'd like to see more platforms develop systems that leave traces of when and why content has been removed or modified—an approach in play at Wikipedia, for instance.

Other experts agree that companies have a responsibility to provide greater transparency. They also need to dedicate more staff to understanding and performing moderation. They need to attract and retain female engineers, programmers, and managers. They need to invite experts in violence prevention to their tables. Whether online or off, there seems to be an increasing consensus, from the NFL to the White House, that misogyny requires a broad societal response. As President Obama put it in mid-September, "It is on all of us to reject the quiet tolerance of sexual assault and to refuse to accept what's unacceptable."

Soon after Hess's piece appeared on *Slate,* a reader posted it on a FARK message board and users filled the comment thread mocking the policy and discussing the best way to slip a thermometer into Hess. So far, that thread has not been removed. As Hess herself put it, "Policing misogyny is fabulous in theory. In practice, it's a bitch."

CRITICAL THINKING QUESTIONS

1. The authors reference Marshall McLuhan who said that television brought the brutality out of war and into the living room. What do the authors claim is happening with women's violence and the internet? Describe three specific examples of this from the article, and make sure to identify the wrongdoing. Why does Anne Collier think this is both a good and a bad thing?

2. Summarize Jillian York's argument. Why do the authors disagree with her on the point of it being a "pet issue"? Do you agree with Jillian York? Why or why not? Whose responsibility do you think it is to ensure that social networks are safe spaces for all?
3. On May 28th, 2014, Facebook released a statement. Summarize that statement. What do the authors argue *caused* that statement? Why do you think those pressures might have been effective when the pressures of many other people, like Thorlaug Agustsdottir, have not?
4. Who is Jake Dorsey? What is the "leadership crisis" he identifies in the article? Use two statistics from the article to prove that it is a crisis. What are three ways this crisis might affect the problems presented in the article?

HOW TO STOP THE BULLIES

by Emily Bazelon

Emily Bazelon is a senior editor for *Slate*. Her articles range from the education system to cyber bullying. Bazelon is a Truman Capote fellow at Yale Law School.

In this 2013 article from the *Atlantic*, Emily Bazelon struggles with what it means to grow up online. Bullying has always been a part of middle school—but with its move online, it becomes a larger threat that reaches more people more often. Her article explores a few ways people are working to try and limit online bullying. Why is online bullying a unique and especially harmful new rite of passage for kids?

• • • • • • • • • • • • • • •

The angst and ire of teenagers is finding new, sometimes dangerous expression online—precipitating threats, fights, and a scourge of harrassment that parents and schools feel powerless to stop. The inside story of how experts at Facebook, computer scientists at MIT, and even members of the hacker collective Anonymous are hunting for solutions to an increasingly tricky problem.

In the annals of middle-school mischief, the Facebook page Let's Start Drama deserves an entry. The creator of the page—no one knew her name, but everyone was sure she was a girl—had a diabolical knack for sowing conflict among students at Woodrow Wilson Middle School in Middletown, Connecticut. "Drama Queen," as I came to think of her in the months I spent reporting at the school to write a book about bullying, knew exactly how to use the Internet to rile her audience. She hovered over them in cyberspace like a bad fairy, with the power to needle kids into ending friendships and starting feuds and fistfights.

In contrast with some other social networks, like Twitter, Facebook requires its users to sign up with their real names. Drama Queen easily got around this rule, however, by setting up Let's Start Drama with a specially created e-mail address that didn't reveal her identity. Wrapped in her cloak of anonymity, she was free to pass along cruel gossip without personal consequences. She started by posting a few idle rumors, and when that gained her followers, she asked them to send her private messages relaying more gossip, promising not to disclose the source. Which girl had just lost her virginity? Which boy had asked a girl to sext him a nude photo? As Drama Queen posted the tantalizing tidbits she gathered, more kids signed up to follow her exploits—a real-life version of *Gossip Girl*. She soon had an audience of 500, many drawn from Woodrow Wilson's 750 students, plus a smattering from the local high school and a nearby Catholic school.

Students didn't just message rumors to Drama Queen; they also commented in droves on her posts, from their own real Facebook accounts, or from other fake ones. As one kid wrote about Drama Queen on the Let's Start Drama page, "She just starts mad shit and most of the time so do the ppl who comment."

Drama Queen was particularly ingenious at pitting kids against each other in contests of her own creation. She regularly posted photographs of two girls side by side, with the caption

"WHOS PRETTIERRR?!" Below the pictures, commenters would heckle and vote. One such contest drew 109 comments over three days. When it became clear which contestant was losing, that girl wrote that she didn't care: "nt even tryinqq to b funny or smart." The rival who beat her answered, "juss mad you losss ok ppl voted me ! If you really loooked better they wouldve said you but THEY DIDNT sooo sucks for you." This exchange nearly led to blows outside of school, other students told me. And they said a fight *did* break out between two boys who were featured on Let's Start Drama, in dueling photos, above the caption "Who would win in a fight?" They reportedly ended up pummeling each other off school grounds one day after classes.

Melissa Robinson, who was a social worker for the Middletown Youth Services Bureau, quickly got wind of Let's Start Drama because, she says, "it was causing tons of conflict." Robinson worked out of an office at Woodrow Wilson with Justin Carbonella, the bureau's director, trying to fill gaps in city services to help students stay out of trouble. Their connecting suite of small rooms served as a kind of oasis at the school: the two adults didn't work for the principal, so they could arbitrate conflict without the threat of official discipline. I often saw kids stop by just to talk, and they had a lot to say about the aggression on Let's Start Drama and the way it was spilling over into real life. "We'd go on Facebook to look at the page, and it was pretty egregious," Carbonella told me. Surfing around on Facebook, they found more anonymous voting pages, with names like Middletown Hos, Middletown Trash Talk, and Middletown Too Real. Let's Start Drama had the largest audience, but it had spawned about two dozen imitators.

Carbonella figured that all of these pages had to be breaking Facebook's rules, and he was right. The site has built its brand by holding users to a relatively high standard of decency. "You will not bully, intimidate, or harass any user," Facebook requires people to pledge when they sign up. Users also agree not to fake their identities or to post content that is hateful or pornographic, or that contains nudity or graphic violence. In other words, Facebook does not style itself as the public square, where people can say anything they want, short of libel or slander. It's much more like a mall, where private security guards can throw you out.

Carbonella followed Facebook's procedure for filing a report, clicking through the screens that allow you to complain to the site about content that you think violates a rule. He clicked the bubbles to report bullying and fake identity. And then he waited. And waited. "It felt like putting a note in a bottle and throwing it into the ocean," Carbonella said. "There was no way to know if anyone was out there on the other end. For me, this wasn't a situation where I knew which student was involved and could easily give it to a school guidance counselor. It was completely anonymous, so we really needed Facebook to intervene." But, to Carbonella's frustration, Let's Start Drama stayed up. He filed another report. Like the first one, it seemed to sink to the bottom of the ocean.

Facebook, of course, is the giant among social networks, with more than 1 billion users worldwide. In 2011, *Consumer Reports* published the results of a survey showing that 20 million users were American kids under the age of 18; in an update the next year, it estimated that 5.6 million were under 13, the eligible age for an account. As a 2011 report from the Pew Internet and American Life Project put it, "Facebook dominates teen social media usage." Ninety-three percent of kids who use social-networking sites have a Facebook account. (Teens and preteens are also signing up in increasing numbers for Twitter—Pew found that 16 percent of 12-to-17-year-olds say they use the site, double the rate from two years earlier.)

Social networking has plenty of upside for kids: it allows them to pursue quirky interests and connect with people they'd have no way of finding otherwise. An online community can be a lifeline if, say, you're a gender-bending 15-year-old in rural Idaho or, for that matter, rural New York. But as Let's Start Drama illustrates, there's lots of ugliness, too. The 2011 Pew report found that 15 percent of social-media users between the ages of 12 and 17 said they'd been harassed online in the previous year. In 2012, *Consumer Reports* estimated that 800,000 minors on Facebook had been bullied or harassed in the previous year. (Facebook questions the methodology of the magazine's survey; however, the company declined to provide specifics.) In the early days of the Internet, the primary danger to kids seemed to be from predatory adults. But it turns out that the perils adults pose, although they can be devastating, are rare. The far more common problem kids face when they go online comes from other kids: the hum of low-grade hostility, punctuated by truly damaging explosions, that is called cyberbullying.

What can be done about this online cruelty and combat? As parents try, and sometimes fail, to keep track of their kids online, and turn to schools for help, youth advocates like Robinson and Carbonella have begun asking how much responsibility falls on social-networking sites to enforce their own rules against bullying and harassment. What *does* happen when you file a report with Facebook? And rather than asking the site to delete cruel posts or pages one by one, is there a better strategy, one that stops cyberbullying before it starts? Those questions led me to the Silicon Valley headquarters of Facebook, then to a lab at MIT, and finally (and improbably, I know) to the hacker group Anonymous.

The people at Facebook who decide how to wield the site's power when users complain about content belong to its User Operations teams. The summer after my trips to Woodrow Wilson, I traveled to the company's headquarters and found Dave Willner, the 27-year-old manager of content policy, waiting for me among a cluster of couches, ready to show me the Hate and Harassment Team in action. Its members, who favor sneakers and baseball caps, scroll through the never-ending stream of reports about bullying, harassment, and hate speech. (Other groups that handle reports include the Safety Team, which patrols for suicidal content, child exploitation, and underage users; and the Authenticity Team, which looks into complaints of fake accounts.) Willner was wearing flipflops, and I liked his blunt, clipped way of speaking. "Bullying is hard," he told me. "It's slippery to define, and it's even harder when it's writing instead of speech. Tone of voice disappears." He gave me an example from a recent report complaining about a status update that said "He got her pregnant." Who was it about? What had the poster intended to communicate? Looking at the words on the screen, Willner had no way to tell.

In an attempt to impose order on a frustratingly subjective universe, User Operations has developed one rule of thumb: if you complain to Facebook that you are being harassed or bullied, the site takes your word for it. "If the content is about you, and you're not famous, we don't try to decide whether it's actually mean," Willner said. "We just take it down."

All other complaints, however, are treated as "third-party reports" that the teams have to do their best to referee. These include reports from parents saying their children are being bullied, or from advocates like Justin Carbonella.

To demonstrate how the harassment team members do their jobs, Willner introduced me to an affable young guy named Nick Sullivan, who had on his desk a sword-carrying Grim Reaper figurine. Sullivan opened the program that he uses for sorting and resolving reports, which is known as the Common Review Tool (a precursor to the tool had a better name: the Wall of Shame).

Sullivan cycled through the complaints with striking speed, deciding with very little deliberation which posts and pictures came down, which stayed up, and what other action, if any, to take. I asked him whether he would ever spend, say, 10 minutes on a particularly vexing report, and Willner raised his eyebrows. "We optimize for half a second," he said. "Your average decision time is a second or two, so 30 seconds would be a really long time." (A Facebook spokesperson said later that the User Operations teams use a process optimized for accuracy, not speed.) That reminded me of Let's Start Drama. Six months after Carbonella sent his reports, the page was still up. I asked why. It hadn't been set up with the user's real name, so wasn't it clearly in violation of Facebook's rules?

After a quick search by Sullivan, the blurry photos I'd seen many times at the top of the Let's Start Drama page appeared on the screen. Sullivan scrolled through some recent "Who's hotter?" comparisons and clicked on the behind-the-scenes history of the page, which the Common Review Tool allowed him to call up. A window opened on the right side of the screen, showing that multiple reports had been made. Sullivan checked to see whether the reports had failed to indicate that Let's Start Drama was administered by a fake user profile. But that wasn't the problem: the bubbles had been clicked correctly. Yet next to this history was a note indicating that future reports about the content would be ignored.

We sat and stared at the screen.

Willner broke the silence. "Someone made a mistake," he said. "This profile should have been disabled." He leaned in and peered at the screen. "Actually, two different reps made the same mistake, two different times."

There was another long pause. Sullivan clicked on Let's Start Drama to delete it.

With millions of reports a week, most processed in seconds—and with 2.5 billion pieces of content posted daily—no wonder complaints like Carbonella's fall through the cracks. A Facebook spokesperson said that the site has been working on solutions to handle the volume of reports, while hiring "thousands of people" (though the company wouldn't discuss the specific roles of these employees) and building tools to address misbehavior in other ways.

One idea is to improve the reporting process for users who spot content they don't like. During my visit, I met with the engineer Arturo Bejar, who'd designed new flows, or sets of responses users get as they file a report. The idea behind this "social reporting" tool was to lay out a path for users to find help in the real world, encouraging them to reach out to people they know and trust—people who might understand the context of a negative post. "Our goal should be to help people solve the underlying problem in the offline world," Bejar said. "Sure, we can take content down and warn the bully, but probably the most important thing is for the target to get the support they need."

After my visit, Bejar started working with social scientists at Berkeley and Yale to further refine these response flows, giving kids new ways to assess and communicate their emotions. The researchers, who include Marc Brackett and Robin Stern of Yale, talked to focus groups of 13- and 14-year-olds and created scripted responses that first push kids to identify the type and intensity of the emotion they're feeling, and then offer follow-up remedies depending on their answers. In January, during a presentation on the latest version of this tool, Stern explained that some of those follow-ups simply encourage reaching out to the person posting the objectionable material—who typically takes down the posts or photos if asked.

Dave Willner told me that Facebook did not yet, however, have an algorithm that could determine at the outset whether a post was meant to harass and disturb— and could perhaps head it off. This is hard. As Willner pointed out, context is everything when it comes to bullying, and context is maddeningly tricky and subjective.

One man looking to create such a tool—one that catches troublesome material before it gets posted—is Henry Lieberman, a computer scientist whose background is in artificial intelligence. In November, I took a trip to Boston to meet him at his office in MIT's Media Lab. Lieberman looked like an older version of the Facebook employees: he was wearing sneakers and a baseball cap over longish gray curls. A couple years ago, a rash of news stories about bullying made him think back to his own misery in middle school, when he was a "fat kid with the nickname Hank the Tank." (This is hard to imagine now, given Lieberman's lean frame, but I took his word for it.) As a computer guy, he wondered whether cyberbullying would wreck social networking for teenagers in the way spam once threatened to kill e-mail—through sheer overwhelming volume. He looked at the frustrating, sometimes fruitless process for logging complaints, and he could see why even tech-savvy adults like Carbonella would feel at a loss. He was also not impressed by the generic advice often doled out to young victims of cyberbullying. "!'Tell an adult. Don't let it get you down'—it's all too abstract and detached," he told me. "How could you intervene in a way that's more personal and specific, but on a large scale?"

To answer that question, Lieberman and his graduate students started analyzing thousands of YouTube comments on videos dealing with controversial topics, and about 1 million posts provided by the social-networking site Formspring that users or moderators had flagged for bullying. The MIT team's first insight was that bullies aren't particularly creative. Scrolling through the trove of insults, Lieberman and his students found that almost all of them fell under one (or more) of six categories: they were about appearance, intelligence, race, ethnicity, sexuality, or social acceptance and rejection. "People say there are an infinite number of ways to bully, but really, 95 percent of the posts were about those six topics," Lieberman told me.

Focusing accordingly, he and his graduate students built a "commonsense knowledge base" called BullySpace—essentially a repository of words and phrases that could be paired with an algorithm to comb through text and spot bullying situations. Yes, BullySpace can be used to recognize words like *fat* and *slut* (and all their text-speak misspellings), but also to determine when the use of common words varies from the norm in a way that suggests they're meant to wound.

Lieberman gave me an example of the potential ambiguity BullySpace could pick up on: "You ate six hamburgers!" On its own, *hamburger* doesn't flash cyberbullying—the word is neutral. "But the relationship between *hamburger* and *six* isn't neutral," Lieberman argued. BullySpace can parse that relationship. To an overweight kid, the message "You ate six hamburgers!" could easily be cruel. In other situations, it could be said with an admiring tone. BullySpace might be able to tell the difference based on context (perhaps by evaluating personal information that social-media users share) and could flag the comment for a human to look at.

BullySpace also relies on stereotypes. For example, to code for anti-gay taunts, Lieberman included in his knowledge base the fact that "Put on a wig and lipstick and be who you really are" is more likely to be an insult if directed at a boy. BullySpace understands that lipstick is more often used by girls; it also recognizes more than 200 other assertions based on stereotypes about gender and sexuality. Lieberman isn't endorsing the stereotypes, of course: he's harnessing them to make BullySpace smarter. Running data sets from the YouTube and Formspring posts through his algorithm, he found that BullySpace caught most of the insults flagged by human testers—about 80 percent. It missed the most indirect taunting, but from Lieberman's point of view, that's okay. At the moment, there's nothing effective in place on the major social networks that screens for bullying before it occurs; a program that flags four out of five abusive posts would be a major advance.

Lieberman is most interested in catching the egregious instances of bullying and conflict that go destructively viral. So another of the tools he has created is a kind of air-traffic-control program for social-networking sites, with a dashboard that could show administrators where in the network an episode of bullying is turning into a pileup, with many users adding to a stream of comments—à la Let's Start Drama. "Sites like Facebook and Formspring aren't interested in every little incident, but they do care about the pileups," Lieberman told me. "For example, the week before prom, every year, you can see a spike in bullying against LGBT kids. With our tool, you can analyze how that spreads—you can make an epidemiological map. And then the social-network site can target its limited resources. They can also trace the outbreak back to its source." Lieberman's dashboard could similarly track the escalation of an assault on one kid to the mounting threat of a gang war. That kind of data could be highly useful to schools and community groups as well as the sites themselves. (Lieberman is leery of seeing his program used in such a way that it would release the kids' names beyond the social networks to real-world authorities, though plenty of teenagers have social-media profiles that are public or semipublic—meaning their behavior is as well.)

I know some principals and guidance counselors who would pay for this kind of information. The question is what to do with it. Lieberman doesn't believe in being heavy-handed. "With spam, okay, you write the program to just automatically delete it," he said. "But with bullying, we're talking about free speech. We don't want to censor kids, or ban them from a site."

More effective, Lieberman thinks, are what he calls "ladders of reflection" (a term he borrowed from the philosopher Donald Schön). Think about the kid who posted "Because he's a fag! ROTFL [rolling on the floor laughing]!!!" What if, when he pushed the button to submit, a box popped up saying "Waiting 60 seconds to post," next to another box that read "I don't want to post" and offered a big X to click on? Or what if the message read "That sounds harsh! Are you sure you want to send that?" Or what if it simply reminded the poster that his comment was about to go to thousands of people?

Although Lieberman has had exploratory conversations about his idea with a few sites, none has yet deployed it. He has a separate project going with MTV, related to its Web and phone app called Over the Line?, which hosts user-submitted stories about questionable behavior, like sexting, and responses to those stories. Lieberman's lab designed an algorithm that sorts the stories and then helps posters find others like them. The idea is that the kids posting will take comfort in having company, and in reading responses to other people's similar struggles.

Lieberman would like to test how his algorithm could connect kids caught up in cyberbullying with guidance targeted to their particular situation. Instead of generic "tell an adult" advice, he'd like the victims of online pummeling to se alerts from social-networking sites designed like the keyword-specific ads Google sells on Gmail—except they would say things like "Wow! That sounds nasty! Click here for help." Clicking would take the victims to a page that's tailored to the problem they're having—the more specific, the better. For example, a girl who is being taunted for posting a suggestive photo (or for refusing to) could read a synthesis of the research on sexual harassment, so she could better understand what it is, and learn about strategies for stopping it. Or a site could direct a kid who is being harassed about his sexuality to resources for starting a Gay-Straight Alliance at his school, since research suggests those groups act as a buffer against bullying and intimidation based on gender and sexuality. With the right support, a site could even use Lieberman's program to offer kids the option of an IM chat with an adult. (Facebook already provides this kind of specific response when a suicidal post is reported. In those instances, the site sends an e-mail to the poster offering the chance to call the National Suicide Prevention Lifeline or chat online with one of its experts.)

Lieberman would like to build this content and then determine its effectiveness by asking kids for their feedback. He isn't selling his algorithms or his services. As a university professor, he applies for grants, and then hopes companies like MTV will become sponsors. He's trying to work with companies rather than criticize them. "I don't think they're trying to reflexively avoid responsibility," he told me. "They are conscious of the scale. Anything that involves individual action on their part, multiplied by the number of complaints they get, just isn't feasible for them. And it is a challenging problem. That's where technology could help a little bit. My position is that technology can't solve bullying. This is a people problem. But technology can make a difference, either for the negative or the positive. And we're behind in paying attention to how to make the socialnetwork universe a better place, from a technological standpoint."

Internal findings at Facebook suggest that Lieberman's light touch could indeed do some good. During my visit to Silicon Valley, I learned that the site had moved from wholesale banishment of rule-breakers toward a calibrated combination of warnings and "temporary crippling of the user experience," as one employee put it. After all, if you're banished, you can sign up again with a newly created e-mail address under an assumed name. And you might just get angry rather than absorb the message of deterrence. Instead, Facebook is experimenting with threats and temporary punishments. For example, the Hate and Harassment Team can punish a user for setting up a group to encourage bullying, by barring that person from setting up any other group pages for a month or two. (If the account associated with the offensive group uses a madeup name, then the site's only leverage is to remove the group.) According to an in-house study, 94 percent of users whose content prompted a report had never been reported to the site before. As Dave Willner, the content-policy manager, put it when he told me about the study: "The rate of recidivism is very low."

He explained, in his appealingly blunt way, "What we have over you is that your Facebook profile is of value to you. It's a hostage situation." This didn't surprise me. In the course of my reporting, I'd been asking middle-school and high-school students whether they'd rather be suspended from school or from Facebook, and most of them picked school.

The hacker group Anonymous isn't the first place most parents would want their bullied kids to turn. Launched a decade ago, Anonymous is best known for its vigilante opposition to Internet censorship. The group has defaced or shut down the Web sites of the Syrian Ministry of Defense, the Vatican, the FBI, and the CIA. Its slogan, to the extent a loosely affiliated bunch of hackers with no official leadership can be said to have one, is "When your government shuts down the Internet, shut down your government." Anonymous has also wreaked financial havoc by attacking MasterCard, Visa, and PayPal after they froze payments to the accounts of WikiLeaks, the site started by Julian Assange to publish government secrets.

Since Anonymous is anarchic, the people who answer its call (and use its trademark Guy Fawkes mask in their online photos) speak for themselves rather than represent the group, and protest in all kinds of ways. Some, reportedly, have not been kind to kids. There was the case, for example, of a 15-year-old named McKay Hatch, who started a No Cussing Club in South Pasadena, California. When the concept took off in other cities, a group referring to itself as Anonymous launched a countercampaign, No Cussing Sucks, and posted Hatch's name, photo, and contact information across the Web; he got 22,000 e-mails over two weeks.

But other people in Anonymous have a Robin Hood bent, and this fall, they rode to the rescue of a 12-year-old girl who'd come in for a torrent of hate on Twitter. Her error was to follow the feed of a 17-year-old boy she didn't know and then stop following him when he posted remarks she found rude. The boy took offense and, with three friends, went after her. The boys threatened to "gang bang" her, and one even told her to kill herself. "I'm gonna take today's anger and channel it into talking shit to this 12 year old girl," one wrote. "Blow up [her Twitter handle] till she deletes her twitter," another one added. The girl lived far from the boys, so she wasn't in physical danger, but she was disturbed enough to seek help online. "I have been told to kill myself alot its scary to think people in the world want you to die :(," she wrote to another Twitter user who asked me to call her Katherine. "He has deleted some of them he was saying things like do you have a rope? and didnt the bleach work?"

Her pleas reached Katherine in the wake of the suicide of a 15-year-old Canadian girl named Amanda Todd. Before Amanda died, she posted a video of herself on YouTube, in which she silently told her story using note cards she'd written on. Amanda said that a man she'd met online had persuaded her to send him a topless photo, then stalked her and released the photo, causing her misery at school. The video is raw and disturbing, and it moved Katherine and a member of Anonymous with the screen name Ash. "It made me choke up," Ash told me. When Katherine discovered that people were still sending the compromising photo of Amanda around online, she and Ash teamed up to help organize a drive to stop them and report offending users to Twitter, which removes pornographic content appearing on its site.

As Katherine and Ash came across other examples of bullying, like rape jokes and suicide taunts, they found that "Twitter will suspend accounts even if they are not in violation of Twitter rules when simply 1000s of people mass report an account as spam," Katherine explained to me in an e-mail. A Twitter spokesperson said this was possible (though he added that if spam reports turn out to be false, most accounts soon go back online). Twitter bans direct and specific threats, and it can block IP addresses to prevent users whose accounts are deleted from easily starting new ones. But the site doesn't have an explicit rule against harassment and intimidation like Facebook does.

While monitoring Twitter for other bullying, Katherine found the 12-year-old girl. When Katherine told Ash, he uncovered the boys' real names and figured out that they were high-schoolers in Abilene, Texas. Then he pieced together screenshots of their nasty tweets, along with their names and information about the schools they attended, and released it all in a public outing (called a "dox"). "I am sick of seeing people who think they can get away with breaking someone's confidence and planting seeds of self-hate into someone's head," he wrote to them in the dox. "What gives you the fucking right to attack someone to such a breaking point? If you are vile enough to do so and stupid enough to do so on a public forum, such as a social website, then you should know this . . . We will find you and we will highlight your despicable behaviour for all to see."

"I informed them that the damage had been done and there was no going back," he explained to me. "They understood this to be an act by Anonymous when they were then messaged in the hundreds." At first the boys railed against Ash on Twitter, and one played down his involvement, denying that he had ever threatened to rape the girl. But after a while, two of the boys began sending remorseful messages. "For two solid days, every time we logged on, we had another apology from them," Ash said. "You hear a lot of lies and fake apologies, and these guys seemed quite sincere." Katherine thought the boys hadn't understood what impact their tweets would have on the girl receiving them—they hadn't thought of her as a real person. "They were actually shocked," she said. "I'm sure they didn't mean to actually rape a little girl. But she was *scared.* When they started to understand that, we started talking to them about antibullying initiatives they could bring to their schools."

I tried contacting the four boys to ask what they made of their encounter with Anonymous, and I heard back from one of them. He said that at first, he thought the girl's account was fake; then he assumed she wasn't upset, because she didn't block the messages he and the other boys were sending. Then Ash stepped in. "When i found out she was hurt by it i had felt horrible," he wrote to me in an e-mail. "I honestly don't want to put anyone down. i just like to laugh and it was horrible to know just how hurt she was." He also wrote, "It was shocking to see how big [Anonymous was] and what they do."

Ash also e-mailed his catalog of the boys' tweets to their principals and superintendents. I called the school officials and reached Joey Light, the superintendent for one of the districts in Abilene. He said that when Anonymous contacted him, "to be truthful, I didn't know what it was. At first the whole thing seemed sketchy." Along with the e-mails from Ash, Light got an anonymous phone call from a local number urging him to take action against the boys. Light turned over the materials Ash had gathered to the police officer stationed at the district's high school, who established that one of the boys had been a student there.

The officer investigated, and determined that the boy hadn't done anything to cause problems at school. That meant Light couldn't punish him, he said. "I realize bullying takes a lot of forms, but our student couldn't have harmed this girl physically in any way," he continued. "If you can't show a disruption at school, the courts tell us, that's none of our business." Still, Light told me he that he felt appreciative of Anonymous for intervening. "I don't have the technical expertise or the time to keep track of every kid on Facebook or Twitter or whatever," the superintendent said. "It was unusual, sure, but we would have never done anything if they hadn't notified us."

I talked with Ash and Katherine over Skype about a week after their Texas operation. I wanted to know how they'd conceived of the action they'd taken. Were they dispensing rough justice to one batch of heartless kids? Or were they trying to address cyberbullying more broadly, and if so, how?

Ash and Katherine said they'd seen lots of abuse of teenagers on social-networking sites, and most of the time, no adult seemed to know about it or intervene. They didn't blame the kids' parents for being clueless, but once they spotted danger, as they thought they had in this case, they couldn't bear to just stand by. "It sounds harsh to say we're teaching people a lesson, but they need to realize there are consequences for their actions," Ash said.

He and Katherine don't have professional experience working with teenagers, and I'm sure there are educators and parents who'd see them as suspect rather than helpful. But reading through the hate-filled tweets, I couldn't help thinking that justice Anonymous-style is better than no justice at all. In their own way, Ash and Katherine were stepping into the same breach that Henry Lieberman is trying to fill. And while sites like Facebook and Twitter are still working out ways to address harassment comprehensively, I find myself agreeing with Ash that "someone needs to teach these kids to be mindful, and anyone doing that is a good thing."

For Ash and Katherine, this has been the beginning of #OpAntiBully, an operation that has a Twitter account providing resource lists and links to abuse-report forms. Depending on the case, Ash says, between 50 and 1,000 people—some of whom are part of Anonymous and some of whom are outside recruits—can come together to report an abusive user, or bombard him with angry tweets, or offer support to a target. "It's much more refined now," he told me over e-mail. "Certain people know the targets, and everyone contacts each other via DMs [direct messages]."

In a better online world, it wouldn't be up to Anonymous hackers to swoop in on behalf of vulnerable teenagers. But social networks still present tricky terrain for young people, with traps that other kids spring for them. My own view is that, as parents, we should demand more from these sites, by holding them accountable for enforcing their own rules. After all, collectively, we have consumer power here—along with our kids, we're the site's customers. And as Henry Lieberman's work at MIT demonstrates, it is feasible to take stronger action against cyberbullying. If Facebook and Twitter don't like his solution, surely they have the resources to come up with a few more of their own.

CRITICAL THINKING QUESTIONS

1. The author argues that social media has, "plenty of upside for kids." What are two benefits of social media for children? Also, provide two reasons why you think social media is a detriment to children. Use evidence from the reading to address both points.
2. Emily Bazelon argues that social media is the new "public square"—but that it has "plenty of upside for kids" over the physical public square. Why could social media be considered a "public square?" Why might bullying be harsher and more prevalent online than in other public spaces, like high schools?
3. According to the author, who should kids on the internet worry about most: "predatory adults" or "other kids?" Why does she believe that group is the larger threat? Explain who you think children should be most worried about by providing evidence from the reading.
4. Who is Dave Willner, and what is his role at Facebook? Emily Bazelon writes that he tries to "impose order on a frustratingly subjective universe." Why does she describe bullying on Facebook as "frustratingly subjective?" Do you think bullying online is more or less subjective than bullying offline? Why do you think that?

A FEMALE WRITER'S NEW MILESTONE: HER FIRST DEATH THREAT

by Annie Gaus

Annie Gaus is a journalist who reports on technology. Gaus previously worked as a technology and science reporter for *Discovery Digital.*

In this 2014 article from *The Daily Beast,* Annie Gaus describes her experiences after receiving her first death threat online. She finds that it is extremely easy to obtain someone's personal information online, and that there are many men out there who will use the tools of the Internet to harass women online. She finds some comfort that most other women with an online presence have also received these threats, but that nothing has happened to them. But the question remains: why are so many women finding threats of physical, emotional, or sexual violence to be so common online?

• • • • • • • • • • • • • • •

65 percent of U.S. adults ages 18–29 have been harassed online—some to the point of their home address posted online, which is easier than ever to track down thanks to shoddy white pages websites.

So much of life can be measured in sentimental milestones. Your first kiss. Your first heartbreak. Your first telephoned rape and death threat from a strange caller. You know, the precious threads in life's shimmering tapestry.

You'll never forget your first: I was at the offices of an Oakland creative agency, in the middle of a conversation about website copy. I normally ignore blocked numbers, but was expecting a number of calls that day so I excused myself and answered anyway.

"Hello?"

"Are you still writing articles and doing videos? Because I have a story for you," said a young, nasally, male voice.

"Who's calling?

"The person that's going to rape and murder you."

"Oh."

This wasn't the first weird call I'd received on my cell. Earlier that year, I'd gotten a pair of voicemails—both from blocked numbers—from a single male caller identifying himself as two different law enforcement officers.

"This is Officer Hernandez," the man introduced himself on one call. "You are guilty of entrapment. We have a warrant. Please turn yourself into the nearest police station."

Recognizing this as a shoddy approximation of how an arrest works (cops generally don't call to warn you), I laughed off the voicemails and filed them away in the "Weird Shit" folder on my desktop. Then I forgot all about them.

But for obvious reasons, the most recent call was different. It was a new voice, and in contrast to the ham-handed posturing of "Officer Hernandez," the threat was direct and more aggressive. Sure, like many people who publish stuff on the Internet—previously I'd been a full-time video journalist covering technology and science—I'd had my share of juvenile insults, pervy remarks, and implausible threats casually lobbed in my direction. But a stone-cold *death threat* to my cell phone—that was a new one. Yet the caller sounded like he was reciting a telemarketing script: prepared in advance, quite possibly practiced on others before me. And as with most unwanted telemarketing calls, the pitch wasn't that effective.

"Okay." I chortled.

Click.

Nonetheless, I analyzed the call in my mind. The caller mentioned my work, which focused primarily on consumer products, mobile apps, emerging start-ups, and web trends. So what piece could have so passionately enraged this caller that I was marked for death? Was it my 2014 CES recap? My comparison of Siri and Google Voice Search? My coverage of the XBox One launch in Fall 2013? My lightly mocking overview of the Facebook Phone? Maybe this person really, really liked the Facebook Phone—who knows.

After talking to some of my peers in tech, science, and gaming journalism, it became clear that these annoying events are not only commonplace, but practically a rite of passage. Among those I know personally, well over half have received messages similar to mine, whether on Twitter, in comments, a phone call, or in some cases even physical letters. The letters, science journalist Trace Dominguez told me in an IM, "are taken more seriously. Because you have to REALLY WANT IT. But comments? Tweets? The barrier to entry for finding a stamp in your DESK is higher [sic]."

The ubiquity of these threats alarms some people, and it's an understandable reaction. After all, we live in a weird time when dozens of female celebrities just suffered a mass nude photo leak, an executive of a major company openly talked about "digging up dirt" on journalists' personal lives, and a nebulous movement called #Gamergate has generated a months-long firestorm of shit-slinging ostensibly around the issue of games journalism. In countless news headlines, Gamergate has been credited with "death threats" and "doxxes" specifically targeting female developers and critics—especially those, like Anita Sarkeesian, who apply feminist views to their work. Well-publicized events like this have led some critics to characterize the movement as gender warfare waged by misogynistic trolls intent on expelling female and progressive voices from the gaming community—in op-eds, in Tweets, and in countless headlines that mash "death threats" and "women" together in a tasty clickbait stew of culture war hysteria.

For what it's worth, I have seldom commented on the status of women in technology or gaming—not because I don't have opinions, but because I'm a tech critic, not a social critic. If you read my Twitter, for instance, I guarantee the only institutions you'll hear me railing against are the iMessage platform and Los Angeles sports teams. So in the event I ended up in the dossiers of a misogynistic activist group, I'd have to assume it was some sort of clerical error.

But fishing for rationale in harassment is almost always a waste of time. The reality is, it is common to the point of mundane. According to Pew Research center, 65 percent of American adults aged 18–29 have experienced online harassment, with 20 percent reporting threats of physical harm. This helps to illustrate why treating harassment as an ideological war can distract from the bigger issue at the heart of it: systemic privacy loopholes.

Should you choose to a few precious hours of your life catching up on #Gamergate media coverage (not that I recommend it), you'll find many breathless accounts of "doxxing"—that is, having one's personal information (e.g., phone number or home address) published online, with the intent to intimidate. This is a common escalation of harassment. Tara Long, a journalist active in the gaming space, described to me a series of incidents in which her home address, along with rape threats, was published using dummy Twitter accounts. After the first was taken down, "the same guy signed up under two other anonymous accounts, even tweeting a picture of my house to me." Surely only an advanced hacker could mastermind such a fiendish act—right?

Hardly. As Tara pointed out, "literally everyone's home address is publicly available online through shitty websites like Whitepages.com and Peekyou.com." As for the picture of her house, "It was obviously taken off Google Maps." (Ultimately, all it took was the mere mention of a lawyer for the perpetrator to delete the accounts and disappear completely.)

If you've ever Googled yourself (which you almost certainly have), you may have encountered listings on "people search" sites like the ones Tara mentioned: Spokeo, Pipl, Instant-Checkmate, PeopleFinder, and many, many others. There are dozens of these engines, and they all do basically the same thing: Use web crawlers to mine existing sites, such as social accounts and other publicly available directories, for personal information associated with a single identity. That information is then indexed, repackaged, and aggressively upsold—you can pay $4.95 for an "Address Check," $9.95 for a "Criminal Check," etc. Unlike the old, printed White Pages of decades past, people search sites are designed to make you to shell out your credit card for the tantalizing, if unlikely, possibility of uncovering someone's juicy private info. More often than not, you'll end up with a hodgepodge of inaccurate or incomplete information; when I paid $2.95 to stalk myself on PeekYou, for example, I ended up with an address that was outdated by several years.

Still, it's nearly impossible to get yourself removed from these sites. You may send an opt-out request to one, but because they rely on crawlers, there's always a chance a listing will crop up again. As it turns out, my cell phone number had been searchable through a GoDaddy domain listing I obtained several years ago. So when you consider that nearly everyone's personal information is discoverable, individual instances of harassment, like the one I experienced, seem a lot less intimidating.

There are indeed cases of serious harassment that warrant both public scrutiny and close attention from law enforcement. Police need to direct resources and expertise shrewdly to address these reports. But in the majority of cases, let's call it what it is: a stupid prank call. At best, these amount to low-level exploits of publicly available information, and are not themselves worthy of special recognition—that would be giving the perpetrators more credit than they really deserve. So to the guy who called me, wherever you are: If you stay on the line and explain why I deserve to be killed, I promise not to laugh in your face next time.

CRITICAL THINKING QUESTIONS

1. Why does the journalist Trace Dominguez think physical letters should be taken more seriously than online threats? When she talks about how the "barrier to entry" is low for online harassment, what does she mean? Draw a connection between this thought and why harassment might be worse online.

2. The author argues that the biggest issue for cyber harassment is "systemic privacy loopholes." What are these loopholes she identifies? Why was it so easy to find out where she lived? Who benefits from these services? What, if anything, do you think should be done about these kinds of websites?

3. Annie Gaus references her death threat as a "new milestone." Explain what she means by this. She also writes that, "after talking to my peers in tech, science,

and gaming journalism, it became clear that these annoying events are not only commonplace, but practically a rite of passage." What does she mean when she writes that they have become a "rite of passage?" What do you think this says about the difficulty of being a female writer on the internet?

4. **Connection.** After receiving her online threat, Annie Gaus calls the cops. Refer back to Amanda Hess' article—why is calling the local cops so ineffective? What is Annie Gaus' experience with law enforcement? Why does Amanda Hess claim it is so common to receive an ineffective response from local law enforcement?

HOW TO RID TWITTER OF MISOGYNY AND MAKE IT FIT FOR DEBATE

by Simon Jenkins

Simon Jenkins is an author and journalist. He writes for *The Guardian* and he is also a BBC broadcaster. He has worked as an editor for the *London Evening Standard*, and he has also chaired the National Trust.

In this 2013 article from *The Guardian*, Simon Jenkins outlines his surprise at the response to Caroline Criado-Perez's treatment online after pursuing more females being celebrated on British currency. He argues that free speech in the real world has limitations—you can't yell "fire" in a crowded theater, for example. And he thinks online speech should be regulated as well. Why has regulation been so long in coming to the internet, and why is it necessary?

Women like Caroline Criado-Perez have suffered a torrent of bigotry on social media. But regulation can stop it.

The great god of the mountain is turning grim. The warm, lovable, liberal dawn of the digital era suddenly seems dark and menacing. E-crime is rife, state snooping is everywhere, hate speech and misogyny howl and cackle in the internet slipstream. People are getting hurt.

Such has been the row over Jane Austen at the Bank of England that we might think Caroline Criado-Perez was running her for deputy governor. The campaign was in genteel line of descent from Wollstonecraft and Pankhurst, but the method used—through social media—opened a flank to sex-crazed, anonymous misogynists, one so offensive as to require police attention.

Criado-Perez is the latest victim in an almost daily litany of woe emanating from the once unblemished internet. Last year Lord McAlpine had to fight off untrue viral accusations about his private life. Mary Beard was abused for her looks on television. The Home Office is obsessed with online paedophilia, David Cameron with internet porn, and Panorama with Facebook entries stolen as profiles for dating agencies. And no one seems to pay any tax.

That Austen had to be championed by a feminist website was sad. Her cause became identified with gender representation rather than with her qualities as a novelist. But any "feminist issue" is still treated by the media as the ring-fenced preserve of female commentary. When reporting, reviewing, profiling or debating women, an editor's instinct is to turn for safety to a woman writer. It was near impossible last week to find any male comment on Criado-Perez and trolling (the Independent's Owen Jones excepted). Women are addressed by women much as cricket is addressed by men.

Most men, dare I use the phrase, have little idea what some women experience when they appear in public or express strong opinions. My postbag may contain abuse, but female colleagues experience real vitriol. Nor is this just writers. Last week's treatment of Theresa May for losing weight—attributed to her ambition rather than her health—was appalling. The MP Stella Creasy received rape threats merely for supporting Criado-Perez. The refusal of many able women to engage in public debate—the BBC has a list of refuseniks—may not help their cause. But the misogynist response makes it understandable.

Social media have given such responses not just an audience but a legitimacy, creating a sewer for anonymous prejudice and hate. Twitter may be a harmless pastime for show-offs and voyeurs, but it is crack cocaine for the commentariat. It reduces the soundbite to absurdity. Shouted rants of thesis and antithesis are a pastiche of American shock jocks. But as victims have found, the rants can be every bit as offensive as newspaper libel or harassment.

Fundamentalists ordain that those who "don't like the heat" should stay out of the kitchen. The essence of the internet is the democracy of the air. We are all members of the global village and villagers supposedly enjoy no privacy. Indeed privacy, like accuracy, is said to be an attribute of yesterday's media. Let the market rule, cry the libertarians. Let good servers drive out bad. As for the trolls, they are just hangers-on. Those who eat in celebrity restaurants should not protest at the presence of paparazzi.

A minute's consideration destroys this argument. Like all advantageous inventions, the internet has strengths but also weaknesses, and the latter need regulating. It may be the apotheosis of the word, but no one really believes that "words can never hurt you". Laws on defamation, privacy, harassment and incitement exist for a reason. If they are not enforced, people will take the law into their own hands. Freedom requires courtesy, and courtesy requires rules.

Britain's mass media has just been through an orgy of self-examination with the Leveson report. It was written as if the digital age did not exist, like an inquiry into transportation that stopped with Stephenson's Rocket. The abuse of electronic surveillance by lawyers, businesses, banks, indeed entire governments, seemed to be of no concern to an inquiry that appeared mesmerised by protecting Hugh Grant's private life.

It is no longer enough to dismiss the exhibitionists of Facebook and Twitter as collaborators in their own downfall. What may be acceptable in the confines of a bigots' club is intolerable in any public domain, including that of the web. I may not know how to regulate cyberspace, but I know that such regulation limps far behind the need for it.

Last month's revelations by Edward Snowden showed the full extent of government prying into our electronic lives under cover of "counter-terror". It also showed an alarming political cynicism towards the dangers implied. That a British minister, William Hague, could dismiss them with "the innocent have nothing to fear" shows how much the innocent have to fear.

Digital innovation pretends to offer user choices while striving to curtail them. No sooner are we warned to read the small print and not tick the cookie box, than we are told it makes no difference. "They" know who we are, what we buy and where we go anyway—and will never forget. As Eric Schmidt of Google points out in his book *The New Digital Age,* our digital footprints are as immutable as our fingerprints. Now we learn that we are vulnerable to drone observation and facial recognition. There is no escaping these demons.

That does not negate all hope of regulating them. Every civilised society has rules for the conduct of free speech. I still find the readiness of platforms to give space to anonymous commentary extraordinary. If I dare to say who I am, why cannot my critics? And what of their "publishers"? As Andy Trotter, of Association of Chief Police Officers, said of the platform providers on Monday: "They can't just set them up and walk away."

Moves by platforms to end anonymity and the progressive demise of internet privacy may diminish the torrent of pseudonymous abuse. So may new editing and security systems. But it is not enough to hope that personalised apps, lock-downs and report buttons will suffice to discipline the millions of words which, in print, are subject to the law.

The internet is a wondrous thing that has changed and liberated people. It also threatens our idea of ourselves as private persons and citizens. It has become a masked ball, whose concealed dancers may be corporations or governments, paedophiles or rapists, weirdos or fools. It must be regulated. This is not a "feminist issue", but we can thank feminism for bringing the threat to the fore.

CRITICAL THINKING QUESTIONS

1. There was a debate in England surrounding currency. Describe that debate. Simon Jenkins argues that, "the misogynist response (to the debate) makes it understandable" that many women did not engage in it. What is the misogynist response he is talking about? Why might that have caused women to opt out of the debate? Why do you think that is a negative thing?
2. In the article, find three ways that social media acts as the "crack cocaine for the commentariat." Do you agree with this analysis? Why or why not?
3. Simon Jenkins summarizes his argument by writing that, "like all advantageous inventions, the internet has strengths but also weaknesses, and the latter need regulating." What are two weaknesses of the internet that he has identified in his article. Do you agree that there should be regulation on this internet? What are two potential downsides to regulation on the internet?
4. **Connection.** Simon Jenkins argues that one thing to do to limit harassment online would be to "end anonymity" online. Both Amanda Hess and Annie Gaus suffered from online harassment by anonymous men. Describe one of their experiences in a few sentences. How might this experience have been different if this person had not been allowed to be anonymous? Do you think we should ban anonymity from the internet? Why or why not?

THE CULT OF OPENNESS ENABLES MISOGYNY

by Astra Taylor

Astra Taylor is a writer and documentary filmmaker. She wrote the book *The People's Reform: Taking Back Power and Culture in the Digital Age.* She is also an activist who helped launch the Strike Debt campaign.

In this 2014 article published in *Mother Jones*, Astra Taylor questions the fundamental assumption of the Internet: that openness is always a good thing. Her reporting demonstrates that the Internet is a remarkably open place—for young white men. And this lack of diversity—from the boardrooms of technology companies to users of reddit—is shaping how the Internet acts. She also demonstrates that the Internet is acting in an exclusive way. Why does a technology that promises equality act in a way that is less equal than the world it is determined to change?

• • • • • • • • • • • • • • •

Social media harassment and "brogramming" culture have become synonymous with the Internet. It doesn't have to be this way.

The Web is regularly hailed for its "openness" and that's where the confusion begins, since "open" in no way means "equal." While the Internet may create space for many voices, it also reflects and often amplifies real-world inequities in striking ways.

An elaborate system organized around hubs and links, the Web has a surprising degree of inequality built into its very architecture. Its traffic, for instance, tends to be distributed according to "power laws," which follow what's known as the 80/20 rule—80% of a desirable resource goes to 20% of the population.

In fact, as anyone knows who has followed the histories of Google, Apple, Amazon, and Facebook, now among the biggest companies in the world, the Web is increasingly a winner-take-all, rich-get-richer sort of place, which means the disparate percentages in those power laws are only likely to look uglier over time.

Powerful and exceedingly familiar hierarchies have come to define the digital realm, whether you're considering its economics or the social world it reflects and represents. Not surprisingly, then, well-off white men are wildly overrepresented both in the tech industry and online.

Just take a look at gender and the Web comes quickly into focus, leaving you with a vivid sense of which direction the Internet is heading in and—small hint—it's not toward equality or democracy.

|

EXPERTS, TROLLS, AND WHAT YOUR MOM DOESN'T KNOW

As a start, in the perfectly real world women shoulder a disproportionate share of household and child-rearing responsibilities, leaving them substantially less leisure time to spend online. Though a handful of high-powered celebrity "mommy bloggers" have managed to attract massive audiences and ad revenue by documenting their daily travails, they are the exceptions not the rule. In professional fields like philosophy, law, and science, where blogging has become popular, women are notoriously underrepresented; by one count, for instance, only around 20% of science bloggers are women.

An otherwise optimistic white paper by the British think tank Demos touching on the rise of amateur creativity online reported that white males are far more likely to be "hobbyists with professional standards" than other social groups, while you won't be shocked to learn that low-income women with dependent children lag far behind. Even among the highly connected college-age set, research reveals a stark divergence in rates of online participation.

Socioeconomic status, race, and gender all play significant roles in a who's who of the online world, with men considerably more likely to participate than women. "These findings suggest that Internet access may not, in and of itself, level the playing field when it comes to potential pay-offs of being online," warns Eszter Hargittai, a sociologist at Northwestern University. Put simply, closing the so-called digital divide still leaves a noticeable gap; the more privileged your background, the more likely that you'll reap the additional benefits of new technologies.

Some of the obstacles to online engagement are psychological, unconscious, and invidious. In a revealing study conducted twice over a span of five years—and yielding the same results both times—Hargittai tested and interviewed 100 Internet users and found that there was no significant variation in their online competency. In terms of sheer ability, the sexes were equal. The difference was in their self-assessments.

It came down to this: The men were certain they did well, while the women were wracked by self-doubt. "Not a single woman among all our female study subjects called herself an 'expert' user," Hargittai noted, "while not a single male ranked himself as a complete novice or 'not at all skilled.'" As you might imagine, how you think of yourself as an online contributor deeply influences how much you're likely to contribute online.

The results of Hargittai's study hardly surprised me. I've seen endless female friends be passed over by less talented, more assertive men. I've had countless people—older and male, always—assume that someone else must have conducted the interviews for my documentary films, as though a young woman couldn't have managed such a thing without assistance. Research shows that people routinely underestimate women's abilities, not least women themselves.

When it comes to specialized technical know-how, women are assumed to be less competent unless they prove otherwise. In tech circles, for example, new gadgets and programs are often introduced as being "so easy your mother or grandmother could use them." A typical piece in the *New York Times* was titled "How to Explain Bitcoin to Your Mom." (Assumedly, dad already gets it.) This kind of sexism leapt directly from the offline world onto the Web and may only have intensified there.

And it gets worse. Racist, sexist, and homophobic harassment or "trolling" has become a depressingly routine aspect of online life.

Many prominent women have spoken up about their experiences being bullied and intimidated online—scenarios that sometimes escalate into the release of private information, including home addresses, e-mail passwords, and social security numbers, or simply devolve into an Internet version of stalking. Esteemed classicist Mary Beard, for example, "received online death threats and menaces of sexual assault" after a television appearance last year, as did British activist Caroline Criado-Perez after she successfully campaigned to get more images of women onto British banknotes.

Young women musicians and writers often find themselves targeted online by men who want to silence them. "The people who were posting comments about me were speculating as to how many abortions I've had, and they talked about 'hate-fucking' me," blogger Jill Filipovic told *the Guardian* after photos of her were uploaded to a vitriolic online forum. Laurie Penny, a young political columnist who has faced similar persecution and recently published an ebook called *Cybersexism*, touched a nerve by calling a woman's opinion the "short skirt" of the Internet: "Having one and flaunting it is somehow asking an amorphous mass of almost-entirely male keyboard-bashers to tell you how they'd like to rape, kill, and urinate on you."

Alas, the trouble doesn't end there. Women who are increasingly speaking out against harassers are frequently accused of wanting to stifle free speech. Or they are told to "lighten up" and that the harassment, however stressful and upsetting, isn't real because it's only happening online, that it's just "harmless locker-room talk."

As things currently stand, each woman is left alone to devise a coping mechanism as if her situation were unique. Yet these are never isolated incidents, however venomously personal the insults may be. (One harasser called Beard—and by online standards of hate speech this was mild—"a vile, spiteful excuse for a woman, who eats too much cabbage and has cheese straws for teeth.")

Indeed, a University of Maryland study strongly suggests just how programmatic such abuse is. Those posting with female usernames, researchers were shocked to discover, received 25 times as many malicious messages as those whose designations were masculine or ambiguous. The findings were so alarming that the authors advised parents to instruct their daughters to use sex-neutral monikers online. "Kids can still exercise plenty of creativity and self-expression without divulging their gender," a well-meaning professor said, effectively accepting that young girls must hide who they are to participate in digital life.

Over the last few months, a number of black women with substantial social media presences conducted an informal experiment of their own. Fed up with the fire hose of animosity aimed at them, Jamie Nesbitt Golden and others adopted masculine Twitter avatars. Golden replaced her photo with that of a hip, bearded, young white man, though she kept her bio and continued to communicate in her own voice. "The number of snarky, condescending tweets dropped off considerably, and discussions on race and gender were less volatile," Golden wrote, marveling at how simply changing a photo transformed reactions to her. "Once I went back to Black, it was back to business as usual."

OLD PROBLEMS IN NEW MEDIA

Not all discrimination is so overt. A study summarized on the *Harvard Business Review* website analyzed social patterns on Twitter, where female users actually outnumbered males by 10%. The researchers reported "that an average man is almost twice [as] likely to follow another man [as] a woman" while "an average woman is 25% more likely to follow a man than a woman." The results could not be explained by varying usage since both genders tweeted at the same rate.

Online as off, men are assumed to be more authoritative and credible, and thus deserving of recognition and support. In this way, long-standing disparities are reflected or even magnified on the Internet.

In his 2008 book *The Myth of Digital Democracy*, Matthew Hindman, a professor of media and public affairs at George Washington University, reports that of the top 10 blogs, only one belonged to a female writer. A wider census of every political blog with an average of over 2,000 visitors a week, or a total of 87 sites, found that only five were run by women, nor were there "identifiable African Americans among the top 30 bloggers," though there was "one Asian blogger, and one of mixed Latino heritage." In 2008, Hindman surveyed the blogosphere and found it less diverse than the notoriously whitewashed op-ed pages of print newspapers. Nothing suggests that, in the intervening six years, things have changed for the better.

Welcome to the age of what Julia Carrie Wong has called "old problems in new media," as the latest well-funded online journalism start-ups continue to be helmed by brand-name bloggers like Ezra Klein and Nate Silver. It is "impossible not to notice that in the Bitcoin rush to revolutionize journalism, the protagonists are almost exclusively—and increasingly—male and white," Emily Bell lamented in a widely circulated op-ed. It's not that women and people of color aren't doing innovative work in reporting and cultural criticism; it's just that they get passed over by investors and financiers in favor of the familiar.

As Deanna Zandt and others have pointed out, such real-world lack of diversity is also regularly seen on the rosters of technology conferences, even as speakers take the stage to hail a democratic revolution on the Web, while audiences that look just like them cheer. In early 2013, in reaction to the announcement of yet another all-male lineup at a prominent Web gathering, a pledge was posted on the website of the *Atlantic* asking men to refrain from speaking at events where women are not represented. The list of signatories was almost immediately removed "due to a flood of spam/trolls." The conference organizer, a successful developer, dismissed the uproar over Twitter. "I don't feel [the] need to defend this, but am happy with our process," he stated. Instituting quotas, he insisted, would be a "discriminatory" way of creating diversity.

This sort of rationalization means technology companies look remarkably like the old ones they aspire to replace: male, pale, and privileged. Consider Instagram, the massively popular photo-sharing and social networking service, which was founded in 2010 but only hired its first female engineer last year. While the percentage of computer and information sciences degrees women earned rose from 14% to 37% between 1970 and 1985, that share had depressingly declined to 18% by 2008.

Those women who do fight their way into the industry often end up leaving—their attrition rate is 56%, or double that of men—and sexism is a big part of what pushes them out. "I no longer touch code because I couldn't deal with the constant dismissing and undermining of even my most basic work by the 'brogramming' gulag I worked for," wrote one woman in a roundup of answers to the question: Why there are so few female engineers?

In Silicon Valley, Facebook's Sheryl Sandberg and Yahoo's Marissa Mayer excepted, the notion of the boy genius prevails. More than 85% of venture capitalists are men generally looking to invest in other men, and women make 49 cents for every dollar their male counterparts rake in—enough to make a woman long for the wage inequities of the non-digital world, where on average they take home a whopping 77 cents on the male dollar. Though 40% of private businesses are women-owned nationwide, only 8% of the venture-backed tech start-ups are.

Established companies are equally segregated. The National Center for Women and Information Technology reports that in the top 100 tech companies, only 6% of chief executives are women. The numbers of Asians who get to the top are comparable, despite the fact that they make up one-third of all Silicon Valley software engineers. In 2010, not even 1% of the founders of Silicon Valley companies were black.

MAKING YOUR WAY IN A MISOGYNIST CULTURE

What about the online communities that are routinely held up as exemplars of a new, networked, open culture? One might assume from all the "revolutionary" and "disruptive" rhetoric that they, at least, are better than the tech goliaths. Sadly, the data doesn't reflect the hype. Consider Wikipedia. A survey revealed that women make up less than 15% of the contributors to the site, despite the fact that they use the resource in equal numbers to men.

In a similar vein, collaborative filtering sites like Reddit and Slashdot, heralded by the digerati as the cultural curating mechanisms of the future, cater to users who are up to 87% male and overwhelmingly young, wealthy, and white. Reddit, in particular, has achieved notoriety for its misogynist culture, with threads where rapists have recounted their exploits and photos of underage girls got posted under headings like "Chokeabitch," "Niggerjailbait," and "Creepshots."

Despite being held up as a paragon of political virtue, evidence suggests that as few as 1.5% of open source programmers are women, a number far lower than the computing profession as a whole. In response, analysts have blamed everything from chauvinism, assumptions of inferiority, and outrageous examples of impropriety (including sexual harassment at conferences where programmers gather) to a lack of women mentors and role models. Yet the advocates of open-source production continue to insist that their culture exemplifies a new and ethical social order ruled by principles of equality, inclusivity, freedom, and democracy.

Unfortunately, it turns out that openness, when taken as an absolute, actually aggravates the gender gap. The peculiar brand of libertarianism in vogue within technology circles means a minority of members—a couple of outspoken misogynists, for example—can disproportionately affect the behavior and mood of the group under the cover of free speech. As Joseph Reagle, author of *Good Faith Collaboration: The Culture of Wikipedia*, points out, women are not supposed to complain about their treatment, but if they leave—that is, essentially are driven from—the community, that's a decision they alone are responsible for.

"URBAN" PLANNING IN A DIGITAL AGE

The digital is not some realm distinct from "real" life, which means that the marginalization of women and minorities online cannot be separated from the obstacles they confront offline. Comparatively low rates of digital participation and the discrimination faced by women and minorities within the tech industry matter—and not just because they give the lie to the egalitarian claims of techno-utopians. Such facts and figures underscore the relatively limited experiences and assumptions of the people who design the systems we depend on to use the Internet—a medium that has, after all, become central to nearly every facet of our lives.

In a powerful sense, programmers and the corporate officers who employ them are the new urban planners, shaping the virtual frontier into the spaces we occupy, building the boxes into which we fit our lives, and carving out the routes we travel. The choices they make can segregate us further or create new connections; the algorithms they devise can exclude voices or bring more people into the fold; the interfaces they invent can expand our sense of human possibility or limit it to the already familiar.

What vision of a vibrant, thriving city informs their view? Is it a place that fosters chance encounters or does it favor the predictable? Are the communities they create mixed or gated? Are they full of privately owned shopping malls and sponsored billboards or are there truly public squares? Is privacy respected? Is civic engagement encouraged? What kinds of people live in these places and how are they invited to express themselves? (For example, is trolling encouraged, tolerated, or actively discouraged or blocked?)

No doubt, some will find the idea of engineering online platforms to promote diversity unsettling and—a word with some irony embedded in it—paternalistic, but such criticism ignores the ways online spaces are already contrived with specific outcomes in mind. They are, as a start, designed to serve Silicon Valley venture capitalists, who want a return on investment, as well as advertisers, who want to sell us things. The term "platform," which implies a smooth surface, misleads us, obscuring the ways technology companies shape our online lives, prioritizing certain purposes over others, certain creators over others, and certain audiences over others.

If equity is something we value, we have to build it into the system, developing structures that encourage fairness, serendipity, deliberation, and diversity through a process of trial and error. The question of how we encourage, or even enforce, diversity in so-called open networks is not easy to answer, and there is no obvious and uncomplicated solution to the problem of online harassment. As a philosophy, openness can easily rationalize its own failure, chalking people's inability to participate up to choice, and keeping with the myth of the meritocracy, blaming any disparities in audience on a lack of talent or will.

That's what the techno-optimists would have us believe, dismissing potential solutions as threats to Internet freedom and as forceful interference in a "natural" distribution pattern. The word "natural" is, of course, a mystification, given that technological and social systems are not found growing in a field, nurtured by dirt and sun. They are made by human beings and so can always be changed and improved.

CRITICAL THINKING QUESTIONS

1. Astra Taylor argues that the internet "reflects and often amplifies real-world inequalities in striking ways." How does the internet *both* "amplify" and "reflect" the real world when it comes to gender inequality? Provide two examples from the article.

2. Compare the gender and racial demographics of the tech industry to our society at large. What are three issues that this difference may cause? Can you think of another field where white men are overrepresented? What are some issues that arise in that field from this lack of diversity?

3. Taylor writes that "some of the obstacles to online engagement are psychological, unconscious, and invidious." For each of these three adjectives, explain what the author means. Provide one example from the reading, and one from your own life experiences of the internet not being an open and free playing field.

4. Describe the University of Maryland Study Astra writes about. What were their findings? Why is this problematic? Why do you think the results turned out that way?

THIS IS WHAT TECH'S UGLY GENDER PROBLEM LOOKS LIKE

by Issie Lapowsky

Issie Lapowsky is a staff writer for *Wired*. She posts articles on topics including finances, hotel and travel deals, social media, and the newest APPs.

Issie Lapowsky interviewed women who were working to start successful businesses in the technology field for this 2014 article from *Wired* magazine. While the other readings describe the ways in which being a woman online is difficult, this article attempts to explain why. Lapowsky finds it is extraordinarily difficult to develop a business if you are female in Silicon Valley. How does the technology industry's "ugly gender problem" operate? And why is it so difficult to fix?

• • • • • • • • • • • • • • •

Shortly after Kathryn Tucker started RedRover, an app that showcases local events for kids, she pitched the idea to an angel investor at a New York tech event. But it didn't go over well. When she finished her pitch, the investor said he didn't invest in women.

When she asked why, he told her. "I don't like the way women think," he said. "They haven't mastered linear thinking." To prove his point, he explained that his wife could never prioritize her to-do lists properly. And then, as if he was trying to compliment her, he told Tucker she was different. "You're more male," he said.

Tucker didn't need to hear any more. "I said, 'Thanks very much,' walked out, and never spoke to him again," she recalled earlier this year, as part of a panel discussion on "fundraising while female" at the annual Internet Week conference in New York.

It was one of many stories shared during a panel that painted the tech world as a place that—for all its efforts to push into the future with apps and gadgets and online services—is still very much stuck in the past when it comes to attitudes involving gender. Rachel Sklar, founder of Change the Ratio, an advocacy group for women in tech, shared the story of an investor who said he doesn't invest in women he doesn't find attractive. Another gave women in the audience a tip for pitching VCs: "Wear a wedding ring."

As unsettling as they were, these stories only begin to describe the obstacles facing women in the tech world. We've all seen the numbers. According to a recent report from Pitchbook, only 13 percent of venture-backed companies had at least one female co-founder. In the software sector, women-run businesses accounted for just 10 percent of all venture capital deals. And that's a drastic improvement.

There are any number of reasons for this. People have argued that because there are fewer women in computer science, there might be fewer women pitching these VCs. But research also shows that gender discrimination of varying degrees—both conscious and subconscious—is alive and well among tech's overwhelmingly white, male investors. And the stories shared by many women—on that Internet Week panel and beyond—bear this out.

Certainly, not all venture capitalists discriminate against female founders. Not all female founders feel they've been discriminated against. Not all female founders deserve to be funded. And yes, there are many stories that will restore your faith in the industry. "I've had only wonderful experiences in pitching investors," says Jessica Mah, founder of the accounting and payroll services startup InDinero. "Most, if not all, have been very supportive and respectful."

But there's another truth to remember: For every story you hear about investors behaving badly, there are far worse stories that many women wouldn't dare to tell. "The most common thing I hear from other women is: "Oh the stories I'll tell once I'm far enough along that I don't have to worry about being shamed,'" says Kathryn Minshew, co-founder of the job search and career advice site The Muse.

For women who have experienced this bias—and there are many—the simple act of talking about it is taboo. There's a notion that acknowledging the problem only exacerbates it. No one wants to be known as the woman who cried sexism for fear of being labeled a tattletale, a liability, or, at the very least, not worth the trouble. And yet, it's only through these stories that we can begin to understand that the statistics aren't the result of some fluke or mass oversight, but a very real problem that needs to be solved.

"I'M SO RELIEVED. I THOUGHT I WAS THE ONLY ONE"

Minshew has a few stories of her own. Two months into fundraising for The Muse, she attended a dinner held by a group of young tech entrepreneurs. The guest of honor was someone Minshew calls a "well-known investor and former entrepreneur." During the dinner, he approached Minshew, one of the only women at the event, to say he found her company interesting and wanted to meet later and dig deeper into the business model.

They swapped cards. She emailed him a pitch deck. And she scheduled a meeting through the investor's assistant for 4 pm the following Tuesday. At the last minute, the investor said his schedule had changed and asked if Minshew was free to meet at the bar in his hotel that night. "That obviously wasn't ideal," Minshew tells *Wired*, "but I felt like he had my deck, and I scheduled it with his assistant." So she went.

It was a typical meeting until the investor asked Minshew to move over to a couch, where he sat down so close to her that his body was leaning against the entire left side of hers, his arm around her back, and his line of questioning, Minshew says, turned personal. "I was pretty upset and trying to direct the conversation back to business. He was definitely not going back to business," she remembers. "I was sitting with my arm in a blocking position because he was so close. I was basically pushing his chest off me. So after not long, I said 'I have to leave' and left."

Afterword, Minshew wondered which warning signs she might have overlooked before the meeting, but would soon come to learn this is an all-too familiar scenario for young female founders. When she tells the story to other women in the field, they typically sympathize. "The biggest response from women entrepreneurs was: 'Oh, I'm so relieved. I thought I was the only one.'"

The most challenging part of all this, she says, is that most early-stage investing is built on camaraderie, and getting drinks and other informal meetings are great ways to build that camaraderie. Male founders generally don't have to make so many mental calculations about an investor's intent before agreeing to meet at a bar. Female founders do. "Guys can say: 'It was great to meet you at that event. Let's go grab a beer,'" says Danielle Weinblatt, who started the video interview platform, Take the Interview, in 2011. "Women just can't do that. We're inevitably always going to be left out of things, because there are certain lines you can't cross and things that are unspoken parts of the boys club."

"WHY DO I HAVE TO GO TO GENDER-SPECIFIC INVESTORS?"

But for Weinblatt, just as frustrating as being excluded from the "boys club" is being funneled toward the "girls club." Throughout her fundraising process, she says, investors have repeatedly directed her to other female investors. She remembers one meeting with a venture capitalist who suggested Weinblatt meet Joanne Wilson, an angel investor who funds primarily female-founders. "Nothing gets under my skin more than when someone says: 'Have you met so and so? She likes investing in women,'" Weinblatt explains. "Why do I have to go to gender-specific investors? Our company is pretty gender agnostic, at this point."

Weinblatt, who closed a $2.2 million Series A funding round last year, knows comments like these are meant to be helpful, and female-focused investors are enabling more women to launch companies. But, she says, being told she needs to find an investor who "likes investing in women" makes her feel like being a woman is something to overcome. "I think that's a terrible way to look at it," she says. "I hate this philosophy that because you're female, woe is you. I don't want someone to feel sorry for me."

When you're a single mother, says Sheri Atwood, founder of SupportPay, it's even tougher to be taken seriously. The child of a divorce and coming out of a divorce herself, Atwood built SupportPay, an online platform to help divorced parents manage and share child support. But almost as soon as she began pitching investors in 2011, she faced a barrage of doubt as to whether she could handle a company and kids at the same time.

Atwood says that while their concern is legitimate, it's also a bit backward. She believes it's because she's a single mother—not despite it—that she's a safe bet for investors. "I'm not doing this as a side project. I don't have a spouse supporting me. I'm putting everything on the line, and I'm responsible for a child," she says. "I'm going to do everything possible to make that work."

But being a single mother wasn't Atwood's only problem. She's also a coder. With all the recent efforts from Google, Square, and other organizations to get young girls interested in coding, it's hard to imagine Atwood's ability to code was a drawback when she was trying to get funded. And yet, she says, when she told her investors she had built SupportPay herself, they repeatedly doubted her. "No one believed me," Atwood says.

"THIS ISN'T A 21-YEAR-OLD-KID-IN-A-HOODIE PROBLEM"

Once, an associate at a venture capital firm even gave Atwood a bit of advice after turning her down for funding. "Hire a young guy in a hoodie," he said. "I laughed," Atwood remembers. "Then I said: 'That's a great point, but the reason why there's no solution on the market today is because this isn't a 21-year-old-kid-in-a-hoodie problem.'"

Luckily for Atwood, after about nine months of getting questioned on everything from her ability to run a business as a single mom to her blonde hair—one investor claimed brunettes are taken more seriously—Atwood landed $1.1 million in funding from several top angel investors, including Draper Associates, Broadway Angels, and Marc Benioff. "They got it," she says. "They saw that my being a woman and my age was an asset."

Indeed all of the women interviewed for this story have found investors who they say have been wholly supportive throughout the process. Even those who have experienced bias, like Tucker, say it's hard to get outraged about outright ignorance. In telling her story, she merely hopes to help convince the investing community that bias does exist, so they can begin to build systems within their firms to "handicap for the bias." "Relying on your gut is not necessarily good business, and they're leaving a lot of money on the table, as a result," she says.

Meanwhile, Minshew says it's been "heartening" to see men in the tech community listen to women's stories and begin to talk about the problem themselves. That, she says, may be the first step toward real change. "Years ago, you could say really horrible, racist things, and people who didn't agree would stay quiet because that was the time we were in. Now, we're in a time where someone says something horribly racist, and other people say: 'Shit, I can't believe you just said that,'" Minshew explains. "My hope is we're moving toward a world in which if one partner at a VC firm knows another partner is behaving inappropriately with female entrepreneurs, it'll be the same sort of shock and outrage. It'll be unacceptable."

CRITICAL THINKING QUESTIONS

1. What does the report from Pitchbook reveal about women in the technology world? These numbers depict a field that is very unequal. In what ways might sexism be keeping women from heading successful technology startups?
2. Issie Lapowsky writes that while many women in the tech industry experience bias, "the simple act of talking about it is taboo." Why is it taboo? Why can women experience difficulty when they confront it? Why does the author claim that talking about it is important in fixing the issue?
3. Danielle Weinblatt's actions to fund her app are described in the article. Where was she continually sent for funding? Why did this bother her? Do you think this is sexism? Why or why not?
4. Sheri Atwood is seeking funding for her app. What does her app do? It is described as fixing something that "isn't a 21-year-old-kid-in-a-hoodie problem." What does she mean by this? What is another social issue that might be difficult to solve if the only people working on it were 21-year-old white men? Why would it be difficult?

TECHNOLOGY'S MAN PROBLEM

by Claire Cain Miller

Claire Cain Miller is a journalist who writes about Google, e-commerce, startups, and technology in general. She has worked for the San Francisco bureau of *The Times* since 2008, and previously she was a reporter for *Forbes*. Miller graduated from Yale University and the University of California at Berkeley's Graduate School of Journalism.

One way to reduce the hostility of the online environment for women is to have women play a significant part in the companies that develop the online space. Claire Cain Miller, in this 2014 *New York Times* article, explains why that goal is difficult. Women who work in the technology industry face sexism that was long ago abolished in other industries. How should we work to change the technology industry, and how does its failing effect everyone's online experience?

• • • • • • • • • • • • • • • •

Elissa Shevinsky can pinpoint the moment when she felt that she no longer belonged.

She was at a friend's house last Sept. 8, watching the live stream of the TechCrunch Disrupt hackathon on her laptop and iPhone. Entrepreneurs were showing off their products, and two young Australian men, David Boulton and Jethro Batts, stood behind the podium to give their presentation. "Titstare is an app where you take photos of yourself staring at tits," Mr. Boulton began, as photographs of women's chests on a cellphone flashed on the screen behind him.

After some banter, Mr. Batts concluded, "This is the breast hack ever."

The crowd—overwhelmingly young, white, hoodie-wearing men—guffawed. Something in Ms. Shevinsky's mind clicked. If ever there was proof that the tech industry needed more women, she thought, this was it.

Ms. Shevinsky, 35, wasn't the only one who was disgusted by the presentation. Twitter lit up with outrage. She joined in, writing a blog-post manifesto: "I thought that we didn't need more women in tech. I was wrong."

Then things got worse. The next day, Pax Dickinson, who was her business partner in a start-up called Glimpse Labs, as well as the chief technology officer of the news site Business Insider, took to Twitter to defend the Titstare pair against accusations of misogyny. "It is not misogyny to tell a sexist joke, or to fail to take a woman seriously, or to enjoy boobies," he wrote.

Ms. Shevinsky felt pushed to the edge. Women who enter fields dominated by men often feel this way. They love the work and want to fit in. But then something happens—a slight or a major offense—and they suddenly feel like outsiders. The question for newcomers to a field has always been when to play along and when to push back.

Today, even as so many barriers have fallen—whether at elite universities, where women outnumber men, or in running for the presidency, where polls show that fewer people think gender makes a difference—computer engineering, the most innovative sector of the economy, remains behind. Many women who want to be engineers encounter a field where they not only are significantly underrepresented but also feel pushed away.

Tech executives often fault schools, parents or society in general for failing to encourage girls to pursue computer science. But something else is at play in the industry: Among the women who join the field, 56 percent leave by midcareer, a startling attrition rate that is double that for men, according to research from the Harvard Business School.

A culprit, many people in the field say, is a sexist, alpha-male culture that can make women and other people who don't fit the mold feel unwelcome, demeaned or even endangered.

"It's a thousand tiny paper cuts," is how Ashe Dryden, a programmer who now consults on increasing diversity in technology, described working in tech. "I've been a programmer for 13 years, and I've always been one of the only women and queer people in the room. I've been harassed, I've had people make suggestive comments to me, I've had people basically dismiss my expertise. I've gotten rape and death threats just for speaking out about this stuff."

She added: "A lot of times that makes me want to leave. But it's hard, because this is basically the only field that I've ever known. And is it right for me to have to leave when I'm not creating the problem?"

Ms. Shevinsky never received death threats, but she experienced her share of come-ons and slights. A few days after Mr. Dickinson's "It is not misogyny" tweet, she quit Glimpse. She had been aware of earlier cringe-making tweets in which her business partner had joked about rape or questioned even the most basic feminist precepts. ("Women's suffrage and individual freedom are incompatible. How's that for an unpopular truth?") Still, she admired Mr. Dickinson's technical skills and work ethic. Married and then 40, he was more experienced and serious about work than many other tech types she knew, and she said he always treated her with respect.

But after the Twitter controversy, she decided that she just couldn't work with him anymore.

Ms. Shevinsky's epiphany, however, wasn't just about Mr. Dickinson or a couple of engineers. It was about computer-engineering culture and her relationship with it. She had enjoyed being "one of the bros"—throwing back whiskey and rubbing shoulders with M.I.T. graduates. And if that sometimes meant fake-laughing as her colleagues cracked jokes about porn, so be it.

"For years, all I wanted to do was work and code and make software," she said in an interview. "That's why I didn't care about feminism. I just wanted to build stuff."

"But Titstare showed me that was no longer a viable option," she said. "We had to address our culture, because something was really not working."

Two days after the TechCrunch show, Business Insider forced Mr. Dickinson to resign. The Australian entrepreneurs and TechCrunch each apologized. But incidents like these aren't exceptional.

"We see these stories, 'Why aren't there more women in computer science and engineering?' and there's all these complicated answers like, 'School advisers don't have them take math and physics,' and it's probably true," said Lauren Weinstein, a man who has spent his four-decade career in tech working mostly with other men, and is currently a consultant for Google.

"But I think there's probably a simpler reason," he said, "which is these guys are just jerks, and women know it."

The choice for people who are uncomfortable with the "bro" culture is to try to change it or to leave—and even women who are fed up don't always agree on how to go about making a change. But leaving can be hard too.

"There was only one thing I wanted to do," Ms. Shevinsky said. "Be the C.E.O. of Glimpse."

A BRIGHT BEGINNING

When Ms. Shevinsky was introduced to engineering culture at Williams College, she got no hint of sexism. A political theory major, she learned to code from a boyfriend, and she described their engineer friends as "forward-thinking feminists."

She worked in product development for a number of start-ups and was a co-founder of a dating site. She settled in New York, where she got to know Mr. Dickinson at tech meet-ups. When she had a new business idea—a kind of Snapchat for adults that prevents people from taking screen shots of private pictures—she sought out his advice.

Last spring, they decided to build the app together. At first, they conceived it as a sexting product, but later they shifted to a service that could be used by anyone concerned about keeping their messages safe from prying eyes. They called it Glimpse.

By August, Ms. Shevinsky had closed her dating site to work on Glimpse. Mr. Dickinson, who had his full-time job at Business Insider, helped when he could.

"I remember thinking just that I was so lucky that Pax was going to work with me," Ms. Shevinsky said. "At the time I was still relatively unknown, and he was one of the best technologists I'd met."

Computer science wasn't always dominated by men. "In the beginning, the word 'computers' meant 'women,'" says Ruth Oldenziel, a professor at Eindhoven University of Technology in the Netherlands who studies history, gender and technology. Six women programmed one of the most famous computers in history—the 30-ton Eniac—or the United States Army during World War II.

But as with many professions, Dr. Oldenziel said, once programming gained prestige, women were pushed out. Over the decades, the share of women in computing has continued to decline. In 2012, just 18 percent of computer-science college graduates were women, down from 37 percent in 1985, according to the National Center for Women & Information Technology.

This lack of women has become of greater concern in the industry for a number of reasons. For one, the products that the tech industry creates are shaping the future for everyone. "Women are increasingly consumers; they're not going to like products that don't work for them," said Londa Schiebinger, a Stanford professor who runs the Gendered Innovations project, which encourages engineers and scientists to consider gender when developing new products.

Perhaps more fundamentally, there are simply more jobs than can be filled by available talent. Some 1.2 million computing jobs will be available in 2022, yet United States universities are producing only 39 percent of the graduates needed to fill them, the N.C.W.I.T. estimates.

Tech's biggest companies say that recruiting women is a priority. "If we do that, there's no question we'll more than double the rate of technology output in the world," Larry Page, the chief executive of Google, said last spring. Yet at Google, less than a fifth of the engineers are women.

That's a typical figure. Twenty percent of software developers are women, according to the Labor Department, and fewer than 6 percent of engineers are black or Hispanic. Comparatively, 56 percent of people in business and financial-operations jobs are women, as are 36 percent of physicians and surgeons and one-third of lawyers.

At tech start-ups, often considered the most desirable places to work, the number of women appears to be even lower. The companies generally don't release these numbers publicly, but an engineer at Pinterest has collected data from people at 133 start-ups and found that an average of 12 percent of the engineers are women.

Sexism exists in many places, but start-up companies have particular qualities that can allow problems to go unchecked. The lines between work and social life are often blurry, because people tend to be young and to work long hours, and the founders and first employees are often friends. And start-ups pride themselves on a lack of bureaucracy, forgoing big-company layers like human resources departments. They say they can move faster that way, without becoming bogged down in protocol.

But a result can be an anything-goes atmosphere, said Julie Ann Horvath, a software designer and developer who publicly quit her job last month at GitHub, the coding website, saying that there was a culture of intimidation and disrespect of women. GitHub, founded in 2008, hired a senior H.R. executive only in January.

"If there is no structure, that's actually more harmful to marginalized people," Ms. Horvath said in an interview while she still worked at GitHub. "It's just unprofessional. Tech needs to grow up in a lot of ways."

At GitHub, Ms. Horvath, who was the only female developer at the company when she started, said she once declined a romantic relationship with one of her co-workers. Then, she said, she discovered that code she had written had disappeared. The man, she said, had ripped it out.

"It makes a hostile environment for me," she said. "But I don't want to raise my hand and call negative attention toward myself, and become the woman who is the problem—'that woman.' In start-up culture they protect their own tribe, so by putting my hand up, I'm saying I'm an 'other,' I shouldn't be there, so for me that's an economic threat."

Ms. Horvath eventually decided that it was worth the risk, and quit. She said the people who mistreated her included a founder of the company.

Chris Wanstrath, GitHub's chief executive and another co-founder, apologized to Ms. Horvath in a blog post and said the co-founder she complained about was put on leave and the company was investigating what happened.

At bigger companies, women say harassment may be easier to stop but that other, subtler forms of sexism persist.

Women often take on the role of product manager, or P.M., which entails the so-called soft skills of managing people and bridging the business and engineering divide. Yet even though this is an essential job, it's the purely technical people—not the businesspeople—who get the respect in the tech industry.

"In engineering, whoever owns the code, they have the power," said Ana Redmond, a software engineer. When she worked as a senior engineer at a big company, Expedia, she said she was constantly underestimated by male colleagues and suffered because she was not willing to leave her children to work the hours needed to "own the code."

In a statement, Expedia said Ms. Redmond had not raised these concerns during her tenure. The company added that it now has programs to develop and retain female talent; it also has a goal to double the number of women in roles at the vice-president level and higher by 2020.

In 2011, Ms. Redmond quit to start her own company, Infinut, that makes educational apps for children, and to teach computer science at the University of Washington—largely, she said, to mentor female students. "For me, what worked best was changing the context," she said, "not conforming to it."

A 'BOY-PUERILE ATMOSPHERE'

After she quit Glimpse, Ms. Shevinsky began looking for a job outside the start-up world. Mr. Dickinson, no longer at Business Insider, made it his mission to persuade her to return. Glimpse had no office and little money, so they met at TGI Friday's and at a dive bar that served $5 beer.

The conversations started at a deadlock.

"There was the one where Pax said, 'I got to keep tweeting, I got to keep tweeting,'" Ms. Shevinsky recalled. "I wasn't going to come back to Glimpse if we both weren't going to be taking it seriously. I remember telling Pax that his tweets were going to be very expensive for us."

Social media, where people carefully build their public personas, often become bullhorns for offensive comments.

After the Titstare presentation, a commenter calling himself White_N_Nerdy wrote on Reddit, "I'm honestly trying to understand why anyone says that females are 'needed' in the tech industry." He continued: "The tech community works fine without females, just like any other mostly male industry. Feminists probably just want women making more money."

Online gathering spots for engineers, like Reddit, Hacker News and 4chan, where people often post anonymously, can feel like hostile territory for women.

"Many women have come to me and said they basically have had to hide on the Net now," said Mr. Weinstein, who works on issues of identity and anonymity online. "They use male names, they don't put their real photos up, because they are immediately targeted and harassed."

That sense of being targeted as a minority happens at the office, too. That is part of the reason nearly a third of the women who leave technology jobs move to nontechnical ones, according to the Harvard study.

"It's a boys' club, and you have to try to get into it, and they're trying as hard as they can to prove you can't," said Ephrat Bitton, the director of algorithms at FutureAdvisor, an online investment start-up that she says has a better culture because almost half the engineers are women.

Writing code is a high-pressure job with little room for error, as are many jobs. But coding can be stressful in a different way, women interviewed for this article said, because code reviews—peer reviews to spot mistakes in software—can quickly devolve.

"Code reviews are brutal—'Mine is better than yours, I see flaws in yours'—and they should be, for the creation of good software," said Ellen Ullman, a software engineer and author. "I think when you add a drop of women into it, it just exacerbates the problem, because here's a kind of foreigner."

"I'm in no way saying that women can't take a tough code review," she added. "I'm saying that no one should have to take one in a boy-puerile atmosphere."

STILL ON THE DEFENSIVE

Late last fall, Ms. Shevinsky and Mr. Dickinson flew together from a tech conference in California back to New York. When Ms. Shevinsky awoke from a nap, Mr. Dickinson asked her to look at a letter he had written on his iPad about the Titstare episode and his comments on Twitter about women.

"It was a lapse in judgment and I'm entirely responsible for that," he wrote. "I sincerely and unreservedly apologize to anyone I offended."

For both of them, the letter was the turning point. "The biggest thing was Pax realizing he was a public figure and the responsibilities that came with that," Ms. Shevinsky said. "He wrote the apology letter, and it was very genuine and moving and impactful for me."

Mr. Dickinson sent his letter to VentureBeat, a tech blog, for publication.

Ms. Shevinsky returned to Glimpse in December. But first Mr. Dickinson had to make some promises. Ms. Shevinsky would be the chief executive and the public face of the company. She would have to sign off on what he said on social media and in press interviews—as she did when he was interviewed for this article. And the company would add a second mission statement supporting women in tech, including through hiring.

"I have come to realize there are problems with sexism in technology through all this," Mr. Dickinson wrote in an interview over email.

Nonetheless, he wasn't retreating from his public tweets. Rather, he said, the media had portrayed him in a way that didn't capture his full personality.

"I am not just my tweets, and I never was," he wrote in the email interview. "The caricature that's been painted of me isn't accurate. I realized after all this that many of my tweets came off meanspirited in a way I never intended, hence my apology."

At Glimpse, Ms. Shevinsky's title is "ladyboss"—which she likes because, she said, it embraces the idea of women being in charge. Three of the six people who work at the company are women, as are two of the three board members. The pair raised a small amount of money, mostly from New York angel investors, and introduced the Glimpse app at the South by Southwest conference in Austin in March.

But the debate isn't over. In fact, Ms. Shevinsky now finds herself in another argument. This time, however, she's on the defensive with other women.

A prominent feminist in tech told her that she was doing a disservice to women by accepting Mr. Dickinson's apology and working with him again. The conversation, Ms. Shevinsky said, was "hateful."

Ms. Shevinsky says that she judges Mr. Dickinson "on his actions, how he is with other people in the company and with me," and said that there was no contradiction in both working with Mr. Dickinson and supporting feminism in tech.

"I care very, very much about women in tech, and I believe the best thing I can do is change the face of what it looks like and be one of the first women to build a billion-dollar social networking company," she said with entrepreneurial brio.

There are strong differences of opinion, even among women in tech, about how to make the culture more welcoming. Many people at tech companies say it's important to hire women as engineers at the founding of a company and include women in management and in all job interviews.

In this vein, there are women-only hacker spaces and programs to increase the number of women and minorities who appear at tech conferences. Ms. Horvath started a program called Passion Projects, at which a technical woman presents her work each month. Amelia Greenhall and Shanley Kane, technologists and writers, started Model View Culture, a publication about technology, culture and diversity, in which Ms. Kane recently wrote about how myths of tech culture work to "exclude and marginalize minorities."

But some women argue that these kinds of initiatives are unhelpful.

"My general issue with the coverage of women in tech is that women in the technology press are talked about in the context of being women, and men are talked about in the context of being in technology," said a technical woman who would speak only on condition of anonymity because she did not want to be part of an article about women in tech.

"I'm also very good at my job, and as a technologist, I want to be recognized for that and not because I have breasts."

Lea Verou, an incoming Ph.D. candidate in electrical engineering and computer science at M.I.T., wrote in a much read essay that women-only conferences and hackathons "cultivate the notion that women are these weak beings who find their male colleagues too intimidating."

"As a woman," she wrote, "I find it insulting and patronizing to be viewed that way."

Another camp discourages emphasizing complaints about sexism. Rather, they try to focus on positive stories, to encourage women to enter the industry.

"I've been doing this 10 years, and myself and everyone I've spoken to who's a female developer has had an amazing experience in the developer community," said Sara Chipps, chief technology officer of the Flatiron School, a coding school in New York, and a co-founder of Girl Develop It, a nonprofit group to help women become software developers.

"People should say something if something bad happens, but I also want people to know that doesn't have to be the case," she said.

For Ms. Shevinsky, the solution was returning to tech and trying to change the culture from the inside. And part of the reason she decided to work with Mr. Dickinson again, she said, was that both believe in another type of diversity: the diversity of thought.

"It's very dangerous for us as a community," she said, "to say we will only work with people who share our beliefs."

CRITICAL THINKING QUESTIONS

1. Ms. Shevinsky and Lea Verou have very different ideas about how women should handle sexism in the tech industry. How do they disagree? Evaluate Lea Verou's argument—do you think her approach helps reduce sexism or not?

2. Pax Dickinson defended the app "titstare" on Twitter. Put his argument in your own words. Do you agree or disagree with his views? How did Elissa Shevinsky respond? Why do you think she responded that way?

3. The author writes that many people in the tech industry think it has a "sexist, alpha male culture that can make women and other people who don't fit the mold feel unwelcome, demeaned, or even endangered." Find three examples from the article that would support why women could feel this way and describe them.

4. What trend does Ruth Oldenziel describe in the field of computer science? Why does she think this trend has occurred? Do you think her argument is valid? Why or why not?

UNIT 4

Health

INTRODUCTION

Food has always been central to human existence. The *Talmud*, a holy text of the Jewish faith, has a saying: "the belly carries the feet." The *Koran*, the holy text of the Islamic faith, has prescribed strict rules for how to handle food, how to prepare food, and what can and cannot be eaten. The Christian *New Testament* has four books describing the life of Jesus; the only miracle described in all four of those books is his feeding of five thousand people. For humanity, food has always been central to our lives, our health, and our culture.

Much has changed regarding food since those religious texts were written. This unit explores those changes to food and their connection to our health.

When Muhammad laid down his rules for eating at some point before his death in 632, there were around two hundred million people on earth. As you read this, there are over seven billion people sharing a planet. To accommodate this, massive cities grew and urbanization became the new norm. According to the United Nations, in 1900, only 13% of people lived in urban areas; now, more than half do. To live in an urban area is to depend on others to supply your food, to remove yourself from the lands where they create what appears on your plate. To enable us to feed a significantly larger population living in large areas without access to farmland, we needed to develop new ways of developing food, and quickly.

An example of this comes from India, a country whose population, the world's second largest, is over one billion people. In the early 1960s, they were on the verge of widespread famine; their food production methods, which had remained rather similar for hundreds of years, were failing to keep up with the increasing demand. Scientists and government officials encouraged the adoption of a rice strain—IR8—that would allow each farmer to produce much more food. IR8 was developed in a lab and marketed without widespread testing. This was a dramatic success—rather than experiencing massive famine, India now exports millions of tons of rice each year.

We have also had a food revolution in America, but its results are more complicated. We have more food than ever, and more food choices. You are able to buy blueberries at any time of the year, not just when they are in season; but people are more likely to buy a blueberry pie that has been processed and frozen at a manufacturing plant and shipped across the country to a local supermarket. Meat was, for most of human history a luxury. Now, McDonald's sells seventy-five hamburgers every second. The meat from these cows needs to be cheap, because fast food workers have the lowest wages of any measured sector of the economy. The cows are given hormones to help them grow quickly. To make the meat as cheap as possible, the feed for the cows needs to be cheap as well. To create large amounts of cheap animal feed like corn, they need to spray the crops with fertilizers so that they don't lose so much to diseases, and so that the crops grow fast and full.

The way we eat, and what we eat, is very different than it was just a few decades ago, and research is just starting to help us determine what the effects of all these changes will be. This unit asks the following questions: *Is how we produce our food making us ill? And what are the social and economic effects of our food production system?*

One third of American adults are obese, and the medical costs for Americans are 150 billion dollars annually. Our food industry employs millions, but—from those who pick the New Jersey blueberries, to those who serve the McDonald's Big Mac—few of these employees makes a living wage. We need to understand why our food industry looks like it does, why we are so ill, and what can be done about it.

IS OBESITY AN ADDICTION?

by Paul Kenny

Paul Kenny earned his Ph.D. in Neuropsychopharmacology from the University of London in 2000. Kenny's research focuses on understanding the neurobiological mechanisms of drug addiction, obesity, and schizophrenia. He has a number of articles published in journals within his field. Additionally, Kenny has earned a number of awards and recognitions for his work, such as the Mathilde Solowey Lecture Award in the Neurosciences for his work in advancing science education.

In this 2013 article from *Scientific American*, Paul Kenny discusses research into how the body deals with modern, calorie rich food. He presents the addiction model, but also why food is significantly different than other substances that cause addiction—namely, we need it. Scientists are studying how changes to our diet brought about by industrialization are affecting how our body receives food. Food is plentiful in America, but it is full of fats and sugars. If one can be addicted to food, do we need to reevaluate how we think about obesity?

• • • • • • • • • • • • • • • •

New brain research is revealing why fats and sugars may be driving more and more people toward obesity.

Would a rat risk dying just to satisfy its desire for chocolate?

I recently found out. In my laboratory, we gave rats unlimited access to their standard fare as well as to a mini cafeteria full of appetizing, high-calorie foods: sausage, cheesecake, chocolate. The rats decreased their intake of the healthy but bland items and switched to eating the cafeteria food almost exclusively. They gained weight. They became obese.

We then warned the rats as they were eating—by flashing a light—that they would receive a nasty foot shock. Rats eating the bland chow would quickly stop and scramble away, but time and again the obese rats continued to devour the rich food, ignoring the warning they had been trained to fear. Their hedonic desire overruled their basic sense of self-preservation.

Our finding mirrored a previous trial by Barry Everitt of the University of Cambridge—only his rats were hooked on cocaine.

So are the fat rats addicted to food? An inability to suppress a behavior, despite the negative consequences, is common in addiction. Scientists are finding similar compulsiveness in certain people. Almost all obese individuals say they want to consume less, yet they continue to overeat even though they know that doing so can have shockingly negative health or social consequences. Studies show that overeating juices up the reward systems in our brain—so much so in some people that it overpowers the brain's ability to tell them to stop eating when they have had enough. As with alcoholics and drug addicts, the more they eat, the more they want. Whether or not overeating is technically an addiction, if it stimulates the same brain circuits as drug use, in the same way, then medications that dial down the reward system could help obese people to eat less.

SUSPICIOUS HORMONES

Until the early 1990s, society viewed obesity solely as a behavioral disorder: overweight individuals lacked willpower and self-control. Since then, the view has changed dramatically, in the scientific community at least.

The first change in opinion arose from pioneering work by Douglas Coleman of the Jackson Laboratory in Bar Harbor, Me., and by Jeffrey Friedman of the Rockefeller University. Experiments with two strains of mice, both genetically prone to obesity and diabetes, determined what drove the mice to overeat. The researchers discovered that one strain had a genetic defect in fat cells that secrete a hormone called leptin. Mice, like humans, normally secrete leptin after a meal to suppress appetite and prevent overeating. The obese mice had a leptin deficiency—and an insatiable appetite. Researchers later found that obesity in the second strain of mice was caused by a genetic defect in their ability to respond to leptin and regulate its actions. The findings seemed to make it clear that hormones regulate appetite and therefore body weight. A hormonal imbalance could lead to overeating; indeed, obesity runs rampant in certain human families that have a genetic deficiency in leptin.

Two observations suggest that viewing obesity as a hormone disorder is too simplistic, however. First, only a small number of obese people in the U.S. and elsewhere have a genetic deficiency in appetite-related hormones. Second, we would expect blood tests of obese people to show either a lower level of hormones that suppress appetite or a higher level of hormones that increase appetite. Yet the reverse is true. Obese individuals generally have a paradoxically high level of appetite-suppressing hormones, including leptin and insulin.

This is where the concept of food addiction comes into play. Appetite-controlling hormones affect certain pathways of neurons—feeding circuits—in the hypothalamus. They also affect systems in the brain that control feelings of reward, which makes perfect sense. If you have not eaten for many hours, you will spend a great deal of time, effort and money to obtain food—and it will taste very good! As the old adage says, "Hunger is the best sauce."

During periods of hunger, hormones heighten the reactivity of food-related reward circuits in the brain, particularly in the striatum. The striatum contains high concentrations of endorphins—chemicals that enhance feelings of pleasure and reward.

As you eat, your stomach and gut release appetite-suppressing hormones that decrease pleasure signals that are triggered by the striatum and other components of the reward system. This process makes food seem less attractive, and you may switch your activity away from eating and toward other pursuits. Appetite-regulating hormones control feeding, in part by modulating the pleasurable experience of consuming a meal.

Yet some modern, appetizing foods—dense in fat and sugar and often visually appealing—affect reward systems strongly enough to override the appetite-suppressing hormones, thus prompting us to eat. These foods activate our reward circuits more powerfully than leptin's ability to shut them down. All of us have experienced this effect: you have just finished a big dinner and could not possibly eat another bite. Yet when the chocolate cake appears, you can miraculously "find room" for one last morsel—one that happens to be the most calorie-laden of the day.

Therein lies the rub. We have evolved an efficient brain system to help maintain a healthy and consistent body weight by signaling when it is time to eat and when it is time to stop. But highly appetizing foods can often override these signals and drive weight gain.

Our body responds to the override by elevating the blood levels of appetite-suppressing hormones such as leptin and insulin higher and higher as body weight increases, yet the hormones become progressively less effective as the body develops tolerance to their actions. Moreover, brain-imaging studies by researchers at Brookhaven National Laboratory and the Oregon Research Institute show that the brain's reward systems in overweight individuals respond weakly to food, even to junk food. These muffled reward circuits depress mood. How does an individual overcome this funk? By eating more delectable food to gain a temporary boost, thereby perpetuating the cycle. Obese individuals may overeat just to experience the same degree of pleasure that lean individuals enjoy from less food.

Obesity, it seems, is not caused by a lack of willpower. And it is not always caused by an imbalance in hormones. In some cases at least, obesity may be caused by hedonic overeating that hijacks the brain's reward networks. Like addictive drugs, overeating creates a feedback loop in the brain's reward centers—the more you consume, the more you crave, and the harder it is for you to satisfy that craving.

But does that make hedonic eating an addiction?

TOLERANCE AND RELAPSE

Drugs of abuse, such as morphine, stimulate the brain's reward systems the way food does. Yet the similarities do not end there. When morphine is injected into the striatum of rats, it triggers bingelike overeating, even in rats that have been fed to satiety. This response shows that morphine and other opiates mimic the effects of neurotransmitters (brain chemicals) such as endorphins that are naturally produced in the brain to stimulate feeding behaviors.

We might expect, then, that drugs that block the action of endorphins could reduce hedonic overeating. Recent studies have shown that endorphin blockers do lessen the activation of reward circuits in humans and rodents that are presented with appetizing food—the subjects eat less. The blockers can also reduce heroin, alcohol and cocaine use in human drug addicts, supporting the idea that common mechanisms regulate hedonic overeating and addictive drug use. Strikingly, rats that binge on food every day display behaviors that closely resemble withdrawal, a symptom of drug addiction, after they are treated with endorphin blockers. This behavior raises the remarkable notion that hedonic overeating can induce a drug-dependence-like state.

These discoveries add credence to the idea that overeating in some circumstances may share core features of drug addiction. We see the same similarities with another basic neurotransmitter: dopamine. All known addictive drugs lead to the release of dopamine into the striatum. Dopamine is central to motivation, spurring people to seek the drug. Most experts maintain that this action drives the development of addiction, although the precise mechanisms are hotly debated. It turns out that appetizing food also stimulates the release of dopamine into the striatum, motivating people to focus on obtaining and consuming food. Imaging studies reveal that the striatum of obese individuals shows low levels of a receptor that responds to dopamine, termed the dopamine D2 receptor (D2R). The same holds true for those suffering from alcoholism or from opiate, cocaine or methamphetamine addiction.

We now also know that people who are born with reduced levels of D2R are at greater genetic risk of developing obesity and drug addiction. The condition results in lower levels of activity in the brain's reward systems, suggesting that these individuals may overeat just to obtain the same level of pleasure from food as those who do not have D2R deficits. These people also tend to have trouble learning to avoid actions that have negative consequences; brain systems involved in suppressing risky yet rewarding behaviors, such as consuming high-calorie food or using drugs, may not work as effectively.

Our lab study of rats backs up this idea. The obese rats that ate the cafeteria food regardless of warnings about being shocked had reduced levels of D2R in their striatum. Our study and others demonstrate that drug use in addicted rats and hedonic eating in overweight rats persist even when the animals face negative consequences. Many obese individuals struggle so badly with their poor food choices that they will voluntarily undergo potentially dangerous procedures, such as gastric bypass surgery, to help them control their eating. Yet very often they will relapse to overeating and gain weight.

This cycle of engaging in a bad habit that gives short-term pleasure, then attempting to abstain from it and eventually relapsing, sounds disturbingly like drug addiction. Given the latest research, it seems that obesity is caused by an overpowering motivation to satisfy the reward centers—the pleasure centers—of the brain. The hormonal and metabolic disturbances in obese individuals may be a consequence of weight gain rather than a cause.

NEW TREATMENTS POSSIBLE

The similarities between obesity and addiction have led certain experts to say that the two conditions should be treated in the same manner. Some of them recommended that obesity be included in the most recent update to the *Diagnostic and Statistical Manual of Mental Disorders*—the bible of psychiatry that provides guidelines for diagnosing mental illnesses, known as the *DSM-5*. This proposal sparked lively debate among neuroscientists and psychiatrists, but arbiters for the *DSM-5* ultimately dropped the idea, largely to avoid labeling obese people, in essence, as mentally ill.

Caution may have been warranted because despite the parallels, obesity and addiction differ in important ways. For example, if food is addictive, then surely it must contain some unique component that drives the addiction—the nicotine of junk food, if you will. Work by Nicole Avena of the University of Florida, the late Bartley Hoebel of Princeton University and others lends some credence to the idea that particular fats or sugars may be responsible. A small study by David Ludwig of Boston Children's Hospital suggests that highly processed, quickly digested carbohydrates could trigger cravings. But research overall indicates that no one ingredient stokes addictionlike behaviors. Rather the combination of fats and sugars, together with calorie content, seems to maximize food's "hedonic impact."

Other experts, including Hisham Ziauddeen, I. Sadaf Farooqi and Paul C. Fletcher of the University of Cambridge, do not think that tolerance and withdrawal occur in obese people the way they do in drug addicts. They argue that obesity and drug addiction are fundamentally different. This view is debatable, however. If obese individuals must eat more and more to overcome reduced activation of reward networks in the brain, that sounds a lot like tolerance. And weight loss can trigger negative mood and depression, much like that experienced by former addicts who try to practice abstinence, suggesting that withdrawal may be in effect.

Other experts have argued that the entire notion of food addiction is preposterous because we are all, in a sense, addicted to food. If we were not, we would not survive.

The difference in obesity, I would suggest, is that modern high-calorie foods can overwhelm our biological feedback networks in a way that other foods cannot. During millions of years of evolution, the major concern of humans was not suppressing appetite but hunting, collecting or growing enough food to persist during lean times. Perhaps our feeding circuits are better at motivating food intake when we are hungry than they are at suppressing food intake when we are full. It is easy to imagine that the brain would regard overeating of high-calorie food as tremendously beneficial if it is unclear when food will again be available. Perhaps this behavior is no longer adaptive and could even be counterproductive in a world where food is bountiful.

The scientists who argue against an addiction model of obesity make reasonable points, and I also fear that the term "addiction" comes loaded with unhelpful preconceptions. Still, compulsive eating and compulsive drug use seem to share obvious features, most notably an inability to control consumption. It is up to scientists to determine if these similarities are superficial or stem from common, underlying alterations in the brain. More important will be determining whether the addiction model is useful. Unless it helps us design new treatment approaches, the debate is simply an academic exercise.

For an addiction model to have value, it should make accurate predictions about treatment options, including new medications. One example comes from Arena Pharmaceuticals, which recently obtained approval from the U.S. Food and Drug Administration to market a drug called Belviq for weight loss in obese or overweight adults. The drug stimulates a brain protein called the serotonin 2C receptor, which reduces the desire to consume nicotine in lab rats.

Another drug is rimonabant, which had been approved in Europe to help curb appetite in obese individuals. The drug exploits the well-known property of cannabis to increase desire for food—the so-called munchies. Cannabis activates a brain protein called the cannabinoid receptor 1, so researchers reasoned that inhibiting that receptor would decrease desire for food. Rimonabant does exactly that. A notable side effect is its ability to decrease tobacco users' desire to smoke. In rats, the drug also decreases the desire to use alcohol, opiates and stimulants such as cocaine.

As with all potentially therapeutic drugs, however, caution is required. Rimonabant has triggered depression and thoughts of suicide in some individuals. This finding led European authorities to suspend its use and prompted U.S. officials to not approve it. Why depression emerged is still unclear. Thus, although an addiction model of obesity could yield unexpected treatments, those modalities must be thoroughly scrutinized.

Before scientists can declare that overeating is or is not an addiction, they will have to identify precisely which networks and cellular adaptations in the brain drive compulsive drug use and then determine if the same mechanisms also motivate compulsive food intake. It is possible, even likely, that addiction networks for cocaine and for food operate in different parts of the brain yet use similar mechanisms. Scientists will also have to determine if common genetic variations, such as those that affect D2R, contribute to drug addiction and obesity. Identifying such genes may reveal new targets for medications to treat both disorders.

Even if scientists prove that obesity can stem from an addiction to food, and we find that antiaddiction medications can help people lose weight, obese individuals will have to struggle with one factor that seems now to be endemic in America: they will probably be surrounded by overweight family members, friends and co-workers who are still overeating, putting them in the same difficult environment they were in before. As we know from recovering drug addicts and alcoholics, environmental cues are a major cause of craving and relapse. Western society, saturated in fat and temptation, will make it hard for any obese person to quit.

CRITICAL THINKING QUESTIONS

1. The author, Paul Kenny, is himself a scientist, and he opens up the article by discussing his experiments with rats and chocolate. Describe his experiment with the rats. What are his findings? Do his findings surprise you? Why or why not? And do you think his research should affect how we look at overweight people?
2. Modern foods are described as "dense in fat and sugar." How do these foods override the body's hormones? What do they activate? How can this lead to weight gain?
3. What is D2R? What are the risks of being born with reduced levels of D2R? Why does a lack of D2R make these consequences more likely? How do people with low levels of D2R relate to the rats in Kenny's research?
4. The author lays out the ways that food could act like an addiction for some people. Then he describes how "obesity and addiction differ in important ways." Describe at least two of the ways they can differ. Based on your reading of the article, do you think obesity can be considered an addiction? Why or why not?

HOW A NATIONAL FOOD POLICY COULD SAVE MILLIONS OF AMERICAN LIVES

by Mark Bittman, Michael Pollan, Ricardo Salvador, and Olivier De Schutter

Mark Bittman is an author, an opinion columnist, and a food writer for *The New York Times*. Michael Pollan teaches journalism at the University of California Berkeley, and wrote the bestselling book, *The Omnivore's Dilemma*. Ricardo Salvador is a senior scientist and director of the food and environment program at the Union of Concerned Scientists. Olivier De Schutter is a professor of international human rights law at Catholic University of Louvain, and he served as the U.N. *special rapporteur* concerning the right to food from 2008–2014.

This 2014 editorial in *The Washington Post* argues for a national policy regarding the growth, distribution, and consumption of food in our country. The authors argue that as we have national policies for the environment, for crime, and for retirement—we should also have a national policy for something all of us use every day: food. What we eat touches so many parts of our economy and our society—the health of our environment, the shape of our communities, how we spend our paychecks, and what the government does with our taxes. For the first time in decades, kids living today are projected to have shorter life spans than their parents. Why is our government so slow to fix our broken food system?

• • • • • • • • • • • • • • •

How we produce and consume food has a bigger impact on Americans' well-being than any other human activity. The food industry is the largest sector of our economy; food touches everything from our health to the environment, climate change, economic inequality and the federal budget. Yet we have no food policy—no plan or agreed-upon principles—for managing American agriculture or the food system as a whole.

That must change.

The food system and the diet it's created have caused incalculable damage to the health of our people and our land, water and air. If a foreign power were to do such harm, we'd regard it as a threat to national security, if not an act of war, and the government would formulate a comprehensive plan and marshal resources to combat it. (The administration even named an Ebola czar to respond to a disease that threatens few Americans.) So when hundreds of thousands of annual deaths are preventable—as the deaths from the chronic diseases linked to the modern American way of eating surely are—preventing those needless deaths is a national priority.

A national food policy would do that, by investing resources to guarantee that:

- All Americans have access to healthful food;
- Farm policies are designed to support our public health and environmental objectives;
- Our food supply is free of toxic bacteria, chemicals and drugs;
- Production and marketing of our food are done transparently;
- The food industry pays a fair wage to those it employs;
- Food marketing sets children up for healthful lives by instilling in them a habit of eating real food;

- Animals are treated with compassion and attention to their well-being;
- The food system's carbon footprint is reduced, and the amount of carbon sequestered on farmland is increased;
- The food system is sufficiently resilient to withstand the effects of climate change.

Only those with a vested interest in the status quo would argue against creating public policies with these goals. Now weigh them against the reality that our current policies and public investments have given us:

Because of unhealthy diets, 100 years of progress in improving public health and extending lifespan has been reversed. Today's children are expected to live shorter lives than their parents. In large part, this is because a third of these children will develop Type 2 diabetes, formerly rare in children and a preventable disease that reduces life expectancy by several years. At the same time, our fossil-fuel-dependent food and agriculture system is responsible for more greenhouse gas emissions than any other sector of the economy but energy. And the exploitative labor practices of the farming and fast-food industries are responsible for much of the rise in income inequality in America.

We find ourselves in this situation because government policy in these areas is made piecemeal. Diet-related chronic disease, food safety, marketing to children, labor conditions, wages for farm and food-chain workers, immigration, water and air quality, greenhouse gas emissions, and support for farmers: These issues are all connected to the food system. Yet they are overseen by eight federal agencies. Amid this incoherence, special interests thrive and the public good suffers.

In the early days of the Obama administration, there were encouraging signs that the new president recognized the problems of our food system and wanted to do something about them. He spoke about the importance of safety, transparency and competition in the food industry.

Since then, the first lady has made childhood obesity her signature issue, elevating food on the national agenda. But as Michelle Obama raises awareness of healthy eating and tries to reform school lunch, she is struggling to undo the damage caused by outmoded agricultural policies that her husband has left largely undisturbed. The result is the spectacle of Michelle Obama warning Americans to avoid high-fructose corn syrup at the same time the president is signing farm bills that subsidize its production.

The contradictions of our government's policies around food become clear as soon as you compare the federal recommendations for the American diet, known as MyPlate, with the administration's agricultural policies. While MyPlate recommends a diet of 50 percent vegetables and fruits, the administration devotes less than 1 percent of farm subsidies to support the research, production and marketing of those foods. More than 60 percent of that funding subsidizes the production of corn and other grains—food that is mostly fed to animals, converted to fuel for cars or processed into precisely the sort of junk the first lady is urging us to avoid.

How could one government be advancing two such diametrically opposed goals? By failing to recognize that an agricultural policy is not the same as a food policy—and that the former does not necessarily contribute to public health.

Our food system is largely a product of agricultural policies that made sense when the most important public health problem concerning food was the lack of it and when the United States saw "feeding the world" as its mission. These policies succeeded in boosting the productivity of American farmers, yet today they are obsolete and counterproductive, providing billions in public support to an industry that churns out a surfeit of unhealthy calories—while at the same time undermining the ability of the world's farmers to make a living from their land.

These farm policies have nourished an agricultural-industrial complex before which the president and the first lady seem powerless. The administration's early efforts to use antitrust laws to protect farmers and consumers from agribusiness oligopolies were quietly dropped. Promises to regulate the use of antibiotics in animal agriculture—widely acknowledged as a threat to public health—resulted in toothless voluntary guidelines from the Food and Drug Administration.

When it came to regulating methane, one of the most potent greenhouse gases, the Environmental Protection Agency proposed stringent rules for the energy industry—and another voluntary program for agriculture, the single biggest emitter of the gas. And in February the president signed yet another business-as-usual farm bill, which continues to encourage the dumping of cheap but unhealthy calories in the supermarket.

These policies and the diet they sponsor threaten to undermine President Obama's Affordable Care Act. The government now finds itself in the absurd position of financing both sides in the war on Type 2 diabetes, a disease that, along with its associated effects, now costs $245 billion, or 23 percent of the national deficit in 2012, to treat each year. The government subsidizes soda with one hand, while the other writes checks to pay for insulin pumps. This is not policy; this is insanity.

The good news is that solutions are within reach—precisely because the problems are largely a result of government policies. We know that the government has the power to reshape the food system because it has already done so at least once—when President Richard Nixon rejiggered farm policy to boost production of corn and soy to drive down food prices.

Of course, reforming the food system will ultimately depend on a Congress that has for decades been beholden to agribusiness, one of the most powerful lobbies on Capitol Hill. As long as food-related issues are treated as discrete rather than systemic problems, congressional committees in thrall to special interests will be able to block change.

But there is something the president can do now, on his own, to break that deadlock, much as he has done with climate change. In the next State of the Union address, he should announce an executive order establishing a national policy for food, health and well-being. By officially acknowledging the problem and by setting forth a few simple principles on which most Americans agree, the introduction of such a policy would create momentum for reform. By elevating food and farming to a matter of public concern rather than a parochial interest, the president can make it much more difficult for the interests of agribusiness to prevail over those of public and environmental health.

The national food policy could be developed and implemented by a new White House council, which would coordinate among, say, the Department of Health and Human Services and the USDA to align agricultural policies with public health objectives, and the EPA and the USDA to make sure food production doesn't undermine environmental goals. A national food policy would lay the foundation for a food system in which healthful choices are accessible to all and in which it becomes possible to nourish ourselves without exploiting other people or nature.

As Obama begins the last two years of his administration facing an obstructionist Republican Congress, this is an area where he can act on his own—and his legacy may depend on him doing so. For the president won't be able to achieve his goals for health care, climate change, immigration and economic inequality—the four pillars of his second term—if he doesn't address the food system and its negative impact on those issues.

There are precedents for such a policy. Already a handful of states are developing food charters, and scores of U.S. cities have established food policy councils to expand access to healthful food. Brazil and Mexico are far ahead of the United States in developing national food policies. Mexico's recognition of food as a key driver of public health led to the passage last year of a national tax on junk food and soda, which in the first year has reduced consumption of sugary beverages by 10 percent and increased consumption of water.

Brazil has had a national food policy since 2004. In the city of Belo Horizonte that policy—coupled with an investment of 2 percent of the local budget in food-access and farmer-support programs—has reduced poverty by 25 percent and child mortality by 60 percent, and provided access to credit for 2 million farmers, all within a decade.

A well-articulated national food policy in the United States would make it much more difficult for Congress to pass bills that fly in its face. The very act of elevating food among the issues the White House addresses would build public support for reforms. And once the government embraces a goal such as "We guarantee the right of every American to eat food that is healthy, green, fair and affordable"—it becomes far more difficult to pass or sign a farm bill that erodes those guarantees.

Think of the food system as something that works for us rather than exploits us, something that encourages health rather than undermines it. That is the food system the people of the United States deserve, and Obama, in his remaining time in office, can begin to build it.

CRITICAL THINKING QUESTIONS

1. The authors claim, "The food system and the diet its created have caused incalculable damage to the health of our people, and our land, water, and air." Provide three examples of how the American food system damages the health of our people, our land, our water, and our air using the article to support your points.

2. How does the food system impact children in today's society? Has the quality of life for children improved due to the food system when compared to previous generations, or has it worsened? Support your response with points from the article.

3. What is the difference between agricultural policy and food policy in America? What reasons do the authors give for linking these two policies? Do you agree with their reasoning? Why or why not?

4. The authors comment on Brazil's food policy. How has this policy helped the country of Brazil? The authors mention that "special interests" and "vested interests" are standing in the way of America developing a national food policy, which they believe could have similar positive outcomes for our citizens. Select and describe one food issue the authors mention that you believe is a problem. Who would be a "vested interest"? Who would work to block a solution to this issue? Why would they not support a solution on that issue that worked for the national good?

STILL A FAST-FOOD NATION: ERIC SCHLOSSER REFLECTS ON 10 YEARS LATER

by Eric Schlosser

Eric Schlosser wrote the widely praised and best-selling book *Fast Food Nation*, where he discusses the fast food and farming industries in the United States. He has written numerous articles relating to farming, disease, and the fast food industry.

In 2001, Eric Schlosser wrote *Fast Food Nation*, which explored how food was created, distributed, and consumed in America. His examination of our often-overlooked food system galvanized many who were unaware of how we treat the animals we eat, the employees who serve us our food, and the children to whom we market our food products. In this essay, he reflects on how things have changed . . . and stayed the same. He writes that while the food industry is as obtuse and profit driven as ever, he sees changes in what matters—the people who buy food. Some Americans are paying more attention to what they eat and where the food comes from. Others, mostly poor and minority consumers, are eating increasingly less nutritional foods while supporting companies whose profits are higher and higher. Can we work on raising food quality and assisting those who struggle to pay for meals?

• • • • • • • • • • • • • • •

Ten years after his seminal book *Fast Food Nation,* Eric Schlosser reflects on how little has changed in the production, safety, and consumption in America—but why he's still hopeful.

More than a decade has passed since *Fast Food Nation* was published, and I'd love to report that the book is out of date, that the many problems it describes have been solved, and that the Golden Arches are now the symbol of a fallen empire, like the pyramids at Giza. Sadly, that is not the case. Every day about 65 million people eat at a McDonald's restaurant somewhere in the world, more than ever before. The annual revenues of America's fast-food industry, adjusted for inflation, have risen by about 20 percent since 2001. The number of fast-food ads aimed at American children has greatly increased as well. The typical preschooler now sees about three fast-food ads on television every day. The typical teenager sees about five. The endless barrage of ads, toys, contests, and marketing gimmicks has fueled not only fast-food sales, but also a wide range of diet-related illnesses. About two thirds of the adults in the United States are obese or overweight. The obesity rate among preschoolers has doubled in the past 30 years. The rate among children aged 6 to 11 has tripled. And by some odd coincidence, the annual cost of the nation's obesity epidemic—about $168 billion, as calculated by researchers at Emory University—is the same as the amount of money Americans spent on fast food in 2011.

Throughout both terms of President George W. Bush's administration, every effort to reform the nation's food-safety system was blocked by the White House and by Republicans in Congress. During the summer of 2002, ground beef from the ConAgra slaughterhouse in Greeley, Colo., was linked to an outbreak of E. coli 0157:H7. The outbreak killed one person and sickened at least 46.

ConAgra voluntarily recalled almost 19 million pounds of potentially contaminated meat, less than a month's worth of production at Greeley. An investigation by the U.S. Department of Agriculture's Office of the Inspector General subsequently found that the plant had been shipping beef tainted with E. coli 0157:H7 for nearly two years. The Greeley recall later seemed minuscule compared to that of the Westland/Hallmark Meat Co. In 2008 Westland/Hallmark agreed to recall 143 million pounds of potentially contaminated ground beef after an undercover video showed downer cows being dragged by forklift into a slaughterhouse. More than one fourth of the recalled meat had been purchased to make tacos, chili, and hamburgers for federal school-lunch and nutrition programs. As of this writing, the USDA still lacks the authority to test widely for dangerous pathogens, to set enforceable limits on those pathogens, and to demand the recall of contaminated meat.

The industry-friendly policies of the Bush administration also reduced government oversight of worker safety. In 2002 the Occupational Safety and Health Administration changed the form that meatpacking companies must use to report injuries. The new form had no space to report musculoskeletal disorders caused by repetitive trauma—thereby preventing a whole category of serious injury from being counted. Instantly, as if by magic, the injury rate in meatpacking dropped by almost 50 percent. "Recordable safety incident rate in plants cut in half since 1996," the American Meat Institute proudly announced in a press release, without ever mentioning that the decline was due to the change in record keeping. In a scathing report on the exploitation of American meatpacking workers, Human Rights Watch suggested that the AMI had deliberately chosen the year 1996, as a basis of comparison, to mislead the public. "A 50 percent drop in meat and poultry industry injury rates in a single year would be implausible," the report noted, "but reaching back six years creates an impressive but fictitious improvement in plant safety."

A few years later the AMI claimed that "recordable injuries" had actually fallen by 70 percent, thanks to the meatpacking industry's concern for worker safety. The claim was made in an AMI pamphlet commemorating the 100th anniversary of *The Jungle*'s publication.

The title of the pamphlet—"If Upton Sinclair Were Alive Today . . . He'd Be Amazed by the U.S. Meat Industry"—was perhaps its most accurate assertion. Sinclair would no doubt be amazed. He would be amazed by how little has fundamentally changed over the past century, by how poor immigrant workers are still routinely being injured, and by how the industry's lies, no matter how brazen, are still said with a straight face.

Despite all the needless harm that continues to be done, much has changed for the better since 2001, when *Fast Food Nation* appeared in bookstores. Issues that were rarely discussed in the mainstream media—food safety, animal welfare, the obesity epidemic, the ethics of marketing junk food to children, the need for a new and sustainable agricultural system—have become inescapable. A food movement has arisen across the country, promoted by authors, activists, and filmmakers. Marion Nestle's *Food Politics* (2002), Frances and Anna Lappé's *Hope's Edge* (2003), Matthew Scully's *Dominion* (2003), Carlo Petrini's *Slow Food* (2004), Deborah Koons Garcia's *The Future of Food* (2004), Morgan Spurlock's *Super Size Me* (2004), Franny Armstrong's *McLibel* (2005), Michael Pollan's *The Omnivore's Dilemma* (2006), Aaron Woolf's *King Corn* (2008), Raj Patel's *Stuffed and Starved* (2008), Robby Kenner's *Food, Inc.* (2008), Barry Estabrook's *Tomatoland* (2011), the reporting of Tom Philpott, the essays of Corby Kummer and Mark Bittman, the many books of Wendell Berry and Alice Waters, Jamie Oliver's televised *Food Revolution*—all of these works have combined to create a new food culture in the United States. That culture rejects highly processed foods, genetically modified foods, and the whole industrial approach to food production. It champions farmers' markets, school gardens, healthy school lunches, and local and organic production. And it has caused a sea change in American attitudes toward food. A decade ago, the idea of an organic garden at the White House would have seemed inconceivable.

Throughout the United States, parents are working to kick fast food, junk food, and soda out of their children's schools. The sale of fruit and vegetable seeds for home gardens is soaring. Idealistic college kids often dream of becoming chefs or farmers, instead of doctors and lawyers. The Food Network has turned cooking into a form of mass entertainment and transformed people who cook well into celebrities. The frozen, reheated, salty, fatty foods served at McDonald's and Burger King and KFC are the antithesis of what this new movement wants. Even the National Restaurant Association, a corporate bastion of the old mindset, now acknowledges the change. Its 2011 "Restaurant Industry Forecast" says that today's top menu trends are "local sourcing, sustainability, and nutrition."

At the moment, the main problem with the food movement is how few Americans can enjoy its benefits. Although the amount of money spent on organic food has increased more than 20-fold since the early 1990s, it currently accounts for only 4 percent of the nation's total spending on food. The annual revenue of McDonald's Corp. is roughly equal to those of America's entire organic-food industry. Organic food is more expensive. Families in which both parents work outside the home often don't have the time to prepare meals from scratch. And more than 23 million low-income Americans now live in "food deserts" that lack supermarkets. As upper-middle-class and well-educated people increasingly reject fast food, the industry has responded much like the tobacco industry once did when that demographic group decided to quit smoking. The fast-food chains, like the tobacco companies, are now aggressively targeting African-Americans, Latinos, and the poor. America's low-income communities now boast the highest proportion of fast-food restaurants—as well as the highest obesity rates and the highest rates of diabetes. Two vastly different food cultures now coexist in the United States. While some Americans eat free-range chicken and organic produce, exercise regularly, and improve their health, most are consuming inexpensive processed foods, drinking large amounts of soda, and reducing their life expectancy. The contrast between the thin, fit, and well-to-do and the illness-ridden, poor, and obese has no historical precedent. The wealthy used to be corpulent, while the poor starved.

Although the food movement originated among the well-educated upper middle class, it is now reaching out to those less fortunate. The Coalition of Immokalee Workers, an organization that campaigns on behalf of migrant farm workers in Florida, has persuaded the leading fast-food chains—after years of protests—to help raise the wages and improve the working conditions in the fields there. The Restaurant Opportunities Centers United is fighting against wage theft, racism, and the abuse of workers in the restaurant industry. The Edible Schoolyard Project and Slow Food USA are trying to bring healthy food to children in low-income communities. And Growing Power, a group led by Will Allen and based in Milwaukee, is demonstrating how agriculture can thrive in the inner city, turning urban food deserts into farms that produce healthy food.

There are inherent limits, however, on how much this thriving new movement can achieve. At a time when unemployment is high, 46 million Americans live below the poverty line, and the minimum wage remains almost 20 percent lower, adjusted for inflation, than it was 40 years ago, changes to America's food system won't be enough. In the previous chapter of this book, I argued that the 21st century would be marked by a struggle to curtail excessive corporate power. I believe that more strongly today than I did a decade ago. The Founding Fathers of the United States believed that absolute power corrupts absolutely. They believed in the need for competing centers of power. They created a system of government with checks and balances so that no branch of government would become despotic. And they were equally convinced that competition was essential in the economic sphere. If they were alive today, like Upton Sinclair they would be amazed by the monopolies and monopsonies that now dominate the American economy, by the corruption of government officials, and by the wide disparities in wealth. The food movement needs to become part of a larger movement with a broader vision—a movement that opposes unchecked corporate power, that demands not only healthy food but also a living wage and a safe workplace for every single American.

Fast Food Nation was my first book, and I had no idea whether anyone would care to read it. The views expressed in the book seemed completely out of step with the views of most people. I certainly didn't expect that it would still be in print more than a decade later. Since the book was published, I've been strongly criticized by fast-food chains, meatpacking companies, and industry-front groups. The criticism has, for the most part, been quite personal. I've been called a communist and a socialist, a "dunce," a "health fascist," an "economics ignoramus," a "banjo-strumming performer at Farm Aid," a "hectoring nanny of the nanny state," and much stronger epithets. Elementary school principals have been contacted and warned that I shouldn't be allowed to visit classrooms or speak with schoolchildren. Extraordinary lies about me have been spread on the Internet. A number of my readings at bookstores and talks on college campuses have been disrupted by industry supporters. At times I've been accompanied at public appearances by police officers. And all of that has occurred because this book describes the business practices of companies that sell hamburgers.

Nevertheless, I've found the whole experience immensely rewarding. Over the years, I've done my best to help groups campaigning for food safety, child nutrition, worker rights, animal welfare, and sustainable agriculture, among other causes. It has felt good to get out of the office and into the world, to try and do things instead of simply writing about them. I've met countless people who are making a difference, whose self-sacrifice makes my work on behalf of change seem insignificant.

Everything that I've learned since *Fast Food Nation* was published has made me more, not less, optimistic about the possibilities for change. I believe, more than ever before, that nothing about our current food system was inevitable. And when things aren't inevitable, that means things don't have to be the way they are. I hope that 10 years from now this book really is irrelevant—and that the world it describes, so full of greed and lacking in compassion, is just a bad memory.

CRITICAL THINKING QUESTIONS

1. Eric Schlosser writes that in America there now exists "two vastly different food cultures." What are these two cultures? What are the two ways in which they are different? Why are these drastic differences problematic? Provide evidence from the reading to support your points.

2. Schlosser writes that the fast food industries are responding to current consumer trends by acting like the tobacco companies. What does he mean by this? Why do you think they are acting this way? Who are they targeting, and do you think they will be successful? Why or why not?

3. The author argues that "the food movement needs to become part of a larger movement." Describe why he thinks a larger movement is needed. How and why would the food movement be connected to these larger concerns?

4. **Connection.** Eric Schlosser places the blame for the increase in obesity and other negative health outcomes on the food industry and its use of an "endless barrage of ads, toys, contests, and marketing gimmicks." Paul Kenny, in *Is Obesity an Addiction*, presents another view—that our own biology might be the most important factor. Which one do you think holds the most influence over the rise in obesity and other negative health outcomes? Why do you think that? Why is the other option less convincing for you?

HOW JUNK FOOD CAN END OBESITY

by David Freedman

David Freeman is a Boston-based journalist for *The Atlantic* and *Scientific American*. He has been a contributor for *The Atlantic* since 1998, and he has authored five books.

In this essay from *The Atlantic* in 2013, David Freedman presents a counter-intuitive argument: that the best way to make America healthy is to embrace the food we have been demonizing for decades. He shows that the natural, wholesome food many champion is not necessarily healthier than the fast food that many despise. What Americans need to do is eat fewer calories—an 800-calorie, all-natural organic smoothie has as many calories as an 800-calorie hamburger from McDonalds. And because fast food restaurants are already so ingrained in the way many Americans eat, they are in the best position to positively affect the diet of many Americans. Their scale allows them to place better food in the hands of the most people. Will we allow science and industry to help us in the fight against obesity?

• • • • • • • • • • • • • • •

Demonizing processed food may be dooming many to obesity and disease. Could embracing the drive-thru make us all healthier?

Late last year, in a small health-food eatery called Cafe Sprouts in Oberlin, Ohio, I had what may well have been the most wholesome beverage of my life. The friendly server patiently guided me to an apple-blueberry-kale-carrot smoothie-juice combination, which she spent the next several minutes preparing, mostly by shepherding farm-fresh produce into machinery. The result was tasty, but at 300 calories (by my rough calculation) in a 16-ounce cup, it was more than my diet could regularly absorb without consequences, nor was I about to make a habit of $9 shakes, healthy or not.

Inspired by the experience nonetheless, I tried again two months later at L.A.'s Real Food Daily, a popular vegan restaurant near Hollywood. I was initially wary of a low-calorie juice made almost entirely from green vegetables, but the server assured me it was a popular treat. I like to brag that I can eat anything, and I scarf down all sorts of raw vegetables like candy, but I could stomach only about a third of this oddly foamy, bitter concoction. It smelled like lawn clippings and tasted like liquid celery. It goes for $7.95, and I waited 10 minutes for it.

I finally hit the sweet spot just a few weeks later, in Chicago, with a delicious blueberry-pomegranate smoothie that rang in at a relatively modest 220 calories. It cost $3 and took only seconds to make. Best of all, I'll be able to get this concoction just about anywhere. Thanks, McDonald's!

If only the McDonald's smoothie weren't, unlike the first two, so fattening and unhealthy. Or at least that's what the most-prominent voices in our food culture today would have you believe.

An enormous amount of media space has been dedicated to promoting the notion that all processed food, and only processed food, is making us sickly and overweight. In this narrative, the food-industrial complex—particularly the fast-food industry—has turned all the powers of food-processing science loose on engineering its offerings to addict us to fat, sugar, and salt, causing or at least heavily contributing to the obesity crisis. The wares of these pimps and pushers, we are told, are to be universally shunned.

Consider *The New York Times.* Earlier this year, *The Times Magazine* gave its cover to a long piece based on Michael Moss's about-to-be-best-selling book, *Salt Sugar Fat: How the Food Giants Hooked Us.* Hitting bookshelves at about the same time was the former *Times* reporter Melanie Warner's *Pandora's Lunchbox: How Processed Food Took Over the American Meal,* which addresses more or less the same theme. Two years ago *The Times Magazine* featured the journalist Gary Taubes's "Is Sugar Toxic?," a cover story on the evils of refined sugar and high-fructose corn syrup. And most significant of all has been the considerable space the magazine has devoted over the years to Michael Pollan, a journalism professor at the University of California at Berkeley, and his broad indictment of food processing as a source of society's health problems.

"The food they're cooking is making people sick," Pollan has said of big food companies. "It is one of the reasons that we have the obesity and diabetes epidemics that we do . . . If you're going to let industries decide how much salt, sugar and fat is in your food, they're going to put [in] as much as they possibly can . . . They will push those buttons until we scream or die." The solution, in his view, is to replace Big Food's engineered, edible evil—through public education and regulation—with fresh, unprocessed, local, seasonal, *real* food.

Pollan's worldview saturates the public conversation on healthy eating. You hear much the same from many scientists, physicians, food activists, nutritionists, celebrity chefs, and pundits. *Foodlike substances,* the derisive term Pollan uses to describe processed foods, is now a solid part of the elite vernacular. Thousands of restaurants and grocery stores, most notably the Whole Foods chain, have thrived by answering the call to reject industrialized foods in favor of a return to natural, simple, nonindustrialized—let's call them "wholesome"—foods. The two newest restaurants in my smallish Massachusetts town both prominently tout wholesome ingredients; one of them is called the Farmhouse, and it's usually packed.

A new generation of business, social, and policy entrepreneurs is rising to further cater to these tastes, and to challenge Big Food. Silicon Valley, where tomorrow's entrepreneurial and social trends are forged, has spawned a small ecosystem of wholesome-friendly venture-capital firms (Physic Ventures, for example), business accelerators (Local Food Lab), and Web sites (Edible Startups) to fund, nurture, and keep tabs on young companies such as blissmo (a wholesome-food-of-the-month club), Mile High Organics (online wholesome-food shopping), and Wholeshare (group wholesome-food purchasing), all designed to help reacquaint Americans with the simpler eating habits of yesteryear.

In virtually every realm of human existence, we turn to technology to help us solve our problems. But even in Silicon Valley, when it comes to food and obesity, technology—or at least food-processing technology—is widely treated as if it is the problem. The solution, from this viewpoint, necessarily involves turning our back on it.

If the most-influential voices in our food culture today get their way, we will achieve a genuine food revolution. Too bad it would be one tailored to the dubious health fantasies of a small, elite minority. And too bad it would largely exclude the obese masses, who would continue to sicken and die early. Despite the best efforts of a small army of wholesome-food heroes, there is no reasonable scenario under which these foods could become cheap and plentiful enough to serve as the core diet for most of the obese population—even in the unlikely case that your typical junk-food eater would be willing and able to break lifelong habits to embrace kale and yellow beets. And many of the dishes glorified by the wholesome-food movement are, in any case, as caloric and obesogenic as anything served in a Burger King.

Through its growing sway over health-conscious consumers and policy makers, the wholesome-food movement is impeding the progress of the one segment of the food world that is actually positioned to take effective, near-term steps to reverse the obesity trend: the processed-food industry. Popular food producers, fast-food chains among them, are already applying various tricks and technologies to create less caloric and more satiating versions of their junky fare that nonetheless retain much of the appeal of the originals, and could be induced to go much further. In fact, these roundly demonized companies could do far more for the public's health in five years than the wholesome-food movement is likely to accomplish in the next 50. But will the wholesome-food advocates let them?

I. MICHAEL POLLAN HAS NO CLOTHES

Let's go shopping. We can start at Whole Foods Market, a critical link in the wholesome-eating food chain. There are three Whole Foods stores within 15 minutes of my house—we're big on real food in the suburbs west of Boston. Here at the largest of the three, I can choose from more than 21 types of tofu, 62 bins of organic grains and legumes, and 42 different salad greens.

Much of the food isn't all that different from what I can get in any other supermarket, but sprinkled throughout are items that scream "wholesome." One that catches my eye today, sitting prominently on an impulse-buy rack near the checkout counter, is Vegan Cheesy Salad Booster, from Living Intentions, whose package emphasizes the fact that the food is enhanced with spirulina, chlorella, and sea vegetables. The label also proudly lets me know that the contents are raw—no processing!—and that they don't contain any genetically modified ingredients. What the stuff does contain, though, is more than three times the fat content per ounce as the beef patty in a Big Mac (more than two-thirds of the calories come from fat), and four times the sodium.

After my excursion to Whole Foods, I drive a few minutes to a Trader Joe's, also known for an emphasis on wholesome foods. Here at the register I'm confronted with a large display of a snack food called "Inner Peas," consisting of peas that are breaded in cornmeal and rice flour, fried in sunflower oil, and then sprinkled with salt. By weight, the snack has six times as much fat as it does protein, along with loads of carbohydrates. I can't recall ever seeing anything at any fast-food restaurant that represents as big an obesogenic crime against the vegetable kingdom. (A spokesperson for Trader Joe's said the company does not consider itself a "'wholesome food' grocery retailer." Living Intentions did not respond to a request for comment.)

This phenomenon is by no means limited to packaged food at upscale supermarkets. Back in February, when I was at Real Food Daily in Los Angeles, I ordered the "Sea Cake" along with my green-vegetable smoothie. It was intensely delicious in a way that set off alarm bells. RFD wouldn't provide precise information about the ingredients, but I found a recipe online for "Tofu 'Fish' Cakes," which seem very close to what I ate. Essentially, they consist of some tofu mixed with a lot of refined carbs (the RFD version contains at least some unrefined carbs) along with oil and soy milk, all fried in oil and served with a soy-and-oil-based tartar sauce. (Tofu and other forms of soy are high in protein, but per 100 calories, tofu is as fatty as many cuts of beef.) L.A. being to the wholesome-food movement what Hawaii is to Spam, I ate at two other mega-popular wholesome-food restaurants while I was in the area. At Café Gratitude I enjoyed the kale chips and herb-cornmeal-crusted eggplant parmesan, and at Akasha I indulged in a spiced-lamb-sausage flatbread pizza. Both are pricey orgies of fat and carbs.

I'm not picking out rare, less healthy examples from these establishments. Check out their menus online: fat, sugar, and other refined carbs abound. (Café Gratitude says it uses only "healthy" fats and natural sweeteners; Akasha says its focus is not on "health food" but on "farm to fork" fare.) In fact, because the products and dishes offered by these types of establishments tend to emphasize the healthy-sounding foods they contain, I find it much harder to navigate through them to foods that go easy on the oil, butter, refined grains, rice, potatoes, and sugar than I do at far less wholesome restaurants. (These dishes also tend to contain plenty of sea salt, which Pollanites hold up as the wholesome alternative to the addictive salt engineered by the food industry, though your body can't tell the difference.)

One occasional source of obesogenic travesties is *The New York Times Magazine's* lead food writer, Mark Bittman, who now rivals Pollan as a shepherd to the anti-processed-food flock. (*Salon*, in an article titled "How to Live What Michael Pollan Preaches," called Bittman's 2009 book, *Food Matters*, "both a cookbook and a manifesto that shows us how to eat better—and save the planet.") I happened to catch Bittman on the *Today* show last year demonstrating for millions of viewers four ways to prepare corn in summertime, including a lovely dish of corn sautéed in bacon fat and topped with bacon. Anyone who thinks that such a thing is much healthier than a Whopper just hasn't been paying attention to obesity science for the past few decades.

That science is, in fact, fairly straightforward. Fat carries more than twice as many calories as carbohydrates and proteins do per gram, which means just a little fat can turn a serving of food into a calorie bomb. Sugar and other refined carbohydrates, like white flour and rice, and high-starch foods, like corn and potatoes, aren't as calorie-dense. But all of these "problem carbs" charge into the bloodstream as glucose in minutes, providing an energy rush, commonly followed by an energy crash that can lead to a surge in appetite.

Because they are energy-intense foods, fat and sugar and other problem carbs trip the pleasure and reward meters placed in our brains by evolution over the millions of years during which starvation was an ever-present threat. We're born enjoying the stimulating sensations these ingredients provide, and exposure strengthens the associations, ensuring that we come to crave them and, all too often, eat more of them than we should. Processed food is not an essential part of this story: recent examinations of ancient human remains in Egypt, Peru, and elsewhere have repeatedly revealed hardened arteries, suggesting that pre-industrial diets, at least of the affluent, may not have been the epitome of healthy eating that the Pollanites make them out to be. People who want to lose weight and keep it off are almost always advised by those who run successful long-term weight-loss programs to transition to a diet high in lean protein, complex carbs such as whole grains and legumes, and the sort of fiber vegetables are loaded with. Because these ingredients provide us with the calories we need without the big, fast bursts of energy, they can be satiating without pushing the primitive reward buttons that nudge us to eat too much.

(A few words on salt: Yes, it's unhealthy in large amounts, raising blood pressure in many people; and yes, it makes food more appealing. But salt is not obesogenic—it has no calories, and doesn't specifically increase the desire to consume high-calorie foods. It can just as easily be enlisted to add to the appeal of vegetables. Lumping it in with fat and sugar as an addictive junk-food ingredient is a confused proposition. But let's agree we want to cut down on it.)

To be sure, many of Big Food's most popular products are loaded with appalling amounts of fat and sugar and other problem carbs (as well as salt), and the plentitude of these ingredients, exacerbated by large portion sizes, has clearly helped foment the obesity crisis. It's hard to find anyone anywhere who disagrees. Junk food is bad for you because it's full of fat and problem carbs. But will switching to wholesome foods free us from this scourge? It could in theory, but in practice, it's hard to see how. Even putting aside for a moment the serious questions about whether wholesome foods could be made accessible to the obese public, and whether the obese would be willing to eat them, we have a more immediate stumbling block: many of the foods served up and even glorified by the wholesome-food movement are themselves chock full of fat and problem carbs.

Some wholesome foodies openly celebrate fat and problem carbs, insisting that the lack of processing magically renders them healthy. In singing the praises of clotted cream and lard-loaded cookies, for instance, a recent *Wall Street Journal* article by Ron Rosenbaum explained that "eating basic, earthy, fatty foods isn't just a supreme experience of the senses—it can actually be good for you," and that it's "too easy to conflate eating fatty food with eating industrial, oil-fried junk food." That's right, we wouldn't want to make the same mistake that all the cells in our bodies make. Pollan himself makes it clear in his writing that he has little problem with fat—as long as it's not in food "your great-grandmother wouldn't recognize."

Television food shows routinely feature revered chefs tossing around references to healthy eating, "wellness," and farm-fresh ingredients, all the while spooning lard, cream, and sugar over everything in sight. (A study published last year in the *British Medical Journal* found that the recipes in the books of top TV chefs call for "significantly more" fat per portion than what's contained in ready-to-eat supermarket meals.) Corporate wellness programs, one of the most promising avenues for getting the population to adopt healthy behaviors, are falling prey to this way of thinking as well. Last November, I attended a stress-management seminar for employees of a giant consulting company, and listened to a high-powered professional wellness coach tell the crowded room that it's okay to eat anything as long as its plant or animal origins aren't obscured by processing. Thus, she explained, potato chips are perfectly healthy, because they plainly come from potatoes, but Cheetos will make you sick and fat, because what plant or animal is a Cheeto? (For the record, typical potato chips and Cheetos have about equally nightmarish amounts of fat calories per ounce; Cheetos have fewer carbs, though more salt.)

The Pollanites seem confused about exactly what benefits their way of eating provides. All the railing about the fat, sugar, and salt engineered into industrial junk food might lead one to infer that wholesome food, having not been engineered, contains substantially less of them. But clearly you can take in obscene quantities of fat and problem carbs while eating wholesomely, and to judge by what's sold at wholesome stores and restaurants, many people do. Indeed, the more converts and customers the wholesome-food movement's purveyors seek, the stronger their incentive to emphasize foods that light up precisely the same pleasure centers as a 3 Musketeers bar. That just makes wholesome food stealthily obesogenic.

Hold on, you may be thinking. Leaving fat, sugar, and salt aside, what about all the nasty things that wholesome foods do not, by definition, contain and processed foods do? A central claim of the wholesome-food movement is that wholesome is healthier because it doesn't have the artificial flavors, preservatives, other additives, or genetically modified ingredients found in industrialized food; because it isn't subjected to the physical transformations that processed foods go through; and because it doesn't sit around for days, weeks, or months, as industrialized food sometimes does. (This is the complaint against the McDonald's smoothie, which contains artificial flavors and texture additives, and which is pre-mixed.)

The health concerns raised about processing itself—rather than the amount of fat and problem carbs in any given dish—are not, by and large, related to weight gain or obesity. That's important to keep in mind, because obesity is, by an enormous margin, the largest health problem created by what we eat. But even putting that aside, concerns about processed food have been magnified out of all proportion.

Some studies have shown that people who eat wholesomely tend to be healthier than people who live on fast food and other processed food (particularly meat), but the problem with such studies is obvious: substantial nondietary differences exist between these groups, such as propensity to exercise, smoking rates, air quality, access to health care, and much more. (Some researchers say they've tried to control for these factors, but that's a claim most scientists don't put much faith in.) What's more, the people in these groups are sometimes eating entirely different foods, not the same sorts of foods subjected to different levels of processing. It's comparing apples to Whoppers, instead of Whoppers to handground, grass-fed-beef burgers with heirloom tomatoes, garlic aioli, and artisanal cheese. For all these reasons, such findings linking food type and health are considered highly unreliable, and constantly contradict one another, as is true of most epidemiological studies that try to tackle broad nutritional questions.

The fact is, there is simply no clear, credible evidence that any aspect of food processing or storage makes a food uniquely unhealthy. The U.S. population does not suffer from a critical lack of any nutrient because we eat so much processed food. (Sure, health experts urge Americans to get more calcium, potassium, magnesium, fiber, and vitamins A, E, and C, and eating more produce and dairy is a great way to get them, but these ingredients are also available in processed foods, not to mention supplements.) Pollan's "foodlike substances" are regulated by the U.S. Food and Drug Administration (with some exceptions, which are regulated by other agencies), and their effects on health are further raked over by countless scientists who would get a nice career boost from turning up the hidden dangers in some common food-industry ingredient or technique, in part because any number of advocacy groups and journalists are ready to pounce on the slightest hint of risk.

The results of all the scrutiny of processed food are hardly scary, although some groups and writers try to make them appear that way. The Pew Charitable Trusts' Food Additives Project, for example, has bemoaned the fact that the FDA directly reviews only about 70 percent of the ingredients found in food, permitting the rest to pass as "generally recognized as safe" by panels of experts convened by manufacturers. But the only actual risk the project calls out on its Web site or in its publications is a quote from a *Times* article noting that bromine, which has been in U.S. foods for eight decades, is regarded as suspicious by many because flame retardants containing bromine have been linked to health risks. There is no conclusive evidence that bromine itself is a threat.

In *Pandora's Lunchbox,* Melanie Warner assiduously catalogs every concern that could possibly be raised about the health threats of food processing, leveling accusations so vague, weakly supported, tired, or insignificant that only someone already convinced of the guilt of processed food could find them troubling. While ripping the covers off the breakfast-cereal conspiracy, for example, Warner reveals that much of the nutritional value claimed by these products comes not from natural ingredients but from added vitamins that are chemically synthesized, which must be bad for us because, well, they're *chemically synthesized.* It's the tautology at the heart of the movement: processed foods are unhealthy because they aren't natural, full stop.

In many respects, the wholesome-food movement veers awfully close to religion. To repeat: there is no hard evidence to back any health-risk claims about processed food—evidence, say, of the caliber of several studies by the Centers for Disease Control and Prevention that have traced food poisoning to raw milk, a product championed by some circles of the wholesome-food movement. "Until I hear evidence to the contrary, I think it's reasonable to include processed food in your diet," says Robert Kushner, a physician and nutritionist and a professor at Northwestern University's medical school, where he is the clinical director of the Comprehensive Center on Obesity.

There may be other reasons to prefer wholesome food to the industrialized version. Often stirred into the vague stew of benefits attributed to wholesome food is the "sustainability" of its production—that is, its long-term impact on the planet. Small farms that don't rely much on chemicals and heavy industrial equipment may be better for the environment than giant industrial farms—although that argument quickly becomes complicated by a variety of factors. For the purposes of this article, let's simply stipulate that wholesome foods are environmentally superior. But let's also agree that when it comes to prioritizing among food-related public-policy goals, we are likely to save and improve many more lives by focusing on cutting obesity—through any available means—than by trying to convert all of industrial agriculture into a vast constellation of small organic farms.

The impact of obesity on the chances of our living long, productive, and enjoyable lives has been so well documented at this point that I hate to drag anyone through the grim statistics again. But let me just toss out one recent dispatch from the world of obesity-havoc science: a study published in February in the journal *Obesity* found that obese young adults and middle-agers in the U.S. are likely to lose almost a decade of life on average, as compared with their non-obese counterparts. Given our obesity rates, that means Americans who are alive today can collectively expect to sacrifice 1 billion years to obesity. The study adds to a river of evidence suggesting that for the first time in modern history—and in spite of many health-related improvements in our environment, our health care, and our nondietary habits—our health prospects are worsening, mostly because of excess weight.

By all means, let's protect the environment. But let's not rule out the possibility of technologically enabled improvements to our diet—indeed, let's not rule out *any* food—merely because we are pleased by images of pastoral family farms. Let's first pick the foods that can most plausibly make us healthier, all things considered, and then figure out how to make them environmentally friendly.

II. LET THEM EAT KALE

I'm a fan of many of Mark Bittman's recipes. I shop at Whole Foods all the time. And I eat like many wholesome foodies, except I try to stay away from those many wholesome ingredients and dishes that are high in fat and problem carbs. What's left are vegetables, fruits, legumes, whole grains, poultry, and fish (none of them fried, thank you), which are often emphasized by many wholesome-food fans. In general, I find that the more-natural versions of these ingredients taste at least a bit better, and occasionally much better, than the industrialized versions. And despite the wholesome-food movement's frequent and inexcusable obliviousness to the obesogenicity of many of its own foods, it deserves credit for paying more attention to those healthier ingredients than does Big Food.

Where the Pollanites get into real trouble—where their philosophy becomes so glib and wrongheaded that it is actually immoral—is in the claim that their style of food shopping and eating is the answer to the country's weight problem. Helping me to indulge my taste for genuinely healthy wholesome foods are the facts that I'm relatively affluent and well educated, and that I'm surrounded by people who tend to take care with what they eat. Not only am I within a few minutes' drive of three Whole Foods and two Trader Joe's, I'm within walking distance of two other supermarkets and more than a dozen restaurants that offer bountiful healthy-eating options.

I am, in short, not much like the average obese person in America, and neither are the Pollanites. That person is relatively poor, does not read *The Times* or cookbook manifestos, is surrounded by people who eat junk food and are themselves obese, and stands a good chance of living in a food desert—an area where produce tends to be hard to find, of poor quality, or expensive.

The wholesome foodies don't argue that obesity and class are unrelated, but they frequently argue that the obesity gap between the classes has been created by the processed-food industry, which, in the past few decades, has preyed mostly on the less affluent masses. Yet Lenard Lesser, a physician and an obesity researcher at the Palo Alto Medical Foundation Research Institute, says that can't be so, because the obesity gap predates the fast-food industry and the dietary dominance of processed food. "The difference in obesity rates in low- and high-income groups was evident as far back as we have data, at least back through the 1960s," he told me. One reason, some researchers have argued, is that after having had to worry, over countless generations, about getting enough food, poorer segments of society had little cultural bias against overindulging in food, or putting on excess pounds, as industrialization raised incomes and made rich food cheaply available.

The most obvious problem with the "let them eat kale" philosophy of affluent wholesome-food advocates involves the price and availability of wholesome food. Even if Whole Foods, Real Food Daily, or the Farmhouse weren't three bus rides away for the working poor, and even if three ounces of Vegan Cheesy Salad Booster, a Sea Cake appetizer, and the vegetarian quiche weren't laden with fat and problem carbs, few among them would be likely to shell out $5.99, $9.95, or $16, respectively, for those pricey treats.

A slew of start-ups are trying to find ways of producing fresh, local, unprocessed meals quickly and at lower cost. But could this food eventually be sold as cheaply, conveniently, and ubiquitously as today's junky fast food? Not even according to Bittman, who explored the question in a recent *New York Times Magazine* article. Even if wholesome food caught on with the public at large, including the obese population, and even if poor and working-class people were willing to pay a premium for it, how long would it take to scale up from a handful of shops to the tens of thousands required to begin making a dent in the obesity crisis? How long would it take to create the thousands of local farms we'd need in order to provide these shops with fresh, unprocessed ingredients, even in cities?

Yet these hurdles can be waved away, if one only has the proper mind-set. Bittman argued two years ago in *The Times* that there's no excuse for anyone, food-desert-bound or not, to eat fast food rather than wholesome food, because even if it's not perfectly fresh and locally grown, lower-end wholesome food—when purchased judiciously at the supermarket and cooked at home—can be cheaper than fast food. Sure, there's the matter of all the time, effort, schedule coordination, and ability it takes to shop, cook, serve, and clean up. But anyone who whines about that extra work, Bittman chided, just doesn't want to give up their excessive TV watching. (An "important benefit of paying more for better-quality food is that you're apt to eat less of it," Pollan helpfully noted in his 2008 book, *In Defense of Food*.) It's remarkable how easy it is to remake the disadvantaged in one's own image.

Let's assume for a moment that somehow America, food deserts and all, becomes absolutely lousy with highly affordable outlets for wholesome, locally sourced dishes that are high in vegetables, fruits, legumes, poultry, fish, and whole grains, and low in fat and problem carbs. What percentage of the junk-food-eating obese do we want to predict will be ready to drop their Big Macs, fries, and Cokes for grilled salmon on chard? We can all agree that many obese people find the former foods extremely enjoyable, and seem unable to control their consumption of them. Is greater availability of healthier food that pushes none of the same thrill buttons going to solve the problem?

Many Pollanites insist it will. "If the government came into these communities and installed Brita filters under their sinks, they'd drink water instead of Coke," Lisa Powell, a professor of health policy and administration at the University of Illinois at Chicago's Institute for Health Research and Policy, told me. But experts who actually work with the obese see a more difficult transition, especially when busy schedules are thrown into the equation. "They won't eat broccoli instead of french fries," says Kelli Drenner, an obesity researcher at Stephen F. Austin State University in Nacogdoches, Texas, which has about four fast-food restaurants per block along most of its main drag. "You try to make even a small change to school lunches, and parents and kids revolt."

Hoping to gain some firsthand insight into the issue while in L.A., I drove away from the wholesome-food-happy, affluent, and mostly trim communities of the northwestern part of the city, and into East L.A. The largely Hispanic population there was nonaffluent and visibly plagued by obesity. On one street, I saw a parade of young children heading home from school. Perhaps a quarter of them were significantly overweight; several walked with a slow, waddling gait.

The area I found that's most chockablock with commercial food options brackets the busy intersection of two main streets. However, like most areas I passed through nearby, this food scene was dominated not by fast-food restaurants but by bodegas (which, like most other types of convenience stores, are usually considered part of the low-income, food-desert landscape). I went into several of these mom-and-pop shops and saw pretty much the same thing in every one: A prominent display of extremely fatty-looking beef and pork, most of it fresh, though gigantic strips of fried pork skin often got pride of place. A lot of canned and boxed foods. Up front, shelves of candy and heavily processed snacks. A large set of display cases filled mostly with highly sugared beverages. And a small refrigerator case somewhere in the back sparsely populated with not-especially-fresh-looking fruits and vegetables. The bodega industry, too, seems to have plotted to addict communities to fat, sugar, and salt—unless, that is, they're simply providing the foods that people like.

Various efforts have been made to redesign bodegas to emphasize healthier choices. I learned that one retooled bodega was nearby, and dropped in. It was cleaner and brighter than the others I'd seen, and a large produce case was near the entrance, brimming with an impressive selection of fresh-looking produce. The candy and other junky snack foods were relegated to a small set of shelves closer to the more dimly lit rear of the store. But I couldn't help noticing that unlike most of the other bodegas I'd been to, this one was empty, except for me and a lone employee. I hung around, eventually buying a few items to assuage the employee's growing suspicion. Finally, a young woman came in, made a beeline for the junk-food shelves, grabbed a pack of cupcakes, paid, and left.

It's not exactly a scientific study, but we really shouldn't need one to recognize that people aren't going to change their ingrained, neurobiologically supercharged junk-eating habits just because someone dangles vegetables in front of them, farm-fresh or otherwise. Mark Bittman sees signs of victory in "the stories parents tell me of their kids booing as they drive by McDonald's," but it's not hard to imagine which parents, which kids, and which neighborhoods those stories might involve. One study found that subsidizing the purchase of vegetables encouraged shoppers to buy more vegetables, but also more junk food with the money they saved; on balance, their diets did not improve. The Centers for Disease Control and Prevention recently found that the aughts saw a significant drop in fruit intake, and no increase in vegetable consumption; Americans continue to fall far short of eating the recommended amounts of either. "Everyone's mother and brother has been telling them to eat more fruit and vegetables forever, and the numbers are only getting worse," says Steven Nickolas, who runs the Healthy Food Project in Scottsdale, Arizona. "We're not going to solve this problem by telling people to eat unprocessed food."

Trim, affluent Americans of course have a right to view dietary questions from their own perspective—that is, in terms of what they need to eat in order to add perhaps a few months onto the already healthy courses of their lives. The pernicious sleight of hand is in willfully confusing what might benefit them—small, elite minority that they are—with what would help most of society. The conversations they have among themselves in *The Times,* in best-selling books, and at Real Food Daily may not register with the working-class obese. But these conversations unquestionably distort the views of those who are in a position to influence what society does about the obesity problem.

III. THE FOOD REVOLUTION WE NEED

The one fast-food restaurant near that busy East L.A. intersection otherwise filled with bodegas was a Carl's Jr. I went in and saw that the biggest and most prominent posters in the store were pushing a new grilled-cod sandwich. It actually looked pretty good, but it wasn't quite lunchtime, and I just wanted a cup of coffee. I went to the counter to order it, but before I could say anything, the cashier greeted me and asked, "Would you like to try our new Charbroiled Atlantic Cod Fish Sandwich today?" Oh, well, sure, why not? (I asked her to hold the tartar sauce, which is mostly fat, but found out later that the sandwich is normally served with about half as much tartar sauce as the notoriously fatty Filet-O-Fish sandwich at McDonald's, where the fish is battered and fried.) The sandwich was delicious. It was less than half the cost of the Sea Cake appetizer at Real Food Daily. It took less than a minute to prepare. In some ways, it was the best meal I had in L.A., and it was probably the healthiest.

We know perfectly well who within our society has developed an extraordinary facility for nudging the masses to eat certain foods, and for making those foods widely available in cheap and convenient forms. The Pollanites have led us to conflate the industrial processing of food with the adding of fat and sugar in order to hook customers, even while pushing many faux-healthy foods of their own. But why couldn't Big Food's processing and marketing genius be put to use on genuinely healthier foods, like grilled fish? Putting aside the standard objection that the industry has no interest in doing so—we'll see later that in fact the industry has plenty of motivation for taking on this challenge—wouldn't that present a more plausible answer to America's junk-food problem than ordering up 50,000 new farmers' markets featuring locally grown organic squash blossoms?

According to Lenard Lesser, of the Palo Alto Medical Foundation, the food industry has mastered the art of using in-store and near-store promotions to shape what people eat. As Lesser and I drove down storied Telegraph Avenue in Berkeley and into far less affluent Oakland, leaving behind the Whole Foods Markets and sushi restaurants for gas-station markets and barbecued-rib stands, he pointed out the changes in the billboards. Whereas the last one we saw in Berkeley was for fruit juice, many in Oakland tout fast-food joints and their wares, including several featuring the Hot Mess Burger at Jack in the Box. Though Lesser noted that this forest of advertising may simply reflect Oakland residents' preexisting preference for this type of food, he told me lab studies have indicated that the more signs you show people for a particular food product or dish, the more likely they are to choose it over others, all else being equal.

We went into a KFC and found ourselves traversing a maze of signage that put us face-to-face with garish images of various fried foods that presumably had some chicken somewhere deep inside them. "The more they want you to buy something, the bigger they make the image on the menu board," Lesser explained. Here, what loomed largest was the $19.98 fried-chicken-and-corn family meal, which included biscuits and cake. A few days later, I noticed that McDonald's places large placards showcasing desserts on the trash bins, apparently calculating that the best time to entice diners with sweets is when they think they've finished their meals.

Trying to get burger lovers to jump to grilled fish may already be a bit of a stretch—I didn't see any of a dozen other customers buy the cod sandwich when I was at Carl's Jr., though the cashier said it was selling reasonably well. Still, given the food industry's power to tinker with and market food, we should not dismiss its ability to get unhealthy eaters—slowly, incrementally—to buy better food.

That brings us to the crucial question: Just how much healthier could fast-food joints and processed-food companies make their best-selling products without turning off customers? I put that question to a team of McDonald's executives, scientists, and chefs who are involved in shaping the company's future menus, during a February visit to McDonald's surprisingly bucolic campus west of Chicago. By way of a partial answer, the team served me up a preview tasting of two major new menu items that had been under development in their test kitchens and high-tech sensory-testing labs for the past year, and which were rolled out to the public in April. The first was the Egg White Delight McMuffin ($2.65), a lower-calorie, less fatty version of the Egg McMuffin, with some of the refined flour in the original recipe replaced by whole-grain flour. The other was one of three new Premium McWraps ($3.99), crammed with grilled chicken and spring mix, and given a light coating of ranch dressing amped up with rice vinegar. Both items tasted pretty good (as do the versions in stores, I've since confirmed, though some outlets go too heavy on the dressing). And they were both lower in fat, sugar, and calories than not only many McDonald's staples, but also much of the food served in wholesome restaurants or touted in wholesome cookbooks.

In fact, McDonald's has quietly been making healthy changes for years, shrinking portion sizes, reducing some fats, trimming average salt content by more than 10 percent in the past couple of years alone, and adding fruits, vegetables, low-fat dairy, and oatmeal to its menu. In May, the chain dropped its Angus third-pounders and announced a new line of quarter-pound burgers, to be served on buns containing whole grains. Outside the core fast-food customer base, Americans are becoming more health-conscious. Public backlash against fast food could lead to regulatory efforts, and in any case, the fast-food industry has every incentive to maintain broad appeal. "We think a lot about how we can bring nutritionally balanced meals that include enough protein, along with the tastes and satisfaction that have an appetite-tiding effect," said Barbara Booth, the company's director of sensory science.

Such steps are enormously promising, says Jamy Ard, an epidemiology and preventive-medicine researcher at Wake Forest Baptist Medical Center in Winston-Salem, North Carolina, and a co-director of the Weight Management Center there. "Processed food is a key part of our environment, and it needs to be part of the equation," he explains. "If you can reduce fat and calories by only a small amount in a Big Mac, it still won't be a health food, but it wouldn't be as bad, and that could have a huge impact on us." Ard, who has been working for more than a decade with the obese poor, has little patience with the wholesome-food movement's call to eliminate fast food in favor of farm-fresh goods. "It's really naive," he says. "Fast food became popular because it's tasty and convenient and cheap. It makes a lot more sense to look for small, beneficial changes in that food than it does to hold out for big changes in what people eat that have no realistic chance of happening."

According to a recent study, Americans get 11 percent of their calories, on average, from fast food—a number that's almost certainly much higher among the less affluent overweight. As a result, the fast-food industry may be uniquely positioned to improve our diets. Research suggests that calorie counts in a meal can be trimmed by as much as 30 percent without eaters noticing—by, for example, reducing portion sizes and swapping in ingredients that contain more fiber and water. Over time, that could be much more than enough to literally tip the scales for many obese people. "The difference between losing weight and not losing weight," says Robert Kushner, the obesity scientist and clinical director at Northwestern, "is a few hundred calories a day."

Which raises a question: If McDonald's is taking these sorts of steps, albeit in a slow and limited way, why isn't it more loudly saying so to deflect criticism? While the company has heavily plugged the debut of its new egg-white sandwich and chicken wraps, the ads have left out even a mention of health, the reduced calories and fat, or the inclusion of whole grains. McDonald's has practically kept secret the fact that it has also begun substituting whole-grain flour for some of the less healthy refined flour in its best-selling Egg McMuffin.

The explanation can be summed up in two words that surely strike fear into the hearts of all fast-food executives who hope to make their companies' fare healthier: McLean Deluxe.

Among those who gleefully rank such things, the McLean Deluxe reigns as McDonald's worst product failure of all time, eclipsing McPasta, the McHotdog, and the McAfrica (don't ask). When I brought up the McLean Deluxe to the innovation team at McDonald's, I faced the first and only uncomfortable silence of the day. Finally, Greg Watson, a senior vice president, cleared his throat and told me that neither he nor anyone else in the room was at the company at the time, and he didn't know that much about it. "It sounds to me like it was ahead of its time," he added. "If we had something like that in the future, we would never launch it like that again."

Introduced in 1991, the McLean Deluxe was perhaps the boldest single effort the food industry has ever undertaken to shift the masses to healthier eating. It was supposed to be a healthier version of the Quarter Pounder, made with extra-lean beef infused with seaweed extract. It reportedly did reasonably well in early taste tests—for what it's worth, my wife and I were big fans—and McDonald's pumped the reduced-fat angle to the public for all it was worth. The general reaction varied from lack of interest to mockery to revulsion. The company gamely flogged the sandwich for five years before quietly removing it from the menu.

The McLean Deluxe was a sharp lesson to the industry, even if in some ways it merely confirmed what generations of parents have well known: if you want to turn off otherwise eager eaters to a dish, tell them it's good for them. Recent studies suggest that calorie counts placed on menus have a negligible effect on food choices, and that the less-health-conscious might even use the information to steer clear of low-calorie fare—perhaps assuming that it tastes worse and is less satisfying, and that it's worse value for their money. The result is a sense in the food industry that if it is going to sell healthier versions of its foods to the general public—and not just to that minority already sold on healthier eating—it is going to have to do it in a relatively sneaky way, emphasizing the taste appeal and not the health benefits. "People expect something to taste worse if they believe it's healthy," says Charles Spence, an

Oxford University neuroscientist who specializes in how the brain perceives food. "And that expectation affects how it tastes to them, so it actually *does* taste worse."

Thus McDonald's silence on the nutritional profiles of its new menu items. "We're not making any health claims," Watson said. "We're just saying it's new, it tastes great, come on in and enjoy it. Maybe once the product is well seated with customers, we'll change that message." If customers learn that they can eat healthier foods at McDonald's without even realizing it, he added, they'll be more likely to try healthier foods there than at other restaurants. The same reasoning presumably explains why the promotions and ads for the Carl's Jr. grilled-cod sandwich offer not a word related to healthfulness, and why there wasn't a whiff of health cheerleading surrounding the turkey burger brought out earlier this year by Burger King (which is not yet calling the sandwich a permanent addition).

If the food industry is to quietly sell healthier products to its mainstream, mostly non-health-conscious customers, it must find ways to deliver the eating experience that fat and problem carbs provide in foods that have fewer of those ingredients. There is no way to do that with farm-fresh produce and wholesome meat, other than reducing portion size. But processing technology gives the food industry a potent tool for trimming unwanted ingredients while preserving the sensations they deliver.

I visited Fona International, a flavor-engineering company also outside Chicago, and learned that there are a battery of tricks for fooling and appeasing taste buds, which are prone to notice a lack of fat or sugar, or the presence of any of the various bitter, metallic, or otherwise unpleasant flavors that vegetables, fiber, complex carbs, and fat or sugar substitutes can impart to a food intended to appeal to junk-food eaters. Some 5,000 FDA-approved chemical compounds—which represent the base components of all known flavors—line the shelves that run alongside Fona's huge labs. Armed with these ingredients and an array of state-of-the-art chemical-analysis and testing tools, Fona's scientists and engineers can precisely control flavor perception. "When you reduce the sugar, fat, and salt in foods, you change the personality of the product," said Robert Sobel, a chemist, who heads up research at the company. "We can restore it."

For example, fat "cushions" the release of various flavors on the tongue, unveiling them gradually and allowing them to linger. When fat is removed, flavors tend to immediately inundate the tongue and then quickly flee, which we register as a much less satisfying experience. Fona's experts can reproduce the "temporal profile" of the flavors in fattier foods by adding edible compounds derived from plants that slow the release of flavor molecules; by replacing the flavors with similarly flavored compounds that come on and leave more slowly; or by enlisting "phantom aromas" that create the sensation of certain tastes even when those tastes are not present on the tongue. (For example, the smell of vanilla can essentially mask reductions in sugar of up to 25 percent.) One triumph of this sort of engineering is the modern protein drink, a staple of many successful weight-loss programs and a favorite of those trying to build muscle. "Seven years ago they were unpalatable," Sobel said. "Today we can mask the astringent flavors and eggy aromas by adding natural ingredients."

I also visited Tic Gums in White Marsh, Maryland, a company that engineers textures into food products. Texture hasn't received the attention that flavor has, noted Greg Andon, Tic's boyish and ebullient president, whose family has run the company for three generations. The result, he said, is that even people in the food industry don't have an adequate vocabulary for it. "They know what flavor you're referring to when you say 'forest floor,' but all they can say about texture is 'Can you make it more creamy?'!" So Tic is inventing a vocabulary, breaking textures down according to properties such as "mouth coating" and "mouth clearing."

Wielding an arsenal of some 20 different "gums"—edible ingredients mostly found in tree sap, seeds, and other plant matter—Tic's researchers can make low-fat foods taste, well, creamier; give the same full body that sugared drinks offer to sugar-free beverages; counter chalkiness and gloopiness; and help orchestrate the timing of flavor bursts. (Such approaches have nothing in common with the ill-fated Olestra, a fat-like compound engineered to pass undigested through the body, and billed in the late 1990s as a fat substitute in snack foods. It was made notorious by widespread anecdotal complaints of cramps and loose bowels, though studies seemed to contradict those claims.)

Fona and Tic, like most companies in their industry, won't identify customers or product names on the record. But both firms showed me an array of foods and beverages that were under construction, so to speak, in the name of reducing calories, fat, and sugar while maintaining mass appeal. I've long hated the taste of low-fat dressing—I gave up on it a few years ago and just use vinegar—but Tic served me an in-development version of a low-fat salad dressing that was better than any I've ever had. Dozens of companies are doing similar work, as are the big food-ingredient manufacturers, such as ConAgra, whose products are in 97 percent of American homes, and whose whole-wheat flour is what McDonald's is relying on for its breakfast sandwiches. Domino Foods, the sugar manufacturer, now sells a low-calorie combination of sugar and the nonsugar sweetener stevia that has been engineered by a flavor company to mask the sort of nonsugary tastes driving many consumers away from diet beverages and the like. "Stevia has a licorice note we were able to have taken out," explains Domino Foods CEO Brian O'Malley.

High-tech anti-obesity food engineering is just warming up. Oxford's Charles Spence notes that in addition to flavors and textures, companies are investigating ways to exploit a stream of insights that have been coming out of scholarly research about the neuroscience of eating. He notes, for example, that candy companies may be able to slip healthier ingredients into candy bars without anyone noticing, simply by loading these ingredients into the middle of the bar and leaving most of the fat and sugar at the ends of the bar. "We tend to make up our minds about how something tastes from the first and last bites, and don't care as much what happens in between," he explains. Some other potentially useful gimmicks he points out: adding weight to food packaging such as yogurt containers, which convinces eaters that the contents are rich with calories, even when they're not; using chewy textures that force consumers to spend more time between bites, giving the brain a chance to register satiety; and using colors, smells, sounds, and packaging information to create the belief that foods are fatty and sweet even when they are not. Spence found, for example, that wine is perceived as 50 percent sweeter when consumed under a red light.

Researchers are also tinkering with food ingredients to boost satiety. Cargill has developed a starch derived from tapioca that gives dishes a refined-carb taste and mouthfeel, but acts more like fiber in the body—a feature that could keep the appetite from spiking later. "People usually think that processing leads to foods that digest too quickly, but we've been able to use processing to slow the digestion rate," says Bruce McGoogan, who heads R&D for Cargill's North American food-ingredient business. The company has also developed ways to reduce fat in beef patties, and to make baked goods using half the usual sugar and oil, all without heavily compromising taste and texture.

Other companies and research labs are trying to turn out healthier, more appealing foods by enlisting ultra-high pressure, nanotechnology, vacuums, and edible coatings. At the University of Massachusetts at Amherst's Center for Foods for Health and Wellness, Fergus Clydesdale, the director of the school's Food Science Policy Alliance—as well as a spry 70-something who's happy to tick off all the processed food in his diet—showed me labs where researchers are looking into possibilities that would not only attack obesity but also improve health in other significant ways, for example by isolating ingredients that might lower the risk of cancer and concentrating them in foods. "When you understand foods at the molecular level," he says, "there's a lot you can do with food and health that we're not doing now."

IV. THE IMPLACABLE ENEMIES OF HEALTHIER PROCESSED FOOD

What's not to like about these developments? Plenty, if you've bought into the notion that processing itself is the source of the unhealthfulness of our foods. The wholesome-food movement is not only talking up dietary strategies that are unlikely to help most obese Americans; it is, in various ways, getting in the way of strategies that could work better.

The Pollanites didn't invent resistance to healthier popular foods, as the fates of the McLean Deluxe and Olestra demonstrate, but they've greatly intensified it. Fast food and junk food have their core customer base, and the wholesome-food gurus have theirs. In between sit many millions of Americans—the more the idea that processed food should be shunned no matter what takes hold in this group, the less incentive fast-food joints will have to continue edging away from the fat- and problem-carb-laden fare beloved by their most loyal customers to try to broaden their appeal.

Pollan has popularized contempt for "nutritionism," the idea behind packing healthier ingredients into processed foods. In his view, the quest to add healthier ingredients to food isn't a potential solution, it's part of the problem. Food is healthy not when it contains healthy ingredients, he argues, but when it can be traced simply and directly to (preferably local) farms. As he resonantly put it in *The Times* in 2007: "If you're concerned about your health, you should probably avoid food products that make health claims. Why? Because a health claim on a food product is a good indication that it's not really food, and food is what you want to eat."

In this way, wholesome-food advocates have managed to pre-damn the very steps we need the food industry to take, placing the industry in a no-win situation: If it maintains the status quo, then we need to stay away because its food is loaded with fat and sugar. But if it tries to moderate these ingredients, then it is deceiving us with nutritionism. Pollan explicitly counsels avoiding foods containing more than five ingredients, or any hard-to-pronounce or unfamiliar ingredients. This rule eliminates almost anything the industry could do to produce healthier foods that retain mass appeal—most of us wouldn't get past xanthan gum—and that's perfectly in keeping with his intention.

By placing wholesome eating directly at odds with healthier processed foods, the Pollanites threaten to derail the reformation of fast food just as it's starting to gain traction. At McDonald's, "Chef Dan"—that is, Dan Coudreaut, the executive chef and director of culinary innovation—told me of the dilemma the movement has caused him as he has tried to make the menu healthier. "Some want us to have healthier food, but others want us to have minimally processed ingredients, which can mean more fat," he explained. "It's becoming a balancing act for us." That the chef with arguably the most influence in the world over the diet of the obese would even consider adding fat to his menu to placate wholesome foodies is a pretty good sign that something has gone terribly wrong with our approach to the obesity crisis.

Many people insist that the steps the food industry has already taken to offer less-obesogenic fare are no more than cynical ploys to fool customers into eating the same old crap under a healthy guise. In his 3,500-word *New York Times Magazine* article on the prospects for healthier fast food, Mark Bittman lauded a new niche of vegan chain restaurants while devoting just one line to the major "quick serve" restaurants' contribution to better health: "I'm not talking about token gestures, like the McDonald's fruit-and-yogurt parfait, whose calories are more than 50 percent sugar." Never mind that 80 percent of a farm-fresh apple's calories come from sugar; that almost any obesity expert would heartily approve of the yogurt parfait as a step in the right direction for most fast-food-dessert eaters; and that many of the desserts Bittman glorifies in his own writing make the parfait look like arugula, nutrition-wise. (His recipe for corn-and-blueberry crisp, for example, calls for adding two-thirds of a cup of brown sugar to a lot of other problem carbs, along with five tablespoons of butter.)

Bittman is hardly alone in his reflexive dismissals. No sooner had McDonald's and Burger King rolled out their egg-white sandwich and turkey burger, respectively, than a spate of articles popped up hooting that the new dishes weren't healthier because they trimmed a mere 50 and 100 calories from their standard counterparts, the Egg McMuffin and the Whopper. Apparently these writers didn't understand, or chose to ignore, the fact that a reduction of 50 or 100 calories in a single dish places an eater exactly on track to eliminate a few hundred calories a day from his or her diet—the critical threshold needed for long-term weight loss. Any bigger reduction would risk leaving someone too hungry to stick to a diet program. It's just the sort of small step in the right direction we should be aiming for, because the obese are much more likely to take it than they are to make a big leap to wholesome or very-low-calorie foods.

Many wholesome foodies insist that the food industry won't make serious progress toward healthier fare unless forced to by regulation. I, for one, believe regulation aimed at speeding the replacement of obesogenic foods with appealing healthier foods would be a great idea. But what a lot of foodies really want is to ban the food industry from selling junk food altogether. And that is just a fantasy. The government never managed to keep the tobacco companies from selling cigarettes, and banning booze (the third-most-deadly consumable killer after cigarettes and food) didn't turn out so well. The two most health-enlightened, regulation-friendly major cities in America, New York and San Francisco, tried to halt sales of two of the most horrific fast-food assaults on health—giant servings of sugared beverages and kids' fast-food meals accompanied by toys, respectively—and neither had much luck. Michelle Obama is excoriated by conservatives for asking schools to throw more fruits and vegetables into the lunches they serve. Realistically, the most we can hope for is a tax on some obesogenic foods. The research of Lisa Powell, the University of Illinois professor, suggests that a 20 percent tax on sugary beverages would reduce consumption by about 25 percent. (As for fatty foods, no serious tax proposal has yet been made in the U.S., and if one comes along, the wholesome foodies might well join the food industry and most consumers in opposing it. Denmark did manage to enact a fatty-food tax, but it was deemed a failure when consumers went next door into Germany and Sweden to stock up on their beloved treats.)

Continuing to call out Big Food on its unhealthy offerings, and loudly, is one of the best levers we have for pushing it toward healthier products—but let's call it out intelligently, not reflexively. Executives of giant food companies may be many things, but they are not stupid. Absent action, they risk a growing public-relations disaster, the loss of their more affluent and increasingly health-conscious customers, and the threat of regulation, which will be costly to fight, even if the new rules don't stick. Those fears are surely what's driving much of the push toward moderately healthier fare within the industry today. But if the Pollanites convince policy makers and the health-conscious public that these foods are dangerous by virtue of not being farm-fresh, that will push Big Food in a different direction (in part by limiting the profit potential it sees in lower-fat, lower-problem-carb foods), and cause it to spend its resources in other ways.

Significant regulation of junk food may not go far, but we have other tools at our disposal to prod Big Food to intensify and speed up its efforts to cut fat and problem carbs in its offerings, particularly if we're smart about it. Lenard Lesser points out that government and advocacy groups could start singling out particular restaurants and food products for praise or shaming—a more official version of "eat this, not that"—rather than sticking to a steady drumbeat of "processed food must go away." Academia could do a much better job of producing and highlighting solid research into less obesogenic, high-mass-appeal foods, and could curtail its evidence-light anti-food-processing bias, so that the next generation of social and policy entrepreneurs might work to narrow the gap between the poor obese and the well-resourced healthy instead of inadvertently widening it. We can keep pushing our health-care system to provide more incentives and support to the obese for losing weight by making small, painless, but helpful changes in their behavior, such as switching from Whoppers to turkey burgers, from Egg McMuffins to Egg White Delights, or from blueberry crisp to fruit-and-yogurt parfaits.

And we can ask the wholesome-food advocates, and those who give them voice, to make it clearer that the advice they sling is relevant mostly to the privileged healthy—and to start getting behind realistic solutions to the obesity crisis.

CRITICAL THINKING QUESTIONS

1. David Freedman compares two groups in his essay—the "wholesome-food movement" and the "processed food industry." Define these two groups. What side would Michael Pollan be on? What side would you place the author on? Where does your diet fall? Where do you think it should fall?

2. David Freedman argues that, "the wholesome-food movement veers awfully close to religion." Why does he think this is the case? Find two examples from the article where the wholesome-food movement makes claims about food that Freedman thinks have no merit. Why do you think people believe these ideas?

3. Authors like Bittman and Pollan are, according to Freedman, remaking "the disadvantaged in one's own image." Who are the disadvantaged he is talking about? How are they disadvantaged? How is the wholesome-food movement remaking them? Why does this hurt the disadvantaged?

4. Fast food restaurants, such as McDonald's, have "quietly been making healthy changes for years, shrinking portion sizes, reducing some fats, trimming average salt content by more than 10 percent in the past couple of years alone and adding fruits, vegetables, low-fat dairy, and oatmeal to its menu." Freedman argues that despite these positive changes, our society has "demonized" the fast food industry. Do you agree that fast food is unfairly targeted? Why or why not? Do you trust the fast food industry to continue to develop and offer more innovative, healthy choices in the future? Or, do you think policy regulations must be passed to ensure our society consumes healthier foods?

ORGANIC SHMORGANIC: CONVENTIONAL FRUITS AND VEGETABLES ARE PERFECTLY HEALTHY FOR KIDS

by Melinda Wenner Moyer

Melinda Wenner Moyer is a science writer based in Brooklyn, New York. She has written articles for *Scientific American, Nature Medicine, Slate, Popular Science, Glamour, Redbook,* and *Men's Journal.* Wenner Moyer is also an adjunct faculty member at the City University of New York's Graduate School of Journalism.

In this essay, the author explores whether there is a connection between pesticides and negative outcomes for children. She spends her first years as a parent feeding her children only organic, locally grown food. Due to the expense, conflicting research, and her child's behavior, she decides to investigate whether this is actually necessary for the health of her child. Her findings are mixed, but they mostly demonstrate that a child is not going to be harmed if fed non-organic food. How should we weigh the costs of healthy foods with the potential risks to our children?

• • • • • • • • • • • • • • •

When my son was a baby, *organic* was a synonym for *edible.* If the apples I found at the grocery store weren't certified, I wasn't buying them. I knew that conventional produce could harbor traces of pesticides, and I'd read that pesticides could affect brain development. Sure, the details of this association were hazy—I didn't know how many pesticides my son might ingest from Shoprite strawberries, nor did I know whether that amount would do him any harm. But in a way, it didn't matter: Shelling out a bit more cash to minimize the risks, whatever they were, seemed worth it to me.

Fast-forward two years and my son is eating Shoprite strawberries for breakfast. I support the principles of organic farming, for sure, but it can be hard to consistently pay $7 for a pint of something he'll go through in two days. Plus, I can't help but wonder whether giving my son organic food really makes a difference to his health, considering that he's been known to lick the bottom of his shoes, kiss my poop-sniffing dog, and eat crackers—someone else's—off of the preschool floor.

Instead of continuing to wonder, I decided to dig into the literature and talk to toxicologists, horticulturists, risk experts, and nutritionists to find out whether the chemicals in conventionally farmed foods could truly pose a risk to my child. What I've discovered has totally surprised me—let's just say I'm going to be a little more relaxed about what I serve kid No. 2.

I want to start off by saying that this column is not about whether organic agriculture is worth supporting for its environmental benefits (I think it is) or whether we as a society should care about the chemicals found in our foods and household products (I think we should). This column is about whether it's worth buying organic produce for your kids *specifically because you think the pesticides on conventional produce could harm them.* (If you're curious about the importance of feeding your kids organic dairy products, meats, and eggs, you'll have to wait because I'm going to tackle that in another column.)

I'm also not going to spend much space addressing the recent debate over whether organic produce has higher concentrations of beneficial nutrients than conventionally-farmed produce does. James McWilliams already did a good job of discussing the nuances of that issue in *Slate;* from the research, it seems fairly clear that organic fruits and veggies don't hold a major nutritional edge over conventional ones except in that they may contain fewer nitrates and more vitamin C, but there's little evidence that these differences translate into actual health benefits. It's also difficult to broadly compare the nutrients found in organically versus conventionally grown foods because geography and individual farm practices can impact growth drastically.

So let's focus on that other major claim about organic food—that is it's healthier, particularly for kids, because it contains fewer pesticides. First, let's start with the fact that *organic* does not mean *pesticide-free.* As scientist and writer Christie Wilcox explains in several eye-opening blog posts over at *Scientific American*, organic farmers can and often do use pesticides. The difference is that conventional farmers are allowed to use synthetic pesticides, whereas organic farmers are (mostly) limited to "natural" ones, chosen primarily because they break down easily in the environment and are less likely to pollute land and water. (I say "mostly" because several synthetic chemicals are approved for use in organic farming, too.)

The assumption, of course, is that these natural pesticides are safer than the synthetic ones. Many of them are, but there are some notable exceptions. Rotenone, a pesticide allowed in organic farming, is far more toxic by weight than many synthetic pesticides. The U.S Environmental Protection Agency sets exposure limits for the amount of a chemical that individuals (including kids) can be exposed to per day without any adverse effects. For Rotenone, the EPA has determined that people should be exposed to no more than 0.004 milligrams per kilogram of body weight per day. Let's compare this toxicity to that of some commonly used synthetic pesticides, like the organophosphate pesticide Malathion. The nonprofit Pesticide Action Network calls organophosphates "some of the most common and most toxic insecticides used today." (Sarin, the nerve gas used in two Japanese terrorist attacks in the 1990s, is a potent organophosphate.) Yet the EPA has deemed it safe, based on animal tests, for humans to be exposed to 0.02 milligrams of Malathion per kilogram of body weight per day. This is five times more than the amount deemed safe for Rotenone. In other words, by weight, the natural pesticide Rotenone is considered five times more harmful than synthetic pesticide Malathion. The EPA's recommended exposure limit for Glyphosate, another widely used synthetic pesticide—you might know it as Roundup—is 0.1 milligrams per kilogram per day, which means it's 25 times less toxic by weight than Rotenone. The synthetic pesticide Captan is 32.5 times less toxic than Rotenone, and another one, Pyrimethanil, is 42.5 times less toxic than Rotenone. Rotenone is also not the only natural pesticide that out-ranks synthetic pesticides in terms of toxicity. The pyrethrins, a class of pesticides derived from chrysanthemums that are approved for use in organic farming, are more toxic by weight than Roundup, Captan, and Pyrimethanil, too.

It's only fair to directly compare toxicities if people are being exposed to similar amounts of these synthetic and natural pesticides. Many organic farmers use pesticides as a last resort—so in theory, exposures to natural pesticides should be low. (Conventional growers don't use pesticides unless they have to, either, though; spraying is expensive.) The problem is that farmers often "have to use a lot of the natural pesticides because they break down faster," explains Linda Chalker-Scott, a professor of horticulture and landscape architecture at Washington State University. "One of the benefits of some of the more traditional synthetic pesticides is that they have been manufactured to be more effective at lower doses."

Indeed, in a 1989 report, researchers at McGill University grew apples using either a mixture of organically approved natural pesticides, including a mixture of Rotenone and pyrethrins, or a synthetic pesticide called Imidan. They found that, using the natural pesticides, they could achieve a 75 percent yield on their apples only if they sprayed the fruit at least six to seven times throughout the growing season; using the synthetic pesticide, they could get a 90 percent yield with just four sprays. Another more recent study compared the efficacy of two natural pesticides to two synthetic pesticides and found the organic ones to be much less effective against aphids (plant lice) than the synthetic ones. Since organic farmers may have to spray crops more frequently with natural pesticides, it's not crazy to think that organic produce could sometimes have just as much, if not more, pesticide on it—*natural* pesticide, yes, but remember that natural isn't intrinsically safe—compared to conventional produce.

Ah, but what about all those studies that suggest that organic fruits and veggies harbor fewer pesticide residues than conventionally farmed produce does? Those studies only tested for synthetic pesticides. In the few studies that have also looked for natural pesticides—the USDA's Pesticide Data Program tested for them on organic lettuce in 2009, the California Department of Pesticide Regulation tested a handful of organic fruits and vegetables for certain natural and synthetic pesticides in 2010, and the USDA did an analysis of organic produce in 2010—scientists have found that between 15 and 43 percent of organic produce samples harbor measurable traces of either natural or synthetic pesticides or both. As far as I can tell, however, no one has published a comparison of the overall amounts of both types of pesticides on organic versus conventional produce, so it's hard to conclude much from these findings other than that, yes, organic produce can be pesticide-tainted, too.

So now the question is: Are these pesticides harmful to your kids? As any toxicologist will tell you, it's the dose that makes the poison. In other words, just because both conventional and organic produce are sometimes laced with pesticides doesn't necessarily mean that they're doing anyone any harm. And an analysis of the numbers suggests they're not. In a 2011 study published in the *Journal of Toxicology*, Carl Winter, a pesticide and risk assessment specialist at the University of California-Davis, and his colleague Josh Katz took a close look at the fruits and vegetables that topped the Environmental Working Group's "Dirty Dozen" list—a top 12 list of what the non-profit group considers the most highly contaminated conventionally-grown fruits and vegetables sold in the United States. (This year, apples, strawberries, and grapes topped the list.) Winter was concerned that the EWG's methodology was flawed; among other things, the non-profit group does not compare actual pesticide levels on fruits and vegetables to the EPA's exposure limits to estimate true health effects of consumption.

To estimate how dangerous the pesticide exposures from the EWG's "Dirty Dozen" actually are, Winter and his colleagues analyzed USDA data to determine the average levels of the 10 most commonly found pesticides on each of the 12 conventionally farmed fruits and veggies. They then used other USDA data to estimate the average amounts of each pesticide that individuals typically ingest from each of the 12 fruits and vegetables in a 24- hour period. Finally, they compared those daily exposure estimates to the EPA's exposure limits for each pesticide.

What did they find? Well, let's start with apples, which the EWG considers the most pesticide-laden fruit or vegetable out there, and look at the pesticide that is most commonly found on them, called Thiabendazole. Winter and his colleagues found that, each day from conventionally-grown apples and apple-based products, Americans typically consume a dose of Thiabendazole that is 787 times less than the EPA's recommended exposure limit. Put another way, you'd have to eat as many apples and apple products as 787 Americans eat in a single day combined in order to be exposed to a level of this pesticide that approaches the EPA's exposure limit.

For other fruits and vegetables, Winter and his colleagues found even less reason to worry. For Captan, the synthetic pesticide most commonly found on conventionally grown strawberries, Americans are exposed to 8,180 times less of the chemical per day than the EPA's limit. Overall, Winter and his colleagues reported that the EPA's exposure limits were more than 1000 times higher than the daily exposure estimates for 90 percent of the fruit and vegetable comparisons they made.

Granted, we're exposed to pesticides through other means, too, and some pesticides may have cumulative effects—but Winter says that even so, Americans won't be ingesting anything close to the EPA's limits for any of the pesticides used in U.S. agriculture. (And if you ever *did* ingest a pesticide at or above the EPA's limit, you wouldn't suddenly keel over and die. The agency sets pesticide limits at least 100 times lower than the lowest dose that caused any sign of harm, however minimal, to animals when they were fed that amount every day for most of their lives.) "We have a tremendous amount of data showing that what we're exposed to in the diet for pesticides is very, very low, and certainly much lower than what would be required to have any even minimal health concern," Winter says. And by the way, in several of these studies, the fruits and vegetables weren't rinsed with tap water before they were tested, yet research suggests that doing so can reduce pesticide exposures significantly. Rubbing the food during rinsing helps, too.*

In light of all this, what should we make of some of the research suggesting that kids exposed to pesticides are more likely to develop ADHD, lower IQs, and autism? Importantly, the latter two studies did not link pesticide exposure from food to these problems; what they found was that pregnant women who were exposed to high levels of pesticides, either occupationally or because they lived close to farms, were at an increased risk for giving birth to babies who went on to have lower IQs or develop autism. The study linking ADHD to pesticides is potentially more concerning: It found that kids ages 8 to 15 who had 10-fold higher concentrations of a pesticide break-down product in their urine had about 1.5 times the odds of having ADHD. It's important to note, however, that the study only took a single urine measurement in the kids, so it's hard to know whether it accurately reflected the children's usual pesticide exposure or whether the day of testing could have been anomalous. Ideally, for a study like this, you want to track urine pesticide levels multiple times to make sure they're consistent. One scientist critiqued the study because it did not control for the fact that ADHD often runs in families; if the researchers had done this, he argued, they probably would have found no association between pesticide exposure and ADHD. Finally, the ADHD study focused on the organophosphate pesticides, which are becoming less and less commonly used by U.S. farmers every year.

There's another important thing to keep in mind about fruits and veggies: They are chock full of many naturally-occurring toxic compounds—things like flavonoids, hydrogen peroxide, and formaldehyde. Research conducted by Bruce Ames, director of the Nutrition & Metabolism Center at the Children's Hospital Oakland Research Institute, has found that Americans

*Correction, Jan. 30, 2014: This article originally misstated that in none of the studies were the fruits and vegetables washed before testing.

consume about 1,500 milligrams of natural toxins from plants a day, which is approximately 16,000 times more than the 0.09 milligrams of synthetic pesticides we get from food every day. These natural toxins are for real, too: According to Ames's work, the natural chemicals that are known to cause cancer in animals and are found in a single cup of coffee are about equal in weight to a year's worth of our exposure to synthetic pesticide residues that are known to cause cancer. In a 1996 report, the National Research Council, a non-profit institution that provides expert advice to the government, noted that "natural components of the diet may prove to be of greater concern than synthetic components with respect to cancer risk," in part because "synthetic chemicals are highly regulated while natural chemicals are not."

If you ask Ames or the National Research Council what all this means, you won't hear anyone say *OMG don't eat plants; they are trying to kill us.* It's Ames's belief that plants are exceptionally good for us *in spite of* the fact that they contain high levels of natural toxins—and that we certainly shouldn't be worried about the minuscule differences in pesticide levels between organic and conventional foods. Indeed, if the research literature is clear about *anything* regarding fruits and vegetables, it's that eating more of them—conventional or organic—does good things for the body. One review concluded that the quartile of Americans who eat the most fruits and vegetables, organic or not, are about half as likely to develop cancer compared to the quartile who eat the least. Fruits and veggies may also prevent heart disease and diabetes. A fascinating 2012 study used research-based models to predict what would happen if half of all Americans increased their (conventional) fruit and vegetable intake by a single serving each day; it predicted that doing so would prevent 20,000 cases of cancer a year. When the authors modeled whether this increased intake might pose risks due to the greater pesticide exposure, they concluded that yes, there might be 10 additional cases of cancer every year in the U.S. Put another way, the benefits far, far outweigh the risks.

What all this means for parents is that we should stop worrying so much about whether the apples we buy are organic or conventional—we should just start giving our kids more apples. (And, sure, wash them when you can.) The Environmental Working Group agrees: In the first sentence of the executive summary of its 2013 Shoppers Guide to Produce, the organization points out that "the health benefits of a diet rich in fruits and vegetables outweigh the risks of pesticide exposure." What's more, irrational fears over conventionally farmed produce can introduce dangerous trade-offs. As University of Michigan decision psychologist Brian Zikmund-Fisher put it to me, "If you don't feed your kid the 'right strawberry,' what *do* you feed him?" I've walked into markets with a hungry kid and been so afraid to buy the conventional apple that I've gotten him a snack pack of Annie's Crackers instead. And I know there are parents who buy the Peter Rabbit Organics Fruit Pouches at Starbucks because they don't know whether the bananas on display are organic. These aren't smart moves. It is far, far better for your kids' long-term health to get them in the habit of eating whole fruits and vegetables, regardless of what type of farm they came from, than to give them pretty much anything else to eat, no matter how organic or all-natural it may be.

CRITICAL THINKING QUESTIONS

1. People often confuse *organic* and *pesticide-free.* Define each of these terms. Can something be organic but still use pesticides? What is the difference between synthetic pesticides and natural pesticides? Which ones are you more comfortable with children consuming? Why do you say that?

2. Describes the three parts of Carl Winters' study in your own words. The author then applies this to apples. What does she find? Should an average American be worried about the pesticides on her apples? Why or why not?
3. Are pesticides linked to the development of ADHD, low IQ, and/or autism? One scientist critiqued the study relating to testing for ADHD, low IQ, and autism. What reasons did the scientist provide for critiquing the study? Do you think that the study is flawed? Provide evidence from the reading to support your responses.
4. **Connection.** In "How Junk Food Can End Obesity," David Freedman describes two groups that have opposing viewpoints about food—the "wholesome-food movement" and people who support the "processed food industry." Which group would be more likely to use Moyer's research to support its views? Why do you think that? How does Moyer's work help their argument?

HORMONES IN FOOD: SHOULD YOU WORRY?

by Carina Storrs

Carina Storrs is a freelance science and health journalist out of New York City. She specifically writes about how science affects our daily lives. Her work has been published in *Scientific American*, *The Scientist*, *Discover*, and *Health.com*.

Food technology has increased our ability to feed the world. As we are on the cusp of a new food technology—genetically engineered meat—Carina Storrs examines what this means for our well-being. In her 2011 article for *Health* magazine, she explores how hormones shape us. She works to understand how natural hormones are working, and how the hormones we add to our animals are affecting us. She finds that much of the research is inconclusive. We are changing our food supply before we are able to study what the effects of these changes will be. Should we be worried, or should we trust the companies whose profits depend on efficient food distribution?

• • • • • • • • • • • • • • •

A salmon that grows to market size twice as fast as normal. Dairy cows that produce 15 percent more milk. Beef cows that grow 20 percent faster.

What do these hyper-productive animals have in common? Thanks to injections and implants (in the case of cows) or genetic engineering (in the case of salmon), they contain artificially high levels of sex or growth hormones.

Are these hormones dangerous to the humans who eat the food or drink the milk? The food industry says no—and the Food and Drug Administration (FDA) agrees, at least when it comes to cows.

The FDA, which regulates the use of hormones in livestock, hasn't yet decided whether it will approve the sale of a genetically engineered salmon patented by the biotech company AquaBounty. If the salmon—which is wired to produce growth hormone year-round, instead of just in the spring and summer—gets an OK from the agency, it will be the first genetically engineered animal to wind up on your dinner plate. (Genetically engineered fruits and vegetables have been around for years.)

The FDA's stamp of approval isn't likely to reassure those who worry that excess hormones in the food supply are contributing to cancer, early puberty in girls, and other health problems in humans. For years, consumer advocates and public health experts have fought to limit the use of hormones in cows, and some support a ban on the practice similar to the one in place in Europe, where food regulations are generally more stringent than in the U.S.

But it's not clear if such hormones truly are bad for our health. Surprisingly little research has been done on the health effects of these hormones in humans, in part because it's difficult to separate the effects of added hormones from the mixture of natural hormones, proteins, and other components found in milk and meat. Buying organic may reassure shoppers, but there's little proof these products are indeed safer.

GROWTH HORMONES

In 1993, the FDA approved recombinant bovine growth hormone (rBGH), a synthetic cow hormone that spurs milk production when injected into dairy cows, and consumer groups have been concerned about it ever since. The manipulation of growth hormone in the AquaBounty salmon has sparked similar concerns.

By itself, rBGH has no discernible effect in humans and is of little concern to your health, and the growth hormone in AquaBounty's salmon is expected to be inconsequential to your health as well. The actual fear is that manipulating growth hormones in cows—or salmon—may increase another hormone, insulin-like growth factor (IGF), which could mimic the effects of human growth hormone in harmful ways. In fact, research has found that milk from rBGH-treated cows contains up to 10 times more IGF than other milk.

Higher blood levels of IGF (regardless of what causes them) have been associated with an increased risk of breast, prostate, and other cancers in humans. In a 2004 study, patients with above-average IGF levels had nearly a 50 percent higher risk of prostate cancer and a 65 percent higher risk of hormone-dependent premenopausal breast cancer than people with below-average levels.

Many factors—including genes, smoking, and fat intake—contribute to these cancers, but "it's very likely that at least part of that [risk] is related to IGF levels," especially where prostate cancer is concerned, says Walter Willett, M.D., chairman of the department of nutrition at the Harvard School of Public Health, in Boston.

While consuming lots of milk and other dairy has been shown to raise blood levels of human IGF, the increase is probably not a direct effect of the animal's IGF level or the IGF found in these foods. That's because the amount of IGF in dairy products—whether or not it's from rBGH-treated cows—pales in comparison to what is naturally in your body.

"Just [to get] the amount of IGF secreted in your saliva and digestive tract in a day, you'd have to drink about 95 quarts of milk," says Terry Etherton, Ph.D., a professor of dairy and animal science at Pennsylvania State University and the author of a blog about food biotechnology.

And you'd have to eat at least 170 three-ounce servings of genetically modified salmon. (The IGF levels in the AquaBounty salmon and regular salmon are comparable, although consumer advocates say the studies that determined this are too small to be reliable.)

So if the amount of IGF in milk is negligible, how does milk consumption increase our IGF levels? Milk in general—and the proteins, sugar, minerals, and non-IGF hormones it contains—may somehow cause the human body to make more of its own IGF, Dr. Willett says.

SEX HORMONES AND EARLY PUBERTY

IGF isn't the only hormone found in the food supply. Ranchers have been fattening up cattle with sex hormones—most notably estrogen—since the 1950s. Today most beef cows in the U.S.—except those labeled "organic"—receive an implant in their ear that delivers a hormone, usually a form of estrogen (estradiol) in some combination with five other hormones. (These hormones are not given to chicken and pigs because they don't have the same growth-promoting effect in these animals, although antibiotics are given to all three species for similar growth-promoting reasons.)

One concern is that such hormones may spur earlier puberty in children, who are, on average, entering puberty at a younger age than they did a generation or two ago, for reasons that are unclear.

But Ann Macrina, Ph.D., a researcher in the Department of Dairy and Animal Science at Pennsylvania State University, says that the amount of estrogen found in meat is vanishingly small compared to the level in our bodies. A three-ounce serving of beef from an estrogen-treated cow contains less than a billionth of a gram of estrogen, a level around 400,000 times lower than estrogen in women and nearly 100,000 times lower than that in men.

However, even miniscule amounts of estrogen could affect prepubescent girls and boys, says Dr. Willett. "[For] a girl who's not producing hormones herself, they could be quite substantial."

A 2009 study found that children who consumed the most protein from animal sources entered puberty about seven months earlier than those who consumed the least. "It doesn't matter so much if it's milk, cheese, or meat—all these animal proteins have a clear impact on [our] IGF system," says Thomas Remer, Ph.D., one of the authors of the study and a professor at the Research Institute of Child Nutrition, in Germany.

Still, hormones added to the food supply are probably not the biggest culprit behind early puberty. It's more likely that meat, milk, and similar foods help trigger earlier puberty because they are rich in protein, calories, and nutrients, says Marcia Herman-Giddens, an adjunct professor at the University of North Carolina School of Public Health, in Chapel Hill, and the lead author of an influential 1997 study on early puberty in girls.

However, Herman-Giddens cautions that more research is needed to untangle the many factors involved. For instance, she says, rising rates of overweight and obesity—and the processed foods, high-calorie drinks, and lack of exercise driving them—are "probably the biggest reason" for the trend toward earlier puberty. (Fat cells stimulate the body to produce estrogen.) Pesticides, flame-retardants, plastics, and other chemicals in the environment that can disrupt hormones may also be partly to blame.

ORGANIC OR NOT?

Organic beef and dairy products certified by the U.S. Department of Agriculture (USDA) come with the guarantee that the cows were not treated with rBGH or sex hormones. They also come with a much heftier price. Is the peace of mind worth the extra cash?

Probably not, says Dr. Willett, who advocates cutting back on meat in general. Most people should eat no more than two servings of red meat per week, Dr. Willett says, and "if you're [only] having a couple of servings a week, it doesn't make much difference whether it's organic or not."

Dr. Willett offers similar advice regarding organic dairy. On the other hand, experts like Herman-Giddens urge consumers to stay away from rBGH-treated milk because of its potentially higher IGF levels, and the fact that it does not have any added health benefits over regular milk. Instead of switching to organic milk, Dr. Willett recommends cutting back on dairy altogether, despite USDA recommendations that call for three servings a day of dairy.

Bruce Chassy, Ph.D., a professor of food microbiology at the University of Illinois at Urbana-Champaign, says "propaganda" from organic farming groups has created misconceptions about—and resistance to—rBGH among consumers. In fact, Chassy argues that manipulating growth hormones has benefits: rBGH-treated cows are better for the environment, not just the bottom line, since farmers can get the same amount of milk with fewer cows. Similarly, the AquaBounty salmon consumes 10 percent less feed during its lifecycle than a regular farmed salmon.

The most lasting effect of the fears surrounding hormones in the food supply may be the value of "organic" or "hormone free" as selling points, Chassy says.

"I think there are a lot of farms that are not using [rBGH] because they perceive that consumers do not want [rBGH]-treated milk," he says. He predicts that the AquaBounty salmon will likely inspire "marketing campaigns for 'hormone-free' fish." It's a ridiculous claim, he argues, since all fish—and all meat and milk—has hormones.

CRITICAL THINKING QUESTIONS

1. Genetically engineered fruits and vegetables have been sold for years. What is the potentially new food category the article states may become genetically engineered? Some "worry that excess hormones truly are bad for our health." What are some of their concerns? Would you buy Aqua Bounty's salmon? Why or why not?

2. Since the 1950s, farmers have been using implants to supply cows with extra estrogen. Why have they done this? Do you think this is a valid reason to give hormones to a cow? Summarize Dr. Willet's view on spending more for beef without added estrogen. Do you follow his advice? Do you want to try to?

3. Puberty has been occurring earlier and earlier in the past few decades. This article presents three reasons why this may be the case. Dr. Walter Willet, Dr. Thomas Remer, and Professor Marcia Herman-Giddens all offer different theories as to why puberty is occurring earlier. Which one makes the most sense to you? Describe the scientist's findings and explain why you find it convincing.

4. **Connection.** In "How a National Food Policy Could Save American Lives," the authors present nine guarantees that they believe would help make our food system work better for everyone. Based upon your reading of this article, write a tenth guarantee that you think would help support effective and sensible use of hormones on animals. Why do you think your guarantee would help make Americans healthy?

DIRTY SECRETS OF THE FOOD PROCESSING INDUSTRY

by Sally Fallon

Sally Fallon is a journalist, chef, nutrition researcher, and activist. Her work and research relates to food and its impact on the human body.

In this blog post, Sally Fallon describes how some commonplace foods—soups, cereals, milk, margarine—come to be in our kitchens. Her work shows how industrialized our food production has become. The margarine you use for your morning toast looks like grey cottage cheese before it is steam cleaned and colored—and the food processing industry works hard to keep you unaware of this. We willingly forgo knowledge about the very foods we eat, some of them daily, for the sake of convenience and cost . . . what are the consequences of our choice?

• • • • • • • • • • • • • • •

We have always processed our food; this is an activity that is uniquely human. We chop, soak, cook and ferment our food—as well as grind and dry—these are all types of processing.

Traditional processing has two functions: to make food more digestible and to preserve it for use during times when food isn't readily available. Nutritious, long-lasing processed foods including pemmican, hard sausage and old-fashioned meat puddings and haggis, as well as grain products, dairy products, pickles—everything from wine and spirits to lacto-fermented condiments. Farmers and artisans—bread makers, cheese makers, distillers, millers and so forth—processed the raw ingredients into delicious foods that retained their nutritional content over many months or even years, and kept the profits on the farm and in the farming communities where they belonged.

Unfortunately, in modern times, we have substituted local artisanal processing with factory and industrial processing, which actually diminishes the quality of the food, rather than making it more nutritious and digestible. Industrial processing depends upon sugar, white flour, processed and hydrogenated oils, synthetic food additives and vitamins, heat treatment and the extrusion of grains.

BREAKFAST CEREALS

Let's look at the processing involved in the typical American breakfast of cereal, skim milk and orange juice. Cold breakfast cereals are produced by a process called extrusion. Grains are mixed with water, processed into a slurry and placed in a machine called an extruder. The grains are forced out of a tiny hole at high temperature and pressure, which shapes them into little o's or flakes or shreds. Individual grains passed through the extruder expand to produce puffed wheat, oats and rice. These products are then subjected to sprays that give a coating of oil and sugar to seal off the cereal from the ravages of milk and to give it crunch.

In his book *Fighting the Food Giants*, biochemist Paul Stitt describes the extrusion process, which treats the grains with very high heat and pressure, and notes that the processing destroys much of their nutrients. It denatures the fatty acids; it even destroys the synthetic vitamins that are added at the end of the process. The amino acid lysine, a crucial nutrient, is especially damaged by the extrusion process.

Even boxed cereals sold in health food stores are made using the extrusion process. They are made with the same kind of machines and mostly in the same factories. The only "advances" claimed in the extrusion process are those that will cut cost, regardless of how the process alters the nutrient content of the product.

With so many millions of boxes of cereal sold each year, one would expect to see published studies showing the effects of these cereals on animals and humans. But breakfast cereals are a multi-billion dollar industry that has created huge fortunes for a few people. A box of cereal containing a penny's worth of grain sells for four or five dollars in the grocery store—there is probably no other product on earth with such a large profit margin. These profits have paid for lobbying efforts and journal sponsorships that have effectively kept any research about extruded grains out of the scientific literature and convinced government officials that there is no difference between a natural grain of wheat and a grain that has been altered by the extrusion process.

THE RAT EXPERIMENTS

Unpublished research indicates that the extrusion process turns the proteins in grains into neurotoxins. Stitt describes an experiment, conducted in 1942 by a cereal company but locked away in the company's file cabinet, in which four sets of rats were given special diets. One group received plain whole wheat grains, water and synthetic vitamins and minerals. A second group received puffed wheat (an extruded cereal), water and the same nutrient solution. A third set was given water and white sugar. A fourth set was given nothing but water and synthetic nutrients. The rats that received the whole wheat lived over a year on this diet. The rats that got nothing but water and vitamins lived about two months. The animals on a white sugar and water diet lived about a month. The study showed that the rats given the vitamins, water and all the puffed wheat they wanted died within two weeks—even before the rats that got no food at all. These results suggest that there was something very toxic in the puffed wheat itself! Proteins are very similar to certain toxins in molecular structure, and the pressure of the puffing process may produce chemical changes that turn a nutritious grain into a poisonous substance.

Another unpublished experiment was carried out in 1960. Researchers at the University of Michigan in Ann Arbor were given eighteen laboratory rats. These were divided into three groups: one group received cornflakes and water; a second group was given the cardboard box that the cornflakes came in and water; the control group received rat chow and water. The rats in the control group remained in good health throughout the experiment. The rats eating the box became lethargic and eventually died of malnutrition. The rats receiving the cornflakes and water died before the rats that were eating the box! (The first box rat died the day the last cornflake rat died.) Furthermore, before death, the cornflakes-eating rats developed aberrant behavior, threw fits, bit each other and finally went into convulsions. Autopsy revealed dysfunction of the pancreas, liver and kidneys and degeneration of the nerves of the spine, all signs of insulin shock. The startling conclusion of this study was that there was more nourishment in the box than in the cornflakes. This experiment was designed as a joke, but the results were far from funny.

Most Americans eat boxed cereals today. Because these are fortified with synthetic nutrients, the USDA can claim that they are as healthy as the grains from which they are made. Many of these cereals contain at least 50 percent of calories as sugar. Those sold in health food stores may be made of whole grains and fewer sweeteners. However, these whole grain extruded cereals are probably more dangerous than their refined grain counterparts sold in the supermarkets, because they are higher in protein, and it is the proteins in these cereals that are rendered toxic by this type of processing.

THE EXTRUSION PROCESS

When we put cereals through an extruder, it alters the structure of the proteins. Zeins, which comprise the majority of proteins in corn, are located in spherical organelles called protein bodies. The scientific literature does contain one study on extruded grains, which investigated changes in protein body, shape and release of encapsulated alpha-zeins as a result of the extrusion processing. Researchers found that during extrusion, the protein bodies are completely disrupted and the alpha-zeins dispersed. The results suggest that the zeins in cornflakes are not confined to rigid protein bodies but can interact with each other and other components of the system, forming new compounds that are foreign to the human body. The extrusion process breaks down the organelles and disperses the proteins, which then become toxic. When the proteins are disrupted in this way, it can adversely affect the nervous system, as indicated by the cornflake experiment.

OLD FASHIONED PORRIDGE

There is only one way to put these companies out of business, and that is not to eat their food. So, what are you going to have for breakfast instead of cheerios and corn flakes? Eggs—any style—are always a good choice. As for grain, old-fashioned porridges made from non-extruded grains provide excellent nourishment at an economical price. Grains such as oats should be cut or rolled and then soaked overnight in a warm, acidic medium to neutralize the many anti-nutrients naturally occurring in grains, such as irritating tannins, digestion-blocking enzyme inhibitors and mineral-blocking phytic acid. This treatment can also gently break down complex proteins in grains. You soak the grains in warm water plus one tablespoon of something acidic, like whey, yoghurt, lemon juice or vinegar. The next morning, your grain will cook in just a few minutes. It's best to eat your porridge with butter or cream, like our grandparents did. The nutrients in the dairy fats are needed in order for you to absorb the nutrients in the grains. Without the fat-soluble vitamins A, D and K2, you cannot absorb the minerals in your food. Furthermore, the fats in butter and cream slow down the release of glucose into the bloodstream, so that your blood sugar remains stable throughout the morning.

MILK

Milk is one of nature's most perfect foods. Most of our milk comes from a sacred animal, the cow. Today, however, in the industrial system, we imprison cows indoors for their entire lives; we give them inappropriate feed such as soy, bakery waste, citrus peel cake and the swill from ethanol production, foods that cows are not designed to eat. The confinement environment and the inappropriate feed make these cows sick, so they need antibiotics and other drugs. We breed them to give huge amounts of milk, and give them hormones to increase milk production as well. These cows produce large quantities of watery milk with only half the amount of fat compared to milk produced by old-fashioned cows eating green grass. Then this milk is shipped to factories for processing.

Inside the plants, the milk is completely remade. As described by Emily Green in the *Los Angeles Times,* centrifuges separate the milk into fat, protein and various other solids and liquids. Once segregated, these are recombined at specific levels set for whole, lowfat and no-fat milks. Of the reconstituted milks, whole milk will most closely approximate original cow's milk. What is left over will go into butter, cream, cheese, dried milk, and a host of other milk products. The dairy industry promotes lowfat milk and skim milk because they can make more money on the butterfat when used in ice cream. When they remove the fat to make reduced-fat milks, they replace it with powdered milk concentrate, which is formed by high temperature spray drying.

Then the milk is sent by tanker trucks (which are not refrigerated) to bottling plants. The milk is pasteurized at 161°F for fifteen seconds by rushing it past superheated stainless steel plates. If the temperature is 230°F (over the boiling point), the milk is considered ultra-pasteurized. This ultrapasteurized milk will have a distinct cooked milk taste, but it is sterile and shelf stable. It may be sold in the refrigerated section of the supermarket so the consumer will think it is fresh, but it does not need to be. The milk is also homogenized by a pressure treatment that breaks down the fat globules so the milk won't separate. Once processed, the milk will last for weeks, not just days.

Processing makes the milk difficult to digest and renders the proteins allergenic. Animals fed pasteurized milk exclusively develop nutrient deficiencies and become infertile after several generations.

Fortunately, Real Milk from pasture-fed cows, milk that is not pasteurized, processed or homogenized, is becoming more widely available. In fact, demand for Real Milk is growing rapidly. To find Real Milk in your area, visit realmilk.com.

In order to make powdered milk, fluid is forced through a tiny hole at high pressure and then blown out into the air. This causes a lot of nitrates to form, and the cholesterol in the milk becomes oxidized. Contrary to popular opinion, cholesterol is not a demon but your best friend; you don't have to worry about consuming foods containing cholesterol, except that you do not want to consume oxidized cholesterol. Evidence indicates that oxidized cholesterol can initiate the process of atherosclerosis.

Powdered milk is added to reduced-fat milks and milk products to give them body. So, when you consume reduced-fat milk or yoghurt, thinking that it will help you avoid heart disease, you are actually consuming oxidized cholesterol, which can initiate the process of heart disease.

ORANGE JUICE

Now, let's turn to the orange juice, part of our "healthy breakfast" of cereal, lowfat milk and juice. An article from *Processed and Prepared Foods* describes a "a new orange juice processing plant is completely automated and can process up to 1,800 tons of oranges per day to produce frozen concentrate, single strength juice, oil extracted from the peel and cattle feed." The new method of producing juice puts the whole orange in the machine. Another abstract states: "Various acid sprays for improving fruit peel quality and increasing juice yield are added to these processed oranges." These compounds are added to extract as much juice as possible, as well as the oil out of the skin. The conventional orange crop is sprayed heavily with pesticides called cholinesterase inhibitors, which are very toxic to the nervous system.

When they put the whole oranges into the vats and squeeze them, all that pesticide goes into the juice. Then they add acids to get every single bit of juice out of these oranges. So commercial orange juice can be a very toxic soup. This may be one reason that consumption of fruit juice is associated with increased rates of dementia.

What about the peel used for cattle feed? The dried, left-over citrus peel from orange juice production is processed into cakes, which are still loaded with cholinesterase inhibitors. Mark Purdey, in England, has shown how this practice correlates with mad cow disease. The use of organophosphates either as a spray on the cows or as a component of their feed, causes degeneration of the brain and nervous system in the cow, and if it's doing it to the cow, there's a possibility it may be doing it to you also.

The U.S. government tries to give the impression that pasteurization of juice is necessary to ensure our safety. However, it might surprise you to learn that researchers have found fungus that is resistant to pressure and heat in processed juices. They found that seventeen percent of Nigerian packages of orange juice and twenty percent of mango and tomato juices contained these heat-resistant fungi. They also found E. coli in the orange juice; it was pressure resistant and had survived pasteurization. So there is plenty of danger from contamination in these pasteurized juices.

In one study, heat-treated and acid-hydrolyzed orange juice was tested for mutagenic activity. The authors found that the heating process produced intermediate products which, under test conditions, gave rise to mutagenicity and cytotoxicity. In other words, there were cancer-causing compounds in the orange juice. In another study, gel filtration and high performance liquid chromatography were used to obtain mutagenic fractions from heated orange juice.

So if you want juice with your breakfast, avoid commercial processed orange juice. Instead, squeeze yourself a couple of organic oranges or an organic grapefruit—in other words, process the juice yourself! Mix that fresh juice with sparkling water and a pinch of salt for a delicious spritzer.

NATURAL NOURISHING BROTHS

In the past, many traditional cultures made use of animal bones to make broth. They recognized the healthgiving properties of bone broth as well as wonderful flavors broth gave to soups, sauces, gravies and stews. Modern science has shown us that homemade bone broths are indeed the healing wonders of the food pharmacopia; they provide minerals in abundance, strengthen bones and sinews, heal the gut and help us detoxify. The gelatin in homemade bone broth is a natural digestive aid.

INDUSTRIAL SOUPS

Most commercial soup bases and sauces contain artificial meat-like flavors that mimic those we used to get from natural, gelatin-rich broth. These kinds of short cuts mean that consumers are shortchanged. When the homemade stocks were pushed out by the cheap substitutes, an important source of minerals disappeared from the American diet. The thickening effects of gelatin could be mimicked with emulsifiers, but, of course, the health benefits were lost. Gelatin is a very healthy thing to have in your diet. It helps you digest proteins properly and is supportive of digestive health overall.

Research on gelatin and natural broths came to an end in the 1950s when food companies discovered how to induce maillard reactions—the process of creating flavor compounds by mixing reduced sugars and amino acids under increased temperatures—and produce meat-like flavors in the laboratory. In a General Foods Company report issued in 1947, chemists predicted that almost all natural flavors would soon be chemically synthesized. Following the Second World War, American food companies discovered monosodium glutamate, a food ingredient the Japanese had invented in 1908 to enhance food flavors, including meat-like flavors. Humans actually have receptors on the tongue for glutamate—it is the protein in food that the human body recognizes as meat—but the glutamate in MSG has a different configuration, which cannot be assimilated properly by the body. Any protein can be hydrolyzed (broken down into its component amino acids) to produce a base containing MSG. When the industry learned how to synthesize the flavor of meat in the laboratory, using inexpensive proteins from grains and legumes, the door was opened to a flood of new products, including bouillon cubes, dehydrated soup mixes, sauce mixes, TV dinners, and condiments with a meaty taste.

The fast food industry could not exist without MSG and artificial meat flavors, which beguile the consumer into eating bland and tasteless food. The sauces in many commercially processed foods contain MSG, water, thickeners, emulsifiers and caramel coloring. Your tongue is tricked into thinking that you are consuming something nutritious, when in fact it is getting nothing at all except some very toxic substances. Even dressings, Worcestershire sauce, rice mixes, flavored tofu, and many meat products have MSG in them. Almost all canned soups and stews contain MSG, and the "hydrolyzed protein" bases often contain MSG in very large amounts.

So-called homemade soups in most restaurants are usually made by mixing water with a powdered soup base made of hydrolyzed protein and artificial flavors, and then adding chopped vegetables and other ingredients. Even things like lobster bisque and fish sauces in most seafood restaurants are prepared using these powdered bases full of artificial flavors.

The industry even thinks it is too costly to just use a little onion and garlic for flavoring—they use artificial garlic and onion flavors instead. It's all profit based with no thought for the health of the consumer.

Unfortunately, most of the processed vegetarian foods are loaded with these flavorings, as well. The list of ingredients in vegetarian hamburgers, hot dogs, bacon, baloney, etc., may include hydrolyzed protein and "natural" flavors, all sources of MSG. Soy foods are loaded with MSG.

Food manufacturers get around the labeling requirements by putting MSG in the spice mixes; if the mix is less than fifty percent MSG, they don't have to indicate MSG on the label. You may have noticed that the phrase "No MSG" has actually disappeared. The industry doesn't use it anymore because they found out that there was MSG in all the spice mixes; even Bragg's amino acids had to take "No MSG" off the label.

HEALTH PROBLEMS

While the industry was adding MSG to food in larger and larger amounts, in 1957 scientists found that mice became blind and obese when MSG was administered by feeding tube. In 1969, MSG-induced lesions were found in the hypothalamus region of the mouse brain. Subsequent studies pointed in the same direction. MSG is a neurotoxic substance that causes a wide range of reactions in humans, from temporary headaches to permanent brain damage. It is also associated with violent behavior. We have had a huge increase in Alzheimer's, brain cancer, seizures, multiple sclerosis and diseases of the nervous system, and one of the chief culprits is the flavorings in our food.

Ninety-five percent of processed foods contain MSG, and, in the late 1950s, it was even added to baby food. Manufacturers say they have voluntarily taken it out of the baby food, but they didn't really remove it; they just called it "hydrolyzed protein" instead.

An excellent book, *Excitotoxins*, by Russell Blaylock, describes how nerve cells either disintegrate or shrivel up in the presence of free glutamic acid if it gets past the blood-brain barrier. The glutamates in MSG are absorbed directly from the mouth to the brain. Some investigators believe that the great increase in violence in this country starting in 1960 is due to the increased use of MSG beginning in the late 1950s, particularly as it was added to baby foods.

INDUSTRIAL FATS AND OILS

The food processing empire is built on industrial fats and oils, extracted from corn, soybeans and other seeds. Crude vegetable oil—which is dark, sticky and smelly—is subjected to horrendous processing to produce clean-looking cooking oils, margarine, shortening and spreads. The steps involved in processing usually include degumming, bleaching, deodorizing, filtering and removing saturates to make the oils more liquid. In the process, the nutrients and antioxidants disappear—but not the pesticides. Most processors also add a hexane solvent in order to squeeze the very last drop of oil out of the seeds. Caustic refining, the most widely used process for oil refining, involves adding very alkaline, chemicals to the oil.

In order to make a solid fat out of liquid oil, manufacturers subject the oils to a process called partial hydrogenation. The oil is extracted under high temperature and pressure, and the remaining fraction of oil is removed with hexane solvents. Manufacturers then steam clean the oils, a process that removes all the vitamins and all the antioxidants—but, of course, the solvents and the pesticides remain. These oils are mixed with a nickel catalyst and then, under high temperature and pressure, they are flooded with hydrogen gas. What goes into the reactor is a liquid oil; what comes out of that reactor is a smelly mass resembling grey cottage cheese. Emulsifiers are mixed in to smooth out the lumps, and the oil is then steam cleaned once more, to get rid of the horrible smell. The next step is bleaching, to get rid of the grey color. At this point, the product can be called "pure vegetable shortening." To make margarines and spreads, artificial flavors and synthetic vitamins are added. But the government does not allow the industry to add synthetic color to margarine—they must add a natural color, such as annatto—a comforting thought. The margarine or spread is then packaged in blocks and tubs and advertised as a health food.

Saturated fat is the type of fat found in such foods as lard, butter and coconut oil. Saturated fat molecules are straight, so they pack together easily. That is why saturated fats are solid at room temperature. Unsaturated fats have a little bend at each double bond, with two hydrogen atoms sticking out on the same side. And when that molecule gets incorporated into your cells, the body wants those two hydrogen atoms to be on the same side of the carbon chain, forming an electron cloud; that is where controlled chemical interactions take place.

During the process of partial hydrogenation, one of those hydrogen atoms is moved to the other side, causing the molecule to straighten out so that it behaves chemically like a saturate—although biochemically it behaves very differently. The original, unsaturated molecule is called a "cis" fatty acid, because the two hydrogens are together, and then it becomes a trans fatty acid, because the two hydrogens are across from each other ("trans" means "across"). Your body doesn't know that this new molecule is something that has never existed in nature before, and when you eat one of these trans fatty acids, it gets built into your cell membranes. Because of the chemical rearrangement, the reactions that should happen can't take place. Enzymes and receptors don't work anymore. The more trans fatty acids that you eat, the more partially hydrogenated your cells become and the more chaos that you are going to have on the cellular level.

All of the margarines, shortenings and even low-trans-fat spreads are made with these harmful ingredients. They're used in chips and crackers, and most restaurants use them for cooking fries. Until the early 1980s, fast food outlets and restaurants cooked the fries in tallow, which is a very safe fat, but now they use partially hydrogenated soybean oil.

In the past, when you made desserts for your kids, at least the sugar they contained came with butter, eggs, cream and nuts—all good wholesome foods. Now manufacturers can imitate the butter, eggs, cream and nuts, so all you have is sugar, industrial oils and artificial ingredients in these instant puddings, pastries and other artificial desserts.

Many diseases have been associated with the consumption of trans fatty acids—heart disease, cancer, and degeneration of joints and tendons. The only reason that we are eating this stuff is because we have been told that the competing saturated fats and oils—butter, lard, coconut oil, palm oil, tallow and suet—are bad for us and cause heart disease. Such assertions are nothing but industry propaganda.

WESTON PRICE

Weston A. Price, DDS, discovered that as populations adopt processed foods, with each generation the facial structure becomes more and more narrow. Healthy faces should be broad. We are all designed to have perfectly straight teeth and not get cavities. When you are eating real, nutrient-dense foods, you get the complete and perfect expression of the genetic potential. We were given a perfect blueprint. Whether or not the body temple is built according to the blueprint depends, to a great extent, on our wisdom in food choices.

When primitive societies abandoned the traditional diet and began to eat processed foods, the next generation developed narrowed facial structure and many diseases. We know that if you continue this diet for three generations, reproduction ceases. This is the terrible price of the West, the Western Price. Civilization will die out unless we embrace the food ways of our ancestors. That means turning our backs on processed foods and getting back into the kitchen, to prepare real foods—containing healthy fats—for ourselves and our families.

OPTIMAL FOOD PREPARATION—MADE WITH LOVE

Food preparation is actually a sacred activity: According to esoteric lore, "If a woman could see the sparks of light going forth from her fingertips when she is cooking, and the energy that goes into the food she handles, she would realize how much of herself she imbues into the meals that she prepares for her family and friends. It is one of the most important and least understood activities of life that the feelings that go into the preparation of food affect everyone who partakes of it. This activity should be unhurried, peaceful and happy because the energy that flows into that food impacts the energy of the receiver.

"That is why the advanced spiritual teachers of the East never eat food prepared by anyone other than their own chelas (disciples). The person preparing the food may be the only one in the household who is spiritually advanced. An active charge of happiness, purity and peace will pour forth into the food from him, and this pours forth into the other members of the family and blesses them."

To be healthy, we need to prepare our own food, for ourselves and our families. This doesn't mean you have to spend hours in the kitchen, but you do need to spend some time there, preparing food with wisdom and love. If no one in the family has time to prepare food, you need to sit down and rethink how you are spending your time, because this is the only way to get nourishing foods into your children. We can return to good eating practices one mouth at a time, one meal at a time, by preparing our own food and preparing it properly.

CRITICAL THINKING QUESTIONS

1. The article discusses a variety of foods that are processed. Select one of the foods referenced in the article and describe how it is processed. What are the negative impacts of such processing? Use specific evidence from the article to support your points.
2. MSG is short for **monosodium glutamate**. Based on the article, what is MSG? When did it enter the American diet, and from where? Describe the production of MSG—how do we create it? Finally, explain why the food processing industry uses it.
3. What does it mean to process food? What is the difference between "traditional" processing? Do we practice "traditional" processing in our modern times, or do we implement other processing methods?
4. **Connection.** Towards the end of this article, Sally Fallon writes that, "to be healthy, we need to prepare our own food . . . this is the only way to get nourishing foods into your children." Using two other articles from this section, defend or attack this claim. Use the other readings to explain either why Sally Fallon is correct, and processed food is unhealthy; or, why Sally Fallon is incorrect, and processed foods can be nourishing to children.

GAP IN DIET QUALITY BETWEEN WEALTHIEST AND POOREST AMERICANS DOUBLES, STUDY FINDS

by Tracie McMillan

Tracie McMillan is a journalist who writes about food politics, policy, and the environment. McMillan won the James Beard Award for Newspaper or Magazine Reporting on Nutrition or Food-Related Consumer Issues in 2013.

In this 2014 article from *National Geographic,* Tracie McMillan summarizes a study from the *Journal of the American Medical Association Internal Medicine.* The sobering report concludes that as our country's economic inequality has grown, so has the inequality in our diets. The foods we serve our children vary with our paychecks. There is some good news—our soda consumption has dropped, as has our use of trans fats—but for the least fortunate amongst us, eating healthy foods is getting harder. What needs to be done so that all Americans can heave a healthy diet?

• • • • • • • • • • • • • • •

Higher costs and limited supermarket access are cited as barriers to health.

The diets of low-income Americans have worsened in the past decade, even as the diets of the wealthiest Americans have improved, according to a new study that is among the first to measure changes in diet quality over time by socioeconomic status. Overall diet quality in the United States remains poor, said the lead author of the study, published Monday in the *Journal of the American Medical Association Internal Medicine.*

Although the study found that the diet of all Americans improved on average between 2005 and 2010, the progress masked a decline in diet quality among the poor. The result: a doubling of the gap in diet quality between the wealthiest Americans and the poorest.

The study attributed the change to the higher cost of convenient and healthy meals, as well as limited access to quality supermarkets in some poorer neighborhoods.

Frank Hu, a study author and co-director of the Program in Obesity Epidemiology and Prevention at the Harvard School of Public Health, cautioned against taking the improvements as a sign that Americans eat well. "This is really almost like an American diet report card," Hu said. "This has the good news that there has been some improvement in overall diet quality, but the report card still doesn't look very good."

The report comes at a time when the food choices of low-income households are in the national spotlight. Legislators and advocates have suggested restricting what foods can be bought with the federal Supplemental Nutrition Assistance Program (SNAP, also known as food stamps) in an effort to promote health. First Lady Michelle Obama has made healthy diets a central part of her campaign to end childhood obesity. Today two-thirds of Americans of all classes are overweight or obese, with higher rates among the poor.

Even with the improvements, Americans collectively scored under 50 out of 110 on the Alternative Healthy Eating Index, according to the study.

The diet quality gap

In the U.S., the gap in the quality of diets has widened between the haves and the have-nots.

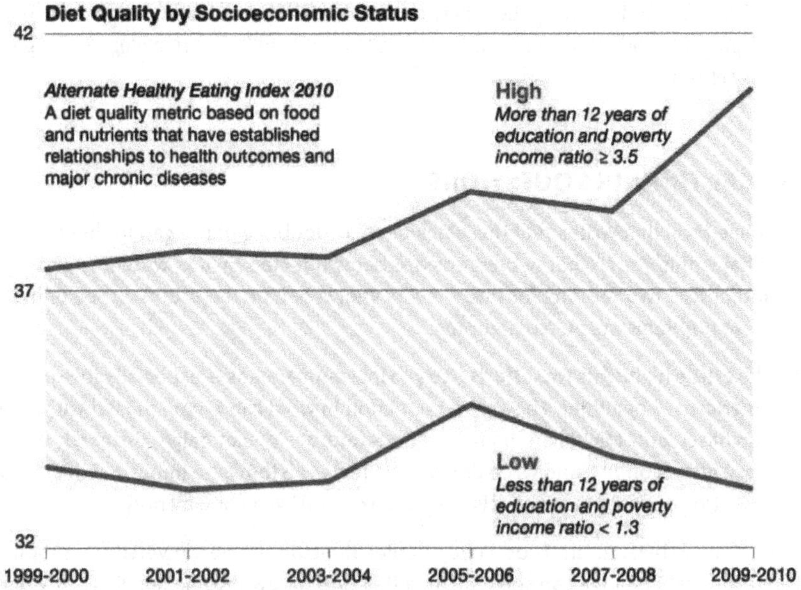

Diet quality scores do not include trans fat component.

Most of the improvement in the American diet, researchers said, was due to a steady decline in the consumption of trans fats. Consumption of sugar-sweetened beverages also dropped, giving a minor boost to overall diet scores. American diets otherwise stayed consistent, with low scores for fruits, vegetables, and whole grains.

Trans fats have been a target of public policy efforts to improve diet. Last fall the Food and Drug Administration announced it was considering banning the fats in processed foods, a decade after the agency required that trans fats be clearly listed on packaged foods. Federal efforts to promote consumption of fruits, vegetables, and whole grains, meanwhile, have largely been confined to education and public service announcements.

The study has implications for efforts to improve Americans' diets, particularly among the poor, experts said. "It really speaks to the evidence that if you want to change the American diet, you have to change the policy," said Marlene Schwartz, director for the Rudd Center for Food Policy & Obesity at Yale University.

"Education will only get you so far," she said, noting that education is often most successful for those who can afford to pay for it. Improving diet among the poor, she said, requires "improving the food supply so people can eat what's there and not be exposed to so many dangerous things."

Jessica Caouette, a nutrition and cooking instructor with Cooking Matters—a national nonprofit—who works with low-income families, echoed that reaction. "All parents are interested in feeding their families healthy meals," she said, but "price is a concern for low-income families."

A survey of Cooking Matters students from 2012 found that 85 percent said they wanted to eat healthfully but that only half were able to do so. More recently a survey from the food bank umbrella group Feeding America found that nearly 80 percent of its clients bought the cheapest food available even though they knew it wasn't healthy. (Related "Study Sheds Light on Broadening U.S. Hunger Problem.")

The best bet for improving the American diet, Hu said, lies in a broad approach. "Without changing the food environment and food system," he said, "education alone is not going to be very effective."

CRITICAL THINKING QUESTIONS

1. Tracie McMillan writes that there has been a "doubling of the gap in diet quality." What is this gap? What two groups are being affected by this widening gap? The author lists two reasons for this growing gap. What are they? Do you see either of these problems in your community?

2. The article highlights two efforts to try to make Americans—especially low-income Americans—healthier. They are a restriction in what can be purchased with SNAP purchases and Michelle Obama's childhood obesity campaign. Research one of these efforts online, and write down three facts you think are important in evaluating it. Do you think these efforts will be successful? Why or why not?

3. Marlene Schwartz, the Food Policy Center director at Yale University, is skeptical that education alone can solve the health issues of low-income families. Why does she think education "will only get you so far?" What are her two recommendations? What do you think is the most effective path for fixing this issue? Why do you believe that path is the best way?

4. **Connection.** In *How Junk Food Can End Obesity*, David Freedman writes about that the "wholesome-food movement" is leaving low-income families behind. Use the evidence this article provides from the *Cooking Matters* survey and the "Feeding America" data to write a paragraph in which you prove David Freedman's point. Then, write a paragraph where you suggest two solutions to this problem.

UNIT 5

Popular Culture

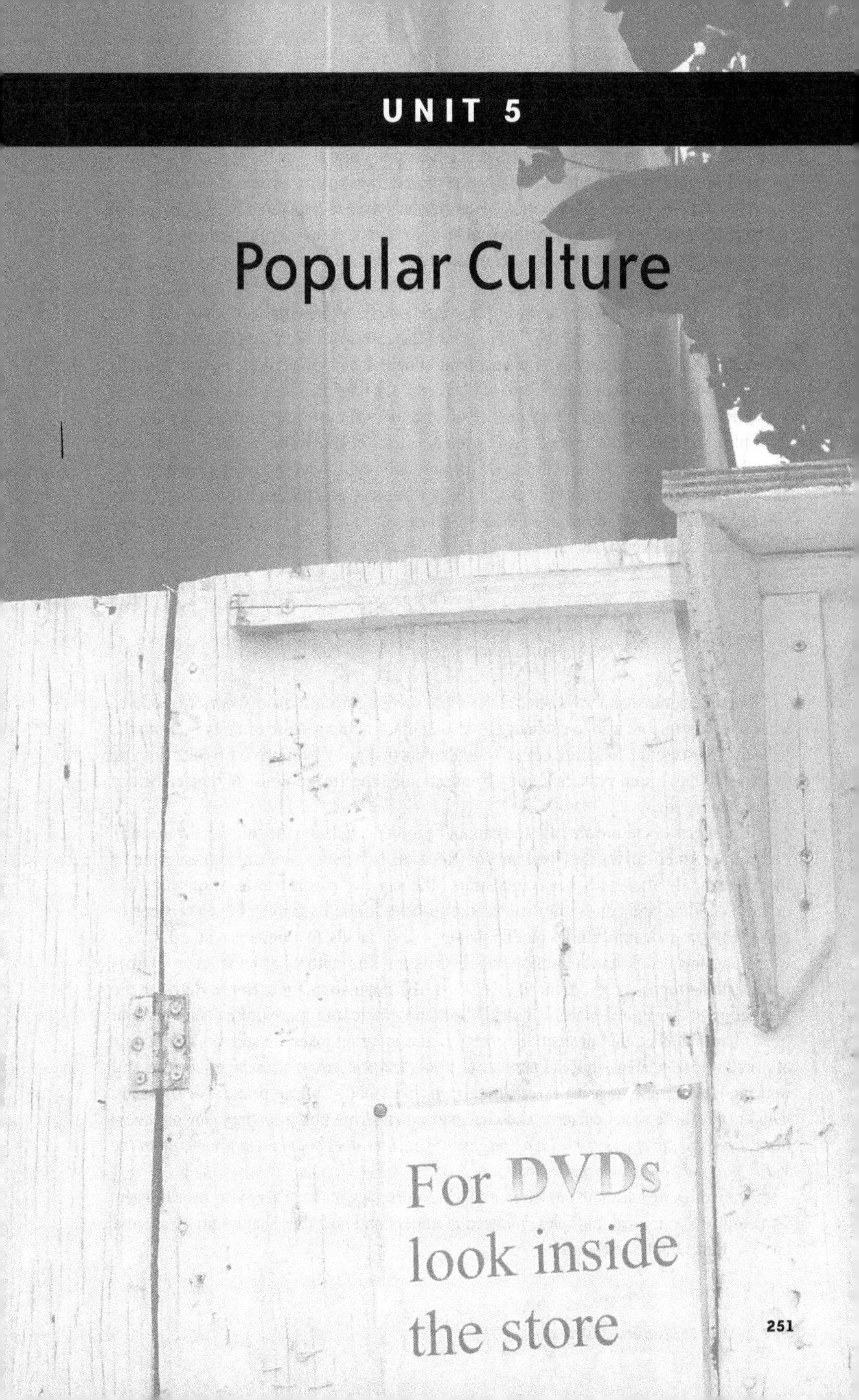
For DVDs
look inside
the store

INTRODUCTION

In the 1940s, Woody Guthrie was at the center of American culture. A folk singer from Oklahoma, he spent the Great Depression traveling the country and seeing the economic devastation and ruin of that era. In the early 1940s, he moved from visiting people at the margins of society to working from the center of it. For a while he moved to New York City, living in one of the trendiest areas of the city. From this spot he used his talents to make appearances on CBS radio, even hosting his own radio program for a time. He sang and broadcast songs people would dance to, sing along with, or hum at work. When the Second World War broke out, he asked the government how he could aid the war effort. He wrote dozens of songs about the fight against fascism. As part of the USO program, the government sent him around the world to entertain soldiers with songs inspiring them to fight against the cruel leaders of the Axis powers. In this way, Woody Guthrie was at the center of a patriotic, wartime culture.

The experiences he had traveling through the barren dust bowl in the 1930s did not leave him, however. While he was upset by the injustices of Hitler and Hirohito, he was also upset by the injustices he saw at home. He then used the cultural power he was given by CBS and the government to critique the media, the government, and the economic system in the United States. The 1945 recording of Woody Guthrie's most famous song, "This Land is Your Land," contains the following lines:

"I'd seen my people,
As they stood hungry, I stood there asking,
Is this land made for you and me?"

Popular culture has always acted in these two seemingly contradictory ways: to reinforce what is in control, but also to challenge it. A song that implies a sense of unity—"from the redwood forests to the New York island"—undercuts that unity by supplying a voice to those who are left out. It undercuts that unity by questioning the great promise of the democracy he was singing for.

The effects of culture are vast and cannot be understated, and they are worthy of study. The average American watches five hours of television each day—poor children watch many more. And study after study has demonstrated the negative effects television watching has on both children and adults. But television also plays a role in shaping better versions of ourselves—from documentaries on PBS that expose social ills, to programs on the TLC network that show people how to remake their bathrooms. The culture has for too long stigmatized certain groups—racial minorities, or the LGBT population, for example. However, the population of the United States is quickly becoming more and more diverse, and cultural trends have matched that diversity. Stereotypes and ignorant jokes are still too large a part of primetime television—but the number of shows featuring women, racial minorities, and working-class families is rising as well. In this way, like Woody Guthrie, prime time television both creates those social currents and challenges them. This unit asks the following questions: *what are the effects of media on our lives?* And, *how does popular culture maintain the status quo, and how does it challenge it?*

The stories we tell about ourselves, and tell to ourselves, matter. Every year, over 120 new films come to your local multiplex. We need to understand how they shape who we are and how we think about ourselves.

WHAT IT MEANS TO BE POPULAR (WHEN EVERYTHING IS POPULAR)

by Adam Sternbergh

Adam Sternbergh is the author of *Near Enemy.* He is also a reporter who has been published in *The New York Times.* Sternbergh won the Edgar Award for Best First Novel by an American Author.

In this 2013 article from *The New York Times,* Adam Sternbergh attempts to understand what "popular" means in the Internet age. He ruminates on what may be lost when subcultures are no longer subordinate, and what we all have to gain from having our cultural choices not being dictated by the media elite. What happens when the way we measure what is "popular" changes? Where do we go for our common cultural experiences if everything is considered popular in its own way?

• • • • • • • • • • • • • • •

"So basically we're doing a whole package about stuff that is terrible." This was a colleague's verbatim reaction to the idea of a culture package devoted to popular things. I don't blame her—after all, it's how we've been conditioned to think for the past century or so. We've seen the rise of mass culture, pop culture, camp culture and trash culture; the cross-pollination of highbrow, lowbrow, middlebrow and nobrow; and, with the advent of the Internet, the introduction of a battalion of shiny new metrics with which we can measure something's popularity to the second, the penny, the click. We are now better equipped than at any time in history to judge, say, the most popular pop song of a given moment, yet we're more confounded by what all this popularity actually means. For example: What constitutes the most popular pop song in a given moment, anyway? The most purchased? The most streamed? The most illegally downloaded? The most ambiently inescapable?

From all this chaos, though, one truism about popularity apparently survives: If something is popular, it can't also be good.

Popularity used to be simple. We had the chart-topping song, the top-rated TV show, the No. 1 best seller, the highest-grossing movie of the year. You could define yourself, taste-wise, as either in league with the popular or against it, and while you didn't have to like what was popular, you certainly were aware of what it was.

Now the concept of cultural popularity has been flayed, hung by its heels and drained of all meaning. For example: "NCIS," the naval-police procedural, is the highest-rated non-football program on television, routinely drawing 17 million viewers a week. By a straightforward accounting, that makes it the most popular show on TV. Yet by a different definition—the extent to which, say, a show saturates the cultural conversation—you could make a case for "Mad Men" as TV's most popular show, even though it draws only 2.5 million viewers. Or "Girls," which draws a paltry 615,000 viewers a week but sometimes feels as if it has generated at least as many essays. By one measure, no one watches "Girls." By another, it's fantastically popular.

We already understand why this is: it's a tenet of faith that we no longer experience culture as one hulking, homogeneous mass. Not that long ago, we had "Thriller," which, at last count, sold about 66 million copies worldwide. Nothing sells 66 million copies anymore. The finale of "M*A*S*H" drew 125 million viewers; no TV broadcast, save the Super Bowl, will ever draw that many simultaneous American viewers again. That's because we've turned off Top 40 and loaded up Spotify; we've clicked away from NBC and fired up Netflix; we, thanks to the increasingly concierge-style delivery system of the Internet, are each sheltered in our own cultural cocoon.

Where does this leave the concept of popularity? Paradoxically, popularity is now both infinitely quantifiable and infinitely elusive. We're awash in cold data even as we try and reconcile how these numbers relate to our larger intuitive sense of what people like. Back in 1940, *Billboard* published a single music chart, simply named the Best-Selling Retail Records, which solely tracked sales. Later, the Billboard Hot 100 collated several factors—radio play, jukebox popularity and sales—into one measure of overall success. Around the same time, the lone tree grew several categorical limbs: R. & B., country, rap and so on, each taking the measure of popularity in a different genre. From one chart grew many. This seemed to make sense.

Then the methodology evolved even further: paid downloads were included in 2005; digital streams in 2007. The top-selling song was no longer necessarily the most popular song in the country. Now it could simply be the song that the most people, somewhere, were listening to, somehow. Then, this year, *Billboard* announced it would include YouTube playbacks as part of its rankings, and the song "Harlem Shake" immediately became the No. 1 song in America. This was thanks largely to a snippet of it being used as the soundtrack for thousands of viral YouTube videos. That meme, like most, burned out quick as a Roman candle. So instead of "Remember the summer of 'Harlem Shake'?" we might one day say wistfully, "Remember the two weeks in February of 'Harlem Shake'?" This is how we ended up with a No. 1 song that isn't even really exactly a song. I'd venture to say that its ascent to that once-hallowed position—the No. 1 song in America!—felt intuitively correct to exactly no one, including the makers of "Harlem Shake."

As for books, we know everything and we know nothing. As any jittery author can confirm, Amazon will now tell you right out in the open where anyone can see exactly where in the vast universe of literature your particular contribution sits. You can watch your sales ranking rise or (more likely) fall in real time, like a stock ticker of public disinterest. On the other hand, *The Times* publishes 17 separate best-seller lists, from Combined Print and E-Book Fiction to Children's Middle Grade to Manga. The purpose of all these different lists is to effectively capture the elusive phenomena of consumer choice—the individual decisions that reflect genuine widespread interest. In contrast, the Nielsen Company offers the BookScan application, which stands as a model of modern bloodless techno-tallying. BookScan will tell you, to the copy, how many books have sold in the past week in 85 percent of the American book market. This includes lots of bulk, discount purchases that aren't so much about people picking books as having books thrust on them. Popularity is something that's no longer just tallied, it has to be curated—and the more-finely-grained measurements seek to differentiate between what people want and what they merely accept out of habit or passivity.

Meanwhile, in the TV world, the old models have more or less gone kablooey. Once upon a time, the Nielsen Company basically polled a handful of households and extrapolated from there. The fundamental question—who's watching what?—remains the same, but measuring it is now exponentially more difficult. Between first-run and repeats and DVRs and downloads and DVD binges and streaming, just how many people watch "Downton Abbey," exactly? Somewhere in there, amid the confusion, "Duck Dynasty," a reality show on A&E about a family of industrious duck hunters that it is entirely possible you are hearing about right now for the very first time, became the No. 1 reality cable program of all time. "Duck Dynasty" T-shirts are the most popular shirts for men, women and girls at Walmart, which is, by some measures, the most popular store in America. So while "Duck Dynasty" may not be the most popular show on TV, it is, by several legitimate metrics, the most popular show on TV.

All of which brings us, inevitably, to "Sharknado," a purposefully campy TV movie on Syfy about a tornado that is full of sharks. It is not, by any known definition, good. And yet, for a few weeks this summer, it was very popular. At one point, the movie generated 5,000 tweets a minute. "#Sharknado" became a nationally trending topic on Twitter. Yet when it was broadcast, it was watched by only slightly more people than watch pretty much anything that Syfy throws on the air on a typical night. So the question is: Was "Sharknado" popular? Syfy proudly called it its "most-social telecast ever," but what does that mean, exactly? It's as if "Sharknado" won a trophy that had been created only for the purpose of being awarded to "Sharknado."

Syfy, by the way, has already approved the production of "Sharknado 2: The Second One." The title was chosen by a vote held on Twitter. It was the most popular choice.

Perhaps the best way to think about the state of popularity is like a kind of quantum element: Both static and in perpetual flux. For example: You can most likely now close the record book on any record that measures how many people did the exact same thing at the exact same time. The movie with the highest box office of all time, adjusted for inflation, is still "Gone With the Wind," released in 1939.

The other metrics of popularity, though—the ones that measure, with increasing exactitude, what we do, when we do them, how long we do them for and how much we enjoyed doing them, are restless and ever-changing. Did you happen to linger for a moment longer on a particular article this morning on the Times Web site? Duly noted and recorded. Did you impulsively skip a particular song on your Gotye Pandora channel? That has been fed back into the algorithm, and good luck ever hearing that song again. You are, to an unprecedented degree, the emperor of a personalized kingdom of popularity, and zillions of bots are working tirelessly to heed your whims and hone your experience.

As a result, we don't live in echo chambers so much as isolation booths. This might be a good time for me to confess that I've never seen an episode of "Duck Dynasty," I can't whistle a single bar of "Radioactive" by Imagine Dragons and I've never read a single page of any of the Harry Potter books, even though I understand all these things are enormously popular. This isn't a question of taste; it's a question of time. When everything's popular by some measure, it's impossible to keep up with everything that's popular.

Or put another way: The old order of popularity is personified by Tom Hanks, a movie star so popular that you could walk a thousand miles in any direction and still not find a human who doesn't know who he is.

The new order of popularity is personified by Pauley Perrette, a star of "NCIS," who is much less well known than Hanks but is so beloved by the fans she does have that, a few years back, she managed to tie Hanks (and Morgan Freeman) as the American celebrities with the highest Q Score (a proprietary ranking that's "the recognized industry standard for measuring consumer appeal of personalities, characters, licensed properties, programs and brands").

For that matter, the new order is exemplified by the existence of Q Scores, which micro-measure the popularity of personalities, characters, brands.

At first inspection, this refraction of the culture into ever-smaller slivers leaves us instinctively with a sense of something lost. Once we listened to the same song together, watched the same show together, argued over the same movies together. Now we're each focused on our own screen, listening to our own playlist, we're bowling alone, etc. A landscape that once featured a few unavoidable monoliths of popularity is now dotted with a multitude of lesser monuments, too many to keep track of, let alone celebrate.

If you're of the sour view, like my colleague quoted above, that popularity is inherently linked to mediocrity, then this development can count only as progress. After all, you can't be held captive by the terribe taste of the masses when there's no such thing as masses anymore.

I subscribe to a more democratic and optimistic view. Popularity may not guarantee artistic quality, but it does confer viability. No matter how it's quantified, popularity ultimately serves as a form of validation, and we all benefit when it's dispersed more generously. I don't mean the kind of judgment-free, trophies-for-everyone mentality that suggests a refusal to exercise critical discretion. In fact, the rise of micropopularity implies the opposite: Things that are good are more likely to be recognized and, on some scale, to thrive. (And things that are absolutely, irredeemably terrible have even fewer excuses.) "Girls" can remain on TV because, on a fundamental level, HBO has a different notion of popularity than CBS does. The sitcom "Arrested Development," which was very good, wasn't popular enough to survive under the old network-TV model. But it's plenty popular enough to resurface in the age of on-demand streaming Internet video. To me, that counts as progress.

Popularity is not just about making cultural products financially viable; micropopularity encourages creativity in more ephemeral ways as well. Maybe your band is not at the top of any Billboard chart, but if you have 1,000 fans on Facebook, that puts some wind in your artistic sails. You might not be writing jokes for Jimmy Fallon, but 500 retweets of your best one-liner will keep you dreaming up punch lines. And 50,000 retweets might just get you a job writing jokes for Jimmy Fallon.

As it turns out, cultural popularity functions best when it's liberally interpreted and freely distributed. If you encounter something that's popular and it turns out not to be to your taste, that's fine, no sweat, move on. In the meantime, get excited for all the new things you might enjoy. I can happily report that my colleague, as a direct result of working on this project, is now a convert to the most popular podcast in the country ("Welcome to Night Vale") and, yes, to "Fifty Shades of Grey." If those don't catch your interest, how about the most popular single rental in the Met Opera's on-demand streaming service? (Elina Garanca in the 2010 production of "Carmen.") I can practically guarantee you that, if you put aside a reflexive aversion to the popular, you'll discover something new that brings you pleasure. So take heart: once we break down the sample sizes into small enough segments, we are all, by some measure, popular.

CRITICAL THINKING QUESTIONS

1. Early in the essay, Adam Sternbergh introduces this paradox: "By one measure, no one watches 'Girls.' By another, it's fantastically popular." How can both be true of the same television show? Prove his statement. Then, think of a piece of culture from your life—a TV show, a musical artist, a celebrity—who is both "fantastically popular" and not widely known. Describe your piece of culture and explain why you think it meets those criteria.

2. In 1940, *Billboard* had a single music chart. Now it has over ten different charts. How does this change reflect the changes Adam Sternbergh is discussing in this article? Describe the changes to the methodology used for the *Billboard* charts since 2005. Sternbergh writes that this lead to the "Harlem Shake" being the number one song in America—something that felt, "intuitively correct to exactly no one." How did those changes lead to the "Harlem Shake," becoming the number one song in America? Do you agree with him that this didn't feel right? Why or why not?

3. Adam Sternbergh's coworker at *The New York Times* is happy that our culture is splintering; Sternbergh says a coworker of his argues that "popularity is inherently linked to mediocrity." What does this statement mean? Do you agree with it? Adam Sternbergh disagrees, writing that popularity does confer "viability," and that is a good thing. What does this mean? What is one example he uses? He also argues that "micropopularity encourages creativity." What does this mean? What is the example he uses? Do you agree or disagree?

4. Some cultural figures—like Taylor Swift or Beyoncé—are still broadly popular amongst wide ranging groups of people. Pick a cultural band—a person, a television show, a movie—that appeals to a diverse audience. Supply three reasons why this cultural brand might have this broad appeal, while much of culture, according to Adam Sternbergh, no longer has mass, broad appeal?

MARSTON, GENDER IDENTITY AND CASTING THE MODERN WONDER WOMAN

by *Noah Berlatsky*, Comic Book Resources

Noah Berlatsky is a contributing writer for *The Atlantic.* He is an editor for *The Hooded Utilitarian,* an online comics and culture website.

Wonder Woman was created to correct the sexist norms in comic books. In this 2014 essay, Noah Berlatsky wonders what it will take to break down the gender-based norms of the 21st century. Does Wonder Women represent all women, or just those thought of as female?

• • • • • • • • • • • • • • •

So, who is the ideal person to play Wonder Woman?

The recently revealed image of Gal Gadot as a Xena-like Wonder Woman has sold a number of folks on her in the role, but artist seraphatonin has presented an unexpected but brilliant alternative: Laverne Cox ("Orange is the New Black"). The idea was first suggested by tumblr poster noottersontheflightdeck, and seraphtonin created a marvelous mash-up image of Cox in a classic version of the costume, looking transcendent, inspiring, strong and ready to take man's world on.

Seraphatonin isn't against Gal Gadot in the role, but as she explained to me, she loves the idea of Cox as Diana for a simple reason. "She represents so much of what Hollywood considers unmarketable—she's black, she's trans, she's a woman . . . Part of what's always drawn me to Diana is her dedication to defending those who can't defend themselves, and that dedication could be so much more complex and personal if she herself experienced the sexism and racism she fights against."

Those are all great reasons to cast Cox as Diana, but here's another one: William Moulton Marston, Wonder Woman's creator, feminist, psychologist and crank, would probably love it.

Marston's been dead for six decades, so he can't speak for himself on this, and there is the unfortunate fact that, even by the ugly standards of his day, his comics could be very insensitive, or even racist. Still, I'd like to think he could have gotten beyond that, and there are other reasons to think he would have been enthusiastic about Cox picking up the golden lasso.

First among these is that the original "Wonder Woman" comics were full nigh-to-bursting with cross-dressing and gender swapping. "Sensation Comics" #2, one of the very first Wonder Woman stories, released in 1942, featured the evil Dr. Poison, a misshapen, green-garbed scientist. At the end of the issue, he is revealed to be a shapely woman—who is swatted on the rear as punishment by Wonder Woman's burly sidekick, Etta Candy. Cross-dressing is not the same as trans identity, of course—but in the context of a comic, where the characters aren't real people anyway, the symbolism is easy to blur. We don't know for sure, after all, whether Dr. Poison considers himself a man or a woman—and indeed that ambiguity seems intentional on Marston's part. (Though he does seem to prefer to live as a man, so I've stuck with the male pronoun.)

This ambiguous gender identity would be a reoccurring theme in Marston's comics. In 1944, Wonder Woman encounters the mustachioed villain Hypnota—only to discover that he's actually the twin sister of his hypnotized servant named (wait for it) Serva. Again, in

"Sensation Comics" #46, from 1946, the Blue Snowman, who seems to have been created in collaboration with Marston's co-writer and assistant Joyce Murchison, pops off his blue cloud head for what is by now a familiar reversal, revealing himself to be a woman. Finally, in the last issue Marston wrote, "Wonder Woman" #28, published after his death, all three of his cross-dressing villains return. Wonder Woman knows who they all are, so there's no reason for disguises, but they still dress as men anyway. Because, why not?

Poison, Hypnota, and the Snowman are villains, and you could arguably see them as in line with such cross-dressing bad guys as Norman Bates in "Psycho" or Buffalo Bill in "Silence of the Lambs," characters whose psychotic impulses are tied to their gender identity. But Marston never links his characters' drag to their villainy. Dr. Poison isn't evil because he had some sort of traumatic relationship with his father; he just likes dressing up as a guy. Hypnota for his part explains that it was great fun for him to switch back and forth, pretending to be his twin sister one minute and the powerful male Hypnota the next. Or, as he says, "Ha! Ha! It was amusing to pose as Serva, hypnotize people and then escape by blaming it on myself!"

All of these characters are drag kings, or (arguably) trans men, but there is one important character who can be seen as a trans woman. Namely, Wonder Woman herself.

Within the narrative of the comic, of course, Wonder Woman is cis[gendered]. But Marston's vision of his creation's gender was complicated. In an article for "The American Scholar," he explained his purpose in creating the character:

"It seemed to me, from a psychological angle, that the comics' worst offense was their blood-curdling masculinity. A male hero, at best, lacks the qualities of maternal love and tenderness which are as essential to a normal child as the breath of life . . . It's smart to be strong. It's big to be generous. But it's sissified, according to exclusively masculine rules, to be tender, loving, affectionate, and alluring. 'Aw, that's girl stuff!' snorts our young comics reader. 'Who wants to be a girl?'

"And that's the point; not even girls want to be girls so long as our feminine archetype lacks force, strength, power."

The phrasing here is telling; "*not even* girls want to be girls." The implication is that girls *should* want to be girls—and that boys should want to be girls, too.

Marston finishes up his discussion by insisting that, if shown a strong enough woman, men will "be proud to become her willing slaves." According to Marston's idiosyncratic theories, women were superior to men because, as he said in a letter to his publisher, they "enjoy submission; enjoy being bound . . . The only hope for peace is to teach people who are full of pep and unbound force to enjoy being bound." So to save the world, women need to teach men how to submit, because women are better at submitting than men. And when men submit, they become like women. The whole point of Wonder Woman, from Marston's point of view, is to teach both men and women to be better women.

Obviously, there aren't many folks, whether feminists, non-feminists, cis, or trans, who would sign onto Marston's particular vision of femininity and submission and gender. But be that as it may, it should be clear at this point why Marston was so enthusiastic about cross-dressing in his comics. The sequence in "Wonder Woman" #23, where the evil cat-headed alien guys riding giant kangaroos invade Paradise Island, only to reveal that under the cat heads they're women, ready to do good and join the Amazons—that's Marston's utopian vision, right there on the comics page. Men turn into women and bliss prevails. Men, women, cat-headed aliens—everyone, everywhere, will become, through Wonder Woman's tutelage, a sister and an Amazon.

"In a world where masculinity is respected and femininity is regularly dismissed, it takes an enormous amount of strength and confidence for any person, whether female- or male-bodied, to embrace their feminine self," Julia Serano, a trans activist and gender theorist, wrote in her book "Whipping Girl." Marston would have agreed with that. And I think he also would have seen Wonder Woman as an expression of his own feminine self; the strong, powerful woman he wanted to be, and wanted everyone, boys and girls, to be as well. Who better to embody that dream than Laverne Cox? Who better to fight for everyone's femininity than a woman like Cox who has fought for, and won, her own?

CRITICAL THINKING QUESTIONS

1. Gal Gadot was cast as Wonder Women in *Batman vs. Superman.* Look up images of Gadot as well as Laverne Cox. Why do you think the movie's producers chose Gal Gadot over someone like Laverne Cox? Summarize why the blogger saraphatonin thinks Laverne Cox would be an exciting choice. If you were producing the movie, who would you choose, and why?
2. William Marston created Wonder Women in the first half of the 20th century. Noah Berlatsky quotes his critique of comic books' "blood curdling masculinity" at the time. What are two reasons he gives for introducing a female comic book character? Think back to your childhood—do you think things have improved for girls? Why or why not?
3. Who is Julia Serano? Paraphrase her quote; how would you explain what she is saying to someone else? Evaluate that statement; is this true? Why or why not? What do you think the effects are on readers when comic books are so focused on the masculine?
4. William Marston created Wonder Woman to serve as a model of a strong woman; he hoped to inspire girls to think of women as equally capable as men. Would casting Laverne Cox, who was born as a biological male, complicate his vision? Do you think Wonder Woman's influence on young girls would lessen if she were played by a trans woman? Why or why not?

IN THEIR OWN TERMS: THE GROWING TRANSGENDER PRESENCE IN POP CULTURE

by Jacob Bernstein

Jacob Bernstein is a staff reporter for *The New York Times*. His father was a writer for *The Washington Post*, and his mother is the late Nora Ephron, a legendary screenwriter. Bernstein wrote a high profile piece about his mother for *The New York Times*, and he is known for his reporting on style and popular culture.

This 2014 piece from *The New York Times* asks us to consider the ways in which we are challenged by disruptions to our perceptions of gender in popular culture. So much of art is personal experience prepared for the audience. What does it mean if the artist is investigating gender in their work? How does this expand our understanding or cause divisions?

• • • • • • • • • • • • • • •

The first time Rhys Ernst saw Zackary Drucker was in 2005 at a bar in the East Village.

At the time, both were aspiring artists. Rhys had recently graduated from Hampshire College and was working for MTV networks. Zackary had graduated from the School of Visual Arts and was appearing on a reality TV show called "Artstar," hosted by Jeffrey Deitch.

But there was one clear impediment to romance: Rhys had never dated a man, and Zackary had never dated a woman.

"I remember thinking," Rhys said, "if I ever dated a boy, that's the type of boy I'd date."

Today, that consideration is not an issue. Over the last five years, Zackary has transitioned from male to female, Rhys from female to male.

And in "Relationship," a photo exhibition currently on view at the Whitney Biennial, the two have chronicled that process and the evolution of their own love affair. (In a recent preview of the Biennial, Holland Cotter of *The New York Times* wrote that the Ernst/Drucker photographs "put queer consciousness on the front burner.")

That a show by two transgender artists should be so prominently featured at the 2014 Biennial should come as a surprise to no one. It is just more evidence of the increasing presence of trans people at the center of popular culture.

In their spring advertising campaigns, the luxury retailer Barneys New York and the award-winning jewelry designer Alexis Bittar feature transgender models. In February, a memoir by Janet Mock, a former editor at *People* magazine, which drew heavily on her transition from male to female, made the *New York Times* best-seller list. Laverne Cox has become a breakout star on Netflix's hit show "Orange Is the New Black," playing a sympathetic character who winds up in prison after using stolen credit cards to pay for her gender reassignment surgery. And Carmen Carrera, a transgender showgirl who first achieved demi-fame as a contestant on the reality television program "RuPaul's Drag Race," has become an in-demand fashion model and muse for the photographer Steven Meisel.

Here are their stories.

LAVERNE COX

Laverne Cox grew up in Mobile, Ala., with her identical twin brother and her mother, a single parent who worked two to three jobs at a time to make ends meet.

She enrolled at Marymount Manhattan College in New York in the late '90s, where by day she majored in dance, took her first acting classes and became immersed in gender studies.

By night, Ms. Cox was a presence on the downtown club scene, hanging out at Flamingo East in the East Village and performing operatic versions of heavy metal songs at Squeeze Box, a Friday night party at Don Hill's. (Among the songs she sang were Iron Maiden's "Be Quick or Be Dead" and Pantera's "Mouth for War.")

At the time, Ms. Cox said, she was in a "gender nonconforming space," no longer living as a man, but still struggling with her own "internalized transphobia" as well as a desire to "be myself and not embody some stereotype of womanhood."

"It was a mess," she said.

After completing her transition, she was cast in 2008 on the VH1 reality show "I Want to Work for Diddy." (Ms. Cox made it halfway through the competition.) Last year, she got her big break with a role on "Orange Is the New Black" on Netflix.

On the show, the major characters appear in prison and then in flashback sequences that show how they got there. So Ms. Cox's twin, a musician who lives in Brooklyn, played her character pretransition.

Ms. Cox has spoken at colleges about the transgender experience. She's also done one now-famous chat on a daytime talk show, where she appeared with Carmen Carrera and gently chastised the host, Katie Couric, for being too focused on questions about genital surgery, which not every transgender person undergoes. After Ms. Couric said to Ms. Carrera, "Your private parts are different now, aren't they," Ms. Cox argued that focusing on this objectifies trans people and prevents a more meaningful discussion from taking place.

"Someone called me a man in the airport today," Ms. Cox said in an interview this week. "Just because there's a few trans folks having lovely careers and having moments of visibility does not mean that a lot of trans folks lives are not in peril. We need to remember those folks who are struggling, particularly trans women of color who are on the margins."

JANET MOCK

Some success stories are neat. Others, like Janet Mock's, less so. She grew up in Hawaii with a mother who had her first child at 16 and a father who battled drug addiction and had numerous children with other women. (One year, Ms. Mock said, her father "had a baby in January, February and April.")

Then, in middle school, Ms. Mock met a transgender girl named Wendi, and at 12 or 13, she began applying lip gloss, wearing makeup and tweezing her eyebrows. At 15, she started hormones.

She was an honor student in high school while she worked as a prostitute on Merchant Street in Honolulu, which is how she saved the money to travel to Thailand and pay for gender reassignment surgery.

After graduating from the University of Hawaii in 2005, Ms. Mock became an editor at People.com, then came out as transgender in a 2011 Marie Claire profile.

This winter, Atria Books (a division of Simon and Schuster) published her memoir, "Redefining Realness," in which she quotes Audre Lorde, James Baldwin and Maya Angelou but wrote that Beyoncé was most responsible for "shifting" how she viewed herself as a woman of color.

"Everyone celebrated her because she was the girl of the moment," said Ms. Mock, 31, who has frizzy, Afro-ish hair with blond highlights, and, on the day I met her, looked effortlessly fashionable in a pair of black Theory jeans and a denim shirt with the sleeves rolled up, showing off her gold-colored infinity bangles. On her arm was a tan leather 3.1 Phillip Lim bag, which she said was a gift to herself after her book became a best seller.

Like Ms. Cox and Ms. Carrera, she has been somewhat offended by the tone of some of her television interviews. Last month, Ms. Mock went on Piers Morgan's CNN show (it has since been canceled), where the host all but began the interview by saying how "amazing" it was that this attractive woman had once been biologically male.

"Had I not known your life story, I would have absolutely no clue," he said, as the scrawl at the bottom of the bottom of the screen read "Born a boy."

Ms. Mock pounced on Twitter, and *Slate* ran a withering piece on Mr. Morgan's performance that evening, chastising him for being "obsessed with appearances" and accusing the show of promoting the segment in a "sensational and ignorant way."

Nevertheless, the interest in Ms. Mock's book and its subsequent sales is an indication that something is changing dramatically. And, no doubt, she appreciates having a platform now.

As a child, she said: "All I knew was gay. All I knew was RuPaul."

VALENTIJN DE HINGH

A Dutch camera crew followed Valentijn de Hingh around for the bulk of her childhood, chronicling her journey from male to female. By the end of high school, she was walking in runway shows for Comme des Garçons and Maison Martin Margiela. In 2012, she gave a talk at a TEDx event in Amsterdam titled "Why Did I Choose?" This year, she is appearing in the Barneys campaign alongside 16 other transgender models.

Having understanding parents helped, she said.

They first read about transgender children in a magazine when Ms. de Hingh was 5 and took her to a hospital in the Netherlands with a program for gender-variant children.

"My parents were looking for answers, and they found it there," she said.

Schoolmates, she said, were largely accepting, though she did experience some taunting. Being openly transgender but preoperative made dating hard, something she struggles with, even after gender reassignment surgery.

"I still have a hard time with dating," said Ms. de Hingh, 23. "I have some figuring out to do."

RHYS ERNST AND ZACKARY DRUCKER

Many of the photographs in Zackary Drucker and Rhys Ernst's show at the Whitney capture them in scenarios most couples can relate to: celebrating anniversaries, lounging around the house while one fights off a cold, sitting poolside on a sunny day.

Others depict circumstances that are perhaps unique to a transgender couple, such as an image of Mr. Ernst's and Ms. Drucker's bandage-covered backsides shortly after taking hormone shots.

According to Ms. Drucker, the exhibition has a couple of aims. One is to show that all relationships are in some way banal. Another, she said, is about "learning to love ourselves and deflect the distortions" that prevent people from doing that.

There weren't a lot of transgender role models for Ms. Drucker and Mr. Ernst growing up. But their parents were progressive and supported their children's gender nonconformity.

In high school, they both became familiar with the writings of Kate Bornstein, a queer theorist whose books "Gender Outlaw: On Men, Women and the Rest of Us," and "My Gender Workbook: How to Become a Real Man, a Real Woman, the Real You, or Something Else Entirely" outlined a way of living that did not ascribe to traditional gender conventions.

"I don't call myself a woman, and I know I'm not a man," Ms. Bornstein once said.

Today, the couple lives in Los Angeles and has been consulting on the pilot of a television show for Amazon called "Transparent." It stars Jeffrey Tambor of "Arrested Development" as an aging man who is beginning a gender transition. (It was picked up on Tuesday.)

They are also part of a wide circle of "gender queer" and transgender creative types that includes Wu Tsang (a filmmaker and visual artist who identifies as "transfeminine" and "transguy") and Amos Mac, a photographer and editor who runs *Originalplumbing*, a magazine and website, that are devoted to hipsterish transgender types.

This pretty much describes Ms. Drucker, 30, who has a penchant for tight leggings, vintage Yves Saint Laurent heels and Grecian tops—and yet has no plans to have gender reassignment surgery, a topic she discusses pretty openly.

The same goes for Mr. Ernst, 31, who sports a light goatee and on Friday was wearing a button-down shirt with high tops and charcoal pants.

Ultimately, Ms. Drucker said, she'd like to get to a point where we "surpass" the binaries of gender altogether.

"That would be the greatest transition of all," she said.

CRITICAL THINKING QUESTIONS

1. Towards the end of the article Zackary Ducker says she would like us to "get to a point where we 'surpass' the binaries of gender altogether." Binary means consisting of two, and only two things. How is gender in this country binary? Towards the end of the article, the author describes what Zackary looks like. How is she surpassing binaries?

2. Rhys Ernst and Zackary Drucker created a photo exhibition of their relationship over the course of five years, as they both underwent gender transition. Drucker tells the author she had two aims: the first was to show the way in which "all relationships are, in some way banal." The second aim was to assist with "learning to love ourselves and deflect the distortions" that prevent people from doing that. Why do you think the artists chose those two aims—why are those important statements to explore in their work?

3. The author describes Ms. Cox's experience by writing, "She was in a 'gender nonconforming space,' no longer living as a man, but still struggling with her own 'internalized transphobia,' as well as desire to 'be myself and not embody some stereotype of womanhood.'" What does this quote mean? What specifically were

Cox's struggles that were referenced in this quote? How can you relate to such struggles?

4. Laverne Cox and Carmen Carrera have both been "somewhat offended by the tone of some of the television interviews" that focus on their experience as transgendered people. Ms. Cox has also been critically acclaimed for her role in the dramatic television series *Orange Is the New Black*. In what way(s) has television and popular culture impacted society's views of transgender people in America? Provide two examples from the reading as evidence of these impacts.

THE EFFECTS OF TELEVISION VIOLENCE ON CHILDREN

by the American Psychological Association

The American Psychological Association (APA) is the largest scientific and professional organization of psychologists in the United States and Canada.

The American Psychological Association went before Congress in 2007 to give this statement. In it, they explain the many ways that violence on television is problematic for children and parents. They make clear that the large amount of violence on television has severe negative impacts on children who watch it, and watch it repeatedly. Who is responsible for controlling this?

• • • • • • • • • • • • • • •

HEARING BEFORE THE U.S. SENATE COMMITTEE ON COMMERCE, SCIENCE, AND TRANSPORTATION

Presented by APA Member Dale Kunkel, PhD
Professor of Communications
University of Arizona

June 26, 2007

I have studied children and media issues for over 20 years, and am one of several researchers who led the National Television Violence Study (NTVS) in the 1990s, a project widely recognized as the largest scientific study of media violence. In my remarks here today, I will briefly report some key findings from the NTVS project, as well as summarize the state of knowledge in the scientific community about the effects of media violence on children.

THE EFFECTS OF TELEVISION VIOLENCE

Concern on the part of the public and Congress about the harmful influence of media violence on children dates back to the 1950s and 1960s, and remains strong today. The legitimacy of that concern is corroborated by extensive scientific research that has accumulated over the past 40 years. Indeed, in reviewing the totality of empirical evidence regarding the impact of media violence, the conclusion that exposure to violent portrayals poses a risk of harmful effects on children has been reached by the U.S. Surgeon General, the National Institutes of Mental Health, the National Academy of Sciences, the American Medical Association, the American Psychological Association, the American Academy of Pediatrics, and a host of other scientific and public health agencies and organizations.

These harmful effects are grouped into three primary categories:

(1) children's learning of aggressive attitudes and behaviors; (2) desensitization, or an increased callousness towards victims of violence; and (3) increased or exaggerated fear of being victimized by violence. While all of these effects reflect adverse outcomes, it is the first—an increased propensity for violent behavior—that is at the core of public health concern

about televised violence. The statistical relationship between children's exposure to violent portrayals and their subsequent aggressive behavior has been shown to be stronger than the relationship between asbestos exposure and the risk of laryngeal cancer; the relationship between condom use and the risk of contracting HIV; and exposure to second-hand smoke in the workplace and the risk of lung cancer. There is no controversy in the medical, public health, and social science communities about the risk of harmful effects from children's exposure to media violence. Rather, there is strong consensus that exposure to media violence is a significant public health concern.

KEY CONCLUSIONS ABOUT THE PORTRAYAL OF VIOLENCE ON TELEVISION

Drawing upon evidence from the National Television Violence Study, as well as other related research, there are several evidence-based conclusions that can be drawn regarding the presentation of violence on television.

1. Violence is widespread across the television landscape.

Turn on a television set and pick a channel at random; the odds are better than 50-50 that the program you encounter will contain violent material. To be more precise, 60% of approximately 10,000 programs sampled for the National Television Violence Study contained violent material. That study identified an average of 6,000 violent interactions in a single week of programming across the 23 channels that were examined, including both broadcast and cable networks. More than half of the violent shows (53%) contained lethal acts, and one in four of the programs with violence (25%) depicted the use of a gun.

2. Most violence on television is presented in a manner that increases its risk of harmful effects on child-viewers.

More specifically, most violence on television follows a highly formulaic pattern that is both sanitized and glamorized.

By sanitized, I mean that portrayals fail to show realistic harm to victims, both from a short and long-term perspective. Immediate pain and suffering by victims of violence is included in less than half of all scenes of violence. More than a third of violent interactions depict unrealistically mild harm to victims, grossly understating the severity of injury that would occur from such actions in the real world. In sum, most depictions sanitize violence by making it appear to be much less painful and less harmful than it really is.

By glamorized, I mean that violence is performed by attractive role models who are often justified for acting aggressively and who suffer no remorse, criticism, or penalty for their violent behavior. More than a third of all violence is committed by attractive characters, and more than two-thirds of the violence they commit occurs without any signs of punishment.

Violence that is presented as sanitized or glamorized poses a much greater risk of adverse effects on children than violence that is presented with negative outcomes such as pain and suffering for its victims or negative consequences for its perpetrators.

3. The overall presentation of violence on television has remained remarkably stable over time.

The National Television Violence Study examined programming for three years in the 1990s and found a tremendous degree of consistency in the pattern of violent portrayals throughout the television landscape. Across the entire study of roughly 10,000 programs, the content measures which examined the nature and extent of violence varied no more than a percent or two from year to year. Similar studies that have been conducted since that time have produced quite comparable results.

This consistency clearly implies that the portrayal of violence on television is highly stable and formulaic—and unfortunately, this formula of presenting violence as glamorized and sanitized is one that enhances its risk of harmful effects for the child audience.

In sum, the evidence clearly establishes that the level of violence on television poses substantial cause for concern. It demonstrates that violence is a central aspect of television programming that enjoys remarkable consistency and stability over time.

IMPLICATIONS FOR PUBLIC POLICY

It is well established by a compelling body of scientific evidence that television violence poses a risk of harmful effects for child-viewers. While exposure to media violence is not necessarily the most potent factor contributing to real world violence and aggression in the United States today, it is certainly the most pervasive. Millions of children spend an average of 20 or more hours per week watching television, and this cumulative exposure to violent images can shape young minds in unhealthy ways.

Given the free-speech guarantees of the First Amendment, the courts have ruled that there must be evidence of a "compelling governmental interest" in order for Congress to take action that would regulate television content in any way, such as the indecency regulations enforced by the FCC. In my view, the empirical evidence documenting the risk of harmful effects from children's exposure to televised violence clearly meets this threshold, and I should note that former Attorney General Janet Reno offered an identical opinion to this Committee when she testified before it on this same issue in the 1990s.

There has been a lot of talk in recent weeks about the U.S. Court of Appeals (2nd Circuit) ruling regarding "fleeting expletives" that were cited as indecent by the FCC (*Fox et al. v. FCC*, June 4, 2007). Some have suggested this ruling threatens the future of any content-based television regulation. While I am not a legal expert, let me draw several important distinctions between this indecency case and the situation policy-makers face with the issue of television violence. First, there is no clear foundation of empirical evidence to document the effects of children's exposure to indecent material in any quantity, much less modest and fleeting examples of it. In contrast, there is an elaborate, solid foundation of evidence regarding the cumulative effects of televised violence on children. While "fleeting expletives" occur occasionally on television, they are generally quite rare. In contrast, violent portrayals are not only common, they are pervasive across the television landscape, and are found in a majority of programs.

Indeed, it is the cumulative nature of children's exposure to thousands and thousands of violent images over time that constitutes the risk of harmful effects. Just as medical researchers cannot quantify the effect of smoking one cigarette, media violence researchers cannot specify the effect of watching just a single violent program. But as exposure accrues over time, year in and year out, a child who is a heavy viewer of media violence is significantly more likely to behave aggressively. This relationship is the same as that faced by the smoker who lights up hour after hour, day after day, over a number of years, increasing their risk of cancer with every puff.

The scientific evidence about the effects of televised violence on children cannot clarify which path is the best for policy-makers to pursue to address the problems that research in this area has identified. That decision rests more in value judgments, based upon the relative importance that each of you place on protecting children's health as contrasted with the other competing interests involved, such as freedom of speech concerns. But when you make that judgment—as each Member of this committee will eventually be called upon to do—it is critical that you understand that television violence harms large numbers of children in this country, and significantly increases violence in our society.

To conclude, the research evidence in this area establishes clearly that the level of violence on television poses substantial cause for concern. Content analysis studies demonstrate that violence is a central aspect of television programming that enjoys remarkable consistency and stability over time. And effects research, including correlational, experimental, and longitudinal designs, converge to document the risk of harmful psychological effects on child-viewers. Collectively, these findings from the scientific community make clear that television violence is a troubling problem for our society. I applaud this Committee for considering the topic, and exploring potential policy options that may reduce or otherwise ameliorate the harmful effects of children's exposure to television violence.

CRITICAL THINKING QUESTIONS

1. The American Psychological Association (APA) groups the harmful effects of television violence for children into three categories. Select a violent TV show or movie. Then describe each category of effect; what does that effect mean, in your own words. Then, apply it to the television show or movie you selected. How could your selected media cause those effects?

2. What does it mean that, on television, violence is "glamorized?" How is this glamorization accomplished? Why do you think the producers of television shows glamorize their violence?

3. In their report before the Senate, the APA stated that, "while exposure to media violence is not necessarily the most potent factor contributing to real world violence and aggression in the United States today, it is certainly the most pervasive." What do they mean when they say media violence is the "most pervasive?" Do you agree with this? Why or why not? The APA believes it isn't the most "potent" factor contributing to violence in America. What do you think is the most potent reason for violent behavior in the U.S.? Why?

4. The article notes that violence on television is harmful to children. Do you think that policy regulations need to be put in place to help with this issue? If so, in what ways? If not, why do you believe that television should not be regulated?

TELEVISION AND CHILDREN

by Kyla Boyse, MS, RN, CPNP

Kyla Boyse earned her Master's degree in Nursing from the University of Michigan. She is a practicing Pediatric Nurse Practitioner, and she has written articles relating to the field of pediatrics.

In the previous reading, the American Psychological Association argued that violence on television has detrimental effects on children. Here, Kyla Boyse collects data that demonstrate many other areas of a child's life that suffer when they are exposed to too much television. Children who watch TV are more likely to smoke, more likely to be overweight, and more likely to sleep less. With television being so harmful, why are Americans watching more and more of it?

• • • • • • • • • • • • • • •

WHAT DO I NEED TO KNOW ABOUT CHILDREN AND TV?

Television (TV) has its good side. It can be entertaining and educational, and can open up new worlds for kids, giving them a chance to travel the globe, learn about different cultures, and gain exposure to ideas they may never encounter in their own community. Shows with a prosocial message can have a positive effect on kids' behavior; programs with positive role models can influence viewers to make positive lifestyle changes. However, the reverse can also be true: Kids are likely to learn things from TV that parents don't want them to learn. TV can affect kids' health, behavior and family life in negative ways.

It's worthwhile for parents to think about what role they want TV to play in their family. Consider:

- A great deal is known about children and television, because there have been thousands of studies on the subject. Researchers have studied how TV affects kids' sleep, weight, grades, behavior, and more. It's worth looking at what the research says when deciding how to manage television in your family.
- Spending time watching TV can take time away from healthy activities like active play outside with friends, eating dinner together as a family, or reading. TV time also takes away from participating in sports, music, art or other activities that require practice to become skillful.
- TV viewing starts earlier than other forms of media—often beginning before age two. In recent years, TV, video and DVD programs geared to babies and toddlers have come on the market—and now even a cable channel for babies. We don't know yet what effect TV-viewing by babies may have on their development. We do know that time spent watching TV replaces time spent interacting with caregivers and other children. Social interaction is critical to a baby's healthy development.

HOW BIG A PRESENCE IS TV IN KIDS' LIVES?

- TV viewing among kids is at an eight-year high. On average, children ages 2–5 spend 32 hours a week in front of a TV—watching television, DVDs, DVR and videos, and using a game console. Kids ages 6–11 spend about 28 hours a week in front of the TV. The vast majority of this viewing (97%) is of live TV.

- 71% of 8- to 18-year-olds have a TV in their bedroom; 54% have a DVD/VCR player, 37% have cable/satellite TV, and 20% have premium channels.
- Media technology now offers more ways to access TV content, such as on the Internet, cell phones and iPods. This has led to an increase in time spent viewing TV, even as TV-set viewing has declined. 41% of TV-viewing is now online, time-shifted, DVD or mobile.
- In about two-thirds of households, the TV is "usually" on during meals.
- In 53% of households of 7th- to 12th-graders, there are no rules about TV watching.
- In 51% of households, the TV is on "most" of the time.
- Kids with a TV in their bedroom spend an average of almost 1.5 hours more per day watching TV than kids without a TV in the bedroom.
- Many parents encourage their toddlers to watch television.
- Find out more about media in the lives of 8- to 18-year-olds, http://kff.org/other/poll-finding/report-generation-m2-media-in-the-lives/

As you can see, if your child is typical, TV is playing a very big role in their life. Here are some key research findings to keep in mind as you decide what kind of role you want TV to play in your family:

- TV viewing is probably replacing activities in your child' s life that you would rather have them do (things like playing with friends, being physically active, getting fresh air, reading, playing imaginatively, doing homework, doing chores).
- Kids who spend more time watching TV (both with and without parents and siblings present) spend less time interacting with family members.
- Excessive TV viewing can contribute to poor grades, sleep problems, behavior problems, obesity, and risky behavior.
- Most children's programming does not teach what parents say they want their children to learn; many shows are filled with stereotypes, violent solutions to problems, and mean behavior.
- Advertisers target kids, and on average, children see tens of thousands of TV commercials each year. This includes many ads for unhealthy snack foods and drinks. Children and youth see, on average, about 2,000 beer and wine ads on TV each year.
- Kids see favorite characters smoking, drinking, and involved in sexual situations and other risky behaviors in the shows and movies they watch on TV.
- More on how television viewing affects children, http://extension.umaine.edu/publications/4100e/.
- For more detailed information on these and other issues, read on.

DOES TV AFFECT CHILDREN'S BRAIN DEVELOPMENT?

With television programs—and even a cable channel—designed and marketed specifically for babies, whether kids under two years of age should be watching becomes an important question. While we are learning more all the time about early brain development, we do not yet have a clear idea how television may affect it. Some studies link early TV viewing with later attention problems, such as ADHD. However, other experts disagree with these results. One study found that TV viewing before age three slightly hurt several measures of later cognitive development, but that between ages three and five it slightly helped reading scores.

The American Academy of Pediatrics takes a "better-safe-than-sorry" stance on TV for young children.

> "It may be tempting to put your infant or toddler in front of the television, especially to watch shows created just for children under age two.
>
> But the American Academy of Pediatrics says: **Don't do it!**
>
> These early years are crucial in a child's development. The Academy is concerned about the impact of television programming intended for children younger than age two and how it could affect your child's development. Pediatricians strongly oppose targeted programming, especially when it's used to market toys, games, dolls, unhealthy food and other products to toddlers.
>
> Any positive effect of television on infants and toddlers is still open to question, but the benefits of parent-child interactions are proven. Under age two, talking, singing, reading, listening to music or playing are far more important to a child's development than any TV show."

In addition, TV can discourage and replace reading. Reading requires much more thinking than television, and we know that reading fosters young people's healthy brain development. Kids from families that have the TV on a lot spend less time reading and being read to, and are less likely to be able to read.

WHAT ABOUT TV AND AGGRESSIVE OR VIOLENT BEHAVIOR?

Literally thousands of studies since the 1950s have asked whether there is a link between exposure to media violence and violent behavior. All but 18 have answered, "Yes." The evidence from the research is overwhelming. According to the AAP, "Extensive research evidence indicates that media violence can contribute to aggressive behavior, desensitization to violence, nightmares, and fear of being harmed." Watching violent shows is also linked with having less empathy toward others.

- An average American child will see 200,000 violent acts and 16,000 murders on TV by age 18.
- Two-thirds of all programming contains violence.
- Programs designed for children more often contain violence than adult TV.
- Most violent acts go unpunished on TV and are often accompanied by humor. The consequences of human suffering and loss are rarely depicted.
- Many shows glamorize violence. TV often promotes violent acts as a fun and effective way to get what you want, without consequences.
- Even in G-rated, animated movies and DVDs, violence is common—often as a way for the good characters to solve their problems. Every single U.S. animated feature film produced between 1937 and 1999 contained violence, and the amount of violence with intent to injure has increased over the years.
- Even "good guys" beating up "bad guys" gives a message that violence is normal and okay. Many children will try to be like their "good guy" heroes in their play.
- Children imitate the violence they see on TV. Children under age eight cannot tell the difference between reality and fantasy, making them more vulnerable to learning from and adopting as reality the violence they see on TV.

- Repeated exposure to TV violence makes children less sensitive toward its effects on victims and the human suffering it causes.
- A University of Michigan researcher demonstrated that watching violent media can affect willingness to help others in need. Read about the study here: http://sitemaker.umich.edu/brad.bushman/files/ba09.pdf.
- Viewing TV violence reduces inhibitions and leads to more aggressive behavior.
- Watching television violence can have long-term effects:
  - A 15-year-long study by University of Michigan researchers found that the link between childhood TV-violence viewing and aggressive and violent behavior persists into adulthood.
  - A 17-year-long study found that teenaged boys who grew up watching more TV each day are more likely to commit acts of violence than those who watched less.
- Even having the TV on in the home is linked to more aggressive behavior in 3-year-olds. This was regardless of the type of programming and regardless of whether the child was actually watching the TV.

What Parents Can Do

- According to the American Academy of Pediatrics, media education can help kids become less susceptible to the bad effects of watching violent TV. Some studies have shown that kids who received media education had less violent behavior after watching violent programs. Teach your kids to be media savvy. Find out more about media literacy.
- Watch with your kids, so if the programming turns violent, you can discuss what happened to put it in a context you want your kids to learn.
- Know what your kids are watching. Decide what programs are appropriate for their age and personality, and stick to your rules.
- To minimize peer pressure to watch violent shows, you may want to talk to the parents of your child's friends and agree to similar rules.
- Visit *YourChild:* Managing Television: Tips for Your Family for more ideas, http://www.med.umich.edu/yourchild/topics/managetv.htm.

For More on TV Violence and Kids

- Key Facts: TV Violence—a report from the Kaiser Family Foundation.
- A 1993 summary of some of the research on TV violence and behavior.
- Television Violence: Content, Context, and Consequences.
- The National Television Violence Study (NTVS).
- Television Violence: A Review of the Effects on Children of Different Ages—a 1995 70-page report and review of the literature.
- Violence in the Media—Psychologists Help Protect Children from Harmful Effects: Decades of psychological research confirms that media violence can increase aggression.
- Comfortably Numb: Desensitizing Effects of Violent Media on Helping Others—This study by a University of Michigan researcher demonstrates that watching violent media can affect willingness to help others in need.
- Joint Statement on the Impact of Entertainment Violence on Children: Congressional Public Health Summit—a statement of the American Academy of Pediatrics, American. Academy of Child & Adolescent Psychiatry, American Psychological Association, American Medical Association, American Academy of Family Physicians, American Psychiatric Association.

CAN TV SCARE OR TRAUMATIZE KIDS?

Children can come to view the world as a mean and scary place when they take violence and other disturbing themes on TV to be accurate in real life.

- Symptoms of being frightened or upset by TV stories can include bad dreams, anxious feelings, being afraid of being alone, withdrawing from friends, and missing school.
- Fears caused by TV can cause sleep problems in children.
- Scary-looking things like grotesque monsters especially frighten children aged two to seven. Telling them that the images aren't real does not help because kids under age eight can't always tell the difference between fantasy and reality.
- Many children exposed to scary movies regret that they watched because of the intensity of their fright reactions.
- Children ages 8–12 years who view violence are often frightened that they may be a victim of violence or a natural disaster.
- Violent threats shown on TV can cause school-aged kids (8–12) to feel fright and worry.
- When the threat is shown as news it creates stronger fears than when it is shown as fictional.

HOW DOES WATCHING TELEVISION AFFECT PERFORMANCE IN SCHOOL?

- TV viewing may replace activities that we know help with school performance, such as reading, doing homework, pursuing hobbies, and getting enough sleep.
- One research study found that TV's effects on education were long term. The study found that watching TV as a child affected educational achievement at age 26. Watching more TV in childhood increased chances of dropping out of school and decreased chances of getting a college degree, even after controlling for confounding factors.
- Watching TV at age four was one factor found to be associated with bullying in grade school.

CAN TV INFLUENCE CHILDREN'S ATTITUDES TOWARD THEMSELVES AND OTHERS?

Let's take a look at what kids see on TV, and how it can affect their beliefs about race and gender:

- Children learn to accept the stereotypes represented on television. After all, they see them over and over.
- When non-whites are shown on TV, they tend to be stereotyped.
- A review of the research on gender bias shows that the gender-biased and gender stereotyped behaviors and attitudes that kids see on television *do* affect how they see male and female roles in our society.
- Television and movies do not often show Asians or Asian Americans, and when they do, they fail to show the diversity in Asian American culture.
- Thin women are disproportionately represented on TV. The heavier a female character, the more negative comments were made about her.

- In 1990's commercials, white men more often were depicted as strong, while white women were shown as sex objects. African American men more often were portrayed as aggressive and African American women, as inconsequential.
- Ads for household items, like cleaning products, usually feature women.
- G-rated movies are commonly viewed by younger children—often over and over on DVD, and perceived by parents as safe for little kids. However, in these movies, whether live action or animated, males are shown more than females, by three to one, they are not often shown in relationships, and do not solve problems peacefully.
- In G-movies, characters of color are under-represented, and are usually shown as sidekicks, comic relief, or bad guys. Male characters of color are more aggressive and isolated.
- Music videos over-represent black males as aggressors, and white females as victims, compared to actual demographic data.
- To learn more, visit the Center for Media Literacy's page on Stereotyping and Representation, http://www.medialit.org/focus/ster_home.html.

HOW ARE CHILDREN PORTRAYED ON TV?

A study by a group called Children NOW of how children are shown on local TV news, found that:

- Almost half of all stories about children focus on crime (45%).
- Children account for over a quarter of the U.S. population but only 10% of all local news stories.
- African American children account for more than half of all stories (61%) involving children of color, followed by Latino children (32%). Asian Pacific American and Native American children are virtually invisible on local news.
- African American boys are more likely than any other group to be portrayed as perpetrators of crime and violence whereas Caucasian girls are most likely to be shown as victims.

CAN TV AFFECT MY CHILD'S HEALTH?

Yes, TV is a public health issue in several different ways. First of all, kids get lots of information about health from TV, much of it from ads. Ads do not generally give true or balanced information about healthy lifestyles and food choices. The majority of children who watch health-related commercials believe what the ads say. Second, watching lots of television can lead to childhood obesity and overweight. Finally, TV can promote risky behavior, such as trying dangerous stunts, substance use and abuse, and irresponsible sexual behavior.

Children Who Watch More TV Are More Likely to Be Overweight

- University of Michigan researchers found that just being awake and in the room with the TV on more than two hours a day was a risk factor for being overweight at ages three and four-and-a-half.
- The effects can carry on into adult weight problems. Weekend TV viewing in early childhood affects body mass index (BMI), or overweight in adulthood.
- University of Michigan researchers and their colleagues who investigated whether diet, physical activity, sedentary behavior or television viewing predicted body mass index (BMI) among 3- to 7-year-old children, found that physical activity and TV viewing are

most associated with overweight risk. TV was a bigger factor than diet. Inactivity and TV became stronger predictors as the children aged.

- Children who watch TV are more likely to be inactive and tend to snack while watching TV.
- Many TV ads encourage unhealthy eating habits. Two-thirds of the 20,000 TV ads an average child sees each year are for food and most are for high-sugar foods. After-school TV ads target children with ads for unhealthy foods and beverages, like fast food and sugary drinks.
- All television shows, even educational non-commercial shows, replace physical activity in your child's life.
- While watching TV, the metabolic rate seems to go even lower than during rest. This means that a person would burn fewer calories while watching TV than when just sitting quietly, doing nothing.
- The food and beverage industry targets children with their television marketing, which may include commercials, product placement, and character licensing. Most of the products pushed on kids are high in total calories, sugars, salt, and fat, and low in nutrients.
- Children watching Spanish-language TV after school and in the evening see lots of ads for food and drink. Much of it targets kids and most of the ads are for unhealthy foods like sugared drinks and fast food. This advertising may play a role in the high risk of overweight in Latino kids.
- Results from recent studies have reported success in reducing excess weight gain in preadolescents by restricting TV viewing.

Childhood TV Habits Are a Risk Factor for Many Adult Health Problems

- One study looked at adults at age 26, and how much TV they had watched as children. Researchers found that "17% of overweight, 15% of raised serum cholesterol, 17% of smoking, and 15% of poor fitness can be attributed to watching television for more than 2 hours a day during childhood and adolescence." This was after controlling for confounding variables.

Children May Attempt to Mimic Stunts Seen on TV

- Injuries are the leading cause of death in children, and watching unsafe behavior on TV may increase children's risk-taking behavior.
- Kids have been injured trying to repeat dangerous stunts they have seen on television shows.
- Many kids watch TV sporting events. Researchers surveyed TV sports event ads to assess what kids might be seeing. Almost half of all commercial breaks during sporting events contained at least one ad that showed unsafe behavior or violence.

Watching TV Can Cause Sleep Problems

- Television viewing is associated with altered sleep patterns and sleep disorders among children and adolescents.
- Regular sleep schedules are an important part of healthy sleep. A recent study found that infants and toddlers who watch TV have more irregular sleep schedules. More research is needed to find out whether the TV viewing is the cause.
- Those sleep disturbances may persist. Teens who watched three or more hours of TV per day had higher risk of sleep problems by early adulthood.
- Find out more in this research brief from the Kaiser Family Foundation: Children's Media Use and Sleep Problems: Issues and Unanswered Questions, http://kff.org/other/issue-brief/childrens-media-use-and-sleep-problems-issues/.

TV Viewing May Promote Alcohol Use

- The presence of alcohol on TV runs the gamut from drinking or talking about drinking on prime-time shows, to beer ads, to logos displayed at sporting events.
- Many studies have shown that alcoholic drinks are the most common beverage portrayed on TV, and that they are almost never shown in a negative light.
- Recent studies have shown that exposure to drinking in movies increases the likelihood that viewers themselves will have positive thoughts about drinking.
- Alcohol has damaging effects on young people's developing brains—and the damage can be permanent. TV ads are a major factor in normalizing alcohol use in the minds of children, adolescents and college students.
- Ads for alcohol portray people as being happier, sexier, and more successful when they drink. Alcohol advertising, including TV ads, contributes to an increase in drinking among youth.
- Television ads for alcohol, such as "alcopop," which combine the sweet taste of soda pop in a liquor-branded malt beverage, may target youth, especially girls and Hispanic and African American kids.
- The Center on Alcohol Marketing and Youth (CAMY) at Georgetown University found that in 2003, the top 15 prime time programs most popular with teens all had alcohol ads.
- Alcohol is increasingly advertised during programs that young people are more likely to watch than people of legal drinking age.

Kids Who Watch TV Are More Likely to Smoke

- Even though tobacco ads are banned on TV, young people still see people smoking on programs and movies shown on television. The tobacco industry uses product placement in films. Smoking in movies increased throughout the 1990s.
- Internal tobacco industry documents show that the tobacco industry purposefully markets their product to youth. The industry uses subtle strategies like logos at sporting events, product placement, and celebrities smoking to get around the ban on TV advertising for their products.
- Kids who watch more TV start smoking at an earlier age. The relationship between television viewing and age of starting smoking was stronger than that of peer smoking, parental smoking, and gender.
- Recent research has shown that exposure to smoking in movie characters increases the likelihood that viewers will associate themselves with smoking.
- Find out more about kids and tobacco, http://www.med.umich.edu/yourchild/topics/tobkids.htm.

Kids Get Lots of Information about Sexuality from Television

- Most parents don't talk to their kids about sex and relationships, birth control and sexually transmitted diseases (STDs). Most schools do not offer complete sex education programs. So kids get much of their information about sex from TV.
- Kids are probably not learning what their parents would like them to learn about sex from TV.
- Sexual content is a real presence on TV. Soap operas, music videos, prime time shows and advertisements all contain lots of sexual content, but usually nothing about contraception or safer sex.

- The number of sex scenes on TV has nearly doubled since 1998, with 70% of the top 20 most-watched shows by teens including sexual content. Fifteen percent of scenes with sexual intercourse depict characters that have just met having sex. Of the shows with sexual content, an average of five scenes per hour involves sex.
- Watching sex on TV increases the chances a teen will have sex, and may cause teens to start having sex at younger ages. Even viewing shows with characters talking about sex increases the likelihood of sexual initiation. (Read more about this study.)
- Watching sexual content on TV is linked to becoming pregnant or being responsible for a pregnancy. Researchers found that even after controlling for other risk factors, the chance of teen pregnancy went up with more exposure to sex on television.
- On the flip side, TV has the potential to both educate teens, and foster discussion with parents. Watch with your kids, and use the sexual content on TV as a jumping-off point to talk with your teen about sex, responsible behavior and safety.
- To find out more, read:
    - The American Academy of Pediatrics' (AAP) Parent Page on Sex, the Media and Your Child, http://pediatrics.aappublications.org/content/suppl/2006/02/15/107.1.191.DC1/p2_191.pdf

HOW CAN I FIND OUT MORE ABOUT KIDS AND TV?

Here Are Some Websites with Helpful Information:

- The Smart Parent's Guide to Kid's TV—from the AAP, https://www.healthychildren.org/English/Pages/default.aspx.
- A guideline from PBS Ready To Learn, http://pbskids.org/island/parents/.
- The Federal Communication Commission's (FCC) page on children's educational TV, https://www.fcc.gov/guides/childrens-educational-television.

Visit These Related Topics on YourChild:

- Managing Television: Tips for Your Family, http://www.healthychildren.org/English/Pages/default.aspx.
- Media and Media Literacy, http://www.med.umich.edu/yourchild/topics/media.htm.
- Video Games, http://www.med.umich.edu/yourchild/topics/video.htm.
- The Internet, http://www.med.umich.edu/yourchild/topics/internet.htm.
- Obesity, http://www.med.umich.edu/yourchild/topics/obesity.htm.
- Sleep Problems, http://www.med.umich.edu/yourchild/topics/sleep.htm.
- Reading, http://www.med.umich.edu/yourchild/topics/reading.htm.

WHAT ARE SOME ORGANIZATIONS THAT WORK ON ISSUES AROUND KIDS AND TV?

- The Center for Media Literacy believes in empowerment through education—that kids need to learn how to think critically about TV and other media, http://www.medialit.org/.
- The Center for Screentime Awareness sponsors National TV Turn-Off Week each year, http://www.screentime.org/. TV-Turnoff Week is supported by over 70 national organizations including the American Medical Association, American Academy of Pediatrics, National Education Association, and President's Council on Physical Fitness and Sports.

CRITICAL THINKING QUESTIONS

1. In four or five sentences, summarize the American Academy of Pediatrics' findings regarding television viewership and young children (infants and toddlers). What is the connection between reading and television viewing? Why would it be problematic for a child to watch television and not read—what would the child be missing out on?

2. The report lists a number of ways that television watching negatively affects health outcomes for children, ranging from sleep issues to obesity to alcohol and drug consumption. Choose three of these health issues and suggest a new law that would help address—try to fix—those three issues. What would your law be? How would it address your three health concerns?

3. Based on this reading, develop five "rules" you think should be in place in most households with children to help regulate television use. Which five of the many negative effects of television on children did you find most troubling? Explain how your plan would address each of those issues in some way.

4. **Connection.** "The Effects of Television Violence on Children" by the American Psychological Association (APA) states that television has a pervasive and troubling effect on children's views about violence. This report supplies data that supports that view. Find five *facts* in this article that support the APA's stance and explain them in your own words.

A complete list of references is included at the end of the book on page 403.

HONG KONG'S POP CULTURE OF PROTEST

by Nury Vittachi

Nury Vittachi is a journalist and author who is based in Hong Kong. He is known for the comedy-crime series *The Feng Shui Detective*, which has been published in many languages. He also writes non-fiction and novels for children. He is the founder of the *Asia Literary Review*, the Hong Kong International Library Festival, and the Man Asian Literary Prize.

This article explores the role popular culture played in protesting China's moves to limit Hong Kong's self-representation in 2014. Writing for *The New York Times*, Nury Vittachi notes that the key cultural elements of protests cross national boundaries. Hong Kong has a complicated ethnic and cultural history, and its relationship with China is tenuous. What role can culture play when people want to protest those in power?

• • • • • • • • • • • • • •

HONG KONG—In the first few days of the pro-democracy protest here, haughty newspaper editorials branded the demonstrators as naïve dreamers. The students responded by daubing a quote from John Lennon's "Imagine" over various parts of the main sit-in site in the Admiralty neighborhood: "You may say I'm a dreamer, but I'm not the only one."

The line turned out to be prophetic: The protesters' ranks soon swelled so much that journalists stopped trying to estimate the numbers. The choice of a Western pop song was also defining. Hong Kong is an international city, and ever since the former British colony was swallowed up by China in 1997, its residents have expected to live by global, not Chinese, standards. That goes for everything, including democracy.

These days the protesters are saying as much, and are rejecting the influence of Beijing over Hong Kong's next election by invoking a combination of local Cantonese cultural references and global musical hits.

The song they most often sing is "Boundless Oceans, Vast Skies," a 1993 ballad by the local Cantonese group Beyond. "Forgive me for loving freedom all my life," goes the band leader Wong Ka-Kui, who, like John Lennon, died before his time. On social media, a sugary 2007 song by an obscure group called the Wokstarz (disclosure: my daughter was a member) had 50,000 Facebook views in three days recently. It is known for celebrating a certain degree of freedom in Hong Kong: "It's true we have no democracy / One day we'll choose leaders / But we can say anything we like / Our free speech has freed us."

In 1964, while China was preparing for the Cultural Revolution, Hong Kong was hosting the Beatles. Today, on the sidelines of the sit-ins, small groups of older people wave the Chinese red flag and sing the Chinese national anthem, with its archaic, ponderous opening: "Arise! All those who refuse to be slaves! Let our flesh and blood forge our new Great Wall!" The protesters bellow back with the stirring "Do You Hear the People Sing?" number from the blockbuster musical "Les Misérables," hoping for a happier ending than in the original.

That song has been used at other demonstrations around the world, but only in Hong Kong is it performed in English and Cantonese. And the version in Cantonese—the dialect of Hong Kong and southern China, whose use Beijing has been working to limit in recent years—was rewritten around the dream of achieving democracy.

Sung by students barricaded in the center of a Chinese city, it gains poignancy from the memory of those other students who died in Tiananmen Square in 1989, and who are mourned publicly in Hong Kong every year, at a huge gathering in Victoria Park. The song's Cantonese lyrics—by an anonymous protester—express the frustrations of an entire community: "Hand in hand, we fight hard for the right to vote for our future. Why is our dream still just a dream?"

As chance would have it, on Oct. 1st, the holiday that commemorates the birth of the People's Republic of China, the song erupted on local news channels and live streams on the Web at the same time that the 2012 Hollywood movie of "Les Misérables" was broadcast on televisions tuned to the local affiliate of HBO. This Oct. 1 was also a day that brought particularly large anti-China crowds out in the streets.

At first, attempts by protest organizers to encourage famous artists to record "Do You Hear the People Sing?" were met by nervous refusals; no one wanted to risk their career. But as the protests grew, the entertainment industry gained a measure of courage. Several popular local singers, including Denise Ho, Kay Tse and Anthony Wong, have been seen standing at the protesters' side. The choice of a Western number depicting a French protest in 1832 adds a soupçon of historical import to the current gathering.

The protesters are also getting their message across the modern, international way by branding their movement with symbols. Many sport umbrellas—real or on stickers, photographs, drawings and in origami—because they have become the ultimate symbol of the movement since protesters began using them for protection against pepper spray and tear gas.

Paul Zimmerman, an elected councilor who was invited to the official ceremony for China's National Day, made himself a hero to students by quietly unfurling a yellow umbrella on that rainless day. And, of course, demonstrators have been breaking into choruses of Rihanna's 2007 hit "Umbrella."

Hong Kong's mixed cultural heritage runs deep even among the police officers now charged with enforcing Beijing's will in the territory. Ethnically, the 30,000-strong force is 99 percent Hong Kong Chinese, but its culture is eclectically Western, from its hierarchical structure to its off-duty rituals. At an official dinner a few years ago, I commented that the ceremonial garb included distinctive plaids from Scotland, including the bright red Mackintosh tartan. An officer next to me shook his head. "No," he said, "that tartan signifies Hong Kong Island officers, and the one over there is from Kowloon." Then a bagpipe player escorted a man carrying a pewter tray with a shot glass of amber liquid—a wee dram not of whisky, but of Chinese tea.

Scientists have long debated the pros and cons of crossbreeding. Botanists mock the bauhinia, the flower that represents Hong Kong on flags and coins, by pointing out that it is a sterile hybrid. But hear the protesters sing "I hope one day you'll join us and the world will live as one" to their police cousins over the barricades, and you know the Hong Kong blend produces beautiful children.

CRITICAL THINKING QUESTIONS

1. Using the internet, research why Hong Kong has a different culture than the rest of China. How does this connect to what happened in 1997? How would this cause the people of Hong Kong to expect "to live by global, not Chinese, standards?" Think of a part of America that might also differ culturally in a similar way. Which area did you select, and why might it differ?

2. The people of Hong Kong were protesting for increased democracy and government accountability. Why might they have chosen to embrace the song, "Do You Hear the People Sing," from the musical *Les Miserables*? Please look up the lyrics to explain your answer.
3. Compare the "ethnic" demographics of Hong Kong versus the "culture" of Hong Kong. How do these parts interact to make Hong Kong unique in its perspective on popular culture? Use evidence from the article to support your points.
4. **Connection.** Nury Vittachi is making an argument that pop culture can be political—that the people in Hong Kong are using music and symbols (like umbrellas) to make changes in society. Select one of the artists Jacob Bernstein profiles in "In Their Own Terms" and explain how that artist is using art to make an argument for societal change.

PUT ME ON TV. I'LL CHANGE. I SWEAR.

by Jon Caramanica

Jon Caramanica is a pop music critic for *The New York Times* and he has written for *Rolling Stone.* He is a journalist who covers music that is underrepresented in mainstream pop culture.

In this 2014 review of reality television programming for *The New York Times,* Jon Caramanica argues that what we want to watch is a projection of ourselves. We want to believe in second chances, so we cast former athletes with a history of unacceptable behavior on a show about living in community on an island. We are overwhelmed by technology and frustrated by the economy, so we want to watch people who live on their own in the woods. We imagine that if we could start things over, we would create a more equitable society; so we watch a Fox show that asks people to design a new society. Will this engagement with our concerns on the television screen yield any changes in the real world?

• • • • • • • • • • • • • • • •

NEW STARTS ON 'LIVE FREE OR DIE,' 'SURVIVOR' AND 'UTOPIA'

Near the turn of the millennium, no man in sports—or popular culture, perhaps—was more reviled than John Rocker.

In a *Sports Illustrated* profile, Mr. Rocker, then pitching for the Atlanta Braves, made derogatory statements—racist, homophobic and more—about New Yorkers. He was colorfully loathsome, a happy villain. And very quickly, a wholly reviled one. The backlash to that article led to more outbursts, and the eventual downward spiral of his career. By the mid-2000s, he'd washed out of the pros, better remembered for his foul mouth than his fastball.

Where else would Mr. Rocker go to be reborn but reality television? He was a contestant on the current season of "Survivor" (CBS), set in San Juan del Sur, Nicaragua. This is one of those seasons in which contestants play the game with (or really, against) a loved one. Mr. Rocker's partner was his girlfriend, Julie McGee. Blistering sun, rationed food, unpredictable personalities in close quarters—how could things go wrong?

What he wanted from "Survivor," most likely, was something of a fresh start, an opportunity to wash away the stains of his professional life and be reborn.

Step in front of the cameras and be free—such is the mantra of a recent wave of reality shows, which take the American impulse toward renewal one step further, by enabling people to shuck off the identities they'd spent decades forming and have a chance at starting anew. This fall, Fox began an ambitious show, "Utopia," which isolated 15 participants on a California ranch with minimal amenities (but dozens of cameras) and tasked them with building a society from scratch. On the National Geographic Channel, "Live Free or Die" follows a handful of people living in extreme anti-modern fashion.

Both of these shows were rooted in the premise that capitalist society is, in effect, broken, and demands a severe head-cleaning to rid oneself of its evils. This is a shift for reality television, which has often been used as a vehicle to a better, more-enhanced self. In the 2000s, reality TV tended toward ubiquitous makeover shows, from the charitable "Extreme Makeover: Home Edition" to the smilingly sinister "America's Next Top Model" to the ghastly theatrics of "The Swan." These were game shows of a different sort: Subject yourself to the cameras, and you would be rewarded handsomely.

Now reality TV is in retreat. Series about those who work hardscrabble blue-collar jobs have given way to series that romanticize those who live with very little, off the grid. You could run a whole network just with shows about living in Alaska—"Life Below Zero," also on Nat Geo, is a worthy recent entry in that category, sharing traits with the newest spate of pioneer shows.

Those programs fetishize a pre-technological, pre-capitalist mode of being. On each, participants often talk about their reasons for leaving civilization behind—some thoughtful, some naïve. "Utopia," which got the ax from Fox after only two months into a planned yearlong run, included Dave, an ex-convict looking to change his life by separating himself from old influences; Bella, an earth mother scared of microwave ovens; and Red, a good ol' boy with deep family demons.

But the real world was never far away. One of the signature tensions of "Utopia"—and there were many—was over whether the society being built on the show should mirror the one out in the real world. More often than not, it did—no one brought any Fourier to inspire something more radical.

Josh, a contractor, got plumbing and electricity up and running fairly quickly. Within weeks, there was private enterprise. Attempts at nondemocratic government systems largely flopped. Utopia, in this case, wasn't much more than the comfort of the familiar.

"Live Free or Die," by contrast, emphasizes experimental living, or at least, choices that were once the norm but feel radical in a modern context. There's Colbert, who walked away from civilization 25 years ago to live on Georgia swampland (though he still likes his morning coffee). He built his home from scratch over 15 years. "I'm way more connected to this house than I am to all the fine houses that I've had," he says.

Thorn is a former schoolteacher—he didn't like "being on someone else's terms"—who has opted to live in a hut he built and makes all his clothes by hand, from available materials.

These are people who have considered what America has to offer, and more or less turned away. And they are keen to spread their message: Thorn's young daughter comes to stay with him, and helps him with projects, while in a recent episode Colbert took on a nephew and tried to guide him in the ways of the wild.

And they try not to poison themselves with money exchange. Colbert traps beaver and raccoon and mails the pelts to be auctioned for money, which doesn't add up to much—his annual expenses are around $2,000, he says. (A spokesman for National Geographic Channel confirmed that the show's stars were paid for their participation in the series, though that income source isn't alluded to in the show itself.)

For these participants, who long ago went rogue, the cameras are there merely to bear witness. In some cases, though, the cameras are an agent of reverse transformation, as on "Living in Secret," which begins Dec. 2 on LMN.

Unlike the former series "Intervention," here the ones who are suffering are choosing to reveal their secret lives. The premiere episode follows Claudia, a shopping addict, and Sophie, a prostitute (those are not their real names) who want to let go of their identities and reclaim their old selves, which they do by confessing to a loved one. The show has a neat conceit—the protagonists' faces are obscured until they reveal themselves, real names included, suggesting that they are not truly whole until they have wiped themselves clean.

Again: this is reality TV as scouring pad, and an argument that the better self is the one who's walked away from society's temptations.

As for Mr. Rocker, his tenure on "Survivor" was short and fraught. He was bitter to teammates and opponents alike. A few other contestants recognized him from the real world and began to poke at him about his past.

After one confrontation with a female member of the opposing team got particularly hot, Mr. Rocker coolly said, "If you were a man, I would knock your teeth out." He was voted out shortly thereafter.

Stripped down to his essence, Mr. Rocker proved to be as bilious as ever. But at least he got what he wanted—everyone saw him for exactly who he was.

CRITICAL THINKING QUESTIONS

1. Jon Caramanica argues that some people, like John Rocker, want to use "reality TV as a scouring pad." Who is John Rocker, and why would he need to be cleaned? The article also describes Claudia and Sophie using reality TV like this. Why would they need this? Do you think a reality television program is a reasonable format to try and be re-born?

2. *Utopia* and *Live Free or Die* follow people who are trying to live in an "anti-modern fashion." Jon Caramanica argues that "both of these shows were rooted in the premise that capitalist society is, in effect, broken." What does this premise mean in your own words? How do both of these shows grow out of the idea that capitalism is broken? Why do you think shows like *Live Free or Die* or *Life Below Zero* are so popular right now?

3. What does the author mean when he writes that "those programs fetishize a pre-technological, pre-capitalist mode of being." What does it mean to "fetishize" something? Why would the producers of this show aim to do this? And why does Jon Caramanica thinks this is actually fake—that the "real world was never far away?"

4. **Connection.** Both this article by Jon Caramanica and "Hong Kong's Culture of Protest" by Nury Vittachi argue that culture arises out of social concerns. In Hong Kong, the protesters were upset about a lack of say in their government. This article argues that people are frustrated by the capitalist and consumerist nature of our economy and society, and that they want to see shows that demonstrate alternatives. What is an example of media that you think is popular amongst your peer group that is responding to a social problem? Why do you think the two are connected?

VOX IS THE CARMELO ANTHONY OF BAD POP-CULTURE METAPHORS

by Benjamin Freed

Benjamin Freed is a Washington, DC, journalist and blogger. He has written and blogged for *Washingtonian* magazine and is the editor-in-chief for *DCist*, an online publication.

Popular culture has a way of infiltrating many parts of our lives—the television show theme song you can't stop humming, or the YouTube video you've watched a dozen times. In this 2014 article for the *Washingtonian* magazine, Benjamin Freed explores a new area that pop culture is attaching itself to—the news. The website *vox.com* attempts to take the news and make it more understandable. What is lost when the news is presented through the lens of popular culture?

• • • • • • • • • • • • • • •

Understanding the news, through pop-culture comparisons that rarely hold up to scrutiny.

Vox's Timothy B. Lee raises a fascinating metaphor in his reading of the Huffington Post's analysis about the latest newsroom buyouts and layoffs at the *New York Times.* Because the *Times* hires younger, presumably cheaper, reporters and editors to balance out attrition caused by divesting itself of older, more expensive staffers, and stays on top of the news business, the paper is—in Lee's estimation—the "LeBron James of the news business."

Metaphors that equate a person or organization with a pop-culture totem make for catchy headlines, but they're also crutches for unimaginative writing. (To wit, consider Brian Stelter's daytime-television treatise *Top of the Morning,* which is riddled with enough metaphorical trusses to hold up Baltimore's Francis Scott Key Bridge.) Such lines, though, are a frequently used device at Vox, where the objective of getting people to "understand the news" seems to be delivered in forcing similarities between newsmakers and cultural icons.

Vox takes a lot of shots at this kind of metaphor, but they rarely connect. If the *Times* is LeBron James, Vox might be Carmelo Anthony, the New York Knicks small forward who puts up decent points, but also throws a ton of bricks. Let's review.

"THE NEW YORK TIMES IS THE LEBRON JAMES OF THE NEWS BUSINESS"

What Is *The New York Times*?

The *Times*, or "Gray Lady," at is sometimes called colloquially, is a New York City-based daily newspaper with global reach. It is also faced with the challenges of remaining financially viable while balancing the costs of a daily, general-interest print product distributed throughout the United States and a round-the-clock digital operation accessed by Internet users around the world.

Who Is LeBron James?

LeBron James is a National Basketball Association forward with a peripatetic relationship to his hometown of Cleveland. James, considered the best active player in the world, recently returned to the Cleveland Cavaliers after a four-year interregnum with the Miami Heat, with whom he won two NBA championships. Since signing with the Cavs, James has also persuaded his team to make other roster moves to lay the groundwork for bringing a major sports championship to long-deprived Cleveland.

Does the Metaphor Hold Up?

No. Founded in 1851, the *New York Times* epitomizes the term "legacy news organization." It is also the namesake property of the New York Times Company, a publicly traded corporation beholden to market swings and shareholder concerns. The *Times* is the peak of the newspaper world, but its editorial supremacy is often contested by the likes of the *Wall Street Journal*, *Los Angeles Times*, *Washington Post*, and *Guardian*, along with newer, online-only competitors. James, entering his 12th season, is a tested NBA veteran, but at 29, he is still very much in his prime and a threat to win more most-valuable player awards and championship trophies. Betting on the Cavs to win the 2015 NBA Finals is safer than wagering on the *Times* to sweep the Pulitzers.

"SOLARCITY IS TRYING TO BECOME THE APPLE OF SOLAR POWER"

What Is SolarCity?

SolarCity, according to Vox's Brad Plumer, is the United States' largest installer of solar panels, devices that absorb energy from the suns rays and convert them to electrical power in order to reduce dependency on expensive, dirty fossil fuels like oil and coal. The company recently purchased a solar-panel manufacturer, giving itself footholds in both the means of production and points of sale for modern electrical technology.

What Is Apple?

Apple is a consumer electronics behemoth known for its computers, phones, music players, and proprietary operating systems that attract cult-like followings. Sometimes it also forces you to own a U2 album you didn't ask for.

Does the Metaphor Hold Up?

No. SolarCity might be a market leader in home solar-panel installations with 25 percent of the national market, but it's no Apple, which commands 42 percent of the US mobile phone market. And before anyone points out that that's a smaller figure than the 52 percent of phones running Android, remember that Apple's share is based on a single family of phones, while Android devices are marketed by numerous different companies. Apple was also just crowned the world's "most valuable brand," at \$118.9 billion. There's not enough Voxsplaining in the world to give SolarCity that kind of monetized ubiquity.

"HOW CBS IS LIKE THE LOS ANGELES LAKERS"

What Is CBS?

CBS is a major broadcast network that fills its prime-time lineup mostly with canned-laughter sitcoms I've never watched and gray-haired cop shows that, well, I've also never watched. While its ratings among crucial 18-to-49-year-old viewers sagged in the 2013–14 television season it still airs, according to Vox's Todd VanDerWerff, several of the most-viewed series thanks to devoted older viewers.

Who Are the Los Angeles Lakers?

The Lakers are the second-most accomplished team in NBA history, with 16 championships, five of which they won between 2000 and 2010. But the 2013–14 Lakers were a bust, hobbled by aging, injury-prone players and missing the playoffs for just the second time in 20 years. But the Lakers, with their history and roster of celebrity fans sitting court-side, are always critical to the sporting zeitgeist. The team has lean years, but never irrelevant ones.

Does the Metaphor Hold Up?

Sort of. CBS faltered as an overall network because, VanDerWerff reasons, strong showings by its legacy shows were worn down by sagging ratings for its younger seasons. The Lakers didn't even fare that well. Besides middling performances by their younger players, the Lakers were also dragged down by lost seasons for their older, ticket-selling veterans Kobe Bryant and Steve Nash. But all things being equal, CBS may one day find its way back to the top of the over-the-air charts, just like the Lakers will probably win another five titles before the Wizards or Knicks even get close.

But Isn't This the Same Metaphor as the *Times*—Lebron James Headline?

Yes! Lee, author of today's "media-as-basketball" story, should have been mindful of his colleague VanDerWerff's deployment of the same metaphor three months earlier.

"JOHN J. MEYER IS ALMOST THE WALTER WHITE OF THE KEY LIME INDUSTRY"

Who Is John J. Meyer?

John J. Meyer is a lime merchant in Key West, Florida, whom Vox's Alex Abad-Santos interviewed for a May feature about spiking lime prices. Meyer stays ahead of the market by buying frozen concentrated lime juice from California to manufacture his citrus-y wares, Abad-Santos writes.

Who Is Walter White?

Walter White is the main character of the television show *Breaking Bad,* which follows the adventures of White, a high-school chemistry teacher who responds to a lung-cancer diagnosis by becoming a massively successful and increasingly diabolical crystal meth kingpin.

Does the Metaphor Hold Up?

No. Walter White cornered the drug market by producing a better product than the competition—or sometimes by literally killing the competition. He also died in the series finale as collateral damage from a revenge contraption he built to kill a gang of white supremacists. Meyer, as he told Vox, is merely trying to insulate himself from lime-market fluctuations. Meyer is very much alive and in charge of a successful lime-product shop.

What Is a Spoiler?

Don't even start. The show's been over for more than a year.

CRITICAL THINKING QUESTIONS

1. Benjamin Freed argues that, "metaphors that equate a person or organization with a pop-culture totem make for catchy headlines, but they're also crutches for unimaginative writing." He then gives five examples of the website Vox.com trying to use metaphors to explain the news. Which one of the five do you feel was the worst at explaining their idea? Why do you think it was ineffective? Rewrite the metaphor so that it helps you better understand the news topic.
2. What is the *tone* of the last entry on John J. Meyer? Why do you think the author chose to approach this section this way?
3. This article is a critique of the website Vox. Benjamin Freed argues Vox acts like "Carmelo Anthony." What does he mean by this? Go to Vox.com and pick an article. Did you find it helpful in understanding the topic? Why or why not?
4. **Connection.** Use a figure from pop culture to describe one of the articles from this unit. (For example, "Hong Kong's Pop Culture of Protest" is the ________________ of readings). Explain why you chose that person. What are the shortcomings of this metaphor? "Does the metaphor hold up?"

UNIT 6

Economics and Sports

INTRODUCTION

In the Fall of 2008, Eric LeGrand started college at Rutgers University in New Jersey. Like most freshmen, he had a major (Labor Relations) and was trying to adjust to the new norms of college. Unlike most freshmen, he was a college athlete, trying to make the football team.

College Athletics has a 150 year history in America, and most of its history bears little resemblance to the situation Eric LeGrand experienced at Rutgers in late 2008. Athletics had always been a part of colleges, as they were seen as ways to form well-rounded students. It seemed natural for competition to form; the first American intercollegiate sporting event was an 1852 rowing race between Harvard and Yale. It took place on a weekend, and the winners took home ceremonial oars; the two schools have held the race annually since then, with the oars going to the victor each year.

In 2014, the ESPN television network paid over 600 million dollars per year to broadcast the last three college football games for the next twelve years. Things have changed considerably.

The first game of Eric LeGrand's sophomore season was against the Cincinnati Bearcats, who flew to Rutgers University on a charter jet. In the offseason prior to the game, Rutgers completed a significant renovation to its stadium. The cost was nearly 100 million dollars, financed almost exclusively through the University's borrowing of money. Not coincidentally, student fees also rose at this time. When Eric LeGrand walked into the new stadium, over 50,000 people were cheering for his team—ticket sales that day alone brought in 1.6 million dollars.

Unlike most other industries, college athletics has flourished during tough economic times. The NCAA signs billion dollar basketball deals, and conferences form their own television networks. One reason they are able to do so well is due to the lack of labor costs. Eric LeGrand didn't make a single dollar from that 1.6 million dollars in ticket sales. For a country that prides itself on success through merit and being paid what the market will bear, this is certainly a unique situation. There are not many other options out there for young people to play sports—the NBA and NFL both require a player to be out of high school for a designated time. In this way, the governing body of college athletics, the NCAA, acts like a monopoly, owning all the available resources for a young person to prove their athletic worth to the professional leagues. If an auto-mechanic is unhappy with her place of employment, she can find work elsewhere; however, this right is not extended to college athletes. If Eric LeGrand had been unhappy at Rutgers, and had wanted to play football at the University of Maryland, he would have had to sit out a year, accepting the risk of injury, the risk of a star recruit taking over his position, or the risk of the coach deciding to pursue a different direction with the team.

If a student not involved in athletics wants supplemental income, she can go find a job at the campus bookstore or a job delivering pizzas. If a student athlete needs additional money, there is little time to work between practices and classes, and here, too, the NCAA limits what they can do to obtain money. Andrew Wiggins, for example, played college basketball for the Kansas Jayhawks in March of 2014 and was given no additional compensation other than a scholarship to that school. In August of that year, the Milwaukee Bucks agreed to pay him 11 million dollars over two years to play for their team.

This unit asks the following questions: *how did this seemingly unjust system come to exist?* And, *what will we do to fix this?*

On October 16, 2010, in a game against Army, Eric LeGrand's career ended with one tackle. On a kickoff return, he tackled the ball carrier, but LeGrand could not get up. He has not walked since, his spinal cord irrevocably injured. His dreams of playing professional football for millions of dollars have become dreams of one day using his arms again. Twenty months later, his coach, Greg Schiano, was given a 15 million dollar, five-year contract to coach in the NFL. When he started his new job Eric LeGrand had yet to graduate from college.

AMERICA'S GAME

by Michael Nelson

Michael Nelson is a former editor for *Washington Monthly.* He is a Fulmer Professor of Political Science at Rhodes College and a senior fellow at the University of Virginia's Miller Center of Public Affairs.

In this 2014 essay for the *Claremont Review of Books,* Professor Nelson explores how the history of "America's Game" mirrors American history. After Theodore Roosevelt saved football, the game changed significantly. It molded itself into the kind of game that modeled the type of country America wanted to be. Now, the sport finds itself in crisis again, and once again, the college game is at the center of the controversy. Can football remodel itself to survive in the 21st century?

• • • • • • • • • • • • • • •

The title of writer Gregg Easterbrook's new book states its theme: *The King of Sports.* "King" is the right word, and no mere figurehead. Super Bowls are Roman numeralized in the manner of monarchs and popes. Super Bowl Sunday has become a de facto national holiday. The 20 most-watched Super Bowls are also the 20 most-watched television programs of all time in the U.S., including the one played on February 2. The Super Bowl's main competition during the coming 12 months will not be from a presidential address or the *Dancing with the Stars* finale but from the first-ever college football championship game on January 12, 2015. (Meta Bowl I?) Condoleezza Rice, former secretary of state, will occupy an even hotter seat as one of the 13 members of the College Playoff Committee who determine which four teams will compete to play in that game. She's not unusual in her love of football: more women now watch the NFL than the Oscars.

NEW RULES

It was not always thus. Football's popular status in the late 19th and early 20th century coincided with a flurry of deaths and a blizzard of disabling injuries on the playing field, triggering calls from prominent educators and Progressive writers to abolish the game. For a time, schools such as Columbia, Northwestern, Stanford, and Cal actually did eliminate it. The *New York Times* ran an editorial in 1903 called "Two Curable Evils." One was lynching. The other was football.

As Hillsdale College's John J. Miller records in his sparkling *The Big Scrum: How Teddy Roosevelt Saved Football* (2011), football then was not the sport it is today. It was entirely a ground game. Five yards in three plays earned a first down and forward passes were illegal. College coaches routinely urged their players to hit and gouge each other within the opacity of the mass pileups that marked every play. They often recruited oversized ringers to pose as student athletes. Players wore minimal equipment; in lieu of helmets, many put their trust in the protective effects of long hair.

"Football is on trial," President Roosevelt—who loved the game for its cultivation of courage, endurance, teamwork, and other warrior virtues—told a summoned gathering of delegations from Harvard, Princeton, and Yale at the White House on October 9, 1905. The

Yale and Princeton coaches nodded but did little more than sign a statement pledging "to carry out in letter and in spirit the rules of the game." Harvard's Bill Reid took the ball and ran with it. Reid formed an alliance with New York University Chancellor Henry MacCracken to press for the formation of a new rules-making body called the Intercollegiate Athletic Association (NCAA) of the United States, soon to be renamed the National Collegiate Athletic Association. For all the NCAA's subsequent (and current) failings, the new rules it ushered in opened up the game by legalizing the forward pass and lengthening first downs to ten yards. The short-term result, Miller writes, was to establish football "as a game that featured high-speed end runs rather than a long series of battering-ram line plunges." The long-term effect, thanks to Roosevelt's intervention, was the game as we know it more than a century later. "Except for this chain of events," said Coach Reid years afterward, "there might now be no such thing as American football."

Easterbrook's and Miller's are just two of a recent flood of ambitious books dealing with football as something more than a subject for team adulation—that is, books unlike (they are legion) *Roll Tide!, 100 Things 49ers Fans Should Know and Do before They Die,* and *God Bless the Vols: Devotions for the Die-Hard Tennessee Fan.* Nicholas Dawidoff's *Collision Low Crossers: A Year Inside the Turbulent World of NFL Football,* which soaked up all the critical rapture available for football books last fall ("an instant classic," gushed the *New York Times Book Review*), actually is closer to the latter genre than the former. Embedded with the New York Jets coaching staff in 2011, Dawidoff's recurring theme may be fairly summarized as: "Isn't it cool that all these manly men seem to like me?" In return for this perceived acceptance, Dawidoff lauds Coach Rex Ryan, 8-8 that year and 14-18 ever since, as "the ascendant figure among headset-and-ball-cap wearers . . . his eyes clear blue, his teeth porcelain tiles, his spirits infectious."

A MODERN GAME

Thoughtful books about football have traditionally been a backwater in the literature of sports. When *Sports Illustrated* published its list of "The Top 100 Sports Books of All Time" in 2002, only 12 concerned football. Forty-two fit author George Plimpton's "Small-Ball Theory" ("the smaller the ball, the more formidable the literature"). Twenty-nine of these were about baseball, eight about golf, two about tennis, two about ice hockey, and one about cricket. Another 18 were about sports that involve no ball at all: boxing (seven books), mountain climbing (three), horse racing (two), and, one apiece: fishing, running, figure skating, gymnastics, body building, and even pro-wrestling.

Why did football, as a subject of book-length excellence, lag so far behind baseball and barely exceed golf? One reason is that technically, writing about football—a game in which 22 men run around a large playing field executing specialized missions at the same time—is extremely hard to do without getting lots of things wrong. Part of what makes Don DeLillo's second novel, *End Zone* (1972), so good, for example, is that he got nearly all the football stuff right.

A second reason becomes apparent only after digging a bit deeper into the list to discover that of the 12 books about football, just two were about the college game. Many talented writers doubtless think it's beneath their dignity to spend precious time describing what teenage males do on playing fields—a disdain felt especially by professors deciding whether to chronicle an activity engaged in by the very large students whom they typically think of as farthest down the great chain of academic being. For similar reasons, it is *infra dig* to write about the coaches who make much more money and sometimes wield far greater influence in university matters than the faculty. When ESPN announces that it wants to televise a Tuesday night game from your campus, for example, expect as a matter of course that all classes from 3:00 pm on will be canceled by order of the college president.

The best explanation, however, may be found in political scientist Michael Mandelbaum's *The Meaning of Sports: Why Americans Watch Baseball, Football, and Basketball and What They See When They Do,* a book that surely would have ranked high on the *S.I.* list if it hadn't been published two years too late, in 2004. Mandelbaum argues that during most of the 20th century, when the Top 100 books were written, baseball was America's leading sport because the game served as a pleasant reminder of an agrarian past to city dwellers who often were just a generation or two away from the farm. (Hence, the national *pastime.*)

Football, according to Mandelbaum, was the right game for the mid- and late-century urban industrial nation. As with modern life in general, and in sharp contrast to baseball, football "is played by the clock" and in disregard of weather. It is, he writes, "the sport of the machine age because football teams are like machines, with specialized moving parts that must function simultaneously."

Television and football rose to prominence hand in hand, which makes sense because "television, with its close-up pictures and its slow-motion replays, can dissect the action and present each slice of it in a way that the naked eye cannot see." Dawidoff, quoting then-New York Jet safety (subsequently a Denver Bronco and Buffalo Bill) Jim Leonhart on the frequent movement of players, coaches, and front office personnel from team to team, describes the NFL as "a corporation with thirty-two branch offices." George F. Will, who dislikes football intensely, nonetheless acknowledges its manifest modernity. "Football," he has written, "combines the two worst things about American life: it is violence punctuated by committee meetings."

RACE AND SEX

To the extent that sport mirrors society, changes in one intertwine with changes in the other—for better and for worse. That is implicitly the theme of *New York Times* reporter Samuel G. Freedman's intelligent and captivating *Breaking the Line: The Season in Black College Football That Transformed the Sport and Changed the Course of Civil Rights.* On its face, *Breaking the Line* is the story of the longtime rivalry between two traditionally outstanding black college football teams, Grambling and Florida A&M, under their legendary former coaches, Grambling's Eddie Robinson and A&M's Jake Gaither. The book is all of that, with riveting descriptions of games played and lives lived.

Underlying the narrative, however, is Freedman's sad account of the world that was lost in the wake of racial integration in the South. The saving grace of that world, riddled as it was with injustice and cruelty, was strong black institutions, from neighborhoods in which, necessarily, African Americans of all classes lived together, to schools in which black principals, teachers, and coaches were respected leaders.

All of these institutions (and more: churches, small businesses, funeral parlors, doctors' and lawyers' practices, and so on) placed young African Americans in a world rich with models of success and virtue. "Your boy will graduate college and your boy will go to church on Sunday," Robinson would tell the sharecropper parents of high school recruits—and they did, in overwhelming numbers. Like Robinson, Gaither prized the "hungry boy"—the poor young man "hungry for recognition" and achievement. Gaither was proud of the 42 team members who later played professional football, but even prouder of the results of an academic study confirming that 89% of his players graduated and 63% went on to earn postgraduate degrees.

No one, least of all Freedman, wants to return to the era of legally mandated segregation. But he laments integration's high price. Black principals and coaches were bucked down to assistant, black professionals and business owners were free to move to previously off-limits parts of town, and—perhaps especially—black football players were scooped up by white colleges and "too often exploited for their football talent and allowed to falter in the classroom." "Even African-American football fans," Easterbrook caustically observes in *King of Sports*, "avert their eyes from the large number of black players used up and thrown away" by modern big-time college football, egged on by coaches to chase the "mirage" of an NFL career at the expense of earning a college degree. "Academics first," LSU coach Les Miles would tell his players when he was at Oklahoma State, then hold up two fingers. "Football second," he'd add, holding up one. The message was clear.

ESPN business reporter Kristi Dosh's *Saturday Millionaires: How Winning Football Builds Winning Colleges* is a much less accomplished book than Freedman's, Easterbrook's, or Miller's. But buried in her clunky prose and tendentious argument that all is well with college football is a solid observation about another social development that has powerfully affected sports. With the enactment by Congress of Title IX of the Education Amendments in 1972, girls and young women were guaranteed equal access to educational programs that receive federal aid. The practical implication for scholastic athletics has been that schools must provide roughly equal opportunities for male and female students to play varsity sports, including athletic scholarships for NCAA Division I and II teams.

Any parent of a girl in the last 40 years knows what a revelation it has been to see daughters playing soccer, basketball, softball, field hockey, volleyball, and other games at a high level from grade school on. As Dosh points out, however, Title IX would smother in its cradle any effort to pay college football players for playing. That idea received its most prominent articulation in an October 2011 *Atlantic Monthly* article in which civil rights historian Taylor Branch argued that "The Shame of College Sports" is a "plantation mentality" that encourages universities "to exploit the skills and fame of young athletes" by perpetrating the "cynical hoaxes" of "'amateurism' and the 'student-athlete.'" The idea received momentum from a September 16, 2013, *Time* cover story called "It's Time to Pay College Athletes" and from an antitrust lawsuit filed against the NCAA seeking compensation for the organization's lucrative licensing of former players' images in commercial products. (E.A. Sports and Collegiate Licensing, companies that lease the images, settled their part of the suit last September; the NCAA has chosen to fight on.)

But, Dosh argues, "Title IX doesn't distinguish among sports based on profit. Even though football and men's basketball make the money, it can't all be spent on them per federal law." Pay all of a school's varsity athletes equally—*Time* suggested $225,047 as a reasonable figure for Texas A&M quarterback Johnny Manziel—and no college would be able to afford to field sports teams at all.

Easterbrook makes an even better point. To be of real value to players, he argues, "reforms must focus on sports' leading to graduation, because a college diploma is substantially more valuable than any pay a college athlete might receive." If college football rankings reflected graduation rates as well as winning percentages, he suggests, coaches would make sure their team members graduated. College football players aren't stupid; if they were they couldn't possibly master the dozens of formations and hundreds of plays that, in contrast to the much simpler game of just 50 years ago, they must know by heart to avoid tripping over their teammates and risk ending up in *SportsCenter's* Not Top 10 Plays of the Week. But coaches currently have little incentive to make their players spend the time it takes to excel in the classroom.

GROWING LITIGIOUSNESS

In addition to debates about race and sex, football also has become caught up in the nation's growing litigiousness. Mark Fainaru-Wada and Steve Fainaru, brothers and ESPN writers, fairly describe the National Football League as for many years a *League of Denial* on the subject of head injuries' severe long-term effects on mental health. Starting on September 28, 2002, the day when the first autopsied brain of a dead ex-NFL player was found to bear evidence of chronic traumatic encephalopathy (CTE), a massive amount of scientific research began to accumulate strongly suggesting that not just severe concussions, but also the cumulative effects of many routine hits, can damage the brain in ways that may later bring on CTE, ALS (Lou Gehrig's disease), Alzheimer's, Parkinson's, dementia, severe cognitive impairment, and other diseases.

A wave of growing knowledge, media attention, grassroots group formation, and congressional hearings began building in a textbook case of how our constitutional system is supposed to work on matters of public concern. More than for the 1,696 men who play pro football in the National Football League at any time, the research raised fears for the roughly 50,000 young men who play college football, the 1.1 million adolescents who play high school football, and the nearly 3 million boys on youth tackle squads down to the pee wee level. After committees of both the House of Representatives and the Senate held hearings, the NFL began taking head injuries seriously as a medical problem with implications both for how the game is played (helmet-to-helmet tackles were banned, kickoffs were moved forward to the 35-yard line) and how injured players are handled. "Shake it off" was out, "no go" for games and practices without an okay from an independent neurologist was in. The Fainaru brothers tell this story with page-turning intensity.

At that point personal injury lawyers took charge, channeling much of the momentum for political and institutional reform into litigation. To the Fainarus, this development seems fine. Their book ends on August 28, 2013, when the NFL and plaintiffs agreed on a $765 million payout from the league to its impaired former players, with another $200 million earmarked for attorneys' fees. But that was "chump change" for the NFL, the authors note, and in return for settling out of court, "there would be no public vetting of what the league knew and when it knew it" concerning the long-term effects of head injuries. In January a federal judge refused to approve the settlement pending proof that $765 million will be enough to cover all the affected players. For the Fainarus, like the judge, the problem was a lousy settlement for the players, not the fact that the issue devolved into a closed-door battle between lawyers. But with the political process short-circuited by litigation, here's what we still don't know: are there contributing factors (genetics? steroid use?) that explain why some former players suffer severe brain damage in later life while most of their teammates do not? Are there ages when, because the braincase is still hardening and necks still thickening, playing organized tackle football should be forbidden? Should additional rule changes be made, like banning the three-point stance for linemen that places their heads directly in the path of collision?

The brain-damage issue aside, marked as it is by the NFL's indefensible concealment of important work-related information from its own front-line employees, it's worth remembering that professional football players are just that, *professionals:* grown men who, with clear knowledge that the game is brutally punishing, choose to pursue a violent career in hopes of receiving massive compensation. Nate Jackson, a retired NFL player who lasted six seasons plus one on the practice squad (about twice the average), writes in a typically lyrical passage from *Slow Getting Up: A Story of NFL Survival from the Bottom of the Pile* that professional players are "pulled toward the mayhem. The feel of the helmet and shoulder pads, the sound of the whistle, the taste of the mouthpiece, the smell of grass and sweat: sacraments for bloodshed." But when the money is gone, he adds, "there is no incentive to continue. There's a reason why you don't see grown men at the park in full pads playing football."

COLLEGE FOOTBALL

The college game is different in some important ways. For one thing, there is such a thing as college football. In a dramatic example of American exceptionalism, our universities differ from those of every other country by making high-level athletic competition a major part of their identity. In 1929 Carnegie Foundation for the Advancement of Teaching president Henry Pritchett imagined a visitor from a European university asking, "What relation has this astonishing athletic display to the work of an intellectual agency like a university?" Critics of big-time college football have been asking the same question, in almost the same words, ever since.

Duke University economist Charles T. Clotfelter is among those critics—at least to a point. In the series of thoughtful empirical studies that constitute *Big-Time Sports in American Universities,* he offers a number of interesting findings. Athletics is absent from universities' own mission statements, a bizarre omission considering how much of a typical campus's money, reputation, and real estate are devoted to sports programs. A major source of revenue for major football programs is tax-deductible "contributions" that are nothing more than fees athletic departments charge for the right to buy good tickets to games. An additional large revenue source is the tickets themselves, which explains why seasons now last into late December or early January instead of ending as they used to before Thanksgiving, in time for fall semester final exams. Success on the field attracts many large donors to the athletic department but few to the university. Judging from various measures of academic quality, universities neither rise nor fall in reputation if they invest in big-time football, according to *Big-Time Sports.* But their students spend "less time in class and studying" and engage "more often in heavy drinking."

Coaches' financial incentives for winning are 12 times greater than any incentives tied to their players' graduation rate or academic performance while enrolled, Clotfelter shows. Players spend much more time on their sports than the NCAA-mandated maximum of 20 hours per week. In addition to practice, travel, and games, they must lift weights, do cardio, watch game film, attend meetings, and get treatment in the training room, among other activities. They often are directed by their coaches to maintain academic eligibility to play by "search[ing] out courses and academic programs that will present a minimum of challenge." At Virginia Tech, for example, a program that Easterbrook celebrates at great length for providing its players with the best of all worlds, Clotfelter finds that 20% of football players major in residential property management, about 40 times the share of other students at the university.

Clotfelter could have added a discussion, as Jeff Benedict and Armen Keteyian do in their well-reported *The System: The Glory and Scandal of Big-Time College Football*, of "the scandals haunting the sport—the bidding wars for top recruits; the booster payoffs; the horrific injuries; the academic cheating; the rising tide of criminal acts." Recently the University of North Carolina was exposed as the latest in a series of prestigious universities whose faculty was offering football players high grades in no-work, even phantom classes. In December the longtime head of the African, African American, and Diaspora Studies department was indicted for taking money to "teach" one such class.

All that said, Clotfelter suggests that because, as economists like to assume, universities are led by "perfectly rational" actors, they must know what they are doing: just look at the facts! "First," he writes, "once a university embarks on big-time sports, it rarely quits. Second, there continue to be universities outside the circle of big-time sports that want to join its ranks."

The saving grace of Clotfelter's argument is that he goes beyond standard microeconomic reductionism to explain what some of the benefits of commercial college sports actually are. One is the enormous pleasure that varsity athletics, "by far the most visible feature of many American universities," provides to millions of people. As writer John U. Bacon points out in his generally admiring account of the Big Ten conference, *Fourth and Long: The Fight for the Soul of College Football*, "College football is one of those few passions we have in common with our great-grandparents." Unlike the professional game, "College teams never threaten to . . . move to Oklahoma City if you don't build them a new stadium." They are woven into the fabric of personal, family, and community life.

Another clear benefit Clotfelter finds in major college sports is the "civic values" they promote. On the playing field, before thousands and sometimes millions of spectators, "the rewards from competition . . . [are] distributed on the basis of merit, not family name, ethnic origin, religious beliefs, or economic status." Beyond that, fans witness enactments of "the possibility and even the desirability of equality and cooperation across identifiable groups in society, in particular across racial lines."

Politically correct writers won't say it, so thanks be to Easterbrook for plainly describing another benefit of college football. The sport's "he-man nature . . . provides balance for left-wing college subjects such as gender studies." And "done properly, football not only helps boys learn to be men, it helps them learn how to cooperate with others and how to express their masculinity within a framework of respect for rules"—the very virtues Theodore Roosevelt was so eager to promote by saving football from itself a century ago.

REDSKINS

Football occupies such a large place in our national life that eventually everything contentious about it overflows into culture, politics, or both at some point. Last fall, for example, an argument arose over the name of Washington's NFL team. For decades (the team got its name in 1933), *Redskins* evoked little or no controversy. More recent resentment of the name stayed well below the horizon, as evidenced by the subject's complete absence from all 11 of the books discussed in this essay, some of which did not go to press until last fall.

Then, in a rush, the Oneida Indian Nation persuaded ten members of Congress to write to Redskins owner Dan Snyder and NFL commissioner Roger Goodell demanding a change; Snyder responded inflexibly; prominent sportswriters and some news organizations declared that they would no longer refer to the Washington squad by name; the president of the United States said that if he owned the team he "would think about changing it"; Goodell altered his public stance from "What's the problem?" to "We need to be listening," and the issue was off and running.

Personally, as one who regards as beyond silly the NCAA rule that forced the removal of admiring team name the Fighting Sioux from the University of North Dakota and mascot Chief Illiniwek from the University of Illinois, I am nonetheless persuaded by Charles Krauthammer's argument that "simple decency" requires that "Redskins" must go. As Krauthammer points out, no one would either publicly call an Indian a redskin or privately use the word in any but a pejorative way. But that's not the point I want to make. My point is that the controversy has unfolded exactly as it should have—and as the concussion issue did not: through open discussion, political organization, consumer pressure, and moral suasion, with plaintiff lawyers for the most part relegated to the sidelines. For a culturally important phenomenon such as football, that way of dealing with the issue, as well as with the other concerns described by these authors, leaves little to be improved on.

BOOKS DISCUSSED IN THIS ESSAY

The Big Scrum: How Teddy Roosevelt Saved Football, by John J. Miller
Collision Low Crossers: A Year Inside the Turbulent World of NFL Football, by Nicholas Dawidoff
The King of Sports: Football's Impact on American Society, by Gregg Easterbrook
The Meaning Of Sports, by Michael Mandelbaum
Breaking the Line: The Season in Black College Football That Transformed the Sport and Changed the Course of Civil Rights, by Samuel G. Freedman
Saturday Millionaires: How Winning Football Builds Winning Colleges, by Kristi Dosh
League of Denial: The NFL, Concussions, and the Battle for Truth, by Mark Fainaru-Wada and Steve Fainaru
Slow Getting Up: A Story of NFL Survival from the Bottom of the Pile, by Nate Jackson
Big-Time Sports in American Universities, by Charles T. Clotfelter
The System: The Glory and Scandal of Big-Time College Football, by Jeff Benedict and Armen Keteyian
Fourth and Long: The Fight for the Soul of College Football, by John U. Bacon

CRITICAL THINKING QUESTIONS

1. According to the author, why was football, "The right game for the mid- and late-century urban industrial nation?" How are the two connected to each other?
2. Provide two examples from the reading that reference how the sport of football directly relates to the social development of the United States.
3. Why have individuals had recent "resentment" toward the Redskins? The team was named in 1933, when there weren't negative feelings about the team name. What happened over time for people to question the Redskins' name? Do you think the team should change its name? Why or why not?
4. College coaches often assist athletes in finding classes that are not rigorous, according to the article. Do you think that athletes should be guided towards those courses? Is this a double standard? Who is harmed when there is a double standard?

COLLEGE SPORTS AREN'T LIKE SLAVERY. THEY'RE LIKE JIM CROW

by Brando Simeo Starkey

Brando Simeo Starkey is a writer and scholar. He graduated from Ohio State University and Harvard Law School. He was a postgraduate Research Fellow at Harvard Law and a Constance Baker Motley Fellow at the Equal Justice Society. He taught law classes at Villanova Law School and the Thomas Jefferson School of Law.

The NCAA controls its athletes like few other organizations in America can. They do not allow student athletes to work outside of the college. They do not allow student athletes to move freely from school to school. They do not allow students to have contact with agents who could help them professionally. Also, unlike almost any other job in America, these student athletes are not paid. In this 2014 article from *New Republic*, Brando Simo Starkey says that the NCAA reminds him of the Jim-Crow South. How long can the NCAA profit off of the labor of student athletes?

• • • • • • • • • • • • • • •

Usually the inventor knows his creation best. Walter Byers, who became the first executive director of the NCAA in 1951, turned a toothless organization into one that controls college sports. He grew disenchanted with his creation, however, writing in his 1995 memoir that the NCAA is "firmly committed to the neoplantation belief that the enormous proceeds from games belong to the overseers (the administrators) and supervisors (coaches). The plantation workers performing in the arena may receive only those benefits authorized by the overseers."

Since then, the slavery analogy has become the favored cudgel of NCAA critics. Comedian Chris Rock, for example, claimed that "college sports are no different than slavery." A.J. Daulerio, then editor-in-chief at Gawker, argued in *The Atlantic* that it's OK to compare college athletes to slaves because it "makes more people turn their heads and openly question the NCAA's policies." Even politically conservative media outlets have endorsed the analogy. *The American Spectator* published a piece, "The NCAA's Slaves," arguing that in some respects slave owners were morally superior to the NCAA. "Even some Southern plantation owners allowed slaves to earn extra cash through self-employment. The NCAA is not so enlightened."

The slavery analogy, however, is wrong: It overstates and misdiagnoses the problem. The NCAA's rules don't mirror slavery but rather the Jim Crow South's legal restrictions on black laborers. In other words, college athletes are exploited like blacks *after* slavery.

In the decades following emancipation, blacks were denied the whole value of their labor and the opportunity to fully compete in the economic marketplace. Southern legislatures enacted laws that allowed former slave owners to limit the economic opportunities available to black workers and increase their own profits. This exploitation was allowed to continue because it harmed blacks, a politically and socially disfavored people. Racism, that is, allowed this labor-market cartel to remain.

That bears a striking resemblance to college athletics today. So-called "student athletes" are likewise denied the whole value of their labor and the opportunity to fully compete in the economic marketplace. The NCAA enacted rules that allowed its member institutions to limit the economic opportunities available to college athletes and increase their own profits. This exploitation is allowed to continue because it supposedly benefits college athletes. The NCAA concocted the term "student-athlete" and wrapped this new phrase in a self-serving mythology that holds that college athletes who profit from their talent are distracted from what should be their first priority: getting a quality education. Many onlookers therefore accept the NCAA's amateurism rules as proper. Paternalism toward "student athletes," that is, allows this labor-market cartel to remain.

The former slave owners, despite their constant attempts after the Civil War, could not enforce a cartel on their own. In spring of 1865, Virginia planters met at the Louisa County Courthouse to fix the price of black labor. They resolved not to pay more than $5 a month and rations, and blacks were to pay for their own clothing and healthcare. "We hope now that the scale of prices having been determined on," the *Richmond Republic* reported, "the negroes will go promptly to work." Such efforts continuously failed because the market for black labor was far too competitive. Southern legislatures, therefore, had to do what planters couldn't do for themselves. The market for college athletes is similarly competitive, thus the NCAA has to maintain the cartel. Whereas the South used anti-black bigotry to keep its cartel alive, the NCAA uses paternalism.

Before exploitation could ensue, though, the targets had to be denied a role in governing.

After the Civil War, in late 1865 and early 1866, newly formed Southern legislatures enacted Black Codes. These laws applied only to freedmen, and, among other things, installed a series of economic regulations to establish a labor-market cartel. During Radical Reconstruction, when blacks voted and served in state legislatures, this cartel dismantled.

But once Democrats recaptured the South, they reinstalled these economic regulations to exploit black labor. To keep blacks from voting by using the power of the state, Southern states drafted new constitutions that disenfranchised blacks mainly through literacy tests. These tests generally required a potential voter to read and understand any section of the state constitution in order to register. "There was a general understanding," wrote historian Vernon Lane Wharton, "that the interpretation of the constitution by an illiterate white man would be acceptable to the registrars; that of a Negro would not."

The Fifteenth Amendment prevented Southern states from passing laws explicitly disenfranchising blacks. Unencumbered by such restraints—the Constitution affords no special protection to "student athletes"—the NCAA implemented a far cleaner solution to the same problem. The NCAA simply denies college athletes a voice in rulemaking, thereby leaving them, like blacks, without a role in the making and enforcement of rules. Voiceless, both groups had the value of their labor fleeced.

The tools of exploitation between the two cartels, moreover, are eerily similar. Southern states passed sunset laws, emigrant agent laws, anti-enticement laws, and contract enforcement laws. These laws, which reduced the slice of the economic pie dished to blacks while enlarging the portion served to white planters, have direct corollaries in the NCAA's meaty rulebook.

"Every man ought to have a right to dispose of his own property," former black Alabama Congressman James Rapier testified in April 1880 during a Senate hearing exploring the exodus of Southern blacks to Kansas in 1879. "I may raise as much cotton as I please," he complained, "but I am prohibited by law from selling it to anybody but the landlord."

Rapier was lamenting an Alabama law that prevented individuals from selling specified agricultural goods from sunset to sunrise. Southern Jim Crow legislatures enacted such "sunset" laws to block the economic avenues for freedmen, most of whom were relegated to field labor, right where the South wanted them. Because landlords often prevented blacks from leaving work during the day, this law limited blacks' ability to do what they wished with what their own hands created.

Today, University of Georgia star running back Todd Gurley, like Rapier in the 1880s, couldn't sell what his hands created: his signature. Gurley is currently suspended for reportedly affixing his John Hancock on eighty pieces of sports memorabilia. In 2010, six Ohio State players including star quarterback Terrelle Pryor were suspended for selling game-worn uniforms, championships rings, and awards. Gurley and Pryor violated NCAA rules prohibiting college athletes from selling memorabilia and profiting off their likeness. Those rules, as did the sunset laws, helped create a monopoly. Both schemes, that is, removed competitors from the marketplace. Indeed, Gurley and Pryor, like Rapier and Alabama blacks, were restrained from selling goods or services on the open market, reducing their economic rewards while boosting that of their plunderers.

"We are bothered by people from other states persuading away our laborers," a North Carolina man told his legislature in the late 1800s, "which [ought] to be a criminal offense." Southern legislatures agreed and enacted emigrant agent laws which required an agent in the business of recruiting laborers for out-of-state work to purchase an exorbitantly expensive license. Emigrant agents were crucial in helping blacks learn of better, but far away, economic opportunities. These laws drove the business of Southern labor agents into the shadows. Planters, though, hired agents of their own to help sell their agricultural products. Their real issue wasn't agents, but rather agents who helped black laborers resist the cartel.

"I hate to say this, but how are [agents] any better than a pimp?" Alabama football coach Nick Saban asked during a 2010 press conference in which he railed against agents having improper contact with college athletes. By prohibiting college athletes from having both meaningful interaction with agents and off-campus economic opportunities, the NCAA devised exploitative rules not unlike the South's emigrant agent laws. Athletes still have contact with agents, but like in the Jim Crow South, it happens in secrecy. Saban, of course, like the planters, employs an agent who benefits him—one who put nearly $7 million a year into Saban's bank account.

Anti-enticement statutes made hiring already employed laborers illegal. Such statutes inhibited competition among employers for employed laborers, weakening the latter's leverage to negotiate for better compensation and working conditions. John Townsend Trowbridge, a northern journalist who toured the South after the Civil War, learned how intolerant Southerners were of black laborers leaving for better opportunities. "I used to think the nigger was the meanest of God's creatures," one South Carolina man told him. "But I've found a meaner brute than he; and that's the low-down white man. If a respectable man hires a nigger for wages, one of those low-down cusses will offer him twice as much, to get him away."

NCAA's tampering rules mimic anti-enticement statutes. Devonte Graham, at the beginning of his senior year of high school in 2012, signed a letter of intent to play basketball for Appalachian State University. But Graham increased his stock after a terrific senior campaign and wanted to play for a better school. "I went on an official visit [to ASU], loved it and loved the coaches," Graham said. "But then I realized I could play at a higher level." ASU, though, refused to release Graham from his letter of intent for over a year, in part because, according to ASU, North Carolina State communicated with Graham without the school's permission, which, if true, constituted tampering.

Tampering rules in professional sports leagues are instituted pursuant to a collective bargaining agreement between owners and players. College athletes, however, had no such opportunity to bargain away such rights. This rule, therefore, prevents athletes from learning about better opportunities from competing institutions—perhaps more playing time or better coaching—information to which free laborers are entitled.

Contract enforcement laws compelled laborers to fulfill their contract under the threat of punishment, typically a fine or imprisonment. Not only did these laws reduce competition for laborers, they helped curtail black laborers' mobility by forcing them to work even if a better deal could be had elsewhere.

The NCAA reproduces contract enforcement laws with its transfer rule policies. Division I football and basketball players seeking to transfer to another Division I school usually must first receive written permission from their current institution to speak to prospective schools. If granted that permission, after transferring, athletes must sit out a year before competing. If not granted permission, athletes can still transfer but must pay for school for a year before being eligible for an athletic scholarship.

When blocking the transfer wishes of freshman women's college basketball star Leticia Romero earlier this year, Kansas State sought to achieve the same ends as the drafters of contract enforcement laws: forcing performance. Romero couldn't fund a year of school, saying that "that's something I can't do. My parents . . . the situation in Spain is really bad right now. They could lose their jobs." Kansas State ultimately relented, allowing her to transfer to Florida State. The NCAA, nevertheless, by punishing those breaking a contract, provides schools weapons to compel performance.

Some will scoff at this comparison between the NCAA and Jim Crow South. Yet the NCAA, through its methods of exploitation, is actually far more effective at snatching money out of its subjects' pockets than even the former Confederacy. Indeed, when courts tossed out the most egregious disenfranchisement laws in the middle of the twentieth century, the NCAA took the Jim Crow South's recipe and spent decades perfecting it. Now, college athletics need its own Civil Rights movement. Schools, coaches, television networks, and corporate sponsors have made a fortune off of college athletes' hard work. It's time those players were allowed to raise cotton for whomever they please.

CRITICAL THINKING QUESTIONS

1. Walter Byers, the first Executive Director of the NCAA wrote in 1995 that the NCAA was "firmly committed to the neoplantation belief that the enormous proceeds from games belong to the overseers (the administrators) and supervisors (coaches). The plantation workers performing in the arena may receive only those benefits authorized by the overseers." In your own words, explain how Byers compares the NCAA to slavery. Do you think it is appropriate to use a slavery metaphor when talking about college athletics?

2. In the Jim-Crow South, what were "sunset laws?" How did they function to keep African Americans economically dependent? Todd Gurley was suspended for selling autographed memorabilia; explain why the author thinks this has parallels with the sunset code. Do you think this comparison has merit? Why or why not?

3. What were anti-enticement statutes in the Jim-Crow South? Why were they created? How did they function to control African American labor? What are the NCAA's tampering rules? How do they function to control athletes? What distinction does the author make between the NFL, which also has an anti-tampering agreement, and the NCAA's tampering policy?

4. The article states, "The NCAA is actually far more effective at snatching money out of its subjects' pockets than even the former Confederacy." Even if one believes that the NCAA is a corrupt organization, is it fair to compare the treatment of athletes to the treatment of African Americans in the Jim-Crow South? Explain your point of view and provide evidence from the text.

PEOPLE ARE MAKING A LOT OF MONEY IN COLLEGE SPORTS, JUST NOT THE ATHLETES

by *Tyler Kingkade*

Tyler Kingkade is a senior editor and reporter for *The Huffington Post.* He is based in New York and covers issues on higher education and Millennials. His previous reporting related to politics for *The Huffington Post* and *The Iowa Independent* and he worked at the *National Journal,* which is a CBS affiliate in Des Moines, Iowa. He has earned national press recognition by the Society of Professional Journalists, the Associated Collegiate Press, and the University of Georgia.

Tyler Kingkade, in this 2014 article for *The Huffington Post,* describes what happens to all the money college sports generates. People wear jerseys from their local state school, buy hot dogs at the games, and fill huge stadiums on Saturdays in the fall. There is plenty of money to go around—but none of it ends up with the students. Coaches make millions, and athletic directors have seven figure salaries, but the students who win national championships, like Shabezz Napier, admit to going to bed hungry at times. Why does college sports reward those who organize the games and not those who play them?

• • • • • • • • • • • • • • •

When it comes to college sports, a lot of money is at stake.

A recent decision by the National Labor Relations Board to allow players at Northwestern University to vote to unionize, coupled with a class-action lawsuit against the NCAA arguing student-athletes should be paid, has shaken the college sports world, threatening to disrupt a multi-billion dollar business.

The NCAA, a nonprofit, has long argued it's an amateur model, the athletes are students first and they are compensated through scholarships.

But that defense is challenged when, after he and his team became the national champions of men's basketball, University of Connecticut player Shabazz Napier opened up about going to bed hungry as a student-athlete.

"We're definitely blessed to get scholarships to our universities, but at the end of the day, that doesn't cover everything," Napier told a group of reporters, adding, "I don't think student-athletes should get hundreds of thousands of dollars, but . . . there are hungry nights that I go to bed and I'm starving."

THE MOST PROFITABLE TEAMS MAKE RIDICULOUS AMOUNTS OF MONEY

Despite UConn winning the national title in both men's and women's basketball this year, Napier plays for a program that actually loses money. According to FindTheBest, a website that collected data submitted to the Education Department's Office of Postsecondary Education, UConn's basketball program ran $2.36 million in the red in the 2013 fiscal year. (Still, UConn men's head coach Kevin Ollie makes $1.25 million annually.)

However, many other hoops teams collect millions in profit. And yet, the *real* money is in college football.

At Northwestern, where players are considering unionizing, football and basketball are the only two sports bringing in cash—and no small amount, either. The Illinois school's football program collects $8.4 million in profits annually, while basketball nabs $3.9 million per year, according to FindTheBest.

To explain how much money is available, see football powerhouse University of Texas at Austin. If the university paid each of its Texas Longhorn football players a salary based off Texas' minimum wage, amounting to $13,920 a year, it would still leave $80 million of profit on the table, according to calculations using FindTheBest's data on profits. If the same were to happen at Northwestern, based on Illinois' current minimum wage, it would still leave almost $7 million in profit untouched.

Of course, players aren't paid a dime, unlike the coaches.

COMPARING COACHING SALARIES WITH THE REST OF THE NONPROFIT WORLD

The head coaches of three football teams—Texas' Charlie Strong, Alabama's Nick Saban and Arkansas' Bret Bielema—all collect more than $5 million a year. Six other head coaches make roughly $4 million annually, ranging $3.9 million to $4.8 million, according to *USA Today's* salary database.

Comparing the salaries of coaches at these "nonprofit" sports programs to those of executives at nonprofits more broadly, Strong, Saban and Bielema each earn approximately twice as much as the "most overpaid" nonprofit executive, according to the Fiscal Times: William and Flora Hewlett Foundation chief investment officer Laurance Hoagland Jr., who pulls in $2.5 million annually.

The roughly $5 million salary these coaches earn is also 12 times more than the median compensation for nonprofit CEOs in 2012: $417,989, according to the Chronicle of Philanthropy. The Chronicle of Philanthropy additionally said that seven nonprofits paid their chief executives in excess of a million last year, along with 27 other groups that provided pay for 2011. No college president in the country earns as much as these coaches, either.

And that's without even mentioning Duke University's head basketball coach, Mike Krzyzewski, who makes nearly $10 million a year, or the 34 other millionaire men's college hoops coaches, or the nine athletic directors making a million or more annually.

THE HIGHEST PAID PUBLIC EMPLOYEE IN ALL BUT 11 STATES IS A COLLEGE FOOTBALL OR BASKETBALL COACH

Assistant coaches make bank, too.

At UT Austin, a number of assistant coaches and coordinators earn close to half a million a year, according to the *Texas Tribune*.

And for good measure, let's not forget that while he's not a public employee, NCAA President Mark Emmert makes over $1.7 million annually, for running a nonprofit.

HOW DO THE EVER-GROWING COACHES' SALARIES COMPARE TO PROFESSORS' PAY?

As the NCAA likes to remind people, the players are in school for an education first and are on the team for the love of the sport. Northwestern head coach Pat Fitzgerald considers himself an educator, "teaching life lessons." Though coaches teach courses at some schools, this isn't true for a majority of universities known for their athletics, or for Fitzgerald.

College professors have salaries that pale in comparison to the coaches of sports teams. Professors earn between $50,032 and $126,981 annually, according to the American Association of University Professors. Adjuncts, or part-time, non-tenure track instructors, make around $20,000 to $25,000 a year.

That pay gap between educators and coaches is also getting worse, and it's not just limited to just basketball and football.

Even the head coaches of NCAA Division I tennis, soccer and golf squads are seeing their pay increase 3 to 4 times faster than the average professor, according to AAUP.

CRITICAL THINKING QUESTIONS

1. How does Tyler Kingkade summarize the NCAA's defense for not paying its athletes? He writes that this defense is "challenged" when players like Shabazz Napier give interviews similar to the one he gave after winning the NCAA championship. How does his story challenge the NCAA? Do you think his story calls for changes to the way the NCAA does business? Why or why not?

2. When Tyler Kingkade is discussing coaches' salaries, he compares them to nonprofit CEOs. What are his findings? Why does he compare them to nonprofit CEOs and not the CEOs of for profit companies?

3. What is the salary range for part-time faculty members at a college? Full-time professors? Compare this to the coaches mentioned in this article—who makes more? Why do you think Tyler Kingkade includes Professors' salaries in this article? Do you think the current situation is acceptable? Why or why not?

4. **Connection.** In "College Sports Aren't Like Slavery, They Are Like Jim Crow" by Brando Simeo Starkey, the author describes students at Ohio State University being suspended for selling their sports memorabilia. In this essay, student-athlete Shabezz Napier argues "I don't think student-athletes should get hundreds of thousands of dollars, but . . . there are hungry nights that I go to bed and I'm starving." Do you think that this is an acceptable situation? Is the NCAA correct to compensate athletes only through scholarships? Should athletes be allowed to have outside income while in school? Defend your argument using at least one quote from each essay.

MYTH: COLLEGE SPORTS ARE A CASH COW

by *David Welch Suggs, Jr., Ph.D.*

David Welch Suggs, Jr. is a professor at the University of Georgia's Grady College of Journalism and Mass Communication. His reporting mainly deals with sports and education.

College sports make a lot of money. ESPN signed a 5.5 *billion* dollar contract with the NCAA to broadcast their football playoffs. In 2012, David Suggs, writing for the American Council for Education, went about explaining why it still might be a poor investment for schools. Most schools, ones unlikely to be featured on ESPN in the large bowl games, lose money on college sports. Why do schools make this investment? And where does all the money go?

• • • • • • • • • • • • • • •

Outside my office door, there it looms. Sanford Stadium, complete with its fabled privet hedges and 93,000 screaming fans on fall Saturdays, lies in the very center of the University of Georgia (UGA) campus, with the humanities and social sciences buildings on the hill to the north and Ag Hill to the south. It's quiet this time of year, but the video advertising boards that flicker on periodically are an LED reminder of the South's year-round love affair with college football.

This is the most visible symbol of the UGA Athletic Association, a not-for-profit organization that in fiscal 2011 recorded operating revenues just shy of $90 million. That money enables the association to send its golf teams to Puerto Rico, track teams to Washington State, and Gym Dogs to Utah. Here and there, the Athletic Association also endows professorships and funds a few campus-wide projects.

As munificent as this is, this kind of spending is typical of big-time college athletics programs at universities across the country. *The Chronicle of Higher Education* recently estimated that college athletics is a $10-billion marketplace. What sets UGA athletics apart is that it can pay for its expenses without turning to the university for help.

Only seven other athletics programs at public universities broke even or had net operating income on athletics each year from 2005–2009, according to data provided by *USA Today* to the Knight Commission on Intercollegiate Athletics (for which I consult). The others were Louisiana State University, The Pennsylvania State University, and the universities of Iowa, Michigan, Nebraska, Oklahoma, and Texas at Austin.

Like these peers, Georgia's athletics department is flush because it can depend on donations, ticket sales, royalties from rights fees and sponsorships, and distributions from lucrative television contracts. It is no surprise that the other members of this elite fraternity belong to the Southeastern Conference, the Big Ten, and (at the time these data were collected) the Big 12.

For almost every other university, sports is a money-losing proposition. Only big-time college football has a chance of generating enough net revenue to cover not only its own costs but those of "Olympic" sports like field hockey, gymnastics, and swimming. Not even men's basketball at places like Duke University or the University of Kansas can generate enough revenue to make programs profitable.

As a result, most colleges and universities rely on what the NCAA calls "allocated revenue." This includes direct and indirect support from general funds, student fees, and government appropriations. In other words, most colleges subsidize their athletics programs, sometimes to startling degrees.

The six elite leagues in Division I are those that participate in the Bowl Championship Series: the Atlantic Coast, Big East, Big Ten, Big 12, Pacific-10, and Southeastern conferences. Even with bowl-game revenues and television contracts, however, public institutions in those conferences provided an average of $5.9 million to athletics in fiscal 2009, including $2.4 million in direct general-fund support and another $2.4 million in student fees.

In other Division I conferences, public institutions subsidized athletics programs with $9.6 million on average in 2009. In the Mid-American Conference, for example, average institutional subsidies rose from $12 million to $16 million between 2005 and 2009. Direct institutional support nearly doubled, from an average of $4 million to $7 million annually, while student fees contributed an average of approximately $7 million.

Why? Cornell economist Robert H. Frank applied his concept of the "winner-take-all" market to college sports in a 2004 white paper for the Knight Commission. "Suppose 1,000 universities must decide whether to launch an athletic program, the initial cost of which would be $1 million a year," Frank wrote. "Those who launch a program then compete in an annual tournament in which finishers among the top 10 earn a prize of $10 million each . . . How many schools will decide to compete?"

In other words, 10 programs will have a net income of $9 million, and the remaining 990 will lose $1 million. Despite the almost certainty of substantial loss, in the past decade only two institutions have left this marketplace—Birmingham-Southern College and Centenary College of Louisiana. In fact, Division I has added 21 member institutions since 2000, bringing its total membership to 337.

Of course, athletics programs foster other, less-clearly defined but important benefits for their institutions. At liberal arts colleges like the one I attended, varsity sports drive enrollment. Should that count as profit? Any number of UGA students will tell you they came here because of the football team. What about goodwill generated among legislators and donors?

These are important considerations. Significant athletics investments may indeed be a good value proposition for building community, spirit, and support. However, no good measures exist for assessing these less-tangible achievements. Most studies find no link between winning teams and measures of institutional success like number and quality of applications, fundraising dollars, or state appropriations.

Justifying institutional spending on athletics is becoming a much more pressing issue for most programs, especially in Division I. Institutions with Football Bowl Subdivision programs have seen subsidies of athletics rise by 53 percent at the median from 2005–2009, according to the Knight Commission. Meanwhile, spending on education and related functions rose only 22 percent. There are similar gaps at other Division I institutions.

If such trends continue, athletics subsidies will continue to grow, both in real terms and as a percentage of institutional budgets. For college presidents and academic leaders, it will be necessary to assess such investments in athletics in terms of opportunity cost. How else could general funds and student fees be spent?

College sports can be a marvelous value experience and a focal point for community-building. But only a few colleges have programs that can provide such benefits without imposing significant costs on their institutions.

CRITICAL THINKING QUESTIONS

1. According to the author, Dr. David Suggs, what sets the University of Georgia's athletic system apart? How many other schools can claim this? What are the benefits of running competitive athletic programs at American colleges and universities? What are the negative aspects of running such programs? Weigh the cost benefit for colleges and universities, especially for colleges whose sports programs are not profitable.

2. Define the word "subsidize." Then, describe how, for most schools, regular students subsidize college sports. Do you think schools should use student funds to subsidize sports? Why or why not?

3. How is college sports similar to a "winner take all" market? Why does this make it surprising that 21 schools added Division One Sports since 2000? Why do you think these schools made that choice?

4. **Connection.** In "People Are Making a Lot of Money Off of College Sports" by Tyler Kinkade, he suggests that paying college athletes minimum wage would allow for profitable athletic organizations to remain profitable. In this article, Dr. Suggs argues that most schools do not make money off of college sports. How do you believe a minimum wage requirement would affect those schools? Do you think that minimum wage is an acceptable amount of compensation for college athletes? Would you support a policy of paying some, or all, college athletes the minimum wage? Why or why not?

NCAA MUST ADAPT OR MOVE ASIDE

by Christopher Gasper

Christopher Gasper is a columnist for the sports section and host of *Boston Sports Live* and *Globe 10.0* on Boston.com. He was an NFL writer from 2006–2009, and he also has covered the Super Bowl, the NBA Finals, the Stanley Cup Final, and the Little League World Series while at *The Boston Globe*.

In the 2014 essay for *The Boston Globe*, Christopher Gasper examines the many contradictions that the NCAA has come to signify. It is a non-profit organization that makes more than most companies in the world; it hosts the enormous sporting events for 80,000 or more fans, but it can't feed the very players the people are watching; it claims its primary focus is education, but premier athletes take meaningless courses and rarely attend class. Can the NCAA adapt, or must it be dismantled?

• • • • • • • • • • • • • • •

The confetti cannons have stopped firing, "One Shining Moment" is but an echo, AT&T Stadium is back to being a soul-less, corporate edifice of excess, not a house of hoops dreams.

The Final Four was a Texas-sized success for the NCAA, one big self-contained, infomercial for the status quo of collegiate athletics with Jim Nantz as narrator. But the state of college sports is shifting, thanks to the Northwestern unionization case, and the NCAA has a choice—adapt or move aside.

The day before the title game, NCAA president Mark Emmert and a few other ambassadors of the current collegiate model addressed the media in Arlington, Texas. They spoke of change, but mostly advocated for the status quo in shiny new packaging. The NCAA is peddling New Coke and telling us they're starting a juice bar.

Much like the term it coined—"student-athlete"—the NCAA is spitting out a lot of contradictions these days.

They have a $10.8 billion deal to televise the NCAA Tournament, but the Most Outstanding Player of the Final Four, the University of Connecticut's Shabazz Napier, said he has gone to bed hungry. Emmert said that most schools don't have the resources to pay athletes, but he would not endorse the idea of athletes getting revenue from a third party via endorsements or for signing their own names. Big 12 commissioner Bob Bowlsby, an articulate and passionate voice of reason, called the NBA "irresponsible" for not providing a legitimate alternative to college for one-and-done players (the NBA D-League doesn't cut it) and then spoke about how the NCAA Tournament covers 85 percent of the association's expenses.

The NCAA can't have it both ways.

It can't say it's a non-profit and have members playing in championships with billion-dollar television deals.

It can't advocate for change in which the primary goal is preserving the lattice of the current model.

It can't say it's an association of 1,100 member schools with common goals and interests and then have 65 power-conference schools that are playing in a different league financially, but forced to follow the same rules.

It can't say its primary mission is educating student-athletes and then have athletes compelled to spend 40 or 50 hours a week in time commitments related to playing their sport.

It can't say it wants student-athletes to have a voice and then want to tell them what issues to speak up about.

The only contradiction that makes sense when it comes to college sports is that it's professional-amateur athletics.

The NCAA Tournament dwarfs the NBA for the month of March. It generates huge revenues. A recent Harris Poll revealed college football was the third-most popular sport in the country, trailing only the NFL and Major League Baseball.

The NCAA Tournament title game between UConn and Coach Cal's Kentucky young'uns was played in front of a record national championship game crowd of 79,238. Everything was handled in a Super Bowl-esque professional way, except the players, the ones pulled from classes and their campuses for the spectacle.

For those who cling to the ideal of amateurism and the sanctity of the scholarship, which is a valuable and significant piece of collegiate athlete compensation, but still just a piece, listen to UConn star guard Napier. During the NCAA Tournament, he was asked about the landmark regional National Labor Relations Board decision that identified Northwestern football players as employees.

Napier told reporters that there are some nights he and his teammates go to bed hungry because of a combination of Draconian NCAA rules stipulations and their impoverished economic backgrounds.

"As student-athletes we get utilized for what we do so well," said Napier. "We're definitely blessed to get a scholarship to our universities, but at the end of the day that doesn't cover everything. We do have hungry nights that we don't have enough money to get food."

Based on Napier's remarks, the NCAA got lampooned by Jon Stewart and "The Daily Show" last Thursday. In a trenchant satire, Stewart called the NCAA a "non-profit monopoly."

The NCAA is becoming a punch line. It's too bad the joke is still on the student-athletes.

Bowlsby, the former athletic director at Stanford, was the lone member of the panel at the Final Four who admitted the NCAA has strayed a bit from its mission. He said the NCAA should be "about degree completion and about getting done what needs to get done on campus."

He is an affable, reasonable, erudite voice. So is Emmert.

But they're trying to defend the indefensible, so they end up making pretzel-logic arguments and sending out talking-points memos.

One simple route for the NCAA, at least with the power conference schools, would be to allow an athlete like Johnny Manziel to do endorsements or sign memorabilia and maintain eligibility.

This way the NCAA can say the payment of athletes beyond the full cost of attendance—the movement to bump up money to pay for basic things like a slice of pizza—becomes a meritocracy.

Let the market decide who gets highly compensated for playing professional-collegiate athletics.

"Yeah, I think that's going to be part of the debate that the membership is going to have to have, whether or not they want to change the basic model," said Emmert. "The principle that I keep hearing again and again from universities is that this has to be about student-athletes, not about paid professionals. People want to make sure that they have the ability and the resources to be successful as students. That includes the debate around miscellaneous expenses and full cost of attendance, and how you fund that, I think, becomes an interesting part of the discussion."

If you're an aspiring musician at the Berklee College of Music, you can take a paid gig to play and still keep attending school. It's not that complicated, NCAA.

Student-athlete might be an oxymoron, but there are too many smart folks in college sports not to see that the current model can't be repackaged.

CRITICAL THINKING QUESTIONS

1. The article begins, "AT&T Stadium is back to being a soul-less, corporate edifice of excess, not a house of hoops dreams." Why is the stadium described as "soul-less" and what is occurring, according to the article, to "shift the state of college sports?"
2. Describe three contradictions of the NCAA referenced in this article. Provide two examples of such contradictions that Christopher Gasper describes, and explain whether or not you think that they are in fact contradictory in nature. Do you think they are, in fact, contradictions? Why or why not?
3. Do you think that the NCAA targets impoverished players purposefully and in an unjust manner? Explain your point of view with supports from the reading. Make sure to reference the concept of "degree completion."
4. **Connection.** In "America's Game," Michael Nelson argues that football had to adapt in the early part of the 20th century or risk losing its place as a sport. Compare that period for football to this period for the NCAA—when writers like Christopher Gasper are saying the NCAA must "adapt or move aside." How are these periods similar? In what ways are they different? Do you think the NCAA can evolve like football did?

NCAA APPROACHING $1 BILLION PER YEAR AMID CHALLENGES BY PLAYERS

by Mark Alesia

Mark Alesia is an investigative reporter for *The Indianapolis Star.* Alesia is a sports business and enterprise reporter. He has also written for *USA Today, The Washington Times* and *The Courier-Journal.*

Mark Alesia looks at the NCAA as it approaches a billion dollars in basketball revenue in this 2014 article for *The Indianapolis Star.* He wonders what is left of true college sports if everyone involved is making money—everyone except the players. The NCAA has grown every year since 2001, but has it become too large to adapt to the pressures being placed upon it?

• • • • • • • • • • • • • •

HOW THE NCAA MAKES AND SPENDS MONEY, 2012–2013

The NCAA made $912.8 million last year, 84 percent of which came from one, three-week event: The Division I men's basketball tournament. Here's a look at where the NCAA's money comes from and how it's spent.

Example: How to Read the Money Flow

Revenue from Division I Men's basketball tournament totaled $769.4 million

NCAA: $527.3 million on cash distributions to schools and conferences

Numbers in millions.

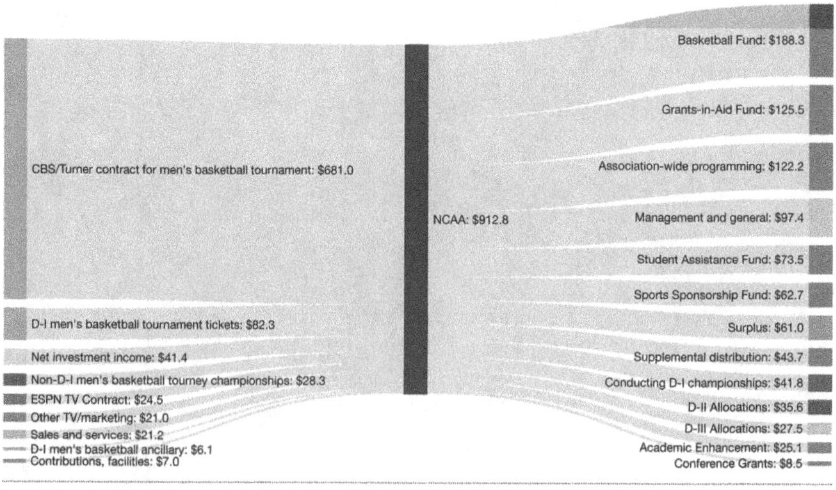

Source: *NCAA tax forms, NCAA bond prospectuses, NCAA financial statements and interviews*
Produced by: Haoyun Su and Mark Alesia/ The Star

Every year since 2001—through the aftermath of the dot-com bust, the Great Recession and the economic stimulus plan—the NCAA has made more money.

Every year, it has given more to the colleges it serves. Every year, it has set aside more money for investments, amassing $627 million. Now, it's poised to top the eye-popping mark of $1 billion in annual revenue.

And it's no secret that one big event, the Division I men's basketball tournament, accounts for 80 percent to 90 percent of that success. What is less clear is how much longer the winning streak will last.

Amid the maze of numbers and legalistic jargon in a recent NCAA bond prospectus, there's an ominous-sounding section on risk.

The Indianapolis-based National Collegiate Athletic Association describes a one-year "financial recovery plan" if anything happens to the money from the basketball tournament. The recovery plan includes drawing heavily from reserve funds, budget reductions, lowering the amount of money distributed to schools and event cancellation insurance.

It sounds extreme, a worst-case precaution bond holders expect, not to be taken as a prediction of doom so much as an insurance plan against loss. But as Indianapolis prepares to begin hosting the Midwest regional semifinals Friday, it's clear the NCAA is in uncharted territory.

The association—once seen as a fearsome monolith—is now the target of increasingly aggressive attacks by high-profile lawyers with deep pockets. On Wednesday, Northwestern University football players won the first round of their effort to become a union, and the NCAA faces a bevy of lawsuits by players who want more of the economic pie.

One high-profile case is scheduled for trial June 9 and, last week, heavyweight sports antitrust lawyer Jeffrey Kessler filed a lawsuit seeking to remove all restrictions on player compensation.

"It's undeniable that the pressure cooker is building," said University of New Haven Professor Allen Sack, a member of Notre Dame's 1966 national champion football team and a longtime critic of the NCAA. "It's a different ballgame. This is not like any other time."

Said Michael McCann, a law professor and legal analyst for SI.com: "This is a transformative era for the NCAA, and at the end, the student-athlete will have a different role. There will be changes to amateurism."

And changes to amateurism could mean changing uses for all that money.

Although he disagrees that pressure is building, even NCAA President Mark Emmert recognizes he's in a battle to preserve the current model of college sports.

In an interview with *The Indianapolis Star*, Emmert was asked if he's apprehensive.

"I'm apprehensive in that the system right now serves 450,000 student-athletes and provides remarkable opportunities for them," Emmert said. "Should that model be blown up, yeah, it would be a significant loss for America. So, of course we want to continue to support the collegiate model of athletics and think it's worth saving. Others disagree."

And, when it comes to the NCAA's future, no city has more at stake than Indianapolis.

SWEETENING THE DEAL

As part of a decades-long strategy to use sports to spur growth, Indianapolis invested heavily in the NCAA.

It took a reported $50 million in incentives for Indianapolis to lure the NCAA from its Overland Park, Kan., headquarters in 1999. Indy and Kansas City, Mo., were the finalists.

THE NCAA'S GROWTH

NCAA's annual revenue has increased every year since 2000-01. It was $912 million in 2012-13, of which about 80 percent comes from television.

The NCAA has grown its net assets to $627 million. They consist of a "quasi-endowment" and operating reserves that are invested. The quasi-endowment --- "quasi" because the principal is available to be used --- was established to protect against the association's dependence on money from the Division I men's basketball tournament.

The net assets dropped in 1997-98 because of a lawsuit the NCAA lost to so-called "restricted earnings" assistant basketball coaches.

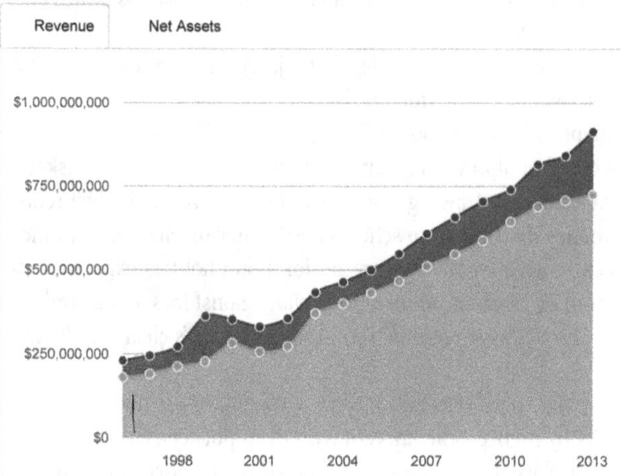

***Source:** NCAA tax reports, bond prospectuses and financial reports, and interviews*

Produced by: Haoyun Su and Mark Alesia/ The Star

The Lilly Foundation kicked in $10 million and private individuals, businesses and organizations raised $15 million. State and city taxpayers picked up the remaining $25 million.

At the time, a member of the Kansas City contingent was quoted as saying Indy "may be a little beyond sane in what they have done."

Indy built the NCAA a 142,000-square-foot headquarters and a 35,000-square-foot "exhibition hall/museum" called the Hall of Champions. The deal included 500 free parking spaces and "first-class landscaping."

The rent: $1 per year.

In 2010, the NCAA and the White River State Park Commission extended the headquarters lease to 2060 with three 10-year options. It included free land for the NCAA to build, with its own money, an expansion of the headquarters.

Rent remains $1 per year for the life of the agreement.

In financial documents, the NCAA listed the true 50-year market value of the rent and land, as determined by outside experts, at $44.5 million.

Taxpayers pick up the tab.

In return, the NCAA's growth has benefited the city.

Since moving to Indianapolis in 1999, the NCAA has gone from about 350 employees to about 500, virtually all of whom live and pay taxes in the area.

NCAA salaries and benefits have jumped from $20 million to $49 million.

In every five-year period until 2060, the NCAA has agreed to stage in Indianapolis the men's Final Four, the women's Final Four, pre-Final Four men's and women's basketball tournament games and the NCAA Convention.

According to an NCAA-commissioned report by professors from Indiana University's Kelley School of Business, the association's headquarters, events and meetings accounted for $161.8 million to Indiana's economy in 2012.

University of West Virginia economics Professor Brad Humphreys had no issues with the report's impact attributed to the headquarters, but he said it "vastly overstates the actual impact of the NCAA sports events."

But there are other intangible benefits.

Allison Melangton, president of the Indiana Sports Corp, calls the NCAA "a perfect fit for Indianapolis."

"They bring a lot of sports leadership to town," she said. "They're a great community partner. . . . The national attention we get in Indy—we have more events here because they're here—elevates our presence nationally, that we're a sports town."

Said Emmert: "Everyone who's involved in NCAA athletics knows the headquarters are here and sees Indianapolis as the epicenter of college athletics."

As the NCAA has grown, so have the benefits to its executives, including Emmert, who makes about $1.6 million a year, according to the latest public records. Those records also note that 86 NCAA employees made more than $100,000.

The NCAA uses consultants to supply salary ranges from comparable organizations, said chief financial officer Kathleen McNeely. She wouldn't name the organizations used by the NCAA but said they are for-profit and nonprofit. A compensation committee of school presidents makes the decisions.

"First of all, we have to compete in the market we're in, which is sports management," McNeely said. "We have a lot of lawyers at the NCAA. A lot of our areas are legislative areas made up of bylaw interpretations and writing bylaws. We have a lot of lawyers in our enforcement division. Our legal counsel—we have lawyers in that area."

The NCAA also relies heavily on outside lawyers who specialize in areas such as antitrust. The NCAA spent $9 million on legal expenses in 2011–12.

It needs lawyers now, perhaps more than ever.

PLAYING DEFENSE

In 2005, the NCAA looked in the mirror, trying to identify its weaknesses.

A risk management consultant identified four main areas of concern. All seem to apply today: federal or state legislative intervention, court decisions, reputation and lack of revenue diversification.

Lack of revenue diversification shows in the NCAA's television money. This year, CBS/Turner will pay about $700 million for the Division I men's basketball tournament.

ESPN will pay $31 million for everything else.

Last year's basketball tournament brought in $81 million of non-television money. Baseball was next at $13.5 million, followed by women's basketball at $4.4 million.

Indianapolis plays a role in helping protect the big money-maker.

In 2004, the NCAA wanted a backup site for basketball tournament games and to extend its lease in Indy. The Indianapolis Colts wanted a taxpayer-financed new stadium. The NCAA also knew that staging events in a big, new hometown stadium would save money.

In exchange for the guarantee of prime NCAA events being staged in Indy, the city extended the dollar-a-year lease and agreed to serve as a contingency site for all men's and women's NCAA tournament games.

The deal was contingent on "substantial improvements to the (old RCA) Dome and/or a new facility."

Lucas Oil Stadium opened in 2008, financed mostly by taxpayers.

The NCAA has never needed to use the contingency agreement. The original "memorandum of understanding" in 2004 is still in effect. It says the Indiana Sports Corp will "use its best efforts" with the city, the Capital Improvement Board, the Pacers and area universities "in the event of an emergency which requires the use of Indianapolis as a backup Event site."

As for the other risk areas, congressional interest in the NCAA creeps up occasionally but isn't a factor now.

Reputation is a constant battle for the NCAA, trying to show it's more than a group that prints money for three weeks every March. It runs 89 national championships, in sports such as rifle and rowing, for more than 1,100 member schools.

The bond prospectus says the NCAA returned 58 percent of its money to members in cash over five years. In 2012–13, the NCAA says it returned more than 90 percent of revenue to members in cash and services.

Legal decisions are by far the biggest current concern, with the capability of radically changing the NCAA model of college sports.

With the basketball tournament bringing in billions over several years and coaches making millions, players have become increasingly bold about fighting for a bigger cut.

Scholarships are worth tens of thousands per year. But critics note that a real education is hard to obtain while working virtually full time as an athlete for coaches whose livelihoods depend on winning.

Star players in the NCAA tournament are worth far more than their scholarships. The latest study of their true value was in *The Atlantic,* which estimated that the true value of freshman star Andrew Wiggins to Kansas was $575,565.

If the NCAA doesn't increase athlete benefits—Emmert says change is coming—the courts might do it instead.

The lawsuit scheduled for trial June 9 was brought by former UCLA star basketball player Ed O'Bannon, who wants athletes, not the NCAA, to control use of their name, image and likeness. That would have implications for production and sales of advertising, DVDs and video games, as well as rebroadcasts of games.

The Kessler lawsuit seeks to remove all restrictions on player compensation.

Another lawsuit also filed this month, by former West Virginia football player Shawne Alston, alleges the NCAA and major conferences illegally cap the value of scholarships at less than the actual cost of attending school.

The players seeking a union have mentioned better insurance and guaranteed multiyear scholarships instead of annual renewals. Lifetime scholarships for players to finish degrees, and get advanced degrees, also has been mentioned.

"Pay for play" is anathema to many fans—two-thirds of the public is against it, according to a recent ABC poll. But Sack, the New Haven professor, contends they've been paid for decades through scholarships.

There used to be additional "laundry money." Athletes can now tap into funds for situations such as buying a suit, traveling home for a funeral, or buying a computer. Bowl games in football, conference tournaments in basketball and the NCAA basketball tournament give players hundreds of dollars in gifts.

"Amateurism is whatever the NCAA arbitrarily decides to call it," Sack said.

McCann sees the possibility of conferences gaining more power and autonomy to define "amateurism." That would mean more benefits to players that smaller schools can't afford. McCann does not foresee the demise of the NCAA.

"I just don't think the country wants that," McCann said.

STRANGE MARRIAGE

It's a strange, enduring marriage, higher education and high-stakes sports. An interview with Emmert ended with a question about whether the NCAA would be around at the end of its lease in 2060.

As he often does, Emmert turned the question around on the interviewer.

"Will the *Indy Star* be here in 2060?" he asks.

The reporter said the company is moving to a modern new office and evolving on different news platforms, adding, "We've been here 100 years and the brand name's pretty strong."

Emmert didn't hesitate.

"I'd say the same thing for the NCAA."

CRITICAL THINKING QUESTIONS

1. Explain how and why the NCAA has been able to make more money since the Great Recession. Specifically, discuss the link between this increase in money and the NCAA Division I basketball tournament, as described in this article.

2. Are you surprised that taxpayers are responsible for some of the costs of stadiums, as referenced in the article? Do you think that such taxpayer money is justified in supporting college and university athletics? Explain your point of view.

3. Professor Alan Sack, who won an NCAA Championship with Notre Dame in 1966, sees the attacks on the NCAA as intensifying. "It's a different ballgame," he says, "this is not like any other time." What are the pressures Sack sees being applied to the NCAA? Why does he feel that the NCAA is no longer a "fearsome monolith?"

4. NCAA President Emmert says, "Should that model be blown up, yeah, it would be a significant loss for America. So, of course we want to continue to support the collegiate model of athletics and think it's worth saving. Others disagree." Do you think that the NCAA model should be salvaged since it is a historic part of America? How do you think the NCAA model should be disrupted? Explain your point of view.

UNIT 7

Criminal Justice

INTRODUCTION

Pierre Samuel du Pont was a French diplomat who served several French governments in the United States. His long correspondence with Thomas Jefferson produced hundreds of letters. In an exchange from 1816, du Pont is discussing a newly written constitution that France is considering. Thomas Jefferson praises the work, but claims it would not work in America; here, he claims, the laws need to be centered on protecting the individual, not the community at large; here, "justice is the fundamental law of society."

What justice means in America has, and always will be, an evolving conversation. In 1640 in the Plymouth Colony, located in what is now Massachusetts, there was a five dollar fine for smoking tobacco if you were a juror on a trial. After independence, and for most of American history, there were no fines for smoking. Then, in 1995, California was the first state to re-introduce fines for smoking in public places. "Justice" may be the fundamental law of our society, but it is an evolving term.

Our system of justice starts with the laws that our government passes—what they determine is legal and illegal, criminal or not criminal. These laws are then enforced by law enforcement officials—police officers and agents of the federal bureau of investigation. Then, we trust our court system—the lawyers, judges, and jurors—to evaluate the merits of each case and ensure justice is served in each situation.

Each of these parts of our criminal justice system is evaluated in this unit, and each has flaws. This unit is designed to evaluate the parts of our criminal justice system that may need to change. Earlier in American history, you could be executed for stealing a horse. In 2014, as the article "Death by Deadline" discusses, you can miss your chance to avoid execution if your lawyer incorrectly files paperwork. It is important that conversations about which laws are just and right, the same conversation Thomas Jefferson was having with Pierre Samuel du Pont, continue to occur.

Our criminal justice system is currently our largest institution housing the mentally ill; half of all executions in American history have been of African Americans, who are less than fifteen percent of the population. Our prisons are the most crowded in the world, creating terrible conditions but also profits for corporations; when people leave prison, their odds of staying out of jail are less than 25% after five years. This unit asks the following questions: *what are the major issues with our criminal justice system?* And, *why do these inequalities exist, and who benefits from them?*

The poet Charles Bukowski said "the only time most people think about injustice is when it happens to them." When Pierre Samuel du Pont was helping Jefferson think through this country's legal system, his perspective was of someone who would never have contact with it. Yet, the justice Thomas Jefferson placed at the center of our system of laws is vital because injustices are spread throughout our society. In fact, in 1997, a criminal court in Pennsylvania found Pierre Samuel du Pont's great, great grandson guilty of murder.

TRIAL BY FIRE

by David Grann

David Grann is a staff writer for the *New Yorker.* Grann is also the author of the bestseller, *The Lost City of Z: A Tale of Deadly Obsession in the Amazon.* Gramm has also written for the *Times Magazine, The Atlantic,* the *Washington Post, The Boston Globe,* and *The Wall Street Journal.*

In this seminal 2009 *New Yorker* essay, David Grann explores the case of Cameron Todd Willingham. He was on Death row in Texas for killing his own children. He is not a sympathetic prisoner—he beat his wife and has a criminal record—but David Grann patiently examines his subject and the case that sent him to the death chamber. After he interviews key witness and examines the evidence, we are left asking if Texas executed an innocent man. And, if so, what does it mean for our justice system if the government kills a citizen who did not commit the crime?

• • • • • • • • • • • • • • • •

DID TEXAS EXECUTE AN INNOCENT MAN?

I

The fire moved quickly through the house, a one-story wood-frame structure in a working-class neighborhood of Corsicana, in northeast Texas. Flames spread along the walls, bursting through doorways, blistering paint and tiles and furniture. Smoke pressed against the ceiling, then banked downward, seeping into each room and through crevices in the windows, staining the morning sky.

Buffie Barbee, who was eleven years old and lived two houses down, was playing in her back yard when she smelled the smoke. She ran inside and told her mother, Diane, and they hurried up the street; that's when they saw the smoldering house and Cameron Todd Willingham standing on the front porch, wearing only a pair of jeans, his chest blackened with soot, his hair and eyelids singed. He was screaming, "My babies are burning up!" His children—Karmon and Kameron, who were one-year-old twin girls, and two-year-old Amber—were trapped inside.

Willingham told the Barbees to call the Fire Department, and while Diane raced down the street to get help he found a stick and broke the children's bedroom window. Fire lashed through the hole. He broke another window; flames burst through it, too, and he retreated into the yard, kneeling in front of the house. A neighbor later told police that Willingham intermittently cried, "My babies!" then fell silent, as if he had "blocked the fire out of his mind."

Diane Barbee, returning to the scene, could feel intense heat radiating off the house. Moments later, the five windows of the children's room exploded and flames "blew out," as Barbee put it. Within minutes, the first firemen had arrived, and Willingham approached them, shouting that his children were in their bedroom, where the flames were thickest. A fireman sent word over his radio for rescue teams to "step on it."

More men showed up, uncoiling hoses and aiming water at the blaze. One fireman, who had an air tank strapped to his back and a mask covering his face, slipped through a window but was hit by water from a hose and had to retreat. He then charged through the front door, into a swirl of smoke and fire. Heading down the main corridor, he reached the kitchen, where he saw a refrigerator blocking the back door.

Todd Willingham, looking on, appeared to grow more hysterical, and a police chaplain named George Monaghan led him to the back of a fire truck and tried to calm him down. Willingham explained that his wife, Stacy, had gone out earlier that morning, and that he had been jolted from sleep by Amber screaming, "Daddy! Daddy!"

"My little girl was trying to wake me up and tell me about the fire," he said, adding, "I couldn't get my babies out."

While he was talking, a fireman emerged from the house, cradling Amber. As she was given C.P.R., Willingham, who was twenty-three years old and powerfully built, ran to see her, then suddenly headed toward the babies' room. Monaghan and another man restrained him. "We had to wrestle with him and then handcuff him, for his and our protection," Monaghan later told police. "I received a black eye." One of the first firemen at the scene told investigators that, at an earlier point, he had also held Willingham back. "Based on what I saw on how the fire was burning, it would have been crazy for anyone to try and go into the house," he said.

Willingham was taken to a hospital, where he was told that Amber—who had actually been found in the master bedroom—had died of smoke inhalation. Kameron and Karmon had been lying on the floor of the children's bedroom, their bodies severely burned. According to the medical examiner, they, too, died from smoke inhalation.

News of the tragedy, which took place on December 23, 1991, spread through Corsicana. A small city fifty-five miles northeast of Waco, it had once been the center of Texas's first oil boom, but many of the wells had since dried up, and more than a quarter of the city's twenty thousand inhabitants had fallen into poverty. Several stores along the main street were shuttered, giving the place the feel of an abandoned outpost.

Willingham and his wife, who was twenty-two years old, had virtually no money. Stacy worked in her brother's bar, called Some Other Place, and Willingham, an unemployed auto mechanic, had been caring for the kids. The community took up a collection to help the Willinghams pay for funeral arrangements.

Fire investigators, meanwhile, tried to determine the cause of the blaze. (Willingham gave authorities permission to search the house: "I know we might not ever know all the answers, but I'd just like to know why my babies were taken from me.") Douglas Fogg, who was then the assistant fire chief in Corsicana, conducted the initial inspection. He was tall, with a crew cut, and his voice was raspy from years of inhaling smoke from fires and cigarettes. He had grown up in Corsicana and, after graduating from high school, in 1963, he had joined the Navy, serving as a medic in Vietnam, where he was wounded on four occasions. He was awarded a Purple Heart each time. After he returned from Vietnam, he became a firefighter, and by the time of the Willingham blaze he had been battling fire—or what he calls "the beast"—for more than twenty years, and had become a certified arson investigator. "You learn that fire talks to you," he told me.

He was soon joined on the case by one of the state's leading arson sleuths, a deputy fire marshal named Manuel Vasquez, who has since died. Short, with a paunch, Vasquez had investigated more than twelve hundred fires. Arson investigators have always been considered a special breed of detective. In the 1991 movie "Backdraft," a heroic arson investigator says of fire, "It breathes, it eats, and it hates. The only way to beat it is to think like it. To know that this flame will spread this way across the door and up across the ceiling." Vasquez, who had previously worked in Army intelligence, had several maxims of his own. One was "Fire does not destroy evidence—it creates it." Another was "The fire tells the story. I am just the interpreter." He cultivated a Sherlock Holmes-like aura of invincibility. Once, he was asked under oath whether he had ever been mistaken in a case. "If I have, sir, I don't know," he responded. "It's never been pointed out."

Vasquez and Fogg visited the Willinghams' house four days after the blaze. Following protocol, they moved from the least burned areas toward the most damaged ones. "It is a systematic method," Vasquez later testified, adding, "I'm just collecting information. . . . I have not made any determination. I don't have any preconceived idea."

The men slowly toured the perimeter of the house, taking notes and photographs, like archeologists mapping out a ruin. Upon opening the back door, Vasquez observed that there was just enough space to squeeze past the refrigerator blocking the exit. The air smelled of burned rubber and melted wires; a damp ash covered the ground, sticking to their boots. In the kitchen, Vasquez and Fogg discerned only smoke and heat damage —a sign that the fire had not originated there—and so they pushed deeper into the nine-hundred-and-seventy-five-square-foot building. A central corridor led past a utility room and the master bedroom, then past a small living room, on the left, and the children's bedroom, on the right, ending at the front door, which opened onto the porch. Vasquez tried to take in everything, a process that he compared to entering one's mother-in-law's house for the first time: "I have the same curiosity."

In the utility room, he noticed on the wall pictures of skulls and what he later described as an image of "the Grim Reaper." Then he turned into the master bedroom, where Amber's body had been found. Most of the damage there was also from smoke and heat, suggesting that the fire had started farther down the hallway, and he headed that way, stepping over debris and ducking under insulation and wiring that hung down from the exposed ceiling.

As he and Fogg removed some of the clutter, they noticed deep charring along the base of the walls. Because gases become buoyant when heated, flames ordinarily burn upward. But Vasquez and Fogg observed that the fire had burned extremely low down, and that there were peculiar char patterns on the floor, shaped like puddles.

Vasquez's mood darkened. He followed the "burn trailer"—the path etched by the fire—which led from the hallway into the children's bedroom. Sunlight filtering through the broken windows illuminated more of the irregularly shaped char patterns. A flammable or combustible liquid doused on a floor will cause a fire to concentrate in these kinds of pockets, which is why investigators refer to them as "pour patterns" or "puddle configurations."

The fire had burned through layers of carpeting and tile and plywood flooring. Moreover, the metal springs under the children's beds had turned white—a sign that intense heat had radiated beneath them. Seeing that the floor had some of the deepest burns, Vasquez deduced that it had been hotter than the ceiling, which, given that heat rises, was, in his words, "not normal."

Fogg examined a piece of glass from one of the broken windows. It contained a spiderweb-like pattern—what fire investigators call "crazed glass." Forensic textbooks had long described the effect as a key indicator that a fire had burned "fast and hot," meaning that it had been fuelled by a liquid accelerant, causing the glass to fracture.

The men looked again at what appeared to be a distinct burn trailer through the house: it went from the children's bedroom into the corridor, then turned sharply to the right and proceeded out the front door. To the investigators' surprise, even the wood under the door's aluminum threshold was charred. On the concrete floor of the porch, just outside the front door, Vasquez and Fogg noticed another unusual thing: brown stains, which, they reported, were consistent with the presence of an accelerant.

The men scanned the walls for soot marks that resembled a "V." When an object catches on fire, it creates such a pattern, as heat and smoke radiate outward; the bottom of the "V" can therefore point to where a fire began. In the Willingham house, there was a distinct "V" in the main corridor. Examining it and other burn patterns, Vasquez identified three places where fire had originated: in the hallway, in the children's bedroom, and at the front door. Vasquez later testified that multiple origins pointed to one conclusion: the fire was "intentionally set by human hands."

By now, both investigators had a clear vision of what had happened. Someone had poured liquid accelerant throughout the children's room, even under their beds, then poured some more along the adjoining hallway and out the front door, creating a "fire barrier" that prevented anyone from escaping; similarly, a prosecutor later suggested, the refrigerator in the kitchen had been moved to block the back-door exit. The house, in short, had been deliberately transformed into a death trap.

The investigators collected samples of burned materials from the house and sent them to a laboratory that could detect the presence of a liquid accelerant. The lab's chemist reported that one of the samples contained evidence of "mineral spirits," a substance that is often found in charcoal-lighter fluid. The sample had been taken by the threshold of the front door.

The fire was now considered a triple homicide, and Todd Willingham—the only person, besides the victims, known to have been in the house at the time of the blaze—became the prime suspect.

Police and fire investigators canvassed the neighborhood, interviewing witnesses. Several, like Father Monaghan, initially portrayed Willingham as devastated by the fire. Yet, over time, an increasing number of witnesses offered damning statements. Diane Barbee said that she had not seen Willingham try to enter the house until after the authorities arrived, as if he were putting on a show. And when the children's room exploded with flames, she added, he seemed more preoccupied with his car, which he moved down the driveway. Another neighbor reported that when Willingham cried out for his babies he "did not appear to be excited or concerned." Even Father Monaghan wrote in a statement that, upon further reflection, "things were not as they seemed. I had the feeling that [Willingham] was in complete control."

The police began to piece together a disturbing profile of Willingham. Born in Ardmore, Oklahoma, in 1968, he had been abandoned by his mother when he was a baby. His father, Gene, who had divorced his mother, eventually raised him with his stepmother, Eugenia. Gene, a former U.S. marine, worked in a salvage yard, and the family lived in a cramped house; at night, they could hear freight trains rattling past on a nearby track. Willingham, who had what the family called the "classic Willingham look"—a handsome face, thick black hair, and dark eyes—struggled in school, and as a teenager began to sniff paint. When he was seventeen, Oklahoma's Department of Human Services evaluated him, and reported, "He likes 'girls,' music, fast cars, sharp trucks, swimming, and hunting, in that order." Willingham dropped out of high school, and over time was arrested for, among other things, driving under the influence, stealing a bicycle, and shoplifting.

In 1988, he met Stacy, a senior in high school, who also came from a troubled background: when she was four years old, her stepfather had strangled her mother to death during a fight. Stacy and Willingham had a turbulent relationship. Willingham, who was unfaithful, drank too much Jack Daniel's, and sometimes hit Stacy—even when she was pregnant. A neighbor said that he once heard Willingham yell at her, "Get up, bitch, and I'll hit you again."

On December 31st, the authorities brought Willingham in for questioning. Fogg and Vasquez were present for the interrogation, along with Jimmie Hensley, a police officer who was working his first arson case. Willingham said that Stacy had left the house around 9 A.M. to pick up a Christmas present for the kids, at the Salvation Army. "After she got out of the driveway, I heard the twins cry, so I got up and gave them a bottle," he said. The children's room had a safety gate across the doorway, which Amber could climb over but not the twins, and he and Stacy often let the twins nap on the floor after they drank their bottles. Amber was still in bed, Willingham said, so he went back into his room to sleep. "The next thing I remember is hearing 'Daddy, Daddy,'" he recalled. "The house was already full of smoke." He said that he got up, felt around the floor for a pair of pants, and put them on. He could no longer hear his daughter's voice ("I heard that last 'Daddy, Daddy' and never heard her again"), and he hollered, "Oh God—Amber, get out of the house! Get out of the house!'"

He never sensed that Amber was in his room, he said. Perhaps she had already passed out by the time he stood up, or perhaps she came in after he left, through a second doorway, from the living room. He said that he went down the corridor and tried to reach the children's bedroom. In the hallway, he said, "you couldn't see nothing but black." The air smelled the way it had when their microwave had blown up, three weeks earlier—like "wire and stuff like that." He could hear sockets and light switches popping, and he crouched down, almost crawling. When he made it to the children's bedroom, he said, he stood and his hair caught on fire. "Oh God, I never felt anything that hot before," he said of the heat radiating out of the room.

After he patted out the fire on his hair, he said, he got down on the ground and groped in the dark. "I thought I found one of them once," he said, "but it was a doll." He couldn't bear the heat any longer. "I felt myself passing out," he said. Finally, he stumbled down the corridor and out the front door, trying to catch his breath. He saw Diane Barbee and yelled for her to call the Fire Department. After she left, he insisted, he tried without success to get back inside.

The investigators asked him if he had any idea how the fire had started. He said that he wasn't sure, though it must have originated in the children's room, since that was where he first saw flames; they were glowing like "bright lights." He and Stacy used three space heaters to keep the house warm, and one of them was in the children's room. "I taught Amber not to play with it," he said, adding that she got "whuppings every once in a while for messing with it." He said that he didn't know if the heater, which had an internal flame, was turned on. (Vasquez later testified that when he had checked the heater, four days after the fire, it was in the "Off" position.) Willingham speculated that the fire might have been started by something electrical: he had heard all that popping and crackling.

When pressed whether someone might have a motive to hurt his family, he said that he couldn't think of anyone that "cold-blooded." He said of his children, "I just don't understand why anybody would take them, you know? We had three of the most pretty babies anybody could have ever asked for." He went on, "Me and Stacy's been together for four years, but off and on we get into a fight and split up for a while and I think those babies is what brought us so close together . . . neither one of us . . . could live without them kids." Thinking of Amber, he said, "To tell you the honest-to-God's truth, I wish she hadn't woke me up."

During the interrogation, Vasquez let Fogg take the lead. Finally, Vasquez turned to Willingham and asked a seemingly random question: had he put on shoes before he fled the house?

"No, sir," Willingham replied.

A map of the house was on a table between the men, and Vasquez pointed to it. "You walked out this way?" he said.

Willingham said yes.

Vasquez was now convinced that Willingham had killed his children. If the floor had been soaked with a liquid accelerant and the fire had burned low, as the evidence suggested, Willingham could not have run out of the house the way he had described without badly burning his feet. A medical report indicated that his feet had been unscathed.

Willingham insisted that, when he left the house, the fire was still around the top of the walls and not on the floor. "I didn't have to jump through any flames," he said. Vasquez believed that this was impossible, and that Willingham had lit the fire as he was retreating—first, torching the children's room, then the hallway, and then, from the porch, the front door. Vasquez later said of Willingham, "He told me a story of pure fabrication. . . . He just talked and he talked and all he did was lie."

Still, there was no clear motive. The children had life-insurance policies, but they amounted to only fifteen thousand dollars, and Stacy's grandfather, who had paid for them, was listed as the primary beneficiary. Stacy told investigators that even though Willingham hit her he had never abused the children—"Our kids were spoiled rotten," she said—and she did not believe that Willingham could have killed them.

Ultimately, the authorities concluded that Willingham was a man without a conscience whose serial crimes had climaxed, almost inexorably, in murder. John Jackson, who was then the assistant district attorney in Corsicana, was assigned to prosecute Willingham's case. He later told the *Dallas Morning News* that he considered Willingham to be "an utterly sociopathic individual" who deemed his children "an impediment to his lifestyle." Or, as the local district attorney, Pat Batchelor, put it, "The children were interfering with his beer drinking and dart throwing."

On the night of January 8, 1992, two weeks after the fire, Willingham was riding in a car with Stacy when SWAT teams surrounded them, forcing them to the side of the road. "They pulled guns out like we had just robbed ten banks," Stacy later recalled. "All we heard was 'click, click.' . . . Then they arrested him."

Willingham was charged with murder. Because there were multiple victims, he was eligible for the death penalty, under Texas law. Unlike many other prosecutors in the state, Jackson, who had ambitions of becoming a judge, was personally opposed to capital punishment. "I don't think it's effective in deterring criminals," he told me. "I just don't think it works." He also considered it wasteful: because of the expense of litigation and the appeals process, it costs, on average, $2.3 million to execute a prisoner in Texas—about three times the cost of incarcerating someone for forty years. Plus, Jackson said, "What's the recourse if you make a mistake?" Yet his boss, Batchelor, believed that, as he once put it, "certain people who commit bad enough crimes give up the right to live," and Jackson came to agree that the heinous nature of the crime in the Willingham case—"one of the worst in terms of body count" that he had ever tried—mandated death.

Willingham couldn't afford to hire lawyers, and was assigned two by the state: David Martin, a former state trooper, and Robert Dunn, a local defense attorney who represented everyone from alleged murderers to spouses in divorce cases—a "Jack-of-all-trades," as he calls himself. ("In a small town, you can't say 'I'm a so-and-so lawyer,' because you'll starve to death," he told me.)

Not long after Willingham's arrest, authorities received a message from a prison inmate named Johnny Webb, who was in the same jail as Willingham. Webb alleged that Willingham had confessed to him that he took "some kind of lighter fluid, squirting [it] around the walls and the floor, and set a fire." The case against Willingham was considered airtight.

Even so, several of Stacy's relatives—who, unlike her, believed that Willingham was guilty—told Jackson that they preferred to avoid the anguish of a trial. And so, shortly before jury selection, Jackson approached Willingham's attorneys with an extraordinary offer: if their client pleaded guilty, the state would give him a life sentence. "I was really happy when I thought we might have a deal to avoid the death penalty," Jackson recalls.

Willingham's lawyers were equally pleased. They had little doubt that he had committed the murders and that, if the case went before a jury, he would be found guilty, and, subsequently, executed. "Everyone thinks defense lawyers must believe their clients are innocent, but that's seldom true," Martin told me. "Most of the time, they're guilty as sin." He added of Willingham, "All the evidence showed that he was one hundred percent guilty. He poured accelerant all over the house and put lighter fluid under the kids' beds." It was, he said, "a classic arson case": there were "puddle patterns all over the place—no disputing those."

Martin and Dunn advised Willingham that he should accept the offer, but he refused. The lawyers asked his father and stepmother to speak to him. According to Eugenia, Martin showed them photographs of the burned children and said, "Look what your son did. You got to talk him into pleading, or he's going to be executed."

His parents went to see their son in jail. Though his father did not believe that he should plead guilty if he were innocent, his stepmother beseeched him to take the deal. "I just wanted to keep my boy alive," she told me.

Willingham was implacable. "I ain't gonna plead to something I didn't do, especially killing my own kids," he said. It was his final decision. Martin says, "I thought it was nuts at the time—and I think it's nuts now."

Willingham's refusal to accept the deal confirmed the view of the prosecution, and even that of his defense lawyers, that he was an unrepentant killer.

In August, 1992, the trial commenced in the old stone courthouse in downtown Corsicana. Jackson and a team of prosecutors summoned a procession of witnesses, including Johnny Webb and the Barbees. The crux of the state's case, though, remained the scientific evidence gathered by Vasquez and Fogg. On the stand, Vasquez detailed what he called more than "twenty indicators" of arson.

"Do you have an opinion as to who started the fire?" one of the prosecutors asked.

"Yes, sir," Vasquez said. "Mr. Willingham."

The prosecutor asked Vasquez what he thought Willingham's intent was in lighting the fire. "To kill the little girls," he said.

The defense had tried to find a fire expert to counter Vasquez and Fogg's testimony, but the one they contacted concurred with the prosecution. Ultimately, the defense presented only one witness to the jury: the Willinghams' babysitter, who said she could not believe that Willingham could have killed his children. (Dunn told me that Willingham had wanted to testify, but Martin and Dunn thought that he would make a bad witness.) The trial ended after two days.

During his closing arguments, Jackson said that the puddle configurations and pour patterns were Willingham's inadvertent "confession," burned into the floor. Showing a Bible that had been salvaged from the fire, Jackson paraphrased the words of Jesus from the Gospel of Matthew: "Whomsoever shall harm one of my children, it's better for a millstone to be hung around his neck and for him to be cast in the sea."

The jury was out for barely an hour before returning with a unanimous guilty verdict. As Vasquez put it, "The fire does not lie."

II

When Elizabeth Gilbert approached the prison guard, on a spring day in 1999, and said Cameron Todd Willingham's name, she was uncertain about what she was doing. A forty-seven-year-old French teacher and playwright from Houston, Gilbert was divorced with two children. She had never visited a prison before. Several weeks earlier, a friend, who worked at an organization that opposed the death penalty, had encouraged her to volunteer as a pen pal for an inmate on death row, and Gilbert had offered her name and address. Not long after, a short letter, written with unsteady penmanship, arrived from Willingham. "If you wish to write back, I would be honored to correspond with you," he said. He also asked if she might visit him. Perhaps out of a writer's curiosity, or perhaps because she didn't feel quite herself (she had just been upset by news that her ex-husband was dying of cancer), she agreed. Now she was standing in front of the decrepit penitentiary in Huntsville, Texas—a place that inmates referred to as "the death pit."

She filed past a razor-wire fence, a series of floodlights, and a checkpoint, where she was patted down, until she entered a small chamber. Only a few feet in front of her was a man convicted of multiple infanticide. He was wearing a white jumpsuit with "DR"—for death row—printed on the back, in large black letters. He had a tattoo of a serpent and a skull on his left biceps. He stood nearly six feet tall and was muscular, though his legs had atrophied after years of confinement.

A Plexiglas window separated Willingham from her; still, Gilbert, who had short brown hair and a bookish manner, stared at him uneasily. Willingham had once fought another prisoner who called him a "baby killer," and since he had been incarcerated, seven years earlier, he had committed a series of disciplinary infractions that had periodically landed him in the segregation unit, which was known as "the dungeon."

Willingham greeted her politely. He seemed grateful that she had come. After his conviction, Stacy had campaigned for his release. She wrote to Ann Richards, then the governor of Texas, saying, "I know him in ways that no one else does when it comes to our children. Therefore, I believe that there is no way he could have possibly committed this crime." But within a year Stacy had filed for divorce, and Willingham had few visitors except for his parents, who drove from Oklahoma to see him once a month. "I really have no one outside my parents to remind me that I am a human being, not the animal the state professes I am," he told Gilbert at one point.

He didn't want to talk about death row. "Hell, I live here," he later wrote her. "When I have a visit, I want to escape from here." He asked her questions about her teaching and art. He expressed fear that, as a playwright, she might find him a "one-dimensional character," and apologized for lacking social graces; he now had trouble separating the mores in prison from those of the outside world.

When Gilbert asked him if he wanted something to eat or drink from the vending machines, he declined. "I hope I did not offend you by not accepting any snacks," he later wrote her. "I didn't want you to feel I was there just for something like that."

She had been warned that prisoners often tried to con visitors. He appeared to realize this, subsequently telling her, "I am just a simple man. Nothing else. And to most other people a convicted killer looking for someone to manipulate."

Their visit lasted for two hours, and afterward they continued to correspond. She was struck by his letters, which seemed introspective, and were not at all what she had expected. "I am a very honest person with my feelings," he wrote her. "I will not bullshit you on how I feel or what I think." He said that he used to be stoic, like his father. But, he added, "losing my three daughters . . . my home, wife and my life, you tend to wake up a little. I have learned to open myself."

She agreed to visit him again, and when she returned, several weeks later, he was visibly moved. "Here I am this person who nobody on the outside is ever going to know as a human, who has lost so much, but still trying to hold on," he wrote her afterward. "But you came back! I don't think you will ever know of what importance that visit was in my existence."

They kept exchanging letters, and she began asking him about the fire. He insisted that he was innocent and that, if someone had poured accelerant through the house and lit it, then the killer remained free. Gilbert wasn't naïve—she assumed that he was guilty. She did not mind giving him solace, but she was not there to absolve him.

Still, she had become curious about the case, and one day that fall she drove down to the courthouse in Corsicana to review the trial records. Many people in the community remembered the tragedy, and a clerk expressed bewilderment that anyone would be interested in a man who had burned his children alive.

Gilbert took the files and sat down at a small table. As she examined the eyewitness accounts, she noticed several contradictions. Diane Barbee had reported that, before the authorities arrived at the fire, Willingham never tried to get back into the house—yet she had been absent for some time while calling the Fire Department. Meanwhile, her daughter Buffie had reported witnessing Willingham on the porch breaking a window, in an apparent effort to reach his children. And the firemen and police on the scene had described Willingham frantically trying to get into the house.

The witnesses' testimony also grew more damning after authorities had concluded, in the beginning of January, 1992, that Willingham was likely guilty of murder. In Diane Barbee's initial statement to authorities, she had portrayed Willingham as "hysterical," and described the front of the house exploding. But on January 4th, after arson investigators began suspecting Willingham of murder, Barbee suggested that he could have gone back inside to rescue his children, for at the outset she had seen only "smoke coming from out of the front of the house"—smoke that was not "real thick."

An even starker shift occurred with Father Monaghan's testimony. In his first statement, he had depicted Willingham as a devastated father who had to be repeatedly restrained from risking his life. Yet, as investigators were preparing to arrest Willingham, he concluded that Willingham had been *too* emotional ("He seemed to have the type of distress that a woman who had given birth would have upon seeing her children die"); and he expressed a "gut feeling" that Willingham had "something to do with the setting of the fire."

Dozens of studies have shown that witnesses' memories of events often change when they are supplied with new contextual information. Itiel Dror, a cognitive psychologist who has done extensive research on eyewitness and expert testimony in criminal investigations, told me, "The mind is not a passive machine. Once you believe in something—once you expect something—it changes the way you perceive information and the way your memory recalls it."

After Gilbert's visit to the courthouse, she kept wondering about Willingham's motive, and she pressed him on the matter. In response, he wrote, of the death of his children, "I do not talk about it much anymore and it is still a very powerfully emotional pain inside my being." He admitted that he had been a "sorry-ass husband" who had hit Stacy—something he deeply regretted. But he said that he had loved his children and would never have hurt them. Fatherhood, he said, had changed him; he stopped being a hoodlum and "settled down" and "became a man." Nearly three months before the fire, he and Stacy, who had never married, wed at a small ceremony in his home town of Ardmore. He said that the prosecution had seized upon incidents from his past and from the day of the fire to create a portrait of a "demon," as Jackson, the prosecutor, referred to him. For instance, Willingham said, he had moved the car during the fire simply because he didn't want it to explode by the house, further threatening the children.

Gilbert was unsure what to make of his story, and she began to approach people who were involved in the case, asking them questions. "My friends thought I was crazy," Gilbert recalls. "I'd never done anything like this in my life."

One morning, when Willingham's parents came to visit him, Gilbert arranged to see them first, at a coffee shop near the prison. Gene, who was in his seventies, had the Willingham look, though his black hair had gray streaks and his dark eyes were magnified by glasses. Eugenia, who was in her fifties, with silvery hair, was as sweet and talkative as her husband was stern and reserved. The drive from Oklahoma to Texas took six hours, and they had woken at three in the morning; because they could not afford a motel, they would have to return home later that day. "I feel like a real burden to them," Willingham had written Gilbert.

As Gene and Eugenia sipped coffee, they told Gilbert how grateful they were that someone had finally taken an interest in Todd's case. Gene said that his son, though he had flaws, was no killer.

The evening before the fire, Eugenia said, she had spoken on the phone with Todd. She and Gene were planning on visiting two days later, on Christmas Eve, and Todd told her that he and Stacy and the kids had just picked up family photographs. "He said, 'We got your pictures for Christmas,'" she recalled. "He put Amber on the phone, and she was tattling on one of the twins. Todd didn't seem upset. If something was bothering him, I would have known."

Gene and Eugenia got up to go: they didn't want to miss any of the four hours that were allotted for the visit with their son. Before they left, Gene said, "You'll let us know if you find anything, won't you?"

Over the next few weeks, Gilbert continued to track down sources. Many of them, including the Barbees, remained convinced that Willingham was guilty, but several of his friends and relatives had doubts. So did some people in law enforcement. Willingham's former probation officer in Oklahoma, Polly Goodin, recently told me that Willingham had never demonstrated bizarre or sociopathic behavior. "He was probably one of my favorite kids," she said. Even a former judge named Bebe Bridges—who had often stood, as she put it, on the "opposite side" of Willingham in the legal system, and who had sent him to jail for stealing—told me that she could not imagine him killing his children. "He was polite, and he seemed to care," she said. "His convictions had been for dumb-kid stuff. Even the things stolen weren't significant." Several months before the fire, Willingham tracked Goodin down at her office, and proudly showed her photographs of Stacy and the kids. "He wanted Bebe and me to know he'd been doing good," Goodin recalled.

Eventually, Gilbert returned to Corsicana to interview Stacy, who had agreed to meet at the bed-and-breakfast where Gilbert was staying. Stacy was slightly plump, with pale, round cheeks and feathered dark-blond hair; her bangs were held in place by gel, and her face was heavily made up. According to a tape recording of the conversation, Stacy said that nothing unusual had happened in the days before the fire. She and Willingham had not fought, and were preparing for the holiday. Though Vasquez, the arson expert, had recalled finding the space heater off, Stacy was sure that, at least on the day of the incident—a cool winter morning—it had been on. "I remember turning it down," she recalled. "I always thought,

Gosh, could Amber have put something in there?" Stacy added that, more than once, she had caught Amber "putting things too close to it."

Willingham had often not treated her well, she recalled, and after his incarceration she had left him for a man who did. But she didn't think that her former husband should be on death row. "I don't think he did it," she said, crying.

Though only the babysitter had appeared as a witness for the defense during the main trial, several family members, including Stacy, testified during the penalty phase, asking the jury to spare Willingham's life. When Stacy was on the stand, Jackson grilled her about the "significance" of Willingham's "very large tattoo of a skull, encircled by some kind of a serpent."

"It's just a tattoo," Stacy responded.

"He just likes skulls and snakes. Is that what you're saying?"

"No. He just had—he got a tattoo on him."

The prosecution cited such evidence in asserting that Willingham fit the profile of a sociopath, and brought forth two medical experts to confirm the theory. Neither had met Willingham. One of them was Tim Gregory, a psychologist with a master's degree in marriage and family issues, who had previously gone goose hunting with Jackson, and had not published any research in the field of sociopathic behavior. His practice was devoted to family counselling.

At one point, Jackson showed Gregory Exhibit No. 60—a photograph of an Iron Maiden poster that had hung in Willingham's house—and asked the psychologist to interpret it. "This one is a picture of a skull, with a fist being punched through the skull," Gregory said; the image displayed "violence" and "death." Gregory looked at photographs of other music posters owned by Willingham. "There's a hooded skull, with wings and a hatchet," Gregory continued. "And all of these are in fire, depicting—it reminds me of something like Hell. And there's a picture—a Led Zeppelin picture of a falling angel. . . . I see there's an association many times with cultive-type of activities. A focus on death, dying. Many times individuals that have a lot of this type of art have interest in satanic-type activities."

The other medical expert was James P. Grigson, a forensic psychiatrist. He testified so often for the prosecution in capital-punishment cases that he had become known as Dr. Death. (A Texas appellate judge once wrote that when Grigson appeared on the stand the defendant might as well "commence writing out his last will and testament.") Grigson suggested that Willingham was an "extremely severe sociopath," and that "no pill" or treatment could help him. Grigson had previously used nearly the same words in helping to secure a death sentence against Randall Dale Adams, who had been convicted of murdering a police officer, in 1977. After Adams, who had no prior criminal record, spent a dozen years on death row—and once came within seventy-two hours of being executed—new evidence emerged that absolved him, and he was released. In 1995, three years after Willingham's trial, Grigson was expelled from the American Psychiatric Association for violating ethics. The association stated that Grigson had repeatedly arrived at a "psychiatric diagnosis without first having examined the individuals in question, and for indicating, while testifying in court as an expert witness, that he could predict with 100-percent certainty that the individuals would engage in future violent acts."

After speaking to Stacy, Gilbert had one more person she wanted to interview: the jailhouse informant Johnny Webb, who was incarcerated in Iowa Park, Texas. She wrote to Webb, who said that she could see him, and they met in the prison visiting room. A man in his late twenties, he had pallid skin and a closely shaved head; his eyes were jumpy, and his entire body seemed to tremble. A reporter who once met him described him to me as "nervous as a cat around rocking chairs." Webb had begun taking drugs when he was nine years old, and had been convicted of, among other things, car theft, selling marijuana, forgery, and robbery.

As Gilbert chatted with him, she thought that he seemed paranoid. During Willingham's trial, Webb disclosed that he had been given a diagnosis of "post-traumatic stress disorder" after he was sexually assaulted in prison, in 1988, and that he often suffered from "mental impairment." Under cross-examination, Webb testified that he had no recollection of a robbery that he had pleaded guilty to only months earlier.

Webb repeated for her what he had said in court: he had passed by Willingham's cell, and as they spoke through a food slot Willingham broke down and told him that he intentionally set the house on fire. Gilbert was dubious. It was hard to believe that Willingham, who had otherwise insisted on his innocence, had suddenly confessed to an inmate he barely knew. The conversation had purportedly taken place by a speaker system that allowed any of the guards to listen—an unlikely spot for an inmate to reveal a secret. What's more, Webb alleged that Willingham had told him that Stacy had hurt one of the kids, and that the fire was set to cover up the crime. The autopsies, however, had revealed no bruises or signs of trauma on the children's bodies.

Jailhouse informants, many of whom are seeking reduced time or special privileges, are notoriously unreliable. According to a 2004 study by the Center on Wrongful Convictions, at Northwestern University Law School, lying police and jailhouse informants are the leading cause of wrongful convictions in capital cases in the United States. At the time that Webb came forward against Willingham, he was facing charges of robbery and forgery. During Willingham's trial, another inmate planned to testify that he had overheard Webb saying to another prisoner that he was hoping to "get time cut," but the testimony was ruled inadmissible, because it was hearsay. Webb, who pleaded guilty to the robbery and forgery charges, received a sentence of fifteen years. Jackson, the prosecutor, told me that he generally considered Webb "an unreliable kind of guy," but added, "I saw no real motive for him to make a statement like this if it wasn't true. We didn't cut him any slack." In 1997, five years after Willingham's trial, Jackson urged the Texas Board of Pardons and Paroles to grant Webb parole. "I asked them to cut him loose early," Jackson told me. The reason, Jackson said, was that Webb had been targeted by the Aryan Brotherhood. The board granted Webb parole, but within months of his release he was caught with cocaine and returned to prison.

In March, 2000, several months after Gilbert's visit, Webb unexpectedly sent Jackson a Motion to Recant Testimony, declaring, "Mr. Willingham is innocent of all charges." But Willingham's lawyer was not informed of this development, and soon afterward Webb, without explanation, recanted his recantation. When I recently asked Webb, who was released from prison two years ago, about the turnabout and why Willingham would have confessed to a virtual stranger, he said that he knew only what "the dude told me." After I pressed him, he said, "It's very possible I misunderstood what he said." Since the trial, Webb has been given an additional diagnosis, bipolar disorder. "Being locked up in that little cell makes you kind of crazy," he said. "My memory is in bits and pieces. I was on a lot of medication at the time. Everyone knew that." He paused, then said, "The statute of limitations has run out on perjury, hasn't it?"

Aside from the scientific evidence of arson, the case against Willingham did not stand up to scrutiny. Jackson, the prosecutor, said of Webb's testimony, "You can take it or leave it." Even the refrigerator's placement by the back door of the house turned out to be innocuous; there were two refrigerators in the cramped kitchen, and one of them was by the back door. Jimmie Hensley, the police detective, and Douglas Fogg, the assistant fire chief, both of whom investigated the fire, told me recently that they had never believed that the fridge was part of the arson plot. "It didn't have nothing to do with the fire," Fogg said.

After months of investigating the case, Gilbert found that her faith in the prosecution was shaken. As she told me, "What if Todd really was innocent?"

III

In the summer of 1660, an Englishman named William Harrison vanished on a walk, near the village of Charingworth, in Gloucestershire. His bloodstained hat was soon discovered on the side of a local road. Police interrogated Harrison's servant, John Perry, and eventually Perry gave a statement that his mother and his brother had killed Harrison for money. Perry, his mother, and his brother were hanged.

Two years later, Harrison reappeared. He insisted, fancifully, that he had been abducted by a band of criminals and sold into slavery. Whatever happened, one thing was indisputable: he had not been murdered by the Perrys.

The fear that an innocent person might be executed has long haunted jurors and lawyers and judges. During America's Colonial period, dozens of crimes were punishable by death, including horse thievery, blasphemy, "man-stealing," and highway robbery. After independence, the number of crimes eligible for the death penalty was gradually reduced, but doubts persisted over whether legal procedures were sufficient to prevent an innocent person from being executed. In 1868, John Stuart Mill made one of the most eloquent defenses of capital punishment, arguing that executing a murderer did not display a wanton disregard for life but, rather, proof of its value. "We show, on the contrary, most emphatically our regard for it by the adoption of a rule that he who violates that right in another forfeits it for himself," he said. For Mill, there was one counterargument that carried weight—"that if by an error of justice an innocent person is put to death, the mistake can never be corrected."

The modern legal system, with its lengthy appeals process and clemency boards, was widely assumed to protect the kind of "error of justice" that Mill feared. In 2000, while George W. Bush was governor of Texas, he said, "I know there are some in the country who don't care for the death penalty, but . . . we've adequately answered innocence or guilt." His top policy adviser on issues of criminal justice emphasized that there is "super due process to make sure that no innocent defendants are executed."

In recent years, though, questions have mounted over whether the system is fail-safe. Since 1976, more than a hundred and thirty people on death row have been exonerated. DNA testing, which was developed in the eighties, saved seventeen of them, but the technique can be used only in rare instances. Barry Scheck, a co-founder of the Innocence Project, which has used DNA testing to exonerate prisoners, estimates that about eighty percent of felonies do not involve biological evidence.

In 2000, after thirteen people on death row in Illinois were exonerated, George Ryan, who was then governor of the state, suspended the death penalty. Though he had been a longtime advocate of capital punishment, he declared that he could no longer support a system that has "come so close to the ultimate nightmare—the state's taking of innocent life." Former Supreme Court Justice Sandra Day O'Connor has said that the "execution of a legally and factually innocent person would be a constitutionally intolerable event."

Such a case has become a kind of grisly Holy Grail among opponents of capital punishment. In his 2002 book "The Death Penalty," Stuart Banner observes, "The prospect of killing an innocent person seemed to be the one thing that could cause people to rethink their support for capital punishment. Some who were not troubled by statistical arguments against the death penalty—claims about deterrence or racial disparities—were deeply troubled that such an extreme injustice might occur in an individual case." Opponents of the death penalty have pointed to several questionable cases. In 1993, Ruben Cantu was executed in Texas for fatally shooting a man during a robbery. Years later, a second victim, who survived the shooting, told the *Houston Chronicle* that he had been pressured by police to identify Cantu as the gunman, even though he believed Cantu to be innocent. Sam Millsap, the district attorney in the case, who had once supported capital punishment ("I'm no wild-eyed, pointy-headed liberal"), said that he was disturbed by the thought that he had made a mistake.

In 1995, Larry Griffin was put to death in Missouri, for a drive-by shooting of a drug dealer. The case rested largely on the eyewitness testimony of a career criminal named Robert Fitzgerald, who had been an informant for prosecutors before and was in the witness-protection program. Fitzgerald maintained that he happened to be at the scene because his car had broken down. After Griffin's execution, a probe sponsored by the N.A.A.C.P.'s Legal Defense and Educational Fund revealed that a man who had been wounded during the incident insisted that Griffin was not the shooter. Moreover, the first police officer at the scene disputed that Fitzgerald had witnessed the crime.

These cases, however, stopped short of offering irrefutable proof that a "legally and factually innocent person" was executed. In 2005, a St. Louis prosecutor, Jennifer Joyce, launched an investigation of the Griffin case, upon being presented with what she called "compelling" evidence of Griffin's potential innocence. After two years of reviewing the evidence, and interviewing a new eyewitness, Joyce said that she and her team were convinced that the "right person was convicted."

Supreme Court Justice Antonin Scalia, in 2006, voted with a majority to uphold the death penalty in a Kansas case. In his opinion, Scalia declared that, in the modern judicial system, there has not been "a single case—not one—in which it is clear that a person was executed for a crime he did not commit. If such an event had occurred in recent years, we would not have to hunt for it; the innocent's name would be shouted from the rooftops."

"My problems are simple," Willingham wrote Gilbert in September, 1999. "Try to keep them from killing me at all costs. End of story."

During his first years on death row, Willingham had pleaded with his lawyer, David Martin, to rescue him. "You can't imagine what it's like to be here, with people I have no business even being around," he wrote.

For a while, Willingham shared a cell with Ricky Lee Green, a serial killer, who castrated and fatally stabbed his victims, including a sixteen-year-old boy. (Green was executed in 1997.) Another of Willingham's cellmates, who had an I.Q. below seventy and the emotional development of an eight-year-old, was raped by an inmate. "You remember me telling you I had a new celly?" Willingham wrote in a letter to his parents. "The little retarded boy.... There was this guy here on the wing who is a shit sorry coward (who is the same one I got into it with a little over a month ago). Well, he raped [my cellmate] in the 3 row shower week before last." Willingham said that he couldn't believe that someone would "rape a boy who cannot even defend himself. Pretty damn low."

Because Willingham was known as a "baby killer," he was a target of attacks. "Prison is a rough place, and with a case like mine they never give you the benefit of a doubt," he wrote his parents. After he tried to fight one prisoner who threatened him, Willingham told a friend that if he hadn't stood up for himself several inmates would have "beaten me up or raped or"—his thought trailed off.

Over the years, Willingham's letters home became increasingly despairing. "This is a hard place, and it makes a person hard inside," he wrote. "I told myself that was one thing I did not want and that was for this place to make me bitter, but it is hard." He went on, "They have [executed] at least one person every month I have been here. It is senseless and brutal.... You see, we are not living in here, we are only existing." In 1996, he wrote, "I just been trying to figure out why after having a wife and 3 beautiful children that I loved my life has to end like this. And sometimes it just seems like it is not worth it all.... In the 3½ years I been here I have never felt that my life was as worthless and desolate as it is now." Since the fire, he wrote, he had the sense that his life was slowly being erased. He obsessively looked at photographs of his children and Stacy, which he stored in his cell. "So long ago, so far away," he wrote in a poem. "Was everything truly there?"

Inmates on death row are housed in a prison within a prison, where there are no attempts at rehabilitation, and no educational or training programs. In 1999, after seven prisoners tried to escape from Huntsville, Willingham and four hundred and fifty-nine other inmates on death row were moved to a more secure facility, in Livingston, Texas. Willingham was held in isolation in a sixty-square-foot cell, twenty-three hours a day. He tried to distract himself by drawing—"amateur stuff," as he put it—and writing poems. In a poem about his children, he wrote, "There is nothing more beautiful than you on this earth." When Gilbert once suggested some possible revisions to his poems, he explained that he wrote them simply as expressions, however crude, of his feelings. "So to me to cut them up and try to improve on them just for creative-writing purposes would be to destroy what I was doing to start with," he said.

Despite his efforts to occupy his thoughts, he wrote in his diary that his mind "deteriorates each passing day." He stopped working out and gained weight. He questioned his faith: "No God who cared about his creation would abandon the innocent." He seemed not to care if another inmate attacked him. "A person who is already dead inside does not fear" death, he wrote.

One by one, the people he knew in prison were escorted into the execution chamber. There was Clifton Russell, Jr., who, at the age of eighteen, stabbed and beat a man to death, and who said, in his last statement, "I thank my Father, God in Heaven, for the grace he has granted me—I am ready." There was Jeffery Dean Motley, who kidnapped and fatally shot a woman, and who declared, in his final words, "I love you, Mom. Goodbye." And there was John Fearance, who murdered his neighbor, and who turned to God in his last moments and said, "I hope He will forgive me for what I done."

Willingham had grown close to some of his prison mates, even though he knew that they were guilty of brutal crimes. In March, 2000, Willingham's friend Ponchai Wilkerson—a twenty-eight-year-old who had shot and killed a clerk during a jewelry heist—was executed. Afterward, Willingham wrote in his diary that he felt "an emptiness that has not been touched since my children were taken from me." A year later, another friend who was about to be executed—"one of the few real people I have met here not caught up in the bravado of prison"—asked Willingham to make him a final drawing. "Man, I never thought drawing a simple Rose could be so emotionally hard," Willingham wrote. "The hard part is knowing that this will be the last thing I can do for him."

Another inmate, Ernest Ray Willis, had a case that was freakishly similar to Willingham's. In 1987, Willis had been convicted of setting a fire, in West Texas, that killed two women. Willis told investigators that he had been sleeping on a friend's living-room couch and woke up to a house full of smoke. He said that he tried to rouse one of the women, who was sleeping in another room, but the flames and smoke drove him back, and he ran out the front door before the house exploded with flames. Witnesses maintained that Willis had acted suspiciously; he moved his car out of the yard, and didn't show "any emotion," as one volunteer firefighter put it. Authorities also wondered how Willis could have escaped the house without burning his bare feet. Fire investigators found pour patterns, puddle configurations, and other signs of arson. The authorities could discern no motive for the crime, but concluded that Willis, who had no previous record of violence, was a sociopath—a "demon," as the prosecutor put it. Willis was charged with capital murder and sentenced to death.

Willis had eventually obtained what Willingham called, enviously, a "badass lawyer." James Blank, a noted patent attorney in New York, was assigned Willis's case as part of his firm's pro-bono work. Convinced that Willis was innocent, Blank devoted more than a dozen years to the case, and his firm spent millions, on fire consultants, private investigators, forensic experts, and the like. Willingham, meanwhile, relied on David Martin, his court-appointed lawyer, and one of Martin's colleagues to handle his appeals. Willingham often told his parents, "You don't know what it's like to have lawyers who won't even believe you're innocent." Like many inmates on death row, Willingham eventually filed a claim of inadequate legal representation. (When I recently asked Martin about his representation of Willingham, he said, "There were no grounds for reversal, and the verdict was absolutely the right one." He said of the case, "Shit, it's incredible that anyone's even thinking about it.")

Willingham tried to study the law himself, reading books such as "Tact in Court, or How Lawyers Win: Containing Sketches of Cases Won by Skill, Wit, Art, Tact, Courage and Eloquence." Still, he confessed to a friend, "The law is so complicated it is hard for me to understand." In 1996, he obtained a new court-appointed lawyer, Walter Reaves, who told me that he was appalled by the quality of Willingham's defense at trial and on appeal. Reaves prepared for him a state writ of habeas corpus, known as a Great Writ. In the byzantine appeals process of death-penalty cases, which frequently takes more than ten years, the writ is the most critical stage: a prisoner can introduce new evidence detailing such things as perjured testimony, unreliable medical experts, and bogus scientific findings. Yet most indigent inmates, like Willingham, who constitute the bulk of those on death row, lack the resources to track down new witnesses or dig up fresh evidence. They must depend on court-appointed lawyers, many of whom are "unqualified, irresponsible, or overburdened," as a study by the Texas Defender Service, a nonprofit organization, put it. In 2000, a Dallas *Morning News* investigation revealed that roughly a quarter of the inmates condemned to death in Texas were represented by court-appointed attorneys who had, at some point in their careers, been "reprimanded, placed on probation, suspended or banned from practicing law by the State Bar." Although Reaves was more competent, he had few resources to reinvestigate the case, and his writ introduced no new exculpatory evidence: nothing further about Webb, or the reliability of the eyewitness testimony, or the credibility of the medical experts. It focussed primarily on procedural questions, such as whether the trial court erred in its instructions to the jury.

The Texas Court of Criminal Appeals was known for upholding convictions even when overwhelming exculpatory evidence came to light. In 1997, DNA testing proved that sperm collected from a rape victim did not match Roy Criner, who had been sentenced to ninety-nine years for the crime. Two lower courts recommended that the verdict be overturned, but the Court of Criminal Appeals upheld it, arguing that Criner might have worn a condom or might not have ejaculated. Sharon Keller, who is now the presiding judge on the court, stated in a majority opinion, "The new evidence does not establish innocence." In 2000, George W. Bush pardoned Criner. (Keller was recently charged with judicial misconduct, for refusing to keep open past five o'clock a clerk's office in order to allow a last-minute petition from a man who was executed later that night.)

On October 31, 1997, the Court of Criminal Appeals denied Willingham's writ. After Willingham filed another writ of habeas corpus, this time in federal court, he was granted a temporary stay. In a poem, Willingham wrote, "One more chance, one more strike/Another bullet dodged, another date escaped."

Willingham was entering his final stage of appeals. As his anxieties mounted, he increasingly relied upon Gilbert to investigate his case and for emotional support. "She may never know what a change she brought into my life," he wrote in his diary. "For the first time in many years she gave me a purpose, something to look forward to."

As their friendship deepened, he asked her to promise him that she would never disappear without explanation. "I already have that in my life," he told her.

Together, they pored over clues and testimony. Gilbert says that she would send Reaves leads to follow up, but although he was sympathetic, nothing seemed to come of them. In 2002, a federal district court of appeals denied Willingham's writ without even a hearing. "Now I start the last leg of my journey," Willingham wrote to Gilbert. "Got to get things in order."

He appealed to the U.S. Supreme Court, but in December, 2003, he was notified that it had declined to hear his case. He soon received a court order announcing that "the Director of the Department of Criminal Justice at Huntsville, Texas, acting by and through the executioner designated by said Director . . . is hereby DIRECTED and COMMANDED, at some hour after 6:00 p.m. on the 17th day of February, 2004, at the Department of Criminal Justice in Huntsville, Texas, to carry out this sentence of death by intravenous injection of a substance or substances in a lethal quantity sufficient to cause the death of said Cameron Todd Willingham."

Willingham wrote a letter to his parents. "Are you sitting down?" he asked, before breaking the news. "I love you both so much," he said.

His only remaining recourse was to appeal to the governor of Texas, Rick Perry, a Republican, for clemency. The process, considered the last gatekeeper to the executioner, has been called by the U.S. Supreme Court "the 'fail safe' in our criminal justice system."

IV

One day in January, 2004, Dr. Gerald Hurst, an acclaimed scientist and fire investigator, received a file describing all the evidence of arson gathered in Willingham's case. Gilbert had come across Hurst's name and, along with one of Willingham's relatives, had contacted him, seeking his help. After their pleas, Hurst had agreed to look at the case pro bono, and Reaves, Willingham's lawyer, had sent him the relevant documents, in the hope that there were grounds for clemency.

Hurst opened the file in the basement of his house in Austin, which served as a laboratory and an office, and was cluttered with microscopes and diagrams of half-finished experiments. Hurst was nearly six and half feet tall, though his stooped shoulders made him seem considerably shorter, and he had a gaunt face that was partly shrouded by long gray hair. He was wearing his customary outfit: black shoes, black socks, a black T-shirt, and loose-fitting black pants supported by black suspenders. In his mouth was a wad of chewing tobacco.

A child prodigy who was raised by a sharecropper during the Great Depression, Hurst used to prowl junk yards, collecting magnets and copper wires in order to build radios and other contraptions. In the early sixties, he received a Ph.D. in chemistry from Cambridge

University, where he started to experiment with fluorine and other explosive chemicals, and once detonated his lab. Later, he worked as the chief scientist on secret weapons programs for several American companies, designing rockets and deadly fire bombs—or what he calls "god-awful things." He helped patent what has been described, with only slight exaggeration, as "the world's most powerful nonnuclear explosive": an Astrolite bomb. He experimented with toxins so lethal that a fraction of a drop would rot human flesh, and in his laboratory he often had to wear a pressurized moon suit; despite such precautions, exposure to chemicals likely caused his liver to fail, and in 1994 he required a transplant. Working on what he calls "the dark side of arson," he retrofitted napalm bombs with Astrolite, and developed ways for covert operatives in Vietnam to create bombs from local materials, such as chicken manure and sugar. He also perfected a method for making an exploding T-shirt by nitrating its fibres.

His conscience eventually began pricking him. "One day, you wonder, What the hell am I doing?" he recalls. He left the defense industry, and went on to invent the Mylar balloon, an improved version of Liquid Paper, and Kinepak, a kind of explosive that reduces the risk of accidental detonation. Because of his extraordinary knowledge of fire and explosives, companies in civil litigation frequently sought his help in determining the cause of a blaze. By the nineties, Hurst had begun devoting significant time to criminal-arson cases, and, as he was exposed to the methods of local and state fire investigators, he was shocked by what he saw.

Many arson investigators, it turned out, had only a high-school education. In most states, in order to be certified, investigators had to take a forty-hour course on fire investigation, and pass a written exam. Often, the bulk of an investigator's training came on the job, learning from "old-timers" in the field, who passed down a body of wisdom about the telltale signs of arson, even though a study in 1977 warned that there was nothing in "the scientific literature to substantiate their validity."

In 1992, the National Fire Protection Association, which promotes fire prevention and safety, published its first scientifically based guidelines to arson investigation. Still, many arson investigators believed that what they did was more an art than a science—a blend of experience and intuition. In 1997, the International Association of Arson Investigators filed a legal brief arguing that arson sleuths should not be bound by a 1993 Supreme Court decision requiring experts who testified at trials to adhere to the scientific method. What arson sleuths did, the brief claimed, was "less scientific." By 2000, after the courts had rejected such claims, arson investigators increasingly recognized the scientific method, but there remained great variance in the field, with many practitioners still relying on the unverified techniques that had been used for generations. "People investigated fire largely with a flat-earth approach," Hurst told me. "It looks like arson—therefore, it's arson." He went on, "My view is you have to have a scientific basis. Otherwise, it's no different than witch-hunting."

In 1998, Hurst investigated the case of a woman from North Carolina named Terri Hinson, who was charged with setting a fire that killed her seventeen-month-old son, and faced the death penalty. Hurst ran a series of experiments re-creating the conditions of the fire, which suggested that it had not been arson, as the investigators had claimed; rather, it had started accidentally, from a faulty electrical wire in the attic. Because of this research, Hinson was freed. John Lentini, a fire expert and the author of a leading scientific textbook on arson, describes Hurst as "brilliant." A Texas prosecutor once told the *Chicago Tribune*, of Hurst, "If he says it was an arson fire, then it was. If he says it wasn't, then it wasn't."

Hurst's patents yielded considerable royalties, and he could afford to work pro bono on an arson case for months, even years. But he received the files on Willingham's case only a few weeks before Willingham was scheduled to be executed. As Hurst looked through the case records, a statement by Manuel Vasquez, the state deputy fire marshal, jumped out at him. Vasquez had testified that, of the roughly twelve hundred to fifteen hundred fires he had investigated, "most all of them" were arson. This was an oddly high estimate; the Texas State Fire Marshals Office typically found arson in only fifty percent of its cases.

Hurst was also struck by Vasquez's claim that the Willingham blaze had "burned fast and hot" because of a liquid accelerant. The notion that a flammable or combustible liquid caused flames to reach higher temperatures had been repeated in court by arson sleuths for decades. Yet the theory was nonsense: experiments have proved that wood and gasoline-fuelled fires burn at essentially the same temperature.

Vasquez and Fogg had cited as proof of arson the fact that the front door's aluminum threshold had melted. "The only thing that can cause that to react is an accelerant," Vasquez said. Hurst was incredulous. A natural-wood fire can reach temperatures as high as two thousand degrees Fahrenheit—far hotter than the melting point for aluminum alloys, which ranges from a thousand to twelve hundred degrees. And, like many other investigators, Vasquez and Fogg mistakenly assumed that wood charring beneath the aluminum threshold was evidence that, as Vasquez put it, "a liquid accelerant flowed underneath and burned." Hurst had conducted myriad experiments showing that such charring was caused simply by the aluminum conducting so much heat. In fact, when liquid accelerant is poured under a threshold a fire will extinguish, because of a lack of oxygen. (Other scientists had reached the same conclusion.) "Liquid accelerants can no more burn under an aluminum threshold than can grease burn in a skillet even with a loose-fitting lid," Hurst declared in his report on the Willingham case.

Hurst then examined Fogg and Vasquez's claim that the "brown stains" on Willingham's front porch were evidence of "liquid accelerant," which had not had time to soak into the concrete. Hurst had previously performed a test in his garage, in which he poured charcoal-lighter fluid on the concrete floor, and lit it. When the fire went out, there were no brown stains, only smudges of soot. Hurst had run the same experiment many times, with different kinds of liquid accelerants, and the result was always the same. Brown stains were common in fires; they were usually composed of rust or gunk from charred debris that had mixed with water from fire hoses.

Another crucial piece of evidence implicating Willingham was the "crazed glass" that Vasquez had attributed to the rapid heating from a fire fuelled with liquid accelerant. Yet, in November of 1991, a team of fire investigators had inspected fifty houses in the hills of Oakland, California, which had been ravaged by brush fires. In a dozen houses, the investigators discovered crazed glass, even though a liquid accelerant had not been used. Most of these houses were on the outskirts of the blaze, where firefighters had shot streams of water; as the investigators later wrote in a published study, they theorized that the fracturing had been induced by rapid cooling, rather than by sudden heating—thermal shock had caused the glass to contract so quickly that it settled disjointedly. The investigators then tested this hypothesis in a laboratory. When they heated glass, nothing happened. But each time they applied water to the heated glass the intricate patterns appeared. Hurst had seen the same phenomenon when he had blowtorched and cooled glass during his research at Cambridge. In his report, Hurst wrote that Vasquez and Fogg's notion of crazed glass was no more than an "old wives' tale."

Hurst then confronted some of the most devastating arson evidence against Willingham: the burn trailer, the pour patterns and puddle configurations, the V-shape and other burn marks indicating that the fire had multiple points of origin, the burning underneath the children's beds. There was also the positive test for mineral spirits by the front door, and Willingham's seemingly implausible story that he had run out of the house without burning his bare feet.

As Hurst read through more of the files, he noticed that Willingham and his neighbors had described the windows in the front of the house suddenly exploding and flames roaring forth. It was then that Hurst thought of the legendary Lime Street Fire, one of the most pivotal in the history of arson investigation.

On the evening of October 15, 1990, a thirty-five-year-old man named Gerald Wayne Lewis was found standing in front of his house on Lime Street, in Jacksonville, Florida, holding his three-year-old son. His two-story wood-frame home was engulfed in flames. By the time the fire had been extinguished, six people were dead, including Lewis's wife. Lewis said that he had rescued his son but was unable to get to the others, who were upstairs.

When fire investigators examined the scene, they found the classic signs of arson: low burns along the walls and floors, pour patterns and puddle configurations, and a burn trailer running from the living room into the hallway. Lewis claimed that the fire had started accidentally, on a couch in the living room—his son had been playing with matches. But a V-shaped pattern by one of the doors suggested that the fire had originated elsewhere. Some witnesses told authorities that Lewis seemed too calm during the fire and had never tried to get help. According to the *Los Angeles Times,* Lewis had previously been arrested for abusing his wife, who had taken out a restraining order against him. After a chemist said that he had detected the presence of gasoline on Lewis's clothing and shoes, a report by the sheriff 's office concluded, "The fire was started as a result of a petroleum product being poured on the front porch, foyer, living room, stairwell and second floor bedroom." Lewis was arrested and charged with six counts of murder. He faced the death penalty.

Subsequent tests, however, revealed that the laboratory identification of gasoline was wrong. Moreover, a local news television camera had captured Lewis in a clearly agitated state at the scene of the fire, and investigators discovered that at one point he had jumped in front of a moving car, asking the driver to call the Fire Department.

Seeking to bolster their theory of the crime, prosecutors turned to John Lentini, the fire expert, and John DeHaan, another leading investigator and textbook author. Despite some of the weaknesses of the case, Lentini told me that, given the classic burn patterns and puddle configurations in the house, he was sure that Lewis had set the fire: "I was prepared to testify and send this guy to Old Sparky"—the electric chair.

To discover the truth, the investigators, with the backing of the prosecution, decided to conduct an elaborate experiment and re-create the fire scene. Local officials gave the investigators permission to use a condemned house next to Lewis's home, which was about to be torn down. The two houses were virtually identical, and the investigators refurbished the condemned one with the same kind of carpeting, curtains, and furniture that had been in Lewis's home. The scientists also wired the building with heat and gas sensors that could withstand fire. The cost of the experiment came to twenty thousand dollars. Without using liquid accelerant, Lentini and DeHaan set the couch in the living room on fire, expecting that the experiment would demonstrate that Lewis's version of events was implausible.

The investigators watched as the fire quickly consumed the couch, sending upward a plume of smoke that hit the ceiling and spread outward, creating a thick layer of hot gases overhead—an efficient radiator of heat. Within three minutes, this cloud, absorbing more gases from the fire below, was banking down the walls and filling the living room. As the cloud approached the floor, its temperature rose, in some areas, to more than eleven hundred degrees Fahrenheit. Suddenly, the entire room exploded in flames, as the radiant heat ignited every piece of furniture, every curtain, every possible fuel source, even the carpeting. The windows shattered.

The fire had reached what is called "flashover"—the point at which radiant heat causes a fire in a room to become a room on fire. Arson investigators knew about the concept of flashover, but it was widely believed to take much longer to occur, especially without a liquid accelerant. From a single fuel source—a couch—the room had reached flashover in four and a half minutes.

Because all the furniture in the living room had ignited, the blaze went from a fuel-controlled fire to a ventilation-controlled fire—or what scientists call "post-flashover." During post-flashover, the path of the fire depends on new sources of oxygen, from an open door or window. One of the fire investigators, who had been standing by an open door in the living room, escaped moments before the oxygen-starved fire roared out of the room into the hallway—a fireball that caused the corridor to go quickly into flashover as well, propelling the fire out the front door and onto the porch.

After the fire was extinguished, the investigators inspected the hallway and living room. On the floor were irregularly shaped burn patterns that perfectly resembled pour patterns and puddle configurations. It turned out that these classic signs of arson can also appear on their own, after flashover. With the naked eye, it is impossible to distinguish between the pour patterns and puddle configurations caused by an accelerant and those caused naturally by post-flashover. The only reliable way to tell the difference is to take samples from the burn patterns and test them in a laboratory for the presence of flammable or combustible liquids.

During the Lime Street experiment, other things happened that were supposed to occur only in a fire fuelled by liquid accelerant: charring along the base of the walls and doorways, and burning under furniture. There was also a V-shaped pattern by the living-room doorway, far from where the fire had started on the couch. In a small fire, a V-shaped burn mark may pinpoint where a fire began, but during post-flashover these patterns can occur repeatedly, when various objects ignite.

One of the investigators muttered that they had just helped prove the defense's case. Given the reasonable doubt raised by the experiment, the charges against Lewis were soon dropped. The Lime Street experiment had demolished prevailing notions about fire behavior. Subsequent tests by scientists showed that, during post-flashover, burning under beds and furniture was common, entire doors were consumed, and aluminum thresholds melted.

John Lentini says of the Lime Street Fire, "This was my epiphany. I almost sent a man to die based on theories that were a load of crap."

Hurst next examined a floor plan of Willingham's house that Vasquez had drawn, which delineated all the purported pour patterns and puddle configurations. Because the windows had blown out of the children's room, Hurst knew that the fire had reached flashover. With his finger, Hurst traced along Vasquez's diagram the burn trailer that had gone from the children's room, turned right in the hallway, and headed out the front door. John Jackson, the prosecutor, had told me that the path was so "bizarre" that it had to have been caused by a liquid accelerant. But Hurst concluded that it was a natural product of the dynamics of fire during post-flashover. Willingham had fled out the front door, and the fire simply followed the ventilation path, toward the opening. Similarly, when Willingham had broken the windows in the children's room, flames had shot outward.

Hurst recalled that Vasquez and Fogg had considered it impossible for Willingham to have run down the burning hallway without scorching his bare feet. But if the pour patterns and puddle configurations were a result of a flashover, Hurst reasoned, then they were consonant with Willingham's explanation of events. When Willingham exited his bedroom, the hallway was not yet on fire; the flames were contained within the children's bedroom, where, along the ceiling, he saw the "bright lights." Just as the investigator safely stood by the door in the Lime Street experiment seconds before flashover, Willingham could have stood close to the children's room without being harmed. (Prior to the Lime Street case, fire investigators had generally assumed that carbon monoxide diffuses quickly through a house during a fire. In fact, up until flashover, levels of carbon monoxide can be remarkably low beneath and outside the thermal cloud.) By the time the Corsicana fire achieved flashover, Willingham had already fled outside and was in the front yard.

Vasquez had made a videotape of the fire scene, and Hurst looked at the footage of the burn trailer. Even after repeated viewings, he could not detect three points of origin, as Vasquez had. (Fogg recently told me that he also saw a continuous trailer and disagreed with Vasquez, but added that nobody from the prosecution or the defense ever asked him on the stand about his opinion on the subject.)

After Hurst had reviewed Fogg and Vasquez's list of more than twenty arson indicators, he believed that only one had any potential validity: the positive test for mineral spirits by the threshold of the front door. But why had the fire investigators obtained a positive reading only in that location? According to Fogg and Vasquez's theory of the crime, Willingham had poured accelerant throughout the children's bedroom and down the hallway. Officials had tested extensively in these areas—including where all the pour patterns and puddle configurations were—and turned up nothing. Jackson told me that he "never did understand why they weren't able to recover" positive tests in these parts.

Hurst found it hard to imagine Willingham pouring accelerant on the front porch, where neighbors could have seen him. Scanning the files for clues, Hurst noticed a photograph of the porch taken before the fire, which had been entered into evidence. Sitting on the tiny porch was a charcoal grill. The porch was where the family barbecued. Court testimony from witnesses confirmed that there had been a grill, along with a container of lighter fluid, and that both had burned when the fire roared onto the porch during post-flashover. By the time Vasquez inspected the house, the grill had been removed from the porch, during cleanup. Though he cited the container of lighter fluid in his report, he made no mention of "the grill." At the trial, he insisted that he had never been told of the grill's earlier placement. Other authorities were aware of the grill but did not see its relevance. Hurst, however, was convinced that he had solved the mystery: when firefighters had blasted the porch with water, they had likely spread charcoal-lighter fluid from the melted container.

Without having visited the fire scene, Hurst says, it was impossible to pinpoint the cause of the blaze. But, based on the evidence, he had little doubt that it was an accidental fire—one caused most likely by the space heater or faulty electrical wiring. It explained why there had never been a motive for the crime. Hurst concluded that there was no evidence of arson, and that a man who had already lost his three children and spent twelve years in jail was about to be executed based on "junk science." Hurst wrote his report in such a rush that he didn't pause to fix the typos.

V

"I am a realist and I will not live a fantasy," Willingham once told Gilbert about the prospect of proving his innocence. But in February, 2004, he began to have hope. Hurst's findings had helped to exonerate more than ten people. Hurst even reviewed the scientific evidence against Willingham's friend Ernest Willis, who had been on death row for the strikingly similar arson charge. Hurst says, "It was like I was looking at the same case. Just change the names." In his report on the Willis case, Hurst concluded that not "a single item of physical evidence . . . supports a finding of arson." A second fire expert hired by Ori White, the new district attorney in Willis's district, concurred. After seventeen years on death row, Willis was set free. "I don't turn killers loose," White said at the time. "If Willis was guilty, I'd be retrying him right now. And I'd use Hurst as my witness. He's a brilliant scientist." White noted how close the system had come to murdering an innocent man. "He did not get executed, and I thank God for that," he said.

On February 13th, four days before Willingham was scheduled to be executed, he got a call from Reaves, his attorney. Reaves told him that the fifteen members of the Board of Pardons and Paroles, which reviews an application for clemency and had been sent Hurst's report, had made their decision.

"What is it?" Willingham asked.

"I'm sorry," Reaves said. "They denied your petition."

The vote was unanimous. Reaves could not offer an explanation: the board deliberates in secret, and its members are not bound by any specific criteria. The board members did not even have to review Willingham's materials, and usually don't debate a case in person; rather, they cast their votes by fax—a process that has become known as "death by fax." Between 1976 and 2004, when Willingham filed his petition, the State of Texas had approved only one application for clemency from a prisoner on death row. A Texas appellate judge has called the clemency system "a legal fiction." Reaves said of the board members, "They never asked me to attend a hearing or answer any questions."

The Innocence Project obtained, through the Freedom of Information Act, all the records from the governor's office and the board pertaining to Hurst's report. "The documents show that they received the report, but neither office has any record of anyone acknowledging it, taking note of its significance, responding to it, or calling any attention to it within the government," Barry Scheck said. "The only reasonable conclusion is that the governor's office and the Board of Pardons and Paroles ignored scientific evidence."

LaFayette Collins, who was a member of the board at the time, told me of the process, "You don't vote guilt or innocence. You don't retry the trial. You just make sure everything is in order and there are no glaring errors." He noted that although the rules allowed for a hearing to consider important new evidence, "in my time there had never been one called." When I asked him why Hurst's report didn't constitute evidence of "glaring errors," he said, "We get all kinds of reports, but we don't have the mechanisms to vet them." Alvin Shaw, another board member at the time, said that the case didn't "ring a bell," adding, angrily, "Why would I want to talk about it?" Hurst calls the board's actions "unconscionable."

Though Reaves told Willingham that there was still a chance that Governor Perry might grant a thirty-day stay, Willingham began to prepare his last will and testament. He had earlier written Stacy a letter apologizing for not being a better husband and thanking her for everything she had given him, especially their three daughters. "I still know Amber's voice, her smile, her cool Dude saying and how she said: I wanna hold you! Still feel the touch of Karmon and Kameron's hands on my face." He said that he hoped that "some day, somehow the truth will be known and my name cleared."

He asked Stacy if his tombstone could be erected next to their children's graves. Stacy, who had for so long expressed belief in Willingham's innocence, had recently taken her first look at the original court records and arson findings. Unaware of Hurst's report, she had determined that Willingham was guilty. She denied him his wish, later telling a reporter, "He took my kids away from me."

Gilbert felt as if she had failed Willingham. Even before his pleas for clemency were denied, she told him that all she could give him was her friendship. He told her that it was enough "to be a part of your life in some small way so that in my passing I can know I was at last able to have felt the heart of another who might remember me when I'm gone." He added, "There is nothing to forgive you for." He told her that he would need her to be present at his execution, to help him cope with "my fears, thoughts, and feelings."

On February 17th, the day he was set to die, Willingham's parents and several relatives gathered in the prison visiting room. Plexiglas still separated Willingham from them. "I wish I could touch and hold both of you," Willingham had written to them earlier. "I always hugged Mom but I never hugged Pop much."

As Willingham looked at the group, he kept asking where Gilbert was. Gilbert had recently been driving home from a store when another car ran a red light and smashed into her. Willingham used to tell her to stay in her kitchen for a day, without leaving, to comprehend what it was like to be confined in prison, but she had always found an excuse not to do it. Now she was paralyzed from the neck down.

While she was in an intensive-care unit, she had tried to get a message to Willingham, but apparently failed. Gilbert's daughter later read her a letter that Willingham had sent her, telling her how much he had grown to love her. He had written a poem: "Do you want to see beauty—like you have never seen? / Then close your eyes, and open your mind, and come along with me."

Gilbert, who spent years in physical rehabilitation, gradually regaining motion in her arms and upper body, says, "All that time, I thought I was saving Willingham, and I realized then that he was saving me, giving me the strength to get through this. I know I will one day walk again, and I know it is because Willingham showed me the kind of courage it takes to survive."

Willingham had requested a final meal, and at 4 P.M. on the seventeenth he was served it: three barbecued pork ribs, two orders of onion rings, fried okra, three beef enchiladas with cheese, and two slices of lemon cream pie. He received word that Governor Perry had refused to grant him a stay. (A spokesperson for Perry says, "The Governor made his decision based on the facts of the case.") Willingham's mother and father began to cry. "Don't be sad, Momma," Willingham said. "In fifty-five minutes, I'm a free man. I'm going home to see my kids." Earlier, he had confessed to his parents that there was one thing about the day of the fire he had lied about. He said that he had never actually crawled into the children's room. "I just didn't want people to think I was a coward," he said. Hurst told me, "People who have never been in a fire don't understand why those who survive often can't rescue the victims. They have no concept of what a fire is like."

The warden told Willingham that it was time. Willingham, refusing to assist the process, lay down; he was carried into a chamber eight feet wide and ten feet long. The walls were painted green, and in the center of the room, where an electric chair used to be, was a sheeted gurney. Several guards strapped Willingham down with leather belts, snapping buckles across his arms and legs and chest. A medical team then inserted intravenous tubes into his arms. Each official had a separate role in the process, so that no one person felt responsible for taking a life.

Willingham had asked that his parents and family not be present in the gallery during this process, but as he looked out he could see Stacy watching. The warden pushed a remote control, and sodium thiopental, a barbiturate, was pumped into Willingham's body. Then came a second drug, pancuronium bromide, which paralyzes the diaphragm, making it impossible to breathe. Finally, a third drug, potassium chloride, filled his veins, until his heart stopped, at 6:20 P.M. On his death certificate, the cause was listed as "Homicide."

After his death, his parents were allowed to touch his face for the first time in more than a decade. Later, at Willingham's request, they cremated his body and secretly spread some of his ashes over his children's graves. He had told his parents, "Please don't ever stop fighting to vindicate me."

In December, 2004, questions about the scientific evidence in the Willingham case began to surface. Maurice Possley and Steve Mills, of the *Chicago Tribune*, had published an investigative series on flaws in forensic science; upon learning of Hurst's report, Possley and Mills asked three fire experts, including John Lentini, to examine the original investigation. The experts concurred with Hurst's report. Nearly two years later, the Innocence Project commissioned Lentini and three other top fire investigators to conduct an independent review of the arson evidence in the Willingham case. The panel concluded that "each and every one" of the indicators of arson had been "scientifically proven to be invalid."

In 2005, Texas established a government commission to investigate allegations of error and misconduct by forensic scientists. The first cases that are being reviewed by the commission are those of Willingham and Willis. In mid-August, the noted fire scientist Craig Beyler, who was hired by the commission, completed his investigation. In a scathing report, he concluded that investigators in the Willingham case had no scientific basis for claiming that the fire was arson, ignored evidence that contradicted their theory, had no comprehension of flashover and fire dynamics, relied on discredited folklore, and failed to eliminate potential accidental or alternative causes of the fire. He said that Vasquez's approach seemed to deny "rational reasoning" and was more "characteristic of mystics or psychics." What's more, Beyler determined that the investigation violated, as he put it to me, "not only the standards of today but even of the time period." The commission is reviewing his findings, and plans to release its own report next year. Some legal scholars believe that the commission may narrowly assess the reliability of the scientific evidence. There is a chance, however, that Texas could become the first state to acknowledge officially that, since the advent of the modern judicial system, it had carried out the "execution of a legally and factually innocent person."

Just before Willingham received the lethal injection, he was asked if he had any last words. He said, "The only statement I want to make is that I am an innocent man convicted of a crime I did not commit. I have been persecuted for twelve years for something I did not do. From God's dust I came and to dust I will return, so the Earth shall become my throne."

CRITICAL THINKING QUESTIONS

1. Describe the changes to both Father Monaghan's and Diane Buffie's testimony over the investigation. Itiel Dror is a cognitive psychologist who studies expert testimony. Summarize why she thinks these changes occur. Do you think her argument is correct? Why or why not? Provide another example of this occurring—either from your own life, something you have seen, or a situation you create for this answer.

2. David Grann writes that, "according to a 2004 study by the Center on Wrongful Convictions . . . lying police and jailhouse informants are the leading cause of wrongful convictions in capital cases in the United States." Elizabeth Gilbert believes Cameron Todd Willingham murdered his children until talking to Johnny Webb. What are three reasons she finds his testimony unbelievable? Do you think his original testimony was accurate? Why or why not?

3. One attempt to reverse Cameron Todd Willingham's conviction was based on the claim that he didn't have a sufficient legal defense. In the article, David Gann compares Willingham's legal defense to that of Ernest Ray Willis, who was convicted in a very similar case. What are some of the ways that the author thinks Willingham's defense failed him? Why did Willis get a better legal defense? What do you think that says about the justice system?

4. John Lentini is a fire investigator and calls the Lime Street Fire, "my epiphany." Describe the Lime Street Fire experiment. What are three ways in which the findings apply to Cameron Todd Willingham's case?

WHAT DEATH PENALTY OPPONENTS DON'T GET

by James Ridgeway and Jean Casella

James Ridgeway is an American investigative journalist. He is the senior Washington correspondent for *Mother Jones*, and a co-editor of *Solitary Watch*. He has authored 16 books, and he has written for *The Village Voice, The Nation, New Republic, Ramparts*, and *The Wall Street Journal*. Jean Casella is a freelance writer, editor, and manager of print and web-based publications. She is co-editor of *Solitary Watch*, and she was named a Soros Justice Media Fellow by the Open Society Institute.

Americans may be split on the death penalty, but few want to appear soft on crime. As a way to justify eliminating the death penalty, many states have made prison life more difficult. In this 2014 article for *The Marshall Project*, James Ridgeway and Jean Casella examine the punishments that the worst criminal offenders face in states without the death penalty. We want justice for victims of crimes, but can justice be had if the punishment is unjust?

• • • • • • • • • • • • • • •

THERE ARE FATES WORSE THAN DEATH

In 1987, when he was 23 years old and in court on a drug charge, William Blake shot two sheriff's deputies in a failed escape attempt, killing one. At his trial, the judge presiding over his case expressed regret that New York did not have capital punishment, so he could not sentence Blake to death.

Instead, for the past 27 years, Blake has lived in extreme isolation in a 7 9 cell. He is fed through a slot in the solid steel door, and on some days he's allowed out for an hour to "exercise" alone in a small, barren pen. Because his sentence is 77 years to life, he is virtually certain to die in prison. Because he is classified as both a cop killer and an escape risk, he may well spend the rest of his life in solitary confinement.

Recently Blake, now 50, described his years in the "Special Housing Units," or SHUs, of New York's state prisons. "If I try to imagine what kind of death, even a slow one, would be worse than twenty-five years in the box—and I have tried to imagine it—I can come up with nothing," he wrote. "Dying couldn't take but a short time if you or the State were to kill me; in SHU I have died a thousand internal deaths."

Opponents of the death penalty have had many occasions to celebrate in the new millennium. Four states have abolished the practice in the past five years, while others have legally or effectively set moratoriums on executions. Support for capital punishment in the United States is at its lowest point in four decades, and seems likely to fall further as the number of exonerations and gruesomely botched executions continues to grow.

But at what cost have these concessions been won? The NAACP Legal Defense and Educational Fund's latest "Death Row U.S.A." report found 3,049 individuals awaiting execution in the United States. According to the Sentencing Project, at last count nearly 50,000 people were serving sentences of life without the possibility of parole—a number that has more than tripled since the early 1990s. Over 159,000 were serving life sentences—many of them, like William Blake, with minimums so long that they might as well be doing life without parole, too.

In many states, the expansion—and the very existence—of life without parole sentences can be directly linked to the struggle to end capital punishment. Death penalty opponents often accept—and even zealously promote—life without parole as a preferable option, in the process becoming champions of a punishment that is nearly unknown in the rest of the developing world.

In California, for example, where the latest attempt to end capital punishment by referendum was narrowly defeated in 2012, voters were urged not simply to abolish the death penalty, but to "replace" it with life without parole. In support of this cause, the ACLU of Northern California made a virtue of the similarity between the two punishments: "The reality is that people sentenced to life without parole have been condemned to die in prison and that's what happens: They die in prison of natural causes, just like the majority of people sentenced to death." Referring repeatedly to life without parole as "death in prison," the ACLU resorts to language far more draconian than one might expect from any liberal organization: life without parole sentences have the advantage of being "certain" and "swift," because "[u]nlike death penalty cases [they] receive no special consideration on appeal" Such sentences are also "severe," since spending a lifetime in "California's overcrowded, dangerous prisons . . . growing sick and old, and dying there, is a horrible experience. This is especially true given the unconstitutional failure to provide adequate health care to California's prisoners."

Kenneth E. Hartman, who is serving life without parole in California, agrees with such an assessment—and for that reason, strongly opposed the referendum to replace capital punishment with life without parole. Hartman runs, from prison, a campaign called the Other Death Penalty Project, on the premise that a sentence of life without parole amounts to "a long, slow, dissipating death sentence without any of the legal or administrative safeguards rightly awarded to those condemned to the traditional forms of execution."

"Though I will never be strapped down onto a gurney with life-stopping drugs pumped into my veins," Hartmann has written, "be assured I have already begun the slow drip of my execution [which] won't come to full effect for 50, maybe 60 years." Like William Blake in New York, he states: "I have often wondered if that 15 or 20 minutes of terror found to be cruel and unusual wouldn't be a better option."

Complicating matters is the fact that life without parole rarely takes its place as simply a one-for-one alternative to the death penalty. In New York State, for example, life without parole did not exist before the state's brief reinstitution of capital punishment from 1995 to 2004. During this period, there were never more than half a dozen men on New York's death row, and no executions took place. Yet today, nearly 250 people are doing life without parole in New York, and more than 1 in 6 of the state's prisoners is serving a life sentence.

Connecticut, in abolishing its death penalty in 2012, legislated a punishment even more harsh than simple life without parole. Thereafter, a new law decreed, those convicted of "murder with special circumstances" would be condemned to live out their life without parole sentences in solitary confinement. The measure was reportedly backed as a way to win enough support for the repeal bill.

Though the requirement that life/LWOP sentences be served in solitary confinement is codified into law only in Connecticut, it exists in practice throughout the nation. An unknown number of lifers have, like William Blake, been placed in permanent or indefinite solitary confinement by prison officials, without benefit of any kind of due process. So have most of the individuals on the nation's death rows, including the supposedly fortunate ones who live in states that have instituted moratoriums, and are therefore unlikely to ever face execution.

Research has confirmed that even brief periods in solitary alter brain chemistry and produce psychiatric symptoms ranging from extreme depression to active psychosis. Some prisoners who have spent longer amounts of time in isolation describe it as a condition that slowly degrades both their humanity and sanity, turning them into blind animals given to interminable pacing, smearing their cells with feces, or engaging in self-mutilation.

"I went days pacing back and forth like a zombie . . . I looked like I was already dead and I had no will to live. Day after day all I saw was gray walls and over time my world became the gray box," Brian Nelson has written of his 12 years in solitary confinement in Illinois. "Every day I went to sleep I got down on my knees and prayed that I would die in my sleep, yet God's will was not mine. When I woke up in the night I prayed harder for death."

Some people condemned to solitary have chosen a swift and certain death over a life of daily torture. Data suggests that as many as half of all prison suicides take place in some form of isolation, and one study in New York found that prisoners in solitary confinement were five times more likely to kill themselves than those in the general population. The disparity exists despite the fact that it's never simple to commit suicide in a bare cell: Some prisoners have resorted to jumping head-first off their bunks; others have bitten through the veins in their arms. Even on death row, some choose to hasten death rather than possibly live out their lives in torturous isolation. In California, where over 700 people languish on San Quentin's death row, just 13 men have been executed since the death penalty was reinstated in 1977. But 22 have committed suicide—eight of them after the state's moratorium on capital punishment went into effect in 2006.

William Blake has said that while he cannot bring himself to take his own life, he would have welcomed the death penalty 27 years ago had he known what a lifetime in solitary confinement would be like. Perhaps the time will come when people like Blake—and the American public—are not forced to choose among such monstrous alternatives. In the meantime, it will be a shame if people who oppose state-sponsored death continue to advocate for state-sanctioned torture.

CRITICAL THINKING QUESTIONS

1. The authors write that "opponents of the death penalty have had many occasions to celebrate" since 2000. What are two things death penalty opponents could have celebrated? Do you celebrate them? Why or why not?

2. Who is Kenneth Hartman? Why might some consider it odd that he is arguing for continuing the death penalty in California? Why does he often wonder if the death penalty "wouldn't be a better option"? Do you think he should be allowed to decide his own fate? Why or why not?

3. What caused Brian Nelson to pray "harder for death?" What are some of the "psychiatric symptoms" and upsetting behaviors that are found amongst prisoners who are in solitary confinement? Do you believe these circumstances qualify as "cruel and unusual punishment?"

4. The authors argue that too often those who oppose the death penalty support "state-sanctioned torture." Why do they consider solitary confinement to be torture? How do you feel about the state "sanctioning" this? What do you think should be done to criminals who are convicted of a serious crime? Why do you think that is the best solution?

BREAKING THE SCHOOL-TO-PRISON PIPELINE: RETHINKING 'ZERO TOLERANCE'

by Bryce Stucki

Bryce Stucki is a freelance writer. His work has been published in *The American Prospect* and *The Bicycle Times*. Stucki writes on topics about safety in public schools, women in the labor force, and graduate legal education.

In this 2014 article from *The American Prospect*, Bryce Stucki talks about how many more schools are trying to embrace "restorative circles" as a countermeasure to discipline problems. There is another circle at work that requires us to rethink the ways our schools punish students: students from disadvantaged backgrounds too often bring violence with them into the school buildings. If they are suspended from school, they are pushed back into the very communities that may have helped develop their behavioral issues. What are the ways in which our schools are grooming students for the criminal justice system, and how can this be changed?

• • • • • • • • • • • • • • •

A new approach to discipline seeks to keep kids in school and, ultimately, out of prison. In one high school, the number of serious incidents of misbehavior plummeted 60 percent, after the start of a "restorative justice" program.

Before 2006, when Debora Borges-Carrera became the principal at Kensington Creative & Performing Arts High School (KCAPA) in north Philadelphia, the school was the scene of pandemonium. Not a day seemed to go by without a fight in the concrete stairwell. Kids sent to the principal's office for disrupting class roamed the hallways. During one visit from the superintendent, a riot broke out in the cafeteria, with students climbing on tables and chucking their meal trays across the room. In Borges-Carrera's first year on the job, the school—where about 90 percent of students are Latino or black and 100 percent are below the poverty line—reported 76 incidents of student misbehavior, more than four times the state average, including 13 aggravated assaults on staff members.

Under KCAPA's "zero tolerance" policy—since the late 1990s, the prevailing approach to discipline in schools across the country—the typical response to student misbehavior was harsh punishment. "Any behavior that got a student sent to the principal's office almost automatically resulted in suspension," says Erin Smith, a teacher at the school since 2004. Under the district's vaguely worded discipline policy, students were routinely transferred for possession of a "weapon," which could be anything from a gun to a butter knife. With an estimated 200 out-of-school suspensions, according to the School District of Philadelphia, and a student body of just under 400, it was clear the system wasn't working.

Within months of coming on the job, Borges-Carrera replaced KCAPA's existing policy with a set of practices collectively known as restorative justice. Rather than punishing students who are out of line, restorative justice aims to help them rebuild their standing in the school community and repair the harm they have caused. The practices vary—peer-mediation programs, empathy training for offenders—but the basic idea is that strong interpersonal and community ties work better than fear of retribution.

The cornerstone of KCAPA's program is the "restorative circle." Drawing inspiration from the American Indian practice of the talking circle, in which a totem is passed around to signal the opportunity to speak, these meetings are convened for all kinds of reasons, from gauging students' moods to addressing acts of serious misbehavior like assault or vandalism. In those more serious cases, all affected members of the community—parents and teachers, police officers, kids from other schools, as well as the perpetrator and victim—are invited to attend. One at a time, without interruption, each participant talks about how the offense has affected him or her. Then the group comes up with a plan to repair the damage. It may sound hokey or mundane, but the results are often striking.

"You get kids where at first glance you think, 'Wow, OK, you seem very hard-core'—full-on crying," says Thalia González, a professor of politics at Occidental College in Los Angeles who studies restorative justice. Many students from neighborhoods with a history of violence, she says, long for a safe environment where they can express themselves. "With restorative justice, school suddenly becomes a place where you can do that. It changes how you view yourself. It changes how you view each other."

Borges-Carrera also instituted a peer-mediation program to resolve conflicts before they escalate. Teachers who come across or hear about students not getting along—an argument in the hall, rumors of an upcoming fight—send them to speak with a designated peer who encourages them to talk out the problem. When the program began, students mostly ended up in mediation by referral, but over time, they have come to recognize its value for themselves. "I've had kids say, 'I really want to fight today,'" Smith says. "They'll ask for a mediation slip, and I'll be like, 'For who?' And they'll be like, 'For me.'"

Borges-Carrera says the students feel attached to one another and their school in a way they didn't before. "For a lot of our kids, we are the only stable family they have," she says. That carries over after they leave; Smith recalls one young man who had graduated from KCAPA a year earlier walking into the school lobby bloodied and badly beaten. He asked to see his 12th-grade English teacher. "I didn't know where to go," he said. "Can you help me?"

By the 2009–2010 school year, four years after the transformation began, KCAPA was a different place. The number of serious incidents of misbehavior had plummeted 60 percent, even with enrollment up by more than 150 students. The 200 out-of-school suspensions per year were down to between 30 and 40. Arrests had decreased by two-thirds.

Spurred in part by the results at KCAPA, the School District of Philadelphia announced it would implement restorative-justice pilot programs in ten schools starting in 2013. If the two-year experiment is successful, the district will likely expand the program across the city. Philadelphia isn't the only metropolis to try this approach—since the late 1990s, Los Angeles, Denver, and San Francisco have also run pilot programs—but it's a bellwether. If restorative justice works in Philadelphia, widely known for rampant problems with violence and for one of the harshest zero-tolerance policies in the country, other major school districts will be encouraged to follow its lead. The most serious obstacle is one faced by local governments everywhere: funding. Governor Tom Corbett removed close to $1 billion from Pennsylvania's education budget shortly after taking office in 2011. Schools like KCAPA have been forced to lay off staff members in droves, leading Borges-Carrera and others to worry that Philadelphia's experiment could be cut short before it's had a chance to demonstrate that restorative justice works better than punitive discipline.

After decades of stability, violent-crime rates began to shoot up starting in the 1960s but escalating in the 1970s and 1980s. Juvenile crime rose in tandem. The percentage of high-school seniors who reported being the victim of a serious assault rose by 18 percent between

1984 and 1994. Overall, arrest rates for violent crime among youth between 10 and 17 jumped 70 percent. The Columbine High School shooting in 1999 solidified the public consensus that drastic measures were needed to keep children safe.

The first federal measure to implement "zero tolerance" in schools was the Gun-Free Schools Act of 1994, which mandated a one-year suspension for students who brought a firearm to school. Across the country, districts expanded on Congress's obligatory punishments to include possession of drugs and alcohol; many began to require one- or ten-day suspensions for minor offenses like cursing or lying to an administrator. The suspension rate soared 87 percent between 1973 and 2006. For the 2009–2010 school year, the most recent for which the Department of Education has released national estimates, more than two million secondary students—one out of nine—were suspended at least once. Most suspensions are for minor infractions; the California Department of Education reported that between 2011 and 2012, more than half the state's suspensions fell under the vague category of "defiance."

Punishments are not doled out evenly. In the 2009–2010 school year, 24 percent of black and 12 percent of Latino kids were slapped with a suspension at least once compared with only 7 percent of white students. This is not because minority students misbehave more than their white counterparts. A 2008 study found that racial and ethnic minorities are disproportionately suspended for the same behavior as their white counterparts.

In the past decade, academic research has come to show what administrators and teachers already know: Suspension may put troubled kids out of sight, but it doesn't alter their conduct. "It's not effective at changing the behavior, and it often contributes to higher dropout rates, higher arrest rates, because they're not supervised," says New York University sociologist Pedro Noguera, a leading advocate of restorative justice. Suspension often marks the beginning of a familiar pattern: Left on their own, kids get arrested, convicted of a crime, and end up incarcerated, feeding what researchers and advocates now call the "school-to-prison pipeline." Here again, the racial disparities are stark: According to a 2009 study from Northeastern University, nearly one in four male African American dropouts between 16 and 24 were in prison. For Latinos, the rate is 6.1 percent, and for whites, it is 6.6 percent.

Even as most school districts across the country were cracking down in the mid-1990s, a different approach was being tried in Minnesota. Alarmed by data showing that most in-school fights ended with a referral to law enforcement, state education administrators implemented a restorative-justice pilot program in 1995. Schools began to use talking circles after fights and replaced suspensions with peer mediations. The results were impressive: Lincoln Center Elementary School in St. Paul saw violent incidents decline from seven per day to fewer than two, while South St. Paul High School had out-of-school suspensions drop from 110 to 65 in one year. By 2001, half of all school districts statewide were using the approach.

As Minnesota's pilots showed promising results, social-justice groups started pushing for restorative justice. The Advancement Project was among the first civil-rights groups to focus on school suspensions. Partnering in Denver with grassroots group Padres y Jóvenes Unidos (Parents and Youth United), the Advancement Project produced a report in 2005 showing that African American and Latino students in the district were 70 percent more likely to be disciplined than white students. Denver started restorative justice in four schools that same year; suspensions were reduced almost by one-third, while attendance went up. Educators across the country began to adopt restorative justice. The San Francisco Unified School District instituted restorative-justice practices in 2009 and saw expulsions fall by 28 percent. The Oakland Unified School District adopted the approach in 2009, which is now in 27 schools; the Ralph J. Bunche Academy, which serves students with behavioral issues, cut suspensions in half in just one year. Newark Public Schools trained its principals in restorative justice last summer, and the Los Angeles Unified School District began to transition to restorative justice in 2012.

The approach has its critics. Chief among them is Annalise Acorn, a law professor at the University of Alberta and author of Compulsory Compassion: A Critique of Restorative Justice. Assailing restorative justice as the product of "new-age thinking," Acorn argues that it takes for granted that the offender is truly sorry rather than just playing along to avoid punishment. Worse, restorative practices can retraumatize victims by mandating further contact with the perpetrator. "You have these really wonderful, moving, sentimental stories about how the victim explains their pain and the perpetrator feels so sorry," Acorn says. "We have this whole veneration of this dramatic, selfless forgiveness, and it's so compelling. It's difficult for victims to say, 'I don't really want to participate in that.' "

Other critics simply think the approach is too soft. Shortly after Philadelphia announced it would be incorporating restorative-justice practices, Philadelphia teacher Christopher Paslay wrote on his blog that it marked "the day discipline officially died in Philadelphia"; without suspensions, Paslay argued, unruly students would be impossible to control.

While they say it's more effective than zero tolerance, supporters acknowledge that the approach can't fix every problem of student behavior. "It's not a panacea," Pedro Noguera says. That's partly because schools are powerless to address the root causes of student misconduct—generational poverty, abusive or neglectful families, gang activity.

Nationally, zero-tolerance policies are still the rule. In 2009, Representative Steve Cohen, a Democrat from Tennessee, introduced the Restorative Justice in Schools Act, which would allow administrators to use federal education funds to train teachers in the method, but the bill never reached the floor for a vote. In 2012, Congress held its first hearing on the school-to-prison pipeline. Earlier this year, both the Department of Education and the Department of Justice recommended that districts consider restorative justice rather than zero tolerance, although the recommendation was nonbinding. None of these efforts, however, has resulted in any change of federal policy, leaving the work of reform up to the states.

But in states like Pennsylvania, budget cuts have endangered districts' ability to dedicate and train staff in new approaches to discipline. Thirty-four states will spend less this year on education than they did before the recession. The School District of Philadelphia lost \$300 million for the 2013–2014 year and had to close 23 schools and fire almost 4,000 staff members, including all its assistant principals, more than 250 counselors, and more than 600 teachers. The district's projected shortfall is estimated to rise to \$320 million next school year.

Restorative-justice programs don't cost a lot to implement—two-year training for faculty runs between \$50,000 and \$60,000—but they do require schools to have sufficient staff. The support staff on which the programs rely—counselors, assistant principals, restorative-justice coordinators—are often the first to go when budget cuts hit.

At KCAPA, much of the staff who assisted with discipline, including two counselors, an assistant principal, and two coordinators, were laid off before the 2013–2014 school year began. "September was bumpy, it was really bumpy," Borges-Carrera says. "We probably had more fights in September than we've seen the past two years." But Borges-Carrera says she and KCAPA are making do. Students are performing the duties of laid-off staff, assisting with peer mediation. Teachers have stepped up to train one another in restorative-justice practices. "We may be dysfunctional at times," Borges-Carrera says. "But we are family nonetheless."

CRITICAL THINKING QUESTIONS

1. What were some of the issues Debora Borges-Carrera was seeing in her school that made her re-think the zero tolerance approach? What evidence does the article provide that a zero-tolerance policy is not effective? What are some of the other issues that have educational leaders turning away from a zero-tolerance policy?

2. What is the concept behind "restorative justice"? How does a "restorative circle" work? University of Alberta professor Annalise Acorn is skeptical that the approach is effective. Summarize her argument. Do you think this would be an effective method for improving schools? Why or why not?

3. Bryce Stucki writes that, "the suspension rate soared 87 percent between 1973 and 2006." What are some of the reasons he gives as to why schools might have been suspending their students at such higher rates? What is another way you think schools could have responded to those factors without suspensions? Why would this alternative idea have been successful?

4. What was the result of the zero tolerance policy in schools where the majority of its students lived at or below the poverty level? Was 'zero tolerance' helping make schools safer? How did the zero tolerance policy mirror racial inequalities in the country? Explain your answer.

DEATH BY DEADLINE, PART ONE

by Ken Armstrong

Ken Armstrong is a former newspaper reporter for *The Seattle Times.* He has won two Pulitzer Prizes for his investigative reporting and for breaking news. Armstrong now works for *The Marshall Project,* a nonprofit journalism organization, covering topics related to criminal justice.

In this 2014 investigation for *The Marshall Project* and *The Washington Post,* Ken Armstrong explores a key change to our criminal justice system. In the 1990s, Congress and President Bill Clinton passed a law limiting the amount of time convicts who were facing the death penalty had to file a federal appeal. It was limited to one year. In too many cases, the deadline passed without their lawyer taking action, even if the person convicted asked them to. Is a justice system just if the deadlines for defense are arbitrary and discriminatory?

• • • • • • • • • • • • • • • •

HOW BAD LAWYERING AND AN UNFORGIVING LAW COST CONDEMNED MEN THEIR LAST APPEAL

In 1992, Kenneth Rouse, an African-American man with an IQ between 70 and 80—"borderline intellectual functioning," in the clinical parlance—prepared to stand trial in North Carolina on charges that he had robbed, murdered and attempted to rape a white, 63-year-old store clerk.

Rouse's lawyers questioned the prospective jurors to try to expose any racial or other bias they might have against the defendant. But several years after the all-white jury convicted Rouse and recommended a death sentence, his defense team made a stunning discovery.

One of the jurors, Joseph S. Baynard, admitted that his mother had been robbed, murdered and possibly raped years before. Baynard had not disclosed this history, he said, so that he could sit in judgment of Rouse, whom he called "one step above a moron." Baynard added that he thought black men ("niggers" was the term he was quoted as using) raped white women for bragging rights.

As claims of juror bias go, the evidence could hardly have been stronger. But Rouse's final appeal was never heard. Under the Antiterrorism and Effective Death Penalty Act of 1996, Rouse's lawyers had just one year after his initial state appeal to petition for a last-resort hearing in federal court.

They missed the deadline by a single day.

A federal appeals judge wrote that it was "unconscionable" for her court to reject Rouse's case because of such a mistake by his court-appointed lawyers. But dozens of lawyers have made the same mistake, and most of their clients, like Rouse, have not been forgiven by the courts for missing the deadline.

An investigation by The Marshall Project shows that since President Bill Clinton signed the one-year statute of limitations into law—enacting a tough-on-crime provision that emerged in the Republicans' Contract with America—the deadline has been missed at least 80 times in capital cases. Sixteen of those inmates have since been executed—the most recent on Thursday, when Chadwick Banks was put to death in Florida.

By missing the filing deadline, those inmates have usually lost access to habeas corpus, arguably the most critical safeguard in the United States' system of capital punishment. "The Great Writ," as it is often called (in Latin it means "you have the body"), habeas corpus allows prisoners to argue in federal court that the conviction or sentence they received in a state court violates federal law.

For example, of the 12 condemned prisoners who have left death row in Texas after being exonerated since 1987, five of them were spared in federal habeas corpus proceedings. In California, 49 of the 81 inmates who had completed their federal habeas appeals by earlier this year have had their death sentences vacated.

The prisoners who missed their habeas deadlines have sometimes forfeited powerful claims. Some of them challenged the evidence of their guilt, and others the fairness of their sentences. One Mississippi inmate was found guilty partly on the basis of a forensic hair analysis that the FBI now admits was flawed. A prisoner in Florida was convicted with a type of ballistics evidence that has long since been discredited.

Just last month, Mark Christeson, a Missouri inmate whose lawyers missed the habeas deadline in 2005, received a stay of execution from the Supreme Court just hours before he was set to die by lethal injection.

In a court brief filed on Christeson's behalf, 15 former state and federal judges emphasized that he had not even met the appellate attorneys handling his federal case until after the filing deadline had passed. "Cases, including this one, are falling through the cracks of the system," they wrote. "And when the stakes are this high, such failures unacceptably threaten the very legitimacy of the judicial process."

The 80 death-penalty cases reviewed here were largely culled from databases of federal court opinions, but they also include other, unpublished rulings that were known to capital defense attorneys and advocates interviewed around the country. They represent just a fraction of the habeas appeals foreclosed by the 1996 law, which also applies to non-capital cases.

Like Rouse, who is still awaiting execution in North Carolina, two other inmates missed the habeas deadline by a single day, and for the most banal reasons. One attorney made the mistake of using regular mail instead of an overnight courier; another relied on a court's after-hours filing system, which turned out to be broken.

But many of the other habeas petitions from condemned inmates were late by hundreds of days, or even thousands. (On average, those lawyers missed the deadline by 853 days, or more than two years and four months.) In one case, the attorney was more than 11 years late.

Some of the lawyers' mistakes can be traced to their misunderstandings of federal habeas law and the notoriously complex procedures that have grown up around it. Just as often, though, the errors have exposed the lack of care and resources that have long plagued the patchwork system by which indigent death-row prisoners are provided with legal help.

The right of condemned inmates to habeas review "should not depend upon whether their court-appointed counsel is competent enough to comply with [the] statute of limitations," one federal appeals judge, Beverly B. Martin, wrote in an opinion earlier this year. Allowing some inmates into the court system while turning others away because of how their lawyers missed filing deadlines was making the federal appeals process "simply arbitrary," she added.

Meanwhile, the problem that the habeas deadline was intended to solve—the ever-lengthening delays in the carrying out of death sentences—has grown steadily. In 1996, the average time from sentencing to execution was 10 years and five months, according to the

Bureau of Justice Statistics. In 2012, the latest year for which the same figure is available, the delay had stretched to 15 years and 10 months.

AVERAGE YEARS FROM SENTENCE TO EXECUTION, 1984—2012

Passing Habeas Reform

The 1996 law that set the one-year statute of limitations on habeas appeals was one of the signal compromises that Clinton forged on domestic policy in the aftermath of the sweeping Republican victory in the 1994 mid-term elections.

Some Republicans had advocated for habeas corpus reform for years, mainly as a way to streamline and limit death-row appeals. The idea struggled to gain traction, but it became a small element of the Contract with America championed by then-Rep. Newt Gingrich (R-Ga.), who was on his way to becoming House speaker. After the Oklahoma City bombing in 1995, the proposal found new life as part of antiterrorism legislation embraced by both parties.

That pairing created political tension, both between the major parties and within them. Some Democrats supported the antiterrorism measures but viewed the habeas restrictions as the unnecessary circumscribing of a fundamental right. Some Republicans backed the habeas restrictions but feared the possible government excesses that might come from expanding surveillance authorities and other law enforcement powers also included in the measure.

"Why is it necessary to link the death penalty and the constitutional guarantees of habeas corpus to a terrorism bill?" Rep. Joseph P. Kennedy II (D-Mass.) asked during the debate in the House. "This is just a political deal. It is a political deal to get votes on the right."

By the mid-1990s, American support for the death penalty had climbed to 80 percent, its highest point since Gallup began polling on the issue in the 1930s. Public patience with the appeals process also was waning as the typical time between sentencing and execution stretched to more than a decade.

"Somehow, somewhere, we are going to end the charade of endless habeas proceedings," the chairman of the House Judiciary Committee, Rep. Henry J. Hyde (R-Ill.), declared in the debate over the antiterrorism law. "And this bill is going to do it."

But important changes in the legal landscape already were raising concerns among some civil libertarians. One opponent of the habeas proposal, Rep. Melvin Watt, a North Carolina Democrat, cited the advent of DNA evidence and the fact that some prisoners were being exonerated up to 15 years after their trials. Congress, he said, was proposing "to compromise the most basic thing—innocence—for political expediency."

Four former U.S. attorneys general who were opposed to the legislation—two Democrats and two Republicans—wrote to Clinton to urge that any filing deadlines on habeas petitions take effect "only upon the appointment of competent counsel."

As supporters of the bill lined up four competing attorneys general behind their position, Hyde announced that he had a "celebrity to trump all of those attorneys general" on the matter. "His name," Hyde said, "is President Clinton."

Clinton, who had initially opposed linking habeas reform to the antiterrorism measures, changed his mind—as he had on key facets of welfare reform, criminal sentencing and other domestic policies. As he began campaigning for reelection, he described the delays in death-penalty litigation as "ridiculous." The streamlining of appeals should begin with the Oklahoma City bombing cases, he announced.

The ranking Democrat on the Senate Judiciary Committee, Joe Biden of Delaware, introduced amendments to soften several of the habeas restrictions in the bill. At one point, he proposed to limit the one-year deadline to only federal prisoners, but he eventually supported the bill that came to the floor without that change.

The legislation passed the Senate by a vote of 91 to 8, and it cleared the House by a margin of more than two to one.

Myriad Mistakes

The hurried and often convoluted draftsmanship of the law's habeas provisions began to come under criticism almost as soon as it took effect. The ambiguities of the measure left a host of questions for the courts to answer, and with each passing year, the relevant case law has grown more complex.

Under the 1996 law, the one-year statute of limitations to file a federal habeas petition is supposed to begin after the conclusion of an inmate's direct appeal, which is filed in the state courts.

The direct appeal—the first of three levels of possible appeals—must focus on the trial record. It can argue, for example, that an important objection by the defense counsel should have been sustained rather than overruled.

Post-conviction petitions, which include federal habeas corpus appeals, can go beyond the trial to deal with anything from new evidence to the discovery of juror misconduct.

Lawyers who do post-conviction work in capital cases face a daunting array of challenges: They must typically reinvestigate the evidence for both guilt and punishment; canvass witnesses called and uncalled; plumb a defendant's criminal, social and family history; and round up and study thousands of pages of records. They must also navigate an ever-shifting landscape of appellate deadlines and procedures, identify promising issues and craft a detailed petition—all while under the pressure of defending a client whose life may depend on their success.

Yet while the law guarantees that indigent death row inmates have a court-appointed attorney in federal habeas corpus proceedings, it does not stipulate that the attorney must be competent. The Constitution guarantees the effective assistance of counsel at trial, but gives no similar assurance for lawyers doing habeas work.

Some of the same federal judges who are responsible for appointing habeas counsel have later traced the failure of such attorneys to meet the filing deadline to their inexperience, indifference, ineptitude or illness—and to myriad combinations thereof.

Motions or petitions filed properly in the state courts can suspend the federal deadline. But sometimes the motions are filed improperly, with lawyers neglecting to secure authorization to practice in a given court or failing to pay a required filing fee.

In at least three cases since 1996, attorneys filed papers in the wrong court. One appellate attorney discovered that his predecessor missed the habeas deadline after failing to even order the client's case file. Another attorney, who insisted that he had read the relevant case file, was later found to have never picked up the voluminous records from a state repository.

In some of the 80 cases, mistakes by judges compounded those of defense attorneys.

The lawyer for Richard Hamilton, who was convicted in 1995 of raping and murdering a 23-year-old nursing student after kidnapping her from a supermarket parking lot in Lake City, Fla., thought Hamilton had more time to file than he really did. So did a local judge, who told Hamilton not to worry. "It has been resolved," the judge said, to which Hamilton replied: "If you say so, that's good enough for me."

In two cases out of Texas, U.S. district court judges granted requests for a filing extension—setting, in effect, what appeared to be a new deadline—then enforced the old deadline after the petition was filed. "Parenthetically, this court may have erred in assuming that it had the authority to extend the statutory deadline," one judge later acknowledged.

Sometimes, courts waited too long to appoint habeas counsel. In California, where the courts have struggled mightily to find attorneys for capital appeals, at least six inmates received an attorney only after their deadline had passed—by more than five years in two cases.

Then there are lawyers who have failed even more basic scrutiny.

Some of the attorneys appointed to the 80 cases include an Alabama lawyer who was addicted to methamphetamine and was on probation for public intoxication, and a Louisiana lawyer who suffered from a neurological and physiological disorder so debilitating that he was asked to leave his firm.

One attorney in Texas had twice before been reprimanded for misconduct, while another Texas lawyer had twice been put on probation by the state bar. Two weeks after being appointed in the capital case, he was put on probation again.

In Mississippi, Willie Jerome Manning's first appointed attorney withdrew, citing his "most limited knowledged [sic] and familiarity with post-conviction proceedings at all." A second attorney also withdrew, citing his lack of qualifications. A third attorney was appointed—by a court order that was misfiled, adding to the delays—seven months after Manning's habeas deadline.

Two other men facing death sentences complained that their lawyer had a drinking problem—and they had the same lawyer. "Damn near fell out of his chair," one of the inmates wrote of the man in a letter to the lawyer's co-counsel.

As deadlines approached, some inmates pressed their attorneys for information. "I'm getting a little worried," one wrote. Another pleaded, "I want to know what's going on!" Chadwick Banks, the inmate executed in Florida on Thursday, wrote his attorney three weeks before his filing deadline, asking about "some date" that he understood could make a "big difference." (Ultimately his appeals deadline was missed by 2,079 days.)

In several cases, courts have shown that prisoners who schooled themselves in habeas law have sometimes demonstrated a better understanding of legal intricacies than their lawyers.

"[P]lease file my 2254 Habeas Petition immediately," one defendant wrote in a typical plea to his lawyer. "Please do not wait any longer . . . again, please file my 2254 Petition at once."

The Supreme Court took note of the phenomenon in the case of Albert Holland, who was sentenced to death for the 1990 murder of a Florida police officer who tried to arrest him.

"Holland was right about the law," the justices wrote. His lawyer, they added, "was wrong about the law."

In the tracing of blame, the case of Mississippi death-row inmate Alan Dale Walker offered a triple bank shot. Attorneys for the state put a wrong date in a court filing. The Mississippi Supreme Court incorporated that error into an opinion. An attorney for Walker then used the opinion to calculate the filing deadline.

Walker had a second attorney who had separately calculated the deadline, without relying on the court's opinion. He came up with a different date—but his date was wrong, too.

Pitfalls and Procedural Issues

The struggle to find capable lawyers for capital cases has been particularly visible in a handful of states with large numbers of death-row inmates.

Since its death penalty was reinstated in 1976, Florida, for example, has bounced from one troubled arrangement to another for the provision of post-conviction counsel. Of the 80 capital cases with a missed deadline, Florida has 37—the most of any state by far.

The state originally asked private lawyers to do the work free; it got few takers. It then established a special government office to do the work, but later shifted much of the load to a registry of private attorneys after lawmakers complained about the delays and the cost. In 1998, the state also set a cap on the number of hours per case those lawyers could bill (840) and the rate they could charge ($100 per hour).

The complexities of habeas law often have challenged even the most conscientious defense attorneys.

Michelle Kraus is an experienced defense attorney in Fort Wayne, Ind., who concentrates almost entirely on trial work. At the request of a lawyer friend, she signed on to assist with a state-level appeal for Gregory Scott Johnson, who had been convicted in 1986 of beating an 82-year-old woman to death. But after her friend left the case, Kraus wound up taking it to federal court, where she confronted a steep learning curve.

"It was overwhelming, getting grounded in it," Kraus says. She got the standard text on habeas practice and procedure—at that point, the two volumes ran to some 2,000 pages—and read it front to back. She also traveled to Atlanta to attend a one-week seminar on capital litigation, taught by some of the country's leading experts.

Kraus devoted long hours to Johnson's petition, which included a claim that prosecutors failed to disclose evidence that might have reduced Johnson's culpability and perhaps spared him the death penalty. She dropped the petition in the mail three days before deadline, but it arrived one day late.

"Counsel bungled the job," the federal appeals court wrote in 2004. Instead of using first-class mail, Kraus should have opted for FedEx or a courthouse messenger, the court said. The person held accountable would be Johnson. " [L]awyers are agents," the court wrote. "Their acts (good and bad alike) are attributed to the clients they represent."

Telling Johnson about her mistake—and how he would be punished for it—"was probably the hardest thing I've ever done," Kraus says. She stayed on the case—"he forgave me," she says—and was with Johnson for his last meal before he was executed in 2005.

But Kraus has declined to do any more habeas work since then.

"The pitfalls are there, and I fell into one," she recalled. "And it was horrible."

Sometimes, even legal organizations that are usually lauded for the quality of their capital work have faced criticism.

In a Georgia case, a federal judge chastised lawyers with the Southern Center for Human Rights, a nonprofit that opposes the death penalty and provides free legal support to prisoners in capital cases. The Southern Center lawyers had left the case well before an inmate's habeas petition was due, but the judge argued that they should have done more to find replacement counsel and to help the inmate determine the filing deadline.

One of the authors of the two-volume legal guidebook on habeas practice, James S. Liebman, a law professor at Columbia University, says the complexity and vagueness of the 1996 law has given lawyers all kinds of procedural nuances over which to fight. An important result has been that prosecutors have more ways to get a petition thrown out on procedural grounds—an advantage that they have seized "energetically and assiduously," Liebman says.

The guidebook, now in its sixth edition, has grown over the years to 2,700 pages. "There are more and more pages," he said, but "less and less justice."

Confronted with late filings, courts have embraced a remedy called "equitable tolling," which allows judges to waive a missed deadline in some circumstances. But courts limit its application to extraordinary situations, and the standard has been applied unevenly around the country.

Plain negligence—or a "simple gaffe," as the court labeled the mistake Kraus made—generally will not merit a judge's forbearance. But abandoning clients or lying to them often will constitute grounds for setting the deadline aside.

In the 80 capital cases, courts have granted equitable tolling in about a third. At least three of the inmates whose habeas petitions were reviewed went on to receive new trials.

The courts usually won't forgive a missed deadline if an attorney misinterpreted the law, a mistake that gets categorized as negligence. But a federal court in Ohio did so in the case of Michael Keenan, a landscaper who was convicted of murdering a young man found in a Cleveland park. "He would have been executed," Keenan's lead defense lawyer, Vicki Werneke, said in an interview. "He came dangerously close to getting his whole case dismissed."

When Werneke came onto the case in 2008, after Keenan had been granted equitable tolling, the state's case was already showing signs of unraveling. In 2012, a U.S. district court judge considered Keenan's habeas petition and ordered a new trial. Citing the state's "egregious prosecutorial misconduct" in withholding evidence, an Ohio county judge later ruled that prosecutors can't retry Keenan, allowing him to go free.

The state's appeal of that ruling is now pending before the Ohio Supreme Court.

Race Against Time

When a deadline is missed, an inmate's federal appeal can be lost—no matter the strength of the argument for a new trial, and even if the late filing can be attributed more to hard luck than ineptitude.

The law requires that prosecutors turn over evidence favorable to the defense before trial. But it wasn't until 22 years after William Kuenzel was condemned in Alabama that his appellate attorney received police notes and grand jury testimony undermining the prosecution's case.

Kuenzel was convicted in 1988 of murdering a convenience-store clerk. But in 2010, the state disclosed that an alleged accomplice originally told police he was with someone else, and that the only eyewitness who identified Kuenzel at trial had told grand jurors she "couldn't really see a face."

With such revelations, Kuenzel's claim of innocence has attracted an array of prominent supporters and generated a polished publicity campaign. Three former district attorneys—Robert M. Morgenthau of Manhattan, Gil Garcetti of Los Angeles and E. Michael McCann of Milwaukee—filed a brief with the Supreme Court saying the newly surfaced evidence "completely eviscerated" a prosecution case that they characterized as "weak, to say the least."

Although Kuenzel now has potentially strong grounds for an appeal, he still lacks a court to hear them—his lawyer missed the federal filing deadline by nearly three years.

When the 1996 law took effect, Kuenzel had one year to file his habeas petition. But the law included a provision that would suspend the normal one-year statute of limitations if an inmate had a "properly filed" petition pending in state court, effectively stopping the clock on the appeals process.

A petition that Kuenzel had filed in an Alabama circuit court had been dismissed as untimely in 1994, but then restored to the docket in May 1996. This led Kuenzel and his attorney to believe he had a "properly filed" state petition pending, and that the countdown toward the appeals deadline had paused.

But three years later, the circuit court reversed itself again at the request of state prosecutors, which was interpreted by a federal court to mean that the clock had been ticking all along.

"It is just the most grievous injustice," says David Kochman, an attorney who has been working on Kuenzel's appeal since 2004. "If any case was crying out for review, it was this case."

The state has written in court files that the newly disclosed evidence "fails to even come close" to exonerating Kuenzel. "It is time for this case to finally come to an end," wrote the state, which two months ago asked for an execution date to be set.

Sentenced to death at 26, Kuenzel is now 52. In a letter to this reporter last month, he wrote that he felt like he was listening to an old grandfather clock as it wound down, knowing he would be killed when it stops. He can't rewind the clock, he said, because "the courts have shut the hole."

Guarding Against Racial Prejudice

On April 17, 1996, as then-Sen. Daniel Patrick Moynihan argued against any weakening of habeas corpus protections in the pending antiterrorism bill, the New York Democrat reminded his colleagues that the matters at hand were more profound than mere legal procedures.

"We are dealing here, sir, with a fundamental provision of law, one of those essential civil liberties which precede and are the basis of political liberties," Moynihan said.

Quoting from a letter that several former attorneys general had written to President Clinton, he cast the federal courts' ability to review state-court decisions under habeas corpus as an essential guarantee: "It has a proud history of guarding against injustices born of racial prejudice and intolerance, of saving the innocent from imprisonment or execution, and in the process, ensuring the rights of all law-abiding citizens."

Two days before Moynihan's speech on the Senate floor, one of the jurors who voted to send Kenneth Rouse to his death, Joseph Baynard, signed an affidavit acknowledging that he had deliberately withheld the fact of his mother's murder so that he could get on the jury.

Baynard, who died last year, acknowledged in the affidavit that his decision in the Rouse case might have been colored by "bigotry." A Duke University law student who interviewed the former juror for Rouse's appeal also filed a separate affidavit detailing Baynard's racial invective.

At that point, Rouse's case was still in the state courts, which ultimately denied him a new trial. His one-year habeas deadline came on Feb. 7, 2000, and his lawyers, who miscalculated the date, filed their petition on his behalf one day too late.

While the American public often complains about criminal defendants winning their legal cases on technicalities, the opposite is often true, says Gretchen Engel, a habeas expert who had advised Rouse's defense team and provided the correct filing date: "What they don't realize is how often people lose on technicalities, or in ways that would offend most people's sense of justice."

Despite the federal courts' refusal to hear his case, Rouse got one more chance in 2009, when the North Carolina legislature passed the Racial Justice Act, allowing condemned prisoners to challenge their sentences if they could demonstrate that racial bias had played a role.

Rouse filed a motion to have his case reviewed under the act. But in 2013—after four other death-row inmates had succeeded in getting their sentences reduced to life without parole under the new provision—the state legislature repealed the law altogether.

Rouse's motion is still pending. It is unclear if it will ever be heard.

This is part one in a series. Read part two.

CRITICAL THINKING QUESTIONS

1. Habeas corpus has been called "the great writ." What does it allow for? And what evidence does the article provide that it is such an effective tool for a defendant?

2. Ken Armstrong provides a number of examples of incompetent lawyers hurting their clients by forgetting deadlines, drinking on the job, and not caring about their appeals process. What evidence does the article provide that Michelle Kraus is not like those attorneys? Yet, despite those reasons, how does she fail Gregory Scott Johnson? He forgives her—could you? Why or why not?

3. In arguing against the bill that limited the habeas corpus appeal timeline, Senator Daniel Patrick Moynihan said the right had a "proud history." Summarize his argument for the strengths of the habeas corpus appeal. Moynihan claims it guards against "racial prejudice." Describe the racial prejudice in Kenneth Rouse's case. Do you think it is fair that Kenneth Rouse's habeas corpus appeal was declined? Why or why not?

4. **Connection.** Habeas corpus is a powerful legal tool that allows defendants to question the legal proceeding that caused their incarceration. If you were to write a habeas corpus argument for Cameron Todd Willingham, from "Trial by Fire," what would be the strongest three arguments you could present that would support his innocence?

DEATH BY DEADLINE, PART TWO

by Ken Armstrong

Ken Armstrong is a former newspaper reporter for *The Seattle Times.* He has won two Pulitzer Prizes for his investigative reporting and for breaking news. Armstrong now works for *The Marshall Project*, a nonprofit journalism organization, covering topics relating to criminal justice.

In part two of this 2014 investigation for *The Marshall Project* and *The Washington Post*, Ken Armstrong explores the lawyers who were responsible for these missed deadlines. He finds that there are few, if any, consequences for a lawyer who misses a key deadline in a capital case. This missed deadline severely reduces the defendants' chances of receiving a new trial. How can our system be considered fair if the system doesn't punish the lawyers who fail the system?

• • • • • • • • • • • • • • •

WHEN LAWYERS STUMBLE, ONLY THEIR CLIENTS FALL

In the fall of 2006, a Florida attorney named Mary Catherine Bonner went before the U.S. Supreme Court to plead for a death-row prisoner whose last-chance appeal had been thrown out because his previous lawyer had missed the filing deadline.

"You know, being lawyers, we always do file at the last minute," Bonner told the justices.

Bonner spoke with some authority. An honors graduate of the University of Miami law school, she had defended some high-profile clients, dealt with complex international legal issues and been admitted to practice in a long list of federal courts.

But barely a month before her Supreme Court argument, Bonner had been upbraided herself by a federal judge who was confronted with two other death-penalty cases where Bonner had missed the filing deadline. In one, she was late by 210 days; in the other, 278 days. In a third case earlier that year, her petition for relief under habeas corpus was 312 days late.

"[I]t is hard for me to fathom how a lawyer who asked for and received the appointment of this Court, could abdicate the most basic function of filing the petition on time," wrote Timothy J. Corrigan, the district court judge in the first two cases.

"I would be remiss if I did not share my deep concern that in these cases our federal system of justice fell short in the very situation where the stakes could not be higher."

Corrigan's frustration has echoed in a series of cases that have come to the federal courts since 1996, when President Bill Clinton endorsed a Republican plan to limit death-penalty appeals by setting a one-year deadline for the filing of habeas corpus petitions.

Those federal appeals, which typically come after claims in state courts have been exhausted, allow inmates to seek a final review of their convictions on grounds ranging from juror misconduct to the suppression of evidence by prosecutors.

Yet an investigation by The Marshall Project has found that in at least 80 capital cases in which lawyers have missed the deadline—sometimes through remarkable incompetence or neglect—it is almost always the prisoner alone who suffers the consequences.

Among the dozens of attorneys who have borne some responsibility for those mistakes, only one has been sanctioned for missing the deadline by a professional disciplinary body, the investigation found. And that attorney was given a simple censure, one of the profession's lowest forms of punishment.

The lack of oversight or accountability has left many of the lawyers who missed the habeas deadlines free to seek appointment by the federal courts to new death-penalty appeals. When Bonner, the Florida attorney, argued before the Supreme Court, the justices said nothing of her being a repeat offender, if they even knew.

The absence of any systematic monitoring or punishment for mistakes on which their clients' lives might depend underscores the uneven quality of publicly funded legal aid to death-row prisoners who turn to the federal courts.

In 17 of the country's 94 federal judicial districts, special teams of government-funded lawyers and investigators monitor the capital cases coming out of their state courts to make sure deadlines are recognized and met. In some other districts, the federal defender's office helps to evaluate the private attorneys who might be appointed to handle those appeals.

But for lawyers outside the government, the work is difficult and often unpopular, with limited funds available for investigators and experts. And in most districts, where judges screen candidates themselves or with the help of review committees, the quality of legal counsel varies widely.

Federal judges sometimes appoint lawyers "who are not good enough to handle these cases," says habeas expert Randy A. Hertz, a professor at the New York University School of Law.

However well-meaning, such lawyers may be inexperienced or overmatched. Some may know the judges who make the appointments, but not the voluminous and complex law surrounding habeas corpus. Others have been found to have mental-health problems, substance-abuse issues or other complications that were missed in their screening.

In about one-third of the 80 cases where habeas deadlines were missed, the federal courts eventually allowed prisoners to go forward with their appeals, often because their attorneys' failures went beyond what the courts would categorize as mere negligence.

Yet even when attorneys have been chastised in federal court rulings for work described as "inexcusable" or "deeply unprofessional," they have managed to evade any discipline from bar associations or other agencies. One lawyer castigated by the United States Supreme Court for "serious instances of attorney misconduct" still has an unblemished disciplinary record.

A prominent death-penalty defense lawyer, Gretchen Engel of the Center for Death Penalty Litigation in North Carolina, offered a simple reason for the discrepancy between the magnitude of some lawyers' mistakes and the paltry consequences they face: "The people who were hurt by it are prisoners."

'A TERRIBLE MISTAKE'

The challenge of finding capable, experienced attorneys to handle the habeas caseload has been especially notable in Florida, which has accounted for 37 of the 80 cases with missed deadlines.

When the state set up a registry of private attorneys in 1998 to help handle capital appeals, it enlisted some lawyers who had little or no idea how to do the work. While these attorneys were contracted to handle appeals in the state courts, many carried their cases on to the final stage of federal habeas corpus, even though the legal issues there could be even more complicated.

One of the attorneys on the registry, Jefferson Morrow, later told a federal judge that he had taken the case of a death-row inmate, Floyd Damren, "because somebody had to."

Morrow was 208 days late in filing his habeas petition. When pressed for an explanation in court, he said he was inexperienced in habeas law, sent a petition to the wrong court and was never able to determine the deadline in the first place.

"I thought I had enough time," he said. "I know that sounds stupid. But I thought I had—I thought there was enough time."

The federal judge called Morrow's work "grossly negligent." Had he "conducted rudimentary legal research," the judge wrote, "he could have ascertained the limitations period."

A year after Morrow testified to missing the deadline, he was elected a trial court judge in Jacksonville, Fla.

Another attorney on the registry, Stuart Mishkin, represented Ronnie Johnson, who had been condemned in two separate cases. Mishkin handled both—and mishandled both, failing to meet either deadline.

"I knew it was specialized, but I did not know to what extent," Mishkin said of the post-conviction appeals process in an interview with the *St. Petersburg Times* in 2000. "It was a terrible mistake for me to get involved."

Mishkin eventually was suspended by the Florida bar for 90 days, though not for his missteps in the capital cases. Other, paying clients had accused him of missing court hearings, failing to file motions and neglecting to keep them informed. When Mishkin failed to respond to their bar complaints in a timely fashion, he was suspended.

Both Morrow and Mishkin have since died.

Despite the early problems with the state registry, Florida's governor at the time, Jeb Bush, pushed in 2003 to close a state death-penalty appeals office and replace it entirely with registry lawyers.

The office, called the Capital Collateral Regional Counsel, was targeted by Republican legislators mainly because it was seen as dragging out death-penalty appeals at public expense. The agency's lawyers were handling about 85 percent of the state's death-penalty cases and had won the exoneration of four death-row inmates over the previous four years.

Opponents of the Bush plan argued that the registry would not be able to find enough competent attorneys and that it would not be able to adequately supervise those whom it hired. Instead of closing the whole agency, the state in 2003 shut down just the northern regional office. But that experiment did not fare well, leading the legislature to reopen the office last year.

LACK OF ACTION

In extreme cases, federal judges may suspend incompetent or unethical lawyers from practicing in their districts. But the primary instruments for lawyer oversight and discipline are state bar associations.

In North Carolina, for instance, the state bar will investigate if it becomes aware of a judicial order suggesting attorney misconduct in a case. "However," the bar counsel, Katherine Jean, stated in an e-mail, the bar's grievance committee "cannot review the hundreds of thousands of court orders entered in the state and federal courts each year to see whether they might contain such information."

The kinds of orders that get entered include one addressing the work of two Raleigh lawyers, Wayne B. Eads and Mark A. Perry. They were appointed to handle the capital appeal for Elton O. McLaughlin, who was convicted in 1984 of killing a man, his wife and a 4-year-old child in a murder-for-hire scheme.

In reviewing the lawyers' failure to file McLaughlin's habeas petition on time, a federal district judge, Terrence W. Boyle, noted in 2000 that they had not taken even "basic, preliminary steps" before the deadline came and went. They had not gathered the complete trial transcript or met with McLaughlin's trial lawyer; other lawyers had telephoned them to warn of the approaching deadline, but Eads and Perry hadn't returned their calls.

The two lawyers "failed to take any action at all," the judge wrote. "The behavior of Eads and Perry in this case is neither 'innocent' nor 'garden variety' and it is certainly not excusable."

So extreme were the attorneys' failures that the judge waived the deadline. McLaughlin received new attorneys and was ultimately spared the death penalty when a court concluded he was mentally retarded.

State bar officials would not disclose whether they ever examined Eads's and Perry's work on the case, but neither lawyer was ever sanctioned. Perry later ran for a county judgeship and lost. Eads said in an interview that he had been diagnosed with cancer not long after taking the McLaughlin case, of which he has "very little memory."

"That was a tough period for me, but I came through it fine, eventually," he said. (Perry did not return calls asking for comment.)

When attorneys in some of the 80 missed-deadline cases have gotten into trouble, it has almost always been for mistakes they made in other, non-capital cases. A North Carolina attorney was disbarred for misappropriating the trust funds of a client. A lawyer in Florida failed to show up for a crucial pretrial conference in a lawsuit against the Boy Scouts; he was later suspended, and eventually disbarred.

In disciplinary matters involving other clients, at least five attorneys in these cases were sanctioned for taking too long to respond to a bar complaint—a deadline involving their law license, not a client's life.

'CHASING AFTER' ANSWERS

In December 2007, a federal judge in Jacksonville held oral arguments in three capital cases.

The judge, Timothy Corrigan, who was appointed in 2002 by President George W. Bush, pulled the cases together because they all raised the same issue: what to do about lawyers' failure to file their clients' habeas petitions on time. In two of the cases, the lawyer who filed late was Mary Bonner.

Corrigan seemed to be in disbelief at what had transpired.

Both of Bonner's clients, William Gregory Thomas and Mark Asay, had directed her to file their habeas appeals before the deadline. Thomas would testify that he had completed a petition on his own, signed it and given it to her. Asay, convicted of a 1987 double murder while on parole, would say he had urged Bonner to abandon an argument she had come up with for why he had more time. "I had days left to file. And I wanted Ms. Bonner to file," he would later testify.

But Bonner did not file either petition in time.

"They knew what they were talking about and the lawyers didn't, right?" Corrigan asked a lawyer for the Florida attorney general's office who was arguing that the deadlines should be enforced anyway.

In Thomas's case, Corrigan had appointed Bonner after she had filed an emergency request to represent him in the habeas appeal. At that point, Thomas, who had been convicted of murdering his wife in 1991 to avoid making payments in their pending divorce, was only three months from his deadline to file.

Corrigan gave Bonner the case with the expectation that she would move as quickly as possible.

Instead, he heard nothing. He was forced to go "chasing after" Bonner for answers, the judge said, and to order an update on the status of the case. Even then, she missed the filing deadline by nine months.

"How is that not either my fault . . . for not appointing a lawyer that was going to file on time, or why is it not Ms. Bonner's fault?" Corrigan asked the state's attorney.

"That's just tough luck?" Corrigan asked.

"That's the statutes," the state attorney said. "I'm not saying that. Congress did."

Bonner told the judge she was "a very, very diligent practitioner" who had run into some hard times. Her husband of 40 years had suffered a stroke and had open-heart surgery, she said. She was hospitalized for a problem with her blood, and also suffered a head injury and broken arm.

"Being a tough old Irish woman, I have believed all along that I could carry what had to be carried and do what had to be done," she told Corrigan.

"I don't know what to tell you, other than, 'I apologize,'" she said. "I am not a bad person."

At another hearing, in 2008, Bonner said she had somehow become confused about the deadline in Thomas's case. She was at a loss to explain what had happened, in part because many of her case files had been destroyed in a hurricane. "I just don't know," she said.

When Corrigan ruled in these cases in 2009, his language was unsparing.

"The terms 'bad faith' or 'dishonesty' capture Ms. Bonner's conduct," he wrote of her work for Asay. In the Thomas case, he wrote, Bonner "engaged in an egregious pattern of misfeasance."

Bonner's failures were sufficiently grave that Corrigan granted both prisoners "equitable tolling," a judicial remedy allowing the missed deadlines to be forgiven.

Bonner was asked to comment for this story in e-mail and telephone messages and letters sent to her office and home addresses in Fort Lauderdale. She did not reply to any of them, and no one answered the door when a reporter made multiple visits to the two locations.

In 2007—four years after Bonner missed the deadline in one capital case, and two years after she missed deadlines in two other capital cases—she was appointed to represent another death-row inmate, Leonardo Franqui.

This time, Bonner filed Franqui's petition on time. But a federal appeals court judge still denounced the quality of her work, saying it reflected either "something more than negligence" or "a level of gee-golly, aw-shucks lawyering that is completely unacceptable in capital cases."

In the three cases where Bonner missed the habeas deadline, there is no record that she ever submitted a request to be paid. In yet another case, in which a habeas deadline had been missed by an earlier attorney, she did seek payment. But that request, which was supposed to be filed with the court within 45 days after the case closed, arrived four years late.

Bonner blamed the delay on a heavy workload and health problems that included four heart surgeries. The judge denied her request, noting a "pattern of untimely pleadings" and "the use of the same or similar health problems and excuses."

In the 80 capital cases with a missed deadline, the inmate who missed the mark by the most was Paul Anthony Brown, whose petition was more than 11 years late. Bonner shows up in that case, too. Brown's federal deadline had already passed when Bonner—who was one of Florida's private registry attorneys—was appointed in the state courts to work on a post-conviction motion.

Court records show that almost seven years passed before she filed the pleading. "Bonner apologized to Brown for the delays and explained that she was hampered by health problems," a court order says.

Despite the criticism she has weathered, Bonner has a spotless record with the Florida Bar. She is still eligible to practice in the federal judicial district where she missed the three deadlines. And she remains on the Florida registry of attorneys for capital appeals, where she has asked to be considered for appointment in every circuit in the state.

Bonner's missed deadlines do not appear to have registered with the Supreme Court, where in 2006 she argued a question of timing in federal habeas cases in *Lawrence v. Florida*.

For the court's purposes, Bonner had put forward the right case at the right time: One that raised a somewhat narrow but important technical question on which lower courts had split.

Bonner commemorated her Supreme Court appearance by commissioning a painting of the event. The work, in watercolor with gouache highlighting, shows her standing at the lectern in a navy blue dress and a strand of pearls, holding forth as the nine justices listen thoughtfully and courtroom illustrators sketch her portrait.

Bonner and her client lost the decision by a vote of 5 to 4.

FACING CONSEQUENCES

Of the 80 federal habeas cases noted here, the one attorney held accountable for the missed deadline did more work for less money than many of his counterparts.

Earle Schwarz, an attorney in Memphis, declined to comment for this story. But his account can be pieced together from a letter he wrote to the Board of Professional Responsibility of the Tennessee Supreme Court, along with other records in the board's file.

A specialist in commercial law and alternative dispute resolution, Schwarz's typical clients included Blue Cross Blue Shield and BellSouth. But in 1998 he agreed to handle a capital appeal—his first—and to do the work free of charge. He hoped for a case in his own state but was persuaded that the need for volunteer counsel was greatest in Alabama.

Schwarz took the case of an Alabama death-row inmate named Robin Myers, who had been convicted of fatally stabbing a woman and stealing her VCR. He picked up the case in the state post-conviction phase, the second tier in the three-tier appeals process.

For more than four years he juggled the appeal with his commercial law practice. Schwarz and his legal team went back and forth to Alabama, to interview "countless witnesses and potential witnesses," Myers's trial attorney and investigator, and Myers himself, according to Schwarz's letter to the board. Together they logged more than 1,200 hours of work on the case. Had the hours been billed, the total would have come to about $145,000 at the law firm's going rates.

While representing Myers, Schwarz changed firms. His old firm had an "enlightened policy" concerning pro bono work and offered support, according to Schwarz's letter. His new firm "did not have a similar commitment."

He made mistakes, Schwarz wrote. He was "mortified" to discover he had missed an important deadline in the state courts, owing to his lack of familiarity with the local rules: Alabama had a 14-day filing requirement while in Tennessee the period was 60 days. Another mistake—perhaps his biggest—was "not remembering" there was a one-year statute of limitations on the filing of Myers's federal appeal.

When Myers lost his state appeal, Schwarz didn't notify his client, nor did he formally withdraw from the case. While Schwarz did nothing, the filing deadline for Myers's federal habeas petition came and went.

At the request of Myers's subsequent attorney, Schwarz later signed a declaration owning up to his mistakes. That declaration then became the source of a disciplinary complaint.

Complaints filed against attorneys by inmates often go nowhere. But the complaint against Schwarz came from the federal magistrate assigned to Myers's appeal.

In 2005, Tennessee's disciplinary board issued a public censure, declaring Schwarz's conduct to be improper but imposing no restrictions on his practice.

Myers is still on death row. Earlier this year, his execution was indefinitely postponed because Alabama ran out of drugs used in lethal injection. But two months ago the state adopted a new drug protocol and resumed its request for execution dates, including one for Myers.

CHANCE FOR REFORM

The rash of missed deadlines has become a source of frustration for some federal judges, and a subject of some concern in the Justice Department.

In an interview, the outgoing United States attorney general, Eric H. Holder Jr., said that before he relinquishes his post, he will deliver a report to President Obama on problems with the death penalty around the country, and that the department will consider the issue of missed deadlines in the filing of habeas petitions.

"When you're talking about the state taking someone's life, there has to be a great deal of flexibility within the system to deal with things like deadlines," Holder said. "If you rely on process to deny what could be a substantive claim, I worry about where that will lead us."

Rosemary Barkett—a former chief justice of the Florida Supreme Court who later sat on the U.S. Court of Appeals for the 11th Circuit—called the courts' practice of stripping inmates of their habeas rights because of the lawyers' failures to file on time both "unconstitutional and immoral."

Earlier this year, after confronting another case where the deadline was overshot, the Eleventh Circuit authorized the establishment of a new unit that would handle habeas appeals in the office of the Federal Defender for the Northern District of Florida. That is the same region where the state of Florida had disbanded its own capital-defense office to rely on the registry of private attorneys.

The Capital Habeas Units of the federal defenders' offices, which now operate in 17 judicial districts spread across 12 states, specialize in habeas corpus and take pains to monitor the progress of death-penalty cases through their state courts.

Dale Baich, an assistant federal public defender in Arizona, says his unit keeps track of legal pleadings and filing dates for each of the jurisdiction's condemned inmates, checking electronic dockets and calling clerks' offices if necessary.

When the unit gets a case, it is assigned a team usually consisting of two lawyers, two investigators, a paralegal and a legal assistant. A single petition can generate that much work, he said.

The federal defenders in the northern district of Florida are now hiring for their new capital habeas unit.

CRITICAL THINKING QUESTIONS

1. In both parts of this essay, Ken Armstrong highlights over six-dozen death penalty cases where lawyers have missed deadlines, causing the defendants to lose a chance to appeal their sentences. On the rare occasions punishments were given, they were minimal. What is the reason that Gretchen Engel gives for this lack of accountability? How would this affect how lawyers are, or are not, punished? Do you believe her argument? Why or why not?

2. "Despite the criticism," Ken Armstrong writes, "Bonner has a spotless record with the Florida Bar." Why would some people be shocked to discover that she still has a spotless record as a lawyer in Florida? Do you think that Bonner and other attorneys who miss habeas corpus deadlines should be punished for such instances? Or, do you think that our justice system is responsible for such circumstances since they do not have "systematic monitoring or punishment for mistakes on which their clients' lives might depend underscores the uneven quality of publicly funded legal aid to death-row prisoners who turn to the federal courts?" Explain your point of view by providing support from the reading.

3. Why is it important for attorneys who deal with the habeas corpus cases to have a depth of experience and knowledge? Why are so many attorneys with a lack of experience and knowledge appointed to such cases and pitted against attorneys with so much experience? Explain why you think this discrepancy occurs by supporting your point of view with evidence from the reading.

4. **Connection.** Using both part one and part two of this essay by Ken Armstrong, suggest three changes that would make the habeas corpus process more fair. Why would these changes create a more equitable system?

THE PRISON INDUSTRY IN THE UNITED STATES: BIG BUSINESS OR THE NEW FORM OF SLAVERY?

by Vicky Pelaez

Vicky Pelaez is a Peruvian journalist and columnist. She is widely known for her work in New York City writing for Spanish language newspapers. She currently works for *The Moscow News*.

In this 2014 report published by the Center for Global Research, Vicky Pelaez observes trends in American prisons. Over the past quarter century, our incarceration rates have skyrocketed; we now have 25% of the world's prisoners, yet we have only 5% of the world's population. She believes that part of the reason for this growth is the money in the prison system. Both the contractors, who can build and run private prisons, and the corporations, which can benefit from the cheap labor, have a financial incentive to grow this system. In seeking efficiency, has our criminal justice system created an economy based on slave-like labor?

• • • • • • • • • • • • • • •

Human rights organizations, as well as political and social ones, are condemning what they are calling a new form of inhumane exploitation in the United States, where they say a prison population of up to 2 million—mostly Black and Hispanic—are working for various industries for a pittance. For the tycoons who have invested in the prison industry, it has been like finding a pot of gold. They don't have to worry about strikes or paying unemployment insurance, vacations or comp time. All of their workers are full-time, and never arrive late or are absent because of family problems; moreover, if they don't like the pay of 25 cents an hour and refuse to work, they are locked up in isolation cells.

There are approximately 2 million inmates in state, federal and private prisons throughout the country. According to California Prison Focus, "no other society in human history has imprisoned so many of its own citizens." The figures show that the United States has locked up more people than any other country: a half million more than China, which has a population five times greater than the U.S. Statistics reveal that the United States holds 25% of the world's prison population, but only 5% of the world's people. From less than 300,000 inmates in 1972, the jail population grew to 2 million by the year 2000. In 1990 it was one million. Ten years ago there were only five private prisons in the country, with a population of 2,000 inmates; now, there are 100, with 62,000 inmates. It is expected that by the coming decade, the number will hit 360,000, according to reports.

What has happened over the last 10 years? Why are there so many prisoners?

"The private contracting of prisoners for work fosters incentives to lock people up. Prisons depend on this income. Corporate stockholders who make money off prisoners' work lobby for longer sentences, in order to expand their workforce. The system feeds itself," says a study by the Progressive Labor Party, which accuses the prison industry of being "an imitation of Nazi Germany with respect to forced slave labor and concentration camps."

The prison industry complex is one of the fastest-growing industries in the United States and its investors are on Wall Street. "This multimillion-dollar industry has its own trade exhibitions, conventions, websites, and mail-order/Internet catalogs. It also has direct advertising campaigns, architecture companies, construction companies, investment houses on Wall Street, plumbing supply companies, food supply companies, armed security, and padded cells in a large variety of colors."

According to the Left Business Observer, the federal prison industry produces 100% of all military helmets, ammunition belts, bullet-proof vests, ID tags, shirts, pants, tents, bags, and canteens. Along with war supplies, prison workers supply 98% of the entire market for equipment assembly services; 93% of paints and paintbrushes; 92% of stove assembly; 46% of body armor; 36% of home appliances; 30% of headphones/microphones/speakers; and 21% of office furniture. Airplane parts, medical supplies, and much more: prisoners are even raising seeing-eye dogs for blind people.

CRIME GOES DOWN, JAIL POPULATION GOES UP

According to reports by human rights organizations, these are the factors that increase the profit potential for those who invest in the prison industry complex:

- Jailing persons convicted of non-violent crimes, and long prison sentences for possession of microscopic quantities of illegal drugs. Federal law stipulates five years' imprisonment without possibility of parole for possession of 5 grams of crack or 3.5 ounces of heroin, and 10 years for possession of less than 2 ounces of rock-cocaine or crack. A sentence of 5 years for cocaine powder requires possession of 500 grams—100 times more than the quantity of rock cocaine for the same sentence. Most of those who use cocaine powder are white, middle-class or rich people, while mostly Blacks and Latinos use rock cocaine. In Texas, a person may be sentenced for up to two years' imprisonment for possessing 4 ounces of marijuana. Here in New York, the 1973 Nelson Rockefeller anti-drug law provides for a mandatory prison sentence of 15 years to life for possession of 4 ounces of any illegal drug.
- The passage in 13 states of the "three strikes" laws (life in prison after being convicted of three felonies), made it necessary to build 20 new federal prisons. One of the most disturbing cases resulting from this measure was that of a prisoner who for stealing a car and two bicycles received three 25-year sentences.
  - Longer sentences.
  - The passage of laws that require minimum sentencing, without regard for circumstances.
  - A large expansion of work by prisoners creating profits that motivate the incarceration of more people for longer periods of time.
  - More punishment of prisoners, so as to lengthen their sentences.

HISTORY OF PRISON LABOR IN THE UNITED STATES

Prison labor has its roots in slavery. After the 1861–1865 Civil War, a system of "hiring out prisoners" was introduced in order to continue the slavery tradition. Freed slaves were charged with not carrying out their sharecropping commitments (cultivating someone else's land in exchange for part of the harvest) or petty thievery—which were almost never proven—and were then "hired out" for cotton picking, working in mines and building railroads. From 1870 until 1910 in the state of Georgia, 88% of hired-out convicts were Black. In Alabama, 93% of "hired-out" miners were Black. In Mississippi, a huge prison farm similar to the old slave plantations replaced the system of hiring out convicts. The notorious Parchman plantation existed until 1972.

During the post-Civil War period, Jim Crow racial segregation laws were imposed on every state, with legal segregation in schools, housing, marriages and many other aspects of daily life. "Today, a new set of markedly racist laws is imposing slave labor and sweatshops on the criminal justice system, now known as the prison industry complex," comments the Left Business Observer.

Who is investing? At least 37 states have legalized the contracting of prison labor by private corporations that mount their operations inside state prisons. The list of such companies contains the cream of U.S. corporate society: IBM, Boeing, Motorola, Microsoft, AT&T, Wireless, Texas Instrument, Dell, Compaq, Honeywell, Hewlett-Packard, Nortel, Lucent Technologies, 3Com, Intel, Northern Telecom, TWA, Nordstrom's, Revlon, Macy's, Pierre Cardin, Target Stores, and many more. All of these businesses are excited about the economic boom generation by prison labor. Just between 1980 and 1994, profits went up from $392 million to $1.31 billion. Inmates in state penitentiaries generally receive the minimum wage for their work, but not all; in Colorado, they get about $2 per hour, well under the minimum. And in privately-run prisons, they receive as little as 17 cents per hour for a maximum of six hours a day, the equivalent of $20 per month. The highest-paying private prison is CCA in Tennessee, where prisoners receive 50 cents per hour for what they call "highly skilled positions." At those rates, it is no surprise that inmates find the pay in federal prisons to be very generous. There, they can earn $1.25 an hour and work eight hours a day, and sometimes overtime. They can send home $200–$300 per month.

Thanks to prison labor, the United States is once again an attractive location for investment in work that was designed for Third World labor markets. A company that operated a maquiladora (assembly plant in Mexico near the border) closed down its operations there and relocated to San Quentin State Prison in California. In Texas, a factory fired its 150 workers and contracted the services of prisoner workers from the private Lockhart Texas prison, where circuit boards are assembled for companies like IBM and Compaq.

[Former] Oregon State Representative Kevin Mannix recently urged Nike to cut its production in Indonesia and bring it to his state, telling the shoe manufacturer that "there won't be any transportation costs; we're offering you competitive prison labor (here)."

PRIVATE PRISONS

The prison privatization boom began in the 1980s, under the governments of Ronald Reagan and Bush Sr., but reached its height in 1990 under William Clinton, when Wall Street stocks were selling like hotcakes. Clinton's program for cutting the federal workforce resulted in the Justice Departments contracting of private prison corporations for the incarceration of undocumented workers and high-security inmates.

Private prisons are the biggest business in the prison industry complex. About 18 corporations guard 10,000 prisoners in 27 states. The two largest are Correctional Corporation of America (CCA) and Wackenhut, which together control 75%. Private prisons receive a guaranteed amount of money for each prisoner, independent of what it costs to maintain each one. According to Russell Boraas, a private prison administrator in Virginia, "the secret to low operating costs is having a minimal number of guards for the maximum number of prisoners." The CCA has an ultra-modern prison in Lawrenceville, Virginia, where five guards on dayshift and two at night watch over 750 prisoners. In these prisons, inmates may get their sentences reduced for "good behavior," but for any infraction, they get 30 days added—which means more profits for CCA. According to a study of New Mexico prisons, it was found that CCA inmates lost "good behavior time" at a rate eight times higher than those in state prisons.

IMPORTING AND EXPORTING INMATES

Profits are so good that now there is a new business: importing inmates with long sentences, meaning the worst criminals. When a federal judge ruled that overcrowding in Texas prisons was cruel and unusual punishment, the CCA signed contracts with sheriffs in poor counties to build and run new jails and share the profits. According to a December 1998 *Atlantic Monthly* magazine article, this program was backed by investors from Merrill-Lynch, Shearson-Lehman, American Express and Allstate, and the operation was scattered all over rural Texas. That state's governor, Ann Richards, followed the example of Mario Cuomo in New York and built so many state prisons that the market became flooded, cutting into private prison profits.

After a law signed by Clinton in 1996—ending court supervision and decisions—caused overcrowding and violent, unsafe conditions in federal prisons, private prison corporations in Texas began to contact other states whose prisons were overcrowded, offering "rent-a-cell" services in the CCA prisons located in small towns in Texas. The commission for a rent-a-cell salesman is $2.50 to $5.50 per day per bed. The county gets $1.50 for each prisoner.

STATISTICS

Ninety-seven percent of 125,000 federal inmates have been convicted of non-violent crimes. It is believed that more than half of the 623,000 inmates in municipal or county jails are innocent of the crimes they are accused of. Of these, the majority are awaiting trial. Two-thirds of the one million state prisoners have committed non-violent offenses. Sixteen percent of the country's 2 million prisoners suffer from mental illness.

CRITICAL THINKING QUESTIONS

1. Why are private prisons such a good investment? What makes them better at producing items like helmets, paints, and home appliances? Consider the difference in pay you would get at a state-run prison versus a private prison. Do you think it is moral to purchase goods made at a prison? Why or why not?
2. The author quotes an article that states that in America we have a "markedly racist set of laws." Provide a fact from the essay that demonstrates that there are racial disparities in our criminal justice system. Summarize Vicky Pelaez's argument that this is connected to our history of slavery. Do you think this argument is valid?
3. The Correctional Corporation of America (CCA) is the largest private prison company in America. Their prisoners lose their "good behavior time" at a rate *eight times* higher than those in state prisons. Why might this be the case? What incentive does CCA have to see that prisoners stay in their prison longer? Who provides their financial incentive—who is paying for it? Do you think this system is fair? Why or why not?
4. Explain how prisoners are paid differently in private prisons or in state-run prisons. Why would the working conditions in these private prisons lead Vicky Pelaez to argue that this is a "new slavery?" Do you think her argument has merit?

CRIMINAL: HOW LOCKUP QUOTAS AND "LOW-CRIME TAXES" GUARANTEE PROFITS FOR PRIVATE PRISON CORPORATIONS

by In the Public Interest

In the Public Interest is a resource center on privatization and contracting. The organization stands by its public officials, advocacy groups, and researchers to ensure that public contracts with private parties are fairly managed in order to meet long-term community needs.

In this report, they examine the key contract clause that private prison companies demand from states: a bed guarantee. The state agrees to pay the prison companies per bed if they are filled or not. This, the article argues, creates both an incentive to create more prisoners, and a company that benefits from laws that create more criminals and supply longer sentences. Is it in the public's interest for states to make deal that incentivizes locking up their citizens?

• • • • • • • • • • • • • • •

MAJOR FINDINGS

- **65 percent of the private prison contracts** ITPI received and analyzed included occupancy guarantees in the form of quotas or required payments for empty prison cells (a "low-crime tax"). These quotas and low-crime taxes put taxpayers on the hook for guaranteeing profits for private prison corporations.
- **Occupancy guarantee clauses** in private prison contracts range between 80% and 100%, with 90% as the most frequent occupancy guarantee requirement.
- **Arizona, Louisiana, Oklahoma and Virginia** are locked in contracts with the highest occupancy guarantee requirements, with all quotas requiring between 95% and 100% occupancy.

STATE-SPECIFIC FINDINGS

- **Colorado:** Though crime has dropped by a third in the past decade, an occupancy requirement covering three for-profit prisons has forced taxpayers to pay an additional $2 million.
- **Arizona:** Three Arizona for-profit prison contracts have a staggering 100% quota, even though a 2012 analysis from *Tucson Citizen* shows that the company's per-day charge for each prisoner has increased an average of 13.9% over the life of the contracts.
- **Ohio:** A 20-year deal to privately operate the Lake Erie Correctional Institution includes a 90% quota, and has contributed to cutting corners on safety, including overcrowding, areas without secure doors and an increase in crime both inside the prison and the surrounding community.

INTRODUCTION

In 2012, Corrections Corporation of America (CCA), the largest for-profit private prison company in the country, sent a letter to 48 state governors offering to buy their public prisons. CCA offered to buy and operate a state's prison in exchange for a 20-year contract, which would include a 90 percent occupancy rate guarantee for the entire term.[1] Essentially, the state would have to guarantee that its prison would be 90 percent filled for the next 20 years (a quota), or pay the company for unused prison beds if the number of inmates dipped below 90 percent capacity at any point during the contract term (a "low-crime tax" that essentially penalizes taxpayers when prison incarceration rates fall). Fortunately, no state took CCA up on its outrageous offer. But many private prison companies have been successful at inserting occupancy guarantee provisions into prison privatization contracts, requiring states to maintain high occupancy levels in their private prisons.

For example, three privately-run prisons in Arizona are governed by contracts that contain 100 percent inmate quotas.[2] The state of Arizona is contractually obligated to keep these prisons filled to 100 percent capacity, or pay the private company for any unused beds.

These contract clauses incentivize keeping prison beds filled, which runs counter to many states' public policy goals of reducing the prison population and increasing efforts for inmate rehabilitation. When policymakers received the 2012 CCA letter, some worried the terms of CCA's offer would encourage criminal justice officials to seek harsher sentences to maintain the occupancy rates required by a contract.[3] Policy decisions should be based on creating and maintaining a just criminal justice system that protects the public interest, not ensuring corporate profits.

Bed guarantee provisions are also costly for state and local governments. As examples in the report show, these clauses can force corrections departments to pay thousands, sometimes millions, for unused beds—a "low-crime tax" that penalizes taxpayers when they achieve what should be a desired goal of lower incarceration rates. The private prison industry often claims that prison privatization saves states money. Numerous studies and audits have shown these claims of cost savings to be illusory,[4] and bed occupancy requirements are one way that private prison companies lock in inflated costs after the contract is signed.

THIS REPORT

This report will discuss the use of prison bed occupancy guarantee clauses in prison privatization contracts and explore how bed occupancy guarantees undermine criminal justice policy and democratic, accountable government. Section 1 explains the for-profit private prison industry's reliance on high prison populations, and how these occupancy guarantee provisions directly benefit its bottom line. Section 2 discusses the prevalence of bed guarantee clauses, drawing on a set of contracts that ITPI obtained through state open records requests. Section 3 describes how occupancy guarantees have harmed states, focusing on the experiences of Arizona, Colorado, and Ohio—three states that have agreed to these provisions to detrimental consequences. Lastly, Section 4 will discuss our recommendation that governments can and should reject prison occupancy guarantees.

SECTION 1: WHY QUOTAS ARE IMPORTANT TO THE FOR-PROFIT PRIVATE PRISON COMPANY BUSINESS MODEL

The private prison industry has promoted policies and practices that increase the number of people who enter and stay in prison. It is no surprise that the two major private prison companies, CCA and GEO Group, have had a hand in shaping and pushing for criminal justice policies such as mandatory minimum sentences that favor increased incarceration. In the past, they have supported laws like California's three-strikes law, and policies aimed at continuing the War on Drugs.[5] More recently, in an effort to increase the number of detainees in privately-run federal immigration detention centers, they contributed to legislation, like Arizona Senate Bill 1070, requiring law enforcement to arrest anyone who cannot prove they entered the country legally when asked.[6] The industry's reliance on a harsh criminal justice system is summed up in a statement from CCA's 2010 annual report: "The demand for our facilities and services could be adversely affected by the relaxation of enforcement efforts, leniency in conviction or parole standards and sentencing practices or through the decriminalization of certain activities that are currently proscribed by our criminal laws."[7]

These companies also spend large amounts of money to lobby federal and state lawmakers to advance policies that protect their bottom line and keep pro-privatization lawmakers in office. The Center for Responsive Politics reports that CCA spent $17.4 million in lobbying expenditures from 2002 through 2012,[8] while GEO Group spent $2.5 million from 2004 to 2012.[9] Similarly, CCA spent $1.9 million in political contributions from 2003 to 2012,[10] and GEO Group spent $2.9 million during the same time period.[11]

While the for-profit prison industry works hard to ensure harsh criminal laws and elect policymakers that support its agenda, bed guarantee contract provisions are an even more direct way that private prison companies ensure that prison beds are filled. These companies rely on occupancy guarantee clauses in government contracts to guarantee profits and reduce their financial risk, since the ability of private prison companies to ensure prison beds are filled generates steady revenues. These contract requirements are an important tool in private prison corporations' efforts to maximize profits. Private prison companies have negotiated these clauses in both older existing contracts and newer amendments. They have even lobbied lawmakers to impose bed guarantees on prison facilities, as the below example from Colorado shows. Private prison companies make no secret that high occupancy rates are critical to the success of their business. During a 2013 first quarter conference call, GEO Group boasted that the company continues to have "solid occupancy rates in mid to high 90s."[12]

By contractually requiring states to guarantee payment for a large percentage of prison beds, the prison companies are able to protect themselves against fluctuations in the prison population. These provisions guarantee prison companies a consistent and regular revenue stream, insulating them from ordinary business risks. The financial risks are borne by the public, while the private corporations are guaranteed profits from taxpayer dollars.

SECTION 2: THE PREVALENCE OF QUOTAS IN CONTRACTS

To understand the prevalence of prison occupancy guarantee provisions in prison privatization contracts, In the Public Interest (ITPI) analyzed numerous contracts between states and local jurisdictions and private prison companies. ITPI identified 77 county and state-level private facilities nationwide and collected and analyzed 62 contracts from these facilities. These contracts each relate to the operation of an individual facility within the state or

Occupancy Guarantee Provision

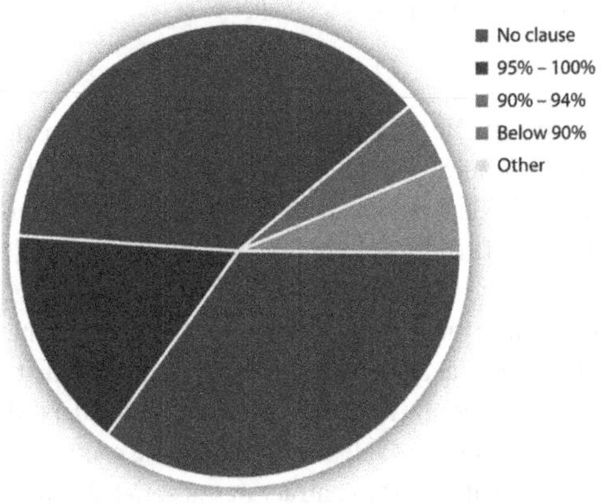

locality. The contracts that we collected were either given to us by state-level organizations that already had the contracts in their possession, or we utilized the open records request process with state and local governments. ITPI is currently following up with states to collect additional information.

Of the contracts that we reviewed, 41 (65 percent) contained quotas. These occupancy requirements were between 80 percent and 100 percent, with many around 90 percent. The highest bed guarantee requirements were from Arizona, Louisiana, Oklahoma, and Virginia. As mentioned above, Arizona has three contracts that contain 100 percent occupancy guarantee clauses. Oklahoma has three contracts with a 98 percent occupancy guarantee provision, while a couple of Louisiana's contracts contain occupancy requirements at 96 percent, and Virginia has one at 95 percent. All major prison companies, CCA, GEO Group, and Management and Training Corporation (MTC), have been successful in negotiating prison quotas in contracts.

Interestingly, prison companies have also been successful at winning bed guarantee promises even after a contract that contains no such provision is executed. Many of these bed guarantee clauses were added after the initial contract was signed, usually in a contract amendment. This is consistent with the prison industry's approach to revenue growth. In CCA's 2010 Annual Report, the company explicitly cites "enhancing the terms of our existing contracts" as one of the approaches it uses to develop its business.[13] Additionally, bed guarantee clauses may be imposed completely outside the contracting process. As discussed in more detail in the next section, CCA was able to insert a bed guarantee requirement for private facilities into the Colorado fiscal year 2013 state budget, completely circumventing the contract amendment process.[14] The percentage of facilities that actually have bed guarantee requirements may be higher than an analysis of their contracts alone indicate.

SECTION 3: IMPACTS OF PRISON QUOTAS

Bed guarantee clauses can have measurable impacts on a state's criminal justice policy, the state budget, the functioning of a specific facility, and the community. This section focuses on the experiences of Colorado, Arizona, and Ohio and describes the specific impacts that bed guarantee clauses have had on their states. All three states have prison facilities operated by private prison companies with occupancy guarantees in their contracts, and all three states have suffered detrimental consequences as a result.

Colorado

Colorado has experienced a sizable reduction in its prison population. In the past decade, the crime rate has dropped by a third, and since 2009, five prisons have been closed. The state projects that two to ten additional prisons could close in the near future, depending on the size of the facilities chosen.[15] This decrease in prison population propelled CCA, which operates three private prisons in the state, to take action. Last year, CCA negotiated the insertion of a bed guarantee provision in the state budget for all three of its facilities for the 2013 fiscal year. Even though all three contracts for these facilities include explicit language specifying that "the state does not guarantee any minimum number of offenders will be assigned to the contractors' facility," the company was able to circumvent the contracting process and mandate occupancy guarantees long after the contract was negotiated and signed.

In 2012, the state began a utilization study to analyze which facilities made the most sense to close, but did not want any to shut down any facilities until the formal analysis was complete. In response to these preliminary discussions, CCA threatened to close one of its private facilities. Behind closed doors and without any public hearings, CCA and the Governor's Office and the Joint Budget Committee negotiated a deal.[16] In exchange for keeping the facility open, the state agreed to a bed guarantee, which required Colorado to keep at least 3,300 prisoners in the three CCA facilities, at an annual rate of $20,000 per inmate for the 2013 fiscal year.[17]

Instead of using empty bed space in its state-run facilities, the Colorado Department of Corrections housed inmates in CCA's facilities to ensure they met the occupancy requirement. Colorado taxpayers must pay for the vacant state prison beds and for the per diem rate for inmates redirected to the CCA facility to fulfill the bed guarantee.[18] The Colorado Criminal Justice Reform Coalition estimates that the deal cost the state at least $2 million.[19] The *Colorado Springs Gazette* notes that the figure could be even higher. As of March 2013, the state already had 1,000 empty beds in various state prisons and that number was projected to increase by almost 100 beds per month.[20] Legislators predicted that the inmate population would drop between 160 to 1,256 people by June 2013, but by February 2013, the total had already fallen by 1,700 inmates.[21] The occupancy requirement not only ensured that CCA continued to receive a guaranteed level of revenue each month despite the decrease in inmates, but also had the effect of diverting inmates away from available public prison beds.

CCA Colorado Total Inmate Population

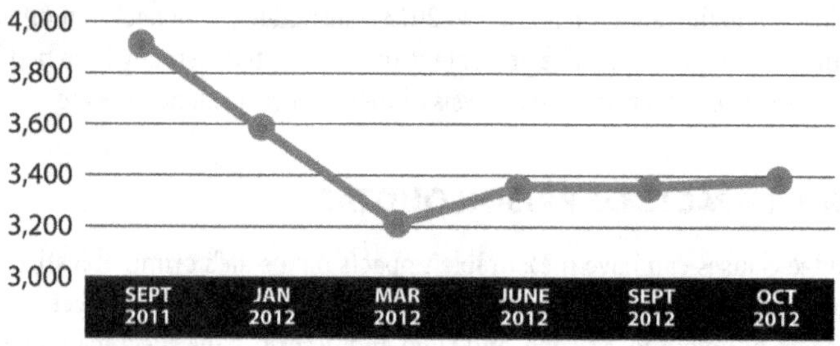

Source: Colorado Criminal Justice Reform Coalition, CO DOC monthly population reports

Colorado originally intended its private prisons to be used for overflow purposes, but the bed guarantee provisions allowed it to become the first priority for placement.

The chart on the previous page shows how the inmate population in CCA facilities decreased as state prison population also decreased until 2012, when the CCA inmate population increased, as a result of the bed guarantee deal.

Arizona

100% Bed Guarantees at Three Facilities

Private prison companies were successful in inserting the highest prison bed guarantee into contract amendments for the three oldest private prison facilities in Arizona: Arizona State Prison–Phoenix West and Arizona State Prison–Florence West, both operated by the GEO group; and the Marana Community Correctional Treatment Facility, operated by Management and Training Corporation (MTC). All three contracts require the state to fill or compensate the company for every available bed. The bed guarantee provisions were the result of an agreement between the Arizona Department of Corrections (ADC) and the private prison companies in 2008. In this "deal," the corporations agreed to lower rates for emergency beds meant to temporarily house an overflow of prisoners, in exchange for the state accepting a 100 percent occupancy guarantee for all regularly-rated beds in all three facilities. Even with the addition of the 100 percent bed guarantee clauses, an August 2012 analysis from Tucson Citizen shows that the per-prisoner, per-day rates for the three facilities have increased by an average of 13.9 percent since the contracts were first awarded. [22]

The details of the contract for the Marana facility reveal an even worse deal for Arizona taxpayers. Amendment 14, signed in June 2011, refers to a dispute between ADC and private prison company, MTC, in which the company claimed that the 5-year contract renewal was not performed in a timely manner. ADC maintained it was. The settlement for this dispute included ADC paying the company for 500 beds, including 50 which were identified as reduced-rate emergency beds, at the full per diem rate with the 100 percent guaranteed occupancy requirement. Incredibly, this agreement was applied retroactively, effectively erasing all but three months of the reduced rate for the emergency beds. The settlement results in an additional $2,659,390 in revenue to MTC through the remainder of the contract, which expires in October 2013.[23]

Despite MTC's guaranteed revenue, the Marana facility has been plagued by safety problems. In a security review in August 2010, state inspectors found broken security cameras, swamp coolers out of commission, insecure doors and windows on housing units, inadequate perimeter lighting, and broken control panels that failed to alert staff when inmates opened exterior doors. When inspectors returned in March 2011 to perform the annual audit, problems persisted, including broken security cameras and control panels.[24]

Arizona State Prison–Kingman

The Kingman facility, a prison with a 97 percent bed guarantee clause, has been troubled with pervasive safety issues, ultimately leading to the escape of three prisoners in July 2010 and the murder of a New Mexico couple. Among the security issues identified at the MTC-operated facility that allowed for the escape were: a broken alarm, burned-out perimeter lights, broken security equipment, and a lackadaisical approach to safety by the private prison staff, including ignoring alarms, leaving their patrol posts, and leaving doors open and unwatched.[25] After the escape, the state pulled 238 high-risk prisoners out of the facility and refused to send any additional prisoners to Kingman until MTC fixed the identified problems. It took MTC eleven months to address the issues, during which time ADC refused to pay the 97 percent bed guarantee. In January 2011, MTC filed a claim against ADC, complaining about the decrease in profits caused by the state's refusal to cover the empty beds. They asked for nearly $10 million to cover their losses. In another poor deal for Arizonans, ADC agreed to return to paying the 97 percent rate on May 1, 2011, even though the empty beds would not yet be filled, in exchange for MTC dropping its claim. ADC ended up paying over $3 million for the empty beds.[26]

Ohio

Ohio's experiences with prison privatization are plagued with stories of mismanagement, violence, and unexpected costs. Though crime rates in the state have been decreasing, the private prison industry continues to ensure that prisons remain as full as possible. In both the Lake Erie Correctional Institution and the North Coast Correctional Treatment Facility, bed guarantees have helped protect the private prison industry's profits.

Lake Erie Correctional Institution

The 2011 sale of the Lake Erie Correctional Institution in Conneaut, Ohio, to CCA was lauded by the private prison industry as an innovative cost-cutting move that would save the state of Ohio money, while improving the quality of services provided to inmates. A look at prison operations after the sale tells a very different story.

Bundled with the sale of the facility was a 20-year contract between the Ohio Department of Rehabilitation and Correction and CCA for operation of the prison. This contract includes a 90 percent bed guarantee clause, which holds Ohio, and ultimately its taxpayers, accountable for ensuring that 1,530 of the 1,700 available beds in the prison are occupied, or for compensating for unused beds. After purchasing the prison, CCA squeezed in an additional 300 beds, even converting an area where prisoner re-entry classes were held into sleeping space.[27] A November 2012 government audit found that the addition of the 300 beds brought the facility out of compliance with minimum square footage per inmate requirements.[28] The high occupancy requirement, especially when applied to a facility not originally designed for the additional 300 converted beds, has contributed to overcrowding, and the deplorable conditions and safety issues that persist in the facility.[29]

Multiple examples of unacceptable living conditions are described in a troubling government audit from September 2012.[30] The report describes a chronically overcrowded facility, with numerous cases of triple bunking, cramming three inmates into a cell designed for two, which left inmates sleeping on the floor, some without mattresses. Recreation areas without secure doors were used for housing inmates and minimum square footage per inmate requirements were not observed. Numerous other health and safety conditions were noted in the audit as well. The overcrowding and mismanagement of the Lake Erie Correctional Institution has led to numerous safety issues, including a rise in violent incidents and disturbances. Both staff and inmates interviewed for the audit reported that personal safety was at risk, and that "assaults, fights, disturbances, and uses of force have all increased in comparison to prior years."[31] Even the city of Conneaut has seen increased crime related to the issues at the prison, as drugs and other contraband materials thrown over the fence for inmates to retrieve have been reported.[32] The occupancy requirement not only creates perverse incentives to encourage the facility to keep as many "heads in beds," but does so at the expense of the health and safety of the inmates and the larger Conneaut community.

North Coast Correctional Treatment Facility

The privatization experiment at the North Coast Correctional Treatment Facility in Grafton, Ohio, also suffered as a result of bed guarantee requirements in its contract. In a 2000 contract between the OHDRC and the private prison company CiviGenics (now part of private prison company Community Education Centers), a 95 percent bed guarantee risked the safety of the facility. Originally intended to house primarily drunk-driving offenders, the bed guarantee ensured that even if the state of Ohio did not convict 665 persons of felony drunk driving offenses, they would pay CiviGenics for that level of operation in their 700-person facility. In an effort to fill North Coast to 95 percent capacity, the state sent inmates who had been convicted of more serious crimes, including sexual battery, assault, arson, manslaughter, and robbery, when it could not fill the facility with drunken-driving offenders.[33] The facility, designed to hold only felony drunken-driving and nonviolent drug offenders, was not properly equipped for these changes in the inmate population, and the facility suffered from riots, safety problems, and other contract violations, as well as unstable staffing, including four different people serving as warden.[34] Ultimately, the contract was taken from CiviGenics and given to another private prison company, Management Training Corporation, and later combined with the Grafton Correctional Institution and returned to public control.

As the three case studies show, these small contract clauses can have enormous ramifications. Bed guarantee clauses bind the state to pay for beds that they may not need or use at the time of contract signing or at any point in the future. Some prison contracts last for up to 20 years. It is virtually impossible for states to predict prison population trends for a few years forward, let alone decades into the future. The state loses flexibility to deal with changing circumstances that a public facility would afford. Furthermore, states may enact policies or engage in practices that keep prison facilities full, in an effort to fulfill bed occupancy guarantees. As the Ohio experience above shows, this can lead to facilities holding more dangerous inmates than they are designed to house. Or prisons may be filled beyond capacity, leaving a facility overcrowded and a breeding ground for violence. The cities in which these facilities are located may feel the effects of the increased violence, as drug use and gang activity overtake prisons and seep into the community.

If the state decides not to keep prison beds filled, bed guarantee clauses can wreak havoc on state budgets. Numerous examples show that these provisions can cost states millions of dollars. At a time when government budgets are shrinking, cities and states cannot afford the financial risk of prison privatization. In the long-term, governments, taxpayers, and communities cannot afford the damage that these provisions cause to the very foundations of our criminal justice system.

SECTION 4: RECOMMENDATIONS

Bed guarantee clauses can have broad negative implications for government entities, even beyond obvious financial concerns. As discussed in the report., these clauses can result in dangerously unsafe conditions, and tie the hands of lawmakers and correctional agencies. Our analysis leads to one clear conclusion: bed guarantee clauses should be prohibited in any private prison contract. We offer the following recommendations on ways to avoid the pitfalls that come with bed guarantees.

Governments Can and Should Reject Bed Guarantee Clauses

As ITPI's analysis shows, there are a number of private prison contracts without bed guarantee clauses. In our review of many Texas private prison contracts, we found that no contract contained a bed guarantee clause. The state's contracts with private prisons specifically state that the payment schedule is based on occupancy levels determined by the official count of the number of inmates who are present at the facility at the end of each day calculated at midnight (what Texas refers to as the "The Midnight Strength Report"). State and local governments should not agree to bed guarantee provisions during the initial contract signing or any subsequent amendment. Instead payments to the contractor should be based on the actual daily count of the number of inmates housed in a facility. Enacting state legislation that prohibits occupancy guarantee clauses allows the government contracting agency to take the discussion of these provisions out of the negotiating process, and reject them based on state law.

Prison occupancy quotas require the government to spend public dollars on housing and supervision of a certain number of inmates, whether a prison is empty or full. With governmental priorities pulling public funds in so many different directions, it makes no financial sense for taxpayers to fund empty prison beds. From a financial standpoint, bed guarantee clauses are insupportable for government entities.

Private prison companies often attempt to lure governments into agreements with bed guarantee clauses by promising a lower per diem cost. However, bed guarantees do not secure jurisdictions lower per diem rates, as evidenced by Arizona's experience of per diem rates rising 13.9 percent even after the bed guarantee was added to the contracts.[35] With better understanding of the per diem rates in private prison contracts in similar facilities in other jurisdictions, governments can negotiate reasonable per diem rates without resorting to bed guarantees.

Bed guarantee clauses can also tie the hands of lawmakers. If lawmakers determine that there are more effective ways of dealing with specific criminal offenses than prison time, bed guarantee clauses may restrict their options. If lawmakers pass rules that have the effect of decreasing the prison population, if law enforcement officials take action that results in a reduced prison population, or if the crime rate simply drops, the government might be responsible for funding empty prison beds. In the words of Roger Werholtz, former Kansas secretary of corrections, "My concern would be that our state would be obligated to maintain these (occupancy) rates and subtle pressure would be applied to make sentencing laws more severe with a clear intent to drive up the population."[36]

Furthermore, private corporations interested in running public prisons should be forced to run a competitive business in the open market. When entering a contract to operate a prison, a private company should be required to take on some risk. If the company fails to perform well, a bed guarantee clause should not serve as the company's financial safety net. In many cases, private prison beds were intended to be a safety valve to address demand that exceeded public capacity. It was never intended that taxpayers would be the safety valve to ensure private prison companies' profits.

Elimination of bed guarantee clauses will allow lawmakers to enact policies that are in the public interest, not in a private prison corporation's financial interest. Corrections agencies should not be forced to direct prisoners to certain private facilities because of bed guarantee clauses. Criminal justice policy and programs should be guided by our public goals, such as reducing the number of people in prison. Rejecting bed guarantee clauses allows public officials to make the best decisions in the public's interest.

APPENDIX

The following chart documents the privatized facilities identified by In the Public Interest, and includes information about which contracts ITPI received and which contracts contained occupancy guarantee clauses.

Facility	Company	Location	Customer	Have Contract?	Expiration Date (if known)	Occupancy Guarantee?
Hudson Correctional Facility	GEO	Hudson, CO	AK	Current	September 2013	Section 4.01 — 80% with exceptions for ramp-up or ramp-down or transportation dates
Arizona State Prison — Florence West	GEO	Florence, AZ	AZ		October 2017	100%
Arizona State Prison — Phoenix West	GEO	Phoenix, AZ	AZ	Current	July 2017	Amendments 7, 9, 11: 100% for emergency/ temporary beds
Central Arizona Correctional Facility	GEO	Florence, AZ	AZ		December 2016	
Arizona State Prison — Kingman	MTC	Kingman, AZ	AZ	Current		97% according to AFSC AZ, Amendment 2 — 90%
Marana Community Correctional Treatment Facility	MTC	Marana, AZ	AZ	Current		Amendment 9 — 100% for specified period
La Palma Correctional Center	CCA	Eloy, AZ	CA	Current	June 2013	Section 3.01 — 90%
North Fork Correctional Facility	CCA	Sayre, OK	CA	Current	June 2013	Section 3.01 — 90%
Tallahatchie County Correctional Facility	CCA	Tutwiler, MS	CA	Current	June 2013	Section 3.01 — 90%
Central Valley Modified Community Correctional Facility	GEO	McFarland, CA	CA	2012		Exhibit 6.14, Amendment 9 — 90%
Desert View Community Correctional Facility	GEO	Adelanto, CA	CA	2012		Exhibit A, G.7, Amendment 9 — 90%
Golden State Medium Community Correctional Facility	GEO	McFarland, CA	CA	Current	June 2016	Exhibit 6.14 — 90%
McFarland Community Correctional Facility	GEO	McFarland, CA	CA	2010		Exhibit B, 1.C — 70%
Red Rock Correctional Center	CCA	Eloy, AZ	CA/HI	Current CA portion	January 2024	Section 3.01 — 90%
Bent County Correctional Facility	CCA	Las Animas, CO	CO	Outdated	June 2013	Included in 2012/2013 budget, guarantee for 3,300 beds for all CCA facilities Contract: 2.1.1. "The State does not guarantee any minimum number of Offenders will be assigned to Contractor's Facility."
Crowley Correctional Facility	CCA	Olney Springs, CO	CO	Current	June 2013	Included in 2012/2013 budget, guarantee for 3,300 beds for all CCA facilities Contract: 2.1.1. "The State does not guarantee any minimum number of Offenders will be assigned to Contractor's Facility."
Correctional Treatment Facility	CCA	Washington, DC	DC			
Bay Correctional Facility	CCA	Panama City, FL	FL	Current	July 2013	p. 93, Section 7.1 — 90%
Graceville Correctional Facility	CCA	Graceville, FL	FL	Current	September 2013	Section 7.1 — 90%
Lake City Correctional Facility	CCA	Lake City, FL	FL	2009	Indefinite	Original contract, section 7 — 90%
Moore Haven Correctional Facility	CCA	Moore Haven, FL	FL	Current	July 2013	Section 7.1 — 90%
Citrus County Detention Facility	CCA	Lecanto, FL	Citrus County, FL	Current	September 2015	
Blackwater River Correctional Facility	GEO	Milton , FL	FL	Current	April 2013	Section 7.1 — 90%
South Bay Correctional Facility	GEO	South Bay, FL	FL	2009	July 2014	Article 7 — 90%
Gadsden Correctional Institution	MTC	Gadsden, FL	FL	Current		p. 98, 7.1 — 90%

continued

Facility	Company	Location	Customer	Have Contract?	Expiration Date (if known)	Occupancy Guarantee?
Coffee Correctional Facility	CCA	Nicholls, GA	GA	Current	June 2013	2011 amendment — 90%
Jenkins Correctional Center	CCA	Millen, GA	GA	Current		Original contract, p. 2, part 2B & 2013 amendment — 90%,
Wheeler Correctional Facility	CCA	Alamo, GA	GA	Current	June 2013	2011, 2012, 2013 amendments — 90%
Riverbend Correctional Facility	GEO	Milledgeville, GA	GA	Current	July 2013	Section — 90% guarantee
Saguaro Correctional Center	CCA	Eloy, AZ	HI		June 2014	
Idaho Correctional Center	CCA	Kuna, ID	ID	Current	June 2014	
Kit Carson Correctional Center	CCA	Burlington, CO	ID	Current	July 2014	Included in 2012-2013 budget, guarantee for 3,300 beds for all CCA facilities. Contract: 2.1.1. "The State does not guarantee any minimum number of Offenders will be assigned to Contractor's Facility."
Idaho Capp Facility	MTC	Kuna, ID	ID	Current		Section 3.2 — No guarantee for the first 6 months and then 80% (320/400 beds)
Marion County Jail II	CCA	Indianapolis, IN	IN		December 2017	
New Castle Correctional Facility	GEO	New Castle, IN	IN	Current	January 2015	Amendment 4 — 90%, also fixed monthly payments for annex
Plainfield Indiana STOP Facility	GEO	Plainfield, IN	IN	Current	March 2015	
Marion Adjustment Center	CCA	St. Mary, KY	KY		June 2013	
Winn Correctional Center	CCA	Winnfield, LA	LA	Current	June 2020	Section 3.1 — 96%
Allen Correctional Center	GEO	Kinder, LA	LA	Current	July 2020	Section 3.1 — 96%
Wilkinson County Correctional Facility	CCA	Woodville, MS	MS		June 2013	
East Mississippi Correctional Facility	MTC	Meridian, MS	MS			
Marshall County Correctional Facility	MTC	Holly Springs, MS	MS			
Walnut Grove Correctional Facility	MTC	Walnut Grove, MS	MS			
Crossroad Correctional Facility	CCA	Shelby, MT	MT		August 2013	
New Mexico Women's Correctional Facility	CCA	Grants, NM	NM	Current	June 2013	Section 4.1 — 580/611 (95%)
Guadalupe County Correctional Facility	GEO	Santa Rosa, NM	NM	Current		Section 4.1 — 90%
Lea County Correctional Facility	GEO	Hobbes, NM	NM	Current		Section 4.1 — 90%
Northeast New Mexico Detention Facility	GEO	Clayton, NM	NM	Current	August 2013	Daily credit for unoccupied beds during initial 60-day ramp-up period
Lake Erie Correctional Institution	CCA	Conneaut, OH	OH	Current	June 2032	Original contract w/ MTC, page 12 — 95%, more recent w/ CCA, noted in attachment 7, cost summary —90%
North Central Correctional Complex	MTC	Marion, OH	OH			
Cimarron Correctional Facility	CCA	Cushing, OK	OK	Current	June 2014	Original contract, Article 7, amndmt 5 & 6 — 98%
Davis Correctional Facility	CCA	Holdenville, OK	OK	Current	June 2014	Original contract, article 7, amndmts 5 & 6 — 98%
Lawton Correctional Facility	GEO	Lawton, OK	OK	Current	June 2013	Amendments 1 & 2, Article 7 — 98%

continued

Facility	Company	Location	Customer	Have Contract?	Expiration Date (if known)	Occupancy Guarantee?
Hardeman County Correctional Center	CCA	Whiteville, TN	TN		May 2015	
South Central Correctional Center	CCA	Clifton, TN	TN	2007		
Whiteville Correctional Facility	CCA	Whiteville, TN	TN		June 2016	
Metro-Davidson County Detention Facility	CCA	Nashville, TN	Davidson County, TN	Current	July 2014	Section 6.1 — 90%
Silverdale Detention Facilities	CCA	Chattanooga, TN	Hamilton County, TN			
Bartlett State Jail	CCA	Bartlett, TX	TX	Current	August 2013	
Bradshaw State Jail	CCA	Henderson, TX	TX	Current	August 2013	
Bridgeport Pre-Parole Transfer Facility	CCA	Bridgeport, TX	TX	Current	August 2013	
Dawson State Jail	CCA	Dallas, TX	TX	Current	August 2013	
Mineral Wells Pre-Parole Transfer Facility	CCA	Mineral Wells, TX	TX	Current	August 2013	
Willacy County State Jail	CCA	Raymondville, TX	TX	Current	August 2013	
Cleveland Correctional Center	GEO	Cleveland, TX	TX	Current	January 2014	
Lockhart Work Program Facility	GEO	Lockhart, TX	TX	2005	January 2013	
Lindsey State Jail	CCA	Jacksboro, TX	TX	Current	August 2013	
Billy Moore Correctional Center	MTC	Overton, TX	TX	Current		
Bridgeport Correctional Center	MTC	Bridgeport, TX	TX	Current		
Diboll Correctional Center	MTC	Diboll, TX	TX	2008		
East Texas Treatment Facility	MTC	Henderson, TX	TX	2005		
Kyle Correctional Center	MTC	Kyle, TX	TX	Current		
Sanders Estes Unit	MTC	Venus, TX	TX	2009		
South Texas Intermediate Sanction Facility	MTC	Houston, TX	TX	Current		
West Texas Intermediate Sanction Facility	MTC	Brownfield, TX	TX	Current		
Lawrenceville Correctional Center	GEO	Lawrenceville, VA	VA	Current		Original contract, Article.6.1.c — 1495 out of 1500 beds, 95%
Lee Adjustment Center	CCA	Beattyville, KY	VT	Current	June 2013	

NOTES

1. Chris Kirkham, "Private Prison Corporation Offers Cash in Exchange for State Prisons," *Huffington Post,* February 14, 2012. http://www.huffingtonpost.com/2012/02/14/private-prisons-buying-state-prisons_n_1272143.html.

2. American Friends Service Committee of Arizona, Cell-Out Arizona Exclusive, "Part II: Arizona For-Profit Prison Costs Rose 14%; Now Guarantee 100% Occupancy," August 3, 2012. http://tucsoncitizen.com/cell-out-arizona/2012/08/03/cell-out-arizona-exclusive-part-ii-arizona-for-profit-prison-costs-rose14-now-guarantee-100-occupancy/.

3. Kevin Johnson, "Private purchasing of prisons locks in occupancy rates," March 8, 2012. http://usatoday30.usatoday.com/news/nation/story/2012-03-01/buyingprisons-require-high-occupancy/53402894/1.

4. A Sept. 2010 report by Arizona's Office of the Auditor General found that privately-operated prisons housing minimum-security state prisoners actually cost $.33 per diem more than state prisons ($46.81 per diem in state prisons vs. $47.14 in private prisons), while private prisons that house medium-security state prisoners cost $7.76 per diem more than state facilities ($48.13 per diem in state prisons vs. $55.89 in private prisons), after adjusting for comparable costs. See: http://www.azauditor.gov/Reports/State_Agencies/Agencies/Corrections_Department_of/Performance/10-08/10-08.pdf.

5. Dina Rasor, "Prison Industries: Don't Let Society Improve or We Lose Business," *Truthout,* April 26, 2013. https://truth-out.org/news/item/8731-prison-industries-dontlet-society-improve-or-we-lose-business-part-i.

6. Laura Sullivan, "Prison Economics Help Drive Ariz. Immigration Law," National Public Radio, October 28, 2010. http://www.npr.org/2010/10/28/130833741/prison-economics-help-drive-ariz-immigration-law.

7. CCA's 2010 Annual Report on Form 10-K.

8. Center for Responsive Politics, http://www.opensecrets.org/lobby/clientsum.php?id=D000021940&year=2002.

9. Center for Responsive Politics, http://www.opensecrets.org/lobby/clientsum.php?id=D000022003&year=2004.

10. National Institute on Money in State Politics, http://www.followthemoney.org/database/topcontributor.phtml?u=695&y=0.

11. National Institute on Money in State Politics, http://www.followthemoney.org/database/topcontributor.phtml?u=1096&y=0.

12. Nicole Flatow, "Private Prison Profits Skyrocket, as Executives Assure Investors of 'Growing Offender Population,'" *Think Progress,* May 9, 2013. http://thinkprogress.org/justice/2013/05/09/1990331/private-prison-profits-skyrocket-as-executives-assure-investors-of-growing-offender-population/.

13. CCA's 2010 Annual Report on Form 10-K, page 10.

14. Colorado WINS, "Imprisoned by Profit: Breaking Colorado's Dependency on For-Profit Prisons, February, 27, 2013. http://coloradowins.org/2013/02/27/imprisoned-by-profit-breaking-colorados-dependence-on-for-profit-prisons/.

15. Ann Imse, "State pays millions as prison populations sink," *Colorado Springs Gazette,* March 9, 2013. http://gazette.com/state-pays-millions-as-prison-populations-sink/article/152065.

16. Ibid.

17. Ibid.

18. Colorado Criminal Justice Reform Coalition, "Prison population update and overview," December 3, 2012.

19. Ann Imse, "State pays millions as prison populations sink," *Colorado Springs Gazette,* March 9, 2013. http://gazette.com/state-pays-millions-as-prison-populations-sink/article/152065.

20. Ann Imse, "State pays millions as prison populations sink," *Colorado Springs Gazette,* March 9, 2013. http://gazette.com/state-pays-millions-as-prison-populations-sink/article/152065

21. Ann Imse, "State pays millions as prison populations sink," *Colorado Springs Gazette,* March 9, 2013. http://gazette.com/state-pays-millions-as-prison-populations-sink/article/152065.

22. American Friends Service Committee of Arizona, Cell-Out Arizona Exclusive, "Part II: Arizona For-Profit Prison Costs Rose 14%; Now Guarantee 100% Occupancy," August 3, 2012. http://tucsoncitizen.com/cell-out-arizona/2012/08/03/cell-out-arizona-exclusive-part-ii-arizona-for-profit-prison-costs-rose14-now-guarantee-100-occupancy/.

23. American Friends Service Committee of Arizona, Cell-Out Arizona Exclusive, "Part II: Arizona For-Profit Prison Costs Rose 14%; Now Guarantee 100% Occupancy," August 3, 2012. http://tucsoncitizen.com/cell-out-arizona/2012/08/03/cell-out-arizona-exclusive-part-ii-arizona-for-profit-prison-costs-rose14-now-guarantee-100-occupancy/.

24. Bob Ortega, "2010 escape at Kingman an issue for MTC's bid," *The Arizona Republic,* August 11, 2011. http://www.azcentral.com/news/articles/2011/08/11/20110811MTC-bid-issue-2010-escape-at-kingman.html.

25. Bob Ortega, "Arizona prisons slow to fix flaws in wake of Kingman escape," *The Arizona Republic,* June 26, 2011. http://www.azcentral.com/news/articles/2011/06/26/20110626 arizona-prison-safety-improvements.html.

26. Bob Ortega, "Arizona prison oversight lacking for private facilities: state weighs expansion even as costs run high," *The Arizona Republic,* August 7 ,2011. http://www .azcentral.com/news/articles/20110807arizona-prison-private-oversight.html.

27. Chris Kirkham, "Lake Erie Prison Plagued by Violence and Drugs After Corporate Take-over," *Huffington Post,* March 22, 2013. http://www.huffingtonpost.com/2013/03/22/lake-erie-prison-violence_n_2925151.html.

28. Ohio Department of Rehabilitation and Correction, 2012 Full Internal Management Audit Report, September 25, 2012. http://www.inthepublicinterest.org/sites/default/files/prison-audit-report%20OHIO.pdf.

29. The ACLU Ohio continues to monitor the conditions at the Lake Erie Correctional Institution. In May 2013, they released a timeline chronicling problems at the facility, which can be found at http://www.acluohio.org/crisis-in-conneaut-timeline.

30. Ohio Department of Rehabilitation and Correction, LaECI Audit Reinspection, November 15, 2012. http://big.assets.huffingtonpost.com/ccareinspection.pdf.

31. Gregory Geisler, Correctional Institution Inspection Committee Report on the Inspection and Evaluation of the Lake Erin Correctional Institution, January 22–23, 2013. http://big.assets.huffingtonpost.com/lakeeriereport.pdf.

32. Chris Kirkham, "Lake Erie Prison Plagued by Violence and Drugs After Corporate Takeover," *Huffington Post,* March 22, 2013. http://www.huffingtonpost.com/2013/03/22/lake-erie-prison-violence_n_2925151.html.

33. ACLU Ohio, "Prisons for Profit: A Look at Prison Privatization." http://www.acluohio.org/assets/issues/CriminalJustice/PrisonsForProfit2011_04.pdf.

34. Policy Matters Ohio, "Selective Celling: Inmate Population in Ohio's Private Prisons" May 2001. http://www.policymattersohio.org/selective-celling-inmate-population-in-ohios-private-prisons.

35. American Friends Service Committee of Arizona, Cell-Out Arizona Exclusive, "Part II: Arizona For-Profit Prison Costs Rose 14%; Now Guarantee 100% Occupancy," August 3, 2012. http://tucsoncitizen.com/cell-out-arizona/2012/08/03/cell-out-arizona-exclusive-part-ii-arizona-for-profit-prison-costs-rose14-now-guarantee-100-occupancy/.

36. Kevin Johnson, "Private purchasing of prisons locks in occupancy rates," March 8, 2012. http://usatoday30.usatoday.com/news/nation/story/2012-03-01/buying-prisons-require-high-occupancy/53402894/1.

CRITICAL THINKING QUESTIONS

1. Summarize what happened at both the Lake Erie correctional institution and the North Coast Correctional Treatment Facility. Describe how for-profit prisons led directly to the situation at each prison.

2. Explain the contractual obligation that the state of Arizona has regarding the prison bed guarantee. What are your thoughts about such a contractual agreement? What are the implications for current and future prisoners in Arizona? How could this agreement affect law enforcement or new laws that may be considered in the state?

3. Why are quotas important to the for-profit private-prison-company business model, according to this article? Why do these quotas run counter to the state's public policy goals?

4. Discuss whether or not you think that, "Governments can and should reject bed guarantee clauses." Supply at least one reason for states to use private prisons. Then explain and evaluate the claim that bed guarantees don't assist the public, but support "prison corporation's private interests."

HOW LACK OF POLICE TRAINING CAN BE DEADLY FOR THE MENTALLY ILL

by Aaron Ernst

Aaron Ernst is an independent producer and multimedia journalist reporting on current and international affairs. Ernst has written numerous articles for *Al Jazeera America.*

In this 2014 article from *Al Jazeera America,* Aaron Ernst writes that police are struggling to deal with the mentally ill. Due to shrinking health budgets, veterans returning from combat, and a growing population, police encounters with the mentally ill are becoming more and more common. Programs are available that can help train police officers, keep them safe, and save lives. Why aren't they more widespread?

• • • • • • • • • • • • • • •

Fifty percent of Americans killed by the police every year are mentally ill; how do we change that?

In the mornings, Keith Vidal-Wilsey would ask his mom if she wanted a cup of hot chocolate. Every night, he would tell her he loved her. He liked banging out hard rock riffs on his drum kit, and enjoyed when it snowed. He was also schizophrenic.

On one occasion, Keith tried to hurt himself. He tried to drink bleach and then wrapped a vacuum cord around his neck. With the help of local police, his mother, Mary Wilsey, got her son to the hospital for treatment. And she wanted to do the same earlier this year.

On Jan. 5, Keith had picked up a small screwdriver and was scaring her. She asked her husband to call 911. Two officers arrived, she said, and started calmly speaking with the 18-year-old. Then, she said a third officer from another police force showed up and escalated the situation, which quickly spiraled out of control. Less than a minute later, Keith had been tased and was struggling with the first two officers to arrive.

"Then, I heard the gun go off and saw my son start bleeding," she said.

The third officer, Bryon Vassey of the Southport Police Department, had shot her son. Keith died in an ambulance on the way to the hospital. Vassey was indicted for voluntary manslaughter. His attorney said his client had to make a split-second decision and was protecting the lives of the other officers.

"When a child gets killed, you not only grieve for their loss, but you also grieve for everything that should have happened," said Wilsey, explaining through tears that she'll never see her son graduate, or get married. "What ended up happening is my son ended up dead because this individual was not trained to handle a mentally ill person."

POLICE BECOME PROVIDERS

According to experts, conventional police training can actually inflame encounters with the mentally ill.

In March, police confronted a homeless man named James Boyd, who was illegally camping in the New Mexico foothills. A helmet camera video released by the police department showed Boyd picking up his belongings when an officer hit him with a flash-bang device, which was followed by screams of "Get on the ground." Then, Boyd pulled out a knife, and the police fired multiple rounds at him. He was pronounced dead the next day.

"Traditional law enforcement tactics are rooted in logic, in reasoning—and in issuing commands for someone to comply so that we can make the situation safe right now by taking a person into custody," said Douglas County Police Capt. Attila Denes, who has spent much of his career in the Douglas County Sheriff's Office in Colorado trying to improve police interaction with the mentally ill. "But barking orders at a person with serious mental illness doesn't work."

And encounters between the police and the people with mental illness have been rising. In the last few decades, mental health hospitals have shuttered and services have been slashed, leaving more of the mentally ill without support and places for treatment. Prisons are now home to 10 times more mentally ill Americans than state psychiatric hospitals. And at least half of the people shot and killed by police in the U.S. every year have mental health problems, according to a 2013 report by the National Sheriffs' Association.

A DIFFERENT APPROACH

WHOA WHOA WHOA WHOA! WHAT THE F**K ARE YOU DOING!?

RELAX, RELAX, RELAX.

I AM RELAXED! YOU RELAX! WHO THE F**K ARE YOU?

ARE YOU OK?

Role-playing is a key part of crisis intervention team training or CIT, in which officers are taught how to better identify and interact with the mentally ill. At this 40-hour training in Colorado, an actor plays a person with mental health problems, and the police officers take what they've learned in class—how to pick up on the signals, how to react—and try to implement them in the heat of the moment.

"Oh, they're very realistic," said Mike Hanifan, an officer in the training. "During one of the scenarios you can actually feel the sweat dripping down inside your shirt, because you put yourself in that situation."

Half of the state's police officers are now trained in the approach, and it seems to be working. Colorado deploys fewer SWAT teams and saves money by diverting the mentally ill from prisons, according to 10 years of data, collected in cooperation with Harvard Medical School, which hasn't yet been published. Nationwide, CIT officers are injured 80 percent less than untrained officers in interactions with the mentally ill.

Officer Chad Walker said the training has clearly helped him in real-life situations, like when he got a call about a 10-year-old with autism, who had a knife.

"He looked at us and started walking toward us with the knife in his hands," Walker recounted. "We knew this person by name, called him by his first name, asked him how he was feeling. And he dropped the knife, and came to us and started listening to us."

But despite this proven track record, only 10 percent of the nation's 25,000 police departments require crisis intervention training. In North Carolina, where Keith was killed, only one in five officers receive the training.

KEITH'S LAW

"That's the kind of training I would like for all my officers to have—at some point," said Montrina Sutton, the chief of police in Burgaw, N.C., a small town a few dozen miles away from where Keith was shot. "But because of my small agency and I have a small budget, it makes it really hard."

Sutton said she's noticed that more veterans are returning to town with mental health issues, and that the officers have to deal with that "the best way we know how."

But she's deeply concerned about the lack of formal training. "That's just like if I am not able to send an officer to the range to learn how to use his weapon," she said. "And if he gets into a situation where he needs to use it, but he didn't know how because he's not trained."

After Keith's death, in lieu of CIT, Sutton's department started a program called Special Awareness Verification Enrollment, or S.A.V.E. Residents can register with the police any household member with a mental illness, and an officer who is dispatched to that home then receives that background information before he or she arrives on scene.

Since her son's death, Mary Wilsey has become a fierce advocate of CIT.

"What happened in my home that day, I felt there was people that were not qualified to handle a mentally ill person," she said. "And if you're not qualified, what the heck are you doing in my home? Get out. You should not be here."

She submitted a proposal for a bill to her state representative called Keith's Law, which would make CIT mandatory for all officers in North Carolina. She called it "common sense."

"Train them so they can handle the population that they deal with every day," she said. "My goal is to prevent another family from going through a terrible tragedy that has ruined our lives."

For Wilsey, she plans on lobbying for the bill for as long as it takes until it's passed.

"And then, I'm going to I'm going to Virginia," she said. "And I'm going to Maryland. And then, I'm going anywhere I can go and get anybody I can to listen to me."

CRITICAL THINKING QUESTIONS

1. Discuss the situation that occurred during Keith Vidal-Wisley's arrest. The author claims that Byron Vassey failed in this situation because he was trained in "traditional law enforcement tactics." Why weren't these effective with Vidal-Wisley? How does his mother plan to address these shortcomings in policing?

2. What is the reason the author gives for the criminal justice system having many more encounters, both in law enforcement and in prisons, with the mentally ill? What did the 2013 National Sheriffs' Association's report find about how these situations are handled? Do these facts confirm or challenge your thinking about police?

3. What is the CIT program? Summarize the findings from the Harvard Medical School. How could CIT training have changed the last few moments of Keith Vidal-Wilsey's life? Why is this training not more common?

4. **Connection.** The author writes that, "prisons are now home to ten times more mentally ill Americans than state psychiatric hospitals." One could argue that instead of treating mentally ill people, like Keith Vidal-Wisley, we have criminalized their behavior. What would Vicky Pelaez, author of "The Prison Industry in the United States" say about this? Why would she argue that we have decided it is better to put the mentally ill in prisons than in hospitals?

CITATIONS FOR INCLUDED WORKS

Alesia, M. (2014, March 27). NCAA approaching $1 billion per year amid challenges by players. *INDYStar.* Retrieved from http://www.indystar.com/story/news/2014/03/27/ncaa-approaching-billion-per-year-amid-challenges-players/6973767/.

Alvarez, L. (2014, November 9). States listen as parents give rampant testing an F. *The New York Times.* Retrieved from http://www.nytimes.com/2014/11/10/us/states-listen-as-parents-give-rampant-testing-an-f.html?emc=edit_th_20141110&nl=todaysheadlines&nlid=62218720&_r=1.

Armstrong, K. (2014, November 15). Death by deadline, part one. T*he Marshall Project.* Retrieved from https://www.themarshallproject.org/2014/11/15/death-by-deadline-part-one.

Armstrong, K. (2014, November 16). Death by deadline, part two. *The Marshall Project.* Retrieved from https://www.themarshallproject.org/2014/11/16/death-by-deadline-part-two.

American Psychological Association. (2007, June 26). The effects of television violence on children. *American Psychological Association.* Retrieved from http://www.apa.org/about/gr/pi/advocacy/2008/kunkel-tv.aspx.

Anyon, J. 1980. "Social Class and the Hidden Curriculum of Work." *Journal of Education* 162 (1): 67–92.

Baptiste, N. (2014, October 14). Them that's got shall get. *The American Prospect Longform.* Retrieved from http://prospect.org/article/staggering-loss-black-wealth-due-subprime-scandal-continues-unabated.

Bazelon, E. (2013, February 20). How to stop the bullies. *The Atlantic.* Retrieved from http://www.theatlantic.com/magazine/archive/2013/03/how-to-stop-bullies/309217/.

Berlatsky, N. (2014, August 5). Martson, gender identity and casting the modern Wonder Woman. *Comic Book Resources.* Retrieved from http://www.comicbookresources.com/?page=article&id=54596.

Bernstein, J. (2014, March 12). The growing transgender presence in popular culture. *The New York Times.* Retrieved from http://www.nytimes.com/2014/03/13/fashion/the-growing-transgender-presence-in-pop-culture.html.

Bittman, M., Pollan, M., Salvador, R., & De Schutter, O. (2014, November 7). How a national food policy could save millions of American lives. *The Washington Post.* Retrieved from http://www.washingtonpost.com/opinions/how-a-national-food-policy-could-save-millions-of-american-lives/2014/11/07/89c55e16-637f-11e4-836c-83bc4f26eb67_story.html.

Buni, C. & Chemaly, S. (2014, October 9). The unsafety net: How social media turned against women. *The Atlantic.* Retrieved from http://m.theatlantic.com/technology/archive/2014/10/the-unsafety-net-how-social-media-turned-against-women/381261/.

Cain Miller, C. (2014, April 5). Technology's man problem. *The New York Times.* Retrieved from http://www.nytimes.com/2014/04/06/technology/technologys-man-problem.html.

Caramanica, J. (2014, November 21). Put me on tv. I'll change. I swear. *The New York Times.* Retrieved from http://www.nytimes.com/2014/11/23/arts/television/new-starts-on-live-free-or-die-survivor-and-utopia.html.

Casella, J. & Ridgeway, J. (2014, November 30). What death penalty opponents don't get. *The Marshall Project.* Retrieved from https://www.themarshallproject.org/2014/11/30/what-death-penalty-opponents-don-t-get?utm_medium=homepage&utm_campaign=site-placement&utm_source=featured-block&utm_content=3-112.

Coates, T. (2014, June). The case for reparations. *The Atlantic.* Retrieved from http://www.theatlantic.com/features/archive/2014/05/the-case-for-reparations/361631/.

Darling-Hammond, L. 1998. "Unequal opportunity race and education." *The Brookings Review* 28–32.

Edwards, D. (2014, October 17). American schools are training kids for a world that doesn't exist. *Wired.* Retrieved from http://www.wired.com/2014/10/on-learning-by-doing.

Ernst, A. (2014, April 21). How lack of police training can be deadly for the mentally ill. *Aljazeera America.* Retrieved from http://america.aljazeera.com/watch/shows/america-tonight/articles/2014/4/23/how-traditional-policinghurtsaandsometimeskillsathementallyill.html.

Fallon, S. (2012, February 10). Dirty secrets of the food processing industry. *Food Matters.* Retrieved from http://www.foodmatters.tv/articles-1/dirty-secrets-of-the-food-processing-industry.

Freed, B. (2014, October 10). Vox is the Carmelo Anthony of bad pop-culture metaphors. *Washingtonian.* Retrieved from http://www.washingtonian.com/blogs/capitalcomment/media/vox-is-the-carmelo-anthony-of-bad-pop-culture-metaphors.php.

Freedman, D. (2013, June 19). How junk food can end obesity. *The Atlantic.* Retrieved from http://www.theatlantic.com/magazine/archive/2013/07/how-junk-food-can-end-obesity/309396/.

Fry, R., Kochnar, R. & Taylor, P. (2011, July 26). Wealth gaps rise to record highs between Whites, Blacks, Hispanics. *Pew Research Social and Demographic Trends.* Retrieved from http://www.pewsocialtrends.org/2011/07/26/wealth-gaps-rise-to-record-highs-between-whites-blacks-hispanics/.

Gasper, C. (2014, April 15). NCAA must adapt or move aside. *The Boston Globe.* Retrieved from http://www.bostonglobe.com/sports/2014/04/14/ncaa-can-have-both-ways/NwEJwcM8oFDseuyFWi1b3K/story.html.

Gatto, J. (2003). *Against School.* Retrieved from http://www.wesjones.com/gatto1.htm.

Gaus, A. (2014, December 1). A female writers new milestone: Her first death threat. *The Daily Beast.* Retrieved from http://www.thedailybeast.com/articles/2014/12/01/a-female-writer-s-new-milestone-her-first-death-threat.html?via=desktop&source=twitter.

Grann, D. (2009, September 7). Trial by fire. *The New Yorker.* Retrieved from http://www.newyorker.com/magazine/2009/09/07/trial-by-fire.

Hannah-Jones, N. (2014, April 16). Segregation now. *ProPublica.* Retrieved from http://www.propublica.org/article/segregation-now-full-text.

Hess, A. (2014, January 6).Why women aren't welcome on the Internet. *Pacific Standard.* Retrieved from http://www.psmag.com/navigation/health-and-behavior/women-arent-welcome-internet-72170/.

Hoagland, E. (2002, July 3). 1776 and all that. *The Nation.* Retrieved from http://www.thenation.com/article/1776-and-all#.

In the Public Interest. (2013, September). Criminal: How lockup quotas and "low crime taxes" guarantee profits for private prison corporations. *In the Public Interest.* Retrieved from http://www.inthepublicinterest.org/sites/default/files/Criminal-Lockup%20Quota-Report.pdf.

Jenkins, S. (2013, July 31). How to rid Twitter of misogyny—and make it fit for debate. *The Guardian.* Retrieved from http://www.motherjones.com/media/2014/04/open-internet-closed-to-women.

Kenny, P. (2013, August 20). Is obesity an addiction? *Scientific American.* http://www.scientificamerican.com/article/is-obesity-an-addiction/.

Kingkade, T. (2014, April 13). People are making a lot of money in college sports, just not the athletes. *Huffington Post.* Retrieved from http://www.huffingtonpost.com/2014/04/13/college-athletes-coaches-salaries_n_5079590.html.

Lapowsky, I. (2014, July 28). This is what tech's ugly gender problem really looks like. *WIRED.* Retrieved from http://www.wired.com/2014/07/gender-gap/.

Madden, V. (2014, September 21). Why poor students struggle. *The New York Times.* Retrieved from http://www.nytimes.com/2014/09/22/opinion/why-poor-students-struggle.html?_r=0.

McMillan, T. (2014, September 1). Gap in diet quality between wealthiest and poorest Americans doubles, study finds. *National Geographic.* Retrieved from http://news.nationalgeographic.com/news/2014/09/140901-american-diet-obesity-poor-food-health/.

Nelson, M. (2014, February 7). America's game. *The Claremont Institute.* Retrieved from http://www.claremont.org/article/americas-game/#.VJRxzsAOC.

Pelaez, V. (2014, March 31). The prison industry in the United States: Big business or a new form of slavery? *Global Research.* Retrieved from http://www.globalresearch.ca/the-prison-industry-in-the-united-states-big-business-or-a-new-form-of-slavery/8289.

Rich, M. (2014, November 10). U.S. to focus on equity in assigning of teachers. *The New York Times.* Retrieved from http://www.nytimes.com/2014/11/11/us/obama-administration-puts-new-focus-on-equity-in-teacher-quality.html?emc=edit_tnt_20141110&nlid=62218720&tntemail0=y&_r=0.

Schlosser, E. (2012, March 3). Still a fast food nation: Eric Schlosser reflects on 10 years later. *The Daily Beast.* Retrieved from http://www.thedailybeast.com/articles/2012/03/12/still-a-fast-food-nation-eric-schlosser-reflects-on-10-years-later.html.

Sen, A. (2001, November 23). A world not neatly divided. *The New York Times.* Retrieved from http://www.nytimes.com/2001/11/23/opinion/a-world-not-neatly-divided.html.

Starkey, B. (2014, October 31). College sports aren't like slavery. They're like Jim Crow. *New Republic.* Retrieved from http://www.newrepublic.com/article/120071/ncaa-college-sports-arent-slavery-theyre-jim-crow.

Sternbergh, A. (2013, September 9). What was, is and will be popular: The driving forces of popular culture. *The New York Times.* Retrieved from http://www.nytimes.com/interactive/2013/09/08/magazine/the-culture-package.html?_r=1&#/#item_14.

Storrs, C. (2011, January 31). Hormones in food: Should you worry? *The Huffington Post.* Retrieved from http://www.huffingtonpost.com/2011/01/31/hormones-in-food-should-y_n_815385.html.

Stucki, B. (2014, June 10). Breaking the school-to-prison pipeline: Rethinking 'zero tolerance.' *The American Prospect.* Retrieved from http://prospect.org/article/breaking-school-prison-pipeline-rethinking-zero-tolerance.

Suggs, D. (2012). *Myth: College sports are a cash cow.* Retrieved from http://www.acenet.edu/news-room/Pages/Myth-College-Sports-Are-a-Cash-Cow2.aspx.

Tavernise, S. (2012, February 9). Education gap grows between rich and poor, studies say. *The New York Times.* Retrieved from http://www.nytimes.com/2012/02/10/education/education-gap-grows-between-rich-and-poor-studies-show.html?pagewanted=all.

Taylor, A. (2014, April 10). How the cult of Internet openness enables misogyny. *Mother Jones.* Retrieved from http://www.motherjones.com/media/2014/04/open-internet-closed-to-women.

The Pew Research Center. (2012, June 19). The rise of Asian Americans. *Pew Research Social and Demographic Trends.* Retrieved from http://www.pewsocialtrends.org/2012/06/19/the-rise-of-asian-americans/.

Vittachi, N. (2014, October, 14). Hong Kong's pop culture of protest. *The New York Times.* Retrieved from http://www.nytimes.com/2014/10/15/opinion/hong-kongs-pop-culture-of-protest.html.

Wenner Moyer, M. (2014). Organic shmorganic. *Slate.* Retrieved from http://www.slate.com/articles/double_x/the_kids/2014/01/organic_vs_conventional_produce_for_kids_you_don_t_need_to_fear_pesticides.html.

Wiley-Little, A. (2014, January 9). How economic inclusion can lead to success. *National Journal.* Retrieved from http://www.nationaljournal.com/next-america/perspectives/how-economic-inclusion-can-lead-to-success-20140109.

TELEVISION AND CHILDREN REFERENCES

American Academy of Pediatrics, Committee on Public Education. Media education. Pediatrics. 1999 Aug;104(2 Pt 1):341-3. Available at: http://aappolicy.aappublications.org/cgi/content/full/pediatrics;104/2/341.

American Academy of Pediatrics, Committee on Public Education. Media violence. Pediatrics. 2001 Nov;108(5):1222-6.

American Academy of Pediatrics, Committee on Public Education. Media violence. Pediatrics. 2001 Nov;108(5):1222-6. Available at: http://aappolicy.aappublications.org/cgi/content/full/pediatrics;108/5/1222.

American Academy of Pediatrics. Television—what children see and learn. Available at: http://www.aap.org/pubed/ZZZNKWJGQ2D.htm?&sub_cat=1. Accessed 11 November 2009.

American Medical Association. Brain Damage Risks. Available from: http://www.ama-assn.org/ama/no-index/physician-resources/9416.shtml. Accessed 30 June 2010.

Bartsch RA, Burnett T, Diller TR, Rankin-Williams E. Gender representation in television commercials: updating an update. Sex Roles. 2000 Nov;43(9/10);735-43.

Bickham DS, Rich M. Is television viewing associated with social isolation? Roles of exposure time, viewing context, and violent content. Arch Pediatr Adolesc Med. 2006 Apr;160(4):387-92.

Bushman & Anderson, 2009.

Bushman BJ, Anderson, CA. Comfortably numb: desensitizing effects of violent media on helping others. Psychological Science. 2009 21(3):273-277.

Caballero B. Obesity prevention in children: opportunities and challenges. Int J Obes Relat Metab Disord. 2004 Nov;28 Suppl 3:S90-5.

Canto J. Mommy, I'm Scared: How TV and Movies Frighten Children and What We Can Do to Protect Them. San Diego: Harcourt Brace;1998.

Center on Alcohol Marketing and Youth. Alcohol advertising on television, 2001 to 2003: more of the same. Executive Summary. Available at: http://camy.org/research/tv1004/report.pdf. Accessed 20 July 2009.

Center on Alcohol Marketing and Youth. Youth exposure to alcohol advertising on television, 2001 to 2007. Available at: http://www.camy.org/research/tv0608/tv0608.pdf. Accessed 20 July 2009.

Chandra A, Martino SC, Collins RL, Elliott MN, Berry SH, Kanouse DE, Miu A. Does watching sex on television predict teen pregnancy? Findings from a national longitudinal survey of youth. Pediatrics. 2008 Nov;122(5):1047-54.

Children Now. The local television news media' s picture of children. October 2001.

Collins RL, Elliott MN, Berry SH, Kanouse DE, Kunkel D, Hunter SB, Miu A. Watching sex on television predicts adolescent initiation of sexual behavior. Pediatrics. 2004 Sep;114(3):e280-9.

Coltrane S, Messineo M. The perpetuation of subtle prejudice: race and gender imagery in 1990s television advertising. Sex Roles. 2000 Mar;42(5/6):363-89.

Cummings KM, Morley CP, Horan JK, Steger C, Leavell NR. Marketing to America's youth: evidence from corporate documents. Tob Control. 2002 Mar;11 Suppl 1:I5-17.

Dal Cin S, Gibson B, Zanna MP, Shumate R, Fong GT. Smoking in movies, implicit associations of smoking with the self, and intentions to smoke. Psychological Science. 2007 18:559-563.

Dal Cin S, Worth KA, Gerrard M, Gibbons FX, Sargent JD. Watching and drinking: expectancies, prototypes, and peer affiliations mediate the effect of exposure to alcohol use in movies on adolescent drinking. Health Psychology. 2009 28:473-83.

Federman, 1998.
Federman J, ed. National Television Violence Study. Vol 3. Thousand Oaks, CA: Sage; 1998.
Fouts GT, Burggraf KK. Television situation comedies: Female weight, male negative comments, and audience reactions. Sex Roles. 2000 May;42(9/10):925-32.
Gutschoven K, Van den Bulck J. Television viewing and age at smoking initiation: does a relationship exist between higher levels of television viewing and earlier onset of smoking? Nicotine Tob Res. 2005 Jun;7(3):381-5.
Hancox RJ, Milne BJ, Poulton R. Association between child and adolescent television viewing and adult health: a longitudinal birth cohort study. Lancet 2004; 364:257-262.
Hancox RJ, Milne BJ, Poulton R. Association of television viewing during childhood with poor educational achievement. Arch Pediatr Adolesc Med. 2005 Jul;159(7):614-8.
Huesmann LR, Moise-Titus J, Podolski CL, Eron LD. Longitudinal relations between children's exposure to TV violence and their aggressive and violent behavior in young adulthood: 1977-1992. Dev Psychol. 2003 Mar;39(2):201-21.
Jago R, Baranowski T, Baranowski JC, Thompson D, Greaves KA. BMI from 3-6 y of age is predicted by TV viewing and physical activity, not diet. Int J Obes (Lond). 2005 Jun;29(6):557-64.
Jernigan DH, Ostorff CR. Alcohol advertising and youth: a measured approach. Journal of Public Health Policy 2005;26:312-325.
Johnson JG, Cohen P, Kasen S, First MB, Brook JS. Association between television viewing and sleep problems during adolescence and early adulthood. Arch Pediatr Adolesc Med. 2004 Jun;158(6):562-8.
Johnson JG, Cohen P, Smailes EM, Kasen S, Brook JS. Television viewing and aggressive behavior during adolescence and adulthood. Science. 2002 Mar 29;295(5564):2468-71.
Kelly, Smith, 2006.
Kelly J, Smith, SL. G movies give boys a D: portraying males as dominant, disconnected and dangerous. See Jane Program at Dads and Daughters. May 2006.
Klesges RC, Shelton ML, Klesges LM. Effects of television on metabolic rate: potential implications for childhood obesity. Pediatrics. 1993 Feb;91(2):281-6.
Kunkel D, Eyal K, Finnerty K, Biely E, Donnerstein E. Sex on TV. Kaiser Family Foundation. November 2005.
Lumeng JC, Rahnama S, Appugliese D, Kaciroti N, Bradley RH. Television exposure and overweight risk in preschoolers. Arch Pediatr Adolesc Med. 2006 Apr;160(4):417-22.
Manganello JA, Taylor CA. Television exposure as a risk factor for aggressive behavior among 3-year-old children. Arch Pediatr Adolesc Med. 2009 Nov;163(11):1037-45.
McDonough P. TV viewing among kids at an eight-year high. Nielsenwire. October 26, 2009. Available at: http://blog.nielsen.com/nielsenwire/media_entertainment/tv-viewing-among-kids-at-an-eight-year-high/. Accessed 11 November 2009.
McGinnis JM, Gootman JA, Kraak VI, eds. Food marketing to children and youth: threat or opportunity? Washington, D.C.: National Academy Press; 2006.
Mekemson C, Glantz SA. How the tobacco industry built its relationship with Hollywood. Tob Control. 2002 Mar;11 Suppl 1:I81-91.
Mok TA. Getting the message: media images and stereotypes and their effect on Asian Americans. Cult Divers Ment Health. 1998;4(3):185-202.
Rich M, Woods ER, Goodman E, Emans SJ, DuRant RH. Aggressors or victims: gender and race in music video violence. Pediatrics. 1998 Apr;101(4 Pt 1):669-74.
Rideout, Foehr, Roberts, 2010.
Rideout VJ, Foehr UG, Roberts DF. Generation M2: media in the lives of 8-18 year-olds. Kaiser Family Foundation. January 2010. Available at: http://www.kff.org/entmedia/upload/8010.pdf. Accessed 30 June 2010.
Roberts, Foehr, Rideout, 2005.

Senate Committee on the Judiciary. Children, violence, and the media: a report for parents and policy makers. September 14, 1999. Accessed 14 June 2006. Previously available at: http://judiciary.senate.gov/oldsite/mediavio.htm.

Snyder LB, Milici FF, Slater M, Sun H, Strizhakova Y. Effects of alcohol advertising exposure on drinking among youth. Arch Pediatr Adolesc Med. 2006 Jan;160(1):18-24.

Strasburger VC. Alcohol advertising and adolescents. Pediatr Clin North Am. 2002 Apr;49(2):353-76, vii.

Tamburro RF, Gordon PL, D'Apolito JP, Howard SC. Unsafe and violent behavior in commercials aired during televised major sporting events. Pediatrics. 2004 Dec;114(6):e694-8.

Thompson DA, Christakis DA. The association between television viewing and irregular sleep schedules among children less than 3 years of age. Pediatrics. 2005 Oct;116(4):851-6.

Thompson DA, Flores G, Ebel BE, Christakis DA. Comida en venta: after-school advertising on Spanish-language television in the United States. J Pediatr. 2008 Apr;152(4):576-81. Epub 2007 Nov 5.

van der Molen JH, Bushman BJ. Children's direct fright and worry reactions to violence in fiction and news television programs. J Pediatr. 2008 Sep;153(3):420-4. Epub 2008 Apr 28.

Vandewater, Bickham, Lee, 2006.

Vandewater EA, Bickham DS, Lee JH. Time well spent? Relating television use to children's free-time activities. Pediatrics. 2006 Feb;117(2):e181-91. Available at: http://pediatrics.aappublications.org/cgi/content/full/117/2/e181 . Accessed 11 November 2009.

Vandewater, EA., et al. When the Television Is Always On: Heavy Television Exposure and Young Children's Development. American Behavioral Scientist. 2005 Jan 01;48(5):562-577.

Viner RM, Cole TJ. Television viewing in early childhood predicts adult body mass index. J Pediatr. 2005 Oct;147(4):429-35.

Yokota F, Thompson KM. Violence in G-rated animated films. JAMA. 2000 May 24-31;283(20):2716-20.

Zimmerman FJ, Christakis DA. Children's television viewing and cognitive outcomes: a longitudinal analysis of national data. Arch Pediatr Adolesc Med. 2005 Jul;159(7):619-25.

Zimmerman FJ, Glew GM, Christakis DA, Katon W. Early cognitive stimulation, emotional support, and television watching as predictors of subsequent bullying among grade-school children. Arch Pediatr Adolesc Med. 2005 Apr;159(4):384-8.